The Supreme Court of Florida, 1917–1972

UNIVERSITY PRESS OF FLORIDA

Florida A&M University, Tallahassee
Florida Atlantic University, Boca Raton
Florida Gulf Coast University, Ft. Myers
Florida International University, Miami
Florida State University, Tallahassee
University of Central Florida, Orlando
University of Florida, Gainesville
University of North Florida, Jacksonville
University of South Florida, Tampa
University of West Florida, Pensacola

The Supreme Court of Florida, 1917–1972

WALTER W. MANLEY II

AND CANTER BROWN JR.

Prepared for the Florida Supreme Court Historical Society
Eric W. Rise, Contributing Scholar

University Press of Florida
Gainesville/Tallahassee/Tampa/Boca Raton
Pensacola/Orlando/Miami/Jacksonville/Ft. Myers

Printed in the United States of America on acid-free paper

11 10 09 08 07 06 6 5 4 3 2 1

A record of cataloging-in-publication data is available from the Library of Congress
ISBN 0-8130-3003-X

The University Press of Florida is the scholarly publishing agency for the State University System of Florida, comprising Florida A&M University, Florida Atlantic University, Florida Gulf Coast University, Florida International University, Florida State University, University of Central Florida, University of Florida, University of North Florida, University of South Florida, and University of West Florida.

University Press of Florida
15 Northwest 15th Street
Gainesville, FL 32611-2079
http://www.upf.com

Contents

Illustrations

Preface and Acknowledgments

This book continues the history of the Supreme Court of Florida series, which commenced with the 1997 publication of *The Supreme Court of Florida and Its Predecessor Courts, 1821–1917.* Sponsored, as was the first volume, by the Florida Supreme Court Historical Society, this second volume describes and analyzes the development of Florida's highest court—and to some extent the state's entire appellate court system—from 1917 to 1972, an era of significant challenges and change during which Florida emerged from relative national obscurity to become one of the nation's largest and most dynamic political subdivisions. No previous work has addressed this subject in the depth or scholarly manner presented here. Nor has any earlier study attempted to place Florida's judicial system during this period within the larger context of state, regional, and national history, an approach that permits emphasis on the close relationship between the Supreme Court of Florida's jurisprudence and the prevailing social, economic, and political conditions of nearly eight decades of the twentieth century.

Following the pattern established by the first volume, this volume's narrative is divided into discrete time periods and, within each such period, contains specific historic, biographical, and jurisprudential material pertinent to the times. The sections include The Roller-Coaster Years, 1917–1932; The Great Depression and World War II, 1933–1945; Peace and Prosperity, 1946–1955; Change and Reaction, 1955–1964; and The Realization of Reform, 1964–1972. Each of these sections offers general historical context, a specific examination of the supreme court's experiences and evolution, biographies of each court member who assumed a seat on the supreme bench during the period, and a review of appellate decisions either typical of or particularly pertinent to that period. The rationale for inclusion of the historical materials is axiomatic given this volume's general purpose. The use of detailed biographical sketches of each justice permits highlighting the importance of individual personalities in shaping the law in Florida. An acute analysis of the court's opinions on the key issues of the day, meanwhile, serves to demonstrate the manner in which the work of the court shaped, and was in turn fashioned by, the competing economic and social interests that transformed Florida.

As intended by the Florida Supreme Court Historical Society in commissioning this work, every effort has been made to offer an objective examination of the court and the men who sat upon it from 1917 to 1972. While incorporating in the book the latest contributions to Florida historiography, the authors have striven to avoid political favoritism or ideological bias. Readers will find within these pages, for instance, frank explorations of the court's role in resisting demands for civil rights advances by minority groups such as African Americans, as well as the impact of personal ambition and of powerful influences brought to bear by political and economic interests. The discussions include relevant interpretation but allow readers themselves to examine and decide the soundness of decisions and the measure of the men who made them. The narrative also makes clear that Floridians may take pride in the honesty and public-mindedness evidenced by most of those men while pointing out the dangers inherent in politicization of such tribunals. Not only does the book offer a context for contemporary understanding of Florida jurisprudence, but also a work suitable for practical use within the judiciary and the bar, as well as one that provides provocative and informative reading for scholars, students, and the general public.

This series, as conceived by the officers and directors of the Florida Supreme Court Historical Society, fills two significant voids in the historical and legal literature. First, despite the rich historiography of Florida's past, the state's legal history, and particularly the history of its judiciary, has been sorely neglected. The leading general histories of the state contain scant reference to the work of Florida's highest court, and even specialized monographs and journal articles focus on the political and social history of the state. Yet, as the book displays, the Supreme Court of Florida often found itself at the center of leading political, social, and economic controversies. In addition, virtually every jurist on the appellate courts held other prominent positions in business or government. The biographical sections of the work establish that the political and jurisprudential philosophies of these men often overlapped in consequential ways.

Second, this history provides an important contribution to the renewed interest in state and local courts spawned by the recent transformation in the influence of state constitutional law. For most of the twentieth century, several circumstances—including the nationalization of the economy commenced with the New Deal, the centralization of governmental authority in response to world war and cold war, and the application of the Bill of Rights to the states through the Fourteenth Amendment—combined to establish the federal courts as the primary arbiters of governmental authority and personal liberty. Today, public institutions play an increasingly significant role in American society. In fact, they have become the loci of power, authority, and responsibility. There is reconstructed interest among lawyers, judges, historians, political scientists, and scholars of jurisprudence in the function and history of the highest state appellate courts because of the state constitutional law revolution that has occurred in the past three decades. There has been an emergence of a "new federalism" and an increased emphasis by civil libertarians and those who oppose the unfettered expansion of individual rights at the expense of the general society on state constitutions as independent sources of civil rights and civil liberties. This trend has spurred lawyers, historians, and political scientists to pay considerable attention to the processes of state constitution-making and to the adjudication of constitutional cases at the state level.

Surprisingly, this renewed interest in state constitutionalism has not produced significant scholarship in the history of state appellate tribunals, despite the fact that during much of the twentieth century state courts were the primary venues for the creation and interpretation of constitutional law. This historical series addresses that void by presenting the most comprehensive historical analysis of a state supreme court during and in the era following this golden age of state constitutional law. Thus, at a time when state courts would assume greater responsibilities, this book will reveal to scholars and policymakers the challenges faced by an earlier court in assuming the burden of arbitrating constitutional struggles over power and liberty.

A number of organizations and individuals played an important role in this book project, either by laying its foundation, by rendering assistance in an extraordinary research effort, or by undertaking thoughtful review of the text. The Florida Supreme Court Historical Society, led by distinguished attorneys and bar leaders Robert M. Ervin, H. Russell Troutman, W. Dexter Douglass, Benjamin Hill III, John A. DeVault III, and Howard Coker, wholeheartedly supported this project. The late circuit judge and regents professor Harold B. Crosby initially led the book project until I assumed that director's role in 1991, and he was assisted by historian Thomas Gillian. Eric Rise was an important contributing scholar. Of course, no one could be more fortunate than I in enjoying as a coauthor the distinguished historian Canter Brown Jr.

The interest in and support of this volume by the following are gratefully acknowledged: Dr. Larry Eugene Rivers, dean of the College of Arts and Sciences, Florida A&M University; Dr. James M. Denham, director, Center for Florida Studies, Florida Southern College; Leland M. Hawes of the *Tampa Tribune*; and the staffs of the Florida Archives, the State Library of Florida, and the Florida Supreme Court Library. Barbara Brown of Tallahassee undertook the painstaking task of searching through decades of daily and weekly Florida newspapers for those bits of historical information that proved essential in the writing of this book.

Moreover, thanks are due to Nancy Dobson, the society's outstanding executive director through June 2001, and Park Trammell, her accomplished successor, for abetting this successful history project. Andrew Edel, research historian for the society, assisted in assembling rare photographs. Also facilitating the work are

Adam Watson, photographic archivist for the State Archives of Florida, Craig Waters, public information officer of the Supreme Court of Florida, and Jackson Maynard, who drew my attention to obscure state supreme court cases.

This book and the authors could not have had a better friend than the distinguished lawyer and bar leader Mark Hulsey, liaison to the project for the society, who spent many hours reading and providing valuable editorial suggestions for the manuscript. The aforementioned Robert M. Ervin joined Mark Hulsey in supporting this project for fifteen years. Moreover, a general grant from the Florida Bar Foundation supported publication of this volume, as did an earlier grant for the first volume. The late justices Stephen C. O'Connell and Richard Ervin, both of whom wrote insightful forewords for the first volume, gave me substantial encouragement, as did the late Raymond Ehrlich, accomplished attorneys M. Lewis Hall Jr., H. Russell Troutman, and Michael Rosen, and former justice Stephen H. Grimes. Moreover, Talbot D'Alemberte, William Reece Smith Jr., the late Chesterfield Smith, former justice Parker Lee McDonald, and former justice Ben F. Overton, Mark Hulsey, and Douglas D. Friedrich, then provost of the University of West Florida, ably served on the original advisory committee established in 1990 to determine the proper course of this book project.

Through her wise experience Meredith Morris-Babb, director of the University Press of Florida, recognized the substantial merit of this book and supported its publication. Her predecessor, Ken Scott, provided invaluable support for the first volume and encouraged the effort that culminated in this volume. Managing editor Gillian Hillis, project editor Susan Albury, production manager Lynn Werts, and editor Hannah Smith improved this book as did proofreader Jody Larson.

Without the foregoing individuals' enormous encouragement, support, assistance, and extremely high standards of excellence, which were consistent with those of the two coauthors, this book would have not been written.

Further, the first volume received over fifteen highly generous reviews, which helped establish it as the finest nineteenth-century state supreme court history and the best legal history of Florida. Certainly, those reviewers helped focus and nourish our efforts (measured in several thousands of hours) in researching and writing this volume. Their thoughtful praise and analyses of the earlier text validated our immense effort and helped us in improving the volume.

Last, I express my love and thanks to my wife, Linda, my children, Marjorie and Ben, and my grandson, Cameron, for their patience and support.

Professor Walter W. Manley II
Director
History of the Supreme Court of Florida Project
Coauthor and Coeditor
Tallahassee, Florida
September 2005

PART ONE

The Roller-Coaster Years, 1917–1932

1

World War I, the Boom, and the Bust

As the year 1917 opened in Florida, the state expectantly awaited the beginning of a new era that promised to usher in marvels and challenges previously anticipated by only a relative handful of individuals gifted with deep insight and great imagination. "The entire country is in a stage of 'Pushforwardedness' in all enterprises," one minister appropriately declared. Especially in the fast-growing peninsula, excitement about future prospects glimmered and pulsed with a rhythm that captured hearts, minds, and souls. "Never in the history of the city has the spirit of optimism been so manifest as now," one south Florida man commented in a typical fashion. "The elements of a center of commercial life and progress are here; the present bears testimony to the unlimited resources and a determination to use them," he continued. "Everywhere there are evidences of steady and permanent growth."[1]

Although Florida remained sparsely inhabited and mostly poor, growth of remarkable proportions had begun to remake the state. Two years earlier the population had reached close to one million, whereas in 1905 it had rested at just over six hundred thousand. During the decade that commenced in 1915, the number of Floridians would jump again, to over one and a quarter million. By 1930 it would near one and a half million, about triple the figure attained at the century's advent.[2]

Increasingly, Florida trended away from its "Old South" roots as the population shifted from a rural to an urban orientation with an increasing dominance of white over black. Jacksonville, the state's largest town, had reached nearly thirty thousand by 1900. That total more than doubled within the next fifteen years. It doubled again by 1930. At the century's commencement, Pensacola had trailed Jacksonville with about seventeen thousand residents, while Key West stood not far behind, a combination that had remained more or less static for the past half century. In 1915, though, Tampa had emerged by far as the state's second city with Pensacola a distant third. The population shift ever deeper into the peninsula became even more pronounced by 1930. Miami, a municipality that had claimed only seventeen hundred denizens in 1900, now offered a home to one hundred ten thousand. Tampa had climbed meanwhile to over one hundred thousand.

Overall, 80 percent of Floridians had claimed rural homes in 1900. The passage of the decades witnessed a near-complete reversal. By 1930, over 60 percent of state residents boasted urban status.[3]

Meanwhile, the population swelled generally, with the number of African American residents increasing as well. White immigration significantly outpaced black immigration, though, and the percentage of blacks in the state plummeted. At the century's turn, African Americans had constituted nearly 44 percent of Floridians. That level slipped during the next fifteen years to 35 percent. Census takers in 1930 recorded continuing erosion. More than 70 percent of the state's inhabitants then were white, while less than 30 percent were black.[4]

As the population edge between the races rose in favor of whites, conditions for African Americans slowly deteriorated. Racial violence had placed Florida, at least on a per capita basis, in the lead as the most lynch-prone state in the nation. Legally mandated Jim Crow racial discrimination also had taken firm hold by 1917. This fact had occurred partly as a result of the state legislature's 1889 decision to impose a poll tax as a prerequisite for registering to vote, an act that drastically cut poor voters, white and black, from the rolls. The "whites-only" Democratic primary, implemented in the late nineteenth and early twentieth centuries, had reinforced the earlier measure's impact. African American leaders had sought to maintain a presence on governing councils, at least in the larger towns and cities, but by 1917 only Palatka's local government included black representation.[5]

Meanwhile, harsh conditions had prompted some of Florida's most talented and most promising young black residents to seek homes and opportunities elsewhere. Among them could be numbered Florida attorney James Weldon Johnson, first executive director of the National Association for the Advancement of Colored People, and his law partner, Judson Douglas Wetmore; A. Philip Randolph, labor organizer and, eventually, the nation's premier civil rights leader; and sociologist and writer Zora Neale Hurston. Mostly these African American émigrés maintained affection for Florida—and hopes for its future—even when they believed that they must live elsewhere. James Weldon Johnson, for one, returned to the state in early 1917 intent upon laying a foundation for improved race conditions. At Jacksonville and Tampa he organized NAACP branches. Aside from organizations at New Orleans and Shreveport, Louisiana, and at Key West, they constituted the first NAACP branches established in the South. Johnson's action, as will be seen, set in motion dynamics that would place Florida in the forefront of civil rights battles a generation afterward.[6]

The tone of Florida's one-party Democratic politics reflected the intensity and pervasiveness of the racial divide while, at the same time, moving away from the mild "progressivism" of departing governor Park Trammell and his predecessors

Albert Gilchrist, Napoleon B. Broward, and William Sherman Jennings. Effective January 2, 1917, Sidney J. Catts served as Florida's chief executive officer and, in doing so, delighted in stirring racial animosities to his own political advantage. Known as the "Cracker Messiah," Catts had achieved election the previous year as the Prohibition Party's candidate after the Florida Supreme Court deprived him of a narrow Democratic primary victory. A series of regular Democrats followed Catts after the expiration of his four-year term, softening the rhetoric but disdaining fundamental social or political change. Suwannee County's Cary Augustus Hardee took office in 1921; Jacksonville's John Wellborn Martin followed in 1925; and Tampa's Doyle Elam Carlton succeeded Martin in 1929. Each to a greater or lesser degree manifested solid conservative and pro-growth attitudes. Florida meanwhile remained a small-government, low-tax state, a fact that found itself engrafted into the state constitution in 1924 when voters approved amendments barring income and inheritance taxes.[7]

Given that the state government's position and philosophy may have limited its ability to spur growth, Floridians owed much to World War I in providing necessary impetus. The Congress at President Woodrow Wilson's request declared war against Germany and its allies on April 6, 1917, only three months after Governor Catts assumed office. Quickly, military planners realized that the state offered ideal conditions for training facilities. This fact especially proved true for the infant air corps. Accordingly, the state came to host seven of the nation's thirty-five flight schools. They ranged from Pensacola's Naval Air Station to Carlstrom and Dorr fields at Arcadia to Miami's Curtiss and Chapman fields. At Key West, another innovative service, the submarine fleet, honed its skills. Camp Joseph E. Johnston near Jacksonville housed army training facilities.[8]

Florida assisted the war effort in a variety of ways beyond providing sites for military posts. Over forty thousand residents either enlisted for military service or answered the call of the draft. More than one thousand paid for their contribution with their lives. Sunshine State farmers produced mass quantities of food, including meat, citrus, and sugar. Forests furnished lumber and naval stores commodities. Meanwhile, workers at the Tampa, Jacksonville, and Pensacola shipyards turned out vessels for the navy and merchant marine service. "Victor Boys" and "Victor Girls" raised morale, home guard units trained and patrolled, and volunteers conducted Liberty Bond drives and war savings stamp sales. These and countless other activities allowed Floridians additional avenues for expression of patriotic support.[9]

As Floridians advanced the war effort, the war effort advanced Florida. Military payrolls and government contracts launched boom conditions in many areas. "The tremendous wages paid by the shipyards induced extravagant living among

Government workers," a Jacksonville historian recalled, "and naturally this had an effect upon all lines of local business." Scholars of the era not only have found similar conditions elsewhere in the state but have noted that the war's end did not end the prosperity. "All segments of Florida's economy experienced a wartime boom," Governor Catts's biographer, Wayne Flynt, discovered. "Even with the closing of some facilities and the rapid dismantling of the federal presence in Florida," Flynt added, "the state's economy did not decline to prewar levels. Wages and salaries more than doubled, and the use of power increased by 40 percent." University of Florida historian Samuel Proctor concurred: "Florida came out of World War I as a growing, prospering state."[10]

By Armistice Day in November 1918 and thanks to the war, Florida had become known to more Americans than ever before. The state's soldiers and sailors had carried news of their home around the globe, while untold thousands of their peers had trained or otherwise served in the state. Beyond that, the press had featured stories of Florida's experience and attributes. The relatively new medium of the movies had opened the eyes of millions to the allure of Florida's sands, palm trees, waters, and pastimes. Whether in newsreel films sponsored by the government and featuring fearless pilot trainees or in commercial features scripted against lush semitropical backgrounds, the state's appeal as translated upon the silver but silent screen proved irresistible to millions once peacetime again prevailed.[11]

Whether those millions desired to relocate to Florida or simply to enjoy a few days or weeks of sun on vacation, they enjoyed the fruits of another World War I by-product: enhanced federal support of road building. The Federal Aid Road Act of 1916 provided the vehicle for distribution of funds, while war's end nudged the government to donate immense quantities of surplus equipment. Thanks in good part to this welcome source of financing, the Dixie Highway, among other improved roads to result, soon linked the metropolis of Chicago with once isolated Miami.[12]

Fortunately, Florida already had organized to lift its roads out of sands and swamps and to help pioneer modern highway construction. Governor Park Trammell in 1915 had achieved creation of the state road department and had aided development of a model "velvet highways" network in his home county of Polk. After trial and error, engineers eventually chose asphalt as the most desirable construction material. The state managed early construction and maintenance of these and other roads thanks in good part to convict labor and local bond issues, but, beginning with a one cent per gallon gasoline tax imposed in 1921, Florida moved closer to a cash contract system. Subsequent administrations furthered Trammell's initiatives and increasingly relied upon the gasoline tax. It rose from three cents per gallon in 1923 to six cents per gallon in 1931. This levy soon provided state and county governments with a principal source of their income.[13]

New and improved highways combined with the availability of inexpensive automobiles such as Henry Ford's Model T Ford literally put Americans on the road. The opening of the decade of the 1920s saw millions annually headed for Florida. By 1925, two and a half million tourists per year selected the state as their destination. Among them came tens of thousands of less affluent families, soon to be called "tin can tourists," who hauled their own lodgings in trailers. "Tourist camps" and "trailer parks" resulted, as did the proliferation of "tourist courts" or motels.[14]

Tourist dollars sparked an unprecedented economic boom that extended past middecade, yet the state's transformation owed every bit as much to those who chose to settle permanently. "Was there ever anything like the migration to Florida?" one northern observer queried. "From the time the Hebrews went into Egypt, or since the Hegira of Mohammed the prophet, what can compare to this evacuation? The Forty-niners did not go out in such great numbers, nor can the gold rush to the Klondike be put in the same class with this flight to Florida. Entire populations are moving away bodily. The personal columns of our local press are unable to chronicle the daily departures."[15]

The boom commenced on the lower Atlantic coast at and near Miami, but it soon progressed northward through the peninsula. Older towns and cities thrived, but newer planned communities such as Coral Gables, Hollywood, and Boca Raton glistened as diamonds in Florida's crown. D. P. "Doc" Davis, Addison Mizner, George E. Merrick, and others divined romantic, inviting, and intriguing worlds molded in concepts and designed in styles that have continued to help define the state to the present day. As would be expected, the transportation system had to expand to link the new and emerging metropolises one to another. Outstanding among the projects, an asphalt highway tied Tampa and Miami to points in between by 1928. The road's opening stood out at the time as a grand symbol of Florida's emergence as a dynamic and modern state. "Perhaps no other project in Florida," one journal declared, "has had as much publicity or been so constantly in people's minds as the Tamiami Trail."[16]

Standing out among other legacies of that golden era are thirteen of Florida's sixty-seven counties. In the last spurt of such actions up to the present time, the legislatures of 1921, 1923, and 1925 authorized creation of Dixie, Union, Gilchrist, Gulf, Charlotte, Glades, Hardee, Highlands, Sarasota, Collier, Hendry, Indian River, and Martin counties. Nine of the new subdivisions stood testimony to the sudden dynamism of central and south Florida, where growth abounded. These lay far distant from the relatively stagnant region of the old north Florida

Panhandle heartland. A majority of Floridians still called north Florida home in 1920, but every year that passed altered the equation in favor of the peninsula.[17]

Boom-time growth brought with it marvelous positive benefits, but it also displayed a darker and less desirable side. Crooks, charlatans, and other fast-buck artists directed themselves to the state with dispatch. They came in a variety of personifications, but the shady real estate agent represented the type to all. "The notorious Florida land boom of the 1920's brought to the state car-loads of realtors and speculators, mostly schooled in California, and well versed in all the arts of subdivision," one student of the subject explained. "Through these men numerous gullible people all over the United States, and in some foreign countries, lost heavily in a gamble which finally collapsed." Urban legends grew around the exploits and extremes of one subgroup of the property salesmen, the "binder boys," twenty-five thousand of whom, it has been reported, labored in Miami alone. Historian William Warren Rogers aptly described them as "fast-talking hucksters, in golf knickers and two-toned shoes." These men hawked lot purchase options literally from street corners, amassing unbelievable paper profits as land prices and their sales pitches soared beyond credibility or control.[18]

Gambling interests, too, flocked to Florida to prey—despite stringent state criminal laws—upon diversion-hungry sojourners. A Cuban-derived numbers game named bolita operated extensively out of Tampa and Miami, while virtually every other type of wager could be placed at some point in the state. Thoroughbred horse races offered one such venue. A track entertained customers between Jacksonville and St. Augustine even before Joseph M. Smoot's Miami Jockey Club (beginning in 1931, Hialeah) opened for business in 1925. With the state awash in gambling opportunities, it seemed fitting to some when, in 1928, Chicago mobster "Scarface Al" Capone, the Federal Bureau of Investigation's "Public Enemy Number One," purchased a Miami home. "The power of money is known," the *Miami Daily News* proclaimed of Capone in 1930. "There is nothing more persuasive, either for good or evil, than gold, and Greater Miami in her indifference has established here one of the most dangerous characters on earth, with all the power of a feudal lord."[19]

Capone's presence in Florida, while highlighting illegal gambling activities, also symbolized unlawful sales of bootleg and moonshine whiskey and other ardent spirits. By a margin of only 350 votes, a state electorate shrunken by the poll tax had approved a Prohibition amendment to the state constitution in 1918 to be effective December 9, giving Florida a lead of well over one year on the federal amendment enacted with the same purpose. An already flawed electoral system thereafter easily facilitated the corruption of law enforcement in many areas. The sheriffs' departments of numerous counties particularly gained a reputation for protecting the liquor trade and its profits. "Did you not know that open saloons, bootlegging joints, and hellholes are flourishing by the hundreds throughout this great county with the full knowledge, consent and apparent protection from the sheriff's office in this county?" one resident asked Governor Carlton in 1930. The letter well reflected complaints received from around the state by all governors of the era.[20]

The sense of moral decay associated with illegal gambling and liquor sales encompassed for some a variety of issues related to women, particularly young women. These included increasing independence of action and emergence into public life as well as changing attitudes toward morality and sexuality. The "Jazz Age" of the 1920s and the lifestyles associated with it brought "flapper" attire and swimming apparel that revealed the female form in shocking detail. The period also encouraged behavior, often fueled by "bathtub gin," viewed by traditionalists as entirely improper. Automobiles afforded mobility unknown to earlier generations, and their "rumble seats" provided a more or less comfortable and private location for intimacy. The era accordingly scandalized and alarmed many Floridians who had chosen paths of less temptation.[21]

Beyond that, many Florida women joined in demands for a role in public affairs. Individuals such as May Mann Jennings, wife of former governor William Sherman Jennings, Jacksonville attorney Gertrude Dzialynski Corbet, and educator Mary McLeod Bethune appealed to Florida's legislature without avail on behalf of a woman's right to vote and otherwise stride officially in the halls of government. Despite the intransigence of some, the Nineteenth Amendment to the U.S. Constitution, ratified in summer 1920, ultimately gifted the women with their demand. On August 27 at Sneads in Jackson County, Fay Bridges became the first woman to exercise the new right in Florida; those in Corbet's Polk County hometown of Fort Meade followed on September 14. Soon women achieved election and appointment to various local offices. The year 1928 proved a turning point in that regard. Orlando's Edna Giles Fuller was elected to the Florida House of Representatives; Monticello's Mamie Eaton Greene won a seat on the Florida Railroad Commission in her own right following a 1927 appointment by Governor John Martin; and Ruth Bryan Owen, daughter of former Democratic presidential candidate and U.S. secretary of state William Jennings Bryan, gained victory in a U.S. House of Representatives contest.[22]

William Jennings Bryan ironically offered Floridians a fitting symbol far removed from his daughter's elevation to the U.S. Congress in that he came to represent the traditional reaction to the era's liberalizing tendencies and trends. Once considered "The Great Commoner," Bryan by the early 1920s lived in Florida and promoted Coral Gables real estate. With the passage of years and three failed attempts at the presidency, he had grown increasingly resolute, especially when it came to "old style" religion and what he perceived as threats to it. The innovative teaching methods propounded by John Dewey and Charles Darwin's theory of evolution offered him especially fetching targets. Despite having carried Florida in landslide proportions during his three runs as the Democratic candidate for president, Bryan's influence failed to achieve passage of a state law barring the teaching of the theory of evolution in Florida's public schools. It did result, however, in approval of a 1923 legislative resolution objecting to Darwin's ideas.[23]

Cautious and traditional leadership such as that embraced by Bryan and others of similar persuasion might not have wrought so profound an impact on the state had it not been for a major technological innovation. The early 1920s, as it happened, proved an appropriate opportunity for the communications revolution known as radio. Perfected during World War I, the medium debuted in the Sunshine State on May 31, 1922, when Tampa's WDAE—one of the nation's first half-dozen stations—came on the air. The city's mayor, Charles H. Brown, barely exaggerated when he marveled at the "wonder of the age that the human voice can be sent broadcast throughout the country." Eventually radio would exert a modernizing trend by opening the lives of rural Floridians to urban culture and mores, but initially it accomplished the opposite by permitting conservative preachers and orators such as Bryan a powerful forum for their views.[24]

Bryan particularly captured state, regional, and national attention in 1925 when, on a pro bono basis, he prosecuted a highly controversial Tennessee criminal case. Authorities had charged teacher John T. Scopes with willful violation of that state's law against the teaching of evolution. The American Civil Liberties Union arranged for renowned attorney Clarence Darrow to defend Scopes and facilitated the trial's broadcast to the nation. Bryan won his guilty verdict against Scopes, endearing himself to religious traditionalists in Florida and elsewhere. Darrow's adept examination of Bryan as an expert on the Bible, though, reduced the famed leader almost to incoherence and likely contributed to his death a short time after the trial's conclusion.[25]

Just as the moral decay "crisis" of the 1920s regenerated Bryan's career, it also gave rise to a serious problem of the boom period. The Ku Klux Klan had not operated in the state in any organized fashion since the 1870s. Just before World War I, however, the organization had been revived at a ceremony on Stone Mountain near Atlanta. Quickly after the war's end, the hooded legions made their entry into Florida. The "100 percent Americanism" philosophy espoused by its members effectively meant opposition to all but reactionary white Anglo-Saxon Protestants. Hoping to enlist supporters not otherwise drawn to its extreme agenda, the Klan publicly presented itself instead as the defender of "Christian morality." It required pledges to swear to "correct evils in my community, particularly vices tending to the destruction of the home, family, childhood and womanhood." Leaders informed those enlisted in the cause: "If the law will not protect our homes, we must. These are strong words, but the times call for stern methods."[26]

Klan activities of the 1920s and early 1930s centered mostly in the fast-changing peninsula. Although klaverns coalesced early on as far north as Gainesville and Perry, most growth was associated with the more southerly locations of Orlando, Tampa, Lakeland, and Miami. A study of one klavern, that at Gainesville, revealed a broad middle-class representation. The local mayor who practiced dentistry and the police chief, for instance, stood in its ranks. Many members perceived the group as little more than a social organization, although a smaller cadre prepared to take direct action. Picnics, barbecues, "Klan days" at county fairs, and a Junior Ku Klux Klan for children polished the social image. Apparently the scheme worked well, for a "minimum" state membership of sixty thousand by the mid-1920s has been reported.[27]

From the beginning, though, and despite attempts to project a more pacific image, some in the group resorted to violence and threats of violence. In just three incidents of many, Klansmen in 1920 endeavored to intimidate black leader Mary McLeod Bethune on the campus of her Daytona girls' school for having urged black women to vote; stoked the Rosewood "massacre" in Levy County during early 1923; and castrated University of Florida instructor and Roman Catholic priest John Francis Conoley at Gainesville later the same year. Items regarding whippings and beatings appeared often in state newspapers. "Bands of masked men said to have worn the regalia of the Ku Klux Klan abducted L. L. Isaac of Isaac's Nest, and the head waiter of El Passaje Spanish restaurant, early Thursday morning, took them into the country several miles, administered severe whippings, and returned them to the city with warnings contained in letters to discontinue the practice of selling liquors," the *Tampa Morning Tribune* offered in a typical report published in November 1923. The account further described Isaac's "wounds" as "severe."[28]

So widespread did Klan violence become by 1926 that Governor Martin courageously took the initiative to combat the secret organization's illegal actions. In September he seized on the opportunity of a Putnam County incident to summon the county sheriff and Palatka's mayor to explain their lack of progress in pursuing charges against the vigilantes despite a record of sixty-three floggings within twelve months. Following outbreaks in Hillsborough, Polk, Volusia, and Monroe counties, he condemned "mobs formed at night to terrorize the community." Seemingly in response to the governor's declaration, the Klan organized a Tallahassee klavern. By December 24 its members had conducted a public Christmas pageant and distributed gifts to "the poor and needy of the city." In future years the group of "several hundred members" would be associated by press reports with the capital city's First Baptist Church.[29]

Although the Klan persisted in Florida, its influence waned after 1926, a moment in time that also saw the implosion of the Florida boom. Unlike the national economic collapse of October 1929, the Florida bust brought its suffering and loss at a slower and more subtle pace. Florida Supreme Court justice Glenn Terrell explained the dynamics at play at middecade during what he characterized as the "sucker's interlude" that led to the economic disaster. "The pots of gold metamorphosed from town lots and cut over lands by the optimism and psychosis of that era changed suddenly [due] to a medley of pyramided mortgages and delinquent tax certificates. The assumed values in the lands were fictitious and existed only in the mind of the claimant. The whole scheme was so fantastic that it made John Law and his Mississippi bubble look tame and innocent."[30]

Terrell's recollection omitted the part played by corrupt collusion among some developers, builders, speculators, public officials, and bankers. Although supposedly supervised by comptroller Ernest Amos, much of the banking system succumbed to the wild excitement and easy money of the era. The coming crash initially came to light at Palm Beach in June 1926 with the first of a chain of bank failures, and as investigations revealed the underlying corruption, Amos and others were indicted. The damage, however, had been done. "It became evident that the era of wild speculation had become a thing of the past," a local historian recorded. "The sudden cessation of real estate activities was at once reflected on all lines of business." A St. Petersburg developer perhaps stated the case with greater piquancy. "We just ran out of suckers. That's all. We got all their money, then started trading with ourselves. That isn't quite correct," he added. "We became the suckers."[31]

After a terrible hurricane struck south Florida in September 1926 at a cost of millions of dollars in damage and hundreds of lives lost, state residents reeled from a combination of troubles that appeared overwhelming and unsolvable by human agency. After a brief respite that permitted rekindling of optimism for some, two more devastating storms in 1928 reinvigorated the sense of calamity only to be followed the next year by a Mediterranean fruit fly epidemic that ravaged the citrus industry. As officials and growers grappled with that assault, the Great Depression descended upon the nation in the wake of the stock market's collapse. By then, some found themselves viewing their world from a perspective that hindsight must label unreal. The capital city's principal newspaper, the *Tallahassee Daily Democrat*, provided an example of that dynamic in the days after the stock market run. "The current antics of the stock market are puzzling enough heaven knows, but they are not half so puzzling as some of the comments . . . by our financial and industrial overlords," the editor opined. "There seems to be a feeling of relief that the small investor is being removed from the scene. Probably it is just as well that the joy ride has ended. It was spreading an unhealthy atmosphere throughout the land."[32]

Into the early 1930s the unreal sense persisted for many, even in the face of authoritative warnings to the contrary. "Florida is in a better economic condition than most other states in the Union and faces a bright business future," one stockbroker would proclaim in December 1930. Countering such claims, respected economist Leroy D. Peavey insisted, "We must realize that our present condition is not one that can be remedied by holding conferences or expressing confident views regarding the outlook. We must face the actual facts."[33]

For those willing to look, the actual facts presented themselves clearly. On the one hand, hundreds of thousands of Floridians survived the era easily. Others proved their ability to do so in luxury. Hordes of tourists continued to visit, and the sun kept shining. Still, suffering, dislocation, and misery could be seen openly in most larger towns and cities. "Hoboes" descended from freight car transports, bread lines formed in front of soup kitchens, and job agencies grew crowded with unemployed workers anxious for any opportunity to support themselves and their families. Local historian Freddie Wright of Bartow made the point succinctly. "It was a desperate time, which only those who lived through it can understand." Consistent with long-established government philosophy, the federal government under President Herbert Hoover offered aid only belatedly and then in insufficient amounts and forms. The state government managed even less. To increase tax revenues, legislators in 1931 turned to the legalization of gambling in the form of pari-mutuel wagering. By New Year's Day 1932 even the *Tallahassee Daily Democrat*'s editor acknowledged the true state of the crisis at hand by running an Associated Press story headlined "Country Faces Huge Problems as 1932 Starts." The fact that, by summer, more than half of the state's financial institutions faced liquidation ratified the editor's newly awakened vision.[34]

The financial crisis hit Florida particularly hard when it came to funding the needs of municipalities, counties, school districts, and other political subdivisions. This situation resulted from two major causes beside the Depression itself. First, local officials intoxicated by the boom had approved issuance of millions of dollars in bonds to fund community improvements. When property values collapsed, so, too, did the governments' ability to service the obligations. As was noted of one community, "The problem of paying its bonded debt [is] a most distressing one." A summer 1932 report highlighted the growing magnitude of the problem.

"The municipalities have been harassed, haunted, and mandamused by individual bondholders until it is impossible to make provision for general liquidation," the *Florida Municipal Record* related. "So-called 'bondholders' protective' committees have sprung up all over the state and added to their woe. Suit after suit, with an ever-increasing tax levy, apparently is their method of procedure."[35]

Local governments might have weathered this financial storm less painfully had it not been for a conscious decision of certain large and financially able taxpayers. The idea came from Consolidated Naval Stores Company, a firm that held one and a half million acres of Florida land. Specifically, after officers expressed concerns to their attorney, E. D. Treadwell, about rising millage rates based upon the demands of bondholder committees and defaults of bankrupted developments and small property owners, he suggested a solution. Why not avoid any problem, he asked, simply by ceasing to make tax payments? The company, after all, would continue to enjoy its right to future redemption. With Consolidated in the lead, others followed. As a result, many local governments—school boards particularly—experienced chaos. Scrip sufficed in many counties for teachers lucky enough to keep their jobs. District officials cut salaries and school terms, eliminated "unnecessary" programs, closed some schools, and otherwise pared costs to the bone. By 1932 one leading state newspaper would declare the state of education in Florida as "disgraceful."[36]

By that time voters in Florida and the nation had determined that if their standing governments could not remedy the economic crisis, then they would change their governments. Desiring relief on many fronts, they also anticipated soon relaxing with a refreshing and legal alcoholic beverage. Accordingly, Prohibition's repeal stood near the top of many an elector's priority list. In a state absolutely dominated by the Democratic Party, primary elections in June decided all electoral contests except the presidential race. In a record turnout, Floridians selected Daytona Beach attorney David Sholtz over former state chief executive John Martin to be their governor. Five months later, three-quarters of those who visited the polls awarded Florida's electoral votes to Democratic presidential nominee Franklin Delano Roosevelt. The nation agreed, and both of the new Democratic administrations undertook final planning for their inaugurations in 1933.[37]

Meanwhile, Floridians waited amid great uncertainty about the future. Often attention focused on what the new president could accomplish in light of his campaign promise of a balanced budget. Since deflation was the primary reason for the continuing economic malaise, increasing taxes to balance budgets would only serve to prolong the Depression until World War II intervened. Doubtlessly many a resident mulled, perhaps less eloquently, the same thoughts about Roosevelt that journalist William Allen White then considered. "He may develop his stubbornness into courage, his amiability into wisdom, his sense of superiority into statesmanship," White recorded in a hopeful vein. He then added, in words that many a Florida politician should have taken to heart, "Responsibility is a winepress that brings forth strange juices out of men."[38]

2

The Supreme Court in Transition

Between 1917 and 1932, the Supreme Court of Florida experienced alterations and encountered unprecedented controversies. While the state rode a roller coaster of fortune from lethargy to prosperity to chilling depression, so, too, did the tribunal find itself and its future ensnared within forces of change often far from its control and, at times, understanding. Meanwhile, the state's growth and the legal complications of boom and bust presented the jurists with a burden of business by the period's end that amounted to triple the caseload they had accepted as normal and appropriate just fifteen years previously. Adding to the court's challenges, its personnel changed dramatically. Six new justices joined the panel, offering fresh energy and perspectives, but the departure of their predecessors also deprived the court of untold depth of experience.

The era would end in controversy for the supreme court, and it commenced that way as well. On January 2, 1917, Prohibition Party candidate Sidney J. Catts prepared at Tallahassee to take his oath of office as the first non-Democrat to serve Floridians as their governor since Redemption of the state in 1877. Plans called for fifty vehicles to carry prominent men and women from across the state to the ceremony, what amounted to the first automobile parade in the capital city's history. Catts, a canny populistic Baptist minister, would follow the procession in his "humble Ford." The plans, however, quickly hit a snag when the supreme court justices refused to participate. After the panel had deprived him of the Democratic nomination the previous year, Catts had blasted the tribunal as "the Court of Supreme Contempt" and promised to impeach "them infernal judges" if elected. The jurists naturally resented the slur. To assuage their anger, Catts dispatched his close adviser and former state senator William W. Flournoy, the attorney who had represented the candidate before the court in 1916. Now Flournoy pleaded, "This motion to join the parade, [the justices] should not deny." When the court announced its consent, Flournoy "brought to their door the finest automobile in town, a six-twin Packard, and the judges loaded in and took their places in the procession."[1]

The maneuver planned by Catts and executed by Flournoy turned out to be a trick. By placing the justices in a luxury car for the parade, the shrewd Catts had portrayed them symbolically as representatives of the wealthy and powerful while he, traveling behind in his humble Ford, stood by the common man. The coup de grace followed once Chief Justice Jefferson B. Browne had administered the oath of office. Standing on the capitol's east steps, the new governor delivered his inaugural address, quickly turning the speech into an attack on his political enemies including the court. Speaking directly to state residents, he declared, "Your triumph is no less in this good hour in beautiful Florida, for you have withstood the onslaughts of the county and state political rings, the vast corporations and the railroads, the fierce opposition of the daily and weekly press, the organization of the negro voters of the state against you, the judiciary of the state partisan to your needs, and the power of the Roman Catholic hierarchy against you. Yet over all these the common people of Florida, the everyday masses of the cracker people, have triumphed, and the day of your apotheosis has arrived."[2]

The justices who listened that morning to Governor Catts's oration represented a court and system conceived in an earlier era. The constitution of 1885, scripted by conservative Democrats to end forever what they considered the excesses of Republican rule under the previous constitution of 1868, had established its structure and jurisdiction. The charter had granted the court broad powers, endowing it with final appellate authority over virtually all cases originating in circuit courts, county courts, and criminal courts of the state. The few exceptions included appeals of criminal misdemeanor convictions and civil lawsuits involving damages of less than one hundred dollars. Further, the constitution empowered the panel to issue a variety of common law writs. They included writs of certiorari, mandamus, and habeas corpus, as well as other writs "necessary and proper to the complete exercise of its jurisdiction." Additionally, the court possessed the authority and the obligation to deliver advisory opinions to the governor under certain circumstances.[3]

The state constitution's provisions mandated the court's size, tenure, and, to some extent, methods of operation. Originally consisting of three justices, Florida's "Progressive era" voters—mindful of a large backlog of appeals then pending—had doubled the panel's size in 1902 while requiring members' election, rather than appointment, beginning in 1904. The backlog of appeals having been eliminated by 1911, the legislature at Representative Glenn Terrell's behest had reduced the number of justices to five. The constitution required the jurists to be "attorneys at law" and to have attained at least twenty-five years of age. Their term of office ran to six years. A chief justice, selected by lot, headed the court. He held the office for the duration of his term. Physically located in the state capitol until 1913, the justices then had relocated their offices and the court itself to a new edifice located on Jackson Square. This ornate structure, the second state government building erected at Tallahassee, would house the court until the late 1940s. The panel shared the facilities with the Florida Railroad Commission.[4]

The two justices who anchored the court shared the constitution's nineteenth-century roots. R. Fenwick Taylor, a Gainesville attorney, had joined the panel in 1891. Although James Bryan Whitfield did not achieve election as a justice until 1904, he already had served as supreme court clerk, state treasurer, and attorney general. Together the highly intellectual Taylor and Whitfield represented a formidable jurisprudential combination. Courts of other jurisdictions frequently cited Taylor's opinions in equity, while Whitfield enjoyed high regard as the leading expert on Florida's statutory law. By the time Taylor retired in 1925, he had participated in more than three-quarters of all cases decided by the tribunal up to that time. Whitfield would go on to write more opinions than any of his predecessors. The more conservative of the two, Taylor perceived his judicial role as protector of private property from any redistributive encroachments of the legislature. Whitfield, more sympathetic to Progressive legislation and a friend to many state officeholders, usually strove to find constitutional justifications for legislative reforms.[5]

Three other men sat with Taylor and Whitfield on the high court. Tampa's Thomas M. Shackleford, a close associate of Progressive governor William Sherman Jennings, had ascended to the bench with a gubernatorial appointment prompted by approval of the 1902 court expansion. William Hull Ellis, Justice Taylor's son-in-law, had won election in 1914. Two years later, Jefferson B. Browne of Key West, a onetime state senate president, had defeated Justice Robert Cockrell in a bitter primary contest. He took his oath of office on January 2, 1917, only hours before Governor Catts did the same. As will be seen, Shackleford would retire later in 1917. Browne and Thomas F. West, Stackleford's replacement, would remain until 1925. Each left behind solid though modest legacies.[6]

The court in 1917 reflected the strong degree to which selection to the judiciary depended upon political acumen rather than formal professional training. Although attorneys and state officials held each justice in high regard as a lawyer, only one of them had attended law school. Four of the men had no prior judicial experience, and Justice Whitfield's tenure as a county judge had lasted less than five months. By contrast, two of the justices had served as attorney general, and one had been a state senator. Taylor and Shackleford had eschewed regular elective public office, although Shackleford had served as one of Florida's presidential electors in 1892 while Taylor had sat as a delegate to the 1885 constitutional convention. To his credit, Whitfield had acted for eight years as supreme court clerk and had written extensively about Florida law. Ellis and Whitfield both had drafted significant pieces of legislation. Ellis also had held appointment as general counsel to the trustees of the Internal Improvement Trust Fund, and Browne chaired the Florida Railroad Commission, two of the most important regulatory agencies in the state. In short, all three men possessed broad knowledge of the workings of Florida's three branches of government and possessed intimate acquaintance with the state's organic, statutory, and common law.[7]

Court life operated at a slow and measured pace in Tallahassee's equally slow and "Old South" atmosphere. The justices typically took a three-month summer vacation, for example, not requiring the time in their efforts to handle the several hundred appeals disposed of each year. As late as 1915, in fact, they disposed of just 217 cases and did so with only 159 opinions.[8] Nonetheless, the jurists occasionally saw themselves as unappreciated for their efforts. "No servants of the people in Florida work harder or are more closely confined than the judges of the supreme court," a newspaper reporter informed the public following a 1917 interview with an unnamed court member:

> Hearing the oral argument is the easiest part: "That is child's play compared to the examination of briefs and citations and the writing of the opinions," said one of the justices. "We are cooped up here working all the time and know little of what is going on about us," he continued, "but it must be that way. We cannot afford to talk politics or anything else much on the streets. I would give anything sometimes to stop and talk with the boys about the latest political move, but it is forbidden fruit. A circuit judge gets out around the circuit twice a year, but we are even denied that little recreation—It is work and study practically all the time with us, with the exception of our vacation in the summer. But we will hardly ever again be able to take another vacation as long as that we enjoyed last summer, the dockets are too crowded and so much time has been consumed in hearing important statewide matters."[9]

It was true that the justices received little aid in carrying out their responsibilities. Court clerk George Talbot Whitfield first had assumed his duties with the tribunal in 1915. A brother to Justice Whitfield, the clerk previously had practiced law at Tallahassee, served as clerk to State Treasurer W. V. Knott and Governors Jennings and Napoleon B. Broward, and acted as secretary to Governors Albert W. Gilchrist and Park Trammell. Compensated very well based upon a fee system, Whitfield paid his employees from his own income. Lawrence Anderson Perkins, born during the Civil War and another scion of a prominent Tallahassee family, had served as court secretary since 1898. Perkins had graduated from Tallahassee's West Florida Seminary and thereafter pursued a business course in Poughkeepsie,

New York. No court marshal or research assistants yet aided the panel's operations.[10]

On the other hand, the court's library constituted a tremendous asset for members in carrying out their duties and served as a source of pride for the tribunal. "Agents for law book companies who have visited the supreme court library here in the magnificent state supreme court and railroad commission building are unanimous in the declaration that Florida has the best library of law in the Southern states, surpassing many of the supreme court libraries of the Northern and Western states and comparing favorably with any in the United States," a journalist proclaimed in 1917. "There are larger libraries, they say, but none containing more valuable books that are necessary to the proper practice of law. Attorneys from Alabama and Georgia have come to Tallahassee to study in the library here because they found books in this collection which are not to be had in the supreme court libraries of their own states." The report concluded, "Clerk of the Supreme Court G. Tolbert [sic] Whitfield says there are some books there that could not be replaced, and that it would require at least $180,000 to buy the books on the shelves in this state library if they had to be purchased over again." As suggested, in the absence of a regular librarian, Clerk Whitfield supervised the collection.[11]

The reluctance of the legislature to interfere with the court's workings also benefited the tribunal in 1917 and the years immediately following. Justice Ellis later explained the situation while taking the opportunity to praise the legal and judicial schemes then in place. "We have in this State an almost perfect system which makes possible an expeditious and inexpensive determination of every litigated case," he asserted. Substantial credit for the situation, Ellis believed, belonged to the legislature. "During the period from 1915 to 1923 inclusive, the Legislature did little or nothing to disturb our practice and procedure Acts." Ellis added, "In other words, the Legislature did not undertake to direct the courts how and in what manner and by what forms justice should be served or the business of the court should be transacted."[12]

Governor Catts, on the other hand, definitely desired to leave his imprint on the court and the judicial system. The reality of a contentious legislature blocked most approaches to the court that he might take. The solons, on the other hand, could not forestall use of his appointment powers, and an opportunity to exercise them appeared shortly. The circumstances arose out of the desire of former legislator Rivers H. Buford, then serving as state attorney at Marianna, to attain a supreme court seat. He announced his intentions one year before the 1918 primary date but found his issue only after reading of the court's plans for its 1917 summer recess. Especially, he learned that Justice Shackleford intended to depart with his family for North Carolina "to spend several months." Buford hurried to Tallahassee's principal newspaper office to vent his sentiments. "To the *Daily Democrat* Mr. Buford was severe in his denunciation of the supreme court for taking a recess for three months, one fourth of the year, and absolutely suspending for that period," the newspaper's account recited. The item then quoted Buford, as follows:

> It is a most serious matter. Lawyers and litigants are greatly inconvenienced, and frequently financially hurt, because they cannot get their cases heard by this court. I have cases now pending before it which should receive immediate attention and I know of many other lawyers who are in the same fix. The truth is, this court should have no adjourned session. I do not mean that individual members of the court should not have a vacation. But there are five members of the court, three constitute a quorum, and it could be easily arranged for only two of them to take vacations and leave the other three in Tallahassee for the transaction of business. This is one of the most needed reforms in Florida.[13]

Meanwhile, Governor Catts endeavored to find a way to rid himself of Attorney General Thomas F. West. An independently elected and powerful figure in his own right, West had short-circuited several of the governor's initiatives. Most recently, in July he had issued an opinion declaring unconstitutional Catts's "selective veto" of appropriations. The governor believed a supreme court appointment just the ticket to entice West to resign and proposed to the legislature that an additional justice be added to the panel. The body declined to accommodate the request, and so Catts bided his time.[14]

The fortuitous moment came for the governor the day after publication of Buford's denunciation of the court. That morning, rumors found their way into print that Justice Shackleford suddenly had resigned. The abrupt action caught everyone by surprise. The jurist insisted simply that he desired to return to Tampa to practice law, given the onset of the world war. "The law firm of Shackleford and Shackleford, two sons of the eminent justice of the supreme court of the state of Florida, had been broken by the call of the country for its stalwart manhood," the *Tampa Morning Tribune* explained. "One son responded, leaving one alone. The father, full of honors and desirous of doing his part in giving of his blood to the cause, comes home from the capital of the state and joins with the son left at home in keeping the firm intact, and in caring for the business of its clients." The timing of the incident, of course, suggested otherwise. Embarrassment from and anger at Buford's charges may have played their roles as well.[15]

Regardless, Shackleford's decision found ready acceptance in the governor's office. The resignation document arrived there on August 27, and Catts immediately appointed West to fill the vacancy. The onetime attorney general had taken up his new responsibilities by September 1. "Judge Thomas F. West entered the supreme court building this morning with an arm full of papers and books, was greeted by Clerk G. Tolbert [sic] Whitfield and those justices who are not spending their vacations out of town, and began to make himself at home in the chambers made vacant by Judge Shackleford, when he left Tallahassee yesterday for Tampa to resume the practice of law," a reporter observed. "Judge West gave his commission to Clerk Whitfield and asked him to lock it up for him. There is no ceremony or public oath for the swearing in of a supreme court justice. The court is not in session now." Most court observers believed West an excellent addition to the tribunal. As the *Tampa Morning Tribune* later noted, "His selection . . . was completely satisfactory to people of all factions."[16]

The fires of political discontent started by Rivers Buford in 1917 continued to flare the next year. The law required Justices West and Whitfield to stand for reelection, with Buford already announced for the race. The challenger chose to face Whitfield, leaving West without opposition. While most court races rarely saw the incumbent leave Tallahassee, Buford made "a strenuous campaign" throughout the state. Whitfield declined to adopt the same schedule but advertised widely. His press notices countered Buford's attacks on the court's pace and vacation calendar by stressing that Whitfield, a native of the capital city, "is noted for being always on duty at Tallahassee." They added: "His style suits the position he occupies. By nature and by experience he is fitted to be a part in the administration of justice." The ads concluded, "He is admired by his fellow justices."[17]

The appeal sufficed and Whitfield, in the words of one newspaper summary, "ran away from his opponent Rivers Buford." The same journal approved the results. "The vote given Mr. Justice Whitfield is, as we believed it would be, one of the handsomest ever polled by a man asking for retention of the seat in this August body. Judge Whitfield made very little active canvas and has been over the state but little in his entire time as justice of the court; but his ability and his worth have become so well known over Florida that we predict it will be many years before the people will consent to exchange him for any young man who offers no more reason for trying to displace him than that of mere personal ambition, no matter how laudable that ambition might be." The newspaper's editorial continued, "As now composed the supreme court of Florida is one of the ablest bodies of its kind in the country, and its opinions are classed among the most convincing and law deciding of any, especially in the South."[18]

The 1918 campaign stood out for an additional reason beyond Justice Whitfield's victory over Rivers Buford, and it involved a theme that would return to bedevil the court in the decades ahead. Anxious to express his patriotic support for the war effort and with time on his hands given a lack of electoral opposition, Justice West took to the stump to build morale and sell liberty bonds around the state. Unfortunately, the veteran public official had yet to accommodate himself entirely to the requirements of a judicial temperament and continued to rely upon the fiery oratory that Florida's political wars had inculcated in him. He told audiences initially that the world conflict boiled down to "Mohammedism against Christianity." He assured them, "We can pray God for help because we believe that the great issue involved is Christian civilization." He would add, "We will not become prussian slaves." Apparently advised that Prussians were Christian, by July he revised his argument to proclaim "that the great issue which is involved is human liberty and Christian civilization." Listeners saw the jurist as "an eloquent speaker, forceful and earnest," but he had set a precedent with his rhetoric that in the future would redound to the court's detriment.[19]

Until 1923, as the excitement of Florida's boom era swung into full volume, the court retained the same personnel, and its members carefully reconstructed a positive public image as hardworking jurists. A steadily building caseload, though, offered a substantial impediment. In 1919 the legislature again considered adding another member to the tribunal but decided instead to allow the use of circuit court judges to aid in clearing the increasingly congested calendar. For the time being the change accomplished its goal. Two years afterward the panel faced 342 new cases on its docket and disposed of 323 appeals. The effort drew praise. "There is nothing like the amount of work pending as has been in years gone by," a widely circulated report averred. "The court was at one time several months behind with their work, but at this time they are practically up with it, and indications are they will be waiting on attorneys for their argument in cases before the fall is gone." The 1921 legislature agreed with the praise and raised the jurists' salaries from forty-five hundred to five thousand dollars per year.[20]

These years passed happily around the court. Governor Catts by January 1921 had departed public office, and new chief executive Cary A. Hardee had proclaimed in his inaugural address that "a free, untrammeled and independent judiciary must ever remain the bulwark of individual liberty." Despite increased workloads, court members enjoyed plenty of opportunity for leisure and other noncourt activities. Justice Browne spent a good deal of time engaged in business as a national officer of the Elks organization, while Justices Ellis and Whitfield served the vestry of Tallahassee's St. John's Episcopal Church. Ellis also honed his golf skills, often aided by young caddy Richard W. Ervin. Justice Taylor sat as a member of the board of electors of New York University, and Justice West labored on behalf of the "Inter-church movement." Vacations of several months duration returned, with the court reconvening in early October.[21]

So positive had the court's image become by 1923 that, at the instance of a new friend who once had been antagonistic, the panel gained even more help. Rivers Buford, fresh from his 1918 court defeat, had rebounded in 1920 to capture the attorney general's office. Having thereafter associated closely with the tribunal and learned firsthand of its workload, Buford recommended in January 1923 that the legislature add a sixth justice. The measure easily passed the senate but ran into unexpected trouble in the house where twenty-six of sixty-six members cast votes against it. Governor Hardee quickly signed the measure, though, and soon designated his old legislative friend Glenn Terrell of Sumter County to the position. A onetime state representative and senator, Terrell also had served as an assistant attorney general and as counsel to the Internal Improvement Trust Fund and the Everglades Drainage District. Terrell accepted the appointment effective May 15.[22]

The addition of the sixth justice meant more in terms of the court's workload than might first catch the eye. Constitutional and legislative authorization in place before the 1911 court reduction had permitted the panel to act in two divisions. That authority remained in effect and later was supplemented. Once Justice Terrell took his seat, the court could utilize it and, within a short time, had done so. The chief justice headed Division B with Division A supervised by the senior justice as "presiding justice." To prevent forum shopping, the clerk assigned cases based on the number affixed to each when he docketed it; even-numbered cases to Division A, odd-numbered to Division B. The court scheduled sessions so that one division could meet in the courtroom for oral arguments, while the other conducted its business in the conference room. As a practical matter, the court now performed almost all of its work in separate divisions and resolved most cases without written opinions. One wit, as a result of this state of affairs, observed satirically that the author of the court's "most intelligent opinions" was "Judge Per Curiam." If a justice determined a written opinion to be necessary, the decision circulated among the justices of both divisions. A final decision required a majority vote of the entire court with any justice permitted to submit a concurring or dissenting opinion. According to law, capital cases and suits involving the interpretation of the state or federal constitutions had to be submitted to the entire court.[23]

The 1923 legislature, probably at Governor Hardee's instance, tried to encourage a second personnel change that year. Senators John P. Stokes and J. Turner Butler pressed legislation that would have permitted Justice Taylor to retire. Born in 1849, Taylor had reached seventy-four years of age and, seemingly, found it increasingly difficult to maintain the court's slightly more demanding pace. In final form the retirement act allowed any justice to leave the court on full salary at age seventy-four and with thirty years' consecutive service. Taylor struggled with the decision. Finally, he announced in September that he would retire January 1, 1924, subject to the right to revoke his decision at any time before that date. Friends, sparked by *Tampa Morning Tribune* editorials, urged the venerable jurist to reconsider. He did so on December 8 without explanation.[24]

It may have been that Justice Taylor simply was awaiting the inauguration of a new governor to tender his final resignation. That event occurred in January 1925 when Jacksonville's former mayor, John W. Martin, succeeded Hardee. On February 28, Taylor resigned. Two days later, Martin replaced him on the tribunal with the governor's own close friend and adviser, Louie W. Strum, Jacksonville's city attorney and previously Senator J. Turner Butler's law partner. At age thirty-five, Strum was hailed erroneously as "the youngest man named to the Supreme Court in the history of the state." Martin described him for Floridians as "an active, virile, energetic man and a capable and efficient attorney." Strum took his seat effective March 2.[25]

The year 1925 proved to be an active one, indeed. In the spring, the legislature answered the call of the Florida State Bar Association for reform of the bar admissions process. Under then current practice, supreme court members individually supervised examinations and decided upon questions of passing and failing. In 1922, though, Miami attorney Armstead Brown had achieved election as the state bar association's president on a pledge to back legislation for the creation of a board of bar examiners. Twice the legislature turned the proposal down, but by 1925 boom-era conditions had swelled each class of bar applicants to the point that the legislature realized the need to act. The measure in final form created a board of nine members, two each from the state's four congressional districts and a chairman. It mandated three examinations per year and required most persons desiring to practice law to go before the board and pass its test. Separate laws, already on the books, exempted graduates of the John B. Stetson University Law School and the University of Florida Law School, affording those individuals a "diploma privilege." In August, Governor Martin designated Jacksonville's Francis P. Fleming as chairman of the new board. Members included Arthur L. Auvil of Dade City; Walter O. Sheppard, Fort Myers; Roy H. Chapman, Lake City; Robert E. Davis, Gainesville; Philip D. Beall, Pensacola; W. W. Wright, Quincy; Ernest Metcalf, West Palm Beach; and Robert H. Anderson, Jacksonville.[26]

The 1925 legislature also took steps to rectify a situation that had become a national embarrassment. The problem concerned the method of selecting the chief justice. Since 1888 the position had been filled by lot. The justices would open a book to a random page, and the one nearest the alphabet's end would win. Sometimes panel members used the Bible, and the man who came closest to a selected verse became chief justice. Whatever the method, the lottery system created perceived inequities. Several court members had served lengthy terms without sitting as chief, some had served multiple terms as chief, and others had been afforded the chance after only a few months' service. Two had gained the honor on their first day in office.[27]

The matter claimed national attention in January 1923, when Justice Taylor prevailed. The method of selection that year had utilized the Bible. Each court member cut to a page division, then took the last digit on the odd-numbered page. The justice with the highest number then won the chief's role. The first concern arose because Taylor's son-in-law, Justice Ellis, believed that his father-in-law had cheated in order to deprive Ellis of the right to preside. "I had never been chief justice, so I was pleased when I cut a '7' page," he later related to law clerk James C. Adkins. "This was the high number and looked like a sure winner. Taylor was the last one to cut. He took the Bible, opened it, and said, 'I have 9.'" The story concluded: "Then he shut the book quickly, before anyone could check it. I know he didn't have a 9!" Ellis declined to voice his concerns publicly. "I couldn't question the honesty of my father-in-law and the dean of the Court."

The matter did not end there. Within a few weeks, the *Louisville Courier Journal*, a major Kentucky newspaper, had deplored Florida's selection method as "lamentable." The editorial, picked up by other journals throughout the country, went on to specify, "Naming chief justices by lottery is based upon the fallacious theory that all members of a supreme court are equally competent to be its head." It added, "The rule of seniority is everywhere and at all times and as to all services a target for criticism, but it is a custom in the business world to consider experience educative and the experienced man valuable upon account of his experience if his general equipment is good."[28]

The 1925 legislature listened and proposed a state constitutional amendment that allowed court members to make their own selection for chief justice rather than be bound by a lottery. Following approval by voters in November 1926, the justices agreed to first award the position to those who had not yet served, beginning with Ellis. Thereafter, the chief justiceship would be rotated every two years in order of seniority. Tribunal members credited this custom with preserving collegiality and "prevent[ing] contests within the Court." It also established that the position of chief justice was honorific and administrative, not substantively different from the positions held by other justices. With occasional deviations, the rotation system has remained the method of selecting chief justices. As fate would have it, Ellis won the lottery to serve a brief interim term between the November 1926 election and the amendment's January 1927 effective date. Happily for him, the deal held and he immediately served a two-year term under the new provision.[29]

Back in 1925, even more changes had occurred that touched upon the court. Governor Martin had won election based upon an aggressive pro-business and development agenda that included enhanced emphasis on transportation improvements, Everglades drainage, and other major programs. The supreme court's tendency to interpret the constitution so as to limit state power appeared as a potentially dangerous obstacle to him. In the circumstances and likely with Justice Strum's guidance, Martin moved to remake the panel into a body more favorable to his "modern" concepts of governmental action. Particularly, he learned that Justice Browne and Chief Justice West never had grown deeply fond of Tallahassee and supreme court life. The former yearned to return to his home in lively Key West, while West preferred to live near his hometown of Milton in west Florida. Seizing upon these circumstances, Martin arranged for new circuit judgeships to be created suitable to the two jurists' desires.[30]

The governor's plan worked well enough, although not exactly according to the timetable he had expected. In June, both Browne and West initially accepted Martin's proffer of a circuit judgeship, and the state senate confirmed both men. West, however, experienced a sudden change of heart and declined to resign from the supreme bench. Nonplussed, the governor replaced Browne with former bar president Armstead Brown, a man of strong pro-business inclinations who enjoyed wide respect among the members of the organized bar and business community. Then the Miami law partner of former state senator John P. Stokes, Brown brought powerful connections to the court including direct ties to the state's most dynamic and booming metropolitan area. He assumed his seat on July 1.[31]

The apparent setback to his plans notwithstanding, Governor Martin persevered in his attempt to replace Justice West and, in so doing, he enlisted two close allies, Attorney General Buford and former state senate president John B. Johnson. In early November, on the eve of a special legislative session, the two men announced their intention to contest the seats of Chief Justice West and Justice Ellis in the 1926 elections. When that pressure failed to accomplish a resignation, the governor went ahead and sent West's name to the state senate for confirmation as circuit judge based upon the jurist's "announced willingness." This action finally sufficed. West submitted the long anticipated resignation on November 23. Martin, at Strum's urging, lost no time in appointing Attorney General Buford to the vacancy. When the new tribunal member joined the panel on December 4, the ensuing court reorganization resulted, almost miraculously, in the advancement of Justice Brown to the chief justiceship. The celebration must have run late and loud that night at the governor's mansion.[32]

As it turned out, though, Governor Martin's dreams mostly were to die aborning thanks to events that soon came near to breaking the supreme court. Within months following Justice Buford's accession to the tribunal, Florida's boom collapsed, state finances plunged alarmingly, a power struggle with the Ku Klux Klan diverted the governor, and a flood of litigation poured into the state's court system. During 1926 alone, 469 new appeals reached the supreme court, a number 125 percent greater than the panel had received in 1915. The next year 624 new appeals added to an increasing backlog, even though the justices disposed of 481 cases. By 1929 the clerk docketed 797 new matters, with 700 cases already pending. And so it went.[33]

Not all of the justices—isolated as they were in Tallahassee and court chambers—believed that their workload problems stemmed from litigants' increased demands. According to Justice Ellis, lawyers deserved blame for most of the court's woes. Inept pleadings, repetitive briefs, longwinded oral arguments, and trial records bloated with irrelevant testimony made it impossible for the court to act with efficiency or justice. "Visualize this situation," Ellis complained in one speech to a local bar. "A judge sits down to his desk with a record of eight hundred or a thousand pages. . . . Can you imagine his dismay if he finds a brief as large as the record?" In most instances, Ellis admonished, "a clear, succinct, statement of the salient points involved in each case may be made on a page of typewritten matter." Justice Terrell concurred. In a 1927 opinion he railed that "the record in this case covers more than twelve hundred pages, the major portion of which is irrelevant, immaterial, and foreign to the issues presented." He added, "It is impregnated from one end to the other with foul, obscene, filthy, scandalous, and lecherous matter that could have had no purpose whatever except to scandalize or embarrass some one connected with the case." If lawyers would stay on point, "they would not only greatly reduce the labors of this court but they would be amazed at the favorable comment they would have on their skill as practitioners and would save their clients thousands of dollars."[34]

Whether from lawyers' inadequacies and incompetence or simple proliferation of litigation, the court found itself overwhelmed with work. The *Florida State Bar Association Law Journal* joked that the shortest time between filing an appeal and getting a decision required "five years and three months, not counting the second petition for a rehearing," whereas the longest time remained "undetermined in this State, as the case is still pending." In fact, the docket had become so crowded by decade's end that as many as two years could elapse between the filing of an appeal and the rendering of a decision.[35]

The 1929 legislature, beset with concerns stemming from the state's dire economic situation, nonetheless made time to seek a solution for the problem. The solons first considered adding a seventh justice by the long and uncertain procedure of constitutional amendment. Taylor County representative Claude Pepper then suggested the creation of an intermediate court of appeals and the vesting of authority in the supreme court for specifying all procedures for practice and pleading. Ultimately, a compromise called for the appointment of three commissioners to evaluate records and render decisions in cases assigned to them by the court. The enabling statute specified that each commissioner should be an attorney "of good moral and professional character . . . and learned in the law." The justices required several secret ballots before selecting the commissioners in late July. The men named were Sam M. Mathews of Jacksonville; Charles O. Andrews, Orlando; and Charles E. Davis, Miami. Having reached that point, the court declared a vacation of six weeks beginning August 1.[36]

The justices did not necessarily welcome the commissioner compromise, but the scheme proved helpful over time. Justice Brown, for one, fulminated into 1930 about the innovation. "This measure . . . has added to the work of the Justices," he informed state bar members, "because, in addition to their own work, they must carefully examine the opinions written by the commissioners, as well as records and briefs in the cases so written, before they can be approved and adopted as the opinions and decisions of the court." As Brown informed his audience, the court made no formal distinction between commissioners and justices in the assignment of cases, and the commissioners' opinions became final only upon the approval of the justices in both divisions. In practice, though, the commissioners focused on cases that could be decided on the record without additional oral argument and did not require a written opinion. Brown's sentiments to the contrary, the commissioners' contributions did make a difference almost immediately. In 1931 the panel disposed of nearly 60 percent of its docketed cases, and for the first time in seven years, case dispositions outnumbered new filings.[37]

Even the achievements posted by the commissioners did not blunt the desire of Justice Brown and others to increase the court's size. Brown campaigned before the bar, for instance, to enlist allies in his cause. He insisted that, based upon the number of appellate judges in each state, "the Supreme Court of Florida turns out more opinions and decisions than any other Supreme Court in this Country." By the legislature's convening in April 1931, he had garnered sufficient support to convince the legislature to propose a constitutional amendment to add the requested seventh justice. It took a fight, however, with court allies battling house opponents intent upon cutting the court to five members and reducing the justices' salaries. "Let them get caught up with their work, and don't pay 'em but $4,000 a year until they do," one Depression-weary legislator argued. Eventually, an informal compromise moved the amendment to approval. The expansion measure went to the voters in November 1932, while the legislature repealed the court commissioners' law effective the same month and cut the justices' then current salaries of $9,600 to $8,500 per year.[38]

As these legislative battles ensued, the panel experienced a surprise change in personnel. On January 13, 1931, the tribunal had chosen Louie Strum as its chief justice. One month and eight days later, President Herbert Hoover nominated Strum to the federal district court, apparently after Justice Terrell had turned down the same offer. The U.S. Senate confirmed Strum on February 28, and he resigned from the supreme court on March 3. This vacancy presented Governor Doyle Carlton with an opportunity. A moderate by Florida standards, Carlton was preparing for the upcoming 1932 Florida elections. It does not seem likely that the governor had already selected a candidate to back, but he knew that he did not want popular and very conservative Attorney General Fred Henry Davis to remain in his cabinet. So Carlton took a leaf from Governor Catts's book and quickly elevated Davis to the supreme bench. Litigation then pending in which Davis was representing the state delayed his departure from the attorney general's office for a few days, placing Davis on the bench March 9.[39]

Now minus one of its most gifted leaders, the court headed into the election year full of hope for ratification of the proposed court expansion amendment. It released statistics on the caseload with which its members dealt, emphasizing 1931 figures that showed an unprecedented 1,018 cases disposed of during the year. It also attempted to educate the public on the nature of its work. "The most common cases are suits regarding foreclosure, of validity of statutes, questions of mortgages, breach of contracts, taxation, enforcement of payment of public bonds, and damage suits for personal injuries," one report explained. Yet these and other efforts found few receptive ears as the agony of Depression gripped the state ever more tightly, and court decisions often appeared to be upholding the rights of the affluent against those of the needy. The result came preordained. Voters "overwhelmingly rejected" the "exceedingly unpopular" amendment by a vote of 78,265 to 38,445 at the same moment that they voted nearly 3 to 1 for Franklin Delano Roosevelt as president of the United States and David Sholtz, who outpolled former governors John W. Martin and Cary A. Hardee, as governor of Florida. Contemporaneously, the court commissioners law expired, and court members suddenly shared at a new and higher level the anxieties of their fellow Floridians about the future.[40]

Jefferson Beale Browne, Supreme Court Justice, 1917–1923; Supreme Court Chief Justice, 1923–1925

Jefferson Beale Browne's tenure on the Florida Supreme Court represented the last gasp of nineteenth-century jurisprudence to reach the tribunal. He had been born at Key West on June 6, 1857. His father, Joseph Beverly Browne, had moved to the island from Virginia at the age of sixteen to join the maritime salvage business of his uncle, the town's mayor. Joseph married Mary Neives Ximinez, the daughter of a prominent Cuban émigré shipowner. Through his family connections, the young man soon emerged as one of the city's governing elite. Before he turned thirty, Joseph B. Browne had served as a delegate to the 1838–39 Florida constitutional convention at St. Joseph and had received appointment as a federal marshal, a post that he held for ten years. He then assumed the position of clerk of court for the federal district court in Key West and also served several terms as mayor. Following the Civil War, Browne won election to the Florida House of Representatives.[41]

As the only son in a prominent middle-class family, young Jeff Browne "enjoyed from birth such social and educational advantages as well-to-do parents of that era could provide." He began his education in public and private schools at Key West, then completed his studies at private academies in Maryland and Virginia. He returned to south Florida about 1876 to prepare for a legal career. He labored briefly as Monroe County surveyor before accepting in 1878 a position as second assistant light keeper at the newly built Fowey Rocks lighthouse near Key Biscayne. The work proved undemanding, permitting the budding attorney ample time to study his law books. After fifteen months, Browne decided to formalize his legal education by attending law school at the University of Iowa. He graduated in 1880 and soon achieved admission to the state and federal bars in Iowa and Florida. Shortly after returning to his native city, he saw his new career well launched when he received appointment to the positions of city and county attorney.[42]

In addition to his duties as a public counsel, Browne built a thriving general practice. His business card proclaimed his willingness "to practice in any court," and he proved open to handling everything from divorces to criminal trials. His client list soon included businesses and financial institutions as well as others with the kinds of legal needs that the unique island might generate. Like most local attorneys, he handled his share of admiralty cases, including one in which he prevented the federal government and a Navy crew from claiming a portion of the prize money awarded to his clients for capturing a vessel during the Spanish American War.[43]

Browne's most notorious case saw him representing three Cubans arrested for murder in 1891. The defendants had come to Key West from Ybor City, having been expelled by Tampans in the wake of cigar factory labor violence. They faced vigilante action as local anti-Cuban sentiment ran high from allegations of gang activity and secret assassinations. Crowds milled daily outside the Monroe County jail, threatening to lynch the defendants. The press published inflammatory articles, and the county commission offered rewards for their conviction. In June 1891, former supreme court justice Henry Laurens Mitchell—then a circuit judge and soon to become governor—ordered the defendants to Tampa. A citizens' committee thereupon warned Charles F. Dupont, the county's African American sheriff, not to allow the prisoners to leave the island. As Dupont protected his charges, a crowd of five hundred or so surrounded the jail until the Tampa steamer left port. The first trial, following in June 1893, ended in a hung jury. Despite hostile public opinion, Browne acted resolutely in requesting a change of venue for the second trial, arguing that the only prospective jurors in Key West capable of rendering a fair verdict would be disqualified because they spoke only Spanish. The court denied his motion, and a jury convicted the men. Browne secured a supreme court reversal. "We do not think it likely," the court held, "that a stronger case [for a change of venue] will ever arise." The justices labeled the failure to grant the motion "a palpable abuse of judicial discretion."[44]

As was true of many ambitious Florida attorneys, Browne's professional interests soon turned to politics. Active in Democratic Party affairs, he received his reward in 1886 when President Grover Cleveland's administration named him Key West postmaster, a plum patronage position. Browne modernized the local postal service, replacing a small mail shed with an ample facility suitable for the state's largest city. The incumbent returned Cleveland's favor in 1888 by serving as a pro-Cleveland delegate to the Democratic national convention at St. Louis, where he joined the committee named to notify the president of his renomination. Browne returned to the convention in 1904 and 1908. Four years later, he cast one of Florida's electoral votes for fellow Democrat Woodrow Wilson. Party work had presented Browne by then with a very special reward. Through Democratic acquaintances he had met Frances Williams Atkinson, grand-niece of General John S. Williams, Mexican War hero and former U.S. senator from Kentucky. The couple wed on June 19, 1889, and their marriage produced a son and a daughter.[45]

The year after his marriage, Browne stepped into state political office by winning election as Monroe County state senator. His tenure coincided with a period of intense rancor within the party. Conservative Bourbon Democrats, aligned with the state's railroad interests, battled the progressive wing supported by Populists and the Farmers' Alliance. A "reform wing" steered a middle course. Led by Senator Wilkinson Call, that faction favored terminating railroad land grants yet balked at the more radical aims of the Populists. Browne aligned himself with this reform wing and, although a neophyte legislator, managed election as state senate president.[46]

In his capacity as senate leader, Browne played a large role in one of the most significant challenges to Bourbon rule in Florida. The election of a U.S. senator ranked high on the legislative agenda. Governor Frances P. Fleming and Pensacola railroad magnate William D. Chipley vehemently opposed Call's reelection. Rules required a two-thirds legislative vote, and nearly two months and eighty-eight ballots passed without a decision. Then, on May 26, seventeen Bourbon state senators fled to Georgia believing that they could stall Call's hopes by depriving the assemblage of a quorum. Browne ruled, though, that a joint session required the presence of only a majority of the total membership of both houses. Call thereupon achieved reelection with only one dissenting vote. The governor refused to issue Call's certificate of election, but Browne enjoyed vindication when the U.S. Senate agreed in June 1892 to seat the incumbent.[47]

Browne's life reached a turning point in 1891 with a casual encounter at Tampa, where the exotic Tampa Bay Hotel was opening to guests. Browne attended the celebration only to find himself buttonholed by railroad baron Henry Flagler, who tried to convince the Key West native that only his railroad could finance and engineer the desirable but difficult route to the island. From that point forward, Browne championed Flagler in the legislature. Among other things, the senate president used his authority to defeat the renewal of Key West extension charters for the three railroads that held them. He also introduced a bill granting the exclusive franchise to Flagler's company.[48]

Other turning points soon appeared in Browne's life. After failing at a bid for the 1892 Florida Democratic gubernatorial nomination, the senator finished his term of office and returned to Key West as collector of customs, another patronage position courtesy of the Cleveland administration. This period witnessed intense revolutionary activity in Cuba. As a result, Browne had his hands full enforcing the American neutrality laws as José Martí and his followers launched numerous expeditions from Key West, sending men, arms, ammunition, and provisions on ships sailing from its port. He also was caught in the middle of controversies concerning the importation of Spanish labor over the objections of Cuban cigar workers, a contretemps that hastened the further removal of the cigar industry to Tampa.[49]

Meanwhile, Browne remained professionally and politically active, although he mostly avoided personal electoral contests. From 1903 to 1907 he served as chairman of the Florida Railroad Commission, and from 1904 to 1908 he served on the Democratic National Committee. He helped to found the Florida State Bar Association in 1907, serving either as president or vice president during its first three years. Also in 1907 he strove unsuccessfully to rid Key West of saloons, running unsuccessfully the following year for governor on a platform of statewide Prohibition. Branded by many voters as a "corporation man," he carried only Monroe and Jackson counties.[50]

Browne proudly boosted his hometown while maintaining active participation in civic life. He sat on the board of public works and helped to establish the Key West Rotary Club, serving as its first president. In 1896 he published a *National Geographic* article touting the advantages that would flow from railroad construction through the Florida Keys and expressing his belief that the city could rival Newport, Rhode Island. When Flagler's line finally arrived at Key West in 1912, Browne issued *Key West, the Old and the New*. It contained both a history of the city and a catalog of its diverse commercial and natural attractions. A genuine love for the city inspired his paeans, but his one-third interest in the eponymous Jefferson Hotel provided a pecuniary motive as well. A prolific poet, Browne frequently celebrated the island in verse. Other poems explored more universal themes including love, beauty, virtue, and, poignantly, his daughter's death. Five of his poems were published in a 1932 anthology edited by Florida poet laureate Vivian Yeiser Laramore. "Perhaps if all our circuit judges were poets," Laramore later commented, "we could hope for justice tempered with mercy."[51]

Beyond all of his other endeavors, Jefferson Browne enjoyed a lengthy judicial career, although its start differed from the norm in the route it took. He commenced with election to the supreme court. The story began in 1916, by which time Justice Robert Cockrell's opinions had angered powerful economic interests. At the time reelection to the court normally appeared a foregone conclusion. Sometimes a member would resign in midterm and permit the governor to name a replacement, but no incumbent had been unseated since the 1885 constitution's ratification. Now, though, railroad owners, familiar with Browne from his days as railroad commissioner, enlisted him to challenge Cockrell in the Democratic primary. Not surprisingly the incumbent proved an inept campaigner, and Browne won easily. On his first day in office, January 2, 1917, the newly seated jurist luckily chose a lot that made him chief justice.[52]

Browne settled, although somewhat uneasily as it turned out, into the judicial role. Comfortable with exercising authority, he insisted on due deference from lawyers and litigants. "[He] demanded recognition," lawyer Leo Foster recalled, and his professional demeanor was "dictatorial" and "very opinionated." Philosophically, he adhered to the classical jurisprudence of the late nineteenth century, a perspective that stressed limited government, laissez-faire economic theory, and the exercise of judicial review to protect individual liberty. He emerged, as a result, as the tribunal's leading champion of property rights. Though principally concerned with threats to property rights, he also criticized the manner in which "the principles of the constitution . . . have been nibbled away by decisions of the courts in order to affirm [criminal] convictions." In Prohibition cases, he construed the state's power very narrowly, holding that the ownership of liquor should be entitled to the same respect as any other property right. He opposed the strengthening of federal power, denouncing prominent nationalists from Alexander Hamilton to Theodore Roosevelt. Unchecked national power, he warned, ultimately could deprive the states of the power to enforce racial segregation, prevent miscegenation, control their own elections, or enact other measures "for the purpose of keeping our white citizens free from mixture with the African race."[53]

Browne reserved his heaviest opprobrium for the police power doctrine, a legal concept invented to "sugar-coat" the "omnipotence and absolutism in the law-making branch of state governments." His critique combined an elitist disdain for democracy with a traditional fear of incipient socialism. "A veritable super-constitution . . . has been enthroned in our jurisprudence," he complained, "something greater than the written constitution, something more sacred than liberty, something dearer than rights of property, something more powerful than the obligations of contract, but something more dangerous than the wildest nightmare of German invasion or the ranting of the Reds whom we are deporting." He excoriated certain activist judges for acceding to "whatever popular fancy or popular prejudice demands." Like many other formalist critics of unrestrained popular rule, he enthusiastically supported the Restatement Project of the American Law Institute. Founded in 1923, the ALI posited that definitive statements of the common law, distilled by experts from the leading law schools and reviewed by other academics and judges, properly could restore the logical taxonomy of legal rules that had been disturbed by ill-advised and contradictory statutory enactments. Such a restatement, Browne asserted, "should come pure gold, and he will be a bold man who will undertake to question it."[54]

As mentioned earlier in this chapter, Browne tired of his duties on the supreme court after only a few years on the bench. The collaborative work of an appellate judge did not suit his personality, particularly after his term as chief justice expired. Accordingly, he explored a circuit judgeship and the delights of a trial court. He loathed Tallahassee and longed to return to Key West. Governor John Martin and the 1925 legislature accommodated him by creating a new Monroe County judicial circuit and making Browne its first judge. Ten years afterward his reach expanded to include Dade County when his jurisdiction was revised to combine that county with Monroe.[55]

Jefferson Browne's rich and long life ended in 1937. He suffered a heart attack on April 12 during a session of his court in Miami. After spending two weeks in a hospital there, he asked for an ambulance to take him back to Key West. He was still working, dictating notes to his secretary, when he died at his home on May 4, a month shy of his eightieth birthday. An unusual provision in his will bequeathed his "entire collection of wines, liquors, cordials, etc." to fifteen friends, including some of the state's most prominent lawyers. "I am not unmindful of the fact, that the gift to each one will be small," he acknowledged, "but I would like for them sometime to pour out a draft and holding it up say, 'Here's to Jeff Browne.'"[56]

Thomas Franklin West, Supreme Court Justice, 1917–1925; Supreme Court Chief Justice, 1925

Where Jefferson Browne's election in 1916 afforded south Florida its first seat on the supreme court since 1868, Thomas West's selection the following year secured tribunal representation for west Florida for the first time since 1904. West was born near Milton on November 23, 1874, and, as such, he represented a younger generation than did Browne. His parents, Leonard F. West and Frances Elizabeth McArthur West, enjoyed a lifestyle substantially more comfortable than did most area residents. A North Carolina native, Leonard stood out among his long-time neighbors. "Mr. West was a native of Santa Rosa county, having been born here about seventy-five years ago," a 1922 obituary incorrectly informed readers. "Throughout the many years of his long life he had taken an active part in the development of this county, working for the promotion of every good and worthy effort, and opposing with equal courage the evils that came up for combat. As a teacher, farmer and capitalist his long life was spent in helping to develop the community in which he lived." Leonard made his living as a banker, with supplemental investments in agriculture, sheep raising, and the lumber industry.[57]

Tom thus enjoyed the benefits of a rural but comfortable upbringing, although his family formed a social as well as an economic exception by adhering to the Presbyterian faith rather than the Baptist church to which most of their neighbors belonged. He grew to six feet in height, and a family friend recalled him as "well built, quite handsome." Despite the rudimentary schooling opportunities then available in Santa Rosa County, West gained a solid educational background thanks to his parents. A happy youth, he would be described in future years as possessing "a delightful personality," an easygoing disposition, and manners that were "uniformly polite." It could not be said, on the other hand, that the youth had enjoyed many experiences with the larger world. Mostly, he lived either on his father's farm twelve miles north of Milton or in the town itself. A report of his venture from Milton to nearby DeFuniak Springs in 1894 to attend the State Normal School recorded the journey as "his first ride on a railway train." The "country boy," a resident reminisced, arrived homesick and feeling as if "he had traveled to the very uttermost limit of the earth."[58]

It seems likely that Tom West's horizons, if not the reality of his daily life, already in 1894 ranged far broader than Santa Rosa County and encompassed a future as an attorney. He remained at DeFuniak Springs only two years before returning home. For two additional years he taught school, meanwhile preparing himself for a more advanced education by reading. Subsequently in 1898, the young man enrolled at Washington and Lee University in Lexington, Virginia, to pursue the law. Within one year he had qualified for an LL.B. degree. His university studies had prepared the budding lawyer well, and he easily gained admission to the bar in Santa Rosa County in 1900. For the next twelve years West practiced his profession at Milton and Pensacola. Colleagues remembered, "His distinctive success and advancement not only attested his powers as a resourceful trial lawyer and well fortified counselor but also set at naught any application of the scriptural aphorism that 'a prophet is not without honor save in his own country.'"[59]

West's rise in these early years doubtlessly came due to his family's position and his own determined efforts. Credit also is due his partner. Shortly after graduation from Washington and Lee, he had married Alma Chaffin at Pensacola, daughter of James Alexander and Virginia Victoria Chaffin. The family enjoyed repute as "one of the most prominent and wealthy families of that city," with Alma's father distinguished as "a well-known banker and lumberman in north Florida." A son, Thomas Franklin West Jr., arrived in July 1900. Daughters Josephine and Alma followed.[60]

Having established himself as a professional and family man, West quite naturally, given his circumstances, turned his attention to Democratic politics. In 1902 he achieved election to the Florida House of Representatives, making his first trip to Tallahassee the following January to assume his duties. During the next election cycle he joined the state senate as a staunch supporter of Progressive governor Napoleon Bonaparte Broward. In the capacity of senate president pro tempore and on the governor's behalf, West in 1905 introduced legislation that created the Everglades Drainage District, an enormous reclamation project and one of Broward's priority issues. One year later Broward recognized West's legal skills by placing the senator on a three-member commission to revise and update the state's statutory law. This task had not been undertaken since 1892, and the well-devised code produced by West and his associates remained in force until 1920. In the 1907 legislative session, the now veteran lawmaker assumed further leadership roles, although he chose in 1908 not to seek reelection.[61]

The retirement from legislative concerns did not last for long. In 1911 West returned for two years to the Florida House of Representatives where, once again, he championed Progressive causes. He pushed two major innovations, initiative and referendum. He easily maneuvered a proposed constitutional amendment through the house, and thereafter achieved a difficult victory in the senate with assistance from that body's president, Frederick P. Cone, and despite the ardent opposition of DeFuniak Springs's William W. Flournoy. Attorney General Park M. Trammell backed West's efforts, while Governor Albert W. Gilchrist joined Flournoy in attempting to forestall them. As events resulted, the voters never managed to have their say. In October 1912 the supreme court by a three-to-two vote ruled the measure off the general election ballot due to technical questions about the resolution's final authentication. Justices James R. Whitfield, R. Fenwick Taylor, and William A. Hocker formed the majority, while Justices Robert S. Cockrell and Thomas M. Shackleford dissented.[62]

As hinted by the initiative and referendum experience, West's legislative career had produced an unexpected result. Beginning in the 1903 house session, he had become closely associated with Polk County's Park Trammell. Both men moved to the state senate at the same time, with Trammell besting West for the body's presidency despite Governor Broward's enthusiastic support for West. This awkward conflict soon matured into friendship, with both men supporting Broward's Progressive agenda. When West left the legislature in 1908, he supported Trammell's successful bid for the attorney general's office. Four years later, Trammell announced for governor and threw his support to West for attorney general. West won the Democratic nomination and election without opposition and served through Trammell's term as governor. In 1916 Trammell, who was departing for the U.S. Senate, offered his friend a chance to return home by way of a circuit court appointment. On that occasion West declined, preferring to run for reelection. Again, he won without opposition.[63]

As attorney general, West distinguished himself. His fellow attorneys offered a solid vote of confidence, for example, when they elected him in 1915 as president of the Florida State Bar Association. "During the period that Mr. West has served in the office of attorney general," the *Jacksonville Florida Times-Union* declared in 1917, "he has represented the state in a number of important cases, and practically all of them have been decided in favor of the state. Mr. West has also done practically all of the state's law business since he has been in office, and it has never been necessary to employ additional counsel at public expense when important cases arose." West, as a matter of course, appeared frequently before the state supreme court, and he argued two cases before the U.S. Supreme Court. In one instance, that tribunal upheld West's contention that a Florida law requiring able-bodied men to devote six days of labor per year to road maintenance (or to provide a substitute) did not constitute involuntary servitude. In his "most noteworthy victory," he convinced the court to overturn a federal district court judgment that a state law imposing special license fees on merchants offering discount coupons and premiums violated the commerce and equal protection clauses of the federal constitution.[64]

Once Catts had succeeded Governor Trammell in 1917, the attorney general's relations with the governor's office quickly soured with the result that, within the year, West left the position. The governor and attorney general clashed to the point that Catts quickly yearned to be rid of West and enjoy the support of his friend William W. Flournoy as the state's legal officer. An attempt to expand the court to fill the purpose failed, but Justice Shackleford's resignation in August created the needed vacancy. West joined the tribunal effective September 1. "'Tom' West, as he is called by nearly every one who knows him, comes to the supreme bench with perhaps as many hearty wishes and congratulations as any man who ever stepped into that scene of a lawyer's ambition," the *Tampa Morning Tribune* offered in praise. "His record as attorney general has stamped him as supreme bench material. His clearness of insight in matters judicial, his ability to express himself clearly and succinctly, and his natural judicial mind all mark him as one of the best fitted men in the state for this high position."[65]

On the supreme bench West's jurisprudence displayed the brand of southern progressivism. As might be expected of someone who had served in every branch of government, he did not share Justice Browne's aversion to the police powers doctrine, retaining instead a Progressive faith in the ability of government to exercise its powers wisely on behalf of its citizens. "This does not mean that the State can do no wrong," he recorded, "[but] it does mean that if authority is abused . . . it should be remedied . . . through the orderly processes of government." West generally favored the prosecution side in criminal cases and scorned those who urged the lax enforcement of Prohibition laws. Nor did he subscribe to a decided preference for individual rights over the rights of the community. Citizenship guaranteed individual liberty, he acknowledged, but it also encompassed a "call to service." The jurist regarded with contempt those who asserted their rights while they skirted jury duty, avoided their taxes, failed to vote, or criticized "movements of community interest for social and moral improvement." Many Floridians regarded him as "one of the ablest orators" in the state, and he frequently espoused his ideas at patriotic celebrations where his talents were always in demand.[66]

As a court member, Justice West maintained an active personal, social, and religious life at Tallahassee. He especially enjoyed participation in the Kiwanis service organization. In March 1923 he helped to found the Tallahassee club and served the group as its first president. He had remained deeply committed as well to the Presbyterian Church. The same year that the Kiwanis Club organized, he presided as moderator of the Florida Presbytery, then in session at his hometown of Milton. In addition, he proudly associated with several masonic branches and with the Benevolent and Protective Order of Elks.[67]

Unfortunately, all did not fare well for the justice during his court service years, and that fact contributed to his early departure from the panel. His father's death in December 1922 capped a period of difficulty with respect to West family home life. He and his wife, Alma, had grown estranged and quietly divorced. More happily, on December 27, 1923, he married Mary McDougall. Yet the allures of Tallahassee life, never capturing West's heart, increasingly appealed less to him. When Governor John Martin proffered a circuit judgeship in Escambia and Santa Rosa counties in early 1925, he nearly accepted but chose to remain with the panel that recently had named him chief justice. By November he had changed his mind. "Judge West is a man of exceptional ability, of broad learning, and a well trained judicial mind," the *Milton Gazette* observed, "and his appointment as Circuit Judge in this Circuit will, we believe, be heartily approved by a vast majority of the people of the entire district." By December 1, the same journal had reported, "Former Chief Justice of the Florida Supreme Court, Thomas F. West . . . is now located in Milton where he is prepared to carry on the work of his position." It added, "While Judge West has not decided where he will be located permanently, he is for the time being located in the petit jury room on the second floor of the courthouse, where he is ready to handle such business as shall come before him."[68]

The business of the circuit court appealed to the former justice. He carried his appellate sensibilities to his new job and was not shy in exercising judicial review even at the trial level. In one of his most notable rulings, he declared unconstitutional a statute that authorized the governor to appoint assistant attorneys general and substitute them for elected prosecutors in criminal trials. The law, he believed, represented "a breaking down of our constitutional system" by threatening democratic rule and the separation of powers. The judge justified judicial intervention because of the legislature's tendency "to pay little attention to the constitution." When African Americans invoked the constitution to assert their political rights, on the other hand, West failed to find sufficient substance in their claims to exercise judicial action. In 1928 he upheld the exclusion of black voters, solely on account of their race, from the Democratic primary at Pensacola. "That a political party . . . is a voluntary association of persons [who] should be allowed to make regulations and restrictions concerning those who are to be admitted into its ranks, without Governmental restrictions, would seem to be obvious," he reasoned.[69]

Judge West's life ended, at age fifty-four, on February 23, 1931, in Pensacola, where he was attending to court duties. He had been recuperating from a brief bout of influenza, and his death "occurred suddenly . . . and was a distinct shock to his many friends." The supreme court suspended its business so that the justices could attend the funeral in Milton, where the body was interred. The justices lauded their departed colleague for "serv[ing] the people of Florida with outstanding ability in each of the three departments of their government." They added, "His passing is a loss to the legal profession and to the state." A newspaper editor offered his own thoughts. "Judge West's life is a fine illustration of the value of doing a service well. He shirked no duty, side stepped no responsibility and performed small tasks so well that larger ones, and greater opportunities, were constantly being opened up to him. His life was so useful to Florida that his name is indelibly printed on the pages of her history."[70]

William Glenn Terrell, Supreme Court Justice, 1923–1964; Supreme Court Chief Justice, 1929–1931, 1938–1941, 1957–1959

William Glenn Terrell served on the Florida Supreme Court longer than any other justice, and his lengthy tenure—combined with a voluminous output of opinions and a colorful personality—ensured him a place as one of the most influential jurists in the state's history. Born at Daleville, Mississippi, on July 24, 1877 (or 1878), he was the son of William Henry Terrell, a Presbyterian minister, and Lizzie Crawford, a schoolteacher. As the younger Terrell matured, he grew increasingly sensitive about his age. As a public official he eventually refused to list his birthday in registers and biographical sketches. When research assistants once asked him directly how old he was, he refused to answer, declaring, "A man who'd tell you his age would tell anything."[71]

When he was still a child, Terrell's family sought greater opportunities in Florida than Mississippi could offer them. In 1882 railroad construction was opening much of the Sunshine State's peninsula to settlement. Although Sumter County remained sparsely populated, the Terrells chose a farm there upon which to begin life anew. They made the journey overland. Justice Terrell later recalled first viewing Florida's capital city as the family made their way east and then south. "[It was winter and] the trees were bare," he recorded. "There was no paving. And the property owners had been sparing of paint." He later boasted that he was "the only justice ever to have first seen Tallahassee from a covered wagon."[72]

At the time, Sumter County's future appeared bright as citrus groves increasingly dotted its hills and glades. "A movement is on foot to introduce white labor into the county, and already several colonies have arrived," a correspondent observed that year. "Indeed Sumter County is at present enjoying a boom unequaled by any of the southern counties. Her people are full of life and vim, and a kind that will make any section of country succeed."[73]

The Sumter County boom soon fizzled, but the Terrells opted to remain and make their way with their neighbors. William Henry Terrell farmed with his son's help and served local Presbyterians and other interested persons as chance allowed. "Most of the pioneers of Sumter County were Protestants to whom religion was very important," a local historian explained. "The south in the mid-1800s had a tradition of evangelical protestantism and those who came here from Georgia and the Carolinas were determined to carry on that tradition, even though the sparse population and rough country made it very difficult. The earliest religious meetings were probably held in the open. People of all denominations worshiped together at first, then as the groups became larger, each denomination built a church of its own." The Presbyterian Church at Bushnell, near the Terrells' farm, would not organize until 1912. When it did, the Reverend and Mrs. Terrell, with son Glenn, signed on as charter members. As it turned out, one of his father's religious duties may well have set Glenn's sights on the path he would take in life. Soon after the family's arrival in Sumter, the minister had received an invitation to open each local term of the circuit court with a prayer. He maintained the tradition for years, taking his son with him to listen to court proceedings.[74]

Although rustic surroundings such as those current in Sumter County during the 1880s and 1890s might have impeded the development of a lad's education, Glenn Terrell benefited well from his mother's teaching skills. At first, she tutored him at home. Then, when Bushnell's first school opened in 1886, Lizzie Terrell served as one of its first two teachers with Glenn joining her class. By the mid-1890s, Glenn himself was teaching near Bushnell at the village of Webster. "He sat behind a desk," an interviewer recorded, "in a pine log school in Florida's backwoods." Before long, the teenager received promotion to principal. Former student Ethel Hawkins Vaughn remembered him walking her to school every day and providing solace after one of her sterner teachers disciplined her. "He would take me by the hand and I would skip along, thinking I was well-protected from all the others." According to another pupil, he handled bullies, "some of whom were as old as he was," by offering to "take off his coat and step outside with them." According to a surviving account, "There were no takers, and no more discipline problem either." At various times thereafter, the young educator instructed students not only in Sumter County but also in Levy and Madison.[75]

While struggling to survive on a rural teacher's salary, Terrell reoriented his professional sights and began to read law. He had attended Hamilton County's Jasper Normal Institute in 1898. From there he had pursued classes at the Georgia Normal College at Abbeville, taking a diploma in 1900. To further his plans, he now entered the law studies program at Tennessee's Cumberland University. He received an LL.B. degree there in 1903. Terrell particularly appreciated the education he had received at Cumberland, where a ten-month curriculum attracted aspiring lawyers from the South. The jurist later would encourage ambitious Floridians anxious to begin their careers, including future governor LeRoy Collins, to take advantage of the school's accelerated degree program.[76]

Law degree in hand, Terrell returned to Bushnell in 1903 to open a legal practice, although he continued to teach at times and within a decade headed the county high school as principal. Judge Rhydon M. Call admitted him to the bar at Starke in the fall following his return. "[With the passage of time] he practiced in all state and federal courts," an early biographer noted, "including the supreme court of the United States." The counselor used his homespun manner to advantage when it came to the law, as his colloquial style and modest demeanor frequently caused opposing counsel to underestimate him. M. Lewis Hall recollected a telling first meeting with Terrell in Fort Lauderdale years after the young attorney had commenced his professional labors. By then, Terrell represented the state's Internal Improvement Trust Fund in litigation against Hall's client. Looking around the Broward County courthouse, a remodeled school building, Terrell drawled, "I feel so much more at home in a school room than I do a court room." Once the trial began, Hall admitted, Terrell nonetheless proceeded to give him "a sound licking." Associated Press reporter Malcolm B. Johnson later described Terrell's manner for readers. "[He] has a friendly dignity and a homely way of speaking and writing that cuts away legal terms and lays the law bare to a layman's understanding."[77]

On December 24, 1907, the now experienced attorney and educator married. His bride, Esther Collins, had taught with him at Webster in 1905. For two years thereafter he had finagled to drive her home in his carriage. The union would become one of the most enduring partnerships in Tallahassee society. Justice Stephen C. O'Connell referred to Esther appropriately in later years as "the Grand Lady of the Court." She entertained often, hosted dinners for the justices and their wives, and prepared meals for Terrell and his clerks, whom he often would bring home for a working lunch. When circumstances forced the jurist to give up driving, she chauffeured him. In 1950 she drove them on an Alaska vacation. Those who knew the justice believed that he obliquely expressed his devotion to his wife in a 1956 opinion upholding the constitutionality of an act that conferred pension benefits to wives of circuit judges. "Whatever the skill or degree of service the judge performed for the state, the wife was his indispensable helpmate." The couple felt blessed with four children: Miriam, Doris, Ruth, and Glenn Jr. Doris Terrell, a lawyer herself, would work for several years as her father's secretary and research assistant.[78]

Small-town lawyering, as so often proved the case with others, also led Terrell into politics. In 1909—and against his wife's wishes—he sought election to the Florida House of Representatives. He thereafter served three consecutive terms. The representative followed his house tenure with two terms in the state senate. Terrell loved the give and take of legislative byplay and championed numerous causes during his years at the state capitol. During 1915 and 1917, in the words of a newspaper reporter, "He was the author of what is known as the anti–race track law, the child labor law, county site election law, the law authorizing special tax school district to bond for school houses and improvements, . . . the law accepting the provisions of the federal aid act for public roads, [and] drainage and other laws." He attempted to eliminate secret ballots for voting and to require candidates to swear loyalty oaths to their parties. The 1915 assembly also saw him striving unsuccessfully to gain passage of a constitutional amendment to institute a "grandfather clause" to restrict African American voting rights. The next session found the senator as one of Governor Catts's few allies in the upper house. Terrell supported the governor's programs and helped to block a senate proposal to limit Catts's appointment powers.[79]

Terrell derived numerous rewards from his legislative endeavors. For two years he acted as an assistant attorney general. From 1915 to 1923 he held the lucrative appointments of counsel to the trustees of the Internal Improvement Trust Fund and to the board of commissioners of the Everglades Draining District. From 1915 to 1917 he assisted Attorney General Thomas F. West in preparing appeals to the supreme court, especially in criminal matters. "During the time he has been counsel . . . all the remaining old land grant cases have been litigated and settled, most of them going to the supreme court of the United States, where they were finally disposed of in favor of the state's contention," a reporter noted in 1923. "The counsel for the trustees of the Internal Improvement fund had full charge of this litigation and they involved land and property worth millions of dollars. He has handled successfully many cases before the supreme court of this state, testing the constitutional validity of taxing and other statutes."[80]

Perhaps Terrell's greatest reward, if not the most lucrative one, came on May 11, 1923, when Governor Cary A. Hardee appointed the veteran official and counsel to a newly created seat on the supreme court. With a commission dated May 15, the new justice simply appeared at the court the next morning and, as a newspaper related, "at once assumed his duties." The journal appended, "There were no specific formalities." That November, Justice Terrell ran unopposed for the seat and won election to a full term. By 1929 he had emerged as the most senior court member who had not yet held the position of chief justice. Under recent court practice his fellow jurists thereupon selected him as their chief. Having declined appointment to the federal district court in 1931, he would again attain the honor of court leadership in 1938 and 1957.[81]

Terrell's jurisprudential style eschewed formalist legal reasoning in favor of resolving disputes based on the equities of a case. "Most of the law I know is the difference between right and wrong," he asserted. "The law was important to him, and he followed that," research assistant Wade Hopping recalled, "but he was more interested in justice." Terrell's judicial style squared neatly with the emerging theory, though radical to most, of legal realism, a concept that viewed law as an instrument of public policy and social reform, tolerated judicial discretion, and insisted on the malleability of legal doctrine. "In a changing world marked by the ebb and flow of social and economic shifts," he observed in 1932, "new conditions constantly arise which make it necessary, that no right be without a remedy, to extend the old and tried remedies." Terrell added: "It is the function of the courts to do this. It may be done by working old fields, but, when it becomes necessary, they should not hesitate to 'break new ground' to do so." Federal judge Joseph Hutcheson, a leading realist thinker, summarized Terrell's approach. "Instead of just taking the law as it was handed down to him by those of old time, he dug and delved, worked and found out, and demonstrated that the law wasn't exactly what it was thought to be aforetime."[82]

Because of his belief in the fluidity of legal doctrine, Terrell did not feel constrained by precedent. Though shocking to some legal scholars, several of his opinions cited no cases. Colleagues sometimes grew frustrated with his propensity for ignoring common law rules that he believed led to unjust results and his blithe indifference to making decisions that, while appropriate to the case at hand, might set severely troublesome precedents for subsequent ones. When a colleague once asked him what he would do if "the justice of [a future] case is in a different direction than your precedent," Terrell replied, "When that case comes along we'll deal with it at that time." Former justice Robert Cockrell, then teaching criminal law to students at the University of Florida, ridiculed Terrell's written opinions and accused him of being a preacher rather than a jurist. Some of the newer generation of lawyers and judges, however, including future justice Elwyn Thomas, acknowledged and appreciated his refusal to submerge his sense of justice "in a tide of technicality." Terrell also found common cause with legislators because of the deference he showed to the political branches. He was much more likely to substitute his moral judgments for common law principles than for statutory pronouncements.[83]

The justice's disregard for classical legal doctrine should not be confused with an embrace of political liberalism. "It was impossible to classify him . . . as a liberal or a conservative, as a progressive or a reactionary," Justice Stephen C. O'Connell commented. "At one time or another, he was each of those things." A fiscal conservative, he disapproved of excessive jury awards and could be parsimonious in the administration of estates. He once disallowed payment for a $5,250 casket because "the charge was grossly excessive and it was neither in keeping with the decedent's station in life nor the value of the estate." He believed that racial segregation "has always been the unvarying law of the animal kingdom" and argued for the slowest possible implementation of the U.S. Supreme Court's 1954 decision in *Brown* v. *Board of Education*. He held similar traditional views about women, preferring to award child custody to the mother because "she is morally, spiritually, and biologically best suited to care for [children]." Also a stern moralist, his decisions often turned on his perception of the individual character of the parties. In one lawsuit he upheld the power of a local school board to dismiss a school bus driver known for frequenting local "jook joints." Such establishments, he felt, were "the arch incubators of vice, immorality, and low impulses." Terrell continued, "It would be too much to presume that a school bus driver who frequents the jook is there to represent the Red Cross or to pick up the children." The driver clearly was "of a moral bent that disqualifies him to be the mentor of little boys and girls."[84]

The son of a minister, the jurist remained a devout Presbyterian who viewed the laws of God and man as mutually reinforcing. He kept a well-thumbed Bible in his chambers, shelved next to his treatises and case reporters. He authored an opinion that kept in force an antebellum statute prohibiting hunting on Sundays, despite a thoroughgoing revision of the fish and game laws in 1929. For over fifty years he taught Sunday school at the First Presbyterian Church. He joined with Justices Rivers Buford and Fred H. Davis as one of the main instructors in a nondenominational men's Bible study class at the local Ritz Theater. "The Magna Carta, the Declaration of Independence, and our United States Constitution," he insisted, "all had their roots in the Christian religion."[85]

In appearance, Terrell stood out as the epitome of the stern jurist. His voice boomed, and others viewed his visage as dour and humorless. "Smiling with him was something rather rare," LeRoy Collins remembered. Yet, despite appearances, the justice's sense of humor earned renown. Joe Butler, a longtime court employee, recalled an incident in which Terrell parked in the space assigned to Justice Ellis. The affronted colleague, whose short temper had achieved legendary status, demanded that the offender move his car forthwith. "Go back down there," Terrell directed Butler, "and tell him that if he can't find any other place, to park on top of my car." Winston Arnow, the first law clerk to the justices, recollected Terrell walking with him to the parking lot one evening. Upon seeing the "old beat-up car" that Arnow drove, the jurist said, "Well, I guess the janitor is working mighty late." According to Doris Terrell, no one appreciated her father's jokes more than he did. "He would get so amused that he could hardly finish the story."[86]

This humor often found its way into judicial opinions. In one instance, a woman appealed her manslaughter conviction and Terrell noticed that her victim had fought back, calling her a "son of a bitch." This led Terrell to remark that "a great many bearing this rustic title have made their way to the Court . . . but none were clothed in female trappings." Void of flowery prose or arcane legal jargon, his writing carried "a light touch," according to Justice O'Connell, "that laymen could read and enjoy." Daughter Doris noted that, because of his writing style, Terrell's opinions "caught the eye of the media" and quotations "appeared in newspapers all over the United States." The judge's folksy musings became known as "Terrellisms." In 1964 M. Lewis Hall compiled them into a popular book.[87]

In his later years Justice Terrell's health began to deteriorate, and he curtailed many of his activities. Around 1945, doctors diagnosed a "minor heart condition" and instructed him to avoid "anything that got him excited and made his heart beat fast." Thereafter, he minimized public speaking. An inner-ear problem affected his ability to maintain his balance, and he stopped driving. As he found it more difficult to keep up with office demands, he allowed research assistants to take a more active role in drafting opinions. By the fall of 1963, he knew that retirement beckoned, but he decided to finish all his assigned opinions. On January 11, 1964, Terrell tersely announced, "I have decided to accept the retirement which is provided by statute, but hold myself available for special service at the recall of the Chief Justice." The following morning, he quietly passed away. Justice Terrell had served for seven consecutive terms, sat on the bench with twenty-one colleagues, and written over twenty-five hundred opinions. He had sat longer on the court, forty years and eight months, than any other justice in its history. Following her beloved husband's death, Esther Collins Terrell remained at the couple's Tallahassee home. She died at Tallahassee on February 12, 1989, at the age of one hundred.[88]

Louie Willard Strum, Supreme Court Justice, 1925–1931; Supreme Court Chief Justice, 1931

Studious, reserved, and slightly built, Louie Willard Strum provided a marked contrast on the supreme bench to colorful personalities such as William Ellis, Glenn Terrell, and Rivers Buford. He arrived in the world at Valdosta, Georgia, on January 16, 1890, the only child of Louis Henry Strum, a hardware and sporting goods merchant, and Dora Ramsey Strum. Sadly, Mrs. Strum passed away at Valdosta when Louie was only six. The lad began his education in the Lowndes County public schools, but when he had reached age fourteen, his father relocated them to Florida. They lived briefly at Tallahassee before moving on to St. Petersburg. Louie then attended St. Petersburg Military High School until graduation in 1906. During his senior year, the maturing scholar achieved selection as captain, Company A, of the school cadets.[89]

Strum's experiences at the military high school led the graduate to service in the U.S. Navy and then a resumption of his education. In 1906 he enlisted as an apprentice seaman, thereafter spending three and a half years "before the mast." Upon discharge in 1910, he enrolled in law studies at Stetson University in DeLand. There he established a reputation as a bookworm. A Sigma Nu fraternity brother remembered him studying "in the corner of the living room of the frat house where the only fire was, where a bull session was going on, or a crap game, and completely shut off his mind to all outside noises and influences." Nevertheless, he managed to participate in many of college life's social aspects. A wiry athlete who "could do hand springs and cartwheels," he played on the football team, captained the debating society, and "enjoyed eggnog parties as much as anybody." Phi Delta Phi legal fraternity also welcomed him to membership.[90]

Strum earned his LL.B. degree from Stetson in 1912 and set out to make his fortune in the practice of law. He immediately departed DeLand for Jacksonville, then the state's largest and most dynamic city. Upon admission to the bar, he associated with the legal partnership of A. D. McNeill and J. Turner Butler, both Stetson alumni. Concerned about Strum's lack of experience, the two men held some reservations about employing him. On the other hand, they decided that he could at least be trusted with handling debt collections for their clients, a task that they both loathed. Their initial misgivings notwithstanding, Strum's employers soon grew impressed with his diligence and his careful efforts to understand the law for its historical and political significance and "not just because it applied to his case." Even at this early stage, they detected a judicial temperament in their protégé. In 1917 Butler retired from the firm to pursue his political interests, and McNeill invited Strum into partnership.[91]

By then, the United States' entry into World War I loomed and that fact commanded a great deal of Strum's attention. He had enjoyed his time at sea and maintained interest in naval service thereafter. In 1914 he had organized the Florida Naval Militia at Jacksonville, the first naval militia in the state's history, and commanded its men until the declaration of war in April 1917 drew Strum into federal service. Commissioned a lieutenant commander, he awaited orders and organized his affairs. One of the matters to which he paid attention concerned him greatly. On June 6, he married Ophelia Wilson Gray of St. Petersburg, the daughter of the Reverend and Mrs. Charles M. Gray. Later that summer, orders dispatched him to the South Seas as commander of a naval vessel, with headquarters at Samoa. Ophelia accompanied her husband to Pago Pago and remained with him for one and a half years. The couple shared the birth of their first son, Louie Jr., there, with son Charles Gray and daughter Ophelia Gray arriving in the postwar era. Eventually Strum commanded the U.S. naval station at Pago Pago and, for a time in 1918, served briefly as acting governor of American Samoa. The newlyweds reveled in the "Eden of the South Seas" and found themselves, as Ophelia later related, "loath to leave the enchanted and fascinating land."[92]

During the summer of 1919, Commander Strum returned to Jacksonville from his stint in the military to resume the practice of law. With his former employer J. Turner Butler now Duval County's state senator, he found ample reason to involve himself in politics. In 1920, for example, he managed John W. Martin's successful mayoral campaign. The next year Martin named Strum assistant city attorney, promoting him to city attorney two years later. In this capacity Strum associated closely with Martin, and the two men grew close. Meanwhile, the city counsel earned tremendous experience in litigation and appeals. During those years he appeared frequently before the supreme court as myriad lawsuits emerging from Florida's boom raised questions of taxation, zoning, home rule, and municipal growth. He began at this time to entertain judicial aspirations, discussing his prospects with acquaintances. When Martin pursued the governor's chair in 1924, Strum campaigned long and hard for his patron. When a vacancy opened on the court with Justice R. Fenwick Taylor's resignation in 1925, Martin hesitated little before naming his friend, supporter, and key adviser to the bench.[93]

More than a few court observers believed that elevation to the tribunal affected Strum significantly. A courteous yet formal demeanor emerged despite his previously warm and gregarious personality. Some saw him as aloof. Other critics believed that elevation to the court stirred in the jurist an inflated sense of self-importance. Friends defended him by attributing the change to an almost obsessive concern for judicial impartiality. "He began early in his career in Tallahassee," court commissioner Giles Patterson recorded, "to separate himself from the friends and acquaintances he had known." To Strum, Patterson believed, such friendships "might create a wrong impression in someone else's mind, of improper connection." There were exceptions. Strum adhered to membership in the Episcopal Church and was "prominently identified" with various masonic organizations. He also valued deeply his connection with the American Legion. He had helped to organize the Edward C. DeSaussure Post No. 9 at Jacksonville and served as its commander in 1922. Among other associations, he especially delighted in Florida's Morocco Temple of the Shrine. In 1928, while on the court, he accepted leadership of the state Shriner organization as its illustrious potentate.[94]

For six years following his appointment, the fledgling jurist labored diligently—even intensively—to learn his craft. He displayed "a keen analytical mind" while striving for precision in the wording of his opinions. This perfectionism resulted in the justice producing substantially fewer opinions than most of his colleagues. "He was never satisfied to release an opinion," Justice Terrell remarked, "until he had exhausted every legal source that would fortify or strengthen his pronouncement." Well versed in municipal law from his days as Jacksonville's city attorney, he wrote notable decisions on the constitutionality of tax and real property legislation. "[Judge Strum's] opinions speak as imperishable evidence of his ability and learning, his exhaustive research, his accurate statement of the law, and his forceful judicial pronouncements," a colleague declared.[95]

Justice Strum seemed poised by 1931 to help lead the supreme court for decades to come when his career suddenly took a different path. In January, the court had honored him with selection as chief justice. In the previous year, the Congress had responded to complaints about crowded federal court dockets in the southern district of Florida, a jurisdiction that extended from Jacksonville to Tampa to Key West, by establishing a third judgeship in the district. The two incumbents were Republicans who originally had hailed from Georgia and Colorado. In the circumstances, Florida's congressional delegation insisted that Republican president Herbert Hoover appoint a Democrat and a Floridian. Presidential aides and Senators Duncan U. Fletcher and Park Trammell examined a list of nearly one hundred applicants, many Republican, and none survived the scrutiny. The *Miami Herald* owner's law partner emerged as a favorite only to be vetoed by Trammell, the *Herald* having opposed the senator's reelection. According to one account, Hoover thereupon inquired of his attorney general, "What sort of man have they down there as chief justice of the supreme court?" Seemingly, this first resulted in an offer of appointment to Justice Terrell, whose term as chief justice had expired. When Terrell rejected the overture, Strum's name surfaced. "According to news from Washington," a report announced, "even the Republican aspirants for the judgeship could bring nothing against Justice Strum."[96]

This series of events sent Strum on to a long and valuable career in the federal court system. The appointment drew praise "in all parts of the state" and resulted in the judge's unanimous confirmation by the U.S. Senate on February 28. On the federal bench, seated at Jacksonville, the jurist earned respect if not affection. When fellow judge Alexander Akerman retired in October 1939, the departure elevated Strum to the position of senior judge for the district. "His knowledge of the law, his steadfast integrity and high sense of duty have distinguished him," the *Jacksonville Florida Times-Union* then observed, "as one of the ablest members of the Federal judiciary." President Harry Truman apparently agreed. When Fifth Circuit Court of Appeals judge Curtis L. Waller, a onetime Tallahassee neighbor, died in 1950, the president designated Strum to fill the vacancy. He remained on that panel until his death.[97]

As a federal jurist, Strum's knowledge of the law, particularly Florida law, proved invaluable. Nowhere did this illustrate itself more profoundly than in diversity cases and litigation involving the reorganization of the Florida East Coast Railway during its bankruptcy in the 1930s and 1940s. Strum also presided over the first case brought under the Fair Labor Standards Act of 1938, which established the federal minimum wage, and the leading case on the power of the federal government to prosecute police brutality under the Civil Rights Acts. He saw several of his opinions as a district judge overturned by the federal circuit court of appeals but then upheld subsequently by the U.S. Supreme Court. This included an influential case expanding the right to counsel. His federal opinions, an observer insisted, "demonstrate[d] Judge Strum's cogency of reasoning and lucidity of statement."[98]

The judge's federal experience, at least when it came to the impressions of some litigants and colleagues, unfortunately appeared to have exacerbated his tendency toward aloofness and stiff formality. Strum's insistence on strict courtroom protocol rankled several prominent Jacksonville attorneys, for instance, who were accustomed to a less deferential style. "They were not even permitted to hand him a memorandum or a book," B. K. Roberts recalled. "They were required to hand it to the Marshal, who would hand it to the Clerk, who would hand it to Judge Strum." Prospective jurors who asked to be excused from jury duty and witnesses who arrived late to the courthouse endured stern lectures about their obligations to their government and the courts. Yet, as another lawyer put it, "His sincerity and courtesy were at all times present and, with his broad understanding, were outstanding indicia of his judicial career."[99]

Elevation to the court of appeals naturally offered Judge Strum a profound sense of accomplishment and merit, but the years of the late 1940s and early 1950s otherwise proved occasionally painful and often challenging. In 1949, to cite an example, Ophelia Gray Strum, his wife of thirty-two years, died at Jacksonville. Following a suitable interlude, the judge married Grace Hilditch Holt, the widow of a Jacksonville neighbor. A friend remembered that she "contributed everything in the way of happiness, comfort, and companionship that a devoted wife could contribute." Strum required those contributions. His health had declined, and he repeatedly faced hospitalization. On the job on June 28, 1954, he quietly returned to the hospital at Jacksonville a few days later. His condition worsened as the days passed, and on July 26 he died. Grace survived her husband by over a quarter century. She died at Jacksonville on March 10, 1980.[100]

Praise for Judge Strum's life and contributions naturally punctuated his death. "I never saw a judge more sensitive to the importance of the judiciary in our democracy than Judge Strum," Justice Terrell proclaimed for the Florida Supreme Court. "To him, the judicial ermine was the symbol of purity and upright purpose and after wearing it for more than thirty years, he laid it down without spot or blemish." His hometown newspaper added, "He had the respect of both lawyers and the citizens generally, and was often referred to as a 'lawyer's judge' because of his intimate knowledge of the law and ability to follow closely and judicially the most intricate cases tried before him." A colleague struck a slightly different chord. "By his pen and public addresses Judge Strum contributed a great deal toward raising educational, ethical, and other qualifications for admission to the bar. He was vitally concerned with the welfare of his country, and although he suffered physically during the late years of his life, he was mentally alert and courageous to the end." The man concluded, "His influence will have its impact on the current of opinion as long as this country continues to be one of laws rather than one of men."[101]

Armstead Brown, Supreme Court Justice, 1925–1946; Supreme Court Chief Justice, 1925–1927, 1941–1943

Armstead Brown, the second of Governor John Martin's three appointees to the supreme tribunal, differed markedly in background from the other justices who served during the era. All of his colleagues had possessed significant experience in public law, either as prosecutors, government attorneys, heads of administrative agencies, or in similar positions. Brown, to the contrary, boasted prowess as a corporate lawyer. To his credit and save for Justice Whitfield, though, he stood out as the only court member with prior judicial experience. Furthermore, unlike his colleagues who had grown up and received their professional training in the state, he had come to Florida after practicing law in another state for fifteen years. He would be the last justice to do so to the present day.

Brown's roots lay at Talbotton, Georgia, where he was born on June 6, 1875, the son of Henry Clay Brown and Susan Dowdell Brown. His maternal grandfather, James F. Dowdell, had served in the U.S. Congress, officered in the Confederate army, and later sat as president of Alabama Polytechnic Institute, the forerunner of Auburn University. Henry Clay Brown, on the other hand, made his living as a merchant and local editor. The times brought difficult economic conditions to Middle Georgia, though, and the Browns soon found themselves, in Judge Vincent C. Giblin's words, "reduced to poverty and hardship." To make matters worse, Armstead's mother died when he was five years of age. Seeking opportunity, his father relocated to Florida, settling on a farm near the rural Alachua County community of Micanopy. There he obtained employment as a railway agent and truck farmer. For several years the lad remained in his grandmother's care at Talbotton. Then at age eleven he joined his father at Micanopy.[102]

The hard times continued for the Browns. Armstead received some training in the public schools of Talbot and Alachua counties. In 1888 his father attempted to break out of the depressing cycle by returning to Georgia and entering the newspaper business at Atlanta. In that city Armstead pursued courses in shorthand and typing. When his father endured further financial reverses, Brown at age fourteen had to help support the family. As one account noted, "From that date to the date of his retirement as a Justice of the Supreme Court of Florida, he carried a man's load and was never permitted to resume his formal education." The teenager managed in 1890 to secure a job as stenographer to Governor John B. Gordon, the former Confederate general who had headed the state's Ku Klux Klan. When Gordon departed office, Brown persisted in his vocation. Beginning in 1892 he worked for several years as stenographer in the Atlanta law firm of King & Spalding. At various times he also labored in his father's newspaper office, as a court reporter, and in a wholesale company.[103]

Perhaps stirred by his exposure to Georgia law and politics while with Governor Gordon, Brown had begun to read law during his tenure at King & Spalding. In 1896 he transferred to Lafayette, Alabama, to continue his studies in the office of his uncle, James R. Dowdell, a judge who later would preside as chief justice of the Alabama Supreme Court. Alabama bar admission then required examination by a judge or two attorneys appointed by a judge. Concerned because "he wanted no partiality," Dowdell insisted on appointing "six lawyers to examine me in open court." The examination, Brown recalled, "lasted nearly two hours." Admitted to practice in 1897, he opened an office at Lafayette. A year later he received appointment as register in chancery and county solicitor for Chambers County and held the positions until 1902. In 1900 Brown also had formed a partnership with J. B. Duke, continuing as a sole practitioner after Duke died two years later.[104]

Wedded bliss and involvement in community affairs additionally occupied Brown's attention during these years. The young attorney married Elizabeth Caroline Dowdell, his cousin and the daughter of Montgomery underwriter James Samford Dowdell, on November 21, 1901. The couple would not share children but remained happily married until Armstead's death. While engaging in numerous worthy causes during their union's first years, they dedicated themselves to the work of the Methodist Episcopal Church, South, and participated in Sunday school programs. In 1906–7, Armstead presided over the Alabama State Sunday School Association. A longtime member of the Alabama Bible Society, he bore responsibility for its presidency between 1909 and 1912.[105]

Brown's career ignited soon after the couple relocated in 1905 to Alabama's capital city. Armstead first practiced at Montgomery with J. Lee Holloway. He handled routine civil litigation, but he also gained valuable corporate experience representing the Western Railway of Alabama. Public office then came calling. In 1909 Governor Braxton B. Comer appointed him to fill a vacancy as associate judge of the City Court of Montgomery, one of two judgeships on the highest trial court of that city. He won the office and a six-year term in his own right during elections the following year.[106]

Chronic health problems suffered by Armstead prompted the Browns to take action in 1915 that changed their lives. "Throughout his career at the bar and on the bench he was plagued by physical frailty," Judge Giblin explained. "But just as his indomitable will and mental strength had enabled him to overcome the handicap of poverty, they supplied the impelling force which he demonstrated in refusing to surrender to his greatest enemy—his bodily weakness." In the circumstances, Brown resigned his judgeship, and the couple relocated to Florida, making a home at Jacksonville. Thanks to professional connections and his background in railroad law, Armstead obtained employment as general solicitor for the Florida East Coast Railway Company, the corporate entity that represented the very considerable interests of the late railroad baron Henry Flagler.[107]

After a two-year interlude at Jacksonville, the Browns headed even further south. They bought a home in Miami Beach and quickly fell in love with the area. "Miami you'll find hard to beat," he declared to out-of-state friends. He extolled the restorative powers of a land of palm trees and sea air "where all microbes the mosquitoes do eat." There Armstead formed the firm of Brown, Twyman, and Scott, eventually renamed Rose, Brown, Twyman, and Scott. In 1923 that firm dissolved, and Brown partnered with powerful former state senator John P. Stokes. "Few, if any, law partnerships stronger or more successful than this association have ever graced the Florida bar," a fellow practitioner recorded. The railroad meanwhile continued as his biggest client. Brown came to represent numerous other corporate clients, including the Miami Electric Light and Power Company.[108]

Brown soon became one of the leading citizens of Miami. He served, for instance, as the first president of the Miami Kiwanis Club and helped to found the Dade County Bar Association. He offered leadership and individual effort on behalf of the Florida State Bar Association, where he grew well acquainted with Justices Browne, West, and Ellis, all past presidents of the group. From 1922 to 1923 as bar president himself, Brown promoted an ambitious agenda that included compulsory bar association membership for all attorneys, reform of jury selection, compulsory instruction about the Constitution for all high school and college students, and the creation of a state board of bar examiners. He also tried to establish a bar journal under the association's auspices. When that venture failed, he ordered the $10 annual bar dues payment cut in half. He energetically supported the Democratic Party and attended its state conventions as a delegate.[109]

Besides bringing him increasing prosperity, Brown's legal skills, pro-business orientation, and advocacy of legal and judicial reforms led him in 1925 to a seat on the supreme court. Governor John Martin desired to fill a vacancy caused by Justice Browne's resignation. Needing a south Floridian to replace Browne, the governor also required someone friendly to his administration's development and growth plans. Brown appeared the ideal choice from all perspectives, and since rumors of his designation surfaced coincidentally with those of Browne's resignation, the matter likely had been settled some time in advance. It took Brown only two weeks to dissolve one of the state's busiest legal partnerships. "I arrived in Tallahassee early on the morning of July 1, called by the Capitol, filed my oath of office and received my commission," he later related, "and by 10 o'clock I joined members of the Court and went to work." In December Justice West resigned, and by a great stroke of good fortune Brown won the lottery to serve out West's term as chief justice.[110]

Justice Brown's heritage was apparent during his court service. He appeared to attorneys as a "southern gentleman, immaculate in dress, courtesy, in all things." His disposition? "Like Justice Whitfield, Armstead Brown was usually cheerful, kindly, and agreeable." His judicial opinions, a law clerk explained, read "like his conversations, lengthy and learned." B. K. Roberts agreed in a slightly more critical tone: "His opinions were too long. He was not the type of justice who would make headlines. He simply reported for work daily, did his work, wrote elegant, erudite opinions, some too long, but always sound." Brown enjoyed conducting his own research, a fact reflected in the copious citations contained in his opinions. Around him sat prolific opinion writers such as Whitfield, Terrell, and Buford, but Brown took his time preparing decisions and frequently fell behind in his work. Not a legal realist in the extreme sense as was Terrell, Brown sometimes embraced novel interpretations and reasoning. Understandably, he often turned to Alabama cases to support his decisions when Florida precedents opposed his position.[111]

Staunchly pro-business, Brown also maintained sympathy—as did Governor Martin—with governmental regulation. Believing that individual liberty could be threatened by state power, he saw danger as well "when any individual or combination of individuals require the power to coerce the public." The justice viewed "private ownership coupled with government supervision and regulation" as the most effective means of ensuring liberty in a modern economy. Still, he insisted on narrowly tailored regulations. He criticized those who lost sight "of their personal accountability [and] cast blame for their sins and failures upon the government or the conditions existing in the society around them." Brown carefully asserted, though, that some rights were so fundamental that government should never encroach upon them. "I might tolerate a statute prescribing the kind of plumbing I shall use in constructing my dwelling," he declared, "but a statute that prescribed . . . the religious doctrine that I must accept, would be intolerable."[112]

During his court tenure Brown emerged as one of the most ardent proponents on the panel for the relief of its workload and improvements in its administration. He argued for an increase in the court's size and the creation of intermediate courts of appeal, with a concomitant reduction of the supreme court's appellate jurisdiction. He urged the tribunal to wield its rule-making power more aggressively in the absence of legislative reforms of the judicial system. In 1930 he drafted revisions of the court's rules governing the form and content of appellate briefs. In the area of criminal procedure, he complained that "we have failed to adapt out legal machinery to the increased volume of crime" and advocated increased speed and efficiency in criminal processing to "increase the deterrent effect of the administration of justice." Later he turned his energies to modernizing the professional standards of the Florida Bar, advocating, as he had as bar president in 1922–23, an integrated bar. He also urged the state bar association to adopt formally the Canons of Ethics promulgated by the American Bar Association.[113]

Twenty-one years of service on the court proved enough for Brown, although his last years on the tribunal, punctuated by health problems, also were marked by distinguished efforts and thoughtfulness. In the latter case, the customary succession practices in place during 1935 again would have made him chief justice. Instead, Brown urged colleagues to support another for the position. "I feared at the time that Justice Whitfield, then seventy-five years of age, was in failing health, and I decided to forego the honor at that time, over Judge Whitfield's protest." Brown's second turn came six years afterward. In January 1941 he accepted the chief justiceship, helping to prepare the panel for the world war that threatened imminently. He awaited World War II's conclusion before retiring. "I am no longer able to do my full share of the work of this busy court," he explained at the time. "I have been eligible for retirement under the statute for a year and a half but have worked on as long as my strength permitted."[114]

Thereafter, the Browns maintained their Tallahassee home. Justice Brown indulged his passion for golf, playing at the Capital City Country Club across the street from his home. On the rare occasions when Brown was not on the links himself, he would ease across the street to the tenth fairway to greet lawyers, friends, and notables who happened to be playing there. Generously, he typically offered critiques of their shots. In October 1951, the Browns decided to share a New York City sojourn in honor of their fiftieth wedding anniversary. Armstead Brown died in that city on October 29 of a heart attack. Recalling his friend, Justice Paul Barns declared of Brown, "As a justice on the bench he displayed an extraordinary knowledge of the law acquired by his own efforts of continuous study even after retirement; and greater than that he understood people with their vices and their virtues." He continued, "He could 'walk with kings and not lose the common touch'; he could apply the law with an equity that made one realize that he well knew that in every lawsuit there were flesh and blood on both sides and it was his constant effort to render justice with an inquiring attitude of mind." Friend F. M. Hudson added, "His life was his best monument."[115]

Rivers Henderson Buford, Supreme Court Justice, 1925–1948; Supreme Court Chief Justice, 1931–1933, 1943–1945

In some respects, Justice Rivers Henderson Buford shared life parallels with Justice Armstead Brown, but the two men represented far different personalities, backgrounds, and perspectives. They first arrived in Florida, by way of similarities, at about the same time and from adjoining southern states. They both found themselves compelled to work for their own support at early ages, and neither attended college or law school. Unlike his colleague, though, Buford represented a throwback to the professional conventions of an earlier era when a lawyer's common sense and rhetorical prowess were prized more highly than formal training or technical knowledge. Where Brown honed his skills in the relatively refined atmosphere of Alabama's capital city, Buford toiled for most of his private career as a lawyer in the rural north Florida Panhandle. While Brown entertained himself with golf and other middle-class pastimes, Buford hunted as his "principal diversion." Rugged, unpretentious, and occasionally profane, Buford earned his reputation as "the most colorful member of the Florida Supreme Court."[116]

Buford arrived in the world at Pulaski, Tennessee, on January 18, 1878. The first of four children, he was the son of Albert Lindley Buford Jr., a farmer and civil engineer, and Martha Bowling Rivers Buford. Ancestors on both sides of his family had helped to settle colonial Virginia, and his mother claimed descent directly from John Rolfe and Pocahontas. Her father, Dr. R. H. Rivers, presided at Martin College in Pulaski and later pastored influential southern Methodist congregations. Providing for his family proved no easier in Giles County for Albert Buford in the early 1880s than it had for Armstead Brown's father in Talbot County, Georgia. As a result, Buford relocated the family on January 2, 1882, to Wewahitchka, then part of Calhoun County, Florida. There he found work as a surveyor and timber cruiser for north Florida logging and lumber companies.[117]

By the age of ten, Rivers was taking any kind of job a boy could find while attempting to obtain the rudiments of an education. He managed to attend classes when offered in the Calhoun County public schools. At age sixteen, the family endeavored to help him further his studies by lodging him with relatives back in Giles County. He enrolled there in public school from 1895 to 1897. Justice Buford related the details of his life immediately thereafter to a newspaper reporter in 1931. "Returning to Florida in 1897, he found work in the log camps along the Apalachicola River," the journalist related. "During the winters of 1897 and '98 he was employed as a laborer in the log camps of the firm of Sheppard & Howard, of which firm Hon. William B. Sheppard, then practicing law in Apalachicola and now United States District Judge for the Northern District of Florida, was the senior partner. It was while so engaged that he was influenced by Judge Sheppard to take up the study of law, and it was Judge Sheppard who made the arrangements with the late Honorable Fred T. Myers of Tallahassee for young Buford to read law in the office of, and under the direction of, Mr. Myers, who was then and for many years thereafter recognized as one of the leaders of the Florida Bar."[118]

The future justice's legal studies commenced at Tallahassee on September 9, 1899, and he quickly mastered his subject and opened several new chapters in his life. After oral examination in open court, Judge John W. Malone admitted him to the bar at Blountstown in October 1900. Already he held the Democratic nomination for state representative from Calhoun County in the upcoming general election, a contest that he won easily. His father had occupied the same seat a decade previously. In 1901 Buford claimed his legislative seat, and when the session ended, he headed for Tennessee to marry his sweetheart, Nora Lee Milliken. The nuptials occurred at Nashville on June 12. The next month the couple located their home at Marianna in Jackson County, where Buford entered a law partnership with J. Walter Kehoe, who then served as state attorney. Sadly, Nora Lee passed away on May 11, 1902.[119]

Within one year or so, Buford attempted to build life anew. In March 1903 he moved to Quincy where a partnership awaited him with William H. Ellis, although only months passed before Ellis accepted Governor William S. Jennings's appointment as attorney general and the association dissolved. Buford nonetheless prospered, gaining new partners over time and a second marriage. At Quincy on September 14, he wed Mary C. Munroe, the daughter of the town's leading physician, Dr. Thomas Freeman Munroe, and his wife, Martha. Eight children would be born to them, although only four survived into adulthood. Those surviving included Martha Hauze, born in 1906; Maxine Francis, 1908; Alice Dismukes, 1910; and Albert Lewis, 1913. The Bufords additionally adopted Bertha Lindley, the daughter of Albert and Bertha Hatton Lindley, in 1911 after her mother died in childbirth.[120]

Mary's well-to-do family enjoyed influential connections not only at Quincy but also at Tallahassee, and Buford capitalized on them in laying foundations for financial security. Meanwhile, the couple attended the local Baptist church and Rivers associated with the Masons, Shriners, Woodmen of the World, and the Elks. By 1909 he had gained sufficient entrée into the cliquish circles of Gadsden County politics to receive appointment as county prosecuting attorney. Within two years, though, an even better opportunity arose. Marianna's William H. Price had been appointed judge for the ninth circuit, and Buford transferred the family to that community to assume Price's profitable client list. In 1911 Governor Albert Gilchrist, whose family ties also ran deep in Gadsden, returned the now veteran lawyer to public office as state attorney for the ninth circuit. Buford held the position until January 4, 1921.[121]

When pursuing private practice, Buford handled the usual variety of cases, with a large volume of his work involving property disputes and criminal defense. A constant reader of legal works, he proved an imaginative advocate. He appeared before the Supreme Court of Florida two dozen times and, as noted earlier, attempted unsuccessfully to gain election to the panel in 1918. The tribunal's decisions usually favored his clients, including cases in which the court overturned the convictions of accused murderers after Buford raised novel claims of self-defense and the admissibility of dying declarations. In another noteworthy victory, Buford convinced the court to reverse the conviction of a reclusive farmer accused of killing his servant's child by arguing that the farmer's failure to notify neighbors about the child's funeral, a key element of the testimony against him, did not comprise sufficient evidence to establish a guilty state of mind.[122]

As a prosecutor, Buford proved in one headline writer's word to be "fearless." He relished the role, seeing himself as "aggressive" and "fair." He proudly recalled averting a lynching and believed that the justice he sought applied to black as well as white persons. During nine years as state attorney he prosecuted 113 defendants and secured 95 convictions. The supreme court overturned only one guilty verdict that he had obtained. In the process, he learned the ins and outs of his responsibilities as well as anyone. Justice Richard W. Ervin agreed. "Justice Buford," he would assert, "no doubt drawing on his excellent service as a prosecutor, was particularly masterful in criminal law."[123]

For the remainder of his life, Buford delighted in telling tales of his days as prosecutor. Always entertaining, the stories ranged far and wide. A thrilling one commenced on the eve of a criminal trial, when the defendant's brother met Buford at his hotel room and threatened to kill the prosecutor if the defendant were convicted. Not wishing to allow the threat to distract him from trying the case, Buford, who always carried a pistol for self-protection, enlisted his friend, Tom Howard, a crack shot, to sit in the courtroom and shoot the defendant's brother when he attempted to execute his murderous intent. Buford and Howard discussed the matter with the trial judge, who instructed Howard to sit near the defendant's table where the defendant's brother would take a seat. The judge, no doubt aware that he sat in the line of fire, advised Howard, "Don't miss!" After court had recessed for lunch, someone took Howard's seat, whereupon the judge ordered the chair vacated so that Howard could resume his defensive position. The defendant's brother, who obviously had figured out that Howard's presence was based on more than curiosity, exclaimed to a friend during court recess that if he "reached for his handkerchief in the courtroom he would surely be shot." At any rate, according to Buford, the deterrence worked, and no homicide resulted.[124]

Buford parlayed more than a decade's experience as prosecutor into a successful 1920 campaign for attorney general, taking office January 4, 1921. Beyond acting as the state's advocate before the court, he urged governmental agencies he counseled to take measures to curb ill effects of Florida's growth. He visited the Everglades in connection with the board of drainage commissioners and advocated reserving the bulk of the reclaimed land for agriculture and grazing. As the pace of investment quickened, he grew concerned with protecting Floridians from fraud. In 1921 he pressed for revisions to state "Blue Sky" laws, insisting that the state claim greater power to regulate securities offerings and transactions in order to "protect the public from impositions practiced by vendors of worthless stocks." Boisterous and extremely popular among voters, the attorney general tended to dominate the cabinet. Even Governor John Martin, Buford's close friend, sometimes found him a difficult person with whom to contend. The two men shared many hopes for the state's future, however, and believed that government should play a role in realizing them. Accordingly, when Justice West resigned in December 1925, Martin seized the opportunity to appoint Buford to the supreme court bench.[125]

Court watchers remembered jurist Buford for his gruff temperament, quick wit, and fair-minded rulings. "Be open, frank, and fair," his longtime rule of conduct, expressed his intentions. He dispatched work expeditiously and wrote opinions marked by brevity and clarity. Unlike colleagues who drafted decisions in longhand, he dictated to a secretary. "Frequently, his first attempt was his final product," a clerk recalled. This practice permitted him to author 2,657 opinions, more than any other justice in Florida court history. His approach to the law could not properly be described as scholarly. Perusing a copy of a bar examination that was about to be administered, he once exclaimed, "My God, I am glad I don't have to take this damn thing." Yet, according to one attorney who practiced before him, Buford "could analyze and see the legal problem quicker than any other judge I have ever known."[126]

Justice Buford prided himself on his intuitive approach to deciding cases. As such, he minimized the technical aspects of lawyering. "It is far more important that Courts should have the mentality and courage to apply the principles of organic law in the light of the existing world conditions," he wrote in the midst of the Great Depression, "than it is that they should be possessed of great learning, as gathered from the writings of the past." He most closely resembled Justice Terrell in his deference to legislative judgments and his reluctance to be "'thought bound' by the fetters of ancient precedents." B. K. Roberts remembered a law professor's comment that "Justice Buford always decided the case right whether or not he knew why he did." Much of the jurist's style stemmed from his comfort with judicial authority. When a young lawyer once approached him with a particularly complicated case and asked him what legal principles would govern it, he replied, "Young man, I don't know the law. I write the law." Of Buford, one justice remarked, "Buford was fearless and dominating on the bench." He added, "Intelligent lawyers strived never to give him an opportunity to jump on them in oral argument."[127]

A homespun but sardonic sense of humor served Buford well. Gazing at the Tallahassee countryside from a large window in the courthouse men's room, he "snorted that the best view from the whole courthouse was from the men's toilet." On another occasion, while an inmate at the Raiford state penitentiary shaved him in the prison barbershop, the inmate introduced himself as having been prosecuted by Buford for murder. The justice often spoke thereafter about his "close shave." He also used sarcasm to good effect. A lawyer once insisted firmly on his right to appear as *amicus curiae* for a defendant in a routine negligence case involving the proper display of warning lights. Opposing counsel objected vociferously. Buford granted the motion. "Let him file his brief. I want to learn all I can about this complicated case of who's totin' the lantern." His quick wit and sense of humor naturally created a demand for Buford as a speaker, a fact that added an interesting task to the duties of his law clerks. James C. Adkins, at least, recalled that Buford instructed him on "how large his drink should be" and charged the young man with inspecting the libations "so his speech would not be boring." One Buford son, on his part, believed the down-to-earth and straightforward Adkins to be the justice who most resembled his father in later years.[128]

As Buford's public service career flourished, he experienced momentous and sometimes tragic changes in his personal life. On September 14, 1924, for instance, wife Mary died unexpectedly at age forty-one on their twentieth wedding anniversary. Apparently, a local doctor had misdiagnosed a pregnancy as a cancerous tumor and operated to remove the growth. The baby died with its mother. For years afterward Buford fumed at the incompetence of the Tallahassee medical community, and when son Rivers's appendix burst, the justice sped to a Thomasville, Georgia, hospital—as he explained to his son—"to save" his life. Another tragedy followed in 1930 when adopted daughter Betty Lindley Page perished in an automobile accident. Two years following Mary's death, though, better times had arrived with remarriage. Mary "Holly" Hollingsworth headed the Department of Speech at the Florida State College for Women (now Florida State University). A native of Greenwood, South Carolina, Holly had joined the faculty in 1921 and would serve until retirement in 1948. As such, she stood out for maintaining a career while her husband sat on the court. They shared one son, Rivers Buford Jr.[129]

Notwithstanding a demeanor so gruff and a physical presence so large and strong that they vividly could be recalled a half-century after Justice Buford's death, within his family the man proved loving, gentle, and devoted. Grandchildren flocked to his home on holidays, and unlike many of his contemporaries, Buford did not shy away from physical affection of loved ones in public. His personal tastes remained human and plain through his years on the tribunal, although he acceded to Holly's wish to enhance their residence, Greenwood, with beautiful antiques and paintings. By contrast, he continued to devote himself to rough-and-tumble hunting trips in the backwoods, including at his old stomping grounds in the "Tate's Hell" area of Calhoun County. Family memory records that, on one such trip, the woods turned out so thick and inhospitable that Buford's dog returned to civilization after one day, leaving the justice behind.[130]

For twenty-two years Justice Buford interpreted, applied, and sometimes made Florida law on the supreme bench, but, as with colleague Armstead Brown, the post–World War II years brought the need for retirement. He had served as chief justice for almost two years following Louie Strum's departure for the federal judiciary, and he took up the responsibility again during the war's final two years. By February 1948, though, a physician had recommended that he distance himself from the demanding workload. Combined with specific health problems that included fading eyesight, this advice prompted him to announced his retirement effective March 1. "Lawyers always accuse supreme court justices of not reading the record or the briefs," he remarked. "I didn't want them to prove it by me." A recent action by his colleagues also may have hastened the departure. The justices had agreed to begin wearing robes when the new supreme court building opened in 1949. Buford objected strenuously, believing that the wearing of ordinary business attire kept the court closer to the people, and he swore never to wear "one of those damnable, black robes."[131]

Over a decade remained to Justice Buford thereafter. He opened a Tallahassee real estate office in preference to a law practice. When friend Robert M. Ervin visited one day, he remarked that Buford must still enjoy perusing the *Florida Reports* that stood on his bookshelves because he had contributed so much to their contents. "Hell, no, Ervin," the retiree scowled. "I'll never read another one of 'em again." Time proved him wrong. In 1953 Buford returned to the supreme bench as a substitute justice. Chief Justice B. K. Roberts lent the venerable jurist his own robe. Later that night, probably at his wife's insistence, Buford sneaked back into the courtroom with a photographer to take the only picture existent of him in a judicial robe. Occasionally thereafter, he returned to fill in for absent or disqualified colleagues, though always in a borrowed robe. Buford served, as well, in 1956 by appointment of Governor LeRoy Collins as a member of the Fabisinski committee. That panel was charged with devising a plan to maintain racial segregation in the wake of the U.S. Supreme Court decision in *Brown* v. *Board of Education*.[132]

Buford died at his Tallahassee home following a lingering illness on March 17, 1959, at age eighty-one. Governor Collins eulogized him for his contributions to state government and the example that he had set. Recalling the justice's humble origins, Collins declared that "his life was an inspiration, especially to young men who had to come up the hard way." The governor added: "I have always thought of Judge Buford as being like Andrew Jackson. They both stood for the right as they saw it and asked for no quarter except fighting room."[133]

Fred Henry Davis Jr., Supreme Court Justice, 1931–1937; Supreme Court Chief Justice, 1933–1935

Humble origins, a pathway to prosperity through the law, and legislative service leading to the attorney general's office marked the life of yet another individual placed on the supreme tribunal not too many years after Justice Rivers's service commenced. Fred Henry Davis Jr. came into the world at Greenville, South Carolina, on May 18, 1894. His father made his living as a typographical machinist, while his mother, Annie E. Pearson Davis, maintained a home for the expanding family. It may have been that Fred Sr. awaited his son's birth before relocating the family to Florida that year. At Jacksonville he had accepted employment with the *Florida Times-Union* newspaper, a job that he maintained until 1907. He then transferred his wife and children to Tallahassee, where he labored for state printer T. J. Appleyard. A Democrat and a Methodist, Fred Sr. believed as well in organized labor. From its creation until his death at Tallahassee on December 5, 1916, he served as president of the Tallahassee Typographical Union.[134]

Fred Jr. matured in circumstances that might be described as modest. He managed to obtain the basics of elementary education in Jacksonville public schools, and when his family moved to Tallahassee, he took up studies at Leon High School. One story recalled by his sister Evelyn Davis Burns illustrated the difficulties faced by the family in those years. "Being the eldest in a large family, he rarely had more than the basic necessities of life," Burns began. "When he was about fourteen, he finally managed to get his very first pair of long pants. Since he could not afford to buy the coat to go with the pants, and coats were a customary part of one's dress in those days, he appeared at school in his long pants and the coat which went with the short pants. One of his schoolmates made great fun of this outfit, and caused a lot of tittering among his class members. Fred took the main culprit aside and offered to engage in a tussle of some sort after school, and, if he won, then the making fun would stop. The bully was afraid he would be beaten and refused to meet Fred. Thereafter, Fred continued to wear his mismatched outfit, but, surprisingly, many others imitated him and long pants and short coats became relatively common."[135]

His family's economic insecurity challenged young Fred to make a way for himself at an early age. The opening came when an uncle, State Representative John W. Davis of St. Johns County, shared a copy of Sir William Blackstone's *Commentaries on the Laws of England*. "Thereafter, he never wanted to be anything else [but an attorney]," Evelyn Burns observed. Likely also through Uncle John's connections, influential Tallahassee lawyer William C. Hodges "took him under his wing." A high school student, Fred nonetheless commenced reading the law with Hodges. As he did so, he spent "every extra hour of his school days" pouring over treatises in the supreme court library. The hard work paid off when he topped the bar examination six months after finishing high school. Justice Richard W. Ervin recalled that Davis's score represented the "best grade ever up till then."[136]

Admission to the bar following the examination temporarily proved problematic, but Davis quickly began to prosper as a lawyer. The problem arose out of the law requiring a candidate for bar admission to have attained twenty-one years of age. As Davis was only twenty, a brief delay ensued before a court order waived the limitation, allowing the young man to take the oath in November 1914. Hodges then guided his able protégé well. He first arranged in 1916 for Davis's appointment as Wakulla County attorney, a position that he retained for nine years. The same year Hodges's law partner, John L. Neeley, assumed office as U.S. attorney for the Northern District of Florida. By 1917 Davis labored as his special assistant. These professional breakthroughs, in light of Fred Sr.'s death in 1916, proved a godsend. The loss left Fred Jr. caring for his widowed mother, a brother, four sisters, and a grandmother. "My father's insurance barely paid for a house for the family," sister Evelyn explained.[137]

The era of the world war brought other trials and more pain of loss for Davis. Even before his father's death, he had endured the death of a high school sweetheart to whom he had become engaged. He suffered as well from asthma. Nonetheless, Davis enlisted in the army in August 1918, soon receiving a second lieutenant's commission at Camp Hancock, Georgia. The war's end in November released him from the potential of duty overseas, but the flu epidemic that accompanied that heralded event brought family tragedy. First, his brother succumbed. Released to attend the funeral, Davis no sooner had returned to duty than word arrived of his mother's imminent death. Unable to travel again to Tallahassee, he found himself left after her demise with "inconsolable" grief. In the circumstances, the young man turned to the Methodist Church for comfort, becoming "a devout Bible student."[138]

Davis's life thereafter quickly took on a brighter tone. Honorably discharged on December 12, 1918, he returned to Tallahassee and the practice of law. William C. Hodges stepped forward once again to assist him, procuring Davis an assignment as prosecuting attorney for Leon County. The two also practiced law together, and in 1920 Hodges urged Davis's candidacy for the Florida House of Representatives from Leon. Elected without opposition, Davis thereafter sought reelection three times, always winning the contest without drawing an opponent. Growing influence and respect for his abilities resulted in Davis's designation as special counsel for the Florida Railroad Commission (1925–27). To cap off this exciting period, on February 3, 1921, Hodges officiated at his Tallahassee home as Davis wed Frances Chambers, daughter of Leon County plantation owner Benjamin R. Chambers and Georgia Chambers. Time's passage blessed the couple with two daughters. Frances Marilyn arrived in June 1924, with Hazel Anice following in October 1925.[139]

The future justice's philosophy as a legislator stressed conservatism and concern for business. "I am opposed to radical legislation of every kind," he insisted. He authored Florida's bad check statute and favored "the passage of laws strengthening the legal remedies for the collections of debts," among many other measures. His energy brought him recognition in his first legislative session for introducing more bills than any other house member, an honor that he strove to maintain. He took special pride in repealing obsolete statutes and "remedying defects which have been found in various statutes by decision of the supreme court." He also endorsed Governor Cary A. Hardee's "Back to the Constitution" movement, going so far as to propose a constitutional amendment that would have carried the effect of repealing the law that created the state road department. On the other hand, perhaps from his own experience with asthma, he also sponsored a bill that resulted in the opening of Florida's first sanatorium for tuberculosis patients. On questions touching upon religion he voted conservatively, although not necessarily from personal conviction. When a bill banning the teaching of evolution in public schools reached the legislature in 1927, for instance, he agreed that the measure was not necessary but also that he could not "vote against a bill of this kind, because my people would approve of it."[140]

As legislative session passed to legislative session for Representative Davis, the respect of colleagues and constituents mounted, with rewards eventually resulting. His friend and protégé Fuller Warren remembered particularly that Davis "was widely regarded as one of the most skillful parliamentarians." A sense of humor aided his effectiveness, and newspapers often quoted his folksy expressions. "Fred Davis says that he has discovered that a pawn-broker won't lend you two cents on your ten million dollar opinion of yourself," one typical item announced. Fellow legislators seemed to agree with the positive assessments. They unanimously elected him their speaker for the 1927 house session.[141]

The up-and-coming politician sensed that preferment lay ahead and prepared well in advance a base from which to contest future elections. "He was often urged to run for governor," sister Evelyn commented, and it was to that office that he began to set his sights. As a veteran, Davis buttressed his military credentials in 1926 by enlistment with the Florida National Guard. Awarded a commission shortly thereafter, by early 1927 he commanded Tallahassee's local guard unit. Eventually he would rise to the rank of major. Meanwhile, the still young legislator participated in a broad variety of civic and social organizations, including several bar associations, the Sons of Confederate Veterans, American Legion, Masons, Elks, Odd Fellows, Lions, Phi Alpha Delta, the Tallahassee Chamber of Commerce, and the Tallahassee Country Club.[142]

Early in 1927, word circulated of a possible run for higher office, and that fact generated a major turning point in Davis's career. An account of the renowned Wakulla Springs annual picnic and political gathering noted in May, for example, that the master of ceremonies "then introduced Speaker Fred Davis, who made a fine talk, pointing out that the voters now had the platforms, or issues of the prospective candidates before them, and we could decide; that everybody seemed harmonious, and while Mr. Davis didn't exactly say so, we felt in our hearts really, that we had not, as yet, learned just what the issues of the campaign really were. We wanted to ask [the master of ceremonies] to introduce Mr. Davis as Florida's Governor in 1932, because that is actually what we think will happen, either then or in 1936." Governor John Martin, on the other hand, guessed that a 1928 gubernatorial bid lay in the offing, one that would conflict with the governor's own plans. One week later, Martin, Davis, supreme court members, and other guests gathered at William C. Hodges's Tallahassee plantation mansion house, Goodwood, for a festive social. Perhaps on that occasion Hodges, now a powerful state senator, furthered discussions about Davis's future with the governor. Whatever the case, on June 4, 1927, Martin surprised the state by designating Davis as Florida's attorney general to fill the unexpired term of J. B. Johnson. Davis would win reelection the following year without opposition.[143]

The new attorney general brought to his position the same indefatigable energy and work habits that his legal and political careers previously had evidenced, but his actions failed to please everyone, and they did so with surprising results. Youth helped. Only thirty-three when he assumed the office, Davis became the second youngest person to hold the post to that time. "He probably rendered more written opinions than any other Attorney General in a like period of time," Fuller Warren believed. "Prodigious worker," Justice Richard W. Ervin declared. Unfortunately, many of Davis's opinions failed to please the state's new governor. "When Doyle Carlton was elected governor of Florida, Fred was attorney general," Evelyn Burns recalled. "It was rumored that he very much wanted Fred off of his cabinet, because if he had any special project he wanted to push before the whole cabinet, the other members would vote with Fred because of their respect for his judgment." Whether other cabinet members favored Davis over Carlton remains uncertain. Clearly, though, Burns remembered correctly a subsequent observation. "Fred and the governor did not always see eye to eye," she recorded, "therefore, when a vacancy appeared on the Supreme Court, he appointed Fred

Davis, and Cary Landis became attorney general." The appointment, announced March 3, 1931, became effective six days later.[144]

Justice Davis brought to the supreme court a well-defined sense of law and jurisprudence. In an address delivered during 1933 he offered insight regarding them:

> The keystone of the law is clarity and consistency in applying its principles. Our scheme of government can only be successfully maintained as a government of law instead of a government of men, by constantly bearing this fundamental truth in mind. Constitutions were written to protect imperishable principles from being departed from in time of excitement and stress. Only to the extent that the fundamental law of the State and Nation is faithfully adhered to at all times and under all circumstances, can the liberties of a people and incidentally the business of the legal profession expect to survive. This is essentially because rights of life, liberty, property, and the pursuit of happiness must be protected from every impairment except by process of due law. Due process of law is a stable and permanent thing. It cannot be a fad like tenet administered by tribunals of justice with chameleon like aspect designed to reflect only the echoes of a rising chorus of yes men or the unreasoning impulses of numberless band wagon riders.

He concluded by appealing for bar aid for the judiciary:

> The courts are helpless to withstand the overwhelming pressure exerted upon them to yield to the policy of judicial noninterference with governmental acts unconstitutionally depriving a portion of the people of their constitutional liberties in the name of emergency, unless they have back of them a united bar reconsecrated to the service of the country in lending their best efforts to preserve the constitution from disintegration and dissolution by tolerating aggressions.[145]

Davis fared well as a member of the court and remained popular in a political sense as well. Voters returned him to the panel for a full term in 1932, and his colleagues joined the next year in naming him their chief justice for the ensuing two years. He thus earned the honor of being the youngest chief justice in Florida Supreme Court history and the youngest then serving in the nation. On the bench Davis worked hard, sometimes departing his chambers for dinner and then returning to labor until midnight. "He was the most brilliant justice I knew before I came to the court," Justice Ervin asserted. Fuller Warren added, "He left as a legacy to Florida some of the soundest judicial opinions ever written by any jurist of any state." Justice Glenn Terrell agreed. "He was a lawyer of splendid ability and one of the keenest judicial minds I ever have come in contact with."[146]

The pace, other stresses, and a weak heart, however, proved too much for Davis. New Deal liberalism and an increasingly compliant judiciary troubled the justice more and more. "He thoroughly believed in the U.S. Constitution," sister Evelyn insisted. "He felt that if this country ever collapsed, it would be because of opinions by the U.S. Supreme Court which were too liberal. He considered Franklin Roosevelt a dangerous president." Another of his protégés, future justice B. K. Roberts, saw a different but equally harmful stress. "He literally worked himself to death," Roberts argued. In any event, while visiting Jacksonville with his wife and friends on June 20, 1937, Justice Fred Henry Davis died in his sleep, reportedly of a heart attack. He was buried in Tallahassee's Old City Cemetery. "All Floridians," Fuller Warren declared, "can be grateful for the consecrated service he rendered in the legislative, executive, and judicial branches of the state government." No one, the future governor believed, had served Florida "more brilliantly" on the supreme bench.[147]

Following her husband's death, Frances Chambers Davis survived for thirty-six years, remaining active in Democratic Party affairs and worthy causes. In 1939 she married Fritz Gordon, who served as a circuit judge before passing away in 1971. She died at Coral Gables on December 24, 1973. Her daughters, Marilyn Davis Childers and Hazel Davis Holley, as well as a son, Robert Gordon, survived her.[148]

3

Court Decisions for a Tumultuous Era

Even for a state that periodically soared with boom times and endured the subsequent busts, the years stretching from 1917 to 1932 presented Florida with truly exceptional and changing circumstances, facts quickly mirrored in the state supreme court's work product. By midway through the era, a jammed calendar reflected virtually every aspect of modern life. Sometimes the jurists found the changes difficult to comprehend. At other times they proved more than willing to embrace the dynamics and moods of the times. As it turned out, the passage of the years tended to turn those moods away from expansiveness and more toward a defensive conservatism.

Naturally, the great events and many of the grand personalities of the times made their appearance in opinions. World War I, for example, raised legal questions at an early date. As the opinion in *Ex parte Marshall* illustrated, though, the panel—or at least a majority of its members—strove to express patriotic support without jeopardizing state's rights. The issue in *Marshall* concerned hackman A. C. Marshall's refusal to pay an auto license tax for vehicles used to ferry servicemen back and forth between Jacksonville and nearby Camp Johnston. Writing for the court, Justice R. Fenwick Taylor quickly distinguished between official governmental activities and those of a private businessman in holding Marshall accountable for the tax: "The case presented is simply of a firm of individuals residing in Jacksonville engaged in and presumably licensed to do a general business of running auto buses and automobiles for hire over the streets of said city who, as an incident of their general business make a side contract so to speak with an officer in command of an encampment of United States soldiers." Chief Justice Jefferson B. Browne, on the other hand, strongly disagreed: "If the services which the commanding officer of Camp Joseph E. Johnston considers essential for the morale, and safety of his men, are not in fact necessary, it is a matter for the National authorities to determine, and is not subject to review by the State courts."[1]

As the 1920s progressed, unprecedented growth and development understandably sparked litigation upon a wide variety of matters. Entrepreneur D. P. Davis, for example, found himself before the court in 1924 over plans to dredge and fill in Hillsborough Bay as part of efforts to create at Tampa the fabled and exotic Davis Islands residential and commercial district. In *State ex rel. Buford* v. *City of Tampa, et al.*, the tribunal pondered whether the state could transfer submerged lands subject to overflow at high tide. Justice William H. Ellis, writing for the majority, found no problem standing in the way of "progress," as understood within the context of Davis's boom-time development plans. "There is no provision in the Constitution of this State expressly or impliedly forbidding the Legislature to dispose of submerged lands lying between high and low water mark," Ellis observed for a three-man majority, "nor declaring any trust in the State in its tide waters, nor the submerged lands that may be subject to overflow at high tide."[2]

As was true for the state generally, not everyone on the court perceived development and change during the 1920s in the same manner as did Justice Ellis in the Davis case. Dissenters James B. Whitfield and William Glenn Terrell, for instance, saw "progress" and the constitution in starkly different terms than did their colleague. "For the purpose of enhancing the rights and interests of the whole people, the States may by appropriate means grant to individuals the title to limited portions of the lands under navigable waters, or may give limited privileges therein," Whitfield asserted, "but not so as to divert them from their proper uses for the public welfare, or so as to relieve the States respectively of the control and regulation of the uses afforded by the land and the waters, or so as to interfere with the lawful authority of Congress."[3]

In any event, the panel could unite on the idea of heavily taxing the real estate agents and brokers who benefited enormously from the chaotic transactions of the boom. Thus, in the 1926 decision in *Gillis ex rel. State of Florida* v. *Croft*, the justices unanimously permitted the City of Fort Lauderdale to levy an occupational license tax on realtors in the considerable amount of $250. The legislature, in authorizing such taxes, set no limits, Justice Rivers H. Buford reasoned. Plus, the realtors offered no showing "that the amount of the tax worked any hardship on the business, or prevents or deters anyone from becoming a real estate broker, or is in any way unreasonable, arbitrary, oppressive or unjust, or discriminatory."[4]

The unanimity seen in *Gillis* but missing from the Davis case reappeared in another key developmental decision rendered in 1928, after the boom had collapsed into bust. The state's economic crisis apparently encouraged the panel to uphold Governor John Martin's ambitious Everglades drainage program. Now development represented jobs and recovery, and Justice Whitfield, speaking for his brethren, waxed eloquently of the plan's positive aspects. "The public improvement is designed for the immediate and potential permanent general benefit to the entire statutory district containing millions of acres," Whitfield explained in

Martin v. *Dade Muck Land Co.*, "by making the lands both public and private that are affected by surplus water fit for improvement and development by growing thereon fruit, vegetables, and staple crops, live stock, and other products, by the erection of commercial, residential, and other structures, by establishing business enterprises, transportation facilities, better flood control, sanitary, health, and general welfare conditions, and by making the lands in the district that are not overflowed more accessible from and over lands to be drained, and more valuable for all useful purposes."[5]

Meanwhile, boom and bust had produced within the state a level of criminal activity that overwhelmed and sometimes corrupted Florida's meager law enforcement network. Seen against this backdrop, the 1926 decision in *Washington* v. *Dowling*, which permitted substitution of death by electrocution for death by hanging, ratified a pro–law enforcement stance. The court in 1927's *Pompano Horse Club, Inc., et al.* v. *State ex rel. Bryan*, with Justices Ellis and Buford dissenting, went further by allowing lower courts to enjoin illegal gambling through recourse to public nuisance statutes. The next year the panel upheld a 1927 "three-strikes law" patterned after a New York statute. The measure considered in *Cross* v. *State* provided mandatory prison terms even when some of the felonies were committed in another state. "Such statutes," Justice Louie Strum advised, "are not modern innovations in the law."[6]

Where criminals felt the court's stern disapproval on many occasions, businessmen often found allies in combating tough times. Three decisions of 1929–30 make the point. In *Folsom* v. *Bank of Greenwood*, owners of bank stock complained of a lack of uniformity in assessment. This state of affairs, Justice Whitfield declared for the panel, constituted denial of equal protection of the laws and rendered the assessment invalid. The court in *Colonial Investment Co.* v. *Nolan* similarly responded to corporate complaints regarding a 25 percent penalty assessed by the 1929 legislature for failure to make a property tax return. With Justices Terrell and Whitfield dissenting, Justice Armstead Brown found the statute invalid based upon a defective title. Finally, mortgage holders breathed a sigh of relief following release of the decision in *Gober* v. *Braddock*. In that opinion, the tribunal for the first time held that a mortgage holder not satisfied by collateral could sue for the balance owed. Commissioner Charles E. Davis penned the judgment with all justices concurring.[7]

The following cases additionally reflect the tone and relevance of the court's attitudes during the era.

Airplanes and Automobiles

Transportation innovations and improvements marked the period and, in key ways, fueled the changes that it brought. Where railroads previously had dominated the area, now the relatively new inventions of the airplane and the automobile increasingly captured attention. In 1929, for instance, the court recognized the legitimate claims of persons injured in airplane calamities as against the interests of insurance companies and the technical wording of their policies. An exclusion of coverage for "accidents of those engaged in aviation," Justice Whitfield determined for a unanimous court in *Price* v. *Prudential Insurance Company of America*, did not apply to the plaintiff's claim for the death of her husband in that, as a passenger, he was not "engaged" in aviation within the full meaning of the term.[8]

By far, the larger number of decisions addressed automobiles and concerns related to them. Already by 1921, the tribunal had extended the dangerous instrumentality doctrine to motor vehicles. "Far from being the enunciation of 'a judicial statute,'" Justice Browne wrote in *Southern Cotton Oil Co.* v. *Anderson*, " . . . it is but the application of an old and well settled principle to new conditions. A locomotive in the roundhouse, a trolley car in the barn, an automobile in a garage, are almost as harmless as canary birds; but in operation they are dangerous instrumentalities and the master who intrusts them to another to operate—the one, on its rights of way; the others, on the public highways—cannot exonerate himself from liability for injury caused to others by the negligence of those to whom they are intrusted." The court in 1924's *State ex rel. Sellars* v. *Parker*, struck a similar chord in placing its stamp of approval on Jacksonville's pioneering drunk driving law, drafted by City Attorney Louie Strum. "The offense defined by the ordinance relates to the operation of an instrumentality that may be peculiarly dangerous in its use," Justice Whitfield commented, "and the ordinance affects the peace, safety, and welfare of persons on the streets of the city, which is a proper subject of municipal regulation even to the extent of imposing imprisonment in the city prisons."[9]

Numerous other decisions similarly stressed the automobile's newly won prevalence and importance. *State ex rel. Bonsteel* v. *Allen*, decided in 1922, witnessed Justice Jefferson Browne sustaining for a united panel the state's motor vehicle license law, even though it dedicated most funds generated by the act solely to road construction. In another example, the opinion in 1929's *Frazee* v. *Gillispie* made clear that due care must be exercised in the operation of a motor vehicle. "Eternal vigilance is in these days the price of safety," Justice Armstead Brown declared. "Due care for the safety of life, limb, and property requires constant and unrelaxing vigilance."[10]

The due care principle was extended within two years to a requirement that persons riding in cars driven by others look to their own safety. The decision in *Florida Motor Lines, Inc.* v. *Ward* afforded relief from some liability claims for common carriers while it specified a passenger's duty to warn the driver of on-coming hazards. "[In] our day with the good road, the motor car, the railroad, and other devices for transporting persons and property and both moving hither and yon in every direction at all times of the day and night the law of the road has assumed a place of unusual importance in our legal code," Justice Terrell observed. "The year preceding this records 33,000 deaths, one half-million accidents, over one million injuries and the loss of other millions in property to the credit of the heedless and incautious driver. Too often those who are circumspect in the observance of the amenities of polite society suddenly become obsessed by the rule of the survival of the fittest the minute they grasp a steering wheel. The law of the road is now embraced in statutes, ordinances, and regulations, is promulgated for the protection of life and property, it is an essential part of the common knowledge of every traveler, and he who goes on the highway and negligently or otherwise fails to observe it does so at his peril."[11]

Although court members proved more than willing to wrap automobile operation within the framework of negligence law, the jurists shied away from generous compensation for injuries, including those sustained in motor vehicle accidents or otherwise on streets and highways. Mamie Davis learned this fact when, in the early 1920s, she sued for the wrongful death of her husband. The court in *Southern Utilities Co.* v. *Moore ex rel. Davis* overturned the $18,000 judgment she obtained as excessive, in the process ruling out recovery for her mental anxiety or distress or for her deceased husband's mental or physical suffering from his injury. In the same vein, when a negligently operated auto killed a child as he alighted from a street car, the panel in *Meeks* v. *Johnston, et al.* directed a verdict for defendants as to damages for the parents' "great mental pain and anguish." Justice Whitfield noted, "If for any reason a parent may recover for the loss of services of a minor child caused by the wrongful death of the child, a right to recover for mental pain and suffering is not necessarily thereby affected." The same year the court considered a $5,000 award for a broken arm and bruises sustained through a fall into an unguarded excavation in a city street to be "manifestly excessive." The jurists suggested that a $2,500 payment would suffice.[12]

Alcoholic Beverage Regulation

The years 1917 to 1932 spanned the heart of the era of Prohibition in Florida and in the nation. Questions and issues of every stripe demanded the attention of state jurists, with the supreme court repeatedly compelled to address matters of controversy and complexity. To inaugurate the period, the panel in *Van Pelt* v. *Hilliard* considered a 1917 state law that attempted to curb social drinking in private clubs. This foray into the private sphere met with the court's approval. Circuit Judge James T. Wills, on behalf of himself and Justices Browne, Taylor, Whitfield, and Ellis, perceived the question of alcohol consumption as one involving a matter injurious to the community. As such, he argued, the police power enabled legislators to act. "Individual interests are not all considered in the exercise of the power," Wills insisted. "They must yield when they are in opposition to the public good."[13]

Not every Prohibition-related measure met with such unanimous approval. A 1918 ruling in *Ex parte Francis*, for instance, saw the tribunal split three to two. There, a new statute limited severely the transportation from a wet county into a dry one of alcoholic beverages for personal use. The majority declared the law invalid. "The discrimination made by this act between the quantity of intoxicating liquor a person may have for his own use in the different counties of the State, finds no justification either in the Constitution or in a valid exercise of the State's police power," Justice Jefferson B. Browne concluded. Justice Whitfield, with Justice West's support, strongly objected. "The police power is governmental authority to regulate personal conduct and property rights for the general welfare," he averred. "It is obvious that the improper or excessive use of intoxicating liquor is regarded by the lawmaking power of the State as being an evil that is detrimental to the general welfare."[14]

The division continued, although the majority reversed, in *Marasso* v. *Van Pelt*. In late 1918 voters had approved a constitutional amendment ushering in statewide Prohibition effective January 1919, even though they did so by a tiny margin and only thanks to an electorate restricted by the poll tax. An Escambia County defendant quickly challenged the ban as a violation of his inalienable right to property. With Justice Ellis switching sides in the debate, a new three-man majority led by Justice Whitfield and including Justice West, rejected the claim. "The sovereign police power of the State extends to all matters that affect the individual and collective welfare of the people, and being universal, it is potentially applicable to all the environments and activities of human life in the family home as well as in the business and public places."[15]

Dissenting in *Marasso* v. *Van Pelt*, Justice Browne questioned the judgment's implications and found them extremely dangerous in a world changed by war and revolution. "If the decision could be limited in its effect to intoxicating liquors it would be harmless as a precedent, as the liquor question will soon be as completely removed from political consideration as the question of slavery. Unfortunately, however, we cannot so limit its scope, and the time is not far distant when it and the decisions by which it is supported will be authority for further inroads upon private ownership of property." Browne concluded, "We cannot bind ourselves to the socialistic conditions prevailing in other countries, and rapidly winning adherents here, whereby the rights of property and the rights of persons are ruthlessly destroyed; justified by the doctrine of public welfare."[16]

Despite support on the tribunal for Prohibition, overzealous enforcement sometimes compelled the jurists to sustain individual rights as opposed to the "public good." One example of this implementation occurred in 1921's *Haile* v. *Gardner*. Officers had searched the defendant's home at night for moonshine whiskey without benefit of a warrant. This invasion, a unanimous court insisted, could not be tolerated. "What is a reasonable or valid search or seizure, is to be determined by the courts upon due consideration of the circumstances and manner in which the search and seizure is made by the officer," Justice Whitfield wrote.

> No search or seizure is permissible under the law without a proper warrant duly issued, except as a reasonable search and seizure may be allowed by law as an incident to a lawful arrest. Where an arrest without a warrant is allowed by law, as for an offense being committed or threatened in the presence of an officer authorized by law to make arrests for such offense, a reasonable search and seizure that is properly incident to a lawful arrest may be made in a reasonable and proper manner by the officer making the lawful arrest; but the search and seizure should not be inappropriate to the reasonable requirements for making effective a lawful arrest. Warrants authorizing a search or seizure may be issued only by the authorized officers and such warrants should not be issued except upon a due showing upon oath or affirmation, indicating a probable violation of the law; and the warrants should particularly describe the person or place or thing to be searched or seized as indicated in the applications duly made for the warrants.[17]

Court members drew careful lines as well when it came to observing proprieties during prosecutions. One illustration of the fact came in 1922's *Hall* v. *State*. The appeal questioned an indictment for illegal possession of rum and moonshine. Justice Whitfield, upon consideration, dismissed the charges. The indictment, he pronounced, was fatally defective for "failing to allege in any way that the rum or moonshine liquor was alcoholic or intoxicating." All members concurred.[18]

As shown in 1922's *Wright* v. *Worth*, on the other hand, the court's majority found flexibility in determining who could enforce Prohibition. The issue came down to whether municipalities possessed the authority. Justice Whitfield easily upheld the municipal position, although Justice Browne once again warned of unintended consequences. "The ordinance of the City of Tampa is but another move in the direction of destroying constitutional guarantees," Browne contended, "and tends to retard the 'back to the constitution' movement, lately inaugurated by the great public thinkers of the country, which is so essential, if anything is to be left of the liberties of the people that the framers of our constitution sought to safeguard."[19]

Corporate Responsibility

Despite its tendency over time to support business interests, as suggested by the following two decisions, the supreme court demanded accountability from corporate officers in an era of corporate license. In 1919's *Beach* v. *Williamson*, Justice Ellis specified some of the standards to be applied. "When one accepts the position of director of a corporation he contracts to give diligent attention to its concerns and to be faithful and honest in the discharge of the duties that the position imposes. He is not supposed to be infallible and does not stipulate against error, but he will not be permitted to speculate with corporate funds or property to his personal gain nor by suppressing information concerning corporate properties [nor] be permitted to acquire them as purchaser at a small price to the consequent injury of the corporation or its creditors." In 1931 the tribunal extended strictures in some instances outside state limits. Officers or stockholders of corporations not authorized to do business in the state are personally liable, Ellis now held, when they sign for their corporation in Florida.[20]

Elections Law

The tumultuous era produced countless chaotic elections and heated election contests. One of the most important decisions to result came in *Darby, et al.* v. *State ex rel. McCullough*, a 1917 case arising out of a Walton County school bond referendum. In *Darby*, the court considered two ballots marked after the words *Against Bonds* rather than before them as required by law. In deciding that the votes should be counted, the panel stressed the "will of the voter" as the determining factor. "Where a ballot is so marked as to plainly indicate the voter's choice and intent in placing his marks thereon," the *per curiam* opinion expressed, "it should be counted as marked unless some positive provision of law would be thereby violated."[21]

By century's end the decision in *Darby* would carry enormous political implications as Florida grappled to decide whether it had voted for a Democrat or a Republican for president of the United States, but seven decades earlier the tribunal already had confronted a similar political contest. *Ex parte Beattie*, decided in 1929, concerned a recent Pinellas County sheriff's election where a Republican candidate had astounded Democrats by securing—it appeared—a victory. In the aftermath, winner Gladstone R. Beattie approached the supreme court asking that it promulgate a writ of prohibition against issuance by Circuit Judge O. L. Dayton of a common law writ of mandamus to compel a recount. Defeated Democrat Roy Booth earlier had petitioned Dayton for the mandamus writ. Justice Terrell declined on the court's behalf to grant Beattie's request. Terrell acknowledged that a writ of mandamus could not be utilized to contest the election. He concluded that it could, however, be used to compel officials to perform their "ministerial duties."[22]

Labor Law

With certain isolated exceptions, organized labor had yet to gain a strong foothold in Florida during the 1920s, yet several court decisions set the stage for significant litigation in the decades thereafter. In 1924's *American Railway Express Co.* v. *Johnson, et al.*, to cite an example, a unanimous panel found that an outlaw strike of railroad switchmen constituted a strike under the law even though the action had not been approved by the labor union's head. The decision effectively released common carriers from liability for damages in the face of an outlaw strike.[23]

Perhaps more significantly, the 1932 decision in *Paramount Enterprises, Inc.* v. *Mitchell* directly considered the legality of labor picketing. The bill of complaint had alleged that "the defendants conspired to injure the plaintiff's business threatening the theatre-going public." For the court, Justice Terrell dismissed the assertion and upheld the legality of peaceful picketing. "It is well settled that employees have a right to combine and fix the amount of their daily wage and to whom they will sell it. It is also true that when under no contract they may quit the service of another at any time they desire. It is alike true that employers have a right to determine the daily wage they are willing to pay and whom they employ." The justice concluded, "Members of a labor organization may presume and confederate not to work except upon payment of an established wage; they may without coercion bring their cause to the note of public opinion in a peaceful manner."[24]

Local Government Powers

With Florida emerging during the 1920s as an ever more urban state, the supreme court year after year addressed issues related to the ability of local governments to govern effectively despite the state's restrictive 1885 constitution and legislators leery of surrendering authority. In quite a number of instances the panel found local actions invalid. The court's 1919 decision in *Ellis* v. *Thiesen*, for instance, declared unconstitutional a municipal ordinance requiring installation of "sanitary cans" in certain buildings. "The ordinance of the City of Pensacola permits an arbitrary discrimination by the city authorities both as to the class of 'buildings' in which privies must be installed," Justice Browne explained, "and as to the time when the penalty provided by the ordinance shall be imposed."[25]

Similarly, when the 1920 legislature permitted county commissions to set the compensation of county officers, the court's majority objected. Although Justices Whitfield and West dissented, Justice Browne insisted that the legislature must act directly rather than authorize local government to do so. "The provision giving the County Commissioners power to fix the salaries of the officers according to the fancy of the Board of County Commissioners, which may vary in each of the fifty-two counties of the State, destroys that uniformity which is contemplated by the Constitution," Browne advised, "and is in direct violation of those provisions of the Constitution requiring the compensation of county officers to be fixed by law."[26]

The power of local government to combat catastrophic economic conditions emerged as an especially critical issue following the 1926 bust. Popular tools for reversing the downward spiral included the sponsorship of attractions and facilities, which the community then would advertise in order to garner more capital, tourists, and new residents. Here again the court found cause to object, as Justice Ellis's opinion in 1931's *Loeb* v. *City of Jacksonville* illustrated. "The idea that our cities, considered as governmental agencies, are vast commercial institutions specializing in pleasure grounds, athletic fields, radio broadcasting stations, music halls, and stadiums is a novel one, especially in view of the powers of government as defined and outlined in our constitution." As such, he argued for a unanimous panel, municipalities were without authority to expend tax dollars for advertising.[27]

In at least one area of interest—land use affected by riparian rights—the court proved more amenable to municipal authority. One example arose in 1918, when the jurists decided *Brickell* v. *Town of Fort Lauderdale*. The litigation involved a suit for injunction by the town against longtime local developers who had laid out the original town site, and it concerned a planned development along the New

River waterfront that would obstruct certain streets. Justice Browne's opinion, concurred in by Justices Taylor, Whitfield, Ellis, and West, required extraordinary evidence to rebut a presumption that the public holds riparian rights appurtenant to a street that ends at a navigable body of water. "It is 'inconceivable' and 'preposterous' to contend that a town would be located on the banks of a navigable river and the inhabitants deprived of the right of access to the river," Browne expounded. The justice pursued the point to assert a municipality's duty to residents as a trustee of the public streets and to authorize the town to bar encroachments of public rights of way.[28]

Three years afterward, the court again endorsed public riparian rights against a developer who sought to limit public access to water. The ruling in *City of Tarpon Springs* v. *Smith* turned on the fact that a dedicator of streets had not reserved riparian rights. "The dedication by the owner under the particular town plat, showing streets, etc., manifestly did not give any easement or other rights beyond the expressly designated limits of the streets and the incidents that are appropriate thereto," Justice Whitfield noted. "Wherever the street, Anclote boulevard, as delineated by line and stated width, touches or approximately touches the body of the Anclote river, the riparian rights that are appropriate to a street easement were also impliedly dedicated as an incident; there being no express or implied reservation by the dedicator of such riparian rights."[29]

Race and Race Relations

Only a few major appeals involving race reached the supreme court during the period beginning with World War I and continuing into the 1920s and early 1930s, even though race relations deteriorated in Florida during the period and incidents of racial violence touched virtually every corner of the state. Overall, the justices remained committed to white supremacy and the racial status quo, attitudes that greatly influenced their legal reasoning. One 1921 appeal, somewhat to the contrary, did express what panel members considered their standards for application of equal justice under the law. The case, *Tillman* v. *State*, involved a black defendant accused of assault with intent to murder a white Manatee County deputy sheriff and the deputy's action in stopping the defendant while walking on a public highway and then seizing a package from him without authority of a search or arrest warrant. Justice Browne's ruling reversed the conviction. "The guarantees of the Constitution protect all classes and races alike," Browne reasoned.

> It is but a step, and a short one, from violating the rights of negroes to violating the rights of white persons. . . . However zealous an officer may be in

> the performance of his duties, he should not forget that his oath to 'support, protect, and defend the Constitution' precludes his seizing property in violation of the Constitution. Eliminate the question of race or color, and the case presented is that of a person walking on a public highway at night and is accosted by another, who assaults him and seeks to take from him by force, without warrant, property in his possession. The assaulted person resists, and in the scuffle shots are fired at the assailant. This would not be an assault to commit murder in either the first or the second degree.[30]

State Regulatory Authority

Two major cases highlighted an important shift in the court's perspective of state regulatory authority from early in the period to its closing years. In 1920, the panel in *State ex rel. Triay* v. *Burr* unanimously upheld the state railroad commission's authority to regulate local transit companies. Justice Whitfield's opinion stressed that any legislative grant of authority in furtherance of the state's police power should be construed liberally and that "all doubts as to the jurisdiction and powers of the railroad commissioners [should be] resolved in their favor."[31]

Eleven years later, following the collapse of the boom and the spread of state and national economic depression, a different climate of opinion prevailed. Now the justices led by Armstead Brown often sought to free businesses of government-imposed restraints. This proved the case, for instance, in *Seaboard Air Line Railway Co., et al.* v. *Wells, et al.*, where the court limited state railroad commission authority to grant permits for truck lines to compete with railroads. Brown justified the ruling, in light of the tribunal's previous stands, by finding that the commission did not always act "for the public convenience and necessity" when making its decisions. Delving into the facts of the matter, Brown determined that the plaintiffs fully and adequately served the territory between Jacksonville and Tallahassee and that no need existed for parallel truck service.[32]

Women's Rights

The Nineteenth Amendment to the U.S. Constitution, effective in 1920, guaranteed the right to vote regardless of sex, fostering revolutionary movement of women into the public sphere. The Florida justices, as was true of most men, struggled to understand the new order of things. As suggested by the opinions in 1924's *State ex rel. Buford* v. *Daniel, et al.*, they followed different paths in doing so, paths that would echo in the women's rights and civil rights crusades of the future. The litigation concerned a state law requiring appointment of women, as well as men, to the Duval County welfare board. The majority accepted this mandate as reasonable and constitutional. "In erecting the office the legislators may prescribe the qualifications of the officers, and the provision requiring both men and women to be appointed to the board merely recognizes the inherent differences between men and women immutably fixed by nature," Justice Whitfield observed, "and also recognizes political equalities imposed by law upon men and women electors for appointment under the act." Whitfield added, "The peculiar nature of the special duties make it appropriate that members of both sexes be appointed."[33]

Justices Ellis and Browne questioned the majority's comprehension and insights, suggesting that its members were limiting, rather than guaranteeing, women's participation in public affairs. "In view of the Nineteenth Amendment to the Federal Constitution there exists no principle in government upon which women, as a class, may be excluded from service as governmental officers," Ellis wrote. "To limit, therefore, her membership on any board, commission, court, or legislature to a minority is to assert the power of reducing her opportunity for service to a negligible quantity. Eligibility to offices does not rest upon considerations of sex nor does woman's qualifications for public service rest upon assumed spiritual endowments, or beauty of soul, nor peculiar faculty for discerning the distinctions, with clearer perceptions between right and wrong than her male compatriot." Ellis concluded, "As a qualified member of the electorate she is, so far as constitutional, logical, legal, physical, moral and intellectual inhibitions are concerned, free and qualified to become an official of government in any of its branches; and being so qualified her activities cannot be limited to that sphere of influence to which she may be assigned by her generous but mistaken fellow citizens of the male persuasion."[34]

PART TWO

The Great Depression and World War II, 1933–1945

4

Economic Calamity and War's Challenge

The period of crisis and challenge that marked Florida's experience from 1933 to 1945 commenced inauspiciously, although several seemingly unrelated events signaled many of the trials that lay ahead. One of them took place January 3, 1933, in Tallahassee. At the state capitol, Chief Justice Rivers H. Buford administered the oath of office to the new governor, David Sholtz. Sholtz's inaugural address touched upon the seriousness of the times. "I am soberly conscious of the responsibility which I assume on this occasion, and I do humbly realize that mine is the obligation to respond with all of the industry and ability that God has given me to the trust and confidence you have reposed in me. You are a patient people because you have borne disappointments and hardships that always attend a national and worldwide depression with fortitude and with hope." The chief executive then cast blame on at least some of those whom he believed responsible for the dilemma. "The unfortunate financial and economical condition in which many of our counties, municipalities, and tax districts now find themselves is, to some extent, a result of the indifference of our people to governmental matters. Until we have a wise, sane, conservative, and economical administration of affairs, there will be no influx of capital here until men with financial means are assured of state administration."[1]

Meanwhile, a second and very different ceremony had just occurred 250 miles distant from the state capital, at Lakeland in the heart of the fast-growing peninsula. On January 2, African Americans had gathered to celebrate Emancipation Day with a parade and speeches. Among the orators, Jacksonville attorney S. D. McGill, who would go on to appear in more cases before a state supreme court than any other black lawyer during his era, stood out. "The colored man is just as intelligent as the white man," McGill proclaimed to eager ears. Calling for political activism and social change, the lawyer added, "We need fifteen more [Oscar] De Priests in Congress." The scene disturbed one white newspaperman greatly, so much so that he perceived "a semblance of communism or bolshevism in the effort." The journalist warmed to his subject. "Many of the people who drop in on a community, are nothing more than advance agents for propagandists that are fighting American principles, and those people who come in and try to make the colored people think they are being held down, that they have rights that are not being given them, have something else up their sleeves besides trying to help this country." The journalist concluded, "Any efforts to stir up the colored people is wrong."[2]

Six weeks then passed before the next event of portent, but when it occurred, all eyes immediately focused on Florida. On February 15, having been welcomed at Miami's Bayfront Park by dignitaries including Circuit Judge Paul D. Barns, President-elect Franklin Delano Roosevelt endured the terror of an assassination attempt. Roosevelt escaped unharmed, but his companion, Chicago mayor Anton Cermak, lay mortally wounded. On March 4, Roosevelt took his own oath of office to assume leadership of a nation in crisis. Sixteen days later, Florida executed Giuseppe Zangara for Cermak's murder. The state's judicial system had taken a mere thirty-three days to exact the ultimate penalty. In the death chamber, though, Zangara remained defiant. When authorities refused to allow photographers to record his death, the assassin shouted at them, "No pictures—capitalists—all capitalists—lousy bunch—crooks."[3]

If the attempted assassination of the president-elect and the murder of Chicago's mayor vividly illustrated Florida's struggle with crime and a level of violence that sometimes seemed pervasive, then one additional happening of 1933, one that proceeded without the glare of publicity that attended Zangara's mad assault, set the stage for a decadelong struggle as the state grappled with the thorny question of the standards of justice appropriate for a tumultuous time. This occurrence was the Isiah Chambers case. It began on the night of May 13 when unknown assailants beat Pompano Beach fish dealer Robert Darsey to death. "Enraged Pompano citizens formed a posse soon after Darsey's body was found," one newspaper reported, "and several lynchings were threatened." Broward County sheriff Walter Clark thereafter arrested several dozen black men for questioning. Over six days authorities relentlessly interrogated the men without allowing them consultations with counsel, releasing one after another until only four remained. The next morning Isiah Chambers, Jack Williamson, Charley Davis, and Walter Woodward confessed and soon found themselves convicted of murder and sentenced to death. The judicial processes that so quickly had terminated Zangara's life slowed only when the Florida Supreme Court in August ordered a stay of execution. As allegations of "torture" and "miscarriage of justice" swirled in the air and in the press, lawyers Daniel W. Perkins, S. D. McGill, and others launched themselves upon a frustrating nine-year journey to reach a final determination of where justice lay in the matter.[4]

Few Floridians, white or black, though, paid attention to the Chambers case, given more immediate and personal distractions. One student of the period described the state of affairs then prevailing. "The entire country was in desperate straits, not just the South, and the pervasiveness of deprivation made it seem more ordinary and natural than it was," John Egerton recorded. "Disparities of race and social class were so much a part of the culture that it was rare to hear them challenged. And, when you consider the region's ameliorating qualities—the strengths of character and personality, the sheltering arms of church and family, the warmth of many personal relationships, the fertility of the fields, the yield of woods and waters, the healing warmth of winter, and all the rest—it's not surprising that some southerners remember the thirties and forties with nostalgic fondness. But hardship there was, and plenty of it, from top to bottom—and the closer you were to the bottom of the economic and social ladder, the worse it got."[5]

For some, desperation came as almost too kind a term. Starvation threatened more than a few, while others begged for employment of any kind. "As a general rule, people want work instead of charity," one commentator observed. "Nine out of ten had rather earn their living than get it from some relief agency. But work is not to be had." Over 107,000 Florida families required charity by October 1933. Crime rates climbed, with youth crime and crime by women grabbing headlines at unprecedented rates. At the social ladder's bottom, the pleas rose with increasing fervor. "I am jobless," a woman informed Governor Sholtz. "I am asking you to help us women get some work. These white folks don't pay us house and washwomen any more than the same 50 cents a day. They don't mean for us to get any more." She closed, "I am afraid to sign my name."[6]

Fears of economic calamity haunted even the more well-to-do, although it should be noted that most Floridians remained employed and relatively secure. Florida's depression by 1933 already had endured for seven years, and many had accommodated themselves to it without undue discomfort. "Those of us in the middle part of the state scarcely realized times were bad until the banks were ordered closed by Roosevelt on March 5, 1933," a survivor of the times recalled. "This brought us up with a jerk!" In fact, the citrus industry had recovered substantially from the 1929 Mediterranean fruit fly infestation, and although hurricane damage and competition undercut profits in 1933, by the following year production and revenues had rebounded. Meanwhile, phosphate industry profits climbed 75 percent from 1932 to 1934. Half a million tourists had returned to the state by winter 1932, a figure that climbed steadily to two million three years later, the largest tourist season in Florida history. "If one would go to Miami now and look around at the crowds of people spending large sums of money for pleasure," University of Florida economist A. Stuart Campbell insisted, "he would not believe that we are just getting over the worst depression in our history."[7]

Florida's problem with poverty related not so much to those whose roots in the state extended so far back even as the 1920s as with the flood of newcomers escaping unemployment and freezing winters in the North, Midwest, and South by flight toward the relatively more plentiful opportunities in the Sunshine State. Even with Depression-era blues, the state's population jumped by almost 30 percent during the 1930s to nearly 1.9 million. Dade County's 142,000 in 1930 swelled to nearly 268,000 ten years later, with Miami by then vying with Jacksonville for honors as the state's largest city. Broward County grew by 50 percent to about 30,000; Palm Beach went to almost 80,000 from 53,000; Hillsborough added almost 30,000; Duval jumped 55,000; and Orange added 40 percent to boast 70,000 by decade's end.[8]

The state's tremendous growth brought with it dynamics that would change Florida permanently, but when combined with rising crime rates and exhausted relief efforts, it sounded alarms of immediate problems as well. The arrival of "hoboes," the erection of tent cities, and the proliferation of trailer camps and trailer parks stirred fears and sparked complaints of "trailer trash" and other problems. Governor Sholtz responded by quarantining the state's borders during the winters of 1935 and 1936 and ordering law enforcement officers to turn back "fundless jobseekers." Governor Fred P. Cone suspended the "border patrol" in 1937 but warned "vagrants, crooks, and 'racketeers in fine limousines and Pullman cars'" that they "had best beware of local police and sheriff's forces."[9]

One group of newcomers especially provoked the ire of some of the state's most affluent and influential residents. Union organizers took up the cause of labor in areas beyond the port cities and phosphate mines where they earlier had carved out bases of power. The citrus groves especially welcomed them as workers reeled from pay cuts and aggravating working conditions wrought by owners anxious to maintain profit levels. Growers combined with local and state governments to resist the incursion. In April 1934 sheriff's deputies kidnapped organizer Frank Norman at Lakeland, after which he disappeared. The Congress of Industrial Organizations (CIO), which one Florida businessman pronounced a "communistic organization seeking power for the Marxian government," entered the picture in 1937. Confrontations, strikes, and countermeasures ensued with labor able to tally few successes. Still, organized labor had served notice of its intention to persist in focusing on Florida.[10]

Hard times, fears of newcomers, of the future, of changes occurring with head-spinning rapidity, and of the unknown, and the support of business interests anxious to preserve their authority offered fertile conditions in the 1930s for a revival of the Ku Klux Klan. Although the organization never had disbanded in Florida, its numbers ballooned in the 1930s as leaders pointed to "bums," "communists," "outside agitators," and others whom, they argued, were responsible for bad conditions or else were intent upon taking away from ordinary folk whatever remained to them. The organization and its members enjoyed a virtual immunity from interference or prosecution by law enforcement authorities, with a number of policemen and sheriff's deputies proudly boasting membership cards. As late as 1939, police escorts protected Klan parades at Orlando, while burning crosses lit up Florida nights on occasions. Whippings and murders stained the state as well. To cite just one of many examples, on July 19, 1935, Klansmen attacked a Fort Lauderdale jail, pulled black prisoner Reuben Stacy from his cell, hanged him from a convenient tree nearby, and then shot him seventeen times.[11]

Klan operations centered mostly in the peninsula where the era's tensions ran highest, but even where the KKK rarely trod—particularly the Panhandle region of north Florida—violence and lynchings punctuated the social and racial climates. Most notably, the lynching of the black man Claude Neal in Jackson County on October 27, 1934, grabbed state and national attention. The tragedy, as described by historian James R. McGovern, "included every element of violence associated with the practice from a public manhunt to the public display of the victim's body." National Association for the Advancement of Colored People (NAACP) spokesman Walter White characterized it as "one of the most bestial crimes ever committed by a mob."[12]

As the times fostered KKK activities and racial violence, so too did they reinvigorate efforts to resist racial prejudice, racial violence, and Jim Crow discrimination. Local branches of the NAACP organized in many locales, while their members raised funds to ensure proper legal defenses for black defendants, as occurred in the Chambers case. NAACP officials also acted directly to save lives, including, unsuccessfully, that of Claude Neal. By 1940, a statewide organization had coalesced as the Florida State Conference of Branches, the first statewide conference in NAACP history. Many of its leaders, including President Harry T. Moore of Brevard County, were teachers who had participated actively in the work of the Florida State Teachers Association. That group, beginning in 1937, launched suits aimed at equalizing teacher salaries. Failing to achieve its goals at first, the organization captured an important prize in 1940 when the Escambia County School Board, faced with principal Vernon McDaniel's demands and S. D. McGill's legal skills, offered a compromise leading to equalization. In July 1942, U.S. District Court judge Louie W. Strum's order requiring equalization in Marion County signaled a new era dawning.[13]

Many of the stresses that tore at Florida's social fabric during the years of depression and war derived from the difficulty of adjusting to a state dramatically altered by time and circumstances. This fact especially proved true for numerous state officials, whose Tallahassee offices lay almost literally a world away from the new Florida being built up in the peninsula. They tended to share the same—and an increasingly outmoded—view of Florida as a rural and slow-paced paradise of limited government. Perhaps Lake City's Fred P. Cone, governor from 1937 to 1941, most typified the stance. He rejected the implications of Roosevelt administration initiatives, calling instead for "a return to the old principles of the Democratic Party." As Cone asserted, "The best government is that which is operated with the least taxes. If we will run our government in that way we will be following one of the oldest principles the Democratic Party has."[14]

The audience most admiring of Cone's stance consisted of Florida's legislative majority. In 1920, more than half of all residents lived less than one hundred miles from the Georgia and Alabama state lines, but the 1930s and 1940s changed the equation markedly as the population center moved southward into the peninsula. Yet, despite constitutional requirements for legislative reapportionment and redistricting, rural north Florida representatives refused to cede power. A 1923 reapportionment had left 27 percent of the population controlling the legislature; from there time's passage had made a bad situation more critical. This fact certainly helps to explain why the 1935 legislature, despite Florida's advancing urban and peninsular orientation, adopted as the state song "Old Folks at Home" or, as it is more commonly known, "Suwannee River." Governors typically maintained a hands-off position on the apportionment question, at least until 1945 when Governor Millard Caldwell demanded action. Titanic political battles fought in summer heat eventually gave south Florida two more seats in the state senate but left power solidly in rural north Florida hands. The governor labeled the action "the best possible under the circumstances."[15]

Some voices did call for recognition and appreciation of the day's changes while urging needed preparation for the future. Dean Walter J. Matherly of the University of Florida's College of Business Administration offered one of them. "While the United States during the first century and a quarter of its existence depended primarily upon agriculture and glorified the occupation of the farmer, the rise of industrialism has pushed agriculture into the background," he instructed audiences over the state. "[Now,] agriculture in America as well as in other leading nations is declining relative to other fields of economic activity. Industrialism triumphant is in the forefront, overshadowing everything else." Although agriculture remained a very strong component of Florida's economy and heavy industry failed to gain a toehold in the state, mining, tourism, transportation, service, and related industries foretold a future not unlike the one Matherly foresaw. Symbolic of this future were modern airports including Miami's, as well as airlines such as Pan American Airways, Eastern Airlines, and National Airlines that called Florida their home.[16]

An occasional voice of progress also could be heard reverberating out of legislative halls. State Representative LeRoy Collins of Tallahassee was such a man. As opposed to leaders who shared Governor Cone's desire to turn back the clock on government, Collins argued for a different path. "The democratic form of government is not a completed structure," he insisted, "but rather it is a structure that each succeeding generation must add to and shape to suit the needs of that generation." In the state senate Dade County's Ernest Graham and Spessard Holland of Polk likewise urged new ways of doing things. Recognizing the corruption that had infested Florida political life since the poll tax's adoption in 1889, they secured its repeal in 1937 in a remarkable political tour de force. Three years later, voters chose Holland to succeed Cone, and they did so with a Democratic primary turnout 50 percent greater than the total of 1936. "The first consideration of state government must be for the people," Holland had told them. "This must be a government which is a democracy of men rather than an aristocracy of money."[17]

As Holland's example illustrates, officials who ran statewide, if they intended political longevity, increasingly did require sensitivity to Florida's demographic and economic changes. No malapportioned district protected them from the tides of popular opinion. The poll tax repeal, particularly, ushered in for them a time of great anxiety as to the nature of the state's electorate. They did not yet, however, need to concern themselves much with the African American vote. The Democratic primary excluded black voters entirely, although many attempted to exercise whatever influence they could, such as voting in Miami's 1939 elections despite KKK intimidation. Then in April 1944, the U.S. Supreme Court in *Smith v. Allwright* ordered the racial barrier to participation in party primaries dropped. Four months later at Lake Wales, Harry T. Moore, Edward D. Davis, and other NAACP stalwarts organized the Progressive Voters' League and launched a statewide voter registration drive. Although totals of registered black voters remained low statewide, by 1945 African Americans truly had begun to make their influence felt in at least some local elections.[18]

However out of touch many state leaders had become, Florida's voters eagerly, happily, and overwhelmingly embraced President Franklin D. Roosevelt and later the "big government" policies he presented as his New Deal. In 1932, Florida, still a one-party Democratic state, switched unexpectedly from its Republican stance of four years previously to hand Roosevelt (who was pledging a balanced budget and reduced federal spending) and the Democrats 75 percent of its vote. Four years afterward, the total edged upward to 76 percent before settling at 74 percent in 1940. As late as 1944, over 70 percent of those who cast ballots in the state still endorsed Roosevelt.[19]

The president's New Deal programs altered Florida significantly. During the famous "One Hundred Days" at the beginning of Roosevelt's first term in 1933, a variety of successful and unsuccessful programs issued forth from the federal government to offer relief, recovery, and reform. The National Recovery Administration's "Blue Eagle" appeared in store and shop windows by the summer. At the same time, Civilian Conservation Corps enlistees—sometimes called "Roosevelt's tree army"—had undertaken work that eventually would result in a $30 million investment in the state's forests, fire protection, rural sanitation, soil conservation, reforestation, and the development of parks and reserves including Highlands Hammock State Park, Florida Caverns State Park, and the St. Marks National Wildlife Refuge. Mosquito and hyacinth control and road repair and construction efforts accelerated as work relief jobs opened for thousands. The Federal Emergency Relief Administration, sometimes aided by the Army Corps of Engineers, also undertook enormous drainage and flood control projects, with the Kissimmee River valley attracting particular attention. Other massive projects drew interest as well, with the period launching construction, for instance, of a Cross Florida ship canal.[20]

The number of initiatives spurred by the New Deal extended well beyond these few examples, and they changed over time as some efforts proved unsuccessful or else were found unconstitutional and others were substituted. The year 1935, for instance, saw passage of the omnibus Emergency Relief Appropriation Act, which gave birth to the Rural Electrification Administration, the National Youth Administration, and the Works Progress (later Works Projects) Administration (WPA). The WPA alone expended the enormous sum of almost $124 million in Florida from July 1, 1935, to December 31, 1940, in carrying out its mission to build and repair roads, bridges, public buildings and facilities, and public parks.[21]

Among the individuals who assisted Florida in benefiting from New Deal largess were Claude Pepper and Mary McLeod Bethune. Upon his election to the U.S. Senate in 1936, Pepper embraced the president and his programs wholeheartedly. "Roosevelt's first hundred days in office, I am convinced," the liberal Pepper later asserted, "saved this country from collapse and preserved our form of government." As Pepper grew close to the president, Bethune-Cookman College president Mary McLeod Bethune's friendship with First Lady Eleanor Roosevelt solidified as well. The first president of the National Association of Colored Women, Bethune accepted appointment as the National Youth Administration's director of Negro affairs. As one biographer noted, "Throughout her tenure in the Roosevelt administration, Bethune's influence remained not only evident, but significant."[22]

One administration initiative, coming during its first year, literally provided cheer for a large percentage of Florida's population. Elected on a pledge to repeal

Prohibition (Eighteenth Amendment), Roosevelt managed to secure congressional approval of an appropriate constitutional amendment (Twenty-first Amendment) by February 1933, before he took office in March. The president's approval of the Beer-Wine Revenue Act on March 22 opened taps in anticipation of liquor sales as soon as ratification occurred. That momentous event came on December 5. Already in early May, though, state newspapers had proclaimed, "Beer came in with a bang." The lawful availability of harder spirits, to the disappointment of many Floridians, awaited voter repeal of the state's constitutional provision on Prohibition in November 1934. Even then, most tipplers faced the hurdle of local option elections to permit sales and possession.[23]

The cheer stirred in some by Prohibition's repeal brightened noticeably as New Deal programs began to energize pained sectors of Florida's economy. By late 1934 and early 1935, spirits definitely had risen, with optimism spreading among the previously depressed. Symbolizing the rekindled spirits, in January 1935 Governor Sholtz and six cabinet members journeyed to Winter Haven to join in dedicating Dick Pope's magnificent Cypress Gardens as, in Sholtz's words, "a new state beauty spot." Not only had tourism rebounded to the extent that it could support such an endeavor but, as historian Stephen E. Branch discovered, the gardens proved "an important element in Florida's late 1930s recovery" by reemphasizing the state's "image as a tropical—and wholly grown—paradise."[24]

With some noticeable bumps in the road, the economy fared relatively well into the late 1930s, but what was true generally did not apply in all cases. As noted previously, numerous large and financially healthy corporate landholders chose not to make ad valorem tax payments in the late 1920s and early 1930s. Given the inability of many individuals to pay taxes, disaster resulted for Florida's local governments and school districts. What amounted to a very large problem swelled beyond the ability of local officials to cope when debt service left over from boom-time bond issues was thrown into the mix. By 1933, over one-third of property taxes went unpaid. One example offers a sense of the result. On February 24, 1933, the Sarasota County School Board closed all public schools, reopening "on a tuition plan" available only to half the student population and with a shrunken school year. The City of Sarasota also cancelled its longtime Sara de Soto Pageant and cut employees' salaries by 10 percent, among other drastic measures. In 1934, the inevitable began to manifest itself when Key West became the first municipal corporation to declare itself bankrupt and "in a state of emergency." The island city by no means was the last. By September of that year, Florida led the national list in defaults by political subdivisions with 328 out of 2,049 political subdivisions and municipalities unable to meet current bills and debt service payments.[25]

State leaders meanwhile pondered how to get taxable property back on the rolls and producing tax revenues. The 1937 legislature adopted a controversial measure known as the Murphy Act, a proposal of Consolidated Naval Stores Corporation, the same company that had initiated the freeze on tax payments in the late 1920s. The new law permitted a purchaser to pay the small amount of state taxes due to gain title to property in default, with local taxes otherwise owing to be forgiven. At Spessard Holland's insistence, some protections for small property owners to redeem their property were built into the bill's language. Nonetheless, Florida's local government officials and ordinary citizens howled in protest. "State Seethes over Tax Sale Auction Issue," one headline blared. "This was the time, if money could be found," one contemporary historian recorded, "to bid on vast acreages." The cattle industry particularly benefited as scores of cattlemen lost no time in claiming grazing lands.[26]

Although cattlemen enriched by the Murphy Act laid foundations for financial empires in the late 1930s and early 1940s, the state's economy unfortunately took a turn for the worse. As late as 1937, the distinguished economist Roger Babson was heralding that he "sees prosperity ahead for the first time in seven years," but forces of man and nature intervened. The nation's economy slumped that year, undercutting tourism. A hard freeze and subsequent drought conditions in 1938 damaged citrus and farm crops. The 1938–39 season ultimately set a record as "one of the most disastrous in the entire history of the Florida citrus industry." World War II's advent in 1939 temporarily sent the phosphate mining industry into a tailspin just before a series of hard freezes in January 1940 created havoc and prompted a citrus embargo. Meanwhile, New Deal dollars dwindled as national defense expenditures began to claim priority. The 1930s ended and the 1940s began with fears of 1932 and 1933 resurrected in the hearts and minds of many Floridians in all areas of the state.[27]

As it happened, the fears proved groundless, for World War II was about to resculpt Florida's landscape, multiply its economy, and send the state on a dizzying boom ride that would last for decades. The state that would emerge from the conflict in 1945 already would differ greatly from the one that had entered it four years earlier.

A taste of events to come had evidenced itself at the decade's beginning even though the general public recognized the fact only slowly. During the year that followed July 1, 1940, the U.S. government spent $125 million on national defense preparations in the state. A ripple effect multiplied the value gained. "This federal priming of business channels overflowed into other fields," one commentator noted, "so that private building operations, gasoline sales, and other business indices climbed to annual records." The results showed themselves nowhere more profoundly than they did at remote Camp Blanding near Starke. "General construction at this army training center, which has risen from a scrub-oak-studded section of woodland to a large city since September, was today from 65 to 72 per cent completed," a report observed in January 1941. Over 1,100 buildings graced the site by spring, and soon the Starke–Camp Blanding vicinity miraculously had been denominated Florida's "fourth largest city."[28]

In addition to Camp Blanding, 171 military installations would find homes in Florida during the war, and given the state's climate and reputation as a center for flying, air bases naturally numbered prominently among them. The Lodwick School of Aeronautics, operated by civilians at Lakeland and eventually Avon Park, had welcomed pilots for training by August 1940. English, Australian, and New Zealander cadets joined the cadre the following summer. By that time, British flyers had been training at Arcadia's Carlstrom Field for months and soon would invade Clewiston. Canadians followed. In the wake of the December 7, 1941, Japanese attack on Pearl Harbor, Hawaii, and the subsequent declaration of war, Lieutenant Colonel Jimmy Doolittle prepared at Eglin Field for his April 1942 raid on Tokyo. Jacksonville Naval Air Station, Pensacola Naval Air Station, Tampa's MacDill Army Air Field, and numerous other such installations unquestionably contributed substantially to the war effort.[29]

While civilian instructors trained pilots, others expressed their patriotic support in countless ways. The agricultural and animal husbandry industries supplied vital food and commodities. Volunteers staffed USO clubs and recreation centers, conducted scrap metal drives, planted victory gardens, and performed other services and duties so varied as to defy any comprehensive listing. Workers—including at Pensacola, Panama City, Orlando, and Tampa—built ships and assault craft. The Florida Defense Council, reactivated by Governor Spessard Holland in 1941, supervised local and county councils that oversaw the labors of more than 300,000 individuals, including air raid wardens, aircraft spotters, and emergency personnel. Notably, Louis Gardner MacDowell, C. D. Atkins, and Edwin Moore, scientists working for the Florida Citrus Commission and the University of Florida Agricultural Experiment Station, developed and then perfected frozen citrus concentrate, with initial shipments of a drinkable product to war-torn England beginning in 1942. Historian Thomas Reilly has pointed out as well the valuable service beginning December 1, 1941, of pilots and support personnel of the Civil Air Patrol. Of 824 Air medals issued nationally to the little recognized CAP pilots, authorities honored Floridians with 205 of them.[30]

Most worthy of mention, about a quarter of a million Floridians served on active duty in the military during and immediately after World War II. They could be found in every branch of service and in every theater of operation. Thousands gave their lives, and thousands received commendations for valor. Fort Meade's

James Henry Mills, for one, received the Congressional Medal of Honor for heroism on the beachhead at Anzio. That First Lieutenant Henry P. Finch of Marianna and First Lieutenant William D. Gahagen of Fort Lauderdale received Silver Stars for bravery in European operations typified the selfless actions of untold numbers of their fellow men and women. The heroism of African Americans deserved the same recognition, but white authorities sometimes declined to make awards or else delayed their presentation, sometimes for decades. Individuals such as Daniel "Chappie" James Jr. and Benjamin O. Davis Jr., both associated with the famed Tuskegee Airmen, nonetheless earned the respect of their comrades and their state.[31]

Although 250,000 or more Floridians entered the military, those numbers paled by comparison to the numbers of servicemen and women who spent time on active duty in the state. Whether training, recuperating, or otherwise engaged in the war effort, two million or more sojourners in uniform visited Florida. Despite military construction that proceeded at a breathtaking pace, the arrivals nonetheless swamped hundreds of resorts, hotels, inns, and other accommodations. By late 1942 in Miami and Miami Beach alone, 300 hotels taken over for military purposes housed 78,000 soldiers, sailors, airmen, and others. Fort Pierce's Naval Amphibious Training Base graduated 150,000 by war's end. So many processed through Camp Gordon Johnston near Tallahassee that the facility leased 160,000 acres to provide sufficient space for the "thousands" of buildings it required.[32]

The presence of so many newcomers understandably created problems for Floridians, and heightened social tensions stood high on the list. Most large communities experienced some disturbance, if not violence. African American soldiers from outside the South resented the restrictions of Jim Crow segregation, not to mention the attitudes of many white law enforcement officers. A 1943 incident at Tampa, to offer one example, resulted in the detention of twelve African Americans for inciting to riot when they protested the arrest of a black soldier. Military authorities had classified an earlier and separate event a "mutiny." The state capital saw a series of events classified as "riots" and "mutinies," and other locales dealt with similar situations. So tense did affairs become by 1944 that military planners at Camp Blanding secretly prepared for the imposition of martial law at Tallahassee, Jacksonville, Miami, Orlando, Tampa, and St. Petersburg.[33]

The picture by no means appeared so grim in every respect. So much federal money poured into the state that, within a few months of the war's commencement, the Great Depression essentially had disappeared. The $400 million or so that Floridians had claimed as income in 1933 almost had quintupled by 1943. Another flood of immigrants thereupon responded to the clarion call of jobs and opportunity. The state's population jumped from 1.9 million in 1940 to 2.25 million five years later. Those statistics fail, though, to reveal the whole story. Twenty-nine counties, mostly in north Florida, lost population. Meanwhile, Dade added almost 50,000; Broward, 20,000; Palm Beach, 32,000; Hillsborough, 27,000; Pinellas, 32,000; Polk, 25,000; Orange, 17,000; and Duval, 64,000. This was the new Florida that prepared to greet the postwar world.[34]

By 1945, what had been the most urban and least rural southern state in 1940 without question had become even more so. Miami, yet the state's second city, stood poised to gain the top ranking, with municipalities such as St. Petersburg, Orlando, West Palm Beach, Fort Lauderdale, and Daytona Beach emerging into the spotlight. Dade, Duval, and Hillsborough alone now contained more registered voters than were voting statewide prior to repeal of the poll tax.[35]

All of the changes left state residents concerned, a little wary, but mostly expectant. The men and women who inhabited those swelling urban environs, or at least the larger portion of them, ached for the future that loomed on the horizon, still remembering the toll and pain of the recent past. Not long after war's end in August 1945, community leader B. H. Alexander reflected on the world around him in terms that he shared with many. "People have money, and now that the war is over, they are itching to spend it," he informed an interviewer. "Twice in my life I think I have seen people with too much money, during the boom and today. There are some money cannot spoil, but I am afraid we have others who cannot take it. I can look back to 1933 and 1934 when good and progressive people were hard up, but we have had good times now for several years, and by and large, any man in this community who has not gotten in good shape has only himself to blame."[36]

5

The Court in Trying Times

The dawning of the New Deal in early 1933 found members of the Supreme Court of Florida as dispirited as much of the rest of the country, although for somewhat different reasons. In November 1932, voters overwhelmingly had rejected the addition of a seventh justice to lessen the panel's workload. That the court would press such a proposal in the Great Depression's depths suggested isolation from current state and national affairs. In future years some court members would highlight just how tight a grip that isolation could have, insisting that the initiative had been sound but was defeated "because of a lack of campaigning on the part of the lawyers." In any event, spirits soon drooped even further when the legislature reduced court salaries from $8,500 to $6,000 per year.[1]

The court's political insensitivity by no means meant that its caseload did not constitute a problem. It did. Florida ranked third in the nation at the time in appellate cases decided, behind only California with twenty-nine appellate judges and Texas with forty-one. In January 1933, 701 cases rested on the docket. During 1932's two terms, the panel had managed to dispose of 780 cases while falling an additional 24 cases behind. In a practical sense, then, the court's docket was running one year behind with no relief in sight. The only solution seen under the circumstances was to hurry cases along. So the wearied justices proceeded during 1933 to exert themselves to new levels, disposing of 1,051 cases and gaining 149 on the docket. Between August 1, 1933, and August 1, 1934, alone, the panel resolved 1,257 matters. Frustrated by mounting appeals, the court by then was including in its press releases a notice that "the Supreme Court of Florida is the only appellate court in the United States which remains in official session from one term to another without taking any intervening vacation adjournment." That statement did not consider the court's annual five- or six-week recess for August.[2]

Court members had themselves partly to blame for the mounting overflow of business. The panel's duties included many matters beyond simple appeals, including consideration of requests for writs of various kinds. Petitions for writs of habeas corpus factored largely in this equation. Individual court members zealously guarded their prerogatives in the granting of such requests, taking pride in the "great liberality" shown, especially in habeas corpus matters. Due to a series of events beginning in 1933, though, the bar at large came to realize just how available such writs could be, a fact previously recognized mostly by the small number of lawyers close to the court. The result, as would be assumed, came in the form of a flood of new petitions.[3]

Briefly, the habeas corpus matter that kindled so much interest concerned the April 1933 killing of Pensacola auto salesman Creel Godwin by Tallahassee slot machine distributor George Deeb. Deeb's Tallahassee attorney, B. K. Roberts—Justice Fred H. Davis's protégé and a friend of other court members including Rivers H. Buford—quickly acted to secure Deeb's release from the Pensacola jail by petitioning Buford for a writ. The justice consented, whereupon outraged Escambia County sheriff H. E. Gandy refused to honor the order. Roberts then demanded that the court hold Gandy in contempt, while Gandy denied the panel's authority. As this tangle ensnared the participants, Roberts, claiming that Deeb was insane, obtained a supreme court writ transferring his client to the Chattahoochee state hospital. Circuit Judge L. L. Fabisinski then ordered Deeb brought to trial in Pensacola, after which Roberts convinced the supreme court to issue a writ of prohibition. By June, five writs had been issued, and newspapers were featuring the "Battle of Writs."[4]

The Deeb case proved for the court a problem that would not go away. Escambia County authorities remained adamant in their desire to prosecute Deeb, finally convicting him of manslaughter in an Okaloosa County courtroom in 1934. Roberts's insanity defense failed to sway jurors, and the judge sentenced the defendant to twenty years in prison. The next year, the supreme court overturned the action, with Justice William H. Ellis denouncing the Pensacola sheriff and judge. A new trial again saw Deeb convicted. Once more, the court set aside the verdict, although now Justices Buford and Roy H. Chapman dissented. A third trial conducted according to the strictures of the court's previous decisions in 1938 finally resulted in Deeb's acquittal. By then the public and the bar had followed the case for five years. Lawyers and more than a few prisoners had come to understand clearly the court's inclinations regarding writs.[5]

A second series of events unfortunately compounded the Deeb case's hint of the appearance of impropriety, reinforcing for some onlookers questions about court access for favorite lawyers and their clients. The situation originated with the best of intentions one Sunday in November 1933 when Justice Glenn Terrell taught a new men's Bible class at Tallahassee's Ritz Theater, where a modern "cooling system" permitted comfortable year-round gatherings. By spring 1934 Justice Armstead Brown had joined Terrell as an occasional class leader. A "full house," including most Tallahassee attorneys, now turned out for the justices' presentations. Justice Fred H. Davis also joined in, on one occasion delighting those present by bringing World War I hero Sergeant Alvin York to the gathering. Davis often taught in association with B. K. Roberts's legal associate Guyte P. McCord, drawing, reports suggested, "a record crowd." Justice Rivers H. Buford associated himself as well and regularly instructed those assembled. The times certainly called for prayer and devotion, but as the years passed, more than a few out-of-town lawyers without access to the classes came to look upon them far differently than did the justices involved.[6]

Such matters as outfall from the Deeb case and whispered concerns about Ritz Bible class coziness among judges and other participants normally would have mattered little to court members, but these times were not normal, and other circumstances built upon already existing tensions and frustrations began to cause real trouble. Embarrassing mistakes, for one thing, played a part. As the justices strove to deal with huge caseloads, they erred in several well publicized instances. Justice Chapman explained the situation years afterward:

> Docketed with the Supreme Court, annually, between the years 1926 to 1940, were approximately 1,200, or more, cases, and six men were required under the then existing machinery, to hear oral arguments four days of each week, and on the fifth to hear and decide our routine motions. Written opinions were required, with the approval of at least a majority of six members. Frequently demands came for opinions in emergency cases from the different sections of Florida, were heard and usually given priority over the other cases. If an error accidentally occurred in the recital of the involved facts, it was of course unpardonable, but if by chance an erroneous legal principle was applied, it was simply hara-kiri. Members of the Court, during these eventful years, worked under pressure, and thoroughness and conservatism of judicial opinions were frequently jeopardized.[7]

Perhaps the most prominent incident involving errors in the "thoroughness and conservatism of judicial opinions" concerned the "KKK flogging cases." There, five Tampa policemen believed to be Ku Klux Klansmen faced charges ranging up to murder. The trials had been transferred to Polk County where Judge Robert T. Dewell presided. Defense counsel Pat Whitaker, a former state senate president, repeatedly found relief in the supreme court, first to influence the course of the original trial and then to overturn guilty verdicts and limit possibilities for retrial. The decision to overturn the guilty verdicts, which had been hailed by U.S. Supreme Court Justice Louis D. Brandeis as "among the most encouraging events of recent years," came in July 1937. In a four-to-one decision, with Justice Brown dissenting and Justice Whitfield absent, the court found reversible error in the judge's admission of conspiracy evidence. The opinion's wording, though, seemed to Dewell to mandate that he direct verdicts of acquittal. Prosecutor J. Rex Farrior then appealed to the court for clarification. The tribunal responded in January 1938 with "an interpretive memorandum." Referred to by the Associated Press as "an unprecedented court document," the memorandum's issuance placed the court in a very critical light. Meanwhile, a frustrated Judge Dewell had quit the case. Within months, his successor, Judge John L. Moore, had dropped all remaining charges. Outraged editors around the state decried the outcome, one commentator insisting that it constituted "about all the disgrace Florida can stand for a while."[8]

The Ku Klux Klan may even have attempted to influence the court's continuing stance on the trials. Less than three weeks after the July 1937 reversal decision and on the morning following announcement that the flogging cases had been set for retrial, Klansmen at Tallahassee lynched two black men, Richard Hawkins and Ernest Ponder. The victims' bullet-ridden bodies were dumped in "a grove of oak trees" that lay "a few yards" from Justice Glenn Terrell's home. Placards adorning the corpses declared, among other things, "This is the beginning, who is next" and "This is your warning." Police were alerted to the bodies' discovery through a telephone call from an otherwise unidentified black woman, likely the Terrell family maid.[9]

During these years the court felt the temporary absence or, at least, distraction of some of its members. In 1934, for instance, Justices Davis and Brown faced reelection contests. Although Brown remained close to Tallahassee, Davis traveled as often as he could to stir support and discourage opposition. He and Brown escaped challenges that year but not without some disruption in the flow of court business. Justice Terrell meanwhile had been laboring as umpire for a time-consuming damage suit involving the state road department. The matter dragged on and on, with Terrell unable to announce a final award until November 1934.[10]

Distractions also came in the form of political ambitions. Justice Davis, for one, seemingly had been weighing a 1932 gubernatorial bid before his appointment to the court, and in the opening months of 1936 he began speaking on public issues in a manner that appeared preliminary to a run that year. He chose, for example, to endorse a controversial plan to mandate that the state fence highways rather than require cattlemen to restrain their herds. Justice Buford actively considered running for the Senate vacancy created by Senator Duncan U. Fletcher's death. Having tested the waters and found them too cool for his liking, Buford withdrew from consideration. Instead, he backed the candidacy of his friend, Tallahassee lawyer Claude Pepper, another regular at the Ritz Bible class.[11]

The direction of politics, as opposed to personal interest in running for office, distracted some panel members. Increasingly, several of the justices looked on in alarm as President Franklin D. Roosevelt launched, as part of his New Deal assault on the Great Depression, initiatives involving huge expenditures and unprecedented governmental intervention in business and daily lives. In 1933, the problem had yet to surface, with Justice Davis able to tell bar members that "the President of the United States has endeavored in every instance to comprehend all emergency measures proposed to the National Congress within the bounds of the national constitution, and not in open usurpation of any of its provisions." By late 1934, though, Justice Terrell had begun to sound alarms about the increasing national debt and to argue for placing "relief and distress work" on a "cash basis." Soon Davis had joined in Terrell's concerns, stressing that "only the people of the nation have the right to change the constitution" and insisting that "the constitution must be followed and changed only by the people if business is to prosper." As mentioned earlier, Justice Davis's sister Evelyn Davis Burns vividly recalled her brother's antipathy to Roosevelt, his characterization of the president as "dangerous," and his staunch opposition to "liberal" supreme court interpretations.

Fairly restrained public criticism gave way to more emotional expressions of concern after announcement in 1937 of Roosevelt's proposal to expand membership on the U.S. Supreme Court, a plan labeled by many critics as his "court packing scheme." At Jacksonville in March, Terrell led by denouncing the Roosevelt initiative as furthering "the possibility of this government drifting into socialism or some other form of the totalitarian state." He added, "It rests on a false premise, is ill conceived, and amounts to a usurpation of power destructive of the orderly system of government." Later the same year Justice William H. Ellis reacted sharply when the president described the Constitution as "not a lawyer's contract" and criticized federal supreme court rulings. "When a person assumes public office and feels he can disregard his oath and the duties devolving upon him," Ellis declared in a Tampa speech, "then I say we have no government of the law."[13]

Comments in this vein reflected not just resentments at national policies but also the tensions of intra-court life at a time when workloads ran high, unfavorable publicity seemed to spring from every direction, distractions abounded, and changed conditions unsettled even if they did not alarm. Persons working within such an environment necessarily would pay a price. It would come due later, if it did not come due sooner.

The first evidence that the stress of court life had begun taking a toll surfaced in 1933 when court clerk George Talbot Whitfield collapsed from exhaustion. Sixty years of age, Whitfield remained away from the court for months while his deputy Ella O'Neill assumed responsibilities. Whitfield's battle with health problems and need for temporary absences persisted until his death on March 29, 1939. To replace the venerable clerk, the justices selected local attorney Guyte P. McCord, then the law partner of Tallahassee's state representative, LeRoy Collins. McCord also assumed Whitfield's duties as secretary to the state board of bar examiners.[14]

The list of the ailing grew. G. T. Whitfield's brother, Justice James Bryan Whitfield, who celebrated his thirty-first year on the court in February 1934, struggled as well. Justice Armstead Brown became concerned about his colleague and took thoughtful action. "I was in line for election to succeed Justice Davis as chief justice in January 1935, but I feared at the time that Justice Whitfield, then seventy-five years of age, was in failing health," he recorded, "and I decided to forego the honor at that time, over Judge Whitfield's protest, and I requested all the Justices to vote for Justice Whitfield, which they did, and he was unanimously elected." Meanwhile, seventy-two-year-old marshal Lawrence Anderson Perkins decided his health required attention. He retired on September 1, 1935, to be replaced by Reuben Williams, the former assistant court librarian.[15]

The low point for health concerns came in 1937. Justice Whitfield's condition worsened to the point that he underwent surgery at Jacksonville, remained in the hospital for two months, and then recuperated slowly at home. Justice Ellis's eyesight had degenerated to the point that his secretary, Leila Cofield, "read all the records, briefs, and cases to him." Although these problems could have been anticipated, another was not. In a Jacksonville hotel room on June 20, Justice Davis suddenly died. Within days Governor Fred P. Cone had named his Lake City law partner and state board of bar examiners chairman, Roy H. Chapman, to fill the vacancy. The act stirred even more controversy for the court when, in the words of clerk James C. Adkins, "many lawyers said it was a political appointment without regard for ability."[16]

Later the same year, three justices—Ellis, Buford, and Chapman—prepared to face voters in the 1938 elections, the first held since repeal of the state's poll tax. Desirous of mustering support from an enlarged electorate of uncertain inclinations, the presumptive candidates ventured out in October on a "south Florida tour." While Buford and Chapman attempted to address court problems, Ellis lashed out at what he termed "mean and unjust criticism." The intemperate remarks undermined his political credibility and the trip's usefulness. Some newspapers bemoaned the whole attempt. The *Tampa Morning Tribune*, for one, did so while labeling the necessity for judicial elections a "statewide disgrace." In an editorial reprinted in the *Florida Law Journal*, the *Tribune* went on to state, "We now witness the humiliating spectacle of three of our Justices, as a matter of political expediency, if not necessity, feeling called upon to make a junketing trip through the state, in order that they may bring their candidacies for reelection to the attention of the people. That must be as distasteful to them as it is derogatory to the dignity and character of the state's judiciary."[17]

If the justices designed their tour to scare off opposition, the effort came up lacking. Tampa's J. Thomas Watson already had announced his intention to run. State senate president D. Stuart Gillis soon followed, charging the tribunal with indecision and confusion. "The court has been unable or unwilling to reach any definite conclusion on many questions vitally affecting the public," he insisted. After Ellis announced for reelection in early November, former state senate president Truman G. Futch of Leesburg and circuit judge Elwyn Thomas of Fort Pierce announced against him. On December 6 Ellis accepted the inevitable, choosing retirement under the provisions of a 1935 statute that permitted justices aged sixty-five or more to retire after twenty years' service. The withdrawal prompted a reshuffling of candidacies, with Watson jumping into the race for the vacancy. As it turned out, voters in May 1938 opted for strong judicial experience over political adeptness and populist appeals, selecting Thomas by a large margin in the Democratic primary runoff.[18]

The remaining races also saw reshuffling following Ellis's withdrawal. Gillis appeared likely to defeat Justice Chapman, given criticisms over qualifications and political favoritism. Justice Buford, however, decided that Chapman deserved better. "When D. Stuart Gillis, a famed state senator from DeFuniak Springs, became disgruntled with the court . . . and decided to run against Judge [Chapman], whom he considered would be the court's weakest candidate," Richard W. Ervin recalled, "Judge Buford had [Chapman] change his qualification to run in the group Gillis would enter so he, Buford, would take on Gillis." Pledging not to leave his office to electioneer until his desk was cleared of all court duties, Buford set about his reelection bid. As the race tightened, though, he distanced himself from his court colleagues. "He has done more to establish and maintain harmony among the justices of the court, to reduce the congestion of the docket, and to speed the disposition of pending cases than has anyone else in the past 12 years," Buford's campaign literature proclaimed. "During the period of his service, only five cases and records have been held or delayed in his office awaiting disposition by him for more than three weeks, and these five cases were delayed because of the large record, extensive briefs, and necessity for independent investigation of legal authorities." The strategy worked. Buford easily bested his opponent in the first primary. The seven counties carried by Gillis understandably centered in the Escambia County vicinity.[19]

Chapman faced Live Oak attorney John Melvin Hearn, a bright turn of fortune for the new court member. To overcome questions about his qualifications, the justice stressed his bar examiner experience. He also prepared press releases explaining court decisions or dissents that he had written, issuing them as the decisions were announced. He followed Buford's early example as well in sticking close to the court and staying busy with court work. Had Hearn lived in south Florida, he might have posed a serious challenge, but to his detriment few people inhabited Suwannee County, and voters elsewhere knew nothing about him. Chapman won the first primary by better than three to one. Hearn carried only his home county.[20]

The difficult 1938 election year passed with only one change in court personnel, but it highlighted another problem of significance. As fatigue, frustration, and stress gripped the court, its members increasingly found themselves divided into equal factions. Three-to-three decisions prompted charges such as those advanced by Senator Gillis that the court either could not or would not act clearly and decisively. Reluctant to generate more of the same, the panel delayed some decisions as the justices searched for solutions. Likely the most prominent such instance involved litigation aimed at voiding the salary rollbacks for state officials mandated by the legislature in the early 1930s. The court lingered for over one year before announcing yet another tie vote, which left the matter unresolved.[21]

The groupings of justices that made up the factions varied from time to time and issue to issue, yet certain general points can be made about them. A corps of justices that often included Terrell, Buford, and Chapman believed the court should seek equitable solutions that, given the state and national emergency, took into consideration the needs of the less fortunate. In an essay published in the *Florida Law Journal* in 1935, Buford insisted that "a Judge who is 'thought bound' by the fetters of ancient precedents not capable of being logically applied to and enforced under the conditions which now obtain, and which did not obtain when those precedents were promulgated, is likely to be more strongly influenced by precedent than by logical application of sound legal principles to present facts and circumstances." Ellis, Brown, and Davis, on the other hand, adhered closely to a pro-business line. As Richard W. Ervin recollected of Brown, "It was said he was a railroad lawyer who didn't rule against them."[22]

This division emerged in a somewhat more sophisticated form following Justice Elwyn Thomas's elevation to the supreme bench in November 1938 by gubernatorial appointment following Justice Ellis's retirement (see p. 115). Experienced as a circuit judge, Thomas believed that only uniformity of approach and procedure could resolve judicial chaos and that the bedrock platform for appellate decision making must be *stare decisis*. "He followed with fidelity those principles which have been tested in the crucible of time and found to represent the most ideal approach to justice under law," First District Judge John T. Wigginton explained. "He abhorred the philosophy of those judicial innovators and activists who constantly strive to substitute their unproven individual concepts of justice for the established products of many fine judicial minds which have preceded us." With important assistance from Justice Brown and, eventually, Justice Harold L. Sebring, Thomas managed to move the court much closer to his views.[23]

For the time being, though, a fractured court continued to deadlock on many key decisions or else attempt to finesse the divisions with opinions that failed to reach or resolve controversial matters in question. It did so with results that could have been expected. The *Tampa Daily Times*, among other state newspapers, held the panel to account in a highly public manner. Even though its words found print late in 1940, they nonetheless reflected sentiments shared within the fourth estate much earlier. The journal first favorably quoted Justice Terrell's direct words in describing a recent lower court conclusion. "Any other [conclusion] would have amounted to a whitewash of fraud and rascality and would have converted a search for justice into a legal snipe hunt," Terrell had written. "Procedural law should not be permitted to so degenerate." The Tampa newspaper then highlighted the "impatience and annoyance which many Floridians have felt when many hair-splitting decisions and highly technical interpretations . . . have allowed indicted public officials and gambling racketeers to go free without even standing trial on the basic question of the guilt or innocence of the charges against them." It added, "It will be reassuring to Floridians if the Supreme Court eliminates these dangers to justice as impressively as it elucidates them."[24]

Justice Thomas took the initiative by enlisting bar support for another attempt to add a seventh justice to the tribunal. His fellow circuit judges already had urged such action, but this time the justification lay in the need to break ties and not in complaints of a heavy workload. Despite expected opposition, the measure met with legislative approval in June 1939. In addition to authorizing a seventh justice, the constitutional amendment also furthered Justice Thomas's interest in more efficient judicial administration. It permitted the court to decide many cases and issues in divisions, with the chief justice sitting as the fourth member. The measure also specified that the chief justice would serve as administrative officer of the court and placed responsibility with him for the dispatch of business and the procuring of consistent opinions. Voters okayed the reforms in November 1940. Governor Fred P. Cone quickly named his supporter Circuit Judge Alto Lee Adams of Fort Pierce to fill the seventh seat.[25]

The addition of a seventh justice did make a crucial difference, and Justice Adams discovered that the tie-vote problem had not been understated. "The first task upon my arrival in Tallahassee . . . was to consider a large number of cases on which the other six justices had been evenly divided in their opinions," Adams remembered. "I had to read and consider all these cases and agree with one side or the other. I did not necessarily have to write an opinion stating the basis for my decision, but it was up to me to cast the deciding vote, based on my interpretation of the law and circumstances." An early friendship with Justice Buford doubtlessly offered the freshman justice helpful direction in some instances. In any event, the three-three split impasse had found a resolution.[26]

By then the justices had resolved the workload crisis. Beginning in October 1938, the court had begun to accept that its rules and policies unnecessarily were adding to its burdens. A series of rule changes late that year and into spring 1939 substantially altered court practices. One such revision authorized the panel to review appeals from interlocutory orders in equity cases by certiorari but provided that opinions would not be written in most such cases. Another specified that applications for extraordinary writs would be heard by the court only on Motion Days and that in mandamus actions the tribunal would accept jurisdiction only where a state officer or agency "authorized to represent the public generally" was named as respondent. Among other revisions, petitions for writs of habeas corpus particularly met with new restrictions. Notice to the attorney general was required, and most writs were made returnable to the circuit court rather than to the supreme court.[27]

Justice Chapman explained the outcome as it appeared by 1945. "Promulgation by the Florida Supreme Court of rules applicable to the extraordinary writs, coupled with a review of interlocutory Chancery orders by certiorari, together with amendments and a general revision of appellate practice rules, have been productive of good results. These rules and the seventh Justice are strong factors in keeping our docket current. A Justice now actually has time to personally make an investigation of the controlling authorities of a litigated cause. We have time to examine a record and know the involved facts." Chapman added, "The members of the Court are trying to do a first class job."[28]

The United States entry into World War II beginning in December 1941 helped as well. For one thing, newspapers typically carried fewer pages and devoted much of the space to war-related news. This fact permitted the court somewhat of a respite from the more intense public scrutiny of the 1930s. While important cases still reached the panel, the amount of work pending slipped considerably. During the January 1943 term, for instance, the court received only 214 new cases for consideration, a dramatic reduction from the previous decade's experience. It disposed of 237 cases, leaving but 160 on the docket. The numbers of appeals increased slightly during the war's remaining years. Even then, the June 1945 term commenced with only 165 cases docketed. The pace had slowed to the degree that members could undertake other responsibilities in support of the war effort.

Justice Elwyn Thomas, for example, accepted Governor Spessard Holland's invitation to chair the Victory Speakers Bureau of the Florida Defense Council.[29]

Mostly the war years passed quietly at the court, with one potentially lethal day offering the principal exception. On Thursday, July 1, 1943, a spray of .50 calibre machine-gun fire suddenly disturbed the otherwise tranquil atmosphere. Military authorities insisted the assault amounted to nothing more than "a freak accident" involving a warplane parked on the line at Dale Mabry Field three miles distant. "Four bullets hit the Supreme court building," a report detailed. "Two knocked small chips from the outside brick wall, and one of them ricocheted and dented the fender of Justice Alto Adams' parked car. One bullet went through the window of the ladies' rest room on the second floor and another broke a window in the railroad commission stockroom on the first floor. Shattered glass was the major damage."[30]

Only one personnel change marked those war years, but it signified a very meaningful changing of the guard. On October 6, 1941, Justice Whitfield announced that he would not seek reelection the next year. Then nearly eighty-one years of age with thirty-seven years of supreme court service behind him, Whitfield's institutional memory stretched back to Florida's constitutional convention of 1885, which he had covered as a newspaper reporter. Through all those years and experiences he had remained, unlike some colleagues, an optimist. "I see no reason why the State should not continue to advance even more rapidly," he had informed an audience during Florida's 1940 economic slump. "We have automobiles, the telegraph, the telephone, the radio, airplanes, and any number of other advantages that were lacking a few years ago." Even announcing his retirement as world war flared, his spirit remained undaunted. "Providence sends troubles to test us," he remarked. "Those who have fortitude will come through."[31]

The contest to determine Whitfield's successor highlighted the politics of old Florida versus those of a new emerging Florida. First to announce was sixty-year-old Theodore T. Turnbull, chairman of the Florida Democratic Executive Committee and onetime state senate president. A resident of Monticello, Turnbull personified north Florida's former dominance of the state and its continuing hold on the legislative process. Pitted against the veteran politician was Harold L. "Tom" Sebring. Forty-three years of age and born outside the South, the world war hero had coached University of Florida football while earning his law degree. Thereafter, Sebring had sought his fortune in urban Florida, specifically Miami and Jacksonville. In a gentlemanly contest, old Florida lost out to the new, with Sebring overwhelming Turnbull. On January 5, 1943, with Justice Whitfield's official retirement, Tom Sebring took his place on the supreme bench.[32]

The crossroads that Florida faced as World War II drew to its close, the choice between old and new, faced the supreme court as well. The future appeared anything but clear, however. In 1945, as Florida celebrated its centennial of statehood, the justices rejected adoption of streamlined federal rules of civil procedure in favor of mild revisions of traditional methods but also upheld the right of African Americans to register to vote in Democratic Party primaries. It saw Justice Brown anxious to retire from the panel, but it also witnessed Justice Terrell's willingness to acknowledge a world changed unalterably. "Whether we realize it or not, the administration of justice in this country has entered a new era," he declared that year. "The world has been marvelously contracted."[33]

Perhaps Justice Chapman best voiced the court's hopes, if not its immediate future, as the tribunal's members looked toward a postwar world. "The march of time suggests to our profession that we are now living in a world quite different from the one of only a few years ago," he began in an essay addressed to the state bar:

> The traditions of our profession have been efficient service to both society and our Nation. If our leadership is to be retained, we necessarily must turn our backs on many idols of the past. The law, based on reason and justice, easily converts its disciples into conservatives. It is possible that the encroachment on the business of the profession is indirectly traceable to the lack of vision or the proper perspective of the practitioners. If errors or mistakes have been committed, then it is our duty and obligation to correct them [so that] we can continue in the rendition of efficient and faithful service to society and the Nation. We can do nothing less.[34]

Roy Harrison Chapman, Supreme Court Justice, 1937–1952; Supreme Court Chief Justice, 1945–1947

Just as had been true of his supreme court predecessor Justice Fred Henry Davis and numerous others of the era, Roy Harrison Chapman came to the tribunal with a strong background in politics and with personal connections in the highest ranks of Florida government. Although at the time of his birth Chapman's family farmed near Lake Butler in Bradford County, he entered the world on July 15, 1883, at Ivalog, near Blairsville in the north Georgia mountains, where his mother was visiting with relatives. Parents William Washington Chapman and Addie Mary Owenby Chapman had been raised in that old gold rush territory and had wed there in the mid-1870s. Justice Chapman reminisced about the reason for their relocation to Florida soon after the marriage. "Their home [place] was in the path of Sherman's march through Georgia," he related. Chapman then quoted his father in observing, "Sherman was awfully careless with fire."[35]

Unlike many boys growing up in rural northeast Florida during the 1880s and 1890s, Chapman benefited from his parents' fervent desire for him to better himself. The Chapmans were proud of their family history and prized education well beyond the standards observed by most of their neighbors. That William Chapman prospered as a merchant as well as a farmer allowed Roy to remain in public schools when others dropped out to work, although he later insisted that the curriculum "consisted largely of a group of well-selected gallberry switches." After graduation from Lake Butler High School, the young man attended the East Florida Seminary at Gainesville beginning in 1902. In 1905 he transferred to the University of Florida at Lake City. The budding scholar's time spent in the latter town coincided with the political turmoil that resulted in the decision to relocate the university to Gainesville. In the circumstances Chapman looked elsewhere for schooling. A few years earlier, Stetson University had opened a college of law, and the school had received widespread publicity in 1905–6 for substantial endowment gifts from the Stetson family, industrialist Andrew Carnegie, and others. Inclined to study law and with the prospects for Stetson appearing so fruitful, Chapman departed for DeLand in 1906. He received an LL.B. degree from Stetson in June 1908.[36]

The young attorney thereafter attempted to pursue his profession from the ground up. Admitted to the bar in 1908, he set up shop in Lake City and strove to make it on his own. Meanwhile, Chapman pursued Democratic Party politics and, through that endeavor, cemented a friendship with Columbia County's state senator Fred P. Cone. Elected to the legislature in 1906 as a strong supporter of Progressive governor Napoleon B. Broward, Cone by 1911 had served as state senate president and was looking ahead to greater opportunities. Seeing in Chapman a young man upon whom he could depend to take care of local business while the senior man pursued possibilities on the broader stage, Cone offered Chapman a partnership in 1912. The business relationship of Cone & Chapman lasted twenty-five years until Cone took office as governor in 1937, and the friendship endured until Cone's death eleven years later.[37]

Although political promotion failed to materialize for Cone in 1912 and the years immediately thereafter, Chapman nonetheless thrived at Lake City. He enjoyed the small town practice of law and later would take pride in calling himself "an average country lawyer." His future court colleague B. K. Roberts would remember him as "a real southern gentleman, ruggedly honest, a little bit rural in his attitude and a hard worker." His never-failing sense of humor and "good hearty laughter" endeared him to townspeople and attracted clients. Chapman loved telling stories on himself. Roberts recalled a yarn that concerned the defense of a man accused of bootlegging whiskey. "He had a hard case so he thought the best thing to do would be to get his local minister to testify that the man was of such character he just couldn't be an ordinary bootlegger. So, without briefing his witness in advance, he put him on the stand and said, 'Now Reverend I want you to tell this jury about this man who is charged with being a bootlegger about his good reputation.'" The minister quickly responded, "Mr. Chapman, I'm glad you asked that. I want to tell you and the gentlemen of the jury, he was the nicest, quietest, most polite bootlegger in our entire area."[38]

Bootlegger clients notwithstanding, Chapman involved himself deeply in civic, social, and religious affairs at Lake City. He joined the First Baptist Church, for instance, and later associated with the Masons and the Shriners. In 1922 he helped to found the local Rotary Club, eventually filling every office available in it. Meanwhile, he hunted, fished, played golf, and otherwise enjoyed himself as a single man. As the years passed, a new passion, the propagation of camellias, added to life's pleasures.[39]

Even the fact that Lake City's economy stagnated in the wake of the University of Florida's removal failed to dampen his spirits. Friends—whether from politics, church, fraternal organizations, or the golf course—saw to it that he fared well financially, even during the difficult times that Floridians faced beginning in 1926. As early as 1912, partner Cone had arranged for Chapman's election as a director of the Bank of Columbia County, a position that he retained until accepting appointment to the bench. Between 1925 and 1927 he acted as Columbia County attorney and held the same position for Lake City from 1931 to 1935. In 1934 and 1935 he also served as Lake City's postmaster.[40]

His contacts soon extended Chapman's reach well beyond Columbia County. In 1916 he represented the state as a delegate to the Democratic National Convention held that year in St. Louis, Missouri. Remaining very active in Democratic affairs, he rendered the party, in his words, "faithful service in each political contest since early manhood days [to 1937]." The activist had emerged by 1935 as a major party leader, chairing the Second Congressional District Democratic Executive Committee. His reward came in 1936 by way of appointment as attorney for the Florida State Racing Commission.[41]

For years Chapman engaged in other public service through application of his administrative and legal skills. Governor John Martin of Jacksonville, for whom the party leader likely campaigned in 1924, recognized Chapman's abilities by appointing him in 1925 as one of three original members of the board of law examiners. Martin's successor Doyle Carlton elevated Chapman to the board's chairmanship, and Governor David Sholtz maintained him in the position. "Under Judge Chapman's leadership the standards of legal education and requirements for admission to the bar were greatly improved," the supreme court later pronounced. "He participated in the examination and certification of a great many applicants to practice law, many of whom are now among the most distinguished leaders of the Florida bar."[42]

Chapman developed a strong commitment to higher standards of professionalism and educational qualification for bar admission, but he retained as well an ability to look at the humor to be found in the time-consuming and often thankless task of weeding out applicants to the bar at a time when examiners possessed no legal right to exclude any applicant from taking the examination "except for moral delinquencies." An example of the problems and the humor arose out of an incident involving a European petitioner. "One day I was interrogating a nice looking young man; he had studied in Spain and had two or three degrees and everything that the colleges and universities could give," Chapman remembered. "He had specialized in giving lectures in some of the different sections on Masonry, and had two special lectures: one that he would give to the brothers only, and a second that he gave to the general public." The story proceeded from there:

> He showed me clippings that he had taken from the newspapers where he had lectured. He stated: "I have trouble with one of the muscles here in my right arm; I can't write well when it gets tired. The thought occurred to me that possibly you could just excuse me in this instance from taking the written examination because of what the newspapers say about me; I think I ought to be admitted without an examination!" I replied: "We apologize for giving you this trouble, but we have no discretion in the matter." A stenographer and typewriter were provided and he was told to take the examination and the board would check his grades. He took the examination but failed to make the required grade. This fellow now stands high in the councils of the Townsend Club and is making a splendid showing.[43]

A controversial political move in 1937 thereafter placed Chapman upon the supreme bench. In the previous year Fred Cone finally had achieved election as governor. Chapman, the new chief executive's closest confidant and adviser, came to Tallahassee with the new administration in January 1937. He played an informal role while his sister Aleen served as one of Cone's private secretaries. That summer Justice Fred Henry Davis suddenly died, and three days later Cone designated his friend as replacement. The new jurist took his seat on July 1.[44]

Criticism from many segments of the bar greeted the appointment. "Many lawyers said it was a political appointment without regard for ability," clerk and future justice James C. Adkins recollected. Chapman responded typically by endeavoring to prove his ability. "When he asked me to do some work for him," Adkins continued, "the conversation would be 'Jimmy, here is a principle of law I'm putting in an opinion. Research this and give me every case you can find sustaining this principle so I can include them in the opinion." Clerk Lamar Warren's memories ran in a similar vein and confirmed the jurist's success. "Justice Chapman had the distinction of having written more decisions by far that appeared in *American Law Reports* as the basis for an annotation than any of the other justices. His characteristic of exhaustively citing decisions of the Court together with those of other jurisdictions may have contributed to this fact."[45]

On the supreme bench, Chapman avoided legalistic approaches, relying instead—and doing so successfully—upon what B. K. Roberts called "pretty sound Cracker logic." The new judge's personal philosophy came simply. In his first speech after taking his seat on the court, he outlined his approach. "Old fashion honesty is the best equipment for life, and hope for the elevation of citizenship lies among young people. The best things in life are not for sale. They are character, integrity, and honor." As a jurist he gave special attention to criminal matters but also proved an excellent administrator. During his term as chief justice from 1945 to 1947, he oversaw the difficult task of planning for the present supreme court building. His fellow panel members came to view him as "a hard worker [who] prepared many very able and lucid opinions for the court." As friend Frank Pepper phrased it, "He completely dug into each case and looked for the meat in the middle!"[46]

Having proven himself to the bar and to the state, Justice Chapman remained on the supreme court until his death at Tallahassee on August 9, 1952. His passing came as the loss of a friend as well as the loss of a colleague. Governor Fuller Warren summed up the man and his life's meaning in words felt by many others. "He had a deeply developed sense of justice. To him, justice was not a cold, legal abstraction. It was the living principle of right and just dealing of men and women with each other." The governor continued:

> He conceived it to be his duty to fully use the great power of his high office to compel people to treat each other fairly and justly. A genuine heartfulness ran like a silver current through all his life. It was the anchor that held him steadfast to all things good and true. His compassionate heart was the furnace where he fashioned the many just and fair opinions he wrote during 15 years as a member of Florida's highest court. He administered justice fairly and impartially to all persons, but he seemed to have a special feeling for the humble, the unfortunate, the under-privileged. He never seemed

> to forget that he was born a sharecropper's son. His judicial decisions have made the burdens of the lowly easier to bear. Many a tear will be shed by those who have been blessed by his just judgments.[47]

Relatively late in life, Roy Chapman married. The event occurred on June 17, 1930, at Kissimmee. His bride, Edith L. Lanier, had been born at Leesburg on June 26, 1890, the daughter of James Cureton Lanier, a railway employee, and Lula Hopson Lanier. Following Justice Chapman's death, his widow lived at Jacksonville. She passed away in that city on April 24, 1970. The couple had no children.[48]

Elwyn Thomas, Supreme Court Justice, 1938–1969; Supreme Court Chief Justice, 1947–1949, 1959–1961

While the path of advancement in the case of Justice Elwyn Thomas bore certain similarities to that of Justice Roy Chapman, the two men otherwise constituted very different human beings. Thomas was born at "the little rural community" of Ankona, near Fort Pierce, Florida, on July 5, 1894. His parents, Hal S. Thomas and Julia Eldred Thomas, hailed from Carrollton, Illinois, although in the 1890s they were attempting to help pioneer pineapple growing in St. Lucie County. Elwyn attended the local public schools at first, but in 1908 his parents acted to ensure a better educational experience for him. They sent the young man to DeLand, where Stetson University maintained a preparatory academy. Once at Stetson, Thomas studied in the preparatory program until 1912, when he matriculated in the College of Liberal Arts. Two years afterward the precocious young man transferred to the law school, from which he graduated in 1915 with an LL.B. degree. He left the campus with a host of contacts through brothers in the Sigma Nu and Phi Alpha Delta fraternities.[49]

A legal career beckoned to Thomas with his 1915 admission to the Florida Bar, and while early contacts proved not so helpful as they might have been, they nonetheless pointed the way toward a bright future. Particularly, Thomas had roomed at Stetson Law School with David Sholtz, a Yale University graduate who, eighteen years later, would become Florida's twenty-sixth governor. For one year the two freshmen barristers attempted a DeLand law partnership before Thomas accepted the necessity to return to Fort Pierce. There he met with better luck. Within one year he had taken on responsibilities as prosecuting attorney for St. Lucie County, holding the office for two years even though he took time out for World War I service in the U.S. Coast Artillery at Key West. Also in 1918 the young lawyer accepted the position of city attorney for Fort Pierce and the next year for Vero Beach. He kept the former retainer until 1925 and the latter until 1923.[50]

The rising legal star immersed himself, just as did Justice Chapman, in local civic, social, and religious activities. He associated with the Episcopal Church; joined the American Legion, several masonic organizations, and the Rotary International; and accepted membership in the Fort Pierce Yacht Club, which he eventually would serve as commodore. He also started a family. On June 18, 1924, he wed Eva Banes at Fort Pierce. Born at Washington, D.C., in 1904, Eva was the daughter of Thomas H. Banes and Eva Stanley Banes. Their first child, Patricia Ann, arrived in April 1925. A second daughter, Pamela, followed.[51]

By the mid-1920s Thomas stood primed for advancement. The moment came in June 1925 when Governor John Martin appointed him as judge of the newly created Twenty-first Judicial Circuit with headquarters at Fort Pierce. Favorable reaction greeted the news. The *Tampa Morning Tribune*, for one, declared, "He has made good, having built up an extensive practice." Thomas retained the judgeship until 1938, compiling experience and polishing his skills. He proudly reminded others that he handled 550 criminal cases during that period with the supreme court reversing only one of his judgments. Meanwhile, the judge's position within the legal community rose with the quality of his work and his participation in bar improvement activities. He additionally offered leadership for Fort Pierce through the local chamber of commerce, serving as its president in 1935–36.[52]

Then, as 1938 approached, Justice William H. Ellis announced his retirement from the supreme court and Thomas decided to run for the seat during what turned out to be a tumultuous election year. While making appearances during the campaign, the candidate refused to offer a "political speech." He preferred, instead, to stress the importance of the judicial branch. In the first primary Thomas narrowly led Tampa lawyer and future attorney general J. Tom Watson with onetime state senate president Truman G. Futch of Leesburg trailing. The May runoff saw the frontrunner stressing "the importance of the Supreme Court in the lives of the average citizen" and "the need for getting people to the polls." The hotly contested election ended with Thomas claiming victory and 59 percent of the vote. He faced no Republican challenger in November. As events transpired, the justice-elect was not required to wait until January 1938 to take his seat. On November 1 Justice Ellis resigned, opening the way for Governor Fred P. Cone to appoint the primary victor to fill out the remainder of the term. Justice Thomas assumed the seat immediately.[53]

Having taken his oath of office, Justice Thomas kept his supreme court seat for thirty years, never drawing opposition and emerging from the experience as one of the most respected individuals to have sat on the tribunal. "He was very dignified in personal appearance, very strict in his courtroom discipline and his personal demeanor," one colleague observed. "Conservative in his philosophy, [he was] a hard working justice." Another saw Thomas as "a scholar" and a "strict conformist to the rules," while a third recalled him as "a stickler for proper judicial behavior" who "thought even a dinner might be considered an improper influence." Justice Richard W. Ervin added his own perspectives. "Justice Thomas respected the amenities. He was punctilious, courtly, a gentleman—a little stuffy and protocolish perhaps but when relaxed exhibited a gruff sense of humor—good speaker—good anecdote and joke teller."[54]

The seriousness and intensity of Thomas's approach to court business found itself well described by law clerk Lamar Warren. "The judge was an intent, tireless worker and took his responsibility seriously. He was greatly interested in well-structured opinions, often resorting to the dictionary for the right word. Drafts of opinions were scrapped and re-written until the last draft bore the clarity and polish for which he was known. He frequently sought comment from the law clerks, invited their criticism and enjoyed lively conferences with them. It was work and more work in his office, and the research that the preparation of decisions demanded caused me to believe—I had just become a lawyer—that research was what it was all about, the name of the game. It is a practice followed by me as a matter of course to this day."[55]

The judge's reputation grew to encompass two very key aspects, as friends and associates have noted. The first related to his approach to counsel appearing before him. "I think that no greater tribute can be paid to a judge," attorney Charles S. Ausley observed, "than to say that any lawyer who appeared before him, did so with full confidence that his case would be carefully and intelligently considered, fairly and objectively decided, based upon sound reasons and clearly expressed legal principles." Others echoed the same sentiment.[56]

Importantly, though, those clearly expressed legal principles—and here is the second aspect—were to be interpreted, unlike Justice Chapman's approach, in a certain and specific manner. "Elwyn Thomas believed implicitly in the doctrine of *stare decisis*," First District Judge John T. Wigginton explained. "He loved and respected the law as a design for the orderly conduct of society and always fought to keep it as pure and uncorrupted as human frailties would permit." Nowhere did Thomas's adherence to the principle of *stare decisis* apply more strongly than in regard to the criminal law, one of his great areas of interest. By the 1960s, that fact, given new federal court mandates for defendants' rights, had come to cause him consternation. "The U.S. Supreme Court has botched [the criminal law] up so," he informed a reporter, "it's made a burden of it."[57]

This is not to say that Thomas did not also merit repute as a legal innovator. What he did was to bring to the court the perspective of a south Florida urban dweller who envisioned the continuing development of that region. He then applied *stare decisis* in a manner that offered a positive response to urban needs and took pride in doing so. "He wrote several pioneer decisions including one upholding the right of a suburban landowner to develop his property into a private airport near Miami despite county restrictions," a journalist noted after speaking with the judge. "Taking cognizance of the importance to Florida of tourism, he was one of the first to establish the principle that beauty, as well as health, safety and morals, may be considered in setting up zoning restrictions." These were two of many examples.[58]

Thomas carried his innovation impulses in other directions as well. Nowhere did this shine through more brightly than in the judge's attempts to restructure the court system and revise its procedures in the interest of efficiency and fairness. As the first chairman of the Florida Judicial Council from 1953 to 1957, he spearheaded efforts to effect change through constitutional amendment. Voter approval of district courts of appeal in 1955 resulted largely from his tireless labors. "The work proceeded with industry and thoroughness, even though no money was available to defray expenses," Thomas recorded. He took special pride in the fact that "for the first time in the United States, a judicial council was created which was composed of more laymen than lawyers" and that "the Council never held a closed meeting."[59]

Long before his successful pursuits of district courts of appeals, Thomas's influence had spread well beyond Florida's borders. From 1950 to 1955 he chaired the American Bar Association's (ABA) Committee on Cooperation with Laymen, working closely with Governor (and subsequent U.S. Supreme Court Chief Justice) Earl Warren of California. In 1956–57 he presided over the ABA's Section of Judicial Administration. Already he had been recognized by designation as a member of the Board of Fellows of the Institute of Judicial Administration. Fittingly, when the Florida Bar awarded Justice Thomas its Distinguished Service Award, it took care to stress his "unique and outstanding contribution of lasting value to the people of Florida and to the nation in improving the administration of justice."[60]

On January 8, 1968, following more than four decades of service on the Florida bench, Elwyn Thomas announced his intention to retire from the Supreme Court of Florida effective January 7, 1969. "I've enjoyed every minute," he remarked at the time, "but I can tell it's been 42 years. I don't like to do it, but the time has come to draw a double line." The Thomases remained in Tallahassee following his departure from the court. Justice Thomas passed away at his home there on February 28, 1971. Eva Banes Thomas continued to maintain her Tallahassee home until her death on January 12, 1998.[61]

Charles S. Ausley found in the writings of Francis Lynde Stetson the words to memorialize Justice Elwyn Thomas:

> His conscience was clear as crystal and never went back on him as it sometimes does on men whose mental vision is less clear than his. Absolute independence was the controlling feature of his life. He was imbued with a high sense of public duty. His power of labor was prodigious. By nature he was warm hearted and magnanimous. He honored and magnified his profession.[62]

Alto Lee Adams, Supreme Court Justice, 1940–1951, 1967–1968; Supreme Court Chief Justice, 1949–1951

Governor Fred P. Cone's 1940 appointment of Alto Lee Adams to the supreme court reflected the north Florida Panhandle roots of so many recent tribunal members, even though the newly minted justice arrived in Tallahassee from Fort Pierce. Adams had been born on January 31, 1899. His parents, farmer Lanyer Adams and Octavia Crosby Adams, then maintained the family in a log cabin overlooking Gum Creek in Walton County. Adams later described them as "poor," although he added, "just like every other family in Walton County is poor." The future attorney's early education derived from two sources. His father, Adams recalled, "taught his eight children to fear God, pay your debts, and vote." More formal instruction commenced at a two-room grammar school in Glendale where the seventeen-year-old principal encouraged the lad to go on to high school by dangling the prize of a forty dollar per month teacher salary. "I figured if a fellow could make that kind of money with an education," Adams reflected, "it was worth trying." Alto Adams Jr. mentioned a second facet of his father's thinking. "He was raised on a farm," he observed, "but did not like farm work."[63]

Once Adams realized that education could lead him toward affluence, he pursued schooling doggedly. He studied at Walton High School in DeFuniak Springs for three years. There he first imbibed a different form of education, encountering backwoods politics played by the hands of a master. This came at a DeFuniak Springs school when Baptist preacher and traveling salesman Sidney J. Catts launched his ultimately successful campaign for governor. "Catts railed against whiskey and the Catholics and told the Crackers they had only three friends—God, Sears Roebuck, and Sidney J. Catts," *Miami Herald* journalist Al

Burt reported. Adams added, "He frightened me to the point where instead of wanting to follow him I thought I'd better hunt up the Catholics and join them." Still, Catts's no-holds-barred style of politics made its impression. During a 1952 statewide race Adams evidenced much the same style. "Although never having participated in a rough-and-tumble political campaign before, he has put on his fighting clothes," one newspaper informed its readers. "He appears to get so sore at his critics that he approaches hysteria when he is shouting back at them from the platform."[64]

Before politics, though, Adams pursued an education in the law, deciding in 1918 to attend the University of Florida Law School because it was "a good idea." Many years afterward as chief justice of the Florida Supreme Court, he shared with Florida State University graduates the philosophy for happiness: "The way to seek it is to plan your life well. The intelligent and thoughtful person will not accept the proposition that each must make his own mistakes. He will profit from the mistakes of others and resolve to build a better and finer life to pass on." In line with his philosophy, the eager student pursued his legal education tenaciously so that he could appreciate when others' mistakes would aid him in building that better life. The only event grand enough to disrupt his plans was World War I. For a time in 1918 he interrupted his studies to enlist voluntarily as an apprentice seaman in the U.S. Navy.[65]

At war's end and back in Gainesville, Adams faced serious challenges but also advanced toward his goals. As to challenges, he particularly grappled with financial problems, one fellow student recalling him as "poor as a church mouse." The veteran worked as a campus janitor, bussed tables in the cafeteria, avoided social life, and became "a loner." The school's yearbook described Adams as "the most serious man now gracing our campus." It also noted, "If he smiles, it is only an accident." But the smiles did not matter as Adams excelled. Receiving his bachelor of laws degree in 1921, he could claim both the trustees' medal for declamation and the presidency of the John Marshall Society.[66]

Then, in launching his legal career, the hungry young professional made a mistake, although he soon managed to extract himself. Adams chose in 1921 to venture to west Florida's largest city to open his practice. There he associated with former congressman J. Walter Kehoe. "He hung up a shingle at Pensacola," one account commented, "[and] three highly unprofitable years ensued." As the bills piled up, an acquaintance suggested Fort Pierce to him, foreseeing "a bright future along Florida's lower east coast." The area, adjacent to some of the state's finest cattle grazing ranges, fit well into Adams's plans. As soon as he could afford it, he planned to marry his childhood sweetheart, Carra Manola Williams, a Florida State College for Women graduate who was the daughter of farmer and rancher

S. L. Williams. The idea of a Fort Pierce home for his daughter and son-in-law appealed to Williams, who encouraged Adams to move Williams's small Wakulla County cattle operation to St. Lucie. When the couple married at DeFuniak Springs on June 13, 1925, Alto Adams already resided at Fort Pierce. The couple would share two children, Elaine and Alto Jr., whom they called "Bud."[67]

The move to Fort Pierce, as it happened, accomplished its purpose once the young lawyer managed to establish himself. "Landing there in the midst of a land boom and a town full of lawyers," reporter Hampton Dunn related, "Adams used as his office a $12-a-month room and his desk was a kitchen table a friend had loaned him." Fortune thereupon shined. "A day later he found a pocketbook someone had lost, took it to the local newspaper, and inserted a small 'found' ad," Dunn explained. "The newspaper seized on the incident and came out with a page one story headlined: 'HONEST LAWYER COMES TO TOWN.'" Even that kind of luck left Adams scrambling for clients, the most notorious of whom were associated with the infamous Ashley Gang. "He represented all classes of clients, poor, rich, and in-between," onetime governor Fuller Warren recorded. "He practiced both civil and criminal law." Alto Adams Jr. provided additional detail. "During the 1920s, he was a trial lawyer and defended minorities when it was neither popular nor profitable." Warren added, "He became known as one of the ablest attorneys of the entire east coast of Florida."[68]

In time, success permitted the beginnings of affluence. By the early 1930s Adams was building a personal fortune, partly by speculating in defaulted bonds and partly by pursuing the citrus and cattle businesses. "I invested in supposedly worthless palmetto flat lands west of Fort Pierce," he informed Dunn, "which have been developed into profitable ranch lands. I had faith in Florida's future, [and] my faith paid off." Passage of the Murphy Act in 1937 permitted Adams to expand his holdings significantly.[69]

The direction of Adams's life changed in 1936 when gubernatorial candidate Fred P. Cone "came to my office in Fort Pierce to talk to me about his candidacy." Having remained relatively inactive politically up to that time, Adams nonetheless agreed to aid Cone. Appreciative for the lawyer's efforts on his behalf, Governor Cone in 1937 placed Adams on the state welfare board. The following year, when Circuit Judge Elwyn Thomas resigned to assume membership on the supreme court, Cone tapped his supporter for the vacancy despite the circuit bar's support of another candidate. When in November 1940 Florida's voters agreed to expand the supreme court to seven members, Cone again expressed his confidence in Adams by appointing him on November 25 to the open seat. The act made Adams the first University of Florida Law School graduate to be elevated to the supreme bench.[70]

Adams served on the court thereafter for eleven years, including a two-year term as chief justice beginning in 1949. Reelection came easily. "I have never solicited a dollar for a campaign and I never received a dollar for a campaign for a judgeship," he later observed, "and I was renominated without opposition." On the tribunal Adams and Justice Rivers H. Buford grew close. The senior jurist influenced the younger man, but Adams's approach to opinion writing remained solely his own. "Justice Alto Adams had the talent of writing short decisions," clerk Lamar Warren recollected. "A study of them show a resolution of the main issue . . . with ample citations of authority." He continued: "He was skilled in real estate and taxation law. Sometimes he and Judge Buford collaborated." B. K. Roberts remembered that the press credited Adams as "the inventor of the one-page opinion." As to Adams's judicial philosophy, Roberts described his colleague as "ultraconservative on fiscal matters and ultraliberal on humane matters."[71]

While Adams performed his responsibilities as required, he never seemed completely comfortable on the supreme bench or, as Justice Stephen C. O'Connell worded it, "he was never dedicated to the public interest." By that, O'Connell meant to suggest that Adams's interest in his business affairs kept him from committing himself solely to the public service. "Judge Adams was a business man type of judge," B. K. Roberts commented similarly. "He always had a keen eye for business." The jurist's financial dealings with Jacksonville businessman Ed Ball also made headlines and, at times, brought demands for his disqualification from cases. Political possibilities intrigued the jurist as well. Rumors published in the *Miami Herald* hinted that he was exploring a 1946 Senate candidacy. Others saw him eyeing a different goal. "He definitely was a politician," a lawyer who practiced before the court averred. "I'm certain that he wanted to be governor."[72]

A run for governor eventually did prompt Adams's resignation from the court on October 22, 1951. Fellow Fort Pierce resident Dan McCarty was preparing for a second run for the chief executive post, and bad blood between the two men prompted Adams with Ball's support to attempt to forestall a McCarty victory. The hot campaign saw inflamed rhetoric that highlighted Adams's wealth and questions about how he had attained it. The candidate later attributed his weak showing to "calumnies . . . perpetrated on me." He returned to Fort Pierce, his family, and his business interests, which prospered for the next fifteen years along with the booming state.[73]

To the surprise of many, Adams resurrected his judicial career in 1967. Republican governor Claude R. Kirk Jr., whose candidacy Adams had supported the previous year, nominated him in October to fill the vacancy created by the resignation of Chief Justice Stephen C. O'Connell, who was assuming the University of Florida's presidency. Immediately before the appointment, Adams switched his party registration from Democrat to Republican, thereby becoming the first Republican member of the supreme court in the modern era. The controversial designation seemingly brought Adams into conflict with the Florida Bar, which reportedly questioned his qualifications and recent experience. Others backed the longtime civic leader and businessman, with Adams insisting that he was "more qualified than ever."[74]

Justice Adams clarified his motives for accepting the appointment, and his subsequent actions bore them out. Specifically, he desired to be able to retire from the bench, which would permit him occasionally to preside as a senior judge. His 1951 resignation otherwise blocked any such assignment. "Judge Adams makes it clear that he has missed this association since he stepped off the bench voluntarily to run for Governor," Malcolm Johnson of the *Tallahassee Democrat* advised. "He probably wouldn't have wanted the appointment (and may not even have been eligible for it) if he had enjoyed the status of other former Supreme Court justices who retire to a sort of emeritus role that allows them to sit temporarily from time to time during illness or absence of active judges." Not surprisingly, in July 1968 Adams announced his departure from the court effective August 1, having qualified for retirement.[75]

The Adamses then resumed their happy lives at their Fort Pierce ranch, which had become one of the showplaces of the Florida cattle industry. Justice Adams died at Fort Pierce on February 20, 1988. Carra Williams Adams passed away in the same community on October 31, 1992. When Justice Adams's death became known, a friend offered a few simple words that touched feelingly upon the judge's life and contributions. "He was a very competent man," former St. Lucie County school superintendent Ben Bryan Sr. commented, "and he worked for the community as well as for himself."[76]

Harold Leon Sebring, Supreme Court Justice, 1943–1955; Supreme Court Chief Justice, 1951–1953

Although Justice Harold Leon "Tom" Sebring boasted "Southern parentage," his background, experiences, and philosophy marked him from the beginning of his judicial service as a man apart from his court colleagues. To begin with, Sebring was born not in Florida or the South but in Kansas. The event occurred on March 9, 1898, at Olathe just southwest of Kansas City. Perhaps more important, the town lay in the heart of the state's pre–Civil War battle zone, where "Bleeding Kansas" took its name. There the deadly excesses of abolitionists and pro-slavery men at Pottawatomie Creek and Lawrence reverberated through the generations that inhabited the land in the conflict's aftermath, tearing some beyond hope of repair and instilling in others a vital sense of the need for balance and justice.[77]

Tom Sebring's youth featured its own forms of disruption and dislocation as his parents—John Thomas Sebring and Anna Lee Hayden Sebring—roved Kansas and Colorado in search of employment. He managed, though, to pursue education and, in 1916, graduated from high school at Gardner, Kansas. Sebring had worked his way through secondary school, and graduation merely meant more of the same, although he combined necessity with a dash of adventure and an interest in seeing more of the world. "He was [a] soda jerker, farm worker, hotel clerk, railroad section worker, Canadian grain harvest hand, carpenter's helper, insurance salesman, [and] oil field laborer," a reporter later revealed. The freedom and the spirit involved with ranch work in the wide open spaces of northwest Canada, however, may have left the most permanent impression.[78]

The freedom of the Canadian range soon yielded to more worldly and dangerous concerns. In 1917 Sebring enlisted in the army as a private. He then served in Europe with the Second Division for twenty-two months, including nine with the army of occupation. During that time he participated in "all the major offensives of the American forces," and circumstances quickly offered lessons in survival. "He discovered on the battlefields of Flanders," one account related, "how to free himself from barbed wire entanglements and to advance from shell hole to shell hole to go over the top." The French and U.S. governments honored his bravery with the Croix de Guerre, the Cord de Fourragere, and the Silver Star with oak leaf cluster.[79]

Released from service in 1919, Sebring determined to pursue education. He entered Kansas State College where he studied mechanical engineering, architecture, and business administration. Besides working to support himself, the future justice also served three times as a class officer, involved himself in campus Greek life, participated in glee club and dramatic performances, and excelled at football. The architecture studies seemed to touch him most personally, a fact that appeared clear when Justice Sebring sat on Florida's supreme tribunal. "He had a great part in the design of the present supreme court building," one of his court colleagues recorded. "I remember that oft' times when we were on the bench and there was a particularly dull argument, he would doodle by drawing pictures of little houses. I don't mean that he wasn't listening to the argument; he was. He was just sort of like doodling. He had the first concept of the present supreme court building."[80]

By the time Sebring received his bachelor of science degree in commerce and banking in 1923, he realized that a business career did not loom in his future.

"I'd been in college for a year," he later observed, "when I knew that I wanted to be a lawyer." Unfortunately, the young veteran—in those days before the GI Bill—did not have the funds to pursue his goal immediately. What he did have was an outstanding record as a football player, a proven track record as a leader, and one very valuable supporter. Major (later Lieutenant General) James A. Van Fleet, a native of Florida's Polk County, was heading the University of Florida's Reserve Officer Training Corps program and coaching football. Whether the two world war heroes had known each other in Europe remains unclear, but Van Fleet recognized Sebring's talent. For two years, as Van Fleet built the university's players into a nationally competitive team, Sebring aided him as assistant. Meanwhile, the young veteran also coached track and field. When Van Fleet departed in 1925, Sebring became head football coach. For three seasons he led the Gator team to distinguished records, although he recalled that "the 1926 team was the greatest I ever coached."[81]

It seems likely that Van Fleet exercised significant influence over Sebring and the development of many of his attitudes and approaches. As football coach, the older man had developed a "will to win" philosophy. By this, he meant, in a biographer's words, "that winning can be willed to come about if the will is strong." Coach Steve Spurrier later would lead from a very similar beginning point, with thanks expressed for Van Fleet's "outstanding leadership." Not surprisingly, as time passed, Sebring enjoyed telling the story "of the frog that fell into the milk until enough cream formed on the top for the frog to jump out." The moral, according to the judge: "We, too, flounder and struggle, but we will prevail."[82]

Winning for Sebring certainly required persistence, but persist he did. Having never lost sight of his legal education goal, he entered the University of Florida Law School in 1925 at the same time he assumed the head football coach's job. He graduated three years later with an excellent record and membership in Phi Delta Phi Fraternity and Florida Blue Key. Having coached mostly from financial necessity, he walked away from football. "I never had any longing for the roar of the crowds," he explained. "I was more interested in helping to develop the character of the boys who played the game." Sebring added, "Football coaching ended when I got my law degree." Still, his love for the University of Florida pulsed deeply. By 1939, after years of service to the school, he had accepted the presidency of the University of Florida Alumni Association.[83]

Graduation brought personal, as well as professional, changes. Now believing that he could support a family, Sebring married. The wedding took place at Gainesville on October 25, 1928. His bride, Elise Bishop, had been born in Jefferson County, Florida, where her physician father, John C. Bishop, numbered as one member of a large and locally prominent clan. Having relocated with her family to Gainesville, Elise had attended Mary Baldwin Seminary at Staunton, Virginia, before returning to the family home and marriage. The couple's only child, Harold Leon Jr., arrived in 1929.[84]

Establishment of a professional career proceeded smoothly, even if not quite so smoothly as the family. Admitted to the bar in 1928 courtesy of the diploma privilege, Sebring briefly attempted to practice in Gainesville before transferring his shingle to more prosperous Miami "for a few months." Then good fortune appeared in the form of an offer to join the Jacksonville firm of Marks, Marks, and Holt. Building his reputation with that partnership, by 1932 Sebring found himself able to organize his own private practice. As these years passed, he immersed himself in good causes at Jacksonville. A devout supporter of the Baptist Church, he also contributed his services to the Red Cross, Community Chest, Tuberculosis Association, Children's Home Society, and numerous other activities of merit. Little wonder that, in 1934, the popular and rising young lawyer easily won the Democratic nomination to represent Duval County in the Florida House of Representatives. He withdrew only because, at the circuit bar's request, Governor David Sholtz on August 17 appointed him to fill a vacancy as judge for the Eighth Judicial Circuit with headquarters in Gainesville. "Judge Sebring," the *Florida Law Journal* offered at the time, "is recognized as a lawyer of ability, courage, and distinction."[85]

For seven years Sebring served with distinction on the circuit bench. He helped lead efforts as vice president of the Florida State Probation and Parole Association to resolve the state's controversial system by creating a Florida parole and probation commission. "Society's responsibility has just begun when the accused is apprehended," he would tell audiences throughout the state. "It has the duty of seeing that he has a fair trial leading up to sentence; a full and fair pre-sentence investigation of the background of the prisoner for the benefit of the court in passing sentence; seeing that proper prison conditions are maintained so that he won't be too much worse when he comes out than he was when he went in; and in some plan of rehabilitation for him when he does come out, to aid him, if possible, to get back into the social order."[86]

Conditions altered for Sebring in 1941, though, when supreme court justice James Bryan Whitfield announced that he would not seek reelection the following year. Aided by Governor Spessard Holland's timely designation of the jurist as trial judge for Miami "divorce mill" disbarment proceedings, an ongoing scandal that the public was following with rapt attention, Sebring announced for the court on December 9. His entry occurred two days after the Japanese attack on Pearl Harbor and one day after the United States' entry into World War II. The race, as it turned out, pitted the onetime football coach against a seasoned politician. Monticello's Theodore T. Turnbull chaired the State Democratic Executive Committee, he had served as state senate president, and he advised the Florida Railroad Commission as counsel. The candidates treated the race and each other respectfully. On primary day, Sebring claimed victory with over twice as many votes as his opponent.[87]

On his part, Sebring had pursued the win by touring the state, speaking to veterans' and civic groups. He had praised President Franklin D. Roosevelt. "In spite of the grumbling and resistance on the part of our people," he observed, "we have had a president who has courage enough and foresight enough, thank God, to go ahead and push things like the C.C.C., selective service, health programs, power projects, all of which have started us along the road to preparation long before the war was ever declared." At the same time Sebring had offered himself as a protector of constitutionally guaranteed rights and liberties in a time of national crisis and in the midst of calls for severe restrictions. "The Axis leaders would like nothing better than to see the American principles of free speech, free press, freedom of assemblage and worship, and all the other freedoms embodied in the Constitution, overthrown as a 'war measure,'" he insisted. "Such a surrender of our freedom would be the first step in the giving up of all we are fighting for." Sebring added, "A sane people need not fear that the complete exercise of their freedom will weaken them or disrupt their war effort. We must be intelligent enough to realize that only by utilizing all of our freedoms and hampering none of them can we build a war machine greater than that developed by the enslaved peoples of our enemies, and win this war which is dedicated to the simple purpose of proving that freedom is better than slavery."[88]

Once upon the supreme bench, the court's newest member pursued the sound of his own drummer. "Judge Harold L. Sebring came to the Court with a determination to be a good judge and he was just that," a former clerk and lawyer long associated with the court recorded. "Not given too much to socializing, he stayed pretty much to his office. His assignments came to his office and he completed them without fanfare; he was thorough, methodical and sort of a no-nonsense individual." He continued: "My recollection of him is that he ground out his opinions day after day without much more than the effort that was usually required. He presented a somewhat hurry-up appearance, yet at the same time he was dignified and reserved."[89]

Sebring especially concerned himself with matters of judicial efficiency, ethical standards, and the dignity of the court. He authored numerous essays and larger works on these subjects that found publication and enjoyed wide circulation. He helped spearhead the movement for constitutional revision and reform of judicial procedure with his closest friend and associate on the court, Elwyn

Thomas. Justice Sebring additionally labored with national organizations, working especially to clarify conflicts in jurisdiction between state and federal courts. His focus aimed directly at the supreme court as well. For one thing, during his 1951–53 term as chief justice, he initiated the practice of preparing a synopsis of each case to be argued with a copy furnished to each justice before oral arguments were heard. But there was much more. "He pushed hard for the formality, the formal rules, the formal conferences, the formal courtroom, the formal drapes," Justice B. K. Roberts recalled. "He pushed hard to put the court in robes, and is generally regarded as being the father of the idea of putting the Supreme Court of Florida in robes. He bought heavy drapes for the courtroom and for the offices." Roberts concluded, "He was so on formality and protocol and he worked hard and he was just a damn good judge." Justice Richard W. Ervin concurred. "With Justice Thomas, Justice Sebring was a strict conformist to the rules [even though] he was a very friendly fellow."[90]

Sebring also furthered his 1942 defense of constitutional liberties. Typically, in 1954—just as calls for disobedience to U.S. Supreme Court desegregation rulings were airing—he reminded law school graduates that the lawyer's oath required support of the Constitution and for maintaining the respect due to courts and judicial officers. "I think all of us are aware that in these times there are people who seem bent on attempting to instill in our citizens a contempt for the laws by which they are governed, and for the judicial institutions that enforce them," he informed the soon-to-be attorneys. Bringing the point down to a "simple truth," Sebring continued, "The law was designed and the courts were set up to protect minority elements, whether criminal or law-abiding; to protect the people against themselves and their passions in rash and turbulent moments; to protect the rights and liberties of the people against the encroachment of government which, if improperly extended, might eventually bring about a condition of political tyranny and despotism that would utterly destroy our free institutions." The justice offered an additional thought with chilling implications for the times in which he spoke. "Reckless and improvident statements that tend to instill in our citizens a contempt for the law, or a mistrust of the judicial exercise of power, will eventually destroy the very source from which such things emanate by destroying the confidence of the people in the free institutions which they have erected."[91]

Eight years earlier, the jurist had seen firsthand the terrible results of the breakdown of respect for civil liberties, due process of law, and courts operated in the interest of justice. In 1946 President Harry S. Truman had designated Sebring as a judge for the Nuremberg trials of German war criminals, and, after facing some disagreement with colleagues on the supreme court, the justice had accepted. Among other cases, he sat on those involving Karl Brandt, Adolph Hitler's personal physician, and Waldemar Hoven, the chief medical doctor at Buchenwald concentration camp. Celebrated for his contributions to the Nuremberg tribunals, Sebring returned to Florida after almost one year to an offer of the University of Florida's presidency and rumors of a 1948 candidacy for governor. He declined in both instances and remained on the supreme court.[92]

Not until the tensions of the mid-1950s exploded in the state and region and, to some extent, on the court did Justice Sebring accept one of the many prestigious or lucrative offers that had come his way. Effective September 15, 1955, he resigned to assume the deanship of the Stetson University College of Law. As a departing gesture, he left a dissenting opinion to the court's October 1955 decision to permit delays in the desegregation of Florida's public schools, beginning with the University of Florida. Joined by Elwyn Thomas, Sebring wrote: "Whatever may be your personal views and desires in respect to the matter, we have the binding obligation imposed by our oath of office to apply to the issue at hand the federal constitution as presently interpreted by the Supreme Court of the United States."[93]

Dean Tom Sebring spent his last years as productively as those that came before. Credited with building his school "to a position of prominence and respect among the nation's law schools," he also kept close ties with national legal and judicial organizations as well as with worthy causes at his new home of St. Petersburg. To cite just one example, from 1958 to 1963 he chaired the Southeastern Association of American Law Schools. When he passed away at St. Petersburg on July 26, 1968, Stetson University president Paul Geren lamented, "We are grief stricken." The *St. Petersburg Times* noted, "In life he prevailed as few men have." The editors of the *University of Florida Law Review* agreed: "The scope and depth of his life defy condensation." Elise Bishop Sebring survived her husband by two decades. She died at Gainesville on June 27, 1988.[94]

6

Case Decisions of the Great Depression and World War II Eras

Between 1933 and 1945, the Supreme Court of Florida faced a caseload that in magnitude far exceeded previous demands placed upon the tribunal, a level of responsibility unprecedented in the panel's century of experience to that point. As would be expected, much of the work involved the evolution of matters of jurisprudential concern that the court had begun to address in earlier days, but some of it grew out of the extraordinary climate of change associated with President Franklin D. Roosevelt's New Deal, the desperate economic circumstances endured by many in those times, and the crisis of world war that began to affect Floridians as early as 1939.

The volatile times produced change, a fact reflected even on the supreme court. Some of its members' attitudes toward national government policies, for instance, altered with the passage of the years as opinions rendered during that era illustrate. The 1934 case of *Adams, et al.* v. *Atlantic National Bank of Jacksonville* offers an example. In that instance, the justices—except William H. Ellis and Armstead Brown—reached to accommodate themselves with New Deal initiatives, finding no problems in federal law governing state trust company and national bank mergers. "Said Act of Congress, properly construed," Fred H. Davis wrote, "does not undertake to deny, destroy nor impair without the consent of the states, any of the legislative and judicial powers reserved by the states with reference to their own corporate creatures."[1]

Yet two years later a different philosophy and four-to-two majority prevailed. Now, with Buford and Terrell dissenting, the court struck down the state's Barber Control Act (known as the "Little NRA") because it permitted price regulation. In *State ex rel. Fulton* v. *Ives, et al.*, Ellis found governmental encroachment on the once-sacred right to contract deeply disturbing. "It is within the power of government to restrain some individuals from all contracts and all individuals from some contracts," he acknowledged, "[but] the truth must not be ignored that a citizen's right to pursue any lawful business is 'property' and the right to contract for personal services as a means for the acquisition of property is one of the privileges of a citizen of the United States of which he cannot be deprived without invading his right to liberty."[2]

The tide of poor migrants that flooded into the state during the Great Depression left its legacy in *Florida Reports* as well. In those years, residents looked on fearfully as strangers seemed to threaten their security, crime rates soared, and new styles of living appeared at odds with typical patterns. "This county is the worse 'hell hole' in America today," one concerned Floridian insisted to Governor Fred P. Cone in an anxious and angry tone not too far removed from the sentiments of many others. Little wonder then that, in 1940, the court in *Watson* v. *Stone* found the need for a "sense of security" sufficient to justify allowing unlicensed firearms to be carried in an automobile glove compartment.[3]

Two other significant cases touched on the same fears and concerns. A unanimous court in 1939's *State ex rel. Green, et al.* v. *Capeheart* upheld Hollywood's ordinance defining a disorderly person and criminalizing disorderly conduct even though the measure's language ranged so broad as almost to defy any clear or specific interpretation of the conduct proscribed.[4] Not too surprisingly, a court increasingly sensitive to new regulatory schemes in 1938 easily accepted regulation of trailer camps and tent cities. As Justice Terrell noted in *Egan* v. *City of Miami*, such power may be exercised as a restraint in protection of sanitation, health, and safety under the police power.[5]

World War II and the years of mounting tensions immediately preceding it similarly brought new issues and, significantly, their contexts before the court. For one thing, school districts began requiring students to recite the pledge of allegiance to the United States flag. In *State ex rel. Bleich, et al.* v. *Board of Public Instruction of Hillsborough County*, decided in 1939, the court viewed the mandate simply as "patriotism in action." When Jehovah's Witnesses complained that the practice violated the biblical command against idolizing graven images, Justice Terrell quickly rejected their claims. "To symbolize the flag as a graven image and ascribe to the act of saluting it a species of idolatry is too vague and too far-fetched to be even tinctured with the flavor of reason," he declared. At that early date, though, two court members held reservations. Writing for himself and Armstead Brown, Rivers Buford saw the need for greater sensitivity to freedom of religion and the need for diversity of opinion. "It occurs to me that in the interest of preserving American ideals, and especially that of religious freedom, we should not by law require one to affirmatively engage in an act, not essential to the public welfare or the support of the government, which he or she conscientiously believes to be contrary to his or her religious tenets." Buford added, "The salute of the flag is, after all, a physical demonstration of respect, and nothing more."[6]

Another question of patriotism reached the court five years later, and now the toll taken by years of terrible war had made itself felt even on Justice Buford. Edward O. Schweitzer, the dean of boys at Dade County's Ada Merritt Junior High School, was a teacher of ten years' experience. The veteran educator also claimed the status of conscientious objector, a fact that prompted district school authorities to terminate his employment. In the resulting appeal of *State ex rel. Schweitzer* v. *Turner, et al.*, a court division consisting of Justices Chapman, Buford, Terrell, and Adams upheld the termination. "[Florida law requires school teachers] to labor faithfully and earnestly for the advancement of the pupils in their studies, deportment and morals," Chapman explained, "and embrace every opportunity to inculcate by precept and example the principles of truth, honesty and patriotism and the practice of every Christian virtue." He continued, "The willingness to bear arms [is] the true test of patriotism."[7]

Here follows a sampling of other opinions of the period, ones that offer a flavor of the times, the court's mood and direction, and a world and state rapidly changing almost beyond understanding.

Airlines, Automobiles, and Tourism

Despite the economic and military challenges of the era, in Florida and elsewhere the world was speeding up. Air travel increasingly linked peoples separated by vast distances, and the Sunshine State, especially Miami, had offered itself as a center for the transportation revolution. Several major airlines by the 1930s called the state its home. One of them in 1939 appeared in the court on a matter that related directly to its ability to construct airports and other necessary facilities. As it happened, the court in *Central Hanover Bank & Trust Co., et al.,* v. *Pan American Airways* agreed with that airline's importance and its request. As Justice Thomas wrote in a pioneering decision, airlines enjoyed the same powers of condemnation as theretofore exercised by railroads.[8]

In 1939, most Floridians had yet to fly in an airplane, but virtually all of them now routinely traveled in automobiles. The court accordingly recognized the automobile's dominance of public ways in the 1935 decision in *Robb* v. *Pike*. "The obsession which seems to possess some people that the right of a pedestrian to the use of the highway is superior to that of the driver of an automobile using the same highway," Justice Ellis intoned, "is without foundation in law or common sense."[9]

Only one interest group could outweigh the auto's heft in Florida law and politics, and tourists eager to spend money soaking up sun and playing in the surf comprised its population. Accordingly, as early as 1937 the court had agreed that Atlantic Beach could close its sands and dunes to automobile traffic to accommodate sun bathers. Justice Terrell's opinion, though, met some heated resistance from dissenting justices Ellis and Davis, who saw the question more as a matter of rich man, poor man. "The people of the State of Florida at large, and not an exclusive class of beach front property owners," Davis wrote, "are entitled to the beneficial enjoyment of the ocean beaches of this state."[10] It took two more years for the court to take the next step. In *White* v. *Hughes* the panel affirmatively declared preferential treatment for ocean bathers over automobiles and their passengers. Justice Brown on that occasion confirmed that bathers have "a superior but not exclusive right to the use and enjoyment of the ocean beach." Floridians have never looked back.[11]

The yearning for tourists' dollars and the snaring of affluent new residents also led Florida and the court into pioneering directions when it came to zoning. After all, an attractive environment would lure and retain desirable visitors and settlers far more effectively than an unattractive one. Early in the period, the tribunal had addressed the subject conservatively. *State ex rel. Henry* v. *City of Miami*, a 1934 decision, had banned "spot" zoning and insisted on the necessity of a general and comprehensive plan.[12] The Sarasota case of *Ex Parte Wise* in 1940 prompted a decision specifying, when a zoning ordinance completely deprived an owner of the beneficial use of his property, that the ordinance should be altered or amended so as to prevent a confiscation of property without compensation.[13] The following year the panel went so far as to order Miami to rezone waterfront property from a classification that effectively would leave it undeveloped to one that permitted hotel and apartment house use. "The purpose of zoning laws," Armstead Brown related, "is to put the land to the uses to which it is best adapted."[14]

Meanwhile, a new theme had begun percolating through the zoning debate. As early as 1935, the court had considered what it referred to as "architectural zoning." *Barton* v. *Moline Properties* that year permitted the use of private covenants to control styles of architecture, bulk and footage of buildings, and other similar aims.[15] Six years later, the court revisited the subject, and its members found themselves willing to go further. *City of Miami Beach* v. *Ocean & Inland Co.* established that the element of "aesthetics" offered a key ingredient to a well-designed zoning plan, particularly when the zoning covered "resort cities and villages." Justice Thomas served notice that the panel thereafter would afford a presumption of constitutionality to any such scheme.[16]

The principle of "aesthetics" soon touched upon a different and normally unappealing aspect of the state's landscape, highway billboards. The same year as the *City of Miami Beach* v. *Ocean & Inland Co.* decision, the court considered the question of billboard regulation. The majority upheld such regulation based upon highway safety considerations, but Justice Brown took matters a step further. "Time has come," his concurring opinion in 1941's *Hav-a-Tampa Cigar Co.* v. *Johnson* expressed, "to make a candid avowal of the right of the legislature to adopt appropriate legislation based upon these so-called aesthetic, but really very practical, grounds."[17]

Increasing concern for aesthetics did not immediately precede increasing sensitivity for protecting the natural environment. The state craved development, welcomed it when it came, and supported it when it could. The 1939 case of *National Container Corporation, et al.* v. *State ex rel. Stockton, et al.* provided an example of how far the court then was willing to go when balancing development against environment. In that decision, Justice Buford accepted that a complaint could be entertained against construction of a wood pulp mill for potential pollution of the St. Johns River. He and his colleagues, on the other hand, would not permit an action based upon the odor that the completed plant would produce.[18]

Alcoholic Beverage Regulation

Prohibition's repeal nationally in 1933 and the following year in Florida brought cheers from tipplers and denunciations from temperance advocates. The supreme court greeted the news cautiously if not with hostility. Several members—most notably Whitfield, Ellis, Terrell, Buford, and Davis—had urged the cause of Prohibition before the public and now feared the results of its demise. Of the numerous decisions taken on the subject, two suggest the majority's attitude and the fact that a minority of members held views vastly different from their colleagues. In 1935's *State ex rel. Atlantic Ice & Coal Co.* v. *Weems*, the court delineated that local jurisdictions could exercise prohibitive control over liquor without fear of judicial intervention; that is, local governments could ban liquor entirely. "There is no inherent right in any one to manufacture alcoholic beverages," Justice James B. Whitfield declared. "There is a vast difference," Justice Brown countered, "between regulation and prohibition."[19] The panel followed up the next year with *State ex rel. Floyd* v. *Noel*. Justice Buford there clearly outlined the "inherent powers" of a municipality "to reasonably regulate the sale of intoxicating liquors," including the power to prohibit the sale of liquors "within certain zones."[20]

Class Action Lawsuits

The troubles of the 1930s, combined with the stresses of a growing population, created a torrent of litigation in Florida's undermanned court system and a deluge of appeals to the supreme court. In those circumstances the tribunal looked very favorably upon the concept of the class action lawsuit, a form of litigation expressly authorized by the 1931 legislature. *Meier, et al.* v. *Johnston, et al.*, considered in 1933, offered one of the first opportunities for the panel to place its stamp upon the concept. Justice Davis found a "true class suit" in that instance, which involved representatives of an unincorporated union bringing foreclosure proceedings on behalf of all union members as co-holders of a mortgage. Since the class members possessed a joint right in the mortgaged property and were too numerous to be joined individually in the action, Davis reasoned, the basic class action requirements had been met.[21]

Several other key decisions thereafter expanded the concept's availability for litigants. Particularly, the opinion in *Allen* v. *Avondale*, a 1938 appeal involving lot owners hoping to cancel a covenant, sustained a class action suit where the plaintiffs shared no joint right or obligation.[22] *Tenney* v. *City of Miami Beach* determined as of 1942 that numbers of plaintiffs alone might suffice to qualify a suit. Justice Terrell held that class litigation could proceed where representatives of over two hundred property owners were seeking to cancel supposedly invalid tax liens on their lands and to recoup taxes already collected. Justice Terrell simply stated, "To have required 232 separate suits here would have been prohibitive and ridiculous and would have deprived many of a remedy."[23]

The Freedoms of Speech, Press, and Religion

The turbulence of the 1930s spawned attacks on many individuals and institutions held dear or even sacred by court members. Politics played out heatedly as charges of improper, if not criminal, conduct filled newspapers and radio broadcasts. Sometimes sharp criticisms focused as well on the courts, including the supreme court. In any number of instances, appeals to the supreme tribunal centered on questions of how far freedoms could protect those on the attack and what limits government could place on the exercise of those freedoms. In some instances, the court appeared willing to nurture and protect the freedoms. In other instances, particularly ones that struck too close to home, it acted otherwise.

Florida's sometimes riotous and often corrupt elections system offered a glorious field upon which to test freedom of speech and of the press. Presumably to rein in some of the most damaging rhetoric, the Florida legislature required that copies of charges to be made against a political candidate must be furnished to that candidate if eighteen days or less remained until the election. In 1936 the local state's attorney and a *Miami Daily News* reporter found themselves accused of violating this "corrupt practices" act. The court through Justice Davis finessed the matter in *Ex Parte: N. Vernon Hawthorne* and *Ex Parte: Dan J. Mahoney*. It upheld the law, describing it as "an aid, rather than a hindrance to free speech and free press." At the same time, the justices tactfully determined that Hawthorne and Mahoney simply had not violated the statute.[24]

As a sidelight to the question of elections, the court considered the same year whether widespread illegal balloting could cause cancellation of an election. The case, *State ex rel. Pooser, et al.* v. *Webster*, involved voting in Jackson County by individuals who had neither registered nor paid poll taxes. The decision probably did not surprise any Floridians. "The rule is settled in this state," Justice Terrell wrote in the matter, "that, where an election is otherwise valid, it will not be held void because illegal votes were cast."[25]

The limits of free speech and a free press reached a court roadblock in a 1935 matter that concerned former justice Jefferson B. Browne, by then a circuit court judge. The governor had assigned Browne to preside at the trial of a state senator accused of gambling violations. *Miami Beach Daily Tribune* personnel published statements, some of which turned out to be inaccurate, about a cozy relationship that supposedly existed between the judge and the case prosecutor. Writing for the court in *Jeans* v. *Coleman*, Justice Whitfield sustained what he saw as a clear case of court contempt. "Such admitted published words are not ambiguous and are necessarily contemptuous of the court and its processes," he insisted. "The apology offered for the mistake of fact contained in the publication and the disclaimer of intent to reflect upon 'the acting Judge' do not deprive the publication of its contemptuous nature, and the Judge had authority to impose appropriate penalties." Justice Buford took strong exception. "I am unable to agree . . . that the acts set forth in the petition for citation of contempt are sufficient to constitute contempt."[26]

A similar situation arose one decade later and resulted in the court receiving a large and undesirable dose of negative publicity. In that affair, Circuit Judges Marshall C. Wiseheart and Paul D. Barns cited *Miami Herald* associate editor John D. Pennekamp after the *Herald* published two editorials and an editorial cartoon that the judges construed as holding them in contempt. The Florida Supreme Court upheld the contempt citations by a vote of five to two. Justice Terrell's opinion, as explained by legal scholar D. Grier Stephenson Jr., found that "the legitimate sphere of operation for both religion and the press was the betterment of society, and presumably when the exercise of these liberties became detrimental to the people, the law would curb their excesses." Justices Buford and Sebring thought otherwise. "As I read the editorials and view the cartoon . . . there is nothing in either which imputes a want of fairness, impartiality or integrity to any Judge or any Court," Buford observed. "If there be those who think it a bad system they have the right to express their views." The U.S. Supreme Court agreed and reversed the Florida decision.[27]

Although the Jehovah's Witness pledge of allegiance case mentioned earlier might have seemed to suggest otherwise, the court tended to react sympathetically to religious freedom questions. Another Jehovah's Witness case, one from 1943, helps to make the point. In that instance the City of Tampa attempted to impose a license tax on the Jehovah's Witnesses for sale of their Watchtower Bible and Trace Society publications. The court in *State ex rel. Singleton* v. *Woodruff* drew the line against Tampa's effort. "A liberated conscience is as essential to a robust democracy as blood is to the human body," Justice Terrell explained. "Enslave the conscience and democracy will perish."[28]

Homestead Exemptions from Taxation

Cash-strapped politicians eager to find some measure of relief for Depression-weary homeowners proposed in 1933 a constitutional amendment providing for a five thousand dollar homestead exemption from taxation. The measure appealed to voters, and they adopted it in November 1934. A court majority thereafter acted, in the words of one commentator, "hostile to the exemption." Within weeks after the amendment's approval, for example, the panel had issued its decision in *Boatright* v. *City of Jacksonville* ruling the exemption inapplicable to taxes levied for payment of existing bonds or authorized refunding bonds unless other revenues sufficient to pay the bonds were guaranteed.[29]

Decisions reached in 1938 and 1939 added new considerations. The first in date, *State ex rel. Ginsberg* v. *Dreka*, broadly construed the amendment's language "except for assessments for special benefits" to permit levies against homesteads for hospital and road and bridge districts.[30] *State ex rel. Clark* v. *Henderson*, on the other hand, denied a school district levy, seeing it merely as a tax in aid of the mandated uniform system of free public schools. A dissent from Justices Buford and Terrell suggested that they could not imagine a school levy not constituting a "special benefit" to a homestead.[31]

Labor Law

Labor organizations have existed in Florida since at least the mid-nineteenth century, but enactment of the New Deal's National Labor Relations Act (Wagner Act) in 1935 spurred union growth and expansion in the state, as well as in much of the rest of the country, on a scale previously unknown. In the years following, the supreme court sent conflicting signals about the activities of organized labor. It ended the period, though, with a controversial decision that placed the panel, at least temporarily, four-square in labor's camp.[32]

Picketing rights occupied the court's attention in several late 1930s appeals. In *Weissman* v. *Jureit*, Justice Chapman in 1938 upheld the right to peacefully picket, at least in circumstances where the court approved of the purpose.[33] Somewhat to the contrary, the next year the tribunal, with Justice Chapman dissenting, barred picketing where no dispute existed between management and its employees. "Peaceful picketing will not be permitted for the purpose of dictating the policy of an owner's business," the opinion in *Retail Clerks Union, Local 779 of Miami* v. *Lerner Shops of Florida, Inc.* read, "to determine whom he will employ or to intimidate him in the management of his business."[34]

World War II helped prompt an almost begrudging shift of sorts in the court's posture. The 1943 case of *Pittman* v. *Nix*, for instance, saw the town of Perry banning all union solicitations on streets and in public or private places within town limits. A unanimous court found that draconian measure improper. "The mere fact that labor unions and their leaders some times, even when our country is in the midst of a great war, abuse their powers and privileges, to the great detriment of the general public," Justice Brown reflected, "should not cause us to deny or impair the well settled legal right of employed workers to organize labor unions and to use their powers of persuasion to induce others to join them, so long as no fraud or coercion is resorted to."[35]

The same year witnessed a much more significantly pro-union ruling. In *International Association of Machinists, et al.* v. *State ex rel. Watson*, a five-member majority upheld the legality of a closed union shop at the Tampa Shipbuilding Company's works at Tampa. In dissent Justices Terrell and Brown spoke to "free enterprise, the right of every man to work for whom he pleases, to hire whom he pleases, to sell his product in the open market whether it be labor or commodity, to save and invest his earnings in any legitimate way he may elect, and take the consequences."[36] Florida's voters agreed. In 1944 they overwhelmingly backed a proposal sponsored by Attorney General J. Tom Watson to write a "right to work" provision into the state constitution. Perhaps not coincidentally, a unanimous court late that year held against the American Federation of Labor in deciding that labor unions could be regulated in Florida "like other organizations."[37]

Local Government Powers

The nightmare of the 1926 Florida bust and the crushing burden of debt borne thereafter by Florida's municipalities and political subdivisions offered background for the court's conservative approach to local government authority during the Depression years. Hundreds of decisions limited taxing and spending authority, even when the initiative in question represented a responsible attempt to revive the local economy or satisfy legitimate obligations. *Brumby* v. *City of Clearwater*, decided in 1933, offered one example. There Justice Buford, writing for a unanimous court, held that a city could not spend public funds to dredge a canal and boat basin for the use of an individual to carry on a private business.[38] Similarly, in 1938's *City of Daytona Beach* v. *King*, only one member dissented from an opinion holding invalid a bond issue to finance a private golf course. If taxpayers' money could be used for such a purpose, Justice Chapman reasoned, then nothing would prevent a municipality from financing "billiard parlors, dance halls, baseball teams, or establishing private drugstores and automobile businesses." Justice Brown insisted to the contrary, "It is not denied that the contract was a benefit to the city."[39]

A few decisions rendered late in the decade augured an eventual change in the court's thinking. The entire court in 1938 joined to validate an act creating a housing authority with power to undertake slum clearance and exercise eminent domain powers. Justice Chapman's opinion in that case, *Marvin* v. *Housing Authority of Jacksonville,* found a legitimate public purpose served in promoting "better citizenship, better notions of necessity for law and order, and a sounder and easier patriotism."[40] World War II–related defense needs helped to justify upholding the Duval County Air Base Authority in 1939. The decision in *State, ex rel. Gibbs* v. *Gordon, et al.*, found merit in the creation of a mechanism to cooperate with the U.S. government in acquiring lands for a naval air station.[41]

Public Records

The corruption that infested many local governments and some state agencies during the eras of the Great Depression and World War II understandably prompted some keepers of public records to attempt to withhold them from public and press scrutiny. When the matter came before the court in 1934's *State ex rel. Davidson* v. *Couch, et al.*, its members unanimously upheld the right of all citizens to examine public records at all times. Justice Ellis cautioned, however, that the right must be exercised "with reason." He added, "A government for the people and of the people is one [in] which the public accounts of revenue collected and expended should show such receipts and expenditures truthfully." Ellis concluded, "It is not a question of what the citizen intends to do with the information when he obtains it."[42]

Race and Race Relations

In key respects race relations deteriorated in Florida during the Great Depression and the war, and the state already labored under the burden of being the most lynch-prone state in the nation on a per capita basis. It seems evident that some court members struggled to find their center on race-related questions, although in 1938 Justices Armstead Brown and Roy H. Chapman appeared more willing than others to challenge prevailing customs. The appeal in *George Washington* v. *State* offers a case in point. There, an African American man from St. Petersburg received a two-year sentence for a routine gambling violation. Justices Buford, Whitfield, and Terrell could find no fault with the punishment, but Brown and Chapman dissented strongly. Chapman's opinion found the sentence "excessive and shocking." After noting that a twenty-five dollar fine or thirty-day jail term would have sufficed, he explained, "To permit or allow this judgment to stand, as I see it, means a miscarriage of justice." Chapman noted further, "It is questionable in my judgment that excessive punishment administered to an obscure and uninfluential citizen will prove much of a deterrent." Before the dissent's publication, though, the court ordered the opinion withdrawn. Press reports suggested that the action came "following protests from Clearwater and St. Petersburg," but court officials denied knowledge of such reports.[43]

U.S. Supreme Court rulings during World War II permitted the Florida court opportunities to acknowledge and define African American rights in a number of respects. Notably, in 1943's *State* v. *Lewis* the panel, with Justice Terrell writing, threw out a rape indictment against an Escambia County man because blacks systematically had been excluded from local grand juries.[44] The tribunal followed in 1945's *Davis* v. *State ex rel. Cromwell*, again an Escambia County case, by upholding the rights of African Americans to register to vote in Democratic Party primaries. The court unanimously joined in Justice Buford's opinion.[45]

The race-related case most prominently associated with the era has come to be known as the Isiah Chambers case. It arose out of the murder of a white man, Robert Darsey, at Pompano on May 13, 1933. Law enforcement authorities eventually centered on four black men as the malefactors. After days of very rough treatment and without being permitted any access to counsel, three of the prisoners offered confessions while Isiah Chambers maintained his innocence. All faced convictions and sentences of death. At that point, attorneys S. D. McGill and Robert Crawford appealed for stays of execution to the Florida Supreme Court alleging coerced confessions and duress. In August the tribunal's decision in *Chambers, et al.* v. *State* granted the stays. "If the trial was had under the circumstances and following the conditions which are alleged in the petition," Justice Buford wrote in concurring, "then it was not a fair and impartial trial."[46]

Thus began a decadelong effort to save the men's lives that repeatedly confronted the Florida Supreme Court and eventually required intervention by the U.S. Supreme Court. The Broward County circuit court first declined to pursue remedies for the men, whereupon the Supreme Court of Florida ordered the issues at question submitted to a jury.[47] The subsequent trial again went against the defendants, and the supreme court once more reversed, holding that the issue of voluntary confessions had not been clearly submitted to the jury.[48] Another trial reaffirmed the guilty verdicts and death sentences. This time, with one dissenting vote, the Florida court upheld the lower court's decisions. "The evidence in the case entitled the petitioners to a verdict in their favor upon the first assignment of error," Justice Brown protested. "These confessions and pleas were not 'freely and voluntarily' made."[49]

At that point, attorneys S. D. McGill, Leon A. Ransom, and Thurgood Marshall took their appeal to the U.S. Supreme Court. The federal tribunal agreed with Justice Brown. In a stinging decision handed down in 1940, Justice Hugo Black speaking for the court in *Chambers, et al.* v. *Florida* reversed the guilty verdicts, finding that "the State of Florida . . . failed to afford the safeguard of that due process of law guaranteed by the Fourteenth Amendment." Explaining his reasoning, Black detailed events leading up to the confessions, determining that acts close to torture had "fill[ed] the petitioners with terror and frightful misgivings." He added: "We are not impressed by the argument that law enforcement methods such as those under review are necessary to uphold our laws. The Constitution proscribes such lawless means irrespective of the end."[50] State's Attorney Phil O'Connell thereafter attempted to retry the defendants, but in March 1942 Circuit Judge C. E. Chillingworth declared Walter Woodward, Jack Williamson, and Charley Davis innocent and dismissed all charges against them. Unfortunately, Isiah Chambers, as a newspaper reported, "had become insane two years ago while in the death house at Raiford and now [was] in the state hospital at Chattahoochee."[51]

Women's Rights

The "women's movement" remained decades in the future in the 1930s and early 1940s, although women occupied numerous elective offices in Florida, including a member of Congress. Increasingly, they involved themselves in business and civic concerns. As to women involved in business and the professions, the court appeared accepting if not encouraging. In 1934, to cite an example, the tribunal unanimously upheld the right of married women to hold employment as teachers in the face of Orange County's policy of hiring only single women. "The effect of such a policy is unreasonable and unheard of in any other business or profession," Justice Terrell proclaimed in *State ex rel. Pittman, et al.* v. *Barker, et al.* "Prevailing policy is to admit women to all professions and businesses on equal terms with men."[52] In 1942's *Merchant's Hostess Service of Florida, Inc.* v. *Cain*, the panel, with Justice Brown dissenting, abrogated the common law rule that commercial contracts could not be enforced against married women.[53]

In certain other respects, court members held tightly to the manners and ways of previous years when it came to women. *Hall* v. *State*, decided in 1939, offers a case on point. There, Mae Hall challenged her criminal conviction by asserting that the failure of the state to impose jury duty upon women deprived her of the equal protection of the laws. The court rejected the assertion. "It is not contended that juries composed of men would be less fair to women defendants than would juries composed of women," Justice Brown pointed out. "Indeed, experience would lead to a contrary conclusion. The spirit of chivalry, and of deep respect for the rights of the opposite sex, have not yet departed from the heads and hearts of the men of this country."[54]

Workmen's Compensation

Another legislative innovation of the 1930s was the Florida Workmen's Compensation Act. As was true in numerous other states, the measure created a workmen's compensation pool, with employers required either to subscribe for their workers in the public plan or else provide essentially the same coverage through private insurers. Employees, in return, could not sue employers for covered accidents. Workmen's compensation cases eventually would present the court with a considerable burden, but in the late 1930s and early 1940s the tribunal's majority looked favorably upon the scheme and sought to extend its coverage. Thus, in 1939's *Sears, Roebuck & Co.* v. *Pixler*, Justices Chapman, Whitfield, and Buford offered eligibility to temporary or casual workers.[55] With Terrell and Adams dissenting in 1943, Justice Thomas in the case of *Tison* v. *Hyer, et al.* included citrus grove workers. He found them to be covered "horticultural" laborers rather than exempted "agricultural" workers.[56] One year later, in *Claude H. Wolfe, Inc.* v. *Wolfe* a court division including Buford, Terrell, Chapman, and Adams covered a company's salaried employee even when that employee was the company's principal owner.[57]

PART THREE

Peace and Prosperity, 1946–1955

7

The Postwar Boom

World War II's conclusion opened Florida to an era of breathtaking transformation, as the formerly poor and underpopulated state evolved at a sometimes reckless pace into an urbanized, air-conditioned Mecca for tourists and transplants. The change came at a substantial price, though. Those who had controlled Florida affairs battled to keep the reins of government and economy in their hands, while tolerating—at times—crime, political corruption, and environmental degradation. Still, a new day was at hand. Eager young veterans of the global struggle returned with a fierce determination not only to make better lives for themselves but also to alter permanently the state of affairs that so many others long had taken for granted.

Which is not to say that the future appeared clearly to Floridians as the veterans began to stream home in late 1945 and early 1946. "The abrupt end of World War II finds Florida in a paradox of pessimism over unemployment resulting from termination of millions of dollars in war contracts," reported a University of Florida economist, "and of optimism over the possibility of greater prosperity in the near future." The uncertainty did not last long. By spring 1947 Florida had emerged as the nation's fastest growing state. "Florida is right in the midst of a postwar building boom which in most cities is breaking all records for the last 20 years," *Florida Builder* observed as early as February. "Leaders in the state's building field agree there would have been even more construction activity during 1946 had materials been more plentiful and building costs cheaper." When federal controls lifted shortly thereafter, the boom quickly burst former records and, despite short intervals to the contrary, reverberated profoundly for decades.[1]

An influx of new residents fueled the boom, and in turn the boom drew ever-greater numbers of new residents. In 1945, Florida's population slightly exceeded 2,250,000 persons, of whom approximately one-quarter were African Americans. By mid-1956, estimates found the state total well on its way to doubling, with 3,937,000 persons already present and an additional half million expected within the following two years. By large numbers the newcomers concentrated in an arc beginning in Orange County and stretching eastward to Volusia and Brevard counties and southward along the Atlantic coast to Dade. They drove the state's ranking among its fellow states from twenty-seventh in 1940 to twentieth a decade later. Well before the 1950s ended, they had pushed the rating to twelfth.[2]

Mostly, the Sunshine State newcomers took up residence in cities, making the South's most urban state even more distinct from its neighboring and rural southern cousins. On the other hand, the kind of cities that Florida nurtured altered substantially from 1945 to the mid-1950s. At the period's beginning, the urban centers remained relatively small, with inhabitants derived mainly from Florida and other southern states. Jacksonville led the list in 1945 with 206,000 inhabitants. Miami trailed with 192,000 and Tampa with 124,000. Within five years, with thousands of arrivals from the North and Midwest, Miami took command while northeast Florida's Jacksonville slumped. The quarter million that in 1950 called Miami home saw their numbers tripled by mid-decade. Meanwhile, cities such as Fort Lauderdale, Miami Beach, Orlando, West Palm Beach, St. Petersburg, and Daytona Beach assumed pride of place among the state's biggest towns.[3]

Many factors drove the population explosion. Historian Tracy Jean Revels explained one of the most important. "World War II accomplished what thousands of tourist campaigns and catchy slogans could not," she observed. "Over two million service personnel had trained in Florida, and many developed lasting impressions of the beautiful, undeveloped area as a perfect site for starting a new life after the war." It certainly did not hurt that technological advances permitted post–World War II residents for the first time to secure affordable air-conditioning units for homes and small businesses. Further, wartime research at Orlando had proved the viability of the pesticide DDT in combating mosquitoes and other irritating bugs. Its liberal application at the behest of thrilled bite victims quickly ensued. Now, besides beguiled veterans, increased waves of retirees accepted a late-life call to the sunshine, assured of comfortable living amid semitropical splendor. Social Security checks flooded banks and businesses, along with annuity payments, stock dividends, and insurance payouts. "Most of the new migrants spoke with northern accents," Revels concluded, "and Florida soon acquired the reputation of being the 'Yankee-est' state in the South."[4]

Jobs proliferated as the economy diversified. Tourists flocked by the millions to beaches and resorts. Businesses and industries of great variety catered to the "snow birds" and flourished in their wake. Increasingly sophisticated financial service firms competed for a share of the suddenly huge cash flow. Even old line sectors of the state's economy boomed. Agricultural applications for DDT multiplied with experimentation, and a state horticultural industry literally blossomed. The building boom catapulted the timber industry into prosperity, just as population increases vastly enhanced the need for newsprint and other paper products. Cattle ranches and dairies struggled to keep up with demand. As to the citrus industry, another World War II innovation promised untold future riches. Specifically, University of Florida Agriculture Experiment Station scientists had developed a process for making frozen orange juice concentrate that did not mar the fruit's natural flavor. Now the nation could enjoy Florida orange juice regardless of the season of the year. Accordingly, the Minute Maid corporation opened its first processing plant in 1946. It took a few years for the product to realize its potential, but killer freezes in California and Texas during January 1949 allowed Florida to dominate the nation's citrus industry.[5]

The boom demanded revolutionary change in many sectors of Florida's economy with transportation needs ranking at the very top. Maintaining the prosperity required easy and cost-effective movement to, from, and around the state. Not surprisingly, airports sprouted on many an abandoned army air base or else in former wasteland. By 1947 Governor Millard Caldwell would proclaim the state as the "capital of international aviation." He also would boast of Miami's Pan American World Airways and the fact that the city's airport had processed over half a million travelers the previous year.[6]

Road and bridge construction competed with airport development for public support. At war's end Florida's internal transportation system neared collapse. Most hard-surfaced roads and bridges, built during the 1920s boom, were crumbling. The narrow width of roads appeared acceptable only when compared to that of the bridges. Many of the latter structures consisted mostly of rotting timber. On the roads, meanwhile, roaming cattle still threatened unwary drivers, a problem that would not be resolved until the early 1950s. With only modest outlays officials attempted to cope with these daunting transportation quandaries, but spending always proved insufficient. Nonetheless, the growth persisted. With demand increasing apace, the state had yet to catch up to its road and bridge needs.[7]

Meanwhile, dreams of greater prospects filled the minds of many. President Franklin D. Roosevelt's administration in 1944 had proposed a vast system of interstate highways, designed on the model of a German *autobahn* and capable of handling motorists at previously unheard-of speeds. Florida stood to gain over one thousand miles of roads. Federal retrenchment following the peace frustrated the plans, but by the early 1950s a taste of the future had become available. A Jacksonville expressway system pioneered the concept in Florida. Quickly, the state's road department proposed a more broadly conceived expressway system to be paid for by tolls. Plans announced in November 1952 called for "limited access" tollways from Jacksonville to Miami and from Daytona Beach to Tampa and Clearwater. The next year the legislature established the Florida State Turnpike Authority to implement first-phase construction from Fort Pierce to Miami.

As these events unfolded, breathtaking bridge and causeway projects awed visitors and residents alike. The Rickenbacker Causeway spanned Biscayne Bay to link Miami with Key Biscayne beginning in 1947. Within months the Courtney Campbell Parkway overcame the waters of Old Tampa Bay to join Tampa with Clearwater and St. Petersburg. In 1949 construction began on the Sunshine Skyway, a visionary span that arched the treacherous waters of Tampa Bay's mouth to connect St. Petersburg with Manatee and Sarasota counties. And by early 1953 the Jacksonville expressways had forged ties with the city's downtown courtesy of the Fuller Warren and John E. Mathews bridges.[8]

Business opportunities on the scale present in Florida during the first postwar decade created fortunes for daring entrepreneurs, probably for none more so than for Edward Ball. The suzerain of duPont family interests in the state, Ball controlled Florida's most powerful chain of banks, eventually twenty-three in number, from a headquarters at the Florida National Bank of Jacksonville. In a postwar economy where start-up cash remained scarce, he found himself positioned to reap immense rewards. "Ball has an ability to see good in something nobody else wants," an observer explained, "a willingness to back his bet with money, and the patience to wait for a return." Only through Ball's decision to purchase otherwise unsalable bonds, for example, could construction proceed on the Rickenbacker Causeway. Through Almours Securities, Inc., the Alfred I. duPont estate, and the St. Joe Paper Company, Ball also held almost one million acres of land in the Panhandle and other investments that touched virtually every corner of the state. Importantly, they came to include the Florida East Coast Railway.[9]

What distinguished Ed Ball from many of Florida's other boomtime millionaires was an intense desire to grab and hold power. "Just as General Motors controls the Automotive Industry; General Electric company, the world of electrical appliances; Standard Oil, the regulation of the oil market; and the E. I. duPont de Nemours Company, the chemical industry," the financier informed the Internal Revenue Service as early as 1931, "Almours Securities, Inc., will, within the next decade rehabilitate, develop and virtually control the State of Florida and become the financial bulwark of the South." To accomplish his goal, Ball interjected himself and the influence he controlled into state and local politics. Generally, he supported men who were pro-business conservatives, and he did so with fervor and tenacity. "Ball is an epic fighter," one reporter noted in 1952. "If he believes he has been wronged, he will fight stubbornly, vengefully, and indefinitely."[10]

Even with the immense fortune available at his command, Ball would not have been able to exercise the power that he came to hold in Florida had he not received good counsel from others. He benefited greatly, for instance, from suggestions received from such politically adroit advisers as Liberty County's George

Pierce Wood. A longtime legislator who had served as the Florida House of Representatives' speaker in 1939, Wood aided the financier in amassing his Panhandle landholdings and ensuring a helpful state government along the way. After Wood joined the staff of Ball's soon-to-be political nemesis U.S. Senator Claude Pepper in 1941, another adviser eclipsed the former speaker. B. K. Roberts, a Tallahassee attorney, had performed legal work for the businessman through the 1930s. The two had cemented their relationship during long conversations over lunch at Jacksonville during the war years. If Ball ever doubted Roberts's counsel, he no longer did so after 1948 when the lawyer quickly obtained a long delayed divorce decree for the business tycoon entered by Tallahassee circuit judge W. May Walker.[11]

Good advice aided Ed Ball to exercise tremendous power in Florida, but his success also must be attributed to his drive, his money and influence, and other factors. Of central importance among them was the nature of Florida's political system and its government, an understanding of which requires a sense of time and place as well as of law and practice. Fact was that Florida existed not as a unified whole but as a loosely joined collection of otherwise separate and distinct parts. Some of the parts changed dramatically while others did not. Within the parts that did not change, as it turned out, were individuals and organizations that found themselves perfectly willing to defy law and constitution to forestall acceptance of the new reality found elsewhere in the state.

A beginning point for gaining a sense of what author Gloria Jahoda called "the other Florida" might be afforded by a look at a few statistics. In 1940, two of the state's six congressional districts encompassed thirty-two counties that ran from Escambia through the Panhandle to Duval and south to Alachua County. Their combined population amounted to 813,637 persons or about 42 percent of the state's total. If urban Duval County is excluded, the region held about 540,000 residents or 28 percent. Of the thirty-one counties remaining, sixteen lost population during the decade and others gained minimally. Other than for military or state government expenditures, the St. Joe Paper Company and its fellow timber companies offered the only substantial props for the local economies. Otherwise, the region sank into the doldrums while the rest of the state boomed. In 1950 the thirty-one counties could claim a mere 21 percent of state residents, a level that continued to decline through the decade.[12]

Politically speaking, these thirty-one counties and a few others like them amounted to even less a factor in statewide elections and far more a power in state government than the statistics would imply. As to statewide elections, it must be borne in mind that almost 30 percent of their population consisted of African Americans who, for the most part, had been excluded from the electorate. On the other hand, the 1885 Florida constitution and subsequent amendments mandated a legislative apportionment scheme that skewed representation toward these counties. The charter compelled reapportionment at the midpoint of each decade, but the 1945 effort—despite intervention by Governor Millard Caldwell—left the thirty-one rural counties mentioned above with sixteen of thirty-eight senators. At the same time, urban jurisdictions such as Duval, Hillsborough, and Dade were allowed but a single senator each. Similar inequities affected the house of representatives.[13]

The problem, given state growth and its distribution by the mid-1950s, soon grew far worse. By 1955 a tiny percentage of Florida's population could elect a majority of the legislature and control state government. Thus, just at the moment in July when Governor LeRoy Collins was recognizing the new Florida by breaking ground six miles west of Fort Lauderdale for "the much talked of Florida turnpike," north Florida politicians were combining to frustrate the governor's insistence on fairer legislative reapportionment. The *Tampa Tribune*'s James Clendinen labeled the core group as "the pork chop gang," and the name stuck. A friendly newspaper described their intention as refusing "steadfastly to permit the delicate balance between north and south Florida, the small counties and the larger counties, to be upset by realignment of Senate districts." In that crusade the porkchoppers succeeded through the decade and well into the 1960s. So long as they did so, Florida's government changed little despite radically altered conditions. "In recent decades two powers have helped to preserve the status quo," remarked one journalist as late as 1965. "One is Ed Ball and his Du Pont empire, the state's largest landowner, bank owner, and grower of pine trees. The other dominating political power is the 'Pork Chop Gang.'"[14]

Moreover, rural north Florida's culture varied dramatically from that of the rapidly growing cities of the central and southern peninsula, a fact that the state's government—headquartered near the Panhandle's heart—naturally reflected. "Any resemblance to the rest of Florida," the *Miami Herald*'s John Pennekamp recalled a friend telling him of the Panhandle, "is purely accidental." In that slow paced and uncluttered world, pine trees vastly outnumbered people, Baptist churches filled on Sundays, and onetime slaves yet lived close to their old plantations. "It is isolated almost beyond imagination, this Florida of the little towns and dim pineland," noted one commentator well after the 1950s. "Its people are just as isolated."[15]

Tallahassee anchored the Panhandle and Florida government, but the contrast between it and the state's dynamic peninsular cities hardly could have been greater. Future Florida Bar director Kenneth Sherouse described the town in this manner: "Post-war Tallahassee as I now recall it was bounded on the North by

Faulkner, on the West by the 19th century, on the East by the Jacksonville *Times Union* and on the South by John McDonald." He added, "The Supreme Court reigned where it could, and the Pork Choppers reigned over everything else." Another resident quoted a friend as declaring: "It's a great place for insomniacs. That's why it's called good old sleepy Tallahassee."[16]

Following World War II, sharp memories of the past—particularly of the "Lost Cause" and its aftermath—yet burned fiercely at Tallahassee as, indeed, they did throughout north Florida. Secretary of State R. A. Gray, for example, loved to regale legislative and social gatherings with details of the tragic death of an uncle at Fredericksburg, "killed by a Federal bullet through the heart." He would share, as well, intimate and inspiring stories of the state's Confederate giants, told to him by the heroes themselves long before during slow moments of shared legislative sessions. Supreme court clerk Guyte P. McCord regularly lectured to area audiences on the more interesting aspects of local history. Former justice James Bryan Whitfield and his friend *Jacksonville Florida Times-Union* editor Willis Manville Ball enlightened legislators and others by recounting details of Reconstruction-era Republican excesses and Democratic election hijinks that occurred in the town during their boyhood. Whitfield had covered the 1885 state constitutional convention as a newspaper reporter. Among his subjects then was delegate Jefferson Alexis Hendley. Since Judge Hendley served in the legislature as late as 1945, he could be counted among those whose own stories drew rapt attention.[17]

For many of those who listened so closely to the tales of the "Old South," the idea of change—they might have labeled it "forced change" demanded by "outsiders"—did not set well. Not only was the disruption of the status quo that was occurring elsewhere in the state resisted by many whites in north Florida, but the very idea of change seemed an outrageous imposition. So the region's voters routinely returned to office conservative legislators who kept state government modeled after their own wishes. The political scientist V. O. Key noted in 1949 that "the search for coherent organized political leadership in Florida seems futile in whatever direction one looks." Instead, a "good old boy" network "got things done." In Governor Millard Caldwell's words, "In politics you reward your friends and punish your enemies." Richard W. Ervin, who served as a reform attorney general beginning in 1949, recalled: "Government was much smaller, more personal than it is today. Back then we were closer to the people and we could get for them the little things they wanted." One scholar concluded his examination of the subject in a more cynical vein. "The conducting of the state's business on the basis of mutual backscratching," he wrote, "has become so habitual that to suggest a different approach to state politics is blasphemous."[18]

Only two governmental forces effectively could limit the rural and regional power that dominated the state legislature and forestalled any different approach to state politics and government. One, the supreme court, will be discussed in chapter 9. The governor was the other. Although the 1885 state constitution drastically limited the executive's powers, the office offered a forum for leadership. Its occupant also could restrain legislative initiatives by exercise of his veto and by other discretionary actions. While funding from businessmen such as Ed Ball could provide a critical edge for a candidate, the decision lay in the hands of registered voters statewide and not just those who lived in north Florida's rural counties.[19]

The trick was to connect with those voters. Campaigning for the office in the mid-1940s still meant traveling the highways and byways soliciting votes on what now would be called a retail basis. No statewide political organization existed in any meaningful sense. V. O. Key summed up the situation as "every man for himself." Radio and "radiothons" permitted some wholesale campaigning, but television did not make a substantive impact until the 1950s. Dwight D. Eisenhower's 1952 presidential race proved the viability of the medium for electioneering, and in 1954 Florida viewers enjoyed the novelty of weighing the appearances of Acting Governor Charley E. Johns, who epitomized Pork Chop leadership, and challenger LeRoy Collins. They did so—much to Collins's benefit.[20]

Whatever restraint governors might impose, the powers that controlled the legislature kept state government weak, especially when it came to criminal law enforcement. As a result, the burden fell on local officials to compel compliance with the law. During the Prohibition era and later amid wartime exigencies, many of these law enforcement authorities had accepted toleration of, if they did not outright support, certain otherwise illegal activities. Gambling and other prohibited vices flourished virtually everywhere. Slot machines lined the walls of service stations, casinos welcomed tourists, and houses of prostitution operated more or less openly. In major cities, newspaper headlines decried the outrage of gangland killings. In the countryside, bootleggers continued to peddle tax-free liquor, and all manner of other infractions passed unchallenged.[21]

To all who opened their eyes to it, lax law enforcement and vice bespoke official corruption. Mostly, its magnitude remained uncertain until U.S. Senator Estes Kefauver opened public hearings on the subject in 1950. Resulting publicity exposed case after case of misconduct by public officials. For his part, Dade County Sheriff Jimmy Sullivan admitted a personal income jump from $2,500 in 1944 to more than $70,000 by 1947. Sullivan's Broward counterpart, Sheriff Walter Clark, told of holding a partnership in a three-quarter million dollar numbers racket.

Many other officials throughout the state joined Sullivan and Clark as targets for exposure.[22]

Soon the disclosures elevated the taint of corruption to the state level. Wealthy businessmen linked to gambling interests acknowledged that they personally had bankrolled Governor Fuller Warren's 1948 campaign. Already, though, voters in many parts of the state had concluded that the disease infected much of Florida's government. In 1947 alone, numerous incidents had left appalled Floridians shaking their heads. Among them, Speaker of the House Thomas D. Beasley of DeFuniak Springs faced a citation for contempt, having shown "gross disrespect" and used "loud and boisterous language" in open court. Then Walton County's state senator, E. Bert Riddle, a school principal, was arrested for fondling a child under fourteen years of age. The year also saw a major bribery scandal hit the legislature when gambling interests were caught improperly attempting to halt restrictive new laws. Many of the affair's details came to light only when, after the solons refused to investigate themselves, West Palm Beach state attorney Phil O'Connell intervened at Governor Caldwell's request.[23]

As the stench of corruption circulated throughout the state, one group of voters already believed that the mess of Florida's political and governmental systems had to be cleaned up and that they were just the people to do it. This mostly unorganized cohort consisted of World War II veterans, and their postwar political activities were not unique to Florida. One student of a neighboring state's experience, for instance, has commented, "Georgia's white veterans returned to mount insurgent revolts against old-guard leadership and political machines sustained by electoral fraud, corrupt patronage, and civic apathy, none of which conformed to the principles of honest and democratic government that many believed they had fought to defend." Future Florida Bar president W. Reece Smith recalled, "The veterans who came out of World War II seemed to think they wanted to make the world better. It may not have been articulated much, but we had common cause nonetheless. We wanted to do good things."[24]

As the Georgia historian intimated, veterans varied as to their goals, especially when it came to the question of black and white. The case of African American returnees will be discussed shortly, but for now the point should be made that white veteran activists—given a wide variety of philosophies—mostly were not what would be described as liberals today. Generally speaking, the breaking down of racial barriers and Jim Crow racial segregation was not their issue. Rather, as William C. Havard and Loren P. Beth have labeled many of those who ultimately would exert the strongest leadership in Florida, they were "urban business conservatives." Of them, the two scholars observed:

> The urban business conservative is usually a governmental reformer; honest government conducted by means of textbook governmental machinery is something of a substitute for a more liberal social and economic policy. On racial questions he leans toward moderation but may occasionally move to extremes. The chances are very much in favor of his being economy-minded and disposed toward consumption taxes for the support of governmental functions, but he does understand the needs of the cities and is willing to take steps to relieve their plight. He is consistently a promoter of business. While making a fetish of the doctrine of free competitive enterprise, he is usually favorable to governmental programs which are designed to aid business at the public expense, and in a good many cases he will go along with legislation which actually restricts competition in order to ensure advantages to existing members of the guild. This type of representative usually supports reapportionment.[25]

One veteran, Stephen C. O'Connell, put it this way. "I never intended to hold public office. I wanted to be a good citizen and help others in politics. I believed in order and honesty. I wanted to help honest people." In later years, LeRoy Collins, another such veteran, would speak of his friend O'Connell's virtues in terms that further helped to summarize these veterans' collective vision. "He came to personify to me what I liked to find in all our people, a keen mind, a love of God and country, sterling character and integrity, compassion, a respect for the rights of all people and a new vision of what our state could become."[26]

It would take several years before the real weight of these veterans began to be felt in local and state politics. O'Connell, Jacksonville's Fuller Warren, Fort Pierce's Dan McCarty, and Tallahassee's LeRoy Collins already had established themselves before the war and either easily resumed political office or else quickly prepared to contest for it. "The returning troops weren't afraid of anybody," remembered one future political activist and judge. "They weren't beholden to anybody for what they had, so they could go after [change]." Most, though, first needed to finalize educations and establish families, which the generous provisions of the GI Bill enabled them to do. The federal government's thank-you programs for veterans "revolutionized home-buying and college-going in America," reported John Egerton. "Within four years, more than four million ex-GIs would flood onto the nation's campuses, and post–high school study would never again be thought of as an elite privilege for the fortunate few."[27]

The GI Bill's provisions did not limit geographically where a veteran might pursue education, but white Floridians often turned their eyes to the University of Florida. The only state institution of higher learning and public law school available in 1946 to white men, the university long had held almost mystical significance to those attracted by its allure. The opportunities the institution afforded for making contacts and launching professional and political careers were unrivaled in the state. Tampa's John Germany recalled, for example, advice he received on the subject from Judge James D. Bruton Jr. "John, don't go to Harvard," Germany quoted the judge as saying. "You've got to go to Florida because that's the network that'll provide your business.'" The situation, while it paralleled circumstances in other states, appears to have bested them. "Graduation from the state university is an important attribute of politicians in a great many states, both from a standpoint of local identity and the personal associations there," one study observed, "but we are not aware of any state in which the affiliation is as close as it is in Florida."[28]

The value of University of Florida connections to a political career could not be underestimated in 1946 and the years immediately following. Campus politics and the university's Florida Blue Key leadership society set countless young men on the road to public office, all within the framework of a very closed, carefully guarded, and special circle. The annual homecoming weekend and football game may have been the single most important state political event in each year. "UF Has Turned Out Many State Leaders" ran the headline of a 1948 news story. The article mentioned that Governor Spessard Holland had served as student body president, while gubernatorial candidates Fuller Warren and Dan McCarty, respectively, had been sophomore class president and student body president. Congressmen George Smathers and Charles E. Bennett likewise had headed the student body. Many others found their names listed as well.[29]

The university's position and its popularity soon resulted in a surprising turn of events, though, one that opened to question the institution's special status and compelled its supporters to redouble their protective efforts. By 1947, facilities planned for 2,500 students were being strained to accommodate 9,000. A Tallahassee campus associated with the Florida State College for Women could not handle the overflow. Accordingly, legislators spoke of making both the Gainesville and Tallahassee schools coeducational. UF student president Harry Parham loudly protested the innovation if the Tallahassee campus attained university ranking. The UF student newspaper explained, "Student body leaders here and alumni groups are still opposed to the bill because, they point out, a second university is established and a loophole is left for the removal in the future of our facilities." Sheer weight of numbers finally made the difference. In May 1947 the governor received the bill creating Florida State University. Millard Caldwell, who had not attended the University of Florida, signed it. That fall, the first FSU Seminole football team took the field. By then, notice had been served that UF no longer stood alone, and the Gators found themselves acting ever more defensively.[30]

While large numbers of veterans pursued education and established themselves preparatory to political activism, some across the South and nation determined to alter a political and social system that relegated blacks to second-class status. Already, National Association for the Advancement of Colored People (NAACP) activists under state conference president Harry T. Moore of Brevard County pushed for substantive change, a crusade greatly assisted by the U.S. Supreme Court's 1944 *Smith* v. *Allwright* decision, which outlawed "whites-only" Democratic primary elections. So while Moore and others registered voters and began contesting local elections, veterans such as Tampa's Robert W. Saunders Sr. used GI Bill benefits to study at Bethune-Cookman College, Florida Memorial College, and other schools. Just as the University of Florida held pride of place among white male students, so too did Tallahassee's Florida Agricultural and Mechanical College for black veterans. Demand for admissions rapidly eclipsed available seats. The porkchopper–dominated state legislature moved slowly at first to provide sufficient funding or to expand graduate programs. Meanwhile, neither Florida A&M nor any other Florida college for African Americans offered a law degree.[31]

Little wonder then that, when the NAACP decided in 1949 to litigate admission of African Americans to Florida's whites-only schools, it chose the University of Florida's graduate and law programs as the first test cases. Filing came in May 1949. Orlando attorney Alex Akerman, the lone Republican in the 1947 legislature, represented five plaintiffs including law student candidate Virgil D. Hawkins. An alarmed state senator, John E. Mathews, "broke the news" in a radio address from Jacksonville. To fight the initiative, he called for six million dollars in supplemental assistance to Florida A&M College. State leaders followed Mathews's lead, appropriating large sums for graduate and law programs at the school in an effort to preserve segregation at the University of Florida. Florida A&M's Law School opened for business in September 1951. Two years later, the legislature redesignated the institution as Florida Agricultural and Mechanical University. Hawkins, meanwhile, persisted in his demand for UF Law School admission.[32]

The attempt to racially integrate the University of Florida set off shock waves at the school and within state government, although the general public seems not to have reacted so strongly. In fact, as late as May 1951 the Florida Student Government Association, upon Florida State University's motion, endorsed desegregation. On the other hand, the move prompted the University of Florida student government to withdraw from the association and to demand continued racial restrictions. One scholar who examined the integration effort offered insights as to why resistance rose so strongly within the university and among its alumni. "The seemingly simple admission of one black to a white state law school was more than that," Algia Cooper commented. "It would symbolize the beginning of the crumbling of a tradition that had been rooted in the history of the state and the hearts of men for decades." As will be seen, the effort eventually would embroil the Supreme Court of Florida for years. By century's end, the University of Florida still would struggle with what one leading newspaper called a "great divide" and would endure a reputation as "one of the least diverse schools in the state's university system."[33]

In those early postwar years and contrary to the reality of the times, Florida enjoyed a reputation for some moderation in racial matters, although the situation altered as the 1940s evolved into the 1950s. Civil rights activists increasingly found themselves bedeviled by the Ku Klux Klan, plus they endured the willingness of some law enforcement personnel either to turn a blind eye to racist outrages or else to abet them. The legislature housed any number of outspoken white supremacists who demanded state action to blunt civil rights efforts. Governor Fuller Warren in 1949 pushed a law to unmask the Klan, but the level of terrorist tactics elevated. On Christmas night, 1951, Klan members assassinated NAACP leader Harry T. Moore and his wife, Harriette, by bombing their Mims home. Veteran Robert W. Saunders returned from studies in Detroit to reassure terrified NAACP members as their new leader. Yet trepidation coupled with financial shortages plagued the organization. In the circumstances, the 1954 and 1955 U.S. Supreme Court decisions commonly known as *Brown* v. *Board of Education* initially resulted in little change.[34]

As Florida's prevailing attitudes in racial matters hardened in the late 1940s and early 1950s, its politics shifted even more markedly. During the immediate prewar and wartime years, the state had elected several liberals to prominent positions, most notably Senator Claude Pepper. Financier Ed Ball and other businessmen had backed the gubernatorial election in 1940 of Spessard Holland and in 1944 of Millard Caldwell, but each had advocated certain progressive causes once in office. Pepper only narrowly escaped a conservative challenge in 1944, but his star seemed to rise in 1948 when his friend Fuller Warren bested Fort Pierce's Dan McCarty for the governor's chair. Interestingly, Ball also had backed Warren, although he did so more to forestall the kinds of anticorruption reforms McCarty demanded than because he liked Warren. The growing strength of south Florida's cities gave McCarty a strong boost that year but was not yet sufficient to overcome Warren's deep connections with north Florida and his support from the emerging block of black voters. In the quixotic world that Florida politics had become by 1948, Warren generally was considered the liberal candidate in the race when viewed against McCarty's businesslike moderate or conservative stance.[35]

The 1950 elections witnessed a fundamental turning point. Ed Ball and other conservative businessmen had decided to oust Pepper from the Senate in favor of a more conservative man. They selected Congressman George A. Smathers of Miami. Previously a Pepper protégé and a moderate, Smathers nonetheless was a south Floridian, veteran, and former University of Florida standout. Ball's faction determined, against the backdrop of the cold war's beginnings and the stirring of conflict in Korea, to paint their opponent as "Red" Pepper and as a supporter of racial integration. The hard-fought campaign polarized a state already grappling with fears of civil rights demands and racial violence. Huge sums were raised and spent to great effect. Although Pepper scored respectably, Smathers triumphed. With his win, the dynamics of state politics shifted to the right. Henceforth anticommunist, anti–civil rights, and pro-business positions routinely marked the platforms of winning candidates.[36]

The political shift did little, however, to heal the north Florida–south Florida electoral split. As south Florida's voting power mounted year by year, candidates attractive to the area's voters—so long as those candidates advocated the litmus test conservative positions in at least a pro forma manner—tended more and more to secure office. In 1952 Fort Pierce's Dan McCarty finally won the governorship, bringing with him to the state capital the conservative reformist impulses of his young, committed veteran backers. When McCarty died during his first year in office, state senate president Charley E. Johns of Starke assumed the executive office in an acting capacity. Effectively, Johns's ascension to office placed the state in porkchopper hands until Tallahassee state senator LeRoy Collins, a close friend and adviser to McCarty, took the job in a special 1954 election. Collins won reelection two years later to a full four-year term. Even Collins, a moderate, who would be considered a traditional conservative by the standards of four decades later, and who is remembered as the shining light of Florida politics during his era, endorsed segregation and resistance. Experience in office would alter his thinking over time, but that story and its impact upon Florida must await a telling in part 4.[37]

Figure 1. The Florida Supreme Court got its own home in 1913, when it moved from the state capitol to this new building constructed on Jackson Square in Tallahassee at a cost of $100,000. The court shared the building with the Florida Railroad Commission until it moved to the new supreme court building in early 1949. Renamed the Whitfield Building in 1952 in memory of Justice James B. Whitfield, the 1913 building was demolished in 1978. Florida Supreme Court Historical Society.

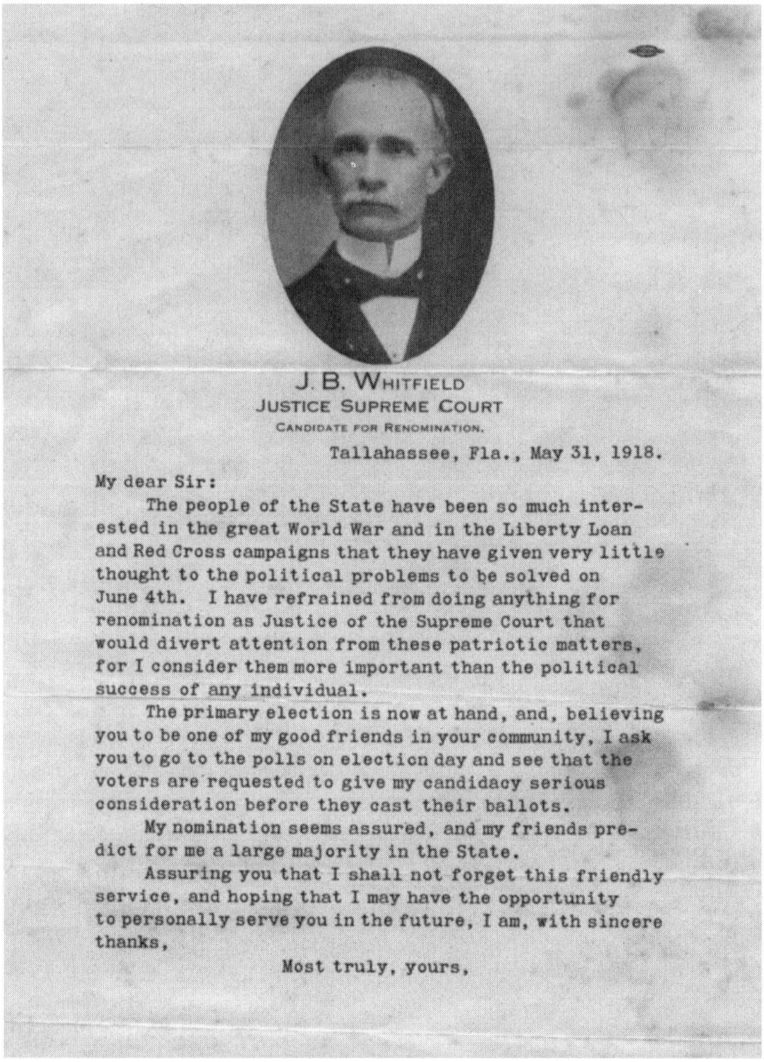

J. B. WHITFIELD
JUSTICE SUPREME COURT
CANDIDATE FOR RENOMINATION.

Tallahassee, Fla., May 31, 1918.

My dear Sir:

The people of the State have been so much interested in the great World War and in the Liberty Loan and Red Cross campaigns that they have given very little thought to the political problems to be solved on June 4th. I have refrained from doing anything for renomination as Justice of the Supreme Court that would divert attention from these patriotic matters, for I consider them more important than the political success of any individual.

The primary election is now at hand, and, believing you to be one of my good friends in your community, I ask you to go to the polls on election day and see that the voters are requested to give my candidacy serious consideration before they cast their ballots.

My nomination seems assured, and my friends predict for me a large majority in the State.

Assuring you that I shall not forget this friendly service, and hoping that I may have the opportunity to personally serve you in the future, I am, with sincere thanks,

Most truly, yours,

Figure 2. As this letter to friends and supporters indicated, Justice James B. Whitfield consciously took a low-key approach to campaigning in his 1918 bid for reelection to the Florida Supreme Court because of the nation's involvement in World War I. Whitfield served on the court for thirty-nine years (1904–43), including three terms as chief justice. Florida Supreme Court Historical Society.

Figure 3. Although considered a "workaholic" by some, Justice Fred H. Davis of Tallahassee took time off to journey with his wife to Tampa to attend the annual Gasparilla festivities. A prodigy in the law, Davis passed the bar exam six months after graduating from high school. Then he successfully petitioned the court to remove the legal restrictions placed on minors so he could begin practicing law at age eighteen. After serving as speaker of the state house of representatives and as attorney general, in 1933 he became the state's youngest chief justice at age thirty-eight. Florida Supreme Court Historical Society.

Figure 4. This photograph of the 1936 Florida Supreme Court was one of the artifacts placed in the cornerstone when the new supreme court building was dedicated in December 1948. Members of the six-member 1936 court were Rivers H. Buford, Glenn Terrell, William H. Ellis, James B. Whitfield, Armstead Brown, and Fred H. Davis. The large portrait hanging above the bench in the old supreme court courtroom was of R. Fenwick Taylor of Alachua County, who served on the court from 1891 to 1925, including three terms as chief justice. Florida Supreme Court Historical Society.

Figure 5. Justice Alto Adams posed for this photograph with his wife, Carra, and children, Alto Jr. (Bud) and Elaine. Adams served on the supreme court from 1940 to 1951—and again in 1967 and 1968. He was chief justice from 1949 to 1951. Born near DeFuniak Springs, he practiced law in Pensacola before moving his practice to Fort Pierce in 1924. He started a St. Lucie County cattle ranch in 1937 that grew to 65,000 acres in three counties, and he is credited with developing the Braford breed of cattle. He also founded an insurance and bond firm in Miami in the early 1950s. Florida Supreme Court Historical Society.

Figure 6. Justice Rivers H. Buford and son, Rivers Jr., were photographed in 1945 at the entrance to the 1913 supreme court building, later renamed the Whitfield Building. Buford "read the law" to prepare for a legal career. He served in the state legislature and as Florida attorney general before being appointed to the Florida Supreme Court in 1925, where he remained until 1948. He twice served as chief justice (1931–33 and 1943–45). By permission of the State Archives of Florida.

Figure 7. Harold L. "Tom" Sebring was "a man for all seasons." He is shown at the far left in this photograph taken while he was on leave from the Florida Supreme Court, serving as a judge in the Nuremberg War Crimes Tribunal after World War II. Heavily decorated for his military service, Sebring served on the Florida Supreme Court from 1943 to 1955 before becoming dean of the Stetson University Law School. Earlier in life he practiced law, served for a time as the University of Florida head football coach, and was trained as an architect. Florida Supreme Court Historical Society.

Figure 8. Campaign advertising by supreme court candidates was commonplace before the implementation of merit selection and retention of appellate judges in the 1970s. In this 1947 campaign ad, candidate Paul D. Barns of Dade County appealed for the support of Spanish-speaking Floridians. Florida Supreme Court Historical Society.

Figure 9. Jefferson Beale Browne, Monroe County, Supreme Court justice, 1917–25; chief justice, 1917–23. By permission of the State Archives of Florida.

Figure 10. Thomas F. West, Santa Rosa County, Supreme Court justice, 1917–25; chief justice, February–December 1925. By permission of the State Archives of Florida.

Figure 11. Louie W. Strum, Duval County, Supreme Court justice, 1925–31; chief justice, January–March 1931. By permission of the State Archives of Florida.

Figure 12. Hal P. Dekle, Dade County, Supreme Court justice, 1971–75. Florida Supreme Court Historical Society.

Figure 13. Governor Millard F. Caldwell and Chief Justice Elwyn Thomas (right) placed a box containing historical documents and photographs in the cornerstone of the new supreme court building at dedication ceremonies on December 28, 1948. Among the artifacts installed in the cornerstone were a copy of General Andrew Jackson's commission as governor of the territories of East and West Florida, a photograph of a painting of French general Marquis de Lafayette, a photograph of a Seminole Indian chief playing golf in Fort Myers, and a copy of the *Tallahassee Democrat*'s March 18, 1945, coverage of the Florida Centennial. Also participating in the cornerstone ceremony were U.S. Supreme Court Associate Justice Stanley F. Reed, who delivered the dedicatory address, and Charles H. Overman, director and secretary of the Florida State Improvement Commission. By permission of the State Archives of Florida.

Figure 14. The new Florida Supreme Court Building was framed by a replica of the nation's Liberty Bell that stood in the park across Duval Street. The bell was relocated within the Capitol Complex during the 1970s when the New Capitol was constructed in the area between the Old Capitol and the supreme court building. Florida Supreme Court Historical Society.

Figure 15. These men sat on the Florida Supreme Court when it moved to its new building west of the state Capitol in 1949. Left to right in this photograph are (*seated*) Glenn Terrell, Chief Justice Elwyn Thomas, and Roy H. Chapman; (*standing*) Alto Adams, Harold L. "Tom" Sebring, T. Frank Hobson, and Paul D. Barns. Terrell served for more than forty years (1923–64), the longest of any justice in Florida history. He served three terms as chief justice. Florida Supreme Court Historical Society.

Figure 16. Incoming Governor Fuller Warren of Blountstown rode in his January 1949 inaugural parade alongside his close friend, B. K. Roberts of Sopchoppy, whom he appointed to the Florida Supreme Court later that year. Roberts's career on the court spanned twenty-seven years and included three terms as chief justice (1953–55, 1961–63, and 1971–73). By permission of the State Archives of Florida.

Figure 17. In April 1955, Chief Justice John E. Mathews (*far right*) attended the opening session of the Florida legislature, shortly before his death on the last day of that month. He was joined for the joint legislative session by fellow justices E. Harris Drew, Glenn Terrell, and H. L. "Tom" Sebring. Florida Supreme Court Historical Society.

Figure 18. Justice Stephen C. O'Connell administered the oath of office to delegates of a young women's organization visiting the state capitol in Tallahassee. By permission of the State Archives of Florida.

Figure 19. Supreme court justices and cabinet members were seated in front of Governor Farris Bryant for the opening session of the 1963 Florida legislature. The justices were (*left to right*) Stephen O'Connell, E. Harris Drew, Glenn Terrell, B. K. Roberts, Elwyn Thomas, Campbell Thornal, and Millard Caldwell. Cabinet members seated behind were (*from left*) Tom Adams, secretary of state; Richard Ervin, attorney general; Ray Green, comptroller; Ed Larson, treasurer; Tom Bailey, superintendent of education; and Doyle Conner, commissioner of agriculture. Florida Supreme Court Historical Society.

Figure 20. In October 1967, Stephen C. O'Connell traded his judge's robe for an academic gown when he resigned from the Florida Supreme Court to become president of the University of Florida. Wishing him well were (*left to right*) E. Harris Drew, Elwyn Thomas, Millard Caldwell (chief justice), B. K. Roberts, Campbell Thornal, and Richard Ervin. By permission of the State Archives of Florida.

Figure 21. The 1968 Constitution Revision Commission included many notable Floridians, including three former or sitting supreme court justices: B. K. Roberts, H. L. "Tom" Sebring, and Stephen C. O'Connell. Other commission members included former governor Charley E. Johns and future governors Lawton Chiles and Reubin Askew. The commission chairman was Chesterfield Smith. By permission of the State Archives of Florida.

Figure 22. The 1968 court was composed of six veteran justices, who averaged over eighteen years of service on Florida's highest court, and a seventh justice, Wade L. Hopping (*far right*), who was appointed August 1 and served only five months. The others were (*left to right*) Richard Ervin, E. Harris Drew, Elwyn Thomas, Millard Caldwell, B. K. Roberts, and Campbell Thornal. Florida Supreme Court Historical Society.

Figure 23. January 7, 1969, was one of the busiest days in the history of the Florida Supreme Court, when three justices left the supreme court and three new ones took the bench. In this photograph, newly elected Justice Vassar Carlton was helped into his robe by retiring justice Elwyn Thomas and Carlton's wife, Grace. In other changes that day, Justice Millard Caldwell retired and Justice Wade Hopping stepped down after losing his reelection bid. Other justices sworn in that day were Joseph A. Boyd Jr. and James C. Adkins. By permission of the State Archives of Florida.

Figure 24. Joseph A. Boyd Jr. of Miami was sworn in on January 7, 1969, by Court Clerk Sid White. Sitting on the bench behind them (*left to right*) were Justices James C. Adkins (who had just been sworn in), Campbell Thornal, and B. K. Roberts. By permission of the State Archives of Florida.

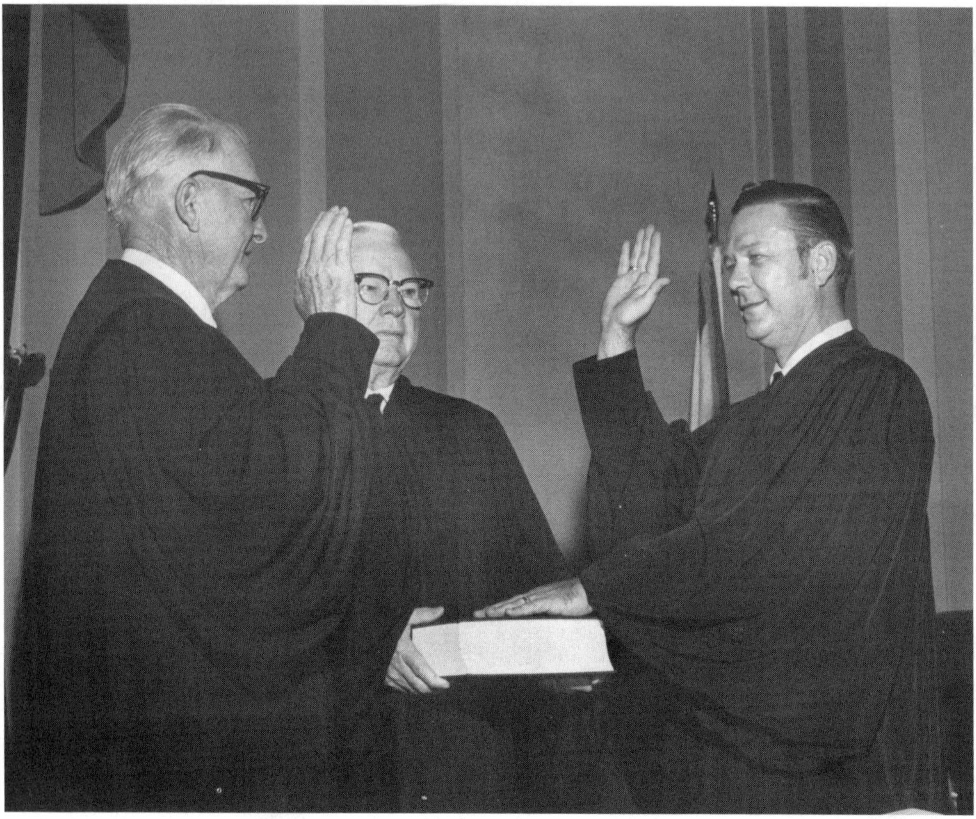

Figure 25. David L. McCain (*far right*) of St. Lucie County was sworn into the Florida Supreme Court in 1970 by Justice Richard Ervin, while Justice Alto Adams held the Bible. He was appointed by Governor Claude Kirk. In 1975 McCain resigned and Justice Hal Dekle retired from the Court while under investigation and facing possible impeachment. By permission of the State Archives of Florida.

8

The Postwar Bar

When peace dawned upon the world in late 1945 and early 1946, the situation of the bar of Florida and of its highest tribunal reflected many of the dynamics at play within the state. Then, as Florida emerged in very different form during the subsequent decade, broad-based reform efforts would transform the practice of law and the judiciary in profound ways, just as similar efforts were attempting to accomplish important alterations in government and society at large. Few of the changes occurred without struggle, though. To some extent within the bar but to a greater measure within the court and the state's political structure, resistance to change handicapped efforts to bring the legal system of a rapidly growing Florida into line with the state's newly emerging needs.

The most forceful agents of the changes to come were World War II veterans. The same youthful energy and determination to transform postwar Florida discussed in the previous chapter were tapped by many of them to force a retooling of the wheels of law and justice. One among them, LeRoy Collins, expressed what many of his peers felt about the matter. "Every lawyer has a duty to be a leader. He is fitted out for such a role. He fails if he ducks the responsibility, just as he fails if he perverts it." Recollect in assessing Collins's words that, in 1946 and the years immediately following, public confidence in and among lawyers ran high. "I think more people had respect for lawyers than they do now," Stephen C. O'Connell observed as the twentieth century closed, "and the trust between lawyers was so great." Gerald Kogan added, "In those days, your word was your bond and your handshake was just as good."[1]

Many older members of the legal profession and judiciary encouraged youthful leadership. Justice Armstead Brown issued a call in the *Florida Law Journal*'s January 1946 issue. "In this thrilling period of the history of the world and of our own country, there are many subjects which we might talk about and think about today, but we, as lawyers and judges here in Florida, must not be diverted from our duties here at home for the advancement and improvement of our profession and of the statutes and rules governing the practice and procedure in our courts of justice. In this, we can count upon those splendid young lawyers who have gloriously served our country during this 2nd and we hope the last world war, and who are now rapidly returning to the ranks of our profession." Future bar president Robert M. Ervin witnessed the situation firsthand. "There was no feeling of hostility about young veterans entering the profession. They were welcomed." That sense of fresh talent not weighted down by unreasonable constraints of the past helped to catapult Ervin's brother, Richard, into the attorney general's job in 1948, an event that showed public, as well as bar, support for fresh leadership. As the *St. Petersburg Times* noted in proffering the young man its endorsement, "He has the vitality and energy of youth in his favor."[2]

With guidance from some older leaders such as Justice Brown, young lawyers developed a sense of real purpose that directed their reform impulses. This drive especially was the case given the context of public concerns for illegality and corruption then current in the state. Campbell Thornal touched on the subject in a talk about his friend and fellow veteran Stephen C. O'Connell. "He had an abiding faith in the rule of law as the ultimate arbiter between right and wrong. He insisted that inefficiency in the administration of the judicial process tended to corrupt the law as a canon of truth. In his view, it generates public suspicions of the very foundation of government." In line with such sentiments, the veterans early on pushed for procedural reforms. "Since the Blount Code of 1829, which adopted as the basic law of Florida the general common and statute law of England as it existed upon the Declaration of Independence," John T. Wigginton explained, "the legal profession of our State has been shackled with the strict, technical common law forms of pleading." He added, "Many years ago England repented, with the result that today it has a greatly simplified code of pleading; yet down through the ages Florida has stubbornly adhered to this time-consuming and archaic system of legal procedure. The only justification for this static condition was evidently ground upon the theory that in law, as in good liquor, age possesses virtue."[3]

While pressing for procedural innovations, the veterans and their colleagues saw numerous other problems that needed attention as well. The quality of legal practice and the competency of some lawyers troubled them. Often they blamed the diploma privilege, which permitted accredited Florida law school graduates to gain bar admission without examination. Following a tough fight but with help from Governor Fuller Warren, a fellow veteran, they succeeded in abolishing the privilege thanks to action by the 1951 legislature. Chapter 26655, *Laws of Florida*, also empowered the supreme court thereafter to prescribe all "requirements, qualifications and standards to be met and procedures to be followed by all persons for admission to practice law in any of the Courts of the State of Florida or its political subdivisions."[4]

The question as to whether the legislature or the supreme court should regulate admission to the practice of law formed a small part of a much larger question, that of constitutional revision. Clifford C. Alloway pointed out the concerns. "The Florida Constitution is quite long, very diversified in subject and poorly written [and] our constitution is definitely antiquated." Few leaders defended the document, but north Florida legislative officers, who controlled the question, refused to call a constitutional convention because delegate selection processes for such an assembly would have reflected statewide population distribution rather than the legislature's malapportioned allotments. In 1947 advocates of change did secure legislative approval of a constitutional amendment that permitted the legislature to propose article by article or section by section amendments. The voters ratified the change in 1948, which set in motion a political tug-of-war over the next two decades regarding the basic charter and its provisions.[5]

Other innovations set important precedents during the period. As talented veterans flooded law schools thanks to support from the GI Bill, standards elevated. Evidence of the fact came when the institutions began contributing to a fixed body of literature that provided analysis and criticism of Florida law and jurisprudence. In March 1947, for instance, the *Miami Law Quarterly* debuted as a University of Miami Law School organ. It not only examined Florida case decisions but also took up the cause of constitutional revision. In 1948, the *University of Florida Law Review* followed. An endorsement of the publication by Chief Justice Elwyn Thomas noted, "The members of the court consider law reviews of great value in the study of cases and the preparation of opinions." He concluded, "Not only are they . . . a valuable contribution to the knowledge which the members of the court gain on the subject, but they save us much time which would be spent by us in research."[6]

Having found a friend in the attorney general's office beginning in January 1949, the lawyers pushed for administrative action to further efficiency and integrity in the making and implementation of law. Richard Ervin responded by enhancing his department's efforts to assist in the drafting of bills and amendments, as well as research for legislators. Unlike the case in later years, the legislature then had virtually no resources upon which to rely other than lobbyists. Ervin also created a program for biennial compilation and publication of the Florida statutes. The idea had predated World War II, but its implementation had been suspended once war loomed. Assistant Attorney General Charles Tom Henderson headed the program for Ervin. When the two-volume 1949 edition of *Florida Statutes* first became available in the summer of 1950, it cost lawyers a mere $12.50 per set.[7]

Paralleling efforts to ensure regular recompilation and publication of the *Florida Statutes* were attempts to recast the nature of published court reports so as to permit greater access while reducing costs. The Florida State Bar Association in 1946 requested that the supreme court limit written opinions generally and published opinions in particular. The court agreed, effective May 7, by announcing that it would "promulgate written opinions only in cases that involve questions that have not been previously adjudicated, or such cases as the facts and circumstances make it advisable that an opinion be written." The panel further specified that "per curiam orders and judgments, as distinguished from opinions expressing or discussing the law of the case, be not published, but that the titles of these cases be carried in the Florida and Southern Reporters under a separate index under the caption, 'Cases determined without opinion,' or some such appropriate heading."[8]

The question of how Florida decisions would appear in print also commanded attention. A bar committee headed by Donald Walker concluded in 1947 that separate publication of *Florida Reports* could no longer be justified in terms of expense. Its recommendation, endorsed unanimously by Florida's justices, followed a Tennessee model. Pursuant to it, a separate volume of *Florida Cases* would be published out of every four or five volumes of the West Publishing Company's *Southern Reporter* series. Delays of various kinds kept the Board of Commissioners of the State Institutions of Florida from contracting with the West Company until 1949. The last volume of *Florida Reports*, numbered 160, carried most Florida Supreme Court decisions through 1948. Subsequent opinions appeared beginning with 37 *So. 2d* 692. The first volume of *Florida Cases* saw publication on December 29, 1949. It cost $10 per book.[9]

The successes enjoyed by activist lawyers could not mask the profession's relative lack of clout and cohesion as it attempted to move state and local governments that often did not welcome significant change. "You had those people from west Florida who just came to Tallahassee to take over the government," observed one lawyer and veteran. "Nobody else would take leadership." Meanwhile, the voluntary Florida State Bar Association could claim only 1,700 of the state's 2,700 lawyers as members. Less than 20 percent of the members participated in bar functions and conventions. Back in 1923, at Armstead Brown's recommendation, an attempt had been made and subsequently revisited time and again to obtain a statute mandating an integrated (nonvoluntary) bar. Each attempt had failed, but the suggestion offered the only apparent method for creating a workable bar organization that could police the profession while representing it effectively in the halls of government.[10]

The possibility of bar integration revived in 1946, and Justice Brown again provided the spark. "It seems that it is only by this method that the bar of Florida can present a united and solid front, in its high endeavors," he declared. State bar association president Julius F. Parker urged action at the organization's convention that year, noting that twenty-seven states already had integrated. Parker and James D. Bruton Jr. subsequently headed a bar integration committee appointed to bring such a plan to the supreme court. By September 1947, its members had polled Florida's lawyers on bar integration and "the payment of $5.00 annual dues and the supervision of the bar's disciplinary action by direct review of the Supreme Court." Of 2,700 attorneys asked the questions, 1,131 responded favorably while 500 expressed opposition. The tally proved heartening enough for bar leaders to endorse preparation of a plan. On December 8, 1948, the bar formally petitioned the court for an integration rule. Oral arguments ensued on January 18, 1949, and the panel issued its favorable decision on June 7. The following March 4 the court implemented its decision by approving rules for integrated bar operations. Within weeks the state bar association had disbanded, and the Florida Bar had become the only statewide organization for all Florida attorneys. In line with the change, in January 1954 the *Florida Law Journal* was renamed the *Florida Bar Journal*.[11]

9

The Postwar Supreme Court

The enthusiastic manner with which World War II veterans embraced the changes and reforms discussed in chapter 7 did not necessarily reflect sentiment on the Supreme Court of Florida. An essentially conservative body, it would witness during the postwar decade a hardening of many of its traditions and positions. Meanwhile, forces beyond its control—and, at times, understanding—rushed the cautious panel pall-mall toward a startlingly new era.

At the supreme court, tradition certainly weighed more heavily than it did among activist lawyer veterans. On the question of bar integration, for example, Justice Paul D. Barns denied the court's authority even to act. Perhaps more suggestively, in 1946 the tribunal had refused to support adoption of the Federal Rules of Civil Procedure as requested by a broad spectrum of bar membership. This reaffirmed a stance proclaimed several times in the 1930s and early 1940s. Tribunal members unanimously denounced the widely accepted and popular rules as "impracticable when taken as a whole." Even the relatively minor revisions looked upon with favor drew dissent from Justices Elwyn Thomas and Harold L. Sebring. Not until November 1949 did the court, thanks to Justice Glenn Terrell's leadership, take substantive steps to adopt a comprehensive revision that reflected the national trend. Effective January 1, 1950, the new code streamlined some procedures, most notably by abolishing common law forms of pleading and replacing them with a simple complaint stating a cause of action. Yet the jurists continued to decline abolishing procedural distinctions between law and equity. John T. Wigginton, the bar's point man on procedural reform, saw the revisions as "an important forward step," but only a step.[1]

To a very great degree, the court of the late 1940s and early 1950s reflected more the old Florida of the Panhandle rather than the new Florida of the booming peninsula. "It was a quiet court," Richard W. Ervin remembered. W. Reece Smith concurred. "It was a court of conservative southern sentiment that was in tune with the legislative governance of the state and the pace of the state at that time." Members took pride in the court's motto *Sat cito si recte*, "Soon enough if correct." The pace of litigation at the war's conclusion permitted that luxury. "The docket of the Supreme Court is right up to date," Chief Justice Roy H. Chapman reported in 1946. "We may have, possibly, 100 cases around the Court that are being worked on and a few cases in which there is a difference of views, or what we frequently refer to as split decisions, but all cases, as a general rule, that have matured are right now being considered, and it is our desire to keep the docket in its present condition."[2]

A reverence for tradition and permanence coexisted among panel members with a certain sense of informality. The justices continued to wear business suits rather than robes. Save for the single addition of Justice Sebring in 1943, the panel's makeup had not changed since before the war. One justice had served since 1923 and two others since 1925. Overwhelmingly, their presence represented the judgment of state chief executives of an earlier era rather than of the state's voters. Only two members had commenced their service through election. Each jurist's tenure theoretically could last as long as he desired. Court races by the 1940s usually received so little attention that, until 1968, no member of that era faced defeat. One critic asserted, "The electoral processes have become in practice little more than casual referenda in which voters periodically go through the motions of endorsing judicial appointments made by our governors."[3]

Court proceedings moved at the unhurried pace typical of Tallahassee's traditional style of life, and tourists often stopped in for a relaxing visit. One itinerary published in 1946 declared:

> Leaving the capitol, you may drop by the supreme court building. Perhaps a hearing will be in progress and—if you're wearing a coat—you'll want to spend a half hour or so listening to lawyers arguing their cases before Florida's seven justices. You may be particularly interested in picking out Judge Glenn Terrell whose sparkling command of language makes many a supreme court opinion merry reading.
>
> Or you might like to have a look at Judge H. L. Sebring, a former University of Florida football coach. Then there are Chief Justice Roy H. Chapman, Judge Rivers Buford—who at the age of twenty was a lumberjack on the Apalachicola river—and Judge Alto Adams who at forty-seven is one of the younger members of the court. The roster is completed by Judge Armstead Brown, who will retire next January, and Judge Elwyn Thomas who was elected to the high tribunal in 1938.[4]

The past remained very much alive at the court building, so much so that stories of ghosts of departed justices roaming hallways and offices could seem plausible. Janitor Frank Batchelor, who commenced his service in 1916, reported in 1947 that Justices Jefferson B. Browne, R. Fenwick Taylor, and Thomas F. West could be seen as apparitions after "first dark." A newspaper story noted, "They move silently among the law books, sit at the desks which were familiar to them many years ago." Batchelor added, "They wear the clothes they used to wear. They want to know how I'm getting along. It doesn't worry me."[5]

As Batchelor's example clearly illustrates, court tradition permitted staff members, as well as justices, to remain as permanently as they desired. Reuben Williams had worked for the tribunal since the century's turn, occupying the marshal's office since 1935. His frugality typified that of the body. Charged with buying and managing court supplies, Williams would test worn-out typewriter ribbons to ensure real need for replacement and buy stationery only a few hundred sheets at a time. "I can't tell when a justice might quit or die," he answered when questioned on the latter practice, "and I would hate for the Court to be left with a lot of stationery that couldn't be used."[6]

Even if not for terms equal to Williams's, others on the small staff also enjoyed employment longevity. Guyte P. McCord, who had served as clerk since 1939, would remain in the position until 1964. The light demands of his office afforded him time to serve as secretary to the state board of bar examiners as had his predecessor. Only in 1945 was McCord's compensation and that of key employees changed from the fee system to a salary. Ella O'Neill Wilkins assisted McCord as deputy clerk. Known to court visitors as "Miss Ella," she began her employment in 1926 and retired from it in 1972. Carson F. Sinclair supervised the court library from 1935 but did not receive the title of librarian until 1957. He held it until retirement in 1977. Joe Butler had undertaken his attaché job seven years prior to Sinclair's starting time. Butler eventually became court messenger. In that capacity, until his 1972 retirement, he "set up the Conference Room, picked up the mail at the post office and located, distributed and replaced the files when they were needed by the justices, the clerk, lawyers, and others visiting the court."[7]

The quiet, the traditions, and the long tenures of office notwithstanding, the postwar years were to work great stresses upon the court and its members; in turn, its image in the public eye—rebuilt during the 1940s after the trying 1930s—would begin to suffer. The resulting damage would stem not only from public perceptions, which will be discussed shortly, but also from the court's inability to sense that problems existed. This situation could arise because, within the small world of the court and the bar, few ever expressed concerns directly. "When I was in the attorney general's office," Richard W. Ervin recorded, "the supreme court judges were revered." A future bar leader added, "Like others, I held all of them in considerable awe."[8]

The reverential treatment accorded by lawyers to justices carried a number of ramifications, one of which should be noted here. Within the court's peaceful and secure environment as the postwar era dawned, members could feel at ease in approaching the law and their decisions less formally than might otherwise have been the case. With distinctions between law and equity remaining significant, several panel members often sought equitable solutions to difficult questions, leaving themselves ample time to construct a legal justification. Justice Terrell explained the philosophy behind the attitude. "The Constitution is what the people intended it to be; its dominant note is the general welfare; it was not intended to bind like a straitjacket but contemplated experimentation for the common good. When it was promulgated, its sponsors thought it the embodiment of the common concept of right and a practical means of insuring justice." With specific reference to a case at hand, Terrell concluded: "We dispel the charge that the Constitutional interpretation is an expression of judicial prejudices or of the judge's social and economic theories. The question here involves new complexes that must be thought through in the light of the purpose designed to be accomplished and not in the light of outworn dogmas that do nothing more than throw our means of administering justice into a stalemate." In 1946 Terrell colorfully added, "A court can no longer interpret the law from the back of an ass."[9]

This flexible approach did not long survive after the court began to battle the effects of Florida's growth and then as controversial cases challenged its and the state's status quo. The boom, with its attendant population surge, understandably caused a tremendous increase in litigation and appeals. As of the mid-1940s, a court term might involve disposition of less than 125 cases, with the same number holding over on the docket until the next term. By early 1949, the yearly load had risen to 750. "The increase in appellate litigation of late, and the probability that in a growing state such as ours it will progressively continue," declared Justice Thomas, "make the problem of dispatch of business, with as little disturbance of settled law as possible, a constant challenge to the profession." Thus the principle of *stare decisis* in the hands of its most outspoken proponent on the court had reasserted itself by 1949 to permit the panel to deal with increased caseloads through "as little disturbance of settled law as possible."[10]

But the caseload crisis merely had reached its launching point. The year 1950 saw a surge to 927 appeals. A total of 941 appeals were disposed of the following year and about the same number in 1952. A stressful situation grew rapidly worse in 1953. The jurists were called upon to process 1,172 matters, a number that harkened back to the court's troubled days in the 1930s. By 1954, when the load had reached 1,251, the Florida tribunal carried a caseload greater than that of any other similar court in the nation. Attempts to streamline procedures and to align them more closely with federal rules helped but did nothing to solve what fast was becoming an overwhelming burden. In 1955 the total dipped slightly to 1,225 with over 600 additional appeals pending. The next year a new record of

1,256 cases made statewide news. Now 1,717 appeals were carried over due to the court's inability to process them.[11]

Even though news of the mounting caseload would spread throughout the state by the mid-1950s, most Floridians back in 1946 had given little thought to the supreme court. To many peninsular newcomers, remote Tallahassee with its court seemed to exist in an altogether different state. Other residents, though, remained very aware of the panel and held impressions that were not favorable at all. Particularly, African Americans—who then composed about one-quarter of the state's population—saw the court as a bastion of privilege and white rule. A positive reaction resulted in 1946 when the panel declared race zoning unconstitutional, but its affects did not linger. A string of decisions regarding matters involving desegregation and rights of criminal defendants further embittered many blacks. NAACP field secretary Robert W. Saunders commented on the general sense. "We felt we were going to face an attitude that pictured the Old South," he observed. "What I'm saying is, look at the Groveland case, the Chambers case, the Shepherd case—all of those cases where the court upheld convictions in rape cases. [The court] was more political than anything else."[12]

The court for the most part failed to perceive the importance of black sentiments about its work, although individual candidates for open seats on the supreme bench found themselves contending by 1946 with the growing power of black voters. Paul D. Barns, W. Raleigh Petteway, James Henry Taylor, and J. L. Lee learned this fact of life while contending that year for retiring Justice Brown's seat. All four candidates voiced conservative stances, with Petteway, the best known of them, insisting, "There are no issues to be discussed." He led Barns in the first Democratic primary by twenty thousand votes. The runoff then went to Barns by six thousand in a low turnout. The winner's support came from the state's largest counties. He had expressed concern for organized labor's needs, and his service as Dade County circuit judge had seen him take care to afford justice to African Americans. These two emerging interest groups, with considerable overlap between the two, provided Barns's margin of victory.[13]

The 1946 court race highlighted additional factors that ultimately would impact the court's reputation—and its cohesion. Petteway and Barns both called Miami home. Barns's election made him Dade County's first son to secure statewide office since the 1920s. The win compelled governors to weigh central and south Florida appointments more heavily. Thus when Justice Buford resigned in 1948, Governor Millard Caldwell looked to the peninsula to find St. Petersburg circuit judge T. Frank Hobson. One downside for the court came from the fact that the appointments challenged its Panhandle orientation and Old South ways, creating tensions that divided its members. Barns and Hobson reveled in the culture and lifestyle of their urban peninsular homes and never truly felt comfortable in Tallahassee. Barns resigned in 1949 to return to Miami. Hobson, whose marriage suffered strain, found it preferable to remain in the capital city even given an atmosphere often cold to him. Separation from his spouse, coupled with an active social life and work habits that strayed from those traditionally associated with court members, prompted most of Hobson's colleagues to distance themselves despite his excellent work product. Mores that would have drawn at most a wary glance in St. Petersburg led Hobson into a sort of quarantine in Tallahassee.[14]

Few residents of the booming peninsula knew of Justice Barns's unhappiness at Tallahassee or of the court's critical view of Hobson's behavior, but other dynamics were being set in motion that would lead many to harbor real concerns. For example, some came to fear—even when careful inquiry might have proven the perception inaccurate—that the court was wrapped up in the corruption Floridians saw all around them in the late 1940s and early 1950s. The justices rarely traveled on business outside the capital city, so public awareness came primarily from news coverage of controversial decisions. Whatever gain the court may have enjoyed among south Floridians when Justice Barns joined the panel, to cite one instance, it quickly lost that advantage when it refused to give constitutional review to the legislature's 1945 apportionment decisions. In 1947, as law enforcement integrity throughout the state came into question amid gambling exposés, the tribunal reversed the conviction of a Marion County sheriff for running a numbers racket, declaring the evidence "not conclusive." In just one of many additional examples, the court in 1951 invalidated corruption indictments lodged against Dade County's Sheriff Jimmy Sullivan, one of the most heavily publicized cases resulting from Estes Kefauver's Florida organized crime hearings.[15]

The ongoing saga of the supreme court's attempt to construct a new building fed the dailies and weeklies with items that caused attentive readers to question its members' collective intentions and good judgment. The project had begun before World War II as a rehabilitation and modernization of the court's 1913 building, a facility that the panel shared with the state railroad commission. A supreme court building commission had been established in 1941 to erect an addition, but Governor Spessard Holland had suspended the entire capital building program following the declarations of war in December. In late 1944 the court revived the project and designated Justice Chapman as liaison. Newly inaugurated Governor Caldwell expressed little interest, though, until contacted on the court's behalf in late January 1945 by industrialist and shipbuilder George Blaine Howell. Swayed by the intercession of his Tampa friend, the governor asked for cost estimates. When they came in at the large sum of $400,000, the thoughts of many turned to the idea of an entirely new building. The legislature obliged by authorizing the project subject to funding. Caldwell then allowed the measure to become law while withholding his own stamp of approval. The architectural firm of Chandler C. Yonge and R. Daniel Hart, in cooperation with James Gamble Rogers II, drew the plans.[16]

The court, especially Justices Chapman and Sebring, desired that the new building express in monumental form the court's eminence and equal standing with the executive and legislative branches. The design costed out initially at $1,200,000. The huge estimate jeopardized the project. Fears of "the attendant publicity that will result relative to the cost of the building" led to a gubernatorial decision to postpone a final decision "until after the land has been acquired because of the wobbly attitude of some cabinet members." The land acquisition process caused more headaches. A site one block west of the capitol and bounded by St. Augustine, Pensacola, Duval, and Bronough streets was selected by April 1946. When property owners sought high compensation, even Chapman declared the demands "out of reason." Condemnation proceedings ensued that took months to result in jury awards of almost $300,000. Aghast, Caldwell labeled the results "excessive" and threatened to shut down the project.[17]

From early 1947 the building initiative rode a very public roller coaster of highs and lows. Fortunately, in January the City of Tallahassee offered $100,000 to be applied against land costs. After a good deal of squabbling and intense lobbying by bar leaders including West Palm Beach's E. Harris Drew, the cabinet in February allotted $1,305,000 for total costs. Bidding resulted by April in an offer from J. A. Jones Construction Company of Charlotte, North Carolina, that ran $400,000 too high, a figure preferable to earlier bids that had pushed the amount up $700,000. Now Caldwell allied himself with opposing cabinet members, only changing his mind after renewed lobbying. This included one official's ultimately successful effort to point out to the governor the fact that the Dade County courthouse lot had cost more than the entire supreme court project. Then north Florida legislative leaders intervened in a political attempt to assert their power over the court by killing construction outright. Only quick thinking that led to a hurried signing of construction contracts foiled the attempt. Senator Claude Pepper thereafter paved the way for necessary federal postwar approvals and assistance. Construction thereupon could begin.[18]

Delays blamed partly on heavy rains highlighted the court building story during the following eighteen months. By November 1947 Caldwell led a chorus of complainants. Through the winter and well into 1948, work crews labored on the building. Sufficient progress had been made by December 29 for laying a cornerstone. As Justice Hobson's father, the Reverend W. A. Hobson, gave the invocation outside the main entrance, a "heavy deluge" fell, compelling those present to remove to the Florida House of Representatives chamber. U.S. Supreme Court Associate Justice Stanley Reed delivered the chief remarks. "May this building stand for decades as a symbol of justice to the rich and to the poor," he declared. "May those whom the people call to labor within its walls feel imbued with the spirit of service. May the people of the state look upon their Supreme Court as a tribunal for the adjustment of differences, a refuge for the persecuted, a haven for the oppressed, a citadel for the weak. If this court remains worthy of popular confidence, Florida can feel secure amid the transient hurricanes of unrest that rock communities where justice is a purchasable or a controlled commodity."[19]

At the time of its dedication, the supreme court building remained unfinished, as it would for decades. When staff and court members began relocating to the facility in March 1949, its main courtroom was not yet ready, no landscaping had been undertaken, no elevator or air conditioning eased the day, painting had advanced little, and not even a flagpole graced the grounds. The panel sat in its new courtroom for the first time on June 7. On that occasion, also for the first time, its members wore robes in line with the desire of several justices, especially Justice Sebring, to elevate and formalize proceedings. The public would not be invited to tour the structure—admired for its beauty and grace despite its yet-to-be-completed status—until late May 1950. Several years afterward, Chief Justice B. K. Roberts arranged for the erection of the flagpole at no expense to the state. He did so as a memorial for the late Justice Fred H. Davis.[20]

While stories about controversial decisions and court building dramas provided provocative fodder for newspaper readers, the reports likely never found the audience that sought out items linking the court to powerful businessman Ed Ball. Early on, a different situation had prevailed. In 1945 the dispatches had noted decisions that blocked Ball's divorce and hampered his takeover of the Florida East Coast Railway, both results perceivable as anti-Ball. Within the year circumstances had reversed. In February 1947 an appellant in a case against Ball asked the court to disqualify Justices Buford and Adams for their ties to the financier. Buford, he pointed out, had received an advantageous lease in 1944 of 18,000 acres of Panhandle pinelands from the St. Joe Paper Company. Adams, the complaint averred, had benefited in 1943 from an $80,000 loan from Ball's Florida National Bank of Jacksonville. Their fellow justices rejected the demand for the disqualifications. Then in October 1948 the same litigant urged another panel member's removal from hearing his case. "I feel I will not receive a fair hearing," he declared, ". . . if Justice Barns sits and participates because of his prejudice against me, as appellant, and against my case and against my counsel, Robert H. Anderson, and in favor of the adverse party." Again, the court declined to act.[21]

Articles about matters such as these laid the groundwork for others to come. The most important series began in summer 1949 when Governor Fuller Warren installed Ball's personal lawyer, B. K. Roberts, on the supreme bench to replace the resigning Justice Barns. In fairness to Roberts, his reputation as an attorney loomed large and the governor held him in the highest personal and professional esteem. Roberts insisted that he had dispensed with all private clients upon taking the oath in August, but some reports hinted that the new judge remained Ball's counsel into the early 1950s if not later. Whether he continued to aid the businessman professionally, Roberts maintained a close personal relationship with Ball and Warren. He also scripted the governor's repudiation of Senator Kefauver's damning investigative conclusions and more or less openly advised the governor on other political and governmental matters.[22]

Meanwhile, Ball's reputation took heavy blows at the same time as his association with Justice Roberts became ever more public. Within a month after Ball's candidate, George Smathers, had bested Senator Claude Pepper in one of the most hotly contested political campaigns in state history, news stories disclosed details of litigation in which the financier was charged with "a cold, ingenious and ruthless plot to pillage an almost insolvent and defenseless State and its taxpaying public." Yet within a few weeks Floridians read a multitude of reports and beheld photographs of Warren, Ball, and Roberts in New York City and Washington, D.C., along with other bankers and businessmen who made up the Florida Chamber of Commerce's Florida Industrial Development Council. Pepper found himself greeting the party in Washington, an encounter that gave rise to one of Florida's great political tales. "I congratulated [Ball] on 'his' victory," the senator recorded. "When he mumbled something to the effect that it was good to have won 'the last round,' I replied that maybe it was not the last round. Ball shrieked so that everyone in the room could hear, 'Claude, if you ever run for public office in Florida again, we'll lick you so bad you'll think this time was a victory.'"[23]

Following the industrial council trip, Roberts took care to distance himself in the press from Ball, but another court member soon found his name again in the headlines. Chief Justice Alto Adams had been invited to accompany the council party on its trip but wisely had declined. Privately, though, Ball and Adams—personally or through intermediaries—began exploring the possibility of Adams contesting the governorship in 1952 against Dan McCarty, with whom Adams shared the same hometown of Fort Pierce. Ball's hostility to McCarty's good government reform agenda had persisted, and the businessman believed that Adams either could beat his fellow townsman or else deprive him of election. As a part of Ball's assistance to Adams, in July 1951 the St. Joe Paper Company purchased the justice's Tallahassee home and surrounding land for $60,000 while permitting

Adams and his family to remain as tenants at a modest rental rate. The transaction became public. The justice in October resigned his court seat after announcing his intention to enter the gubernatorial campaign. Although Adams spent generously, the run failed to stem the McCarty election tide. The onetime judge then returned, at least for the time being, to private life.[24]

As if these various publicity problems were not enough, Governor Warren's designation of a successor to Justice Adams set off a real firestorm. The growing power of Duval County's black voters and resentment of his support for a sales tax had resulted in 1950 in State Senator John E. Mathews's defeat for reelection. Warren, believing that Mathews's loyalty to the governor had caused the loss, saw supreme court service as an ideal way to usher his friend back into public life. As it happened, though, the announcement's timing on October 17, 1951, proved unfortunate. News reports had buffeted the governor as well as the court. Kefauver's *Crime in America* had been published in August, placing Warren and Florida in a very poor light. Although the governor dismissed its importance, Attorney General Richard W. Ervin declared that, in fact, a "state of emergency" existed. Then Warren stirred the political pot by designating Ed Ball's sister Jessie Ball duPont as the first woman to serve on the state board of control, which oversaw higher education. Quickly, Sanford's J. Brailey Odham announced his candidacy for governor with a backhanded slap at Warren by pledging "to throw the commercialized gambling racketeers, legal and illegal, out of our state and local governments."[25]

Odham's announcement came less than two weeks before Mathews's appointment, leaving the state's political air highly charged. It fairly exploded when the Mathews news reached the state's black community. "We bitterly oppose your appointment of Mr. John E. Mathews to the State Supreme Court bench," one "disgusted" Jacksonville resident informed the governor, "because he (Mathews) has a deep and abiding prejudice against Negroes." NAACP head Harry T. Moore, a longtime Mathews foe who would suffer assassination within two months, decried the new justice as a "companion and bed-fellow of the Ku Klux Klan." Soon segments of the mainstream press entered the fray. The *St. Petersburg Times*, for one, reached nearly the same level of hyperbole by insisting that Mathews was "one of the worst bigots" in Florida history. Dan McCarty announced his gubernatorial campaign days later, alluding vaguely to "deals and combinations and manipulations and conspiracies involving the governorship."[26]

The controversy, in turn, created a tradition. Warren and Mathews's friends—with the organized bar and the supreme court's members—rallied around the new justice. Where a simple, private oathtaking previously had marked the advent of court service, now an elaborate swearing-in ceremony was decided upon to permit a public display of support. Accordingly, on October 30 the new jurist placed his hand on the Bible in the court chamber. "High dignitaries of bench and bar were on hand to honor Mathews at the brief, solemn ceremony," one report noted. Bar president John M. Allison administered the oath. "The form of today's induction ceremony was the most impressive in the State's history," the report continued, "and is expected to become traditional as future justices are sworn in the same manner."[27]

The bar's cooperation in buttressing the Mathews appointment carried with it another result. Anxious to avoid any repetition of such a backlash and thankful for bar aid, Warren pledged in February 1952 to make any future supreme court appointments based upon the bar's recommendation. His action related specifically to a proposed court enlargement to be voted on later in the year, but when Justice Chapman passed away in August, the governor honored his commitment by selecting West Palm Beach bar leader E. Harris Drew, who had scored highly in a bar-conducted poll. "No lawyer in the state would have been more cordially received by the legal profession," declared bar president William McRae of Bartow.[28]

The appointment of an individual of Drew's standing came at just the right moment for the court. As mentioned, bar pressure had compelled the 1951 legislature to approve a constitutional amendment designed to address rapidly escalating problems of court administration and caseloads. The solution involved increasing the number of justices from seven to ten, while creating a unified court system for the state with the chief justice as its administrative head. The measure also vested in the supreme court full authority over civil procedure rules. Seemingly, court members felt little concern over the amendment's passage at the upcoming November 1952 general election, although the negative publicity of recent years should have provided ample room for doubt. In any event the bar's enthusiasm over the Drew appointment suggested similar enthusiasm for the amendment.[29]

It was not to be. The timing of Justice Chapman's death and the Drew appointment thrust the new justice immediately into a reelection campaign. Dade County circuit judge Vincent C. Giblin took on Drew in what became one of the hottest judicial races in Florida's experience. The challenger's August announcement proclaimed that he would "expose and condemn in no uncertain terms the evils in our judicial system," a system which Giblin labeled "one of the worst in America." He blasted the proposed court enlargement especially. The challenger charged that the panel was "the least respected court of last resort in America today" and insisted that "the confidence of the people is seriously impaired." Rather than an enlarged court, Giblin argued, "Florida needs more competent supreme court justices." Several major newspapers endorsed the challenger, including the *Miami Herald*. Among those backing Drew and the amendment, only lukewarm support for the court issued forth. "The membership of our supreme court today probably could be stronger," the *Orlando Sentinel* opined. "However, the court as presently constituted is competent, if political." Drew declined to take any position on the court expansion, limiting himself to advocating the necessity of "civil attitudes" for justices. On October 14, Drew squeaked ahead of Giblin by less than 2,000 votes. On November 4, 1952, voters, as bar president Horner C. Fisher put it, "emphatically rejected" the constitutional amendment.[30]

The stunning defeat vividly symbolized the damage done to the supreme court by years of adverse publicity coupled with the panel's isolation from population centers, and it spurred the Florida Bar and the McCarty administration to reorient the direction of its judicial reform efforts. "The bar had had enough of half-baked, high-pressured, ill-considered, piecemeal projects for the amendment of the Judiciary Article," President Fisher explained. Now the bar sought and, in 1953 with McCarty's help, obtained the statutory creation of the independent Judicial Council of Florida as a mechanism for bringing about "needed changes." A supreme court justice, a circuit court judge, a probate judge, the attorney general, four bar members, and nine laymen appointed by the governor made up its membership. Justice Thomas served as founding chairman. Over the following years the council labored patiently, developing plans and nurturing support for streamlining and modernizing the court system.[31]

A breakthrough finally arrived in 1955. Failing in its attempt to find sufficient support for a truly unified three- or four-level court system, the judicial council decided to focus on the creation of three district courts of appeals to relieve the supreme court of its caseload crisis. With help from one of Thomas's close friends—the new governor, LeRoy Collins—the council gained legislative approval for a constitutional amendment. The final language reached well beyond simple authorization for the new courts to limiting the supreme court's power. Under its terms, the courts of appeals would obtain final appellate jurisdiction in all matters excepting judgments imposing the death penalty, construction of state and federal statutes or treaties, constitutional questions, bond validations, matters certified by the district courts to be of great public interest, and cases where district courts stood in conflict on the same point of law. The chief justice would administer and coordinate the work of all state courts, but the amendment also mandated compulsory retirement for all justices and judges (except those then in office) at age seventy. Voters, eager for mandatory retirement and the new courts, endorsed the initiative by a large margin in November 1956. It became effective the following year.[32]

LeRoy Collins in 1955 wrote one additional installment of the supreme court's story, and its message provides a suitable end for this discussion on the first decade of the postwar era. That year, circumstances enabled the governor to begin placing his stamp on the panel by naming two justices. Aide John Germany remembered that, in doing so, "quality was the theme." The first opening arose out of the sudden death in late April of Chief Justice John E. Mathews, exhausted from efforts to manage the tribunal's workload. For the seat Collins named Orlando's Campbell Thornal, a close associate of the governor and of the late Dan McCarty. The second came about when, in July, Justice Sebring announced his resignation to become Stetson University Law School dean. For that position the governor turned to another well-regarded peninsular resident who lacked judicial experience but who enjoyed a reputation for honesty, temperance, and hard work. Fort Lauderdale's Stephen C. O'Connell also had backed the McCarty and Collins reform candidacies. The governor summed up the qualities he saw in Thornal, but the words expressed well the kind of man he believed was needed on the supreme court as Florida swirled into the modern era. "He was clean living, a leader with strong Christian values," Collins observed. "He demanded more of himself than of others. He saw public office not as a goal in itself, but as the means and a source of power to get good things done."[33] The questions that remained grew out of the governor's words. What good things needed to be done? And who would decide what they would be?

Paul Dryden Barns, Supreme Court Justice, 1946–1949

A man of unbending integrity and one of Florida's most seasoned judicial veterans, Paul Dryden Barns achieved a seat on Florida's supreme court only to surrender his prize in order to return to his adopted hometown of Miami. Even before his arrival on the supreme bench Barns had marked the court with his contributions. For decades following his departure, he would continue his professional efforts with much the same affect.

The Barns family arrived in Florida during the early boom days of 1880s railroad construction. It already could trace its early roots to South Carolina and Hope, Arkansas, when its members traveled during 1882 in a covered wagon to still-frontier Hillsborough County. Soon Dr. Augustus Mitchell Barns and his wife, Martha Griffin Barns, had put down roots at Plant City, where he practiced medicine and planted orange groves. Eventually the family, including son John Augustus Barns, turned to merchandising, produce shipping, hotel keeping, and newspaper publishing to solidify the family's fortune. On December 31, 1889, John married Ida Pemberton. Paul Dryden Barns was born on March 20, 1894.[34]

Paul D. Barns passed his youth in the midst of relative affluence, either at his family home centered within an orange grove near Plant City or else with relations in the town's most desirable residential quarter. He attended Plant City public schools but credited his mother as his life's great influence. She had attended college before her marriage and encouraged her son's pursuit of education and professional life. She also gave him a sense of social conscience that derived from an upbringing at Bristol, in Unionist and Republican east Tennessee. With it came a somewhat different perspective on racial concerns than was held by many of their Plant City neighbors. As Paul D. Barns Jr. commented, "Dad stood on the liberal side of social questions."[35]

In line with his mother's desire, Paul Barns pursued higher education following his 1913 graduation from Plant City High School. He first attended Washington and Lee University but transferred to the University of Florida law program in 1915. His funds soon ran out, though. Accordingly, in 1916 Barns decided to drop out of school and take the bar examination early. The future justice easily achieved admission to the Florida Bar and relocated to Miami where relatives were prospering in association with developer George Merrick. World War I thereafter interrupted his professional life with enlistment in the Army Air Corps. Sergeant Barns eventually assisted the war effort by teaching aerial gunnery at Kelly Field, Texas. There he contracted pneumonia, which damaged his lungs with long-lasting consequences. Released from service following recuperation, he chose to return to the University of Florida Law School to finish his studies. Barns earned his LL.B. degree in 1920. By then he boasted membership in Phi Delta Phi, Phi Kappa Phi, and Phi Kappa Alpha fraternities.[36]

A legal practice beckoned Barns back to Miami in 1920, but he yearned to broaden his life by starting a family. First, the still young attorney joined the Rand and Kurtz law firm at the princely salary of $75 per month. "I was happy to get it," he later told his children. As soon as he could get his finances in order, he turned to personal matters. Barns first knew Mattie Victoria Coleman in the fifth grade. She had just moved to Plant City from Brunswick, Georgia, and as Mary Barns Pruitt recalled, "He fell for her immediately." She was a woman of great intelligence. Daughter Mary recalled a telling incident of the couple's formative years. In the seventh grade, their teacher heard that students were criticizing her teaching skills. The struggling educator snapped at the class, "Any of you who think you're so smart, you can just get up and leave and go to the eighth grade." Victoria's response came quickly. She grabbed her friend by the arm and declared, "Come on Paul, let's go." At the time, Barns proved reluctant to follow his girlfriend into early promotion. So Victoria graduated a year ahead of her future husband in 1912, following which she attended Florida State College for Women. After one year's study, "Miss Vick" took the state teachers' exam. She qualified to teach mathematics, returned to Plant City, and pursued her new vocation until a letter arrived from Miami proposing marriage. The couple wed on May 23, 1923, subsequently establishing their home in Coconut Grove. The next year, Paul Jr. arrived, to be followed in 1933 by Mary Elizabeth.[37]

Meanwhile, the young attorney's life blossomed. On the personal front, he delighted in the semitropical pleasures of the Miami area. He evidenced a flair for horticultural experimentation, raised honey bees, and took every opportunity to swim, sail, and hunt the nearby Everglades. When an accidental gun discharge left his face pocked with buckshot, Barns refused to let the incident deny him the sport's enjoyment. He took to more serious pursuits as well. His mother's social conscience manifested itself through his work with a local family service organization, which assisted homeless and divorced persons in need of counseling and other social services.[38]

Barns's professional life quickly prospered along with his personal life. In Miami in the early 1920s, he built a lucrative legal practice while earning a reputation for strict integrity. As such, he appealed to Governor John W. Martin in 1926 when the state's chief executive sought a reliable man to fill a vacancy on the Dade County Civil Court of Record. So successful did Barns's service in the unsolicited position prove to be that the governor elevated him the following year to an eleventh circuit judgeship. Barns would serve in that capacity, drawing opposition only once, until his election to the Florida Supreme Court in 1946. Reportedly, during the period of his circuit judgeship he adjudicated more than 17,000 cases, signing 57,000 judgments and orders.[39]

The work of dispensing justice honed Barns's already substantial capacity for common sense and for analyzing the needs of the legal profession and the judiciary. He helped to author the 1940 constitutional amendment that expanded the Florida Supreme Court to a membership of seven. He also emerged as a leading force for simplification of procedural rules. A conservative man by temperament, he nonetheless urged change in the interest of "making justice simpler and quicker," the theme that he eventually would adopt for his successful 1946 supreme court race. With the passage of time, the tribunal's members often would call upon him to serve on the supreme bench in a temporary capacity, relying upon what Justice B. K. Roberts would describe as his "incisive mind" and his inclination not to "hesitate to disagree." In the process, Judge Barns developed a reputation, as one lawyer who practiced before him noted, "for being very strict and straight-laced." The lawyer added, "I was scared of him."[40]

As would be expected for such a lengthy period of judicial service, Barns's experiences came in a variety of forms, leading him at times into danger and often provoking others to fright. As to danger, the judge sat defenseless on the Miami Bayfront Park stage on February 15, 1933, when gunman Giuseppe Zangara attempted unsuccessfully to assassinate President-elect Franklin D. Roosevelt. Barns escaped without injury, but Chicago mayor Anton Cermak sustained fatal wounds and others suffered less serious injuries. On another occasion the judge threw a bit of fear into Al Capone's lawyer. The event occurred after the attorney offered Barns a bribe in a nuisance action. According to one account, Barns quickly fined the lawyer $1,000 for contempt of court. Believing the equity to lie on Capone's side in the matter at hand, though, Barns thereafter ruled in the gangster's favor.[41]

Repeated temporary service on the supreme court, a desire to further procedural reforms, and a sense that south Florida deserved representation on the statewide judiciary helped to compel Judge Barns in 1946 to seek elevation to the supreme court after Justice Armstead Brown announced retirement plans. The Miami judge expressed his philosophy in these words: "I never could bend judgment to public demand. I have decided cases on their merits and in accordance with the law in order that all litigants would receive justice." Forced into a runoff with his fellow Miami attorney W. Raleigh Petteway after finishing second in Democratic primary voting, Barns captured a narrow win with large margins in the state's most urban counties. The victory, which at that time ensured general election ratification, saw Barns triumph as the first Dade County resident elected to statewide office since the 1920s. The honor actually came to him early. Before his term otherwise would have begun, Governor Millard Caldwell appointed the justice-elect to replace Justice Brown, who had resigned. He took the oath of office on December 2, 1946.[42]

Once in Tallahassee, Justice Barns never truly came to feel at home. He craved Miami's splendors more than north Florida's rural calm. To some extent he found himself out of place on the court as well. "He was the more urbane member of the court," one attorney explained. Another onlooker added, "He was unhappy living in Tallahassee and could never get the Miami sand out of his shoes." Yet Barns worked hard and, by common agreement, wrote "good sound opinions." As would be expected, he stressed procedural reforms and met with some success. He attempted to move the court toward more formality in its operations, insisting on "severe" courtroom discipline. He also demanded that lower courts strictly enforce rules in civil and criminal proceedings. "He was very tough," acknowledged Richard W. Ervin. Added Stephen C. O'Connell with a large measure of respect, "He was a feisty little fellow."[43]

Justice Barns's court tenure ended September 1, 1949, following his resignation in June. His specific reasons have remained unclear. The action came within days after the court ordered an integrated bar for Florida (as opposed to a voluntary bar) over Barns's sharply worded objections. Additionally, some published reports later suggested that Barns believed himself in line for appointment to the federal bench. Clearly, though, the jurist desired to return to Miami. His tenure had run slightly less than three years.[44]

Well over two decades remained to Justice Barns upon his departure from Tallahassee. Quickly, he accepted a full-time teaching position at the University of Miami Law School. He also made himself available for and enjoyed substitute service on the bench, including the state supreme court. He continued to advocate procedural reforms, although he opposed creation of district courts of appeals in favor of an expanded supreme court. He remained active despite increasing discomfort from the respiratory problems that arose out of his wartime service. He finally succumbed to them at Miami on September 22, 1973. Victoria Coleman Barns outlived her husband by nine years. She passed away at Orlando while visiting her daughter on December 3, 1982.[45]

Numerous attempts have been made to sum up the life and career of Justice Paul D. Barns. When the University of Miami dedicated its 1959 lawyer yearbook to him, the school offered one tribute. "Some men we have known in Law School are remembered for their wit and charm, others for their sharp intelligence, for the ability to see through detail to underlying realities. Some men are admired for their unswerving integrity, their honesty, and essential fairness. . . . Judge Barns belongs to all of these groups." The jurist's son offered additional perspective. "As a young lawyer I can remember another lawyer telling me that he didn't need a receipt from me since I was Paul Barns's son. I didn't have to earn a reputation for integrity. I inherited it."[46]

Tolbert Francis Hobson, Supreme Court Justice, 1948–1962; Supreme Court Chief Justice, 1953

Justices T. Frank Hobson and Paul D. Barns shared several life parallels, while parting company when it came to length and nature of service on the Florida Supreme Court. Both rose from prominent and respected families, enjoyed reputations for honesty and legal craftsmanship, served extended apprenticeship periods on the circuit bench, represented peninsular Florida on the state judiciary, and suffered from chronic health problems. Where Justice Barns preferred an early return to south Florida, though, Justice Hobson opted to spend the remainder of his life at Tallahassee where, for fourteen years, he occupied a seat on the supreme bench.

While the Barns family boasted Arkansan roots, the Hobsons looked back to Alabama. Justice Hobson's father, William Andrew Hobson, was born there in Bibb County during the Civil War. In the years following the peace, W. A. Hobson graduated from Howard College and the Southern Baptist Theological Seminary. Soon afterward, he married Lou Alma Cheek in Alabama. The son, grandson, and great-grandson of Baptist ministers, the Reverend Hobson presided over several Alabama churches before accepting a call in 1900 to head Jacksonville's First Baptist Church. Pregnant at the time, Mrs. Hobson quickly returned to her parents' home at Hagler, Alabama, where she delivered a boy, Tolbert Francis Hobson, on August 1. He would be raised as an only child due to the accidental death of his sister at a tender age.[47]

The Hobson family flourished in Florida. The Reverend Hobson earned a well-deserved reputation for inspired leadership and hard work as he rebuilt his Jacksonville church following the city's terrible 1901 fire. In subsequent years he served as catalyst for the establishment of fourteen additional churches in the Jacksonville vicinity. He associated closely as well with the *Southern Baptist Witness* and the *Florida Baptist Witness*, a fact that assisted in spreading his renown throughout the region. W. A. Hobson soon constituted a power within the Southern Baptist Convention and the leadership circles of Stetson College. From 1911 to 1928, he presided over the Florida Baptist Convention.[48]

T. Frank Hobson enjoyed a happy childhood as his father's ministry took on such weighty proportions. He attended Jacksonville public schools until the family decided that the prep school division of North Carolina's Mars Hill Junior College offered better opportunities. Then, with U.S. participation in World War I looming, the Reverend Hobson prevailed upon his son to transfer to Marion Military Institute. In case his son was sent to war, Hobson desired that he have proper training that would lead to a commission. Frank joined the institute's Reserve Officer Training Corps and at one point received an appointment to the U.S. Naval Academy. As it turned out, he was not called to active duty nor did he relocate to Annapolis. Instead, Hobson entered Wake Forest College, where he earned a bachelor of arts degree in 1922.[49]

Back in Florida after graduation, the future justice determined upon several courses of action. One was marriage. Hobson had met Mabel Keller Miller in school at Jacksonville. Their daughter Frances Hobson Simmons recalled that the event occurred while the two teenagers were standing in separate lines during a graduation ceremony. As her father said of her mother, he "liked her looks." So he got a friend to change places in line so that he would be opposite the young woman and able to gain her attention. Their relationship took time to warm, with both dating "a lot" of other people. Nonetheless, following Mabel's graduation from Converse College, the two made plans for marriage. Timing of the event came courtesy of mother Lou Alma Hobson's insistence. According to family lore, she and the Reverend Hobson were taking a retirement trip to the Holy Land and to Europe as a gift of the Jacksonville First Baptist Church. She wanted to make sure that her son was well married—and not running around single—before she departed. The couple recited their vows at Jacksonville on June 14, 1923. A daughter, Frances Burt, arrived in 1926, to be followed by T. Frank Jr. in 1928 and Lucyann Keller in 1939.[50]

By the time of his marriage, Hobson already attended the Stetson University Law School, likely from his father's encouragement. He fared well there. On the other hand, a great passion during the time was playing basketball for the college along with classmate E. Harris Drew. Hobson long remembered with pride a game against the University of Florida where his shot to the basket at the buzzer carried the day for Stetson. Graduation came in 1924.[51]

Justice Hobson's legal career began at Jacksonville but soon veered southward. His parents had retired to St. Petersburg and missed their son and his wife. The Reverend Hobson arranged with local Democratic power broker James Booth, who would represent Pinellas County in the 1927 legislature, to welcome Frank into a partnership of Booth and Hobson. The relationship worked well for three years. Then, in 1926, W. A. Hobson prevailed upon Governor John W. Martin to name his son to the state board of bar examiners. Appointment to a county judgeship followed in August 1927. In February 1928, Martin elevated him to a seat on the sixth circuit bench. The action made Hobson the youngest circuit judge in the state.[52]

For two decades following his appointment to the circuit bench, Hobson served with distinction and without electoral opposition. Already by 1929 he would be praised by a local historian. "Successful to a degree that would be envied by many men of more mature years and experience, Judge Hobson has so carved his career as to enjoy the respect and esteem of his constituents, and all are proud of his record on the bench." During the period Hobson earned broad credit for having a lower percentage of his decisions overturned on appeal than any other circuit judge. His philosophy was described as "middle of the road," and his declared ambition was "to be a good judge." His growing reputation resulted in many requests that Hobson sit on the supreme bench on an interim basis, a fact that may have played a part in his and his father's plans for the future.[53]

Meanwhile, the judge participated fully in community life with his growing family. His children saw him as a wonderful father. He loved hunting and fishing. His associations with local civic, social, professional, and fraternal organizations were diverse, and his friendships numerous. It was said that many relied upon his advice and good judgment, although he was reluctant to venture an opinion unless asked. Not surprisingly, he delighted in a large measure of local popularity. Hobson fit well with the fast-paced lifestyle enjoyed by many affluent Pinellas County residents, although he also spent time as deacon and trustee of his father's Disston Avenue Baptist Church.[54]

Supreme court service for T. Frank Hobson commenced April 6, 1948, after Governor Millard Caldwell appointed him to replace retiring justice Rivers H. Buford. Based upon previous history, W. A. Hobson probably played a role in the designation. Also, the first appointment of a Pinellas County resident to statewide elective office served the governor's politics well, coming as it did in the primary election season when he was backing a south Florida candidate as his gubernatorial replacement. In any event, Hobson quickly found himself in political crisis. Faced with the immediate necessity of running for election, he learned to his chagrin that J. Tom Watson, who just had lost the gubernatorial primary, had opted to challenge the new justice. Initial voting found Hobson trailing the colorful but erratic state attorney general, although he managed to force a runoff election. At that point, the organized bar and organized labor lent critical support, while W. A. Hobson and Florida State Bar Association president Robert J. Pleus conducted "radiocasts." The effort proved sufficient, as Hobson bested his opponent by better than twenty thousand votes thanks to large majorities in the state's urban counties.[55]

As a member of the supreme tribunal, Justice Hobson found himself experiencing the same difficulty as had Justice Barns in fitting in comfortably with his colleagues, only more so. His south Florida urban lifestyle, one that included a more relaxed approach to public life than prevailed in the north Florida Panhandle, affronted several court members and their wives. Public consumption of alcohol constituted one factor in the equation, while unorthodox work habits (he enjoyed working at home or else coming late and staying late) added another. Additionally, strains in the Hobson marriage had resulted in a decision that he and Mrs. Hobson would lead separate lives. In small-town Tallahassee, the arrangement challenged prevailing mores. One onlooker, sensitive to local conditions, described him as "sort of a Lord Byron type." Another opined, "There was turmoil about him."[56]

What could not be denied was Justice Hobson's remarkable qualities as a jurist. His legal assistant, Wade L. Hopping, saw him as "probably the most brilliant person on the court." Hopping also noted, "He was tough. He was bright. He was a beautiful, laborious writer." Others concurred. "He had as good a judicial mind and was as good a writer as I experienced on the court," recalled Stephen C. O'Connell. "As a judge, he was superb." A practitioner before the court also remembered the justice's talent. "He became a great chancellor with a great view of equity," Hal P. Dekle remarked. "He was such a pleasant person, had a human side. He was one you could talk to." B. K. Roberts saw Hobson similarly. "He had a brilliant mind. His philosophy was definitely liberal. He could take a set of facts and reach down and get the equitable solution of the matter. He loved equity."[57]

Although Justice Hobson's strengths were great, they could not overcome the personal disdain felt by some colleagues. This manifested itself in few invitations to socialize with court members and with the reluctance of some members to support him for election as chief justice under the rotation system. In 1953, for example, he achieved election against opposition but resigned the position within a matter of months due to health concerns and prearrangement. In 1961 he declined to contest the matter. Stress joined with other factors to compound existing health problems. Within weeks of assuming the chief justiceship in 1953, he suffered attacks of vertigo and other ailments that compelled him to seek treatment out of state. A heart attack followed in 1955. By February 1962, chronic concerns had reached the point of crisis. From a Tallahassee hospital bed, Hobson penned a resignation letter to Governor Farris Bryant. "I believe that I have, after almost 35 years of service as a judicial officer, earned my retirement."[58]

Tallahassee remained home for T. Frank Hobson after he took his retirement. He took particular pride in the accomplishments of his son, a second district court of appeals judge. The retired justice also sat occasionally on various courts, including the Florida Supreme Court, where attitudes slowly had begun to change by the 1960s. He wrote the court's landmark decision limiting the authority of the legislature's witch-hunting Johns Committee. The judge's health concerns persisted. He entered Baltimore's Johns Hopkins Hospital in July 1966 for treatment. He died there on August 3 with his son at his side.[59]

Mabel M. Hobson had continued her residence at St. Petersburg, where she emerged as one of the community's strong supporters of charitable causes. She especially concerned herself with furnishing clothing and milk to poor families and volunteering at a clinic for infants. Mrs. Hobson remained at her adopted hometown into her ninety-third year. She passed away there on March 8, 1994.[60]

T. Frank Hobson's life and career proved controversial at times, but they also evidenced great merit. Upon his death the *St. Petersburg Times* spoke of "a prodigious legal career begun brilliantly and sustained through 34 years on the bench." It added, "Pinellas County and St. Petersburg were particularly proud of Justice Hobson. He was the first Pinellas citizen to hold high state elective office. But the yardstick by which he was measured was not merely local pride. The principles of justice, the integrity of purpose, and the courage to carry these things forward were what made Tolbert Francis Hobson a great judge. And so it was not merely his home town and county which benefited from his achievements—it was all Florida."[61]

Bonnie Kaslo Roberts, Supreme Court Justice, 1949–1976; Supreme Court Chief Justice, 1953–1955, 1961–1963, 1971–1973

Few individuals have left so profound a mark on the Supreme Court of Florida as did B. K. Roberts. He served through a time of revolutionary change, bringing to the court impressive leadership skills and legal abilities. Often provocative, seldom at a loss for opinion, Roberts more than any other justice dominated the court from the mid-1950s through his resignation in 1976. Three times chief justice, he was heralded for his accomplishments. Still, Roberts struggled early with human concerns and found himself, as was everyone else, subject to human frailties.

B. K. Roberts's story began in the isolated north Florida village of Sopchoppy, located thirty-five miles southwest of Tallahassee near the Gulf of Mexico, where he was born on February 5, 1907. The family had helped to pioneer Wakulla County, arriving from South Carolina in the early 1840s. Given generally poor conditions in the region following the Civil War, the Robertses enjoyed modest prosperity. B. K.'s father, Thomas, and mother, Florida Morrison Roberts, also a descendant of area pioneers, possessed little formal education. Yet they owned a farm of several hundred acres and, at various times, kept a store and benefited from several government and railroad positions that Thomas was able to obtain. Other relations buttressed the family's position in the county, including uncle Angus Morrison, who presided over local affairs first as sheriff and later as state representative.[62]

Education for the lad came at first in a two-room Sopchoppy school. From the third through the eleventh grades he received instruction primarily from teacher Mattie Revell. "You know," Roberts recounted, "when they had us all in the room and called out the class, you know it's amazing we learned anything, but we did." He added, "I was usually the number one in the class." Roberts's intelligence could not be missed. His mother loved to tell whoever might listen "that B. K. was so smart and asked so many questions that the neighbors would close their doors when they saw him coming." At age thirteen he passed the basic level teachers' examination despite blindness in one eye caused by an air rifle accident. By 1921, at age 14, he had achieved a first class certificate. This accomplishment came to the state school superintendent's attention, as a result of which Roberts was invited to take special summer classes at Florida State College for Women. Word of the young man's ability then reached the ears of Thomas D. Bailey, a future state school superintendent but then the principal of a Methodist school at DeFuniak

Springs known as the Thomas Industrial Institute. Bailey recruited Roberts, affording him the opportunity to make more connections that would serve him mightily in the future. He knew well, for instance, future governor Bob Graham's mother, Hilda Simmons. More significantly, he befriended a young man from Blountstown, Fuller Warren.[63]

The future justice faced greater challenges when it came to higher education. His graduation from the Thomas Industrial Institute behind him, Roberts took a Wakulla County construction job. Clearly, the work did not suit the young man. He thereupon decided that teaching offered better prospects. The pay was better, and as he told a friend, "they work in the shade." A four hundred dollar state teaching scholarship underwrote partial costs of two years at the University of Florida. A temporary downturn in the family's fortunes limited his parents' ability to contribute at first, with the result that Roberts eventually was compelled to camp in a tent until the kindness of a Catholic priest permitted him to stay at the university's Crain Hall. While work remained a necessity for the young scholar, his father "picked up a little economically" and conditions soon eased.[64]

Although better times arrived, Roberts's experience with poverty had imprinted an indelible mark upon him. This impression occurred because a "committee" of three University of Florida students approached him at the time he was living in the tent. "[They] advised me to drop out of school and move back to Sopchoppy and become a farmer," he recollected. "They said that I wasn't college material and that my clothes were so shabby 'til I was the source of embarrassment to the other people from West Florida." The event haunted Roberts as the "lowest point" in his life. If anything, his anger and humiliation thereafter drove him to success. This fact evidenced itself when he, Fuller Warren, and others seized control of the student government association. Roberts ultimately would pledge Delta Chi social fraternity. He also accepted membership in Florida Blue Key and Alpha Delta honorary scholastic fraternity.[65]

Along the way Roberts's professional interest evolved from teaching to the law. He credited his father for pressing the idea, but memories of Wakulla County's sometimes arbitrary justice haunted him. Plus, the camaraderie of University of Florida law students such as H. L. "Tom" Sebring and roommate Richard W. Ervin drew him toward the school. He explained the results. "Law was a five-year course then—two years pre-law and three years law. I would have finished in two-and-a-half years, but I wasn't old enough. One had to be twenty-one to graduate because you didn't take the bar exam then, you automatically became a lawyer when you graduated from the University of Florida." That day finally arrived in 1928.[66]

First, though, two events occurred that dramatically altered the course of Roberts's life and career. For one, his social fraternity decided to improve their fraternity house. Needing a loan to finance the project, Roberts approached Jacksonville businessman Edward Ball. He did so at the suggestion of his Wakulla County sheriff uncle, who believed that Roberts could benefit professionally from the acquaintance. Ball represented the growing Florida interests of his brother-in-law, Alfred I. duPont, and recently had begun to acquire huge tracts of land in the north Florida Panhandle. Among the places he was assessing for future purchases was Wakulla County. As it happened, Ball referred Roberts elsewhere for his loan, but he did not dismiss the young man. "Ball liked the young attorney-to-be," reported one biographer. "It was the beginning of a lasting relationship between the two."[67]

The second fortuitous event saw blessings flow out of tragedy. During his senior year at the University of Florida, Roberts's kneecap was shattered when a drunk driver rammed an automobile in which the law student was riding. The injury proved serious, and an insurance company anxiously desired to settle. Three months later, just as he turned twenty-one and prepared to graduate, the carrier delivered a check for $4,000. It represented a princely sum in a state that already floundered in economic depression. With it Roberts could launch a law practice.[68]

Just where that law practice might be located posed an interesting question for the young lawyer in 1928. Three years earlier, a childhood friend from Sopchoppy, Carra Williams, had married a north Florida lawyer recently settled at Fort Pierce named Alto Adams. The two men had become friends, and Adams now offered Roberts employment in his south Florida law office. Instead, the recent graduate harkened to the advice of attorney general and future justice Fred H. Davis, a man with close Wakulla County ties. "Roberts's earliest impressions of the responsibilities of a lawyer to the public, the bench, and his clients," the local newspaper would remark, "was instilled by [Davis]. That relationship continued until Davis's death; and, as an indication of their relationship, Roberts was attorney for his estate." Perhaps reinforcing Davis's effort to influence the young man to select Tallahassee for a home, another of Roberts's uncles, E. C. Roberts, then stood out as the capital city's premier industrialist and a leader in the town's politically powerful First Baptist Church. Such connections could prove fortuitous indeed.[69]

In any event, Roberts listened well to the advice he received. At a time when Tallahassee contained only slightly more than one dozen lawyers, he built a general practice that included clients ranging from the poorest Wakulla County criminal defendants to Ed Ball and the duPonts' expanding St. Joe Paper Company. He earned headlines and legal business by successfully defending his uncle Angus from charges that the sheriff failed to enforce Prohibition laws properly in

Wakulla County and by eventually securing a not-guilty verdict in client George Deeb's multiple-trial murder case. Thanks to Attorney General Davis, he also succeeded with appellate work. "Judge Davis took me over to the old Supreme Court building on South Adams and personally introduced me to all the justices," Roberts later recalled. As the 1930s progressed, he particularly began to represent clients before the tribunal on retainer from downstate firms that could not justify the expense of travel at a time of economic depression. "I would often go to the Supreme Court and listen to the arguments made by the masters from whom I learned much about the work there," he explained. "Those arguments day after day inspired me to want some time to be a member of that court." The increasingly prosperous attorney took on associates, but he chose not to offer any a partnership.[70]

For Roberts, court service lay well in the future because he felt a greater drive to build a personal fortune that would provide him appropriate standing and security. He invested widely in land and businesses in Tallahassee and vicinity. He also combined a longtime love of politics with the growth of his investments. Soon he could claim close connections with Governor David Sholtz (1933–37), Justice Fred Davis (1931–37), Davis's successor Roy Chapman (appointed 1937), and Chapman's former law partner, Governor Frederick P. Cone (1937–41). Roberts later recounted that, when in November 1940 voters approved expansion of the supreme court to seven members, Cone offered him the seat. At that time, the increasingly affluent and influential lawyer declined. Instead, he recommended his friend Alto Adams.[71]

Although the lawyer did not feel the time was right in 1940 to accept a supreme court seat, he already had agreed to a different sort of long-term commitment. He had married. Mary Newman, formerly of Dowling Park near Live Oak, had graduated from Florida State College for Women. Direct and outspoken, she accepted few limits on her rights to an opinion and glowed with enthusiasm for life. She worked briefly in the secretary of state's office before agreeing to serve Roberts as his secretary. Soon smitten, Roberts could not resist this fascinating woman. The couple wed on August 20, 1937. They would adopt two children, Mary Jane and Thomas Frederick, both orphaned during World War II.[72]

The Second World War furthered Roberts's goals while permitting him to serve the country. His blind eye kept him from the draft, but he pulled strings that resulted in an officer's commission in the U.S. Coast Guard. Stationed at Jacksonville, he presided as shipping commissioner for the Port of Jacksonville from May 1, 1943, to December 5, 1945. He and Mary lived in Fuller Warren's home while its owner served abroad. During the period Roberts met often with his mentor and client Ed Ball. The two men grew closer. Roberts also established valuable connections with the labor unions that worked Jacksonville's docks. His deft handling of labor concerns cemented union support in his future elections while affording Roberts a sensitivity to union problems that would evidence itself in his Florida Supreme Court opinions.[73]

War's end saw the soon-to-be justice back in Tallahassee, buttressing his financial and business positions while reestablishing his influence within the state government. In 1948 he assisted Fuller Warren's successful gubernatorial campaign and looked with delight upon the election of his college roommate, Richard W. Ervin, as the state's attorney general. Warren felt so close to the Robertses that he lived in their home during his administration's initial months. Then when Justice Paul Barns resigned from the state supreme court in June 1949, Warren insisted that Roberts accept the appointment. Reportedly, the governor signed the document before informing the new justice of his action. "I never did get around to giving Fuller an answer," Roberts recorded. "He just assumed that once the announcement was made I wouldn't make a liar our of him." He took the oath of office on August 10, 1949. The newly minted jurist would remain a member of the tribunal until retirement in December 1976.[74]

The story of Justice Roberts's service on the Florida Supreme Court and his continuing impact upon the state's government and politics could fill volumes. His friend Chesterfield Smith spoke to the subject: "I know of no other person who over the years has worked so effectively in securing and implementing needed improvements in both the civil and criminal courts in our justice system." Symbols of those contributions included establishment of district courts of appeal, creation of the public defender system and the judicial qualifications commission, the work of the Florida Judicial Council from 1962 to 1980, and state constitutional revision in 1968 and 1972. Roberts looked with particular pride on the fact that so many of his legal opinions were held out as illustrations of excellent writing. The *American Law Reports* published thirty-six of his opinions, a record for his time. Three times chief justice, he directed the court through difficult and even tumultuous years. Justice Hal P. Dekle during one such period expressed the sentiments of many about Justice Roberts's leadership. "I take this opportunity to thank and commend Justice B. K. Roberts, the dean of our court," he commented, "for the calm stability and administrative assistance he has provided to the court in time of crisis and his objectivity in keeping the process of the court going in an orderly manner. No person could have done more than he has done."[75]

Beyond his impact on the court, Roberts touched Florida in numerous other manners during his years in judicial office. By way of example, he provided indispensable assistance in the creation and establishment of the Florida State University College of Law. Its principal building carries his name. The university subsequently awarded him the honorary degree of doctor of humane letters. Other services prompted a myriad of similar awards and recognitions. He served as intimate counselor to Governors Fuller Warren, Hayden Burns, and Reubin Askew. "Every governor should have been fortunate enough, within the context of separation of powers," Askew observed, "to have had a Chief Justice like B. K. when he assumed that responsibility." Perhaps closest to Roberts's heart, though, was the Edward Ball Wildlife Foundation, a nonprofit organization he designed to manage and preserve Wakulla Springs, in his beloved Wakulla County, together with the surrounding waters and forest lands. For these and other reasons, the State of Florida honored Justice Roberts in 1990 with its distinguished service medal as the year's "Great Floridian."[76]

Having noted such accomplishments and recognitions, it should be mentioned that Justice Roberts's zeal for success at every endeavor, when coupled with seemingly inexhaustible energy, provoked controversy and sometimes raised questions as to the proper limits of propriety for action by a judicial officer. His "Great Floridian" award brought forth spirited opposition from some African Americans, who believed his insensitivity to racial concerns argued against his receipt of that honor. His business dealings at times prompted troubling questions, especially his continued relationship with and counsel to Ed Ball. As one colleague noted, "He particularly respected the value of the business community." Some court members chafed at occasional attempts to sway their votes on key matters, and others believed that Roberts crossed lines in a manner that tended to politicize the court, including his counsel to various governors. Rumors regarding his actions, many likely unfounded, hit at the court's integrity. "He wanted to get things done," concluded a longtime friend. "He was absolutely political." A newspaperman added, "There was a sense at times that B. K. was where all the shenanigans were going on."[77]

One incident, by way of illustration, helps to make the point. In 1969, lawyers representing the Florida Bar in support of amendments to the Florida constitution clashed during an oral argument before the supreme court with legal counsel for a committee in opposition to those amendments. Before the hearing Ed Ball, accused by the press of being the "behind the scene leader" of the committee, vigorously had denied any such connection. Immediately, at the hearing's conclusion, the distinguished Jacksonville attorney Fred Kent was overheard by Florida Bar president Marshall Criser and its president-elect, Mark Hulsey, who represented the bar at the proceedings, directing a colleague to "call Mr. Ball and tell him the hearing went well and that B. K. asked some friendly questions."[78]

These types of concerns failed to dim the luster of Justice Roberts's record. He never hesitated to confront his critics, nor did he allow criticisms to dissuade him from any course of action he deemed the correct one. He certainly did not shy away from business or the practice of law. Following his retirement from the court in December 1976, he waited a mere three weeks before founding the Tallahassee firm of Roberts, Miller, Baggett & LaFace. When that firm merged with another in the early 1990s, he persisted on his own course. By the late 1990s, though, age began to slow him, and his health declined. He passed away at Tallahassee on August 4, 1999, at the age of ninety-two. Mary Roberts followed her husband in death at Tallahassee on November 17, 2005.[79]

The tributes poured into Tallahassee at the news of Justice Roberts's death. "It certainly can be said of B. K. Roberts that he left an indelible mark on the legal affairs of this state," one newspaper opined. "His passing mirrors the end of an era that he considered more personal and dignified." Former governor Askew proclaimed, "In the legal profession, he was a giant. He did so much for the rights of people. It would be hard for me to think of anything but the good side of Judge Roberts." It might be, though, that the tribute that would have meant most to Roberts, other than his wife's love, had been given to him one-half century earlier by his hometown newspaper upon his appointment to the supreme court. "B. K. Roberts measures up to that high standard of professional competence and personal integrity that Floridians long have demanded of the justices of their Supreme Court," the *Crawfordville Wakulla County News* declared. "If that fact were not already apparent from his public record, then let the people of Wakulla County— those who should know him best—testify in behalf of this neighbor, friend, kinsman. We who have known him the best and the longest vouch for his integrity and ability." The item concluded, "We of his home county have gloried in the recognition which has come to the man we familiarly know as 'B. K.'"[80]

John Elie Mathews, Supreme Court Justice, 1951–1955; Supreme Court Chief Justice, 1955

In some respects John Elie Mathews appeared unlikely to lend to the Supreme Court of Florida the probity and objectivity expected of a jurist, yet he served the tribunal in excellent, if sometimes unexpected, ways. A political being whose nature compelled him to urge his causes with passion, he emerged as a moderating force during one of the court's and the state's most challenging times. Controversial, he was. But Mathews also was one who strove with all his being to make a difference and who paid the price of his life for the effort.

Unlike Justices Barns, Hobson, and Roberts, John E. Mathews could not claim Florida nativity or the benefit of a Florida legal education. He was born at Gray's Landing, Tatnall County, Georgia, on July 19, 1892. His parents, John W. and

Ava Ophelia McNatt Mathews, were considered to be "prominent, influential, and well-to-do" within their community's context, his father having prospered in merchandising, steamboating, cotton raising, and other endeavors. Young John, the eldest of five children, was raised in the Methodist Episcopal Church, South. He attended local public schools and graduated in regular order from Vidalia High School in Toombs County. He then enrolled at Emory University, located at that time in Oxford, Georgia. There the young man pursued literary and law studies before graduating with a bachelor of science degree in 1913. At Emory, he embraced debating and politics, skills that facilitated his election as student body president.[81]

At the time of his graduation, Mathews already perceived his future to lie in the practice of law. First, however, he accepted employment in 1913 as principal of the high school at Eastman, Georgia. This employment permitted the eager pupil to read the law with Judge Myrick Clements. With the judge's assistance, Mathews achieved admission to the Georgia bar in 1914. He followed on November 24 by wedding his Vidalia sweetheart, Alice Schumpert. Their subsequent vacation trip to Jacksonville, Florida, then proved a momentous excursion. As John Jr. recalled, "[Dad] became impressed by the city while spending his honeymoon here." The couple returned to Eastman where Mathews completed his principal's contract in 1915, whereupon they packed for Florida. At Jacksonville, they would share three children who survived infancy. John Jr. arrived in 1920, William Hugh in 1921, and Helen in 1925.[82]

Jacksonville brought professional good fortune to the novice lawyer. He first arranged employment with William R. Bostwick, one of the city's leading attorneys. In 1919 Mathews changed positions, associating himself with former U.S. Senator Nathan P. Bryan for a time. When Bryan accepted appointment to the U.S. Fifth Circuit Court of Appeals, his young protégé established his own office. Word circulated that Mathews was "an indefatigable student, as well as a voracious reader," conveying a seriousness of purpose and a drive for success. Corporate and real estate law business brought him into contact with Jacksonville's most prominent businessmen and politicians. He devoted considerable time to masonic and fraternal orders, actions that extended the transplant's network of connections. By 1921 he felt sufficiently prepared to launch himself into politics. This initial foray fared none too well. Future governor John W. Martin easily bested Mathews in his reelection bid as Jacksonville's mayor. Surprisingly, the two men emerged from the contest as friends.[83]

Although Martin had drubbed him politically, Mathews's name had extended itself broadly throughout the city, and he had gained many friends. They joined in 1922 to urge his designation as attorney for Duval County, a post he held for eight years. Mathews now delved deeply into the law of road construction, revenue bonding, and related public improvement matters. He began to urge the cause of better roads. Particularly, he pressed for construction of a bridge to connect downtown Jacksonville with its Arlington suburb. In 1928 he campaigned on the bridge issue for election to the Florida House of Representatives. This time he won. When the span he advocated finally opened in January 1953, it carried the name John E. Mathews Bridge in tribute to his efforts, which had required over a quarter of a century.[84]

For a short while Mathews's political career shone brilliantly, then he endured years of disappointment and frustration. In the legislative sessions of 1929 and 1931, he emerged as a champion of urban counties and their right to a proper share of governmental assistance, specifically a fair apportionment of gasoline tax revenues. With only a few allies, he battled small county representatives such as Santa Rosa's Millard F. Caldwell. Reporter Allen Morris noted, "Those who faced the bare-knuckle orator knew they had been in a fight even when they won." In 1930 Mathews defeated Fuller Warren to achieve reelection to the house. As had been the case with John W. Martin a decade earlier, he earned a friend along the way. Two years later the legislator tried unsuccessfully for Duval County state's attorney. In 1938 he ran for state senator against the incumbent J. Turner Butler, the senate president designee. Again Mathews lost. Meanwhile, the future justice hunted and fished, developed a farm and orange grove, and involved his legal practice more heavily in appellate work. And he waited for the right opportunity to come along.[85]

The onetime lawmaker's political fortunes reversed in 1942 when he finally won a state senate seat. Under Governor Spessard Holland he bided his time, perhaps—according to one observer—"because issues did not present themselves." The advent of Governor Millard Caldwell's administration in 1945 changed this state of affairs. Mathews labored as a floor leader for his former colleague and political rival. He fought along with the governor that year for a legislative apportionment reflecting the dramatic growth of urban counties. He found an even more intense spotlight in which to bathe in 1947. As the civil rights era began to dawn, he took a leadership role in the fight for a legally mandated whites-only Democratic primary and in opposition to the U.S. Supreme Court's landmark 1944 decision in the case of *Sweatt* v. *Painter*. His labors fell far short of success. Historian William Warren Rogers concluded that the legislature "repudiated" Mathews's initiative, sending a message that "We are not going to follow the demagogic path of Georgia, Alabama, and South Carolina." Nonplussed, Mathews vowed to take his crusade "into the highways and byways and crossroads" by running for governor in 1948.[86]

The "fiery, red-headed legislator" had taken his place, in Richard W. Ervin's words, as one of Florida's "political giants," but the senator's plans did not eventuate as he hoped that they would. B. K. Roberts recalled that, in a Florida still moderately warm to New Deal liberalism, Mathews's philosophy did not yet resonate with the intensity that it would beginning about 1950. "Mathews was a strong conservative and a great believer in the free enterprise system," Roberts commented. "He was not friendly toward give-away social programs. He was of the unreconstructed type." Unable to stir enough popular enthusiasm for his projected gubernatorial campaign, the senator instead supported his friend Fuller Warren. Once in office, Warren, in turn, adopted Mathews as his own legislative floor leader in the senate.[87]

The senator's support for Governor Warren paid off in the short term, but political disaster lay in wait. First, Mathews aided the chief executive in securing approval of much of his legislative program. For his help, the Warren administration backed development of a Duval County expressway system, including construction of what would become the John E. Mathews and the Fuller Warren bridges. Mathews also took up the reins of legislative leadership on his own account after six African American youths applied for admission to the University of Florida. He demanded protection of racial segregation at the university, urging both resistance to integration and added financial support for Florida A&M University. On another key issue, the senator sided with Jacksonville businessman Ed Ball and against the governor. In that instance, he advocated a sales tax in lieu of an income tax to make up the state's critical revenue shortage. Warren ultimately agreed to a sales tax, but Duval County voters reacted in fury. They ousted Mathews from office in 1950 in favor of antisales tax candidate Wayne Ripley. Ironically, John E. Mathews Jr. would later oust Ripley from the same senate seat.[88]

Following his 1950 defeat, Mathews returned to Jacksonville to practice law with his son, but his departure from public life proved short-lived. When in October 1951 supreme court justice Alto Adams resigned to campaign for governor, Fuller Warren quickly tapped his old friend for the seat. The resulting furor apparently shocked both Warren and Mathews, compelling their friends and allies to gather in public support. The experience seems to have touched Mathews deeply. His statement upon taking the oath of office stressed moderation and judicial discretion. "The executive and legislative departments may at times cater to the passions of the mob," he declared. "They may yield to pressure groups or to the whims of some passing moment. At times the legislative and executive departments are prone, by laws, rules and regulations to invade or deny to the citizens, fundamental rights guaranteed to them by the constitution. The judicial department of the government must exist at all times and stand guard for the protection of the people against usurpation and tyranny on the one hand and for the protection and preservation of our government on the other."[89]

The stress attendant upon his appointment found little release as Justice Mathews assumed the duties of office. With state growth the court's workload increased by the month. He plunged into the tasks at hand to the point that his colleagues came to see him as "one of the Supreme Court's hardest workers." In less than four years he prepared over four hundred opinions that received court approval. One area of his expertise concerned local government spending and bonding authority. In line with his orthodox reading of Florida's constitution, he enunciated strict limitations on public support for innovative programs. Mathews also maintained a schedule of public appearances reflective of his former political life. Within months after his appointment, he began warning of what he considered the "usurpation of the rights of the states and the people" by federal courts. Those demanding societal change he characterized as "following the Communist line."[90]

In January 1955 the court's rotation system elevated Justice Mathews to the position of chief justice, and at that point he accepted a public role involving less emphasis on controversial political questions and more emphasis on positive court leadership. "I deeply and humbly appreciate the opportunity you have given me to serve as Chief Justice of the Supreme Court of Florida," he informed the tribunal. "While I fully realize that my selection is due more to custom and tradition than to any outstanding ability or achievement, I accept the position with deep gratitude and with an abiding sense of the responsibility that the position entails." He called for procedural reforms to expedite appeals. With his close friend Justice H. L. "Tom" Sebring, he crafted new court rules that found implementation in March. The chief justice also endorsed the creation of district courts of appeals. He prepared to work closely with Justice Elwyn Thomas and the Florida Judicial Council to gain legislative approval of an appropriate constitutional amendment.[91]

The effort required by his new duties strained the chief justice severely. Upon his acceptance of the position, former justice Paul D. Barns had warned of the onerous responsibilities. "If he attempts to serve as a jurist too," Barns observed, "he will handicap himself as an administrator." Justice B. K. Roberts likewise had sought to protect his friend. "I urged Mathews to reject the chief justiceship because of his health or at least to serve maybe a month and then give it up," he recalled. "In his own way he said to me, 'I would rather die doing what I was supposed to do than to duck my obligation and live.'" The demands of office quickly told on Mathews's health, which had been poor for one year or more. Soon he was discovered in his office bleeding "profusely." Briefly hospitalized, he returned to his responsibilities in short order.[92]

The end lay not far distant. On Saturday, April 29, the chief justice remained at his court desk until 6:00 p.m. He returned home for dinner and began to experience acute pain. Rushed to the Tallahassee hospital, he spent a restive night. The following morning he suffered a stroke before lapsing into a coma. Death came slightly after 8 p.m. following an intestinal hemorrhage. John E. Mathews was only sixty-two years of age. "Selection to the highest position in the highest court of the state was of course the crown of Justice Mathews' career," Jacksonville's leading newspaper informed readers. "To a man versed as he was in the traditions of the law, possessed of a deep respect for law as the cornerstone of our American liberty, no distinction could have meant more than this one."[93]

Edward Harris Drew, Supreme Court Justice, 1952–1971; Supreme Court Chief Justice, 1955–1956, 1963–1965

Governor Fuller Warren's first two Supreme Court of Florida designations had generated controversy, a fact that encouraged him in 1952 to seek an individual for appointment who enjoyed the highest regard of the legal profession, eschewed politics, and carried with him a reputation for unquestioned probity. In E. Harris Drew he found his man. With Drew's arrival on the court, the rising generation of Florida's lawyers sensed the coming of a new era of judicial professionalism. In Justice Drew's case, they were not disappointed.

Although born at Fargo, Georgia, Justice Drew's background lay deep in Florida soil. His grandfather, James E. Drew, began life in the family's Madison County log cabin in 1838, seven years prior to statehood. James's wife, Charlotte Watts Drew, born in 1844, was a native as well. Before their marriage, though, James had stood among the first to volunteer for Confederate service from Florida. Following hospitalization for illness, he learned of Robert E. Lee's surrender at a rest stop in North Carolina before he could return to army duties. Back in Madison County, the couple married and moved into a new "double pen" log cabin. There, William Thomas Drew first took breath. With time's passage he wed a local girl, Florence Idella Edwards.[94]

As proud a family as were the Drews, they were not well-to-do. As a result, Bill ventured wherever employment beckoned, a fact that explains the family's presence in Georgia on October 28, 1903, when Edward Harris was born. Soon they had relocated near relatives at Live Oak. The family grew to include one brother for Harris and two sisters, and at a young age, Harris was called upon to help out financially. While living in St. Augustine, for instance, he managed a newspaper route while keeping up schooling and family chores. In 1914 the Drews moved for a final time, to south Florida and the growing town of West Palm Beach.[95]

Bill Drew died at a relatively young age, leaving his eldest son to shoulder serious responsibilities. The young man made money as best he could, but already he burned with a desire for a better life. Although the specific inspiration is not known, from an early day Harris yearned for a legal education and, his family believes, saw the epitome of lawyerly success to be a seat on the Florida Supreme Court. He successfully completed a basic public education at West Palm Beach. Then he managed to enroll at Stetson University, benefiting, some evidence suggests, from support from West Palm Beach's chapter of Rotary International. Compelled to work at Stetson, Drew nonetheless found time for studies and for sports. He excelled at basketball, playing forward with his future supreme court colleague T. Frank Hobson. He pledged Delta Sigma Phi social fraternity and Phi Alpha Delta legal fraternity. Precocious from the beginning, the young scholar completed work for his bachelor of law degree in 1923.[96]

Drew's return to West Palm Beach brought challenges and major changes. At age twenty he was too young to take the bar examination. Fortunately, Circuit Judge C. E. Chillingworth sympathized with the young man and ordered removal of the disabilities of his nonage. Quickly, Drew successfully sought bar admission. Before long, he also had decided to marry. Edith Mae Turner hailed from Cleaton, Kentucky. She had moved to West Palm Beach after her parents passed away and an older sister had made a place for her. A mutual friend suggested that the couple meet. Nature took its course, and they were wed at West Palm Beach on June 10, 1927. Daughter Melanie May arrived on May 3, 1938.[97]

Decades of financial struggle now evolved into prosperity for the future justice. As Melanie Drew Mitchell recalled, "He got to Palm Beach when the town was just beginning to grow. He was in the right place at the right time." The good fortune began when, just out of law school, he obtained the job of town attorney for West Palm Beach. He would hold the position for twenty-nine years. Through the 1920s and 1930s he utilized contacts made through this connection to build a lucrative private practice. Before long, Palm Beach and Boca Raton developer Addison Mizner numbered among his clients and friends, as did members of the powerful Mellon family and Miami investor J. Meyer Schine. Within ten years of his practice's beginning, Drew would preside over the Palm Beach County Bar Association. In years to come he would add the titles of attorney to the Jupiter Inlet District and to the Everglades Drainage District to his ever lengthening resume.[98]

As his fortunes brightened, Drew made certain to devote a portion of his time to community service. He spent countless hours in raising funds for his alma mater, and in 1941–42 he was elected president of the Stetson alumni association. He participated in Kiwanis Club activities and the various programs of the Holy Trinity Episcopal Church. He aided the Florida League of Municipalities for years. Perhaps his greatest service contribution came with his work on behalf of the bar of Florida. In 1943–44 he acted as president of the Florida State Bar Association. He helped to draft the constitution and by-laws for an integrated Florida Bar and sat as first chairman of its committee on judicial administration. In the process, he penned numerous articles on various aspects of local government law for respected legal periodicals.[99]

This recitation of Drew's accomplishments might suggest that he neglected personal and family life. Not so. Melanie found him "about as good a father as you could ask for." Friends delighted in his company. "He was a lively, energetic type," Richard W. Ervin recalled. "He had a good sense of humor," added LeRoy Collins. "He was just fun to be around." Drew's short physical stature later prompted Justice Stephen C. O'Connell teasingly to label him "Grumpy," but Drew was quick to respond, "If we both sat down, I'd be taller than you!" He loved cabinet making and mechanical tinkering. His true passion, though, lay in outdoor life. Hunting and touring by automobile were fine by him, yet boating, swimming, and fishing offered the true delight. He built or purchased a series of boats. The first he called *Melanie*. Later, *Amicus Curiae* took pride of place on many a transom. Drew's love of boating eventually would lead Justice B. K. Roberts jokingly to complain: "I wonder what's happened to Drew. Has he quit or has he been lost at sea?"[100]

Little wonder, given Drew's community position, that Fuller Warren would seek his support during the 1948 gubernatorial election, a fact that soon would lead the West Palm Beach lawyer toward his lifelong dream. It would take a while, though. Warren first rewarded his ally with appointment in 1949 as secretary to the board of pilot commissioners for the Port of Palm Beach. Two years later, the governor offered a Game and Fresh Water Fish Commission seat. Meanwhile, a constitutional amendment circulated that would have expanded the Florida Supreme Court by three members. The Florida Bar polled its members as to which lawyers deserved appointment. The name selected first in his judicial circuit and congressional district was that of E. Harris Drew. The governor found it expeditious to promise to appoint based upon the results. As it happened, the amendment failed in November 1952, but on August 12 Warren already had designated Drew to fill a vacancy caused by Justice Roy Chapman's death. The governor thus was able to keep his promise to the bar, place a friend on the court, and serve his political prospects by affording southeast Florida its first representation on the court since Justice Paul D. Barns's resignation in 1949. "No lawyer in the state," commented Florida Bar president William McRae, "would have been more cordially received by the legal profession."[101]

The appointment involved more of a commitment from the new justice than simply agreeing to serve on the court. Pursuant to a supreme court advisory opinion, a special Democratic primary election for his seat was called for October 14. Dade County Circuit Judge Vincent C. Giblin prepared to wage a spirited campaign and did so. Thanks to the intensity of Giblin's campaigning, one historian labeled the race "a very dramatic one." The challenger charged not against Drew but against the proposed court expansion. Governor Warren, the organized bar, and the Florida League of Municipalities backed the incumbent, though, with Drew emerging with a victory margin of only a handful of votes. Fortunately for the victor, a special legislative contest in Suwannee County had brought many of Drew's old Live Oak friends and relations to the polls. As B. K. Roberts noted, "The Drew name was very popular over there." The Suwannee turnout made the difference.[102]

Comfortably seated on the court following the near upset of his short tenure, Justice Drew began to earn a reputation as one of the tribunal's steady workmen. Eventually specializing in municipal law, public financing, and workmen's compensation matters, he wrote opinions in a manner that one court advocate described as "sharp and concise." Justice Richard W. Ervin recollected that Harris was "a fast worker—wrote his opinions speedily" and "had a great analytical mind." He added, "He tried to follow the norm and respected precedent most of the time although now and then he would innovate if he thought the law tended away from old precedent." In one such diversion from precedent, the jurist became one of the nation's earliest critics of cigarette smoking and urged application of liability upon manufacturers for their sale.[103]

The once-poor lad whose dream had come true delighted in court service. "I think he thought they had the best court in the land," observed his daughter. In turn, court members came to regard their fellow justice highly. "He was a great personal friend of mine, a fine colleague, impeccably honest," declared B. K. Roberts. "We relied on him a great deal." During his first term on the court, its members demonstrated their respect by naming Drew chief justice upon John E. Mathews's death. During that period and afterward, the justice grew close to many individuals of wealth or power; he cemented deep friendships on the court with Glenn Terrell, Campbell Thornal, and his fellow West Palm Beach resident, Stephen C. O'Connell. Still, he did not forget his origins or the responsibilities that he believed accompanied public service. "I think it takes a certain degree of humbleness, a certain degree of wondering how the hell you got there and whether you have the ability to do the job," he once commented. Pointing out the sacrifices he saw as a necessary condition of being a public servant, Drew continued: "He gives up the right to be the town drunk or appear in public drinking. I think one of the rights I gave up was, if some guy did something to me, to sock him in the snoot." He refused to lock his office door. "I had no secrets," he asserted, "and my files were open to anyone who wanted to look at them."[104]

Whatever pleasure Justice Drew took from court service, drawbacks and unfortunate consequences presented themselves as well. While serving his second term as chief justice beginning in 1963, he was called upon to preside over the impeachment trial of Circuit Judge Richard Kelly. Court duties already strained its members, and the added constitutional requirement for participation in an impeachment trial compounded the problem. Then this difficult situation trended even more extremely when defense attorneys subpoenaed several justices, including Drew. The combined stresses led to a heart attack shortly after conclusion of the proceedings, and the justice's health thereafter remained of considerable concern. Consequently, in January 1969 he announced that he would not be a candidate for reelection. He retired from the court as of January 5, 1971.[105]

Despite Justice Drew's announced intention to spend his retirement pursuing his hobbies of "boating, fishing, hunting, and cabinet making," his days of public service certainly had not ended. At Governor Reubin Askew's request, in 1974 he agreed to serve on the new Florida Ethics Commission, of which he became the second chairman. He remained on the panel for its crucial first two years. When the governor pressed for voter approval of a measure calling for strict financial disclosure requirements for public officials, Drew stepped in as co-chairman of the petition drive. And he continued to delight in sitting on various courts as a retired justice. As his daughter put it, "Dad stayed active on court matters right up to the day he died."[106]

Justice Drew died at Tallahassee on February 9, 1978, as a result of an automobile accident. Edith Drew remained in the capital city, struggling in her last years with the effects of blindness. She passed away there on January 17, 1990. "She was a caring person," her daughter reflected. "She would go out of her way to help someone." Of Justice Drew, LeRoy Collins sounded the sentiments of many. "The thing that sticks out in my mind about Judge Drew is his willingness to undertake all kinds of efforts for the public good. He was one of the finest public officials I've ever known."[107]

Benjamin Campbell Thornal, Supreme Court Justice, 1955–1970; Supreme Court Chief Justice, 1965–1967

Governor LeRoy Collins continued the trend toward the new vision of legal and judicial professionalism in supreme court appointments begun with Justice E. Harris Drew's selection by naming as his first designee Campbell Thornal. Parallels abound between Drew and Thornal. Both men essentially were self-made. Living in an increasingly urban state, they boasted similar backgrounds of service to municipalities and other local government agencies, yet they built private practices that brought them widespread attention and respect for their professional integrity. They shared interest in community service, and both advocated reforms in the administration of justice. Each had backed a friend's gubernatorial campaign, and each received other rewards of office prior to selection for the tribunal. Not surprisingly, they became each other's best friend on the supreme court. The differences, subtle as they were, came in Collins's desire for appointees who reflected his own moral and philosophical outlook and with whom his core political supporters could identify. Thus he turned to Thornal. In him, Collins found a deeply religious man and a World War II veteran. Perhaps more important, he gained an individual, as the governor put it, "tenacious in purpose."[108]

Campbell Thornal was born at Charleston, South Carolina, on October 15, 1908, to Benjamin Campbell Thornal and Henrietta Fischer Wagener Thornal. Both parental families had resided in Charleston for a considerable time, and Henrietta's prided itself on a distinguished and long-lasting place in the city's history. On the other hand, their family heritages did not necessarily equate with financial security. Benjamin worked in the insurance industry while young Campbell and his siblings attended local public schools. Charleston's sluggish economy held little promise, though. So in 1922 Benjamin agreed to accept a transfer to the Florida city of Orlando. There he hoped better times lay in store.[109]

If the Thornal family dreamed of wealth arising out of the Florida boom of the 1920s, they found themselves disappointed as were other state residents. Orlando never really entered heady days, but when the bust came in 1926, it suffered along with most other communities. The Great Depression that began in 1929 deepened the doldrums. In those conditions, Campbell Thornal matured, expecting to work and hoping to find security and a measure of personal peace. His first job was delivering newspapers for the *Orlando Reporter-Star*. During Christmas holidays he stood at the post office's parcel post window to add a few more dollars to the family's slim coffers. Meanwhile, the tall, slim, reddish-blond young man proved himself a quiet scholar. He so excelled at Orlando's Memorial High

School that its faculty awarded him the Guernsey Good Citizenship Award as the outstanding graduate in his class.[110]

Despite financial difficulties, Thornal pursued education and improvement by entering the University of Florida and, eventually, its law program. He paid his way by assisting in the library, waiting tables, washing dishes, stoking furnaces, and occasionally playing the violin. Summer breaks saw him helping the Orlando survey crew. "Red" Thornal, as he was known to fellow students, came to love the university. He found time for the varsity debating team and a staff job on the student newspaper. The university returned the affection. Thornal achieved admission to membership in Florida Blue Key and numerous other social and professional fraternities. Having excelled at his course work, he graduated with the degree of juris doctor in 1930.[111]

Prospects for opening a legal practice at Orlando appeared dim for any beginning lawyer in 1930. Fortunately, Thornal's local reputation resulted in an offer from the Giles and Gurney law firm. Three years afterward, he joined with John G. Baker in the firm of Baker and Thornal. The partners remained together until Thornal's supreme court appointment. "No meritorious person in trouble and needing his aid and counsel was denied his counsel and assistance regardless of either their financial condition or his own," Baker reminisced. "He was a true idealist of his chosen profession." Thornal's legal abilities impressed area residents and officials. In 1938 the City of Orlando named him its attorney, and Orange County followed suit in 1941. Community service already had led to his election in 1939 as president of the Florida Junior Chamber of Commerce.[112]

By the mid- to late 1930s, the young lawyer prospered sufficiently to start a family. Alyce Carolyn Letton, daughter of Lake County tobacco farmer Jesse Daniel Letton and Alice McCormick Letton, had just moved to Orlando from Leesburg. She and a friend entered a local restaurant where Campbell Thornal happened to be seated with a friend. Thornal, usually a man of caution, found himself smitten. As he related to his son Ben, "I turned to my friend and said, 'I'm going to marry her.'" Alyce did not share the overpowering attraction at first, although she noticed that "he had a nice sense of humor and was romantic!" Time took care of the rest. The couple wed at her uncle's Orlando home on November 7, 1936. They would share two children, Benjamin Campbell Thornal and Alyce "Leecy" Thornal.[113]

The Thornals' life together proceeded on a very desirable course. They shared Methodist church membership, in which Campbell found great comfort and personal satisfaction. Later he would serve on the official board of Tallahassee's Trinity United Methodist Church, on various committees and boards of the regional and national church, and as a member and officer of the board of trustees of Florida Southern College. Justice Stephen C. O'Connell eventually would nickname him "Deacon," when he could resist calling his friend "Slim." The couple deferred to each other's needs and desires. "I guess I'm thoroughly domesticated," he asserted at one point. Alyce responded, "We'll do whatever Campbell wants." They listened to "symphonic music" together, watched television, and took beach vacations, as did countless other families of the time. Campbell also would read—biographies, history, and sea stories were favorites—but fishing topped his list of extracurricular activities. When he could, he would fish every Saturday. As Wayne Todd Jr., Florida senate sergeant-at-arms and one of north Florida's leading outdoorsmen, observed, "Justice Thornal was a superb fisherman; if the fish were there he would find a way to catch them even during his terminal illness." A reporter noted in 1955, though, that "he was always back to teach his Sunday school class of young marrieds at Broadway Methodist Church."[114]

The 1940s and early 1950s found Campbell Thornal a very busy man. In addition to other responsibilities, he served as a legislative aide to Governor Spessard Holland from 1941 to 1943. In Tallahassee, he made the acquaintance of Leon County's young state senator, LeRoy Collins. They and their wives remained lifelong friends. Then Thornal entered the U.S. Naval Reserve with a lieutenant's commission, serving with credit until discharged. Following the peace, the veteran supported reform movements in Florida politics, particularly those of Dan McCarty. Disappointed by McCarty's failed gubernatorial campaign in 1948, he exulted at his friend's 1952 victory. The new governor sought Thornal's counsel as a legislative aide and soon named him to the Florida Turnpike Authority. In that position, the Orlando attorney shunned traditional gifts and otherwise illustrated patterns of strict honesty and integrity. Suspended from office by Acting Governor Charley E. Johns following McCarty's death, Thornal labored tirelessly on behalf of LeRoy Collins's campaign in 1954. Collins thereafter named Thornal to the powerful state road board. The governor later announced Thornal's appointment to the supreme court on May 4, 1955, following Chief Justice John E. Mathews's sudden death. The move delighted many of Florida's young and reform-minded World War II veterans. "We thought he was of a different cut," recalled W. Reece Smith. "His appointment was important to young bar leaders."[115]

Campbell Thornal's tenure on the Supreme Court of Florida extended for slightly more than fifteen years, including two years' service as chief justice. He expressed his philosophy early on in these words: "The law is a progressive science that develops with the needs and customs of the people. The Constitution should be construed exactly as it is written and it isn't up to the court to undertake to rewrite the Constitution." He added, "The wisdom of statutory law is a legislative function, and it is merely the responsibility of the court to apply the law as it is written." Quickly, though, Thornal's strong stance moderated somewhat as his sense of morality asserted itself in his work. By 1957 he would declare, "Judicial consistency loses its virtue when it is degraded by the vice of injustice." Fairness became a touchstone. "He was so fair," his friend John Germany remembered, "that he almost stopped reading the newspapers so that he wouldn't be swayed." Nonetheless, he stuck closely to the principle "that this nation is a nation of laws and not a nation of men." As his longtime assistant Elizabeth Pierson noted, "He did not believe in bending the law."[116]

Thornal's contributions as a court member ranged widely. Some saw him as the panel's intellectual leader. Recognized as "an excellent legal writer," his opinions evidenced, according to a fellow jurist, "a keen, analytical mind." His gift involved understanding complicated issues in simpler terms. Comparing him to Abraham Lincoln, LeRoy Collins said, "Both could find the basic issue of a controversy and solve it by applying fundamental principles gleaned from Bible study or other ancient literary or legal precedents." Thornal stood among the first to sound an environmental alarm, declaring, according to Florida Bar executive director Kenneth Sherouse, "that he would live to see Florida limited by the shortage of potable water and the surplus of solid waste." The justice added, "Central Florida is afloat on a cesspool, and in the long run it will be more important to the lawyers than faculty salaries at Stetson, admissions at Miami, and discrimination cases at Gainesville." Of greater concern to him were the rights of indigent criminal defendants. "He was a very humane man," reflected Richard W. Ervin, "in the sense that he always wanted to see that persons charged with crime had a fair trial and were not in any way denied their rights." He also found time to help ensure the integrated bar's survival, support multistate bar examination implementation, nurture "government in the sunshine," encourage the University of Florida Law School's moot court competition program, and further many other worthy endeavors.[117]

Many law clerks recalled Thornal fondly, adding significantly to any understanding of the man and the jurist. "Thornal was a humorous, witty, and forthright gentleman," William C. Owen remembered. "He would often invite law clerks for other justices into his inner office and solicit their opinions about published cases in a free discussion in which he made every clerk feel like an equal." Owen added, "The justice revealed a humorous side, including his observation that B. K. Roberts would 'crab-walk' anytime he was coming to ask a favor of Thornal."[118]

Despite personal conservatism and a deeply southern heritage, Thornal also stood out during the mid-1950s for his insistence on "effective law enforcement without regard to race, color, or creed." In January 1956, as public fury aroused by U.S. Supreme Court desegregation decisions and the awakening of the modern civil rights movement headed toward a fever pitch, he chose to lecture Florida's sheriffs on their duty. "The administration of justice is the firmest pillar of government," he declared to the lawmen at their annual state convention. "The impartial and effective enforcement of the law is an essential foundation stone in that pillar."[119]

News arriving in March 1969 that Justice Thornal suffered from pancreatic cancer shocked colleagues and friends lulled by his boundless energy, sense of humor, and pleasant demeanor. An emergency operation at Duke University hospital left surgeons frustrated at the impossibility of removing the entire tumor. He recuperated at the home of his daughter and son-in-law, Dr. Thomas Wyatt, a resident physician at Duke, although the experience had taken a serious toll. Justice Thornal returned to the court, but the disease's aftermath taxed him severely, and he could participate only irregularly. The ailing jurist periodically returned to Duke for further treatments, but in October 1970 his physicians operated again. He struggled for two weeks thereafter before passing away on November 4.[120]

The days following Justice Thornal's death brought forth tributes from throughout Florida. The *Orlando Sentinel*, for one, declared that "if a man is judged in this life by his good deeds, then Campbell Thornal leaves a rich legacy." His dear friend LeRoy Collins, several years afterward, summed up his own sentiments: "Campbell loved his God. He loved the law. He found in both inspiration, direction, and prescriptions for living a good life and working for a better state. All of those who knew him sensed this profoundly, were strengthened by the wise counsel he so generously shared and left with us as a precious heritage."[121]

Another friend also chose to preserve insight into Justice Campbell's life. "Campbell Thornal was in all important things a rare uncommon man with a warm and generous heart and a quiet unassuming manner that lent a common touch, making him equally welcome and appreciated in a fishing camp . . . as in the company of high officials or at a sophisticated social event," Stephen C. O'Connell asserted. "If any one of his many admirable traits outshone the others, it was a compulsion to serve, to construct, to improve, to make things work as they were intended and ought to be." He concluded: "As counselor, advocate, civic leader, aide to governors and other leaders, a leader in the bar, a justice and a servant of his Lord, he sought only the opportunity to serve, never seeking personal recognition or acclaim. In all the many years of public service, remarkably, never was there attributed to him a taint of dishonor, selfishness, or improper motives. He invited confidence, radiated character, and inspired trust in himself and the causes he served."[122]

Stephen Cornelius O'Connell, Supreme Court Justice, 1955–1967; Supreme Court Chief Justice, 1967

When a second vacancy opened on the Florida Supreme Court in 1955, Governor LeRoy Collins already had in mind an individual cut from the same cloth as Campbell Thornal. "I think he is ideally suited for the job," the governor said of Stephen C. O'Connell. "He has a sterling character, a brilliant mind and will work hard and devotedly to do an outstanding job." As was true of Thornal, O'Connell boasted a distinguished World War II service record, was a devoted family man, had excelled at the University of Florida, enjoyed a successful private legal practice, had never run for public office but had supported his friend Collins for governor, and held firm religious beliefs that anchored moral values very close to those held by the governor. Of course, the fact that O'Connell was a Roman Catholic and a south Florida resident did not harm the governor's political viability.[123]

The new justice matched Thornal as well in that he arrived in Florida as the boom of the 1920s commenced to rage. His family on both sides had come to the United States from Ireland before settling at Savannah and, subsequently, Macon, Georgia. At Macon Justice O'Connell's parents, Daniel Joseph O'Connell (born June 23, 1873) and Ann Nora McKenna (born January 30, 1879) married in 1904 and commenced a family of their own. When Stephen Cornelius was born on January 22, 1916, the O'Connells temporarily were living at West Palm Beach, Florida, although they returned to Macon shortly thereafter. Steve was the family's fifth child and fourth son.[124]

Childhood was to hold terrible trials. When he was four, his mother died suddenly. The 1920s event proved "catastrophic" for the widower, as Justice O'Connell later recalled. Rent with grief, Daniel O'Connell quickly lost his farm and business. A desperate search for work brought him to south Florida to labor for an Everglades development project. "It was a pioneering existence," remembered sister Leonora M. O'Connell. "Our settlement of three houses was reached only by a little packet boat which came by once a week to bring mail and take us to Carter's Trading Post . . . to do the weekly shopping." After one year O'Connell relocated the family to Brevard County, eventually settling near Mims. Soon he had erected a "filling station" with an apartment located above.[125]

The O'Connells' tiny Brevard County apartment remained Stephen's home until the early 1930s. He attended grade school at LaGrange and high school through the junior year at Titusville. Over time, though, visits from older brother Phillip began to open the young man's eyes to a broader world. Phil had remained in Georgia where relations had aided him to attend Mercer University, then the University of Florida Law School. At Gainesville, he not only succeeded but excelled. Among other things, he fought on the UF boxing team. In 1930 he had won the Southeastern Conference Lightweight Championship. Graduation from law school in 1931 had led him to West Palm Beach, where the following year residents elected Phil O'Connell their municipal judge. Within eight years he would achieve the position of state attorney for the fifteenth judicial circuit, a post that he would retain until 1965.[126]

Problems at home prompted Stephen O'Connell at age seventeen to change his life. He had worked at the filling station and at odd jobs since age twelve, but his strict disciplinarian father often seemed displeased. Also, his father had remarried. Stephen's stepmother brought with her four additional children to live in the tiny apartment. In the end, Stephen simply decided to hitchhike to West Palm Beach, where he took up residence with Phil and enjoyed close proximity to two nurturing aunts, his sister Leonora, and his brother Gerald. With Phil's example before him, he undertook to prepare for a better life. He finished his high school education at Palm Beach High School, where he favored studies in English and Latin. Even more enjoyable were boxing lessons at Woody Norwood's gym and the amateur matches that followed. Unknown to him, he had begun to attract attention from fight fans. Among them was future justice E. Harris Drew, then West Palm Beach's town attorney. O'Connell took odd jobs in his spare time and worked construction during the summer after graduation in 1934. He saved and looked forward to pursuing his education.[127]

What that education might entail changed over time. O'Connell desired to follow Phil's path to the University of Florida. "At that time you could go to the U. of F. even though you had no money if you were willing to work," he reminisced. "Almost all of the students were working for at least part of their expenses." At the school he intended to pursue a dental degree rather than one in law. Despite the pay of various campus jobs and working construction during summers, by sophomore year financial concerns had convinced him to switch to business administration. Encouraged by the Catholic Student Center's Father Jeremiah P. O'Mahoney, he persisted. During his sophomore year, though, he won election as class president, and the victory kindled a fascination with politics. That interest—coupled with an engaging personality and determination—led to his election as student body president, president of Florida Blue Key, president of Alpha Tau Omega fraternity, president of the Newman Club, and other honors. In 1938 he extended his political interests by agreeing to serve as co-chairman with his friends George Smathers and John McCarty of the Florida Supreme Court campaign of Elwyn Thomas. Meanwhile, O'Connell repeated Phil's success on the boxing team, eventually working as an assistant coach. In his spare time, he served as commanding officer of the campus Reserve Officer Training Corps detachment.[128]

The thrill of politics softened O'Connell's determination to pursue business as a career. Instead and with encouragement from Phil, Stephen began to look toward law school. Once enrolled he never looked back. He quickly accepted a love not only for the University of Florida but for the law. "O'Connell was an energetic and hard working undergraduate who knew how to make the best use of his time," Professor Manning Dauer recorded. "He combined a remarkable record of attention to study, earning his way through school, student leadership, athletics, and undergraduate leadership." Dauer concluded, "He showed the same qualities of leadership that were to lead him to be a successful law practitioner . . . and then to selection to the Florida Supreme Court, and finally to the Presidency of the University of Florida." At the law school, O'Connell was elected to Phi Alpha Phi legal fraternity and later would be inducted into the Order of the Coif. He graduated in 1940 with business administration and law degrees.[129]

Then he set out on his own. He gained admission to the bar, but chose not to set up a West Palm Beach practice. Instead he headed for Fort Lauderdale, a community he knew little about but that afforded him the chance to "not be a little brother to Phil." With only a borrowed $75 to call his own, he failed to find employment. Fortunately, Judge Albert McMillan permitted him to use vacant office space and his legal library. The novice attorney boarded, thanks to friends, at the Pine Crest School, exchanging for the boon his work as boxing and tennis coach. The situation lasted about six months.[130]

At that point, the army came calling. With World War II raging in Europe, army preparedness lagged, but officials were striving to reverse the situation. Recruited as the civilian director of physical training for the Third Air Force, by 1942 he wore the bars of a commissioned officer. He served through the conflict in a variety of capacities, first as special service officer for the Fifth Air Force in the southwest Pacific and then as executive officer of the 312th Bomber Group as it moved from Australia to Okinawa. Discharged from the air corps in April 1946, he wore the oak leaves of a major.[131]

Thirty years of age by the time he had arrived back in Fort Lauderdale, the tested veteran set about establishing a regular life. As he described it, "I wanted to be a good citizen and help others in politics." He began by helping to organize the legal partnership of Saunders, Buckley, and O'Connell, the headquarters for which was an abandoned church building. "We took out the pews and made our offices," the future justice explained. He also met and courted Rita Mavis McTigue. The daughter of M. R. and Ruby I. Moore McTigue, she was a native of Estherville, Iowa, in her mid-twenties. The couple wed on November 6, 1946, in Fort Lauderdale. They would adopt four children: Rita Denise, Stephen C. Jr., Martin Robert, and Ann Maureen.[132]

O'Connell's legal practice expanded with the postwar boom, but with prosperity came increasing commitment to community and public service. In 1947 he accepted the position of city attorney for the City of Hallendale, which further extended his area of professional expertise and his local contacts. He associated with the Knights of Columbus, the Elks, the chamber of commerce, local and state bar associations, and other worthy causes. He stepped also into the world of Broward County politics. Building on the University of Florida alumni network, by 1947 he had achieved the chairmanship of the county Democratic executive committee. He perceived his philosophy as "middle of the road," although others described him as "a conservative with high moral values." He disdained office for himself. He particularly worked hard to elect his college friend John McCarty's brother Dan as governor in 1948. O'Connell saw McCarty as "straight as an arrow," a man who would return "order and honesty" to government. Four years later, he served as county chairman for McCarty's second campaign. In return, the new governor appointed his ally as general counsel to the state road department.[133]

Governor McCarty's sudden death interrupted O'Connell's record of public service, but not for long. Acting Governor Charley Johns demanded personal loyalty. O'Connell resigned as Johns was attempting to fire him. He was already determined to oust Johns in favor of LeRoy Collins, another close McCarty ally. Their opportunity came in 1954. In concert with others such as Orange County's Campbell Thornal, they prevailed. The triumph led O'Connell to accept the role of counsel to the state racing commission. When Justice H. L. "Tom" Sebring resigned later in 1955, Collins turned to his campaign aide to fill the seat. The O'Connells declined, reluctant to part from their comfortable and increasing affluent Fort Lauderdale life.[134]

Collins pressed them. "I never considered anybody but Steve for this position," he recalled. "There was then no justice on the court domiciled in the Broward-Dade area of the state, Florida's heaviest populated. I had previously appointed Campbell Thornal, and the two of them could have been cut from the same mold. They were close friends, and their energy fueled their outstanding talents." Collins saw much more in O'Connell than his place of residence or friendship with Justice Thornal. "He came to personify to me what I liked to find in all our people: a keen mind, a love of God and country, sterling character and integrity, compassion, a respect for the rights of all people, and a new vision of what our state could become," the governor later declared. "All these values were reflected by him, with a personality of rare and sparkling wit and endearing charm." The governor's own charm prevailed. O'Connell called it "the most difficult decision I have ever had to make." Still, he acceded to his friend's request. On October 21, 1955, Chief Justice E. Harris Drew administered the oath of office as Collins and friends looked on.[135]

For twelve years O'Connell sat upon the state bench. Within six months he had impressed some critics as well as friends. "[He] has won the esteem of both lawyers and laymen," observed the *Tampa Tribune*, "for the manner in which he has conducted himself on the bench." One practitioner denominated him "a grand justice" who showed "tremendous leadership." By 1957 a "mild boom" seemed to be projecting him toward the 1960 gubernatorial primaries. The *Miami Herald* assessed the justice as "a powerful political personality." Yet O'Connell, after adjusting to the different realities of court life as opposed to legal practice, happily chose to remain on the supreme tribunal, bringing to it a measure of humor and humanity. One attorney recorded the details of his first court appearance. "When I went to the podium with knees shaking I looked up and one of the justices smiled and winked at me. That small gesture gave me great comfort, and I managed to get through my oral argument without passing out. You were that justice, and I have never forgotten that act of kindness throughout my career." As time passed, O'Connell accepted additional responsibilities. In 1957 he succeeded Justice Elwyn Thomas as chairman of the Florida Judicial Council, bearing the weight of pressing for judicial reform for the next four years. He also would serve in the mid-1960s as a member of the constitution revision commission. In 1967, he rose to become chief justice.[136]

Unexpectedly, O'Connell's tenure as chief justice ended soon after it began. At a time when dissent within American society had begun to reverberate in campus protests and sometimes disruption, the Florida board of regents called O'Connell back to his alma mater to guide the University of Florida through the troubled waters that seemed to lie ahead. Serving as university president for six years beginning in 1967, his hand proved steady. "In addition to bringing the university safely through this turbulent period," explained onetime university system chancellor E. T. York, "the university continued to make great strides in the quality and effectiveness of its programs during Steve's term as president." He concluded: "I've never been associated with a person for whom I have greater respect than Steve O'Connell."[137]

The path of O'Connell's life took some unexpected turns following his departure from the University of Florida. He and Rita O'Connell returned to Tallahassee, where he involved himself in banking and legal practice. Sadly, Mrs. O'Connell became ill and died on August 26, 1977. The former justice remained in the community, although he retired from banking in 1983 to spend more time managing his nearby farm and cattle ranch. On October 11, 1997, he remarried. Cynthia Faye Bowling already was well known in Tallahassee circles through community service and public relations activities. Three years later, Justice O'Connell succumbed to cancer, passing away at Tallahassee on April 13, 2001.[138]

How can one sum up such a diverse, prodigious, and significant career of a man who represented the reform element that overwhelmed the less public-minded? Campbell Thornal penned his analysis of the man he believed to be "one of the bright luminaries of the Florida judiciary" at the time O'Connell approached his inauguration as president of the University of Florida. His words offer much to consider. "He had an abiding faith in the rule of law as the ultimate arbiter between right and wrong. He insisted that inefficiency in the administration of the judicial process tended to corrupt the law as a canon of truth. In his view it generates public suspicions of the very foundations of government. His decisions were complete[ly] impersonal. He listens courteously to disagreement with his view, but when convinced that he is right, he clings to his position with the tenacity that typifies his Irish forebears."[139]

10

Case Decisions of the Postwar Era

Florida's appellate decisions during the decade that commenced with the end of World War II hinted at the cross-currents of trends and influences then actively affecting state and local affairs during a period of dramatic growth and unprecedented change. As usually occurs, change stirred anxieties and resentments in some, while inspiring or motivating others. Conflicts and complexities within society at large saw reflections within the hearts and minds of individuals, including the men who sat on the state's supreme court. The tribunal's rulings, in turn, grappled immediately with the changes at play and attempted to influence their direction.

Although not unaware of the evolving needs of an ever larger population and pool of voters, the panel's members nonetheless often aired sentiments of concern for what its members perceived as excessive government growth and intrusion into life, especially into business affairs, stemming from New Deal and World War II initiatives. Several decisions related to New Deal–type "Fair Trade" laws illustrate the point. In 1949 the tribunal by a four-to-three margin overturned as "arbitrary and unreasonable" one price regulation statute. "This legislation is a species of the relatively recent national recovery legislation," Justice Adams related in *Liquor Store, Inc., et al.* v. *Continental Distilling Corp*. "It was conceived at a time when there were surpluses and general need for such a law in certain basic commodities. The courts approving similar acts scarcely had an opportunity to observe its effects other than as its proponents visualized its operation in futuro." Adams concluded, "We are in a more favored position as we have the benefit of the actual consequences flowing from its application."[1]

When the 1951 state legislature attempted to rewrite the fair trade law to pass constitutional muster, the court with only one dissent rejected legislative findings of fact to dispose of the measure once more. Justice Terrell's opinion in *Miles Laboratories, Inc.* v. *Eckerd, et al.* rapped the price fixing concept in words so adamant that they prompted one legal scholar to comment, "*Definitely*, in Florida, the legislative police power is restricted by the judicial power, which in turn is dependent upon the prevailing economic philosophy of the Supreme Court."[2] Within five years, though, the court found it necessary to step back in response to popular opinion. For the panel in *Shiver* v. *Lee*, Justice Terrell agreed that it should sustain a legislative conclusion as to the desirability of price administration for Florida milk sales.[3]

By the same token, court members recognized many of the urgent needs brought on by the immediate demands of growth and for services and at times proved willing to make every effort to uphold new initiatives. Thus in 1950's *Gaulden* v. *Kirk* the tribunal unanimously upheld the state's new sales tax. "The tax provided in the Revenue Act of 1949 is not a property tax as . . . prohibited by Article IX, Section 2 of the Constitution of Florida," Justice Hobson declared. "This being true, it matters not whether it be classified as a state privilege or a state occupation tax for we know of no constitutional provision inhibiting the levy of either as such if it be reasonable and not unjustly discriminatory or arbitrary."[4] Similarly, 1952's *Overman* v. *State Board of Control* approved public subsidies of the state's first medical school, located at the private University of Miami.[5] In one other example, the jurists in 1956's *Gray, et al.* v. *Golden, et al.* unanimously sustained a proposed constitutional amendment providing home rule for the state's new premier county, Dade.[6]

Important to recall, as the years passed one after another, the cold war and the civil rights movement commanded greater attention and sparked increasingly intense emotions and frustrations. These themes will be revisited shortly, but for now two slander-related decisions will aid in emphasizing the point. First, in 1949 six years remained before the U.S. Supreme Court's *Brown* v. *Board of Education* opinions launched "massive resistance" to racial desegregation in the South. Tempers yet, for the most part, remained calm. Ruling that year in *Mann* v. *Roosevelt Shop, Inc.*, the court could find no actionable slander when a shop clerk declared to a white customer: "You are not as good as a Negro. I was hired here to see that Negros were not pushed around. Negroes have a kind, loving heart and you came from Georgia and you are not as good as a Negro." Justice Adams for the court related, "Redress in court does not extend to spoken words constituting a personal insult only."[7] On the other hand, the court reached a different conclusion in 1953's *Joopanenko* v. *Gavagan*. For the court, Justice Mathews held that an oral charge that a person was a communist constituted slander per se.[8]

Among the period's thousands of other decisions, the following offer a sense of the times and of the changes and complexities with which Floridians and their supreme court were required to deal.

Consumerism and Consumer Protection

Florida's expanded electorate naturally demanded that public institutions respect the needs of individual consumers of goods and services, a circumstance that served as context while the court mulled decisions in a variety of related areas. One of them, liability for damaged or dangerous products, commanded attention early in the period. In 1947's *Starke Coca-Cola Bottling Co.* v. *Carrington*, to cite an example, the panel's Division B found itself headed in a direction different from that followed by Division A three years earlier. In the first case (*Hughs* v. *Miami Coca Cola Bottling Co.*) Justices Sebring, Buford, Terrell, and Chapman had declined to apply the doctrine of *res ipsa loquitur* to soda pop manufacturers.[9]

Now Justice Buford, writing for himself and Justices Thomas, Adams, and Barns, held otherwise. In doing so, Buford quoted from a Georgia appellate decision. "The bottle exploded. Inferentially someone was negligent. . . . Someone is prima facie to blame. By process of elimination, we get back to the manufacturer who sets the dangerous agency in motion, and upon whom the blame ought inferably to be fastened." Buford then distinguished *Hughs* because, in the earlier case, there was "no affirmative showing on the part of the plaintiff that the bottle after it left possession of the bottler was not subjected to any unusual atmospheric changes, or changes in temperature, or that it was not handled improperly up to the time of the explosion."[10]

By 1949 the panel had found an implied warranty of fitness in the sale of food by a restaurant. Writing in the Seminole County case of *Cliett* v. *Lauderdale Biltmore Corp*, Justice Sebring observed, "We can perceive no substantial basis for holding a restaurant keeper who serves food for immediate consumption on the premises to a less degree of responsibility than that imposed upon a retailer who sells food for immediate consumption off the premises."[11]

Two other decisions typify the numerous additional consumer-related matters considered during the era. Sunday retail closing laws came under the tribunal's collective eye in 1952, setting the stage for a series of similar decisions as the decade progressed. In that initial case, *Henderson, et al.* v. *Antonacci, et al.*, Justice Hobson for a unanimous court invalidated one such statute as offensive to the state constitution. One commentator, by 1960, saw that opinion and its successors as making it "impossible, under the Florida Constitution, for the Legislature to enact a valid Sunday Law."[12] In 1956 the panel acted to protect consumers while also safeguarding one of the state's premier economic mainstays. Justice Thornal's opinion in *Florida Citrus Commission* v. *Golden Gift, Inc.* upheld the state's authority through one of its agencies to specify by regulation what constituted "chilled orange juice."[13]

Environmental Protection

While the years immediately following the war saw creation of the Everglades National Park, most Floridians and government officials remained focused far more on growth and development than on environmental protection. The 1946 decision in *Holland, et al.* v. *Fort Pierce Financing and Construction Co.* came against that backdrop. Acting Associate Justice George W. Whitehurst, writing for the court, invalidated a special legislative act that attempted to transfer title in submerged lands in the navigable Indian River to the Trustees of the Internal Improvement Trust Fund. Whitehurst reasoned that the riparian owner, having completed bulkheading and filling in a lawful manner and having converted the property to gainful use, deserved no less.[14]

The passage of almost a decade, though, ushered in the hint of attitudinal changes to come. Justice Terrell, writing for himself and Justices Roberts, Sebring, and Mathews in 1954's *Duval Engineering and Contracting Co.* v. *Sales*, specified that the state could withdraw a provisional legislative grant to bulkhead and fill at any time before the owner had complied with the improvement provision of the grant. Of the decision, an analyst noted, "Hence he who hesitates to bulkhead and fill toward the channel may lose his legislative permit at any time the state decides to devote the offshore shallows to some public use, leaving the upland owner with only his ancient rights of access, view, and use."[15]

Labor Law

As Florida grew more complex in the postwar years, questions of labor's rights and duties naturally continued to present matters for litigation and appellate decision. For example, in 1944 a state constitutional amendment had achieved voter approval that guaranteed an "open shop" for workers. The issue of its constitutionality came before the tribunal in 1950. In an opinion concurred in by Justices Adams, Chapman, and Hobson, Justice Sebring in *Local Union No. 519* v. *Robertson* blunted efforts by a Miami local of the plumbers and pipefitters union to compel a business owner to sign a closed shop contract. The state constitutional amendment, Sebring determined, could withstand scrutiny, since the activities of labor unions constituted a matter of public interest.[16]

As also had been true during the previous decade, questions of union picketing rights presented the court with justiciable issues. In 1948 Local No. 222 of the American Federation of Labor in Miami decided to test a state law requiring a secret ballot and approval by a majority of employees at any plant before declaration of a lawful strike, as well as the validity of a circuit court injunction forestalling its strike. A bare majority of the court in *Whitehead* v. *Miami Laundry Co.* sided with the union. Its opinion written by Justice Chapman abrogated previous case law to hold the right to picket to be a part of the constitutional guarantee of free speech and that picketing could be utilized at any time by a labor union to "announce their dispute to the world." The decision, which effectively overturned the 1939 decision in *Retail Clerks Union, Local 779 of Miami* v. *Lerner Shops of Florida, Inc.*, came in the face of dissents from Justices Terrell, Adams, and Barns.[17]

The next year the panel again considered the subject of picketing rights, this time in circumstances where the union did not represent a majority of employees and no majority vote had authorized a strike. With Justices Chapman and Barns taking an opposing stance, Justice Sebring in *Moore, et al. v. City Dry Cleaners & Laundry* specified that "a decree that attempts to condition the right of any person to express his views fully with respect to a labor difficulty or dispute by any form of publication unattended by violence, force, coercion, or other unlawful or oppressive conduct, or to make the right of the expression dependent upon the exercise of 'a labor dispute' or 'strike' in which such person may have a direct interest runs counter to the Constitution."[18]

Justice Sebring's reference to a "publication unattended by violence" took on special meaning in the 1952 case of *Miami Typographical Union No. 430, et al.* v. *Ormerod, et al.* There, on behalf of himself and Justices Sebring, Terrell, and Thomas, Justice Hobson declared that, where violence and picketing proved so intertwined that they could not be separated, a permanent injunction could be granted. Hobson specified this to be the case even in the absence of direct evidence of union involvement in the violence. He also upheld the right of nonunion employees to enjoy injunctive relief.[19]

Legal Practice

The veteran-based reform efforts of the late 1940s and early 1950s touched the legal profession as well as other facets of state life. Particularly, when combined with concerns regarding the intensifying cold war and the rise of the civil rights movement, it encouraged the concept of an integrated bar, a result previously resisted by some supreme court members. In 1949 the panel acceded to requests for action and in *Petition of Florida State Bar Association, et al.* ordered creation of a mandatory universal bar for the state. "There was a time when bar integration would not be supported as strongly as it can at the present," Justice Terrell noted for the court. "The reason for it now is not discipline for unethical conduct, but to alert the bar to professional and public responsibility." He added, "We cannot shut our eyes to the fact that, like the institutions of our country, [the bar] is under attack and that we have a duty to meet the attack courageously. We think this duty devolves on the bar as a whole rather than on a minority organization." He concluded, "The assault on our institutions which the bar is expected to take the leading role in challenging also requires the impact of the full man power of the bar." Arguing against the move, Justice Barns insisted, "The Court is without power to compel the members of the bar to become members of a pseudo-organization called the integrated bar, and it is ill-becoming for this Court to do anything that would tend to coerce such membership."[20]

That the court ordered creation of an integrated bar reflected an assertion of the panel's power rather than a cession of its ultimate decision-making authority. This fact appeared clearly in a number of decisions, including 1954's *State ex rel. Florida Bar* v. *Murrell.* There the court, against the sentiments of Justices Drew and Sebring, refused to follow a strong recommendation of the Florida Bar to disbar an attorney for solicitation of clients. The majority believed, to the contrary of the bar's position, that mere solicitation, if not repeated, failed to provide sufficient grounds to justify so strong a punishment.[21]

Besides providing one backdrop for bar integration, the cold war also affected the practice of law in other ways. In 1955, for instance, the court's decision in *Sheiner* v. *State* touched upon the question of whether a communist could belong to the state bar. Justice Terrell's opinion found that refusal to answer charges of communism did not constitute sufficient grounds for disbarment without other evidence to sustain the charge. Terrell added, however, that "no lawyer . . . can become a member of the Communist Party or other subversive organization without forfeiting his privilege to practice law."[22]

Local Government Powers

Court members recognized Florida's expanding population and accepted certain steps as necessary for coping with the growth, but several remained wary of expanding the powers of local government, particularly when it came to borrowing money for improvements. As Justice Adams later commented, "At that time the judges were sharply divided on the question of approving revenue bonds to build public facilities. It seemed that some of them did not distinguish between a public facility and a facility that would benefit the public." Early in the period, though, a somewhat more permissive attitude prevailed. In the 1946 decision in *State* v. *Dade County*, for example, five panel members reaffirmed, with Justices Brown and Buford dissenting, that air transportation and airport construction and maintenance served a public and municipal purpose even when most of the facilities were to be leased to private concerns. Writing for the majority, Justice

Terrell observed, "Constitutional mandates are wise in proportion to the manner in which they respond to the public welfare and should be construed to effectuate that purpose when possible. The law does not look with favor on social or progressive stalemates."[23] Similarly, *State* v. *Escambia County*, considered in 1951, permitted expenditures—even very large expenditures—to develop recreational facilities including, possibly, a resort.[24]

Soon a different mind-set prevailed, as suggested by two important 1952 decisions. In *State, et al.* v. *Town of North Miami*, Justice Mathews conveyed the sentiments of a unanimous panel in restricting interpretations of previous decisions by specifying that municipal spending and eminent domain powers could be used only for a "public" utility or service, not a private one.[25] Two months later, in August, a nearly united tribunal backed Mathews's opinion in *Adams* v. *Housing Authority of City of Daytona Beach, et al.* The decision held the 1945 Municipal Housing Authority Law unconstitutional and otherwise limited spending and use of eminent domain powers for slum clearance. The majority, by then, seemed to view such projects, as one scholar put it, "as a real estate promotion scheme disguised as a redevelopment plan." Obviously chagrined at the change in attitude, Justice Terrell observed in dissent, "I do not think the makers of the constitution ever intended that instrument to be construed so as to make it a barrier to any community in removing filth, unsanitary places or other conditions that contribute to crime, deteriorate the public morals or which cause an inordinate drain on the tax revenues for police protection to counteract these and kindred influences."[26]

The tenor of the court's language grew even more severe in the years immediately following. Justice Mathews again drafted a key decision, this time in 1954's *City of Clearwater, et al.* v. *Caldwell, et al.* With Justice Terrell dissenting once more, the majority barred municipalities from leasing property to private, profit-seeking persons. "It may be argued that it is desirable for the City . . . to enter into the real estate business and lease its property for hotels, drug stores [etc.]," Mathews commented. "Such a change in policy may well threaten the entire free enterprise system. Why not extend it to . . . collective farms under the system of Communism?"[27]

Already some court members seemingly felt that Justice Mathews's leadership on these issues had taken the court too far. The same year as the *Clearwater* decision, the panel—or at least a division composed of Justices Roberts, Thomas, Drew, and (in a return court appearance) Buford—sidestepped the 1952 *Town of North Miami* precedent by permitting the City of Miami to borrow for limited private purposes under certain circumstances.[28] Within months, Justice Terrell commanded a six-member majority with Mathews dissenting in holding that the "definite possibility" of an "illegal public purpose" did not bar a court from validating a bond issue.[29]

The extent of the zoning power, including several cases related to aesthetic considerations, likewise occupied a good deal of court time and energy. A narrowly divided panel first decided *City of Miami Beach* v. *First Trust Co.*, for instance, in 1949. Justice Thomas then wrote for himself and Justices Adams, Terrell, Sebring, and Hobson to reaffirm the legitimacy of decisions based upon aesthetics. After a rehearing, Terrell and Hobson changed their minds, reversing the initial decision and focusing attention elsewhere. "There must be a positive showing of physical, economic or social change rather than aesthetic or group caprice to justify the release of zoning regulations," Justice Terrell found. "They will not be released at the behest of community or group pressure, if in doing so, constitutional guarantees are undermined."[30]

What a difference three years can make. In 1953 the panel revisited the subject in *Merritt* v. *Peters, et al.* Justice Thomas by then had returned as representative of the majority with only Justice Barns dissenting. At least insofar as resort communities were concerned, the court now saw aesthetics as an integral part of the general welfare. "The attractiveness of a community like Miami Beach was of prime concern to the whole people," Thomas wrote, "and therefore affected the welfare of all." Summing up the decision's impact, one observer declared, "This represents a dramatic lowering of barriers for aesthetic considerations."[31]

Race and Race Relations

Given the World War II "Double-V" campaign signaling that African American men and women were fighting for victory against the enemy overseas and for victory against racism at home, the early postwar period found black veterans and their allies endeavoring to make inroads against Jim Crow discrimination including by the pursuit of litigation. Federal courts encouraged the attempts with landmark rulings. Among them were the U.S. Supreme Court's 1950 decisions in *Sweatt* v. *Painter* and *McLaurin* v. *Oklahoma State Regents* that held inadequate graduate and professional school opportunities, as well as on-campus discrimination, a denial of equal protection of the law. By the issuance in 1954 and 1955 of rulings in *Brown* v. *Board of Education of Topeka, Kansas* (a related case derived from Florida), the legal foundations of the "separate but equal" doctrine had been demolished and public schools everywhere had been ordered to desegregate "with all deliberate speed."[32]

The Supreme Court of Florida found itself involved in this litigation as early as 1950. In a series of decisions rendered in late summer it addressed access to the

University of Florida's graduate and professional programs. The lead case, *State ex rel. Hawkins* v. *Board of Control, et al.*, concerned Virgil Hawkins's attempt to enter the UF Law School, and the trail of litigation that followed generally captured attention as the *Hawkins* case. In the first decision, Justice Sebring for a unanimous court agreed that, pursuant to U.S. Supreme Court mandates, sending black students out of state for graduate and professional training violated their right to equal protection. Sebring insisted, though, that programs at Florida A&M University could substitute for those at the University of Florida or, if not, then FAMU could "loan" the students temporarily for classes elsewhere.[33]

Hawkins returned to the supreme tribunal within one year. The Board of Control, the state's university governing authority, refused Hawkins's renewed attempt to enroll at the UF Law School. In 1951, Justice Sebring again authored the court's opinion in the matter, dismissing the appeal by suggesting that Hawkins had not applied formally for UF admission and had made no showing that its facilities had not been made available to him. "The Court's opinion seemed somewhat incongruous," one scholar of the subject observed, "because in *Hawkins I* it had already found as a matter of law that he had previously applied, was qualified, and was denied admission solely because of his race and color."[34] On his third appellate attempt, Hawkins in 1952 again found little sympathy on the panel. Writing for a unanimous court, Sebring declared that the U.S. Constitution did not demand integration of the UF Law School if another law school for black students has been established in the state. The federal tribunal's 1896 ruling in *Plessy* v. *Ferguson*, he reasoned, required only equality of treatment, not access to the same facilities and programs. Other and more recent decisions, he argued, had not found that "any segregation was unlawful."[35]

The 1952 decision brought the U.S. Supreme Court actively into the legal fray. Shortly after issuing its 1954 *Brown* v. *Board of Education* ruling, the federal panel ordered Florida's tribunal to review its *Hawkins* decision in light of *Brown* and the related cases just decided in May.[36] State reaction came in an opinion issued late in 1955 after the federal court's *Brown* implementation ruling. Justice Roberts on behalf of a five-member majority acknowledged racial segregation to be unconstitutional but insisted that the availability of a law school at FAMU negated the need to admit Hawkins to UF. He distinguished the circumstances in the *Brown* cases and stressed his belief that Hawkins's admission to UF would cause serious public problems. The implementation decision for *Brown*, he observed, did not require "immediate" action but only "all deliberate speed." Meanwhile, Justice Terrell's concurring opinion, as will be discussed in chapter 12, defended racial segregation as providentially ordained. Justice Sebring, on the other hand, could no longer maintain the court's traditional stance. With Justice Thomas's concurrence, he dissented with a call for immediate desegregation of all Florida public schools. For the time being, there the matter stood.[37]

As the *Hawkins* cases wound their way through state and federal courts, the Florida Supreme Court dealt with numerous additional desegregation cases and other matters of litigation more generally related to race and race relations. Although they might not specifically come under the rubric, several criminal decisions were viewed by the state's minority community as being of direct concern, with the Groveland or *Shepherd* case taking top priority. The prosecution originally concerned four Lake County men—Samuel Shepherd, Walter Irvin, Charles Greenlee, and Ernest Thomas—who had been accused in 1949 of kidnapping and raping a white woman. Shepherd came before the supreme court (with Irvin pursuing a companion appeal) as *Shepherd* v. *State* in 1950 when he challenged his sentence of death based upon an absence of blacks from local juries and a prejudicial trial atmosphere. Justice Chapman spoke for the court in rejecting all complaints. "The evidence adduced fails to establish an unconstitutional, intentional and systematic discrimination by the officials against the Negroes of Lake County . . . when selecting the names of persons for jury duty. Our study of the record reflects the view that harmony and good will and friendly relations continuously existed between the white and colored races in all other sections of Lake County. All legal rights of the appellants were ably and thoroughly presented in the lower court."[38]

The U.S. Supreme Court soon reversed its Florida counterpart in what several legal scholars described as "a blistering opinion." The *Shepherd* v. *Florida* decision overturned the convictions after determining that the prejudicial atmosphere would have prohibited a fair trial even if African Americans had sat on the jury. Associate Justice Robert Jackson denominated the pretrial publicity as "one of the best examples of one of the worst menaces to American justice. It is hard to imagine a more prejudicial influence than a press release by the officer of the court charged with defendants' custody stating that they had confessed [especially when the statement] unsworn to, uncross-examined and uncontradicted, was conveyed by the press to the jury." Jackson added that he could not understand "how any Negro on the jury would have dared to cause a disagreement or acquittal."[39]

Despite their victory in the U.S. Supreme Court, Shepherd and Irvin faced lethal consequences. In November 1951 Lake County Sheriff Willis McCall shot both of them, killing Shepherd and seriously wounding Irvin. McCall, who originally had intervened to save the defendants from a mob, claimed that the two men had assaulted him and tried to escape his custody while he was changing a flat tire. Irvin in 1953 again appealed to the Supreme Court of Florida asking for a change of trial venue due to community bias in Lake County that prevented the seating of an impartial jury. In *Irvin* v. *State* Justice Thomas declined to order the trial relocation, having rejected a public opinion survey as a basis for determining bias. "Such a trial," Thomas averred, "cannot be expected to be a pure procedural gem."[40]

One additional case also carried significant implications for black, as well as white, defendants in Florida criminal cases. A petition for a writ of habeas corpus arrived at the supreme court in 1953 from a poor, young, uneducated Palm Beach County defendant. Justices Sebring, Roberts, Terrell, and Mathews having delved into the circumstances of the case, Sebring authored an opinion in *Sneed* v. *Mayo* that, in the case of such a defendant when the court record failed to reflect a waiver of jury trial, the writ should be granted, given serious doubts about the legality of the trial.[41]

The Right to Counsel

Increasingly in the postwar years, questions of the right to counsel tested the court. In 1946's *Johnson* v. *Mayo*, a unanimous ruling found no requirement for appointment of counsel in noncapital cases. "We recognize the fact that in a great number of cases in other jurisdictions courts have construed provisions of respective State Constitutions similar to ours to guarantee to a defendant charged with a felony the benefit of counsel," Justice Buford acknowledged. "We are also cognizant of the rule in the Federal Courts, but we are of the view that those decisions do not control in Florida."[42] By the mid-1950s and given a variety of federal court decisions, a shift of sorts could be seen. With Justices Drew, Terrell, and Hobson concurring, Justice Thornal in *Sheffield* v. *State* reaffirmed that a trial court did not have to furnish a noncapital case defendant with counsel, but he added these caveats: *unless* the defendant makes a specific request therefore or *unless* the court determines that the accused is unable to represent himself because of his age or mental state.[43]

Women's Rights

The modern feminist movement had yet to appear on the state or national scene in the late 1940s and early 1950s despite the labor and sacrifices of women in the effort to secure victory during World War II. Rather, the era saw men returning to old jobs as undisputed heads of households and found many women, whether accepting or not, relegated to a homebound life as wife and mother. The court's few decisions during the period that touched upon women's rights seemed to ratify this basic state of affairs. The 1949 case of *Bacom* v. *State*, for example, unanimously reinforced the exclusion of women from juries, finding that their absence did not constitute a denial of due process for a male defendant.[44]

Meanwhile, sexual mores and women's sentiments regarding them remained, in the eyes of many, a subject not appropriate for public consideration. In those circumstances, the panel, with only Justice Terrell's dissent, declined in 1952's *Ripley, et al.* v. *Ewell* to approve a wife's right to recover for loss of consortium. "If we were to adopt the rule asserted by appellant," Circuit Judge Hugh M. Taylor wrote in his capacity as acting associate justice, "all such cases, when the husband was the injured party, and within the statute of limitations, would be reopened." Taylor added, "We should not by judicial fiat make changes in established law that will injuriously affect many persons who could not possibly foresee or anticipate such action on our part."[45]

Workmen's Compensation

The period witnessed the Florida court setting a national precedent in the area of workmen's compensation. In the 1952 decision in *Gray* v. *Employers Mutual Liability Insurance Co., et al.*, Justice Roberts writing for a deeply divided panel—with Justices Thomas, Mathews, and Drew dissenting—permitted an "accident" claim even in the absence of blood, bruises, or broken bones. The decision angered the insurance industry and produced a veritable flood of new workmen's compensation claims. The Florida legislature, though, eventually ratified the decision by statutory enactment, and other states soon followed Florida's lead.[46]

PART FOUR

Change and Reaction, 1955–1964

11

The Civil Rights Era

The second decade following World War II witnessed the continuation and acceleration of trends set in motion in Florida during the previous ten years. Changes that had begun to rock the state after 1945 now reverberated profoundly. As its population swelled seemingly by the day, Florida's social, economic, and political complexities multiplied, although state government remained shackled to past compromises and constraints. Within the state's borders, frustrated racial minorities demanded faster recognition of their rights and needs, and from the outside came waves of refugees that would impress an indelible mark upon its future. For many, the occurrences of the postwar period threatened traditionally held beliefs. Resistance to change accordingly hardened. Sensitivities made themselves heard with stronger voices. A troubled time evolved into a truly turbulent one.

Many portents of what lay ahead for Florida in the second postwar decade evidenced themselves for those who would see them as early as 1954. The state's movement toward the modern world, for instance, found its herald that year at Tampa Bay in the opening of the magnificent Sunshine Skyway. Called by some "the greatest single highway improvement ever created in Florida," the $21 million fifteen-mile span linked, as one commentator noted, "the southern tip of the hitherto dead-end Pinellas peninsula with the Manatee County mainland and a Southwest Florida primed for development." Two years afterward and at President Dwight D. Eisenhower's urging, Congress authorized the interstate highway system, allocating to Florida 1,126 miles of limited access roads. Then other projects such as the Pensacola Bay bridge illustrated anew what technology and an increasingly affluent state could accomplish. The shining promise of the future literally gleamed with the installation of reflectorized colored highway signs and white road markings to guide motorists safely to their destinations.[1]

Where transportation innovations pushed the state forward quickly, politics witnessed the beginnings of a historic struggle between the old Florida and the new. The focal point involved a gubernatorial contest between Acting Governor Charley E. Johns, whose policies and attitudes harkened back to earlier small-state, north Florida ways, and State Senator LeRoy Collins, a World War II veteran determined, as he saw it, to move the state ahead while cleaning up past corruption. The massive flow of new voters into central and south Florida proved the deciding factor. A huge Collins vote in Dade and other urban counties doomed Johns's candidacy and secured the governor's chair for the challenger. "God's will be done," Johns exclaimed. "God's will was that we lose." Collins declared, "Florida stands on the threshold of greatness. Our future is limited only by the range of our vision, the quality of our leadership, and the desire of our people."[2]

The elections of 1954 told another story, one overlooked for the most part in the excitement over the gubernatorial contest. In 1945 no Republicans had served in the state legislature. Two years later, Orange County's Alex Akerman provided the only such representation by claiming a house of representatives seat. Now the Grand Old Party announced its permanent presence as a factor in state and local politics. William Cato Cramer wrested a Tampa Bay area congressional seat away from a Democratic incumbent. As the *Tampa Tribune* later remarked, "In the beginning there was the party, and the party was Bill Cramer." Already, though, Eisenhower had carried the state easily in 1952. With Cramer's help, the president would best his earlier general election poll in 1956. Eight years further on, the party only narrowly would fail to deliver Florida to Barry Goldwater's presidential quest. The same year, an unknown Claude Kirk would take well over one-third of the vote running against popular Democratic senator Spessard Holland. The years ahead certainly seemed to hold tremendous promise for the long-ignored Republicans.[3]

Although their circumstances did not always show such promise, African Americans also intended great strides forward after 1954. In that year, the U.S. Supreme Court inspirited the civil rights movement with its *Brown* v. *Board of Education* decision, which held racially segregated schools to be unconstitutional. The court's 1955 order specifying implementation "with all deliberate speed" dealt immediate integration demands a sharp blow, but the final challenge to lawfully mandated race discrimination had been engaged. During the next decade, marches, boycotts, sit-ins, swim-ins, bloody clashes, and countless other incidents and initiatives kept the cause alive and moving forward. At the same time, white supremacists and others wedded to the status quo fought the civil rights revolution step by step. Whether in legislative halls or on city streets, some whites reacted defiantly to desegregation demands and to the temerity of U.S. courts in backing the calls for change.[4]

Opposition notwithstanding, the civil rights crusade achieved any number of victories. For one thing, it influenced segregationist governor LeRoy Collins to exercise leadership in support of rights advances. A breakthrough came in November 1957, months after integration of Little Rock, Arkansas, schools had resulted in heated racial strife. On that occasion Collins declared to a gathering of southern newspaper publishers, "The disease of racial intolerance is the greatest roadblock in the way of southern progress." He continued, "We must revitalize the simple precepts of Christian love and understanding of one's fellow man in searching for the answer to the racial problem. Screaming abuse at the Supreme Court will avail us nothing."[5]

Among other victories that civil rights workers could claim by the mid-1960s—in addition to the desegregation of countless transit services, lunch counters, beaches, and theaters—was the forging of a breech in the segregationist wall that protected Florida's white public schools. Although virtually all primary and secondary schools remained one race in 1964, the same could not be said of institutions of higher education. With National Association for the Advancement of Colored People attorneys Thurgood Marshall and Constance Baker Motley spearheading a class action lawsuit, federal judge Dozier Devane in June 1958—in a decision hailed by Governor Collins—ordered the University of Florida's graduate programs opened "to all qualified Negroes." Curiously, Devane excluded from his order's protections longtime plaintiff Virgil Hawkins, whom the judge found was "unqualified." Still, on September 15, Orlando's George H. Starke, an Air Force veteran and Morehouse College graduate, desegregated the University of Florida Law School. Undergraduate programs and university housing at the same school first achieved desegregation in 1962, as did undergraduate programs at Florida State University.[6]

Important to these and other civil rights advances was the fact that Florida's activists drew legal support from an increasingly large cadre of dedicated young lawyers, a number of them trained at Florida A&M University's new law school. With leadership from Dean Thomas Miller Jenkins, that educational facility had received Florida Supreme Court accreditation in 1954. It soon attracted talented teachers such as Robert L. Williams, a New York University alumnus, and Leander J. Shaw Jr., a graduate of the Howard University Law School. A score of students had completed its requirements by the early 1960s, with many more swelling classes by middecade. Among them were Bernice Gaines Dorn and Gwendolyn Sawyer Cherry, the first two black women admitted to the Florida Bar. Dorn graduated in 1958 and subsequently taught at FAMU. Cherry followed in 1965 to become Dade County's first black female lawyer and then, in 1970, the state's first black female legislator.[7]

By the mid-1960s, Florida nonetheless remained for the most part a racially segregated society in which color-based tensions boiled openly, yet the time did mark a great dividing point in the civil rights struggle. In January 1964, a federal constitutional amendment—one that had been urged by Florida's Senator Spessard Holland and that outlawed the poll tax—achieved ratification. Sadly, during the following two months a series of bombings, demonstrations, and riots rattled Jacksonville. All the while, festering racial conflict at St. Augustine neared its crisis point. The explosion came in March and succeeding months as the Ancient City erupted in violence. Local and imported white supremacists buttressed the posturing of the Ku Klux Klan and other organizations. Seeking confrontation, these individuals and groups clashed with the NAACP and its agents such as Robert W. Saunders Sr., G. Frank Pinkston, Leander Shaw, and Joseph Hatchett, as well as with Dr. Martin Luther King Jr. and other Southern Christian Leadership Conference members. As television viewers across the nation watched in alarm, pressure built for Congress to act. In July it responded with passage of the Civil Rights Act of 1964, followed in 1965 by approval of the Voting Rights Act. The death knell of legal protections for racial segregation had been sounded.[8]

Meanwhile, housing—while still racially segregated—nonetheless had undergone revolutionary changes of a very different sort. Not only did air conditioning by then keep a large proportion of Floridians chilled against summer's heat but residents had begun to live with concepts of housing that differed greatly from past realities. Following World War II, developer William J. Levitt had turned a Long Island, New York, potato field into the nation's first preplanned suburban community on a grand scale. Levittown set the pattern for Florida to follow. With steady backing from state and local government officials, businessmen such as Leonard and Jack Rosen platted huge, almost self-contained subdivisions and entire communities. The Rosens' Cape Coral development near Fort Myers offered one of many examples, with the Marco Island project of the Mackle brothers' Deltona Corporation providing another. A single new development, Port Charlotte, anticipated that it would house a population by 1965 of fifty thousand people. Tract homes, high-rise condominiums, finger lakes, boating canals, and shopping centers ate up what formerly had been wetlands, prairies, and semitropical forests.[9]

Unrecognized by many at the time, unbridled development was destroying much of what made Florida special for its residents and visitors. Dredged and filled coastal marshes and other wetlands no longer offered extensive habitat for wildlife. Sewage and pesticide runoff tainted the water. Beauty dissolved into dreariness. Discerning critics had seen the environmental disaster looming by the mid-1950s, if not before. Orlando's Campbell Thornal, for one, predicted the fact and the consequence for his profession. "Central Florida is afloat on a cesspool," he informed legal colleagues about the time of his appointment to the Florida Supreme Court in 1955, "and in the long run it will be more important to the lawyers than faculty salaries at Stetson, admissions at Miami, and discrimination at Gainesville." Thornal shot pretty close to the mark.[10]

The waves of immigration that were feeding Florida's development frenzy received added impetus during the late 1950s and early 1960s from two key sources. As to the first, television brought the excitement of Florida to viewers all over the world thanks to the Soviet Union's launch in October and December 1957 of the first two space satellites. Thereafter, eyes turned to Florida's Cape Canaveral where the United States had built its space launch facilities. Actually, the first rocket had taken off from the cape as early as July 24, 1950. Eight months later, the United States answered the Sputniks with Explorer I, causing a media sensation. Six months later, in July 1958, Congress created the National Aeronautics and Space Administration (NASA) to supervise the space program. Its first manned flight, by Alan B. Shepard Jr. on May 5, 1961, guaranteed that, for years to come, the thoughts and curiosity of hundreds of millions would turn to Florida on a regular basis.[11]

The second source of fresh immigration could be traced to Cuba. The revolution of 1959 reignited a longtime pattern of emigration from the island to Florida. Cities such as Key West, Tampa, and Miami had housed Cubans for generations, but Fidel Castro's victory created a tide that one historian described as involving "astonishing numbers." In the early years Dade County would feel the greatest impact, but with time the influx would spread throughout the state. Among other things, the island exodus would transform local cultures and economies in Florida while rewriting the book on state political coalition building.[12]

As all of these factors combined to stir the state, politicians divided bitterly as to what it all meant and what should be done about it. The legislature—dominated by the "Pork Chop Gang" of rural north Florida representatives and senators—tended to resist Governor Collins's leadership while acting to keep central and south Floridians as far from the levers of power as possible. Threatened by civil rights demands and federal court decisions, the body had begun to react by 1957 with a flurry of legislation aimed at stymieing advances if not turning back the clock. An interposition resolution passed by a near unanimous vote that year, as did a measure vetoed by the governor that would have shut down public schools rather than allow them to be integrated. At sessions in 1959, 1961, and 1963, the fury seemed unable to spend itself, as leading political figures such as former governor Millard F. Caldwell urged the solons to greater lengths in an effort to overcome the failings of a legal profession that was not "standing up" against "judicial tyranny."[13]

In the heat of the civil rights battle, the legislature also attempted to extend its reach by creating a powerful and mostly independent investigative committee. Popularly known after its second chairman, onetime acting governor Charley E. Johns, the Johns Committee first targeted the NAACP. The legislators strove unsuccessfully to expose communists within the organization. Then they acted, again without success, to make public NAACP membership rolls and contributor lists. Frustrated in that quest by federal court opposition, the committee subsequently turned its attention to the possibility that communists, homosexuals, and other "undesirables" might be lurking on university campuses. Its publication *Homosexuality and Citizenship in Florida*, popularly known as the "purple pamphlet," eventually embarrassed the committee and the state with its graphic language and photographs. The panel nonetheless survived until the mid-1960s, helping to set a tone of reaction and fear that permeated state politics through the era.[14]

To combat Pork Chop power, Governor Collins pressed for reform in what had become the nation's most malapportioned legislature. "Progress in business, industry, and human welfare can only go so far with a ward-healing, back-scratching, self-promoting political system," he warned. The battles reached the level of the titanic, but Collins left office in 1961 having failed to achieve satisfactory results. The state's political system simply refused to reconfigure the old Florida power-holding formula. In 1962 *Harper's* magazine described the situation. "A place of dazzling contradictions, Florida is moving fast into the ranks of the big-time, urbanized states. Yet its government is still paralyzed by a little clique of backcountry Senators—relics from a smug, sleepy, rural past." That year, though, change proved to be on the way. As it had begun to do frequently, the U.S. Supreme Court acted to correct the failure of local democracy. Its *Baker* v. *Carr* decision established "one man, one vote" as the rule in apportionment of legislative districts. In July, a federal district judge ordered the Florida legislature to redistrict itself by August 13, but the body rejected all plans in a November special session. The mid-1960s would pass without a final resolution of the reapportionment war.[15]

The second postwar decade thus ended amid ongoing racial conflict and political war, and, as it did so, a different kind of philosophy prevailed at the top. By the late 1950s, Governor Collins had become a force for racial peace and correcting legislative abuses, but the state's executive leadership took a turn with his departure in 1961. In line with the continuing conservative political trend that had begun in 1950 and taken on even greater emphasis with the civil rights crusade, a defender of the "old ways" moved into the governor's mansion in 1961. Marion County's C. Farris Bryant, a Harvard Law School graduate and former speaker of the Florida House of Representatives, had bested a crowded Democratic primary field based upon a pledge to "maintain segregation by every honorable and constitutional means." An advocate for Florida's business development and the jobs that it would bring, Bryant stressed an ambitious highway construction program while keeping his anti-integration promise as best he could. During the 1964 campaign his successor, Haydon Burns, followed Bryant's earlier lead. Having earned a reputation as a racial "hardliner" while serving as Jacksonville mayor, Burns easily had established his pro-segregation credentials, taking special pleasure in denouncing the proposed Civil Rights Act of 1964. As governor, Burns would seek to frustrate passage of the Voting Rights Act of 1965. As will be seen, though, by the time Burns and other state politicians next faced the voters, Florida had begun to swing in distinctly new directions. The days of Pork Chop power and one-party rule finally were coming to an end.[16]

12

The Supreme Court, Federal Judicial Activism, and the Civil Rights Era

During the second decade following World War II, the Supreme Court of Florida for the most part experienced stability in its membership but traveled a more challenging road when it came to its reputation for objective decision making and engendering respect for the constitutional system. The era's social and political stresses touched the court as directly as they did the state. Unfortunately, they came at a time when panel members found themselves poorly prepared to respond to them. Under the circumstances, the results sparked the commencement of a process of reassessment by influential court supporters. Little by little, a sense began to evolve among those supporters, as well as among the tribunal's critics, that fundamental changes in Florida's judiciary needed to be recognized as a matter of urgent public policy.

Just as was true of the statewide situation, warnings of the problems to come had sounded as early as 1954. Court members already staggered beneath a growing burden of appeals. Some of the jurists—used to the slower, more relaxed pace of prior days—found themselves frustrated. Tempers sometimes grew frayed. The U.S. Supreme Court's antisegregation decision in *Brown* v. *Board of Education* sparked headlines and heated debates, with many southern political leaders expressing open disdain for the tribunal. Former governor Millard F. Caldwell, for example, labeled the federal justices "Communist."[1] Florida Supreme Court justice Harold L. Sebring, on the other hand, insisted that attorneys live up to their oath to "support the Constitution of the United States." To Miami law school graduates, he warned:

> Reckless and improvident statements that tend to instill in our citizens a contempt for the law, or a mistrust of the judicial exercise of power, will eventually destroy the very source from which such things emanate by destroying the confidence of the people in the free institutions which they have erected. In simple truth, the law was designed and the courts were set up to protect minority elements, whether criminal or law-abiding; to protect the people against themselves and their passions in rash and turbu-

lent moments; to protect the rights and liberties of the people against the encroachment of government which, if improperly extended, might eventually bring about a condition of political tyranny and despotism that would utterly destroy our free institutions.[2]

This type of thinking, which might have received approval from all or most of the Florida court's members a decade earlier, no longer could pass without challenge. The messenger of the tribunal's response proved to be Justice Glenn Terrell. Although considered a "leveling influence on those around him," Terrell, as also was true of several other court members, reeled from the *Brown* decision. It was not that the ruling surprised him, for, as Attorney General Richard W. Ervin recalled, "There had been indications that way." Rather, the aged justice could find no way to accept the thought of such fundamental alteration, being a man who, in Ervin's words, "clung to the Old South views." He simply found himself unable "to reconcile." Though surrounded by sympathetic colleagues, Terrell now found himself tired, upset, and having difficulty maintaining balance.[3]

The moment for Terrell's first response to *Brown* and to Sebring came in November 1954. The occasion concerned the issuance of the majority opinion in a school bond validation action. Having penned the decision, Terrell added dictum—written in an even tone—to the effect that the *Brown* decision was "a great mistake." He went on to comment, "Whether or not the doctrine of 'separate but equal' has a place in the field of public education is a question of policy determinable by the Legislature. It is not a judicial question as I understand the canons of interpretation. Likewise, the question of segregation is for the same reason a legislative rather than a judicial question."[4]

Having effectively resigned judicial authority for constitutional interpretation, Terrell within one year defended segregation publicly and forcefully with a tone grown passionate. The "all deliberate speed" implementation decision for *Brown* had been released, and the desegregation issue had become ever more contentious for the court because in October 1955 the specific case at hand involved the University of Florida's Law School. Justice Sebring with Justice Thomas's concurrence demanded an immediate integration order. A court majority of five recognized the *Brown* decisions as "the law of the land" but temporized as to timing. Terrell concurred but, in doing so, took his prose to unfortunate places. First the jurist insisted that segregation "is and has always been the unvarying law of the animal kingdom." He then commented, "When God created man, he allotted each race to his own continent, according to color: Europe to the white man, Asia to the yellow man, Africa to the black man, and America to the red man, but we are now advised that God was in error and must be reversed." Terrell thereupon bluntly criticized the U.S. Supreme Court for revisiting prior rulings on the issue, even though the justice in earlier years himself had discounted the importance of *stare decisis*. He then argued that the federal jurists were meddling "in the face of the fact that there is no agitation for the change, the whites and Negroes are as a rule satisfied with what they have and have made remarkable progress with it."[5]

As Governor LeRoy Collins and Attorney General Ervin were attempting to calm public reaction to the *Brown* decisions, Terrell's statements instead fanned emotions within and outside the supreme court. Beloved by many members of the state's legal profession, Terrell—with his immense influence—essentially had committed the court to a course from which it would find it impossible to backtrack so long as he remained on the bench. That commitment came with a price. For one thing, it seemed to place the panel again in the position of appearing to be a "political court." Matters in that regard took a turn for the worse when Sumter County residents—Justice Terrell's home folks—tried to launch a Terrell-for-governor campaign for this "ardent foe of racial mixture in public schools." The court also paid a price in the minds of lawyers disappointed by the intemperate tone of Terrell's statements. Their numbers, seemingly few if judged by local criticism, primarily centered in Dade County. There, the *Miami Law Quarterly* gently rebuked Terrell by reprinting Justice Sebring's cautionary remarks "because of the significance of his address, both to law students and to attorneys in these times." As will be seen, the number of disaffected attorneys began to grow.[6]

As this sense of unease slowly circulated through at least some segments of the state bar, rumors of another court problem also began to find a few receptive ears. Earlier in the decade Justice B. K. Roberts's close connections with Governor Fuller Warren and with powerful businessmen such as Ed Ball had given rise to vague fears that *ex parte* communications might be influencing the court or, at least, one or more of its members. A troubled Justice Alto Adams warned his friend Roberts to take care. "Decide what is right, then go ahead," Adams directed Roberts, "and don't ever surrender your judicial independence to any person or because of any outside influence." Still, Roberts's public friendships with Ball, Warren, and others kept the rumors at play whether or not they contained elements of truth. As one leading attorney put it, "If one party [to an appeal before the supreme court] was an Ed Ball corporation, then look out."[7]

Paralleling the tribunal's purported acceptance of a more political role in the late 1950s and early 1960s, the rumors about *ex parte* communications multiplied. "Over time, the court's image changed," one practitioner recalled. "You always knew some lawyers fared better than other lawyers." Another appeals specialist recollected his frustration at a loss before the court as the new decade began. The court's rationale in his case did not make sense to him. Matters clarified, he related, only when "I learned later that opposing counsel had discussed the matter with the justice who wrote the opinion."[8]

Even if the rumors rested on no firm foundation, they posed a serious enough dilemma to attract attention from some court members and other influential opinion makers. Justice Campbell Thornal, for one, expressed concerns "about the court and its reputation" to close relatives and friends. Of the problem, one of those individuals observed, "Yes, I think he was aware of it. I think everybody in the state was aware of it." Some political reporters smelled smoke even if they did not find fire, and Justice Roberts was a focus for their attention.[9]

Interestingly and of importance to the future, the influence of Justice Terrell's court leadership declined after his expressions following the *Brown* decision while that of Justice Roberts increased. By the early 1960s Roberts, more than any other member, dominated the panel. "During the last fifteen years of his tenure on the Florida Supreme Court, because of seniority, changes in personnel of the Court, his recognized judicial ability, personal magnetism, and pervasive influence," Richard W. Ervin recorded, "he was able to command a majority vote for his views in practically every case in which he participated." Thus empowered, Roberts would help to set the tribunal's tone and guide its direction until 1976. His skillful leadership often served the state and its people well. Yet a lack of sensitivity to avoiding the appearance of impropriety, particularly when it came to *ex parte* communications, unfortunately produced seeds that later would bear bitter fruit for the court.[10]

Despite his many successes as the panel's leading member, at least until the mid-1960s one area of affairs confounded Roberts as he set about influencing court direction. This domain involved the single question that personally divided the panel most deeply, that of jurisdiction. It will be recalled that Florida's voters in 1956 had approved a constitutional amendment creating district courts of appeals. Its provisions limited supreme court jurisdiction after July 1, 1957, and specified any number of matters of which the courts of appeals would have final say except under specified circumstances. Barring conflict between two district courts, the supreme court could exercise little corrective control when a lower appeals court decided a question in any manner at odds with the supreme tribunal's majority. Justice Roberts especially chafed when such a decision appeared to him to stray from a pro-business position and often urged interpretations that would expand the supreme court's review authority.[11]

Roberts's problem stemmed from the fact that at least four of his colleagues were united to deny any review that lessened the impact of the constitutional amendment's delegation of jurisdiction to the district courts of appeal. Justice Elwyn Thomas had chaired the Florida Judicial Council while that body drafted the court of appeals plan. Justice E. Harris Drew had worked closely with Thomas, as had Thomas's friend LeRoy Collins. Collins's two court appointees—Campbell Thornal and Stephen C. O'Connell—shared his and Thomas's concern for the continuing integrity of the reforms. O'Connell's role strengthened in 1957 when he succeeded Thomas as judicial council chairman. So long as these four men stood together, the combined weight of Justices Roberts, Terrell, and (sometimes) T. Frank Hobson seemingly could not turn back the reform clock.[12]

With Governor C. Farris Bryant's 1961 inauguration, circumstances slowly began to change. The judicial council, with O'Connell's leadership, had been planning a major reorganization that would have remodeled a hodgepodge of a dozen or more different kinds of courts in various Florida counties into a statewide four-tier court system. Council initiatives had received Governor Collins's strong backing in the past, but now Governor Bryant stood aloof. Into the vacuum thus formed stepped legislators determined to kill the reforms and the judicial council, asserting that they did so at the behest of the state's circuit judges. The legislative ambush succeeded. The reforms died aborning, and the council found itself without funding. O'Connell resigned his chairmanship in quiet protest upon the legislature's adjournment.[13]

While the judicial council survived the 1961 legislative session, it did so as a changed organization. Governor Bryant designated Chief Justice Roberts as its new chairman, but the funding problem slowed the group's reorganization for one year. Roberts's willingness to serve nonetheless drew praise. As Tampa's John Germany explained, "B. K. continued it when others would have let it go." Even Roberts's vaunted energy, though, could not quickly revive the council's influence or ambitions. He managed with council backing to obtain legislative approval in 1962 for a public defender program for indigent persons accused of felonies, but the council would not for the time being present any broader-based reforms. By late 1963 Justice O'Connell had decided to speak out. He told Floridians that they could "take pride in the job being done by their judicial system but [that] they have no right to be proud of its organization." He called for "a better method" for judicial selection than partisan elections, noting that "the present method does not guarantee that the best qualified candidate will win." The next year Roberts joined in the call for nonpartisan selection of judges and nonpolitical disciplinary processes. The judicial council backed the initiatives, but the second postwar decade concluded without legislative action.[14]

Governor Bryant's arrival in office affected the court in other ways as well. His use of the gubernatorial appointment powers noticeably changed the panel's public and professional image. Justice T. Frank Hobson's health had waxed and waned for years. By February 1962 he felt compelled to resign. Bryant immediately designated former governor Millard Caldwell to fill the vacancy. The act sent a political message loudly and clearly. During the 1950s Caldwell had emerged as one of the state's most vocal defenders of the status quo. Beginning in 1957 he had served as chairman of the pro-segregation, white supremacist Florida Commission on Constitutional Government, a body sometimes referred to as a "state agency" that was sending financial contributions out of state to block civil rights legislation as late as 1964. The onetime governor had come to loathe his successor, LeRoy Collins, and Collins's moderate civil rights stances. Accordingly, the new justice had labored long on behalf of Bryant's candidacy in a bid to secure a different philosophy in the governor's chair. "Caldwell is strictly conservative," reported state newspapers of the appointment, "and has been an outspoken critic of the U.S. Supreme Court."[15]

As chance would have it, within one month of Caldwell's appointment, the U.S. Supreme Court began issuing a series of rulings that were sure to infuriate Caldwell. In March 1962 the tribunal held in *Baker* v. *Carr* that state legislatures must comply with a "one man, one vote" principle. Among many other decisions, it ruled within the next thirty months that prayer and Bible readings in public schools were unconstitutional; in the Florida case of *Gideon* v. *Wainwright*, that felony defendants had a right to appointed counsel; that the state of Florida improperly had convicted Father Theodore Gibson, an NAACP activist targeted by the legislature's Johns Committee; and that its "one man, one vote" decision applied even to the center of conservative power in Florida, the state senate.[16]

Many of the federal decisions angered some members of the Florida Supreme Court, who repeatedly saw their own opinions overturned. More than any other justice, though, Millard Caldwell felt a responsibility to share his outrage with the public. To cite one example, in December 1963, according to a newspaperman, he "flayed" the U.S. Supreme Court in a Jacksonville address. The following February the jurist declared that the federal court "had destroyed the rule of law and substituted the rule of man." The civil rights act then pending before the Congress, he insisted, was "blatant but understandable political sophistry," the purpose of which was to "lead the sheep to the pen for a shearing." Soon he condemned to the Florida Bar's annual gathering "the effete establishment which for some years [has] dominated national affairs." He also informed his audience that "our Republic has, in a major sense, been converted to a collectivist sort of principality over which we, as citizens, have lost control."[17]

Caldwell's public pronouncements found many thousands of receptive ears at a time when conservative Republican presidential candidate Barry Goldwater hoped to sweep the South, but his attacks on the U.S. Supreme Court quickly accelerated to an untenable point. That position arrived in September 1964. The

Florida tribunal was hearing an appeal related to legislative apportionment when Tampa attorney W. Reece Smith pointed out that "the Florida court had always been bound by decisions of the federal tribunal." Caldwell thereupon demanded to know by what authority "you say a supreme court decision is the law of the land." Justice Roberts supported his colleague by asserting that "the U.S. Constitution makes no reference to Supreme Court decisions being the law of the land." Smith and many other Florida lawyers reacted with dismay at the assertions. "I was surprised to hear my Florida Supreme Court, which I held in awe, saying this," Smith remembered. "The electioneering, the speech making, the negative politicking were degrading the bench and the bar that we were devoted to."[18]

Caldwell's tone and questioning of U.S. Supreme Court authority in Florida offered the state's increasingly sophisticated voters a portrait of a court that had drifted away from its proper moorings. Even the *University of Florida Law Review* joined the small but growing circle of its critics. "Apparently the Supreme Court of Florida is saying," the journal declared in 1964 of a series of decisions, "that if the plaintiffs wish to have their civil rights determined they must go to the federal courts. This is strange language from those who most loudly profess a desire to minimize federal intervention." A hardening attitude about precedent and "the sound rule of *stare decisis*" had led the court into a collective state of mind that resembled a siege mentality. From that intellectual vantage point, its members simply could reject the "distorted interpretations" of the national judiciary. That circumstance, in turn, had permitted federal courts to assume control of many jurisprudential matters that impacted directly upon Florida and Floridians. The state would never be the same.[19]

Actually, the state and the court already had begun to change by the time of Justice Caldwell's September 1964 address. Just as Barry Goldwater narrowly would fail to carry the state in November, the whispers of a slightly different trend had begun to sound earlier in the year. Federal courts had set the stage for the breaking of Pork Chop power in the legislature and also had ordered enforcement of civil rights laws at troubled St. Augustine. For the court, the fact that an era had passed had been symbolized back in January with the sudden death of Justice Glenn Terrell. As an obituary properly noted, "The bench will hardly see his like again." Then Governor Bryant surprised the state by appointing Attorney General Richard W. Ervin to the court. Of distinctly less traditional leanings than any of his fellow justices, Ervin had not received the designation because the governor desired him on the supreme bench. Rather, Bryant sought a more amenable attorney general in the person of his young protégé, former University of Florida football star James W. Kynes. Still, a different voice now joined tribunal debates, and any sense of comfortable unanimity among the justices soon became a thing of the past. Winds of change had begun to blow.[20]

Millard Fillmore Caldwell, Supreme Court Justice, 1962–1969; Supreme Court Chief Justice, 1967–1969

Millard Fillmore Caldwell's 1962 appointment to the Florida Supreme Court stood in contrast to those of his immediate three predecessors, E. Harris Drew, Campbell Thornal, and Stephen C. O'Connell. Since their designations in 1952 and 1955, the cold war, the civil rights movement, and federal court decisions had revolutionized Florida's legal and political landscapes. By the early 1960s a state that had prided itself on its political moderation had polarized, a transformation that had ushered in an era of conservative dominance of state affairs. As exemplified by Governor Farris Bryant's 1960 election, political views now ranked higher in priority as a criteria for public office than the pragmatic professionalism and reformist political instincts evidenced by Drew, Thornal, and O'Connell. Further, where these three men each represented a tale of a talented but poor young man who had struggled in south Florida to emerge into a position to offer contributions through public service, Caldwell harkened back to the days when wealthy middle and west Florida planters pursued the law as a kind of noblesse oblige. Not since Justice John E. Mathews's appointment in 1951 had the court welcomed such an individual.

Millard F. Caldwell began life on a plantation. The event occurred at Beverly near Knoxville, Tennessee, on February 6, 1897. His parents, Millard F. Caldwell Sr. and Martha Jane Clapp Caldwell, traced their ancestry through distinguished southern lines. Caldwell Sr. owned farms and cotton plantations in various parts of the South and Southwest. He also wrote, practiced law, and edited a literary magazine. He preferred, nonetheless, the bucolic life. Young Millard's early education thus came in a rural three-room schoolhouse to and from which he walked one mile each day. Although as an adult he preferred not to identify with any church or denomination, the lad received Presbyterian instruction. Caldwell Sr. also took an active part in his son's preparation for life. He declined using corporal punishment, for instance, in favor of discussion and reasoning. Young Millard's life was not a stable one, though, as his father shifted the family from his properties in Tennessee to ones in Texas, Arkansas, California, Virginia, and Louisiana.[21]

Millard Jr. broke out of the family orbit in order to pursue higher education. During 1914–15 he attended Tennessee's Carson-Newman College where he excelled in football and baseball. He evidenced there a fighting spirit, if not a degree of hotheadedness. An illustration occurred when a melee broke out at the end of a game with Maryville College. The fight, with Caldwell front and center, moved from the field, through the gymnasium, and all the way to the train station where Caldwell and his cohorts finally made their escape. Likely upon the faculty's recommendation, Millard soon returned to his family. He remained with them for two years before continuing his studies at the University of Mississippi in 1917. Now tennis, track, and basketball joined football and baseball to occupy his time and interest. Still, a year at school once again sufficed before Caldwell moved on.[22]

This time the young man attempted to serve his country before again pursuing education. The United States had entered World War I, and Caldwell enlisted. At Jefferson Barracks, Missouri, authorities offered him the chance to play baseball or draw kitchen police duties. He opted for baseball, which soon opened the door to officer training. Commission in hand, Caldwell then served in various capacities at Camp Taylor, Kentucky, and Columbia, South Carolina. By discharge time in 1919, he carried the rank of second lieutenant of field artillery. Caldwell returned to civilian life by enrolling in the University of Virginia. He attended some classes in 1919, 1921, and 1922 before taking the Tennessee bar exam. He passed the test but chose to engage in Mississippi cotton planting.[23]

Caldwell's life and subsequent Florida history changed in 1924. As he explained it, "The price of cotton went down and taxes went up." So he and his father endured the travails of driving through north Florida to examine land Caldwell Sr. owned in Santa Rosa County. At Milton, his father introduced him to former state senator and judge Sheppard Walter Clark, who offered to take the young man in as a partner. Anxious for an alternative to cotton planting, Millard agreed and quickly returned to settle. The new arrival achieved Florida Bar admission in 1925. Within one year he had set up his own practice based upon retainers as Milton town attorney, Santa Rosa County attorney, Santa Rosa School Board attorney, and counsel to the First National Bank of Milton. In record time, Caldwell advanced to the front ranks of local professionals and began to enjoy financial security despite the plunge Florida's economy had taken in the 1926 bust.[24]

Healthy professional prospects soon permitted Caldwell to marry. He had known Mary Rebecca Harwood, the daughter of Joseph Walter and Sallie Jones Purkins Harwood, before World War I when his family had enjoyed several years' stay at a plantation across Virginia's Rappahannock River from the Harwood estate. Young though they were, Millard would wait after school to walk Mary home over an ancient, rickety bridge. Once the Caldwells moved away, the young people kept in touch, plus Millard would return to the area in the summers. Meanwhile,

Mary attended Mary Washington College and became a teacher. She remained, as one account described, "gracious and charming, with a great deal of poise." By the early 1920s she had become Virginia's first female county school superintendent. It was thus no ordinary young woman to whom Millard Caldwell proposed in late 1924. Following their February 14, 1925, wedding at Saluda, Virginia, she would teach and eventually serve as a home demonstration agent in Santa Rosa County. They would have three children together: Millard Fillmore III in 1926, Sally Purkins in 1928, and Susan Beverly in 1929.[25]

Caldwell launched himself into politics a few years after the marriage and, in doing so, proved soon enough to be a man of his own thinking. "I was practicing law in Milton in 1928 and ran for the Legislature just for the fun of getting some things off my mind," he recalled. "I made everybody mad and got elected." Caldwell refused to engage in "back-slapping" and "baby kissing." He declined to spend funds other than his own. He believed that he could get votes whether people agreed with him or not; candor, he felt, meant far more to most people than expedient political conformity. Once in office, he reveled in the legislative experience, later asserting that, of all his political offices, it was "the most fun." His approach to campaigning remained unchanged as he battled for the interests of west Florida's underpopulated counties against urban legislators such as Duval County's John E. Mathews. "I was an obstructionist and that probably isn't good," he remembered, "but all my efforts were against serious wrongs and I loved the fights." So effectively did he fight his battles that, in the small county-dominated house, he presided by 1931 over the important rules committee.[26]

After two legislative sessions, the state solon chose not to seek reelection, but his plans, somewhat redirected, soon changed. On the spur of the moment in 1932, he opted to run for a vacant congressional seat that extended through much of north Florida's panhandle. His reasons for making the race have remained a mystery. "I didn't want to go to Congress and when I got there, I didn't want to stay." Yet go to Congress he did, continuing along the way his own personal style of electioneering and officeholding. His friend Congressman Bob Sikes admired the fact that Caldwell was "the most independent successful politician I have ever known. Usually that kind doesn't last. Millard was an exception."[27]

In four terms lasting from 1933 to 1941, Caldwell came to exercise substantial congressional influence, although the conservative Democrat opposed many of President Franklin D. Roosevelt's New Deal programs. Thanks partly to the intercession of school friends such as Sam Rayburn and Joe Byrnes, he gained a place on the powerful House Appropriations Committee, the first of Florida's representatives to do so, as well as one on the prestigious Foreign Affairs Committee. Among his positive accomplishments, he expressed concern over protection of forest resources. He arranged for the cut-over West Florida lands of the Bagdad Land and Lumber Co. to be designated a national forest, an act that led to the Blackwater River State Forest's creation. But world affairs occupied his central focus. He feared European and Asian developments, railing against isolationists in heated calls for military preparedness. The congressman paid from his own funds to tour Germany "to see what made Mr. Hitler tick." He also spurred transfer of the Choctawhatchee National Forest to the U.S. Army, preparing the groundwork for the eventual creation of Eglin Air Force Base. Still, Caldwell chafed at Washington life and "liberal" politicians. After his son died in a District of Columbia automobile accident in 1939, his departure from Congress became only a matter of time. In 1941 he, Mary, and their two girls returned to north Florida. They settled at an historic 800-acre plantation near Tallahassee that he named Harwood.[28]

Rejected for World War II military service, the retired congressman took on another political task. In 1944 friends, including Jacksonville financier Ed Ball, approached him to run for governor. They feared that someone who advocated New Deal–type reforms might seize state government control. The former congressman agreed to run provided that the friends raised necessary campaign funds. "I do not to this day really know who contributed the money to that campaign," he asserted a quarter century later. As a candidate he declared: "My appeal will be based on ability and fitness for the job without emotional and political leapfrogging. Government must be simplified and brought back to the people in Florida." He continued, "I will not swap promises for votes." Following a tumultuous campaign, Caldwell clinched the office in a spirited Democratic primary runoff.[29]

Governor Caldwell's administration (1945–49) recorded several substantive accomplishments. Though a dedicated conservative with longtime north Florida ties, he pushed hard for fairer legislative apportionment, as well as for flood control, water conservation, and state mental hospital reforms. Advances in the field of education probably showed him at his best. "He revolutionized public education in Florida," concluded historian William Warren Rogers. "Although he had many critics as an ultraconservative, he was on education ahead of his time and a pioneer among southern governors in the area." The Minimum Foundation Program and the Southern Regional Education Board stood as memorials to his efforts. Critic John Egerton assessed Caldwell's approach, by comparison with Georgia governors Ellis Arnall and Eugene Talmadge, as "stick[ing] somewhere in the middle between Arnallian reformism and Talmadgeite reaction." Egerton noted that Caldwell refused to join the rightist Dixiecrat Party in 1948.[30]

Out of the governor's mansion in 1949, Caldwell stayed in the public eye. While spurning entreaties by Ed Ball and others to contest Claude Pepper's highly vulnerable Senate seat in 1950, he served at President Harry S. Truman's request as first director of the Federal Civil Defense Agency. He later insisted that he did so only after an arm-twisting poker game with Sam Rayburn and Senator Lyndon B. Johnson. The experience, as it turned out, heightened Caldwell's distaste for Washington and his concern at the threat posed by international communism. Back in Florida after 1952, the onetime governor emerged as a strong anticommunist voice, spreading alarm also at what he termed *internal dangers*. Here Caldwell pointed to "the pampering and protection of Communists by the Supreme Court and Federal Courts." He added, "The most dangerous thing that has happened in this country is the encroachment by the Supreme Court into the executive and legislative branches—and the usurpation by the court of rights which the Constitution reserved to the states." Caldwell concluded, "We are now living in the first years of a judicial tyranny."[31]

Caldwell backed his rhetoric with political action, a step that led to his supreme court appointment. He looked with stern disfavor on many of Governor LeRoy Collins's policies and hoped to ensure that such policies would not be pursued by the next governor. In 1960, he endeavored with his law partners Leo L. Foster and Julius F. Parker Sr. to raise funds and seek support for conservative Farris Bryant for governor. Then, when Justice T. Frank Hobson resigned in February 1962, Governor Bryant immediately turned to his mentor and friend. Although already sixty-five years of age, Caldwell quickly accepted the court appointment. He took the oath before "a crowded courtroom" on February 14.[32]

Because of mandatory retirement requirements, Justice Caldwell would be limited to only one full term on the supreme court. As he had as governor, he approached his work in a relaxed manner. "He prided himself on the fact that most of his opinions were one page," Justice Stephen C. O'Connell recalled. The justice would inform those who questioned his schedule, "If you can't make a living practicing law from nine to noon and two to five, you shouldn't be a lawyer." His Rolls-Royce became a common sight as it whisked the governor—everyone still called him "Governor"—to lunch at the Capital City Country Club. Yet Caldwell occupied a central position on the court and in the politics of the day. He continued to speak out as an anticommunist and a believer in the destructive force of federal court activism. "I don't really think he was much of a judge," one conservative admirer declared, "but I loved him." As longtime secretary of state R. A. Gray put it, "He was firm and expressed his views without hesitation."[33]

Once retired from the bench in early 1969, Caldwell resumed his former law practice and personal interests at Tallahassee. As a professional associate explained, "His life was long and full." He lived into his eighty-seventh year, passing away at Tallahassee on October 23, 1984. On that occasion, the *Miami Herald* joined other newspapers and individuals in praising him. Acknowledging that Caldwell had "served capably as a justice of the Florida Supreme Court," the editorial continued: "He laid the foundation that enabled subsequent leaders to build a modern system of education. In doing so, he secured for himself a lasting place in Florida's history." Mary Harwood Caldwell followed her husband within less than two years. Her death came at Harwood Plantation on February 24, 1986.[34]

Richard William Ervin, Supreme Court Justice, 1964–1975; Supreme Court Chief Justice, 1969–1971

When it comes to the back-to-back supreme court appointments of Millard F. Caldwell and Richard W. Ervin, it remains remarkable that so great a difference could result from two designations by the same governor. The circumstances were these. In 1962 Farris Bryant had desired to place a strong conservative voice on the state panel in the person of his mentor Caldwell. Two years afterward he similarly desired to install a strong conservative in office, but this time the position already was occupied by Attorney General Ervin. So Bryant offered Ervin the chance to interpret—rather than enforce—the law. Ervin accepted. Of dramatically different background and temperament from Caldwell, Ervin in the succeeding thirteen years would bring a dissenting voice to a mostly conservative court and he would live to see many of his dissents emerge as the law of the land. Some called him "the justice for the underdog."[35]

Justice Ervin's family story varied markedly from that of Justice Caldwell. Instead of a plantation birth and upbringing, Ervin came into the world breathing the humbler atmosphere of the isolated Gulf fishing village of Carrabelle, located in Franklin County southwest of Tallahassee. Twenty miles northeast lay Justice B. K. Roberts's hometown of Sopchoppy, a fact of more than passing interest, since the two men would be linked through friendship, politics, and court service. Ervin's birth preceded Roberts's by almost two years, coming on January 26, 1905. Father Richard W. Ervin Sr., a high school principal, came from Marion County pioneer stock, spending his boyhood at Moss Bluff. Mother Carolyn Marvin Phillips Ervin also derived from a Marion County family. She had met and married Richard Sr. while she was teaching and he was acting as principal of the county's Fellowship school.[36]

What Caldwell and Ervin shared was a peripatetic childhood. Always seeking better professional opportunities, Richard Sr. moved the family from Carrabelle to Weirsdale, then on to Green Cove Springs, Hudson, Crystal River, Fellowship, and Winter Garden. In 1919 Richard Jr. accepted an invitation to attend ninth grade at Arcadia High School while living with his aunt Jessie Stuart and family near DeSoto County's Fort Ogden, but the youth's less-than-strict reverence for Bible reading saw him soon returned to Fellowship. In 1921 Richard Sr. took a job with state government at Tallahassee, the first of two key positions that he would hold. His son enrolled at Leon High School, where he graduated in 1922. To the extent that he claimed a hometown, it was Fellowship. "All we had was a three-teacher school, a Woodman of the World lodge, and a Baptist church," he recalled. "But they were good people there." Whatever place he called home, Ervin had spent his youth seeing and experiencing much of Florida. He would not forget the lessons or the contacts, as his future career would illustrate.[37]

Although others also made a difference in the young man's life, the greatest influence came from his father. "An energetic, optimistic individual," Richard Sr. could not accomplish the professional goals to which he had aspired but desired more for his eldest son (for that matter, for all of his children). "You'll have to hit the road and make a dollar," he told Richard Jr. He also opened the door to higher education. At Florida State College for Women teacher-training schools, Richard Sr. had come to know the college's president, A. A. Murphree, who had moved on to the University of Florida's presidency in 1909. Thirteen years later, Richard Sr. took his son to see Murphree, who steered the lad toward the university's law program. Ervin admitted that he was "not an exceptional student," but he fared well. The affable fellow made numerous enduring friendships. One of them was with B. K. Roberts, with whom he roomed his senior year. Among the professors who caught Ervin's imagination at the University of Florida was Robert Spratt Cockrell. The "thin emaciated" former Florida supreme court justice appeared "wizened" to his student. Still, Cockrell opened Ervin's ears and eyes, using ribald jokes and stories "quite shocking to middle-class morality Baptist students in the class."[38]

Exposure to the challenges of college life and professors such as Cockrell produced profound changes in young Ervin's attitudes about the world around him, with telling significance for the future. "I've always somehow or another been living in the present as it occurred," he explained to interviewer Russell Troutman. Ervin went on to mention his pride in the fact that "both my grandfathers served as Confederates during the Civil War." He noted that his childhood world rested not too distant from that past. Regarding Tallahassee as he first saw it, for example, Ervin recalled, "I used to see Judge [Robert Fenwick] Taylor coming and going in that [old-style horse and] buggy." Still, the future justice came to see things differently than did many of his contemporaries. A self-proclaimed "product of southern culture," he asserted nonetheless, "Well, in a way, maybe I deviated from it. I thought after I had been through college that we, the South, had made a great mistake by rebelling. It was emotional and not thought out, and bad, of course, for the people of all the United States. I decided for my career that I was going to try to be a true United States citizen."[39]

It took until 1928 for Ervin to graduate from law school because financial concerns forced time out for work. Whenever the legislature was in session, for example, he served as engrossing clerk for the Florida House of Representatives. His father first had helped him to obtain the elective position in 1921 at age sixteen. Numerous other part-time jobs filled in the monetary gap. He labored on farms and road construction projects. He helped staff a laundry. In the summer of 1922 he found a job in the courthouse at Bristol. The following two summers he joined a survey crew that was laying out routes for Everglades drainage canals. His network of contacts grew all the while.[40]

If Ervin's childhood saw repeated movement, so too did his early legal career. In a state already mired in economic depression, his first employment—with Clearwater's Charles Ware—lasted only five months. Soon he was off to Fort Myers and then to Palatka. In the latter town, he eventually found a place in the state attorney's office. That job lasted until 1935 when he transferred to the state road department as a right-of-way attorney. The change returned him to Tallahassee. By 1939 Ervin's responsibilities had expanded to include those of counsel for the Overseas Road and Toll Bridge District and first attorney for the Florida Department of Public Safety. He accepted the position of assistant attorney general under J. Tom Watson in August 1943 and served there until January 1, 1945. After six months as secretary for the Florida Railroad Commission, he then returned as counsel to the state road department. These experiences once again stretched his web of friendships, one that had come to include road and bridge contractors as well as county commissioners. The proximity to Watson, who allowed Ervin to attend cabinet meetings with him, also worked its effect on the maturing lawyer's life and career. He came to know all the state's leading political figures. Beyond that, the colorful attorney general's personality offered a model. "His forthrightness may have had some impact upon me," Ervin acknowledged.[41]

Mention should be made, before pressing further along in the future justice's professional life, of two important happenings during his Palatka stay. For one thing, Ervin met and, on November 23, 1933, married Frances Blois Baker of Jacksonville. Her mother was Frances Seton Blois Baker, and her father was banker James M. Baker, known around Jacksonville as "Gentleman Jim." Welcomed into the Baker family, Ervin would find that their connections would assist greatly in furthering his legal and political careers. The couple would have two children: Richard William Ervin III, born October 16, 1934, and Sarah Eve Ervin, born December 13, 1944. While Ervin maintained a lifelong connection with the Baptist Church, his wife and children adhered to the Presbyterian.[42]

Also at Palatka, Ervin delved deeply for the first time into state and national politics. The 1928 elections were the first significant ones since he turned twenty-one in 1926. "As a lawyer in Palatka, I was for Al Smith and [later for] the New Deal and against the Ku Klux Klan," he recollected. He considered himself a "liberal" and admired individuals with "social conscience." His father's influence, his own experiences, and the poverty all around him resulting from Florida's 1926 crash stirred his feelings that government should serve "that poor devil in trouble, the underdog." Stated another way, he felt that "government's highest calling was to improve the human condition." Ervin wholeheartedly embraced President Franklin D. Roosevelt's initiatives and supported with enthusiasm his friend Claude Pepper. To a civic club in 1951, he attempted to explain a part of his philosophy. "We must pay more than lip service to our Bill of Rights. We can obtain peace if we are fair, tolerant, patient, enlightened, and good citizens."[43]

Having become one of the state's most traveled and best known public employees, Ervin rode the wave of postwar desire for the leadership of a younger generation into the attorney general's office. He could thank J. Tom Watson (who had decided to run for governor), his family, and his many friends. "I never would have run for attorney general if it had not been for Papa's insistence," he recorded. "I really thought my background as a state government attorney was not enough to qualify me as the state's chief legal officer." His brother Robert, back home from World War II service in the Marine Corps and just admitted to the Florida Bar, served as campaign manager. Having ranged throughout the state pressing flesh, renewing old acquaintances, and making new ones, Ervin led a field of four in the Democratic primary before besting runoff opponent L. Grady Burton to win election. Reelection campaigns in 1952, 1956, and 1960 either saw Ervin unopposed or else an easy winner.[44]

During fifteen years as head of Florida's Law Department, Ervin energized its staff and greatly expanded its fields of endeavor. His office began continuous statutory revision and professionalized the legislative bill drafting service. He pressed for consumer protection programs, openness in government, and conservation laws. "The legislature said I was a wild man," he boasted. He and his staff handled thousands of criminal appeals and issued volumes of legal opinions, including ones to the effect that African Americans could not be excluded as jurors (1950) and that no Florida law barred hotels and motels from accommodating African Americans (1956). He also battled crime, especially illegal gambling, by setting up the Anti-Bookie Anti–Organized Crime Vice Squad. "By the time I reached the attorney general's office in February of 1952," remembered Justice Ben C. Overton, "General Ervin, in three short years, had established a reputation for the office as a truly fair and objective legal advisor to state government and multiple public officials throughout the state. He made sure that his office was staffed with senior assistants of integrity and outstanding legal ability in their respective fields." As to Ervin's role in state government, LeRoy Collins commented: "Dick Ervin as a cabinet member was a man possessed by great ideas, and his whole life has revolved around them."[45]

When it came to civil rights and racial integration, Ervin's record, while respectable in light of actions by his colleagues in other southern states, dims somewhat. On the positive side, he fought efforts to close public schools after the U.S. Supreme Court ordered desegregation in the mid-1950s. "Some of the state's most prominent lawyers wrote us that we should tell the Supreme Court to go to hell," he noted. He did not advocate racial integration. Instead, the attorney general helped to author Florida's program of "gradualism," which the federal court adopted in essence in 1955. Following a segregationist challenge in the 1956 elections, he backtracked somewhat by proposing laws to prevent integration. Still, he would be remembered by many Floridians along with Governor LeRoy Collins as an apostle of moderation. "Mr. Ervin rejected the emotional and demagogic tactics of some other Southern officials and presented temperate, well-reasoned defenses of the state's position," asserted the *Tampa Tribune*. "His sound advice was an important influence in dousing fiery legislation which could have shut down public schools."[46]

By 1964 Richard Ervin's continuance as attorney general seemed assured, but Governor Farris Bryant desired a less independent voice as the state's chief lawyer. Preliminary discussions ensued between the two officials, but Ervin learned that Bryant had appointed him to the supreme court by way of a newspaperman. "I wanted the working man, the little man to get his day in court," Ervin offered as explanation of his decision to accept the seat. One major newspaper headed its editorial on the exchange with the words "Court Gains, Cabinet Loses."[47]

Justice Ervin took the court's oath of office on January 17, 1964, but the tribunal he found left him feeling somewhat the odd man out. "I finally decided after a few months that if I was going to be my own man, I just had to go ahead and disagree." Within two years a University of Florida study would place him alone on the court's moderate-to-left side, with Justice Caldwell firmly anchoring the right. "I found out very soon that some of the judges had special interests. Some favored business, some of them didn't particularly care to take on and decide momentous questions affecting rights, civil rights, and the like, that was just not a part of their tradition." In the atmosphere, Ervin quickly fell to work. He would pen in excess of 600 majority opinions during the following eleven years. His 220 written minority opinions brought him the title "dissenter." Although he was inclined to side with any state regulatory agency against the individual, for instance, in other circumstances Ervin preferred individual right over rights of the community. Most famously, he eventually came to oppose the death penalty, believing that "even for the most heinous crime, governmentally decreed death has a debasing effect on a human society."[48]

Although the experience proved a frustrating one at times for Ervin, he enjoyed service on the court tremendously. He fought to extend the court's jurisdiction, and he forced his colleagues to reexamine some of their ideas. Justice James C. Adkins, for one, noticed the difference in himself. Arriving on the bench a "hard-nosed conservative," he found on the other side of the spectrum Chief Justice Ervin. "He was very prolific and wrote beautifully," Adkins remembered. One after another of Ervin's opinions touched Adkins. He later would acknowledge that "some of my old opinions still haunt me." Of Ervin, Adkins would observe: "He spent his tenure on the Court maintaining his belief that humanitarian principles were the most important. He believed in access to the courts, that every human being had a right to be heard. He believed in openness in government." Adkins concluded, "When he left the Court, I found that we needed his thoughts, [and] we needed his philosophy."[49]

The mandatory retirement age caught up with Justice Ervin in early 1975. The limit did not suit him. "I didn't really want to go," he told an interviewer. "I enjoyed the work over there, and I had been there a long time, long enough in order to really like the people, the personnel on the court, and I really liked the judges who disagreed with me, to tell you the truth." Still, in February 1974 Ervin alerted Governor Reubin Askew that he would depart the panel in accordance with the law. The early notice, he felt, would permit the election of his successor by the people. The retirement became official on January 6, 1975.[50]

Many productive years remained thereafter to the venerable jurist. Into the twenty-first century Ervin continued to stand up for his beliefs. Also, the end of his court tenure permitted him to indulge his passion for golf. Onetime clerk William C. Owen recalled that the retired justice evidenced the same confident decision making on the course as on the court. "He played quickly and never second-guessed himself after a shot," Owen observed. Never one to hang around after a round for a drink or a hand of gin rummy, Ervin played at the five handicap level in his prime. On the links he demonstrated the kindness, encouragement, and graciousness that he had extended to lawyers, law clerks, and his other fellows in years past. "I caddied for him at the George Washington Tournament at Capital City Country Club, and mistakenly advised him to use a six iron instead of the five iron he had selected," Owen added. "The judge hit the golf ball short after taking a fine swing and, in customary equanimity, remarked, 'I must have not hit it solidly.'"[51]

Professionally, he accepted "of counsel" status with the Tallahassee law firm of his brother Robert. Former governor LeRoy Collins would find himself in the same status at the same time. As late as 1995 Ervin continued to appear at his law office every day. A reporter noted, "Justice Ervin is living proof that age is nothing but a number." On May 9, 1997, Florida State University conferred upon Justice Ervin an honorary doctor of laws degree. Soon the Florida Bar had presented to him its foundation's lawyer medal of honor award. Meanwhile, he enjoyed the esteem of at least one U.S. Supreme Court associate justice. "When the judge attended a reception in Tallahassee for Justice Sandra Day O'Connor," Owen commented, "we stood at the end of a line at least 50 yards long, the judge dressed in his seersucker suit so old the stripes bled into one another. When Justice O'Connor recognized Judge Ervin, she immediately rushed to him and brought him next to her."[52]

Justice Richard M. Ervin's life ended at age ninety-nine on August 24, 2004, at Tallahassee. Friends and colleagues joined in their praise of the man. "Truth was central to his life and service," former attorney general Bob Butterworth noted. "As with truth, so it was with justice." Onetime chief justice Ben Overton added: "This was a special man who contributed more to the betterment and welfare of this democracy than any of us can hope to achieve." Overton concluded, "Richard W. Ervin—this special man—was not looking for accolades or recognition but was working to make this a better place." For her colleagues on the supreme court, Chief Justice Barbara Pariente also proclaimed her measure of the man and the meaning of his career. "Justice Ervin was Florida's legal visionary," she observed. "He leaves a legacy that is with us to this day and for all the future."[53]

13

Case Decisions of the Civil Rights Era

The years that stretched roughly between the mid-1950s and the mid-1960s ushered controversy and frustration into Florida Supreme Court life and activity at a level of intensity that overwhelmed previous records. Repeatedly, the state panel clashed with the U.S. Supreme Court and lower federal tribunals, with some state justices resenting what they considered to be intrusion on their jurisdiction and infringement of their prerogatives, not to mention a threat to the way of life that they and many other white southerners previously had taken for granted. In the process, as will be seen, rhetoric sometimes replaced sound reasoning as Floridians opted increasingly to secure their rights through action in the federal courts. As also will be seen, though, in certain respects the Florida judges nonetheless advanced the cause of justice and furthered efforts to ensure modern and fair governmental structures and protections. The story contains depth and diversity and deserves attention for such.

Whatever directions the court took during the period, one issue of national and world importance—it should be remembered—always lurked in the background. The threat of nuclear annihilation, resulting from cold war confrontation between the Soviet Union with its adherents and subject powers and the United States and its allies, presented itself without cease day after day, week after week. Anticommunist hysteria, grounded in understandable fear, sometimes gripped the nation. The phenomenon touched Florida along with the rest of the South and the country. The already threatening cold war took on increasing urgency in the late 1950s following Soviet detonation of a hydrogen bomb, that nation's triumph in launching the world's first artificial satellite, and the takeover of Cuba by a communist government under Fidel Castro.

Lawmakers, in turn, reacted to cold war threats with a variety of new laws that soon made their way to a court system staffed by jurists just as cognizant of and alarmed by world dangers as other citizens. One such law, for example, required a loyalty oath of public school teachers. Educator David Alton Cramp Jr. tested that measure in 1960. In *Cramp* v. *Board of Public Instruction of Orange County*, a united supreme court rejected his appeal, although it reaffirmed limits on the law's application to "knowing" membership in proscribed organizations. "There is a reasonable relationship," Justice Campbell Thornal proclaimed, "between the vital profession of teacher in the public school system and past association with subversive organizations."[1]

Deliberations on such questions required sensitivity and compelled the justices to weave their way carefully through the political bombast then current to reach factual considerations. Many opponents of the civil rights movement, for example, blasted activists as communists and "dupes of the international communist conspiracy." The Florida legislature's Johns Committee, supposedly formed to ferret out communist members of the National Association for the Advancement of Colored People, interrogated officers and demanded membership lists. Arrested for refusal to answer the question "Are you presently a member of the NAACP?" Edward T. Graham appealed to the supreme court in 1960. Justice Thornal's opinion in *Graham* v. *Florida Legislative Investigative Committee* upheld such refusal unless the state could prove a necessity for disclosure. In doing so, Thornal distinguished between membership in the Communist Party, which he saw as connected with "the violent overthrow of the established government," and participation in NAACP initiatives. "In the instant case the objectives of the organization are shown to be legitimate," he observed, "and there is an absence of any showing of a compelling public need that would support encroachment on appellant's constitutionally guaranteed private rights."[2]

When the issue came closer to the fact of Communist Party membership, however, the court trended in a different direction as illustrated by 1960's *Gibson* v. *Florida Legislative Investigative Committee*. In that instance, NAACP officer Father Theodore R. Gibson had been held in contempt for refusing to divulge whether a membership list in his possession included names of persons already identified as communists. For the court, Thornal upheld the contempt order. "The appellant as the official custodian of the subject records can be required to refer to them in order to authenticate his testimony," he remarked. "We do not construe the order of the circuit judge as directing that the records be publicly exposed or delivered to the committee or to anyone else or to be filed in this cause."[3] Ultimately, the U.S. Supreme Court by a five-to-four vote reversed the Florida decision and released Father Gibson from the contempt citation. The majority concluded that the Johns Committee had laid no adequate foundation for its demands. Justice Arthur Goldberg related that essential freedoms may not be curtailed without the showing of some relationship between the NAACP's Miami branch, with which Gibson was associated, and subversive or otherwise illegal activities.[4]

The number of controversial issues decided by the court within the context of the times mounted year by year during the period, and not infrequently, as noted above, judicial tempers flared. The matter of what constituted obscenity and how to regulate it offers a good example. In 1958 the tribunal tersely accepted the U.S. Supreme Court decision in *Butler* v. *State of Michigan* as requiring Florida's obscenity law to be held unconstitutional.[5] The five participating members—Justices Glenn Terrell, B. K. Roberts, E. Harris Drew, Campbell Thornal, and Stephen C. O'Connell—issued the one-paragraph ruling in *State* v. *Tracey* as a *per curiam* opinion.[6] By no means did that response constitute the end of the matter. In 1959 the legislature enacted a revised statute that came under scrutiny in 1961's *Tracey* v. *State*. A unanimous panel, still chafing under the federal court's previous directive, now strained to uphold a statute that banned possession of materials deemed "immoral," "degrading," "sadistic," "masochistic," "obscene," "lewd," "lascivious," "filthy," or "indecent." The court unanimously desired to support the measure while avoiding another adverse appeal. Justice O'Connell found the key. "Scienter [intent or knowledge] is an essential element to the offenses proscribed by the statutes," he declared, "and should be alleged and proved." O'Connell then applied his test to the case at hand and found the appellant guilty nonetheless because he "waived the failure by the State to allege scienter in the information by not attacking [the prosecution] on this issue by motion to quash," "the absence from the information of an allegation of scienter did not render the information void for failure to charge a crime," and "the evidence amply supports the conviction."[7]

Despite a tendency to resist change and to resent directives to alter past perspectives and courses of conduct, the court's members still could evidence a recognition that times had changed. Justice Drew did so, for instance, while concurring in the 1961 decision in *Trustees of the Internal Improvement Trust Fund* v. *LoBean*. The ruling permitted legal estoppel against the state in certain transfers of submerged lands, but Drew's words ranged further and carried a sense of the need to look at jurisprudence in new ways. "In the dim, distant past when the State and its subdivisions were concerned almost exclusively with the business of government," he reflected, "the argument advanced here that the doctrine of legal estoppel is not applicable to the State would have been sound. In this age, however, when the sovereign is engaged in almost every business activity known, from selling aspirin to operating vast industrial complexes, such argument falls by its own weight."[8]

Many arguments, sooner or later, fell by their own weight during the civil rights era, with the supreme court's caseload stretching well beyond ten thousand cases. Here follows a discussion that illustrates the types of appellate litigation significant during the period and that offers a flavor of the tribunal's attitudes toward them.

Anti-Semitic Discrimination

An era that witnessed an explosion of litigation concerning the protection of rights and extensive redefinition as to exactly what those rights were offered the Supreme Court of Florida an opportunity to consider discrimination against the state's fastest growing minority of the 1950s, the Jewish community located mostly in Dade County. The major case, 1959's *Harris* v. *Sunset Island Property Owners*, concerned covenants that restricted purchase and occupation of certain residential properties by a person "not of the Caucasian race, or who is not a Gentile, or who has been convicted of a felony." Without dissent, the tribunal negated enforcement by the state and its agencies of such restrictions as they applied to Jews. Relying upon the U.S. Supreme Court's 1948 opinion in *Shelley* v. *Kraemer*, Justice Thornal agreed that "the right to own, use, occupy, and dispose of property is a privilege guaranteed to a citizen within the contemplation of the provisions of the Fourteenth Amendment" and that restrictive covenants insofar as they were applied to Jewish citizens restrained that right.[9]

Consumer Protection

In 1963, thanks to supreme court action, Florida became the first state in the nation to impose strict liability on cigarette manufacturers for the results of defective or unwholesome products. Justice Drew's opinion in *Green* v. *American Tobacco Company*, from which Justices Thomas and Caldwell dissented, found an implied warranty of fitness irrespective of the manufacturer's knowledge of the product's condition. "To hold that prevailing industry standards supplant the ordinary standard of objective truth and proof, and should be conclusive on the issue of a product's reasonable fitness for human use or consumption, would be to shift to the purchasers the risk of whatever latent defectiveness may ultimately be proven by experience and advancement of human knowledge," Drew commented, "a risk which we are convinced was from the inception of the implied warranty doctrine intended to be attached to the mercantile function."[10]

Environmental Protection

Public sensitivity toward despoliation of Florida's natural beauty and resources gradually began to build as the 1950s progressed into the 1960s. Although major court involvement in furtherance of environmental protection would await the passage of time, the 1962 case of *Gies, et al.* v. *Fischer, et al.* arguably served as a harbinger of future actions. The Florida legislature had enacted new restrictions on bulkheading that the appellants claimed constituted a taking of their property without due process of law or compensation, a denial of equal protection of the law, an impairment of contract, and an unlawful and unconstitutional delegation of legislative authority. On the court's behalf, Justice Drew rejected the claims and upheld the restrictions. "There can be no doubt that in the absence of some overriding necessity a conveyance of public lands or rights in lands which actually results in the impairment of the public servitudes . . . must fail." The *University of Florida Law Review* termed the ruling "perhaps as strong a pronouncement of the trust doctrine as has been made to date." Its commentator added, "It leaves no doubt that private property rights in submerged lands previously granted and sold to private citizens may be infringed in favor of the public servitudes."[11]

Freedom of the Press

As mentioned in earlier chapters, the Florida court traditionally guarded judicial prerogatives when they collided with press freedom questions. The concerns that lay behind the attitude grew with the expansion of television coverage in the 1950s and early 1960s. The medium's broad reach, many jurists believed, posed an imminent threat to the right of a defendant to a fair trial. This issue came to the fore during 1958 in *Brumfield* v. *State*. Writing for a five-man panel that included Justices Terrell, T. Frank Hobson, Thornal, and O'Connell, Justice Drew upheld Circuit Judge Vincent C. Giblin's authority to restrict press photographs and television coverage during a controversial rape trial. "When the conduct involves the exercise of a constitutionally protected right or freedom, as of speech, press, or religion," Drew averred, "then a differed test may reasonably be applied before such restraint or control is warranted. But it does not follow that a court is governed by the same rules in restricting access to its proceedings."[12]

Labor Law

The rights of labor required attention during the period just as did the rights of minority groups. At a time when conservative winds blew briskly through Florida's government corridors and within the supreme court, the panel erected what one scholar called "a harsh, judicially imposed procedural obstacle course" for a union determined to exercise picketing rights. Justice Terrell articulated the new tests in the 1957 decision in *Fontainebleu Hotel Corp.* v. *Hotel Employees Union,*

Local No. 255, et al. "When a bona fide industrial grievance arises, legal and orderly picketing may be indulged in, but the law places limitations on it," he wrote after specifying the limitations. "It condemns violence, manhandling, the use of the club or the Black Mafia," Terrell continued. "It provides an orderly process to conduct it and it contemplates that both parties will cooperate to bring about a solution advantageous to all concerned."[13]

The passage of five years brought a challenge to the state's 1944 constitutional amendment proclaiming the "Right to Work." In order to circumvent this bar to the closed shop, unions had begun to rely upon "agency shop" agreements that required nonunion members as a condition of employment to pay to the union an initiation service charge and a monthly service fee. The tribunal rejected the scheme absolutely in *Schermerhorn* v. *Local 1625, Retail Clerks International Association*. "Such an arrangement," Justice Hobson declared, "is palpably and totally inconsistent with the freedom of choice contemplated by our Declaration of Rights."[14]

Legislative Reapportionment and Redistricting

Florida's often bitter struggle with questions of civil rights to some extent owed its intensity to a legislature reflective of "Old South" north Florida as opposed to the increasingly populous and more easygoing peninsula. Governor LeRoy Collins endeavored to rectify the gross malapportionment that underlay the situation, but final resolution remained years away. In 1956 the issue confronted the supreme court when its members were asked whether the house of representatives could be reapportioned without, at the same time, requiring a reapportionment of the state senate. Justice Thornal, writing for his colleagues in *Brewer* v. *Gray*, declined to intervene. Constitutionally mandated reapportionment and redistricting, he insisted, constituted an exclusively legislative function that could not be reviewed by any other branch of government.[15]

The panel proved more willing to exert its authority in 1962 when congressional, rather than state, reapportionment offered a subject for inquiry. In *Lund, et al.* v. *Mathas, et al.*, Justice Millard Caldwell rebuffed a challenge to the state's twelve recently drawn congressional districts that ranged in population from 237,235 to 660,345 persons. Neither the state nor the federal constitution, he reasoned, required numerical equality; rather, a number of factors including population could be considered.[16] Two years afterward, the U.S. Supreme Court effectively overturned *Lund* in *Wesberry* v. *Sanders*, a decision that applied the "one man, one vote" principle to congressional apportionment and districting questions.[17]

Local Government Powers

With Florida's growth, the complexities facing municipal corporations and other local governments had proliferated tremendously in the twentieth century as had opportunities for harm to arise out of municipal activity. The court recognized this fact increasingly during the late 1950s and early 1960s, as was evident in 1957's *Hargrove* v. *Town of Cocoa Beach*. The case dealt with municipal tort liability, and Justice Thornal's ruling dramatically altered the doctrine of sovereign immunity in light of changed circumstances. "We are here faced squarely with an appeal to secede from our previously announced rule which immunizes a municipal corporation against liability for torts committed by police officers," he explained. Thornal then examined the historical division of municipal functions between governmental and proprietary activities before questioning whether the distinction continued to have merit. "Our own feeling," he noted, "is that the courts should be alive to the demands of justice. We can see no necessity for insisting on legislative action in a matter which the courts themselves originated." Thornal concluded, "We hold that a municipal corporation may be held liable for the torts of police officers under the doctrine of respondeat superior. When an individual suffers a direct, personal injury proximately caused by the negligence of a municipal employee while acting within the scope of his employment, the injured individual is entitled to redress for the wrong done."[18]

Justice Thornal's interest in modernizing local government concepts also evidenced itself in 1957's *DeGroot* v. *Sheffield*. The issue concerned dismissal of a Duval County school district employee when his position was abolished by the district without approval of the civil service board. Thornal found that, when notice and a hearing are required and the decision of an agency is contingent on the showing made at the hearing, the agency's decision becomes judicial or quasi-judicial in nature and, as such, is subject to appropriate judicial review. "Procedural formalities are not necessarily sacrosanct," he observed, "merely because they are time-honored." As one commentator noted, "This decision . . . marked the dawn of modern administrative law concepts in Florida, concepts that were followed in later decisions and embodied in the Administrative Procedure Acts enacted in 1963 and 1974."[19]

Once again Thornal's influence could be seen in the 1959 decision in *Grubstein* v. *Urban Renewal Agency of City of Tampa*. A divided court—with Justice Roberts writing for a four-man majority that included Justices Terrell, Hobson, and Thornal—backed away from the highly restrictive 1952 ruling in *Adams* v. *Housing Authority of City of Daytona Beach*. Particularly, the *Grubstein* decision permitted certain urban redevelopment activities ("slum clearance" as opposed to "blight clearance") to be undertaken where the public purpose served outweighed limitations on public use. "I would broaden the scope of our present holding," Thornal's concurring opinion observed, "by unequivocally receding from the judgment in the Adams case to the extent that it was determined that [the 1945 Municipal Housing Authority Law] was unconstitutional in its entirety."[20]

Thornal's participation in 1960's *Sunad Inc.* v. *City of Sarasota* found him less successful in swaying the court, as a second four-man majority backed away from another earlier decision. This time the case combined questions of aesthetic zoning and billboard regulation. Justice Thomas, on behalf of himself and Justices Terrell, Hobson, and Roberts, accepted that a city such as Sarasota could regulate outdoor advertising based upon aesthetics if the ordinance was grounded upon a solid foundation having a reasonable relation to the community's general welfare. As it turned out, the majority did not believe that Sarasota's ordinance sufficed. "We agree that the City of Sarasota is reasonably placed in the same category as Miami Beach so far as its appeal on the ground of attractiveness is concerned," Thomas accepted. "But we do not concur in the view that the ordinance under attack defines a pattern calculated to protect and preserve the city's beauty. It is, in our opinion, unreasonable and discriminatory and for those reasons invalid."[21]

Race and Race Relations

Public school desegregation, beginning with whites-only universities, constituted a top priority for civil rights activists. The principal litigation, involving Virgil Darnell Hawkins and the University of Florida Law School, was discussed in chapter 10. The case reappeared in the Florida Supreme Court in 1957 after the U.S. Supreme Court the previous year had instructed its Florida counterpart that "there is no reason to delay."[22] Hawkins now asked for immediate admission, and in *State ex rel. Hawkins* v. *Board of Control, et al.* the tribunal again refused to act. Justice Roberts wrote for himself and Justices Thornal, O'Connell, Terrell, and Hobson. "Our study of the results of the survey materials to the question here, and other material evidence," he insisted, "leads inevitably to the conclusion that violence in university communities and a critical disruption of the university system would occur if Negro students are permitted to enter the state white universities at this time." Roberts also expressed resentment at the federal court's assertion of authority. "It is a 'consummation devoutly to be wished' that the concept of 'states' rights' will not come to be of interest only to writers and students of history. We cannot assume that the Supreme Court intended to deprive the highest court of an independent sovereign state of one of its traditional powers, that is, the right to exercise a sound judicial discretion as to the date of the issuance of its process in order to prevent a serious public mischief."[23]

Hawkins's petition did reach receptive ears on the court, though, even if they did not constitute a majority in 1957. "It seems to me that if this court expects obedience to its mandates," Justice Thomas declared, "it must be prepared immediately to obey the mandates from a higher court . . . regardless of our lack of sympathy with the holding." Justice Drew added, "It is a fundamental truth that justice delayed is justice denied. This case has now reached the point where further delay will be tantamount to a denial of a constitutional right of relator."[24]

Race-related appeals involving criminal prosecutions and criminal procedures came before the court as well. In 1956's *State ex rel. Copeland* v. *Mayo*, an appellant argued that the death penalty imposed upon him for murder was discriminatory. He utilized statistics to point out that, of seven executions within his age group (fifteen to nineteen) within the previous twelve years, all victims of execution were black. Justice Terrell dismissed the argument as of "an inconclusive nature" and denied the appeal.[25] The next year, Terrell writing in *Thomas* v. *State* upheld a Duval County rape conviction. With regard to the appellant's argument that, over twenty years, twenty-three blacks had been executed for the crime and only one white man, Terrell found no grounds for reversal and a new trial. "It is settled law that all such cases turn on the peculiar facts of the case," he noted. "The facts in none of these cases are given us. In sum, it may be stated that about all these statistics show is that more Negroes have been tried and convicted for rape than white defendants."[26] In a similar case decided in 1963, *Porter* v. *State*, the court rejected a claim of grand jury discrimination where 10.8 percent of the population consisted of African Americans and only 1.2 percent of the grand jury list was black. For the unanimous court, Justice O'Connell characterized the statistical evidence as "inconclusive." He added, "In this case appellant has not met the burden of overcoming the presumption that the selecting officials proceeded properly."[27]

Interracial cohabitation offered a question for consideration in the 1963 case of *McLaughlin, et al.* v. *State*. A Florida law prohibited racially mixed couples from habitually living in and occupying "in the nighttime the same room." Two defendants argued that the statute violated equal protection rights because it related only to persons of different races and that it imposed higher penalties than other cohabitation laws. Justice Caldwell's opinion upheld the law, finding the punishment the same for guilty parties regardless of race. "This Court is obligated by the sound rule of stare decisis and the precedent of the well written decision in [*Pace* v. *Alabama*]," he wrote. "The Federal Constitution, as it was when construed by the U.S. Supreme Court in that case, is quite adequate, but if the new-found concept of 'social justice' has out-dated 'the law of the land' as therein announced and, by way of consequence, some new law is necessary, it must be enacted by legislative process or some other court must write it."[28] The U.S. Supreme Court took up the challenge and reversed the Florida decision in 1964.[29]

Religion in Public Schools

Among the many civil rights tested during the late 1950s and early 1960s could be numbered the right to resist state-approved religious activities, especially within the public schools. The 1962 case of *Chamberlin, et al.* v. *Dade County Board of Public Instruction* brought the issue four-square to the court. A unanimous panel turned to Justice Caldwell to author its opinion upholding the constitutionality of mandatory prayer, Bible reading, and other religious activities within the context of public education. "We are sensible of the extent to which the sophistries of agnosticism have gained credence," Caldwell began. "And we acknowledge the trend toward the preference of minorities over the majority and toward the requiring of the majority, which seem never to suffer psychological trauma, to yield up its cherished customs and rights. Although we concede the duty to turn the other cheek to the enemy and to deal gently with the weak, we do not agree that it is our function to subvert the purpose and intent of the Constitution to those ends, nor do we feel impelled to indulge in flights of fanciful philosophy. When we subscribed to our official oaths it was with 'no mental reservations and with no purpose to construe the Constitution by hypercritical rules.'"[30]

For Caldwell, as for many others, the attack on religion in schools struck deeply as an attack on the American way of life, and he perceived the enemy clearly within a cold war geopolitical context. "For all practical purposes there are now in the world just two forms of government, loosely denominated Democracy and Communism," he instructed. "The vital difference between the two is that the Democracies accept religion and guarantee its free exercise, in one form or another, as part of the day to day lives of their people, whereas Communism has banished religion, except as it may be bootlegged in the dark and hospitable corners." Caldwell concluded: "A consequential distinction, as the major difference is applied to these United States, is that here we prohibit the governmental establishment of religion but guarantee to all the free exercise thereof while, under Communism, religion is denied and those who profess religion are hounded underground. We feel it equally imperative that we preserve the safeguards of the Constitution against all violations of the 'establishment' and 'free exercise' clauses and, at the same time, preserve those clauses and the rights of the States and the people thereunder against weasel-worded constructions and distinctions designed to impute to them either more or less than was originally intended."[31]

It took the U.S. Supreme Court one year to vacate the Florida judgment and to remand *Chamberlin* for reconsideration in light of the federal panel's recent rulings on the subject.[32] Justice Caldwell again offered the court its unanimous voice. His opinion reaffirmed the constitutionality of Florida's mandated religious observances, this time based upon the legislature's intent in requiring them. "It is our conclusion," Caldwell observed, "that the statute was founded upon secular rather than sectarian considerations." He then allocated responsibility for any confusion to the senior court. "We have, without avail, endeavored to find, in the diverse views expressed by the several justices of the U.S. Supreme Court who participated in these decisions, a clear course for us to follow," Caldwell argued. He added, "It seems, therefore, more fitting that the responsibility for an enlargement be left to that Court." "Apparently the Supreme Court of Florida is saying," the *University of Florida Law Review* observed of the opinion, "that if the plaintiffs wish to have their civil rights determined they must go to the federal courts."[33] The U.S. Supreme Court seemingly agreed and overturned the second opinion as well, at least with respect to Bible reading and prayer.[34]

The Right to Counsel

The question of when counsel should be supplied to a criminal defendant at taxpayers' expense brought Florida's court into the national spotlight in the early 1960s. The train of events commenced when Clarence Earl Gideon, arrested for the felony offense of breaking and entering a Panama City poolroom with intent to commit a misdemeanor, requested counsel from the circuit court. The judge declined, noting that he could lawfully designate counsel only to represent persons charged with capital offenses. Gideon petitioned for a writ of habeas corpus based upon the denial, and in October 1961 the Florida Supreme Court declined without opinion in *Gideon* v. *Cochran* to grant the writ.[35] Gideon thereupon appealed to the U.S. Supreme Court, which responded to his call. In early 1963 the tribunal reversed the Florida decision in *Gideon* v. *Wainwright*. In so doing it established a landmark of legal history. Particularly, Justice Hugo Black determined that the Sixth Amendment right to counsel was a fundamental right applicable to state prosecutions pursuant to the Fourteenth Amendment. "Any person haled into court, who is too poor to hire a lawyer, cannot be assured of a fair trial unless counsel is provided for him," Black declared. "The importance of the *Gideon* decision, which the Court decided unanimously," one legal scholar explained, "was that it totally applied the incorporation doctrine, meaning that nationally every defendant in a felony trial had a right to counsel and that, if a person was indigent, then the state had to provide counsel."[36]

The Supreme Court of Florida then stood only at the beginning of a series of cases dealing with the right to counsel, although its members believed by the time of the *Gideon* ruling that they already had acted to resolve many related issues. Particularly, they had promulgated on April 1, 1963, Criminal Procedure Rule No. 1, a measure that relieved the panel of some of the burden related to postconviction relief by establishing procedures closely following the pertinent federal statute. When *Gideon* returned for reconsideration, the justices simply declined to grant the requested writ of habeas corpus but did encourage Gideon to proceed under the new rule.[37]

Soon, though, a series of appeals tested the new standard. In *Fish* v. *State*, the court considered misdemeanor cases. The state recently had adopted a public defender system for felony cases only, and the panel declined, in Justice Roberts's words, "to overturn the legislative declaration of the policy of this state." *Gideon*, Roberts determined, applied only to felonies.[38] *Weeks* v. *State* followed two months later, in March 1964. The unanimous court with Justice Thornal writing held the appointment of counsel discretionary where an indigent collaterally was attacking a prior criminal conviction.[39] The next year the panel in *Montgomery* v. *State* declined once more to extend the right, this time to persons undergoing police investigation but against whom charges had yet to be filed.[40]

Women's Rights

As suggested by the 1959 decision in *Hoyt* v. *State*, the Florida court's acceptance of feminist tenets remained for the future during the civil rights movement of the 1950s and early 1960s. The litigation involved a subject—jury duty—that the panel had considered earlier, although the issues had been altered somewhat. Now the legislature permitted women to serve on juries but only if they previously had registered the desire to be placed on the jury list. Justice Drew found the scheme acceptable as an expression of legislative policy that recognized the benefit of keeping women at home. "The statute, in effect, simply recognizes that the traditional exclusion was based not upon inherent disability or incapacity," he wrote, "but upon the premise that such demands might place an unwarranted strain upon the social and domestic structure, or result in unwilling participation of those whose conflicting duties, while not amounting to actual hardship, might yet be expected, as a general rule, to affect the quality of their service as jurors." Justice Hobson, with Justice Thomas's support, disagreed. "No one in this enlightened age would question the fact that if a limitation such as is placed upon women by our statute with reference to jury service were engrafted into our statutory law in regard to some of the so-called minority groups comprising our citizenry, it would be stricken down as violative of constitutional guarantees of due process and equal protection of the law." Hobson added, "There can be no question that women as a class have been discriminated against by the statutory limitation."[41]

Similarly, in 1963 the panel upheld Florida's law criminalizing abortion. The 1868 statute, Justice Drew concluded for the court in *Carter* v. *State*, met constitutional standards and did not deny a woman her inviolable rights. Justices Thomas and Roberts dissented. They did so, however, not out of conviction that the law suffered constitutional defect but because they believed the case to involve "a classic instance of entrapment."[42]

PART FIVE

The Realization of Reform, 1964–1972

14

A Peaceful Revolution of Earthquake Proportions

The Sunshine State's story, as it played out from 1964 to 1972, involved transformations every bit as breathtaking as those of the immediate post–World War II era. A new visionary appeared on the scene to recast ideas as to Florida's development and character, just as a hard-driving upstart redrew the political map while breaking the longtime Democratic hold on state government. Excitement filled the air as new forces pushed, pulled, and tugged at the state. Against the backdrop of a divisive war in Vietnam and violence on the campuses and in the streets of the United States, Floridians held their breath while they grasped the handrail of the powerful roller coaster that was propelling them at sometimes heart-stopping speed toward the future.

Perhaps much of what was to come can be traced to a 1964 airplane flight over the pinelands and swamps of the central peninsula. The key participant was Walter Elias Disney, a man determined to make good on his family's Florida legacy by revolutionizing the entertainment and tourism industry. The Disneys had farmed in Volusia County during the early 1890s. There, one of the state's legendary "busts"—the one that followed the Great Freeze of 1895—had driven them in poverty to seek a new start in Missouri. Now Walt Disney was back to select an immense tract of land upon which to build a magnificent new version of his California attraction, Disneyland. About fifteen miles south of Orlando, he found what he wanted. A spread of some 30,000 acres of what one commentator called "nothing land," which straddled the new Interstate 4, seemed perfect. "Great, buy it," Disney instructed a staffer. Another aide later observed, "If he could have, he would have bought 50,000 acres."[1]

Disney's grand vision for Walt Disney World excited Floridians when it was announced in 1965, and few perceptive residents failed to appreciate its tremendous implications. Governor Haydon Burns, as a strong proponent of economic expansion, declared, "This is the most significant day in the history of Florida." The *Miami Herald* soon concluded that "the potential is enormous." As enhancements of the plans found their way into the spotlight, anticipation grew apace. Newsmen were "taken aback" when the entrepreneur guessed in 1966 that he would spend $500 million on the project. Within one year the figure had reached

$600 million. "It staggers the imagination," a state senator proclaimed. "It's bigger, better, greater." By opening day in October 1971, the tide of money flowing into the state washed throughout the peninsula. One study projected $6.6 billion in added income over the following decade, plus 50,000 new jobs, 19 million visitors, 27,000 more hotel and motel rooms, and 37,000 new homes. The estimates, as it turned out, undershot the mark. The *Tallahassee Democrat* summed up the situation well. "Florida," it asserted, "will probably never be the same again."[2]

The code words for Florida's future, heard seemingly everywhere, became "bigger, better, greater." Optimism of grander proportions greeted word of each new attraction, each new resort, and each new community. Tourists flocked to the glamour and the beaches, and many returned to live. The state's 1960 population of just under 5 million previously had seemed an almost impossibly large jump over the 1945 figure of 2.25 million. Now it lurched ahead within the decade to almost 7 million. By 1980 a total of 10 million would appear close at hand. At the same time, trends away from north Florida predominance had accelerated. In 1950, roughly 34 percent of residents had lived in that region, with 38 percent in central Florida and 28 percent in south Florida. Thirty years later, only 20 percent called north Florida home, with 43 percent living in the central region and 37 percent in the south. A state that had been 35 percent rural in 1950 already had become 82 percent urban by 1970.[3]

The state's surge had manifested itself in many facets of life, including the growth of its university system. At World War II's end, three small public institutions of higher learning served Floridians: the University of Florida at Gainesville for white men, the white-only Florida State College for Women at Tallahassee, and the Florida Agricultural and Mechanical College at Tallahassee for male and female African Americans. Both white schools were made coeducational in 1947, with the Tallahassee campus becoming Florida State University. Florida A&M reached university status in 1953. A fourth institution, the University of South Florida at Temple Terrace near Tampa, thereafter received its first freshman class in 1960. Four years later, Boca Raton's Florida Atlantic University opened for students, with the University of West Florida at Pensacola following in 1967. Orange County's Disney World–inspired population explosion led in 1968 to Florida Technological University at Orlando, a facility designed also to service the growing space industry at Cape Kennedy (formerly Cape Canaveral). Finally, Miami's Florida International University and Jacksonville's University of North Florida debuted in 1972. The mushrooming growth of the higher education system seemed little short of phenomenal, as also was the fact that all its member institutions—to greater and lesser degrees—were racially integrated.[4]

Tens of thousands of students, products of the postwar "baby boom," crowded the university campuses, developing attitudes a generation apart from those of their parents. Racial integration had begun to take hold in public primary and secondary schools by the mid-1960s, and the new generation accepted the change, even if it did not completely embrace it. But there was more. The Beatles had created a worldwide sensation after 1964. As its four members and a wave of bands and musicians that followed altered the sound of music, they also popularized longer hair for men and new fashion concepts for both sexes. Other national and international influences also touched younger Floridians and many older ones. Important among them, author Betty Friedan in 1963 had published *The Feminine Mystique*, helping to launch the feminist movement. Three years later, the National Organization for Women provided an organizational framework for furthering women's demands for an end to workplace discrimination, legalized abortion, and an equal rights amendment to the U.S. Constitution.[5]

The period also witnessed the birth of what came to be called the "New Left" partly in reaction to the parental conservatism of the late 1940s through the early 1960s. Free speech demonstrations held at the University of California at Berkeley in 1964 launched years of protests at colleges throughout the nation. A good number of Florida's students—particularly those at Florida State University, Florida A&M University, and the University of Florida—urged the causes of civil rights, social justice, and free speech. At times, the schools found themselves in turmoil, threatened from without and from within. An FSU historian labeled the period "Crisis: Par for the Course." Through it all, no issue inflamed the youth of the mid-1960s to the early 1970s as much as did American involvement in the Vietnam War. Black and white activists joined to force the conflict's end. As University of Florida president Stephen C. O'Connell explained, "Things were reasonable until the Vietnam War broke out and all hell broke loose on university campuses everywhere." Following the bombing of North Vietnam sanctuaries in Cambodia in April 1970 to force North Vietnam to the bargaining table, the universities witnessed a renewed groundswell of protest. After students were shot by National Guardsmen at Ohio's Kent State University in May, protests erupted again. Days later, Mississippi highway patrolmen riddled a Jackson State College dormitory with bullets, killing two more young people. The war's end remained nowhere in sight.[6]

Shifting attitudes, changes in hairstyles and clothing, and the advocacy of controversial issues by some provoked reaction from many of Florida's older residents as well as from its still conservative state government. Civic groups and alumni associations demanded expulsion of activists from campuses. Church leaders called for moral reform, while a member of Florida's Board of Regents described Florida State University dormitories as "taxpayers' whorehouses." Where the color line had marked the state's social split only a few years previously, now age distinctions tended to blur those of race. Still, the societal rent proved painful and, for the time, enduring.[7]

All the while, the nature of Florida's politics and government underwent fundamental change. One key aspect of the transformation concerned the increasingly moderate stance of many Democratic voters statewide. The influx of black electors accounted for an important part of the change, but so too did the demographics of growth. Urban areas such as Dade County tended to vote more liberally than did suburban and rural precincts. Thus, in 1964, Miami's Earl Faircloth narrowly managed to grab the attorney general nomination from the incumbent, Governor C. Farris Bryant's conservative protégé James W. Kynes. The gubernatorial primary of 1966 illustrated the trend even more vividly. Where Miami mayor Robert King High—widely regarded as moderate if not liberal—had run a poor second two years earlier to party winner Haydon Burns after endorsing racial integration, now High trumped Burns in a bitterly contested runoff by nearly ninety thousand votes.[8]

Although a candidate such as High could take a statewide Democratic primary by 1966, Floridians soon discovered that such a victory no longer ensured a general election win. Swelling Republican ranks paralleled the gains of moderates in the Democratic Party. The GOP's 1964 candidates—including Senate hopeful Claude R. Kirk, a Palm Beach businessman—had contested their races credibly. In the months and years that followed, numerous Democrats, resentful of changes in their party and of the politics of Democratic presidents John F. Kennedy and Lyndon B. Johnson, increasingly saw their future in the party of presidential contender Barry Goldwater. Meanwhile, the Arizona senator's narrow 1964 loss of the state had brought to the forefront a new generation of GOP leaders determined to grasp power. Since population growth was creating the potential for thousands of new votes in Republican strongholds such as Sarasota, Pinellas, Hillsborough, Orange, Brevard, Palm Beach, and nearby counties, their aspirations by no means appeared unrealistic. The results of election day 1966 proved them on target. Gubernatorial nominee Kirk, an artful campaigner, drew in conservative Democrats by pounding High's racial attitudes and labeling him an "extreme liberal." On the other hand, Kirk also cast himself as a government reformer, a man who would react aggressively to Pork Chop rule. The tactics won Kirk a 55 percent victory and made him the state's first Republican governor since 1877. The Democrat carried only eleven of the state's sixty-seven counties. By then, twenty-two years had passed since a liberal Democrat, Claude Pepper, had won a race in Florida for the Senate or the governor's office.[9]

A new day clearly had come to light, not that Florida's Democratic Party had collapsed or that other Republicans had joined Kirk at the higher elected ranks of state government. But the new governor did control some executive power, and he soon enjoyed a stroke of luck. Just as his first legislature began in January 1967 (Kirk had called a special session to demand constitutional revision), the U.S. Supreme Court declared the body illegal due to malapportionment. A court-determined reapportionment resulted in the long-sought demise of Pork Chop power by April. *St. Petersburg Times* associate editor Martin Dyckman, one of the state's experienced political reporters, remembered covering his first legislative session that year. "Florida was enjoying a peaceful revolution of earthquake proportions. The Supreme Court's reapportionment decisions had put an end to rural rule, replacing 'Pork Chop' legislators with energetic newcomers from the suburbs and cities and giving rise to the two-party system. I was nervous as any rookie before that 1967 session, but I needn't have been. Two-thirds of the legislators were rookies, too."[10]

With urging from the governor, the new legislature began the process of distancing itself and Florida from the effects of Pork Chop rule. One important measure strove to open state and local government deliberations to the public. This "government in the sunshine law" aimed to stem corruption by blocking what one commentator described as "behind-the-scenes manipulation" and "secretive government practices." Similarly, the solons backed an initiative to create the first statewide law enforcement agency, the Florida Bureau of Law Enforcement. Kirk's "War on Crime" aided passage of this measure, and his positive environmental initiatives led to long overdue attempts to stem environmental despoliation and illegal development. Dredge and fill operations came under scrutiny, while a state pollution control board regulated waste discharge and enforced air and water quality standards.[11]

Remarkable reform prizes were showered on Floridians by the legislators, but as the governor declared, the most important one was constitutional revision. The 1965 legislature had created a constitutional revision commission to be appointed by the governor, the president of the senate, the speaker of the house of representatives, and the state's chief justice. Chaired by Bartow lawyer Chesterfield Smith, the body had fared well until late 1966, when the question of streamlining the judiciary and controversies over selection, discipline, and removal of judges stalled its progress. A subcommittee including Escambia County state senator Reubin Askew, Polk County state senator Lawton Chiles, and Justice Stephen C. O'Connell persisted, and in December they agreed to a sweeping reorganization measure that consolidated the existing fifteen trial courts into two courts in the eleven largest counties and three in the remaining counties.[12]

Hopes ran high that constitutional revision finally was on its way in January

1967, eighty-two years after the state's antiquated 1885 charter had rolled back Reconstruction-era reforms by limiting government generally and weakening the governor's power specifically. Governor Kirk backed the effort strongly, assigning aides such as Wade L. Hopping—the former Florida Bar continuing legal education director—to prod reluctant legislators and help build consensus. The Florida Bar also joined the crusade, working cooperatively with constitutional revision commission members and other reform advocates.[13]

Still, success did not come easily. Even given the benefit of court-mandated legislative reapportionment, the debates dragged on through 1967 and 1968. Three special legislative sessions failed to achieve a suitable compromise despite the best efforts of leaders such as Duval County state senator John E. Mathews Jr. Issues including whether to forbid a state income tax, homestead exemptions from taxation, the legislature's size, and executive department reorganization offered grist for argument, but judicial reform proved the ultimate sticking point as circuit judges rebelled at the thought of additions to their numbers and a prohibition on local salary supplements. Finally, in July 1968 the solons broke the stalemate by eliminating the judicial article from further consideration at that time. The results attracted many critics, including revision commission member B. K. Roberts. The jurist objected strongly to provisions for a lieutenant governor, aid to cities, eminent domain, sovereign immunity, and constitutional amendment by initiative. Voters nonetheless approved the new charter in November. As it happened, the victory owed partial thanks to one of the governor's clever stratagems. When a business coalition formed to block the reforms, Kirk charged that tycoon Ed Ball stood behind the effort. "People said, 'We don't know whether we're for what Kirk wants,'" the governor observed, "but we know we don't want anything that Ed Ball wants."[14]

The results of the 1968 elections seemed full of portents, but many of the signs ultimately proved misleading. The voting ratified not only the new constitution but many of the remarkable changes that residents had been experiencing. Dade County voters, for instance, elected Joe Lang Kershaw, a Coral Gables Junior High School civics teacher, as the first black to sit in the Florida legislature since 1889. Two years later, Gwen Sawyer Cherry, also from Dade County, would join Kershaw, but no African American would sit in the state senate until 1982. Republicans also saw the 1968 returns as highly promising. Richard M. Nixon had captured the presidency, and Orange County's Edward J. Gurney soundly defeated former governor LeRoy Collins for an open Senate seat, becoming the first person in Florida's electoral history to receive more than a million votes. Yet the Florida Republican ascendancy thereafter stalled. The governor, who increasingly practiced what a biographer called "the politics of confrontation," saw his popularity drain during the next two years. Meanwhile, a new generation of moderate Democratic leaders had stepped forward to reclaim the state. In 1970, Reubin Askew snatched the governor's chair from Kirk, and Lawton Chiles similarly bested Congressman William C. Cramer for the Senate.[15]

As the decade turned, Floridians who exulted in the state's economy expressed very different sentiments when it came to questions of personal safety and law and order. The tumult of the previous few years had combined with rising crime rates and increasing usage of illegal drugs to create deeply felt apprehensions. Urban riots, such as those occurring at Tampa in 1967 and in Miami's Liberty City section the following year, stoked the fears, as did exaggerated news coverage of Florida's campus protests. A flood of ever tougher new laws resulted in clogged court calendars and overcrowded prisons. Judicial reform seemed more urgently needed than ever, but urban voters in November 1970 provided the margin that defeated a proposal to revise the constitution's Article V (Judiciary) because they saw it as failing to honor the promise of real reform.[16]

Revision advocates tried again. With Governor Askew's support, a special session in November 1971 produced a new document that created a uniform and streamlined two-tier trial court system, while also providing new mechanisms for judicial selection and discipline. The plan's provisions are explained in greater detail in chapter 15. Optimism for its ultimate approval heightened in January 1972 when Florida Bar president John McCarty announced bar backing for what had been a goal of his late brother, Governor Dan McCarty. Askew named an eighty-seven-member citizens' committee headed by Chesterfield Smith to ensure a favorable vote. Notable among those included were onetime justices Wade L. Hopping and Stephen C. O'Connell, Chief Justice B. K. Roberts, and future justice Ben F. Overton. Former governor Claude Kirk added his endorsement. Serious concerns for the outcome remained evident. "It is now or (almost) never for judicial reform," house judiciary chairman Talbot "Sandy" D'Alemberte warned his fellow lawyers. As it turned out, the news proved good. At a special election held March 14, 1972, the voters enthusiastically embraced the changes, sounding at last a victory call that reformers had hoped to hear since 1945.[17]

The world, the nation, and the state had changed so much in the fifty-five years that reached back to 1917. Then, Floridians prepared for European war against the monarchies of Germany and Austria-Hungary; now they were fighting communism in southeast Asia. In the meantime, a poor, underpopulated state had emerged as one of the nation's most dynamic centers and had begun to shake off inequities of the past and, many of its residents thought, governmental corruption. Given the successes, it should not surprise anyone that the future, rather than the past, commanded attention in 1972. Man first had walked the moon's surface in 1969, and he had traveled there from Florida. Two years later, Walt Disney's dream of restoring his family's Florida legacy had come when he opened the gates of Disney World. Who knew what other dreams might come true? The excitement of the era stirred and beguiled. As it turned out, though, Floridians should have taken a little more care. They might well have kept closer to mind some of the lessons of those fifty-five years, although that story and Florida's post-1972 experience lie beyond the limits of this work. Without doubt, though, that fascinating tale will require a future telling.

15

The Supreme Court and Its Own Revolution

Although in 1964 only one member of the Supreme Court of Florida could boast service on the panel stretching back to World War II, the tribunal remained a conservative one that, in important respects, closely resembled its immediate postwar incarnation. During the next eight years, however, the court would undergo significant alteration in personnel. The changes in some respects reinforced the conservatism of past days, but they also bespoke differences of perspective and attitude that distanced the jurists from their predecessors. The changes also heralded the coming of an era when problems once discussed in a whisper would now become distinctly public.

The court's general philosophy at the period's beginning seemed evident to its members and to others. "If I were asked to categorize the Court of my day and its philosophy," Stephen C. O'Connell recorded, "a couplet, I believe one of Pope's, would seem to fit and describe the philosophy of that Court: 'Be not the first by whom the new are tried, nor yet the last to lay the old aside.'" He added, "It was on balance a conservative one." Scholars agreed. In 1966 the *University of Florida Law Review* assessed the court's spectrum of opinion based upon several categories of appeals decided during the previous two years. "The final ideological pattern shows Justice [Richard W.] Ervin as the 'left wing' of the Court and two 'right wings' consisting of Justice O'Connell and, substantially further to the right, Justice [Millard F.] Caldwell," the study determined. It declared further, "The center of the Court is made up of Justices [Campbell] Thornal, [B. K.] Roberts, [E. Harris] Drew, and [Elwyn] Thomas in descending order of 'liberalness.'" Justice Millard Caldwell took issue with some of the characterizations. "Compared to me," he told friends, "Thornal and O'Connell are liberals."[1]

That is not to say that most Floridians in 1964 maintained any significant awareness of the court or its philosophy. The state capital remained remote from population centers, and the degree of media coverage of court happenings certainly did not risk overexposure for the jurists. If asked who served on the tribunal, residents most quickly would have named Justices Caldwell and Roberts. Their often-provocative public pronouncements and activities made good copy, and they traveled widely throughout the state on personal and court business.

Even lawyers, as a general matter, held little knowledge of the justices' individual philosophies or of the court as a whole. Why this would be the case intrigued two University of Florida scholars. "The absence of serious scholarly study of the Florida Supreme Court is striking," Patrick Brown and William A. Haddad began. "Probably the greatest reason for the lack of research on Florida's Supreme Court is the natural tendency not to tamper with courts. Research is inhibited by the traditional ideas that courts are sacred and impervious institutions that dispense justice according to unquestionable standards, and that if their workings are exposed somehow, their mysterious power will be unveiled for all to see." The same rationale might have applied to journalists' similar lack of penetrating attention to court affairs.[2]

In conducting its business, the court still echoed the practices of a generation past. True, its building offered modern facilities and the jurists now wore robes and enjoyed formal swearing-in ceremonies. On the other hand, no professional administrator yet handled the panel's internal affairs, and its small staff had barely grown since the 1953 legislature authorized employment of seven research assistants. When Sid White succeeded longtime clerk Guyte P. McCord on October 1, 1964, he discovered just how persistent were the old ways of doing business. "The highest level of technology at the court," he recalled, "consisted of typewriters and carbon paper." Computers were a matter for the future. "We did everything by hand until 1980," White added.[3]

Some additional assistance, at least for the chief justice, arrived in 1965 courtesy of that year's legislature. For almost ten years the chief justice had acted under constitutional authority as the administrator of the state judicial system. Now a judicial administration commission coordinated the system's financial operations. Chief Justice Thornal led the panel as its first chairman, although he quickly pointed out the very limited nature of the commission's responsibilities. "We are purely a fiscal service agency," he noted. In late July, Thornal designated the commission's first executive director. J. H. Guerry previously had served the state comptroller's office as a budget expert.[4]

Thanks to the opening of district courts of appeals in 1957, the pace of court life, at least for the time being, ran as slowly in 1964 as it had before the case escalation of the late 1940s and early 1950s. "There is a great esprit de corps among the Supreme Court justices and they lunch together almost every day at a special table at the Tallahassee Country Club," one account observed. "The judges say they can't discuss politics but they are allowed to listen on the subject. They also have a self-imposed rule that an absent member may be discussed at the luncheons only by unanimous vote of those present." The peaceful conditions proved only an interlude, though. Florida's population explosion following announcement of Walt Disney World plans quickly enhanced court filings and appeals. During 1969 the panel would be called upon to dispose of 1,210 cases. Two years later, Chief Justice Roberts declared that "the problem is reaching crisis proportions." Roberts explained, "If we project this year's caseload at its current ratio, the Supreme Court case level will reach a record of 1,500 in 1971, or 50 percent more than the crisis year [of 1952]."[5]

Even before tensions elevated along with the caseload rise, some appeals presented to the justices had sparked great sensitivities and concerns. Through the late 1950s and into the 1960s, the U.S. Supreme Court and other federal tribunals repeatedly had overridden the state panel on several civil and criminal rights issues. Irate at the temerity, the justices had believed that sacrosanct principles of *stare decisis* and judicial reluctance to legislate public policy had been violated. Some thought that a nadir of sorts was reached when the Florida court refused, in a case involving "freedom riders," to carry out a federal court order because it was not authorized to do so by the state constitution.[6]

Resistance of this sort seemed logical to many at the time and pleased much of the bar and public, at least those members who were paying attention. It did not please everyone, though. In September 1966, liberal U.S. Supreme Court Associate Justice William J. Brennan Jr., at a University of Florida Law School function, admonished his local brethren:

> It is not surprising that the state judge faced with a case presenting a conflict of state interests and the national constitution and laws will sometimes react in a way that reflects zealousness to maintain the integrity of his state's sovereign powers. Nor is it surprising that he is occasionally stirred to resentment when the U.S. Supreme Court reaches a different judgment on the question whether the state action he approves must give way to the commands of the national constitution and laws. Nevertheless, it must be remembered that in ratifying our national constitution, the founding states accepted the express constitutional provisions that provide for supremacy of the national constitution and national laws in proper cases.[7]

The *University of Miami Law Review* similarly took the justices to task. "At best, the Florida Supreme Court could be described as slow to recognize the range of Fourteenth Amendment protection," it opined in the fall of 1966, "at worst, the court might be suspected of foot-dragging."[8]

The court's actions by 1966—as the examples mentioned suggest—were attracting critics who were not reluctant to voice their concerns publicly, but the tribunal's problems had not yet come near to the degree of severity that they were about to approach. Claude Kirk deserves credit for starting the ball rolling. The

Republican governor did so because he wanted to stamp his influence on the panel just as had his predecessors. The opportunity arose in September 1967 when Chief Justice O'Connell resigned his seat to accept the University of Florida's presidency. Kirk wanted to fill the vacancy by appointing his protégé and political aide Wade L. Hopping, a former supreme court research assistant and Florida Bar executive. Unfortunately, Hopping had not held membership in the Florida Bar for the legally requisite ten years. So Kirk turned to another supporter and aide, former supreme court justice Alto Adams, who had switched his party registration in anticipation of the eventuality.[9]

The appointment switch blossomed into a statewide shower of bad press for the supreme court. Newspapers carried the details of Kirk's machinations, including the fact that the Florida Bar privately had insisted to the governor that Adams was not qualified. They also reported rumors that Adams would hold the seat only until mid-1968, when Hopping would be able to meet the requirements. "Governor Kirk's appointment of Alto Adams as a justice of the State Supreme Court is an affront to the Bar and a setback to the campaign to take judgeships out of politics," blustered the *Tampa Morning Tribune*. Adams had his defenders. The *Tallahassee Democrat* observed, "We've never heard Alto Adams claim to have become one of Florida's great judges in his few years on the bench; but he served with such patriarchs of jurisprudence as Glenn Terrell, J. B. Whitfield, Armstead Brown, and Rivers Buford, and contributed his share of judicial decisions." It added, "His opinions, it might be observed, are cited by every member of the Bar's Committee as legal precedent when it serves their purpose in court." Overall, a Jacksonville headline writer summed up the prevailing sentiment: "Democrats Must Have Jumped with Joy at Kirk Naming Adams."[10]

The Adams designation ignited controversy, but the resultant publicity also drew attention to the fact that, in 1968, three court seats likely would require filling by election. Adams's seat counted as one open to contest, and Justice Caldwell was barred from seeking a new term due to the constitutional mandatory retirement age of seventy. Then in January, Justice Thomas announced his retirement after forty-three years on the bench, citing advancing years and frustration. "The U.S. Supreme Court has botched [criminal law] up so," he asserted, "it's made a burden of it." A wide range of candidates quickly lined up to vie in party primaries. They included Hopping, who opted to run for Adams's seat. The crowded field winnowed to six party nominees in the May elections: Dade County commissioner Joe Boyd faced Republican C. Richard Leavengood of St. Petersburg; Gainesville circuit judge James C. Adkins, a Democrat, vied with appeals court judge David McCain of Ft. Pierce; and Brevard County circuit judge Vassar B. Carlton carried the Democratic banner against Hopping.[11]

The partisan scramble, on the heels of Adams's appointment, transmitted to Floridians only dimly aware of their supreme court a sense that the tribunal's existence was infused with politics. The situation soon got worse. A sort of one-upmanship led candidates to stake out increasingly conservative positions on hot-button issues in a manner that, not many years earlier, would have been thought highly inappropriate. Another factor complicated matters. In July, Adams suddenly resigned from the court, permitting Kirk to place nominee Hopping on the bench. All the old Adams appointment stories discovered new life. Hopping, at the same time, found himself forced to balance campaigning with brand-new court duties. The voters failed to be amused. In November they cut short Hopping's court career. While Republican Edward J. Gurney carried the state decisively over former governor LeRoy Collins, they handed victory to the three Democrats. "I think a lot us thought there would be coattailing," a frustrated Hopping commented, "but there was no transfer of votes from the head of the ticket down."[12]

The nature of the 1968 court races left many onlookers deeply chagrined. Hopping, for one, immediately called for "a new method of selecting judges." He explained, "What it means is that some day—a day not too far off—good experienced judges are going to be swept out of office because of their political party." In January, *Jacksonville Florida Times-Union* political editor Hank Drane passed on reports that "there will be a strong movement during 1969 by some members of the judiciary to change the present method of electing justices of the Florida Supreme Court, judges of the courts of appeals and, possibly, circuit court judges." Expanding on his story, Drane noted, "There is a suspicion that the three new justices, although all are honorable men with fine records of public service, may have won their seats because they are Democrats and also because they were listed first on the ballot in the Democratic primary by reason of their names beginning with A, B, and C."[13]

Only a bare majority of the court of early 1967 remained on the bench in January 1969, and even that statistic quickly changed when Justice E. Harris Drew expressed his intention not to seek reelection in 1970. Tallahassee attorney Leo Foster, Justice Caldwell's former law partner, announced his bid for the seat in August. "I think it's time the supreme court had a lawyer on it," he declared. "I mean a lawyer who has had extensive experience in all of civil and criminal law and would tend to observe those laws." Dade County circuit judge Hal P. Dekle, an unsuccessful contender in the 1968 Democratic primary, stood to oppose Foster: "School desegregation is being pushed too fast and . . . people are sick and tired of not being safe in their homes and on the streets." This time, no Republican candidate remained in the contest long enough to appear on the general election ballot. Accordingly, Democratic nominee Dekle took Drew's seat in November 1970. Two months earlier in a classic contest of north Florida against south Florida, he had bested Foster almost two to one in the party primary.[14]

The personnel changes had not yet run their course. The day following the 1970 general election, Justice Thornal died of cancer. Having seen the rapid and controversial reworking of the supreme court during the previous two years, reporters jumped on the story in a manner that reinforced concerns that Florida suffered from a "political court." The governor, who had been defeated November 3 by Democrat Reubin Askew, waited well over a month to announce his selection. In the meantime journalists aired a series of intriguing possibilities. One bizarre alternative had Kirk giving the court seat to Senator Ed Gurney, a Harvard Law graduate, the governor appointing himself to the resulting Senate vacancy, and Lieutenant Governor Ray Osborne stepping into the executive office for the remaining few weeks of the term.[15]

As the rumors swirled, other influences touched the appointment process. Pursuant to a previous agreement, the governor asked the Florida Bar to screen one of the defeated 1968 Republican court nominees, David McCain. Bar president Burton Young designated a three-member committee to investigate McCain, with the panel returning a report, as Young described, "replete with suggestions, not only [of] legal improprieties committed by Judge McCain, but of his *suspected* criminal activities and enterprises in which McCain *may* have been involved." When Young presented the report, Kirk reportedly "became livid with rage." Young picked up the story from there. "The governor then rapidly read the report and then looked up and said words to the effect that I should not be surprised as to what he does. I remarked that if he appointed McCain it would be a serious error of judgment. I was then dismissed with a curt 'thank you.' Leaving the governor's office, I met retired Supreme Court justice Alto Adams, who was waiting to see the governor. It was common knowledge that Justice Adams was championing the appointment of Judge McCain."[16]

Action quickly ensued. On December 9, soon after his encounter with Young, the governor moved to place David McCain on the supreme bench. To fill McCain's appeals court position, Kirk tapped his chief legal aide Gerald Mager. Asked by reporters his reasons for appointing McCain, the governor explained that his designee had proven himself "a good judge" and that the new justice "would make a good statewide candidate, and that is important. He will make a good race." Taking the oath on December 14, 1970, McCain claimed seniority over Dekle, who did not join the tribunal until January 5, 1971.[17]

As these events occurred, more controversy flared. Under the rotation system previously in place, Justice Carlton would have assumed the chief justiceship in January 1971. As he was preparing for his new duties, though, Carlton learned that in May 1967, prior to his election, the court quietly had modified its rotation policy to specify that—beginning January 5, 1970—a new rotation scheme would begin with the most senior justice. That man was B. K. Roberts. Newspaper reports quoted "a court source" to the effect that "the election of the veteran of 22 years was a move to assure experienced leadership in 'crisis years' ahead and establish the court as a strong partner with executive and legislative branches of government." The source cited a new constitution and a new governor as requiring mature leadership on the bench, but the individual added, "There is growing interest in criminal procedures brought about by the 'law and order' issue and in court room reform, particularly in the legislature." The apparent slight to Carlton in favor of Roberts, though groundless, stirred segments of the press and bar. As a result, in a quick decision the court opted to forego its new scheme by naming Carlton chief justice effective in January 1973.[18]

As if that were not enough, Justice McCain came under intense scrutiny within days of his appointment as a result of allegations that he had accepted "large unreported campaign contributions" during his 1968 court race. An eyewitness fed details to the Dade County state attorney, who pressed the matter before a grand jury. That body in January 1971 called for a "thorough" investigation by the judicial qualifications committee. McCain denied all charges, and there the matter rested.[19]

All of these happenings helped to set the stage for and added context to the voters' decision in November 1970 to turn down a proposed revision of the constitution's judiciary article as not honoring the promise of real reform. They also help to explain the sense of urgency felt by many reformers to ensure that acceptable action was taken quickly. Governor Askew took a large step in September 1971 when he created judicial nominating councils to advise him supposedly on a nonpartisan basis in making judicial appointments based upon specific criteria. He convened a special legislative session two months later to craft a substantially reorganized and modernized state judicial system. After spirited debate, a revised Article V was approved and set for a ratifying election on March 14, 1972.[20]

The new proposal radically altered Florida's hodgepodge judicial system. Allegedly to remove politics from the judicial selection process, vacancies on courts thereafter were to be filled by the governor from nominations made by nonpartisan judicial nominating commissions. Fourteen trial courts were consolidated into two: circuit courts and county courts. The measure placed ultimate administrative responsibility for the state's court system with the chief justice but also provided for chief judges in each circuit. Unless vetoed by two-thirds vote of the legislature, supreme court rules of practice and procedure would reach all courts. Specialized divisions within any court but the supreme court were authorized, as were branch courts. The plan required all judges to work full time and to be lawyers. At the same time, judicial qualifications commission procedures were made applicable to all judges, and the state assumed responsibility for all judicial salaries. Public defenders were called for in each circuit, among other things. The revised article thus encompassed the hopes of reformers over the entire post-World War II period.[21]

Floridians embraced the court changes with enthusiasm. In March 1972 they approved the proposed constitutional amendment overwhelmingly. Looking ahead to its implementation on January 1, 1973, judicial officials, bar representatives, and legislators joined to lay a firm foundation for change. The legislature had accomplished its part by mid-April 1972. The supreme court took steps as well. Among the changes, the new judicial article established a position of chief court administrator. In announcing the appointment of former Central Intelligence Agency attorney James Ueberhorst to the post in late May, Chief Justice Roberts described his duties as "trouble-shooter for the court on administrative problems involving the judiciary in 20 circuits." Ueberhorst was directed to assume day-to-day administrative responsibility of the state court system under the chief justice, including assignment of cases, assignment of judges, and balancing of caseloads. The newly appointed official acknowledged that his task would be "a tremendous challenge." The court finalized its preparatory work in December by issuing its last transition rules for the changeover.[22]

By 1972's close, the supreme court had witnessed changes in its personnel, its operations, and the state court system that would have seemed highly unlikely to occur eight years previously. Now tribunal members, Florida lawyers, and Floridians generally looked forward to a new day for the judiciary and for justice in the state. Many of the reforms would stand the test of time, while others would require revision and amendment. Legacies of the past proved difficult to overcome, though. Problems of politics (including within the judicial nominating system), intracourt rivalries, *ex parte* communications, appearances of improprieties, and other aspects of human fallibility remained in place, just beneath the surface of public notice. The court's triumphs of past years stood for time to test, but the passing months and years also would gauge how long other legacies would remain unseen just beneath of the surface.

Wade Lee Hopping, Supreme Court Justice, 1968–1969

Wade Lee Hopping's arrival on the Supreme Court of Florida in 1968 spoke volumes about the changes that had occurred in the state within the previous generation. Traditionally, justices had hailed either from Florida (often the Panhandle area) or from a nearby southern state. They trained for the law at the University of Florida, Stetson University, or some well-regarded law school elsewhere in the South. With the exception of Justice Alto Adams's brief second stint on the tribunal, each was a Democrat. But in Florida, change swirled in the air and many assumptions no longer could be trusted. Where white conservatives once rested comfortably within the Democratic Party, for instance, the Republicans now had begun to make inroads that, within another generation, would lead them to control state government. Still, it came as a surprise in 1968 when Wade L. Hopping—a northern-born, northern-educated, conservative Republican—brought to the court a preview of what lay ahead in Florida's future.

Justice Hopping's family represented solid midwestern and middle Atlantic stock. Mother Mildred VanScoyk Hopping was the child of a Pennsylvania Dutch family that had immigrated into Ohio a generation or more earlier. Strict Pentecostals, the VanScoyks held prominent positions at various Ohio locales, including the office of postmaster. The Hoppings also had lived in Ohio for several generations. At Dayton, father Paul Wade Hopping operated a restaurant and bar, while participating actively in community and fraternal organizations. Wade Lee was born in Dayton on August 12, 1931.[23]

Hopping's childhood did not turn out to be the happy one that his parents had anticipated at his birth. Their marriage was troubled, and when he reached age eleven they divorced. The impact of the split fell heavily on the youth. As he recalled, "At one point I was on the way to becoming a juvenile delinquent." Compounding this difficult situation, he spent the remainder of his childhood shifting between the homes of his father, mother, and grandparents, all of whom possessed starkly different attitudes toward life. At one point, in 1947–48, the shifts took Hopping away from Dayton to Chicago, where his mother had remarried. As might be expected, he struggled in school. A high school guidance counselor discouraged him from even considering college.[24]

Fortunately, life did hold positive aspects for Hopping. Soon after his parents divorced, he became involved with Dayton YMCA programs. The local director, Dr. Robert Young, took an interest in Wade. Among other things, Young saw to it that Hopping attended summer camp, where Young designated the lad as a junior counselor. As years passed, the relationship and Hopping's YMCA participation made a substantial difference. "I learned about responsibility," Hopping recalled.

"Dr. Young helped put discipline back into my life, got me back on track." At the camp, Hopping also developed interests that would stay with him through life, among them tennis, boating, sailing, and swimming. Physical activities at the camp encouraged the young man to pursue other sports in high school. Here he excelled. By the time he received his diploma from Dayton's Fairview-White High School in 1949, he had lettered in football and tennis, while also competing well in basketball and track.[25]

The self-esteem and discipline learned from Dr. Young and through sports allowed Hopping to pursue higher education. Despite his grades, state law permitted the high school graduate to attend a state university. He chose Ohio State, where he thrived. Hopping credits his social fraternity, Sigma Chi, for offering him structure and encouraging him to be active. He not only competed on the varsity lacrosse team but also achieved election to the student senate, was an officer of his fraternity and campus political party, and presided over the Pre-Law Club. Most surprising to the young man, he succeeded academically. "If you work hard," he came to believe, "good things can happen." His academic interests evolved as time passed from political science to law. A campus program permitted him to enter law school as a senior and to receive his bachelor of arts degree after successful completion of the first year. Accordingly, he earned a political science degree in 1953 and an LL.B. degree in 1955.[26]

Another milestone occurred for Hopping at Ohio State. During his first year of law school, he married LiAnne Heckman. They adopted Steve and Judson, born in 1959 and 1962. Hank was born to them in 1964.[27]

Following law school graduation, Hopping easily passed the Ohio bar examination, but work other than the law lay in store for his immediate future. During law school he had enrolled in Ohio State's Reserve Officer Training Corps program. His commitment provided for two years' service, as a result of which in August 1955 he reported for active duty in the U.S. Army. Following training courses, he served as tank platoon leader for the 6th Tank Battalion and, later, as division defense counsel and legal assistance officer for the 24th Infantry Division in Korea. A first lieutenant when discharged in May 1957, he returned to Columbus, Ohio, where he engaged in the general practice of law with the firm of Adams & Hopping.[28]

An Ohio legal practice did not suffice to bind Hopping to his home state; rather, he soon directed himself south to Florida. "I didn't have any work to do," he explained about the Ohio experience. Partner Bill Adams practiced during the winter at Fort Lauderdale and encouraged him to take the Florida Bar examination in 1958. Further, Adams enjoyed Democratic Party associations that opened a door for Hopping to meet Justice T. Frank Hobson. The fact that the young lawyer studied for the bar exam in Florida's supreme court library allowed the connection to mature. As a result, Hobson encouraged Hopping to become his research assistant in August 1958. In 1960, he opted for a potentially more lucrative private practice at Palm Beach, although, as it turned out, the town and its social and professional lifestyles did not suit him. Justice Glenn Terrell's wife, Esther, invited Hopping back to Tallahassee to assist her husband in the same manner that he had served Justice Hobson. He remained with Terrell from January 1962 until the justice's death in January 1964.[29]

By the time Hopping served Justice Terrell, his life had begun to change in fundamental ways. For one thing, he searched for a faith that held personal meaning for him. Raised a Pentecostal by his maternal grandparents, at Tallahassee he joined Trinity United Methodist Church. Justice Campbell Thornal furthered his participation in the church's various activities to the point of guiding Hopping into service as a lay preacher to rural congregations. Hopping also taught Sunday school classes for young people, a vocation that he enjoyed intensely, and sat on Trinity's official board.[30]

The changes soon touched Hopping's political perspectives. "I had been a Republican in Ohio," he recalled, "and it was a more liberal Republicanism, a Taft-type, a progressive bullmoose, a get-things-done kind of Republicanism as opposed to the super-conservative southern Democrat." He added, "Being liberal on social issues and conservative on fiscal and economic issues used to be traditional." In Florida, though, the newly transplanted lawyer had registered as a Democrat "in order to vote in local elections." He also found himself becoming more conservative. When Arizona senator Barry Goldwater lost the 1964 presidential election to Lyndon B. Johnson, it proved the last straw for Hopping. "I decided the country was going to hell in a hack," he explained. As a result, he reregistered as one of Florida's growing number of Republicans.[31]

Political affiliation did not mean much professionally to Hopping in 1964, but it soon would. In that year he was working for the Florida Bar as director of Continuing Legal Education, a position that he had assumed after Justice Terrell's death. By 1966, however, Florida had elected Claude Kirk as its first Republican governor since Reconstruction. Hopping had seen Kirk during a Tallahassee campaign stopover but otherwise held no connection with him. Kirk, though, required the services of an expert on the Florida constitution and the constitutional revision process. Former bar president Chesterfield Smith recommended Hopping for a sixty-day loan. When the governor's principal adviser fell victim to a heart attack, Kirk asked his borrowed expert to remain with him. The Republican lawyer and Republican governor found themselves well suited for each other. Before long, Hopping had become one of Kirk's favored aides, with "government" as his area of responsibility.[32]

It did not take Kirk or Hopping long to begin thinking of the now experienced lawyer as a potential supreme court member. When Stephen C. O'Connell resigned from the panel in September 1967, Kirk planned to appoint his aide until the two men discovered the state constitution's requirement of ten years' membership in the Florida Bar. Instead, Kirk designated former justice Alto Adams, perhaps with the understanding that Adams would resign as soon as Hopping qualified. Then in March 1968 Hopping, with Kirk's blessing, announced for the Republican nomination to contest Adams's seat, given that the incumbent could not run again due to the constitution's mandatory age limitation for court members. The candidate quickly presented himself to the public as "a constitutional conservative," insisting that "it was not the duty of the court to change laws." Four months later, Adams sent Kirk a resignation letter. The governor took only a few days to designate his protégé. "His background in constitutional law and his penchant for hard work will serve him well on Florida's highest court," Kirk declared of his appointee. Hopping quietly took the oath of office on August 1, although he repeated the event in a more formal and ceremonious manner on September 10.[33]

Justice Hopping's court tenure ended shortly after it began. In November 1968 Democrat Vassar B. Carlton bested the incumbent by an easy majority and succeeded him in January 1969. Still, Hopping participated in scores of appeals. He wrote opinions in a dozen or more cases, and *American Law Reports* later featured one of them. Hopping remembered his court colleagues affording him a "fine" reception. "They were respectful, if not overly enthusiastic," he explained. "Politics was never an issue. We had some philosophical rows, particularly over jurisdiction." The former justice concluded, "I was a flaming liberal on the court" when it came to questions of jurisdiction.[34]

Having departed the court in early 1969, Justice Hopping pursued his legal career at Jacksonville, where his wife had family connections. The weight of politics and public service had added too much burden to an existing strain on the couple's marriage, though, and it dissolved. More happily, on June 6, 1971, Hopping married Mary Monroe. With her came two children, Kiff and Mary Beth Mendoza.[35]

By the early 1970s, Hopping had relocated his law practice to Tallahassee. Already in 1969 he had decided to pursue legislative representation. Over the following three decades he emerged as one of Florida's premier lobbyists. He has advocated the interests of business and development so successfully that opponents have labeled him the "Darth Vader" of environmentalism. Yet Hopping sees himself as an environmental lawyer and has taught the subject at Florida State University's Law School. He argues that he fights too much government rather than environmental protection. "I think the government is like kudzu," he insists. "You have to prune it back every year." He has remained active in the Florida Bar and the American Bar Association. In 1986–87 he became the first attorney to preside over the Florida Chamber of Commerce. His law firm of Hopping Green Sams & Smith, founded in 1979, continues to offer client services at Tallahassee.[36]

Vassar Benjamin Carlton, Supreme Court Justice, 1969–1974; Supreme Court Chief Justice, 1973–1974

In 1968 Republicans made substantial gains in Florida politics. But, as evidenced by Vassar B. Carlton's election to the state supreme court, old Democratic Florida also proved that it retained enough vitality to push back the political tides much of the time. The contrast between Carlton and his Republican opponent, Wade Hopping, appeared stark. Hopping symbolized the Florida arrival of a tide of northern-born and northern-educated members of the Grand Old Party unburdened by racial divides of the old South. Carlton, on the other hand, traced family roots well into Florida's past, claiming kinship with a governor, a rich frontier heritage, and easy relationships with black voters who were coming to exercise significant influence in the Democratic Party and state elections. Still, Carlton's connections with the past would haunt him on the court, and his stay there would prove less than happy.

His family name suggested wealth and power in Florida, but Carlton came into the world poor. He was born November 13, 1912, to Benjamin Franklin and Zeffie Ergle Carlton. B. F. Carlton's grandfather, Alderman Carlton, had been killed during an 1856 Indian raid near Fort Meade, but his children had gone on to help pioneer southwest Florida and its cattle industry. One descendant, Doyle Elam Carlton, served as Florida governor from 1929 to 1933. Most of the family had prospered given the time and place, but not so with Alderman's son W. T. and his grandson Benjamin Franklin. Similarly, Zeffie Carlton's family had struggled to survive. Her grandfather, James R. Terrell, had been killed during Florida's largest Civil War engagement, the Battle of Olustee. Her parents, John Isaiah and Malvina Sylvester Terrell Ergle, had failed at farming in Putnam County before moving on to Alachua.[37]

In 1912 the B. F. Carlton family lived in rural Alachua County at Island Grove, which lay east of Gainesville and three miles southeast of Cross Creek, the community made famous by writer Marjorie Kinnan Rawlings. Their home had no running water or electricity. An outhouse, or "half-mooner," sufficed for a bathroom. Father Carlton worked local citrus groves and tried to farm as he could. When the Florida bust came in 1926, he relocated the family to nearby Hawthorne where parents and children joined to help operate a café. Its failure in 1927 led to a citrus job at Plant City, where the Carltons first enjoyed indoor plumbing. Then it was on to Fort Meade and, finally in 1929, to Merritt Island.[38]

Vassar Carlton thus matured in a rural world where daily life required both interdependence and self-reliance. As was true of his siblings (he was the third of four sons and a daughter), Vassar performed farm chores and odd jobs from an early age. "I was raised in the country milking cows by lantern light, eating breakfast by lamplight, and plowing fields by daylight. My days numbered from the horse and buggy days to the moon walkin' days." Carlton's parents—strict disciplinarians though they were—provided inspiration, but so did onetime slave Uncle Jack, who helped watch over the lad and delighted him with stories of Florida's past. The Baptist Church also played a part. His parents took their religion seriously and imparted the same commitment to their son. In the rough-and-tumble world in which he grew to manhood, fighting to protect oneself made up another rite of passage. Out of it Carlton developed a lifelong interest in boxing. In the same vein, he came to love outdoors life. Hunting and fishing offered sustenance coupled with pleasure. To benefit properly from the sports, he learned to cook. Quail stew became a specialty.[39]

Given his family's financial circumstances, repeated relocations, and the standards of Florida's rural schools, Carlton's education suffered. Although he would graduate from Cocoa High School in 1931, he could barely read and write. Instead, he had thrived on his athletic ability. He played football, baseball, and basketball while also delving into boxing and bowling. The future judge's affable personality also lent itself to making friends and exercising leadership. Within one month of arriving at Merritt Island, he had achieved the captaincy of the Cocoa High School football team. A few weeks later, the student body elected him general athletic manager for the school. He would star as well in the junior and senior class plays.[40]

Neither of Carlton's parents had graduated from high school, and they yearned for their children to progress beyond their economic limitations. Carlton attempted to attain a University of Florida football scholarship, but none remained unallocated. So Carlton waited tables, solicited dry cleaning, and, with his brother Doyle (not Governor Doyle Carlton), opened a boarding house in an attempt to stay at the University of Florida long enough to prepare to follow his dream, a medical degree. He came close to failing. The course work at times exceeded his ability to cope with it. Carlton and his brother also raised the ire of Professor Robert Spratt Cockrell, a former supreme court justice, thanks to Doyle's challenge of the professor's methods. Vassar paid for the confrontation with a failing grade. It would not be forgotten. "He caused many students to change law schools; he wouldn't let them pass the subjects which he taught," Carlton recalled years later. "Once he even told a crippled student who had to use crutches that he had no business being a lawyer and gave him a failing grade."[41]

Cockrell's enmity, coupled with the offer of a football scholarship at Stetson University, changed the course of the struggling student's education and career. At Stetson, he enrolled in the law school but dropped out of the football program in order to take a lucrative job managing a nearby hotel. The regimen of work and study lasted for two and a half years. Once again Carlton experienced problems balancing work and study, particularly in light of his weak educational background. Stetson's small classes and nurturing faculty made the difference. He graduated with his thirteen-member class, which included brother Doyle, in June 1937.[42]

Law school graduation meant for Carlton a return to Merritt Island, but his career barely stumbled along. Failing to obtain suitable employment, in 1937 he opened for business at Cocoa in offices shared with Hubert Griggs, an established attorney who allowed the neophyte to use his floor space and library. No secretary assisted the budding lawyer, and fees appeared few and far between. He made many friends, though, and by late in the decade he had been elected president of the town's junior chamber of commerce. Some financial relief arrived in 1939 when Florida Power and Light Company of Miami contracted with the young man to obtain right-of-way clearances for power lines in Columbia and Baker counties. Electricity remained a novelty for many, and the job sometimes called upon Carlton's considerable aptitude for negotiation and friendly discourse.[43]

Back at Cocoa in 1940, Carlton faced a professional and financial dilemma that he resolved by deciding to run for county judge. In later years he spoke proudly of his longtime ambition to sit on the Florida Supreme Court, and perhaps he envisioned the race as a first step. More likely, he needed the steady work and four thousand dollars per year compensation. Already popular in the community and carrying the well-known Carlton name, he squared off against an incumbent who took reelection for granted. With five hundred dollars in borrowed campaign funds, the candidate traveled Brevard County's back roads and trails, politicking the old-fashioned way. He won at age twenty-seven. Upon taking office in January 1941, he basked in renown as the state's youngest judge.[44]

By all accounts Carlton's tenure as county judge, lasting almost fourteen years, proved very successful. Reelected without opposition in 1944 and 1948, he easily bested an opponent in 1952. The judge dispensed his brand of justice with a common touch. Insisting that he based judgments upon the "Golden Rule," he believed that he "could always be forgiven for a mistake of the head but could never be forgiven for a mistake of the heart." Carlton worked hard at the job and never lost touch with his electorate. "He's simply the greatest politician I've ever known," one friend declared. "I've learned much from the judge about treating people right." For his part, Carlton loved the position, considering it to be his career's highpoint. "To me the county judge is the closest person to the people," he explained. Carlton especially enjoyed working with young people, even though his methods by today's standards might seem unorthodox. "In those days, when you had a juvenile you could take them home with you or try to find somebody else to take him home with them or you could send them off to the boys' school," he recorded. "It was really a challenge." He must have done it well, or at least many local residents thought so. "He has worn the mantle of the law with dignity and with knowledge, from his first days as county judge of Brevard," observed the *Cocoa Tribune*. "But, perhaps more important, he has worn a second mantle—that of humanity—in a profession more demanding of a man's love of his fellow man than perhaps any other."[45]

One secret to Carlton's electoral success involved support from African Americans. From his childhood relationship with Uncle Jack, the judge had worked with and lived close to black families. At times he labored as the only white man on work crews, yet he found acceptance from other crew members once he proved a willingness to work hard. This meant something important to the poor youth, for such jobs were difficult to obtain and could be lost if he could not get along with others. He felt that he reciprocated the acceptance, believing that, as a judge, he treated African Americans fairly and honestly. Available evidence suggests that Carlton did make efforts that some other jurists of his time did not. He credited his first election, for example, to black votes—no mean feat in a county wherein lived Harry T. Moore, president of the Florida National Association for the Advancement of Colored People and later head of the Progressive Voters' League. When Ku Klux Klansmen assassinated Moore on Christmas night 1951, Judge Carlton quickly empanelled a coroner's jury, taking care that two black men, including one from Moore's community of Mims, served on the panel alongside white members.[46]

The changes that Carlton initiated following his election as county judge, once some financial security seemed assured, included starting a family. In December 1940, shortly before taking office, he married Mary Lee Hardin of Clearwater. Their daughter Mary Carol would be born on December 25, 1941, to be followed by Martha on August 29, 1944, and Barbara on April 21, 1948. The union did not remain a happy one, though, and the couple divorced in 1958. The difficult experience left Carlton ailing and, even though he had moved up to a circuit judgeship in 1955, financially troubled. The healing process finally advanced when he began dating a young woman who worked in the county clerk's office. He and Grace Ramer married in September 1959. Her six-year-old daughter, Pam, joined the family as well.[47]

Through the early 1960s, the circuit judge delighted in family life, community activities, and his work, but politics soon altered matters irrevocably. In 1966, Florida had elected its first Republican governor since Reconstruction, and he soon acted to place his protégé Wade Hopping on the state's supreme court. Public reports of Governor Claude Kirk's plan circulated at the same time as Brevard County Republicans pushed Carlton for an appellate judgeship. The governor's office responded with a directive that the judge change his party registration from Democrat to Republican. Angrily, he declined. He grew more wary when Kirk returned former justice Alto Adams to the court as a Republican. His pique provided whatever additional incentive he needed to announce his own race for the supreme court seat. Basing his campaign upon his judicial record, the candidate boasted twenty-eight years' service on the bench and thirty-five thousand cases processed. In May 1968, he defeated Hal P. Dekle for the Democratic nomination and in November easily outpaced Hopping in general election voting.[48]

Justice Carlton's supreme court career began January 7, 1969. He described himself as "a liberal on human rights and a conservative on the constitution." He added that he saw "the duty of judges to interpret the law, not write it." Critics who felt they represented the "New Florida" questioned his "Old Florida" style. "He could get along with the good old boys in Tallahassee," one of them explained, "and could be talked to." Carlton's greatest challenge arrived in January 1973 when he was elected chief justice following the November 1972 ratification of a revised judicial article for the Florida constitution. He held ultimate responsibility for implementation of the major judicial overhaul, and his success at the task brought praise. "History will indicate," Richard Ervin declared, "that Chief Justice Vassar Carlton was one of the most effective chief justices in the history of the Supreme Court of Florida."[49]

While taking pride in his accomplishments, Carlton found that he did not relish his supreme court service. He often discovered himself in the minority, and he did not form close attachments with his colleagues. Court socializing he considered "very impersonal." He described himself as "very optimistic" when looking forward to his chief justiceship, but Justice Joseph Boyd later insisted that Carlton "hated" the position. One reason concerned grief. On January 17, 1973, his wife, Grace, died, a victim of leukemia. The loss almost overwhelmed the chief justice. Then rumors of court scandals swirled, including published reports that the Judicial Qualifications Commission was investigating Carlton. The Carlton reports proved unfounded, but, when added to other frustrations, they prompted the chief justice to resign. He did so effective February 28, 1974.[50]

In the year of his resignation, Vassar Carlton began restructuring his life. He commenced on February 16, 1974, by remarrying. Bartow native Sue Collins had worked for the state's division of consumer affairs. They had found common ground in talking about hunting, fishing, and cooking quail. Of Carlton, his wife observed: "He listens to people. I mean really listens." He soon returned to the practice of law, while also serving as a director of a large insurance company. In 1988 he helped organize a prepaid legal plan. By the 1990s, he had finally decided to retire for good, as a result of which he and Sue moved to Franklin, North Carolina. Justice Carlton died there on August 31, 2005. Back in 1973, Justice Joe Boyd already had summed up for others his colleague's unique contribution to Florida. "Chief Justice Carlton knew and understood the ordinary citizen a long time before he became a county judge. His years on the bench never caused him to lose sight of the problems confronting the ordinary citizens."[51]

James Calhoun Adkins Jr., Supreme Court Justice, 1969–1987; Supreme Court Chief Justice, 1974–1976

Justice James C. Adkins Jr.'s life and career reflected many of the same aspects as those of Justice Vassar B. Carlton, his fellow victor in the court elections of 1968. Both claimed families with distinguished Florida heritages. Each had attended a Florida law school, and each boasted longtime service as a judge before his election to the Florida Supreme Court. Adkins and Carlton shared a basic conservatism, and both were Democrats. Carlton willingly resigned his seat in 1974, but Adkins would fight to keep his as late as 1987.

Gainesville claimed the Adkins family as its own. Adkins was born there on January 18, 1915, to James Calhoun Adkins Sr. and Elizabeth Edwards Adkins. While Carlton's family coped with rural poverty only a few miles to the east, the Adkinses enjoyed comfort and prominence. At the time of Adkins's birth, his great-uncle Andrew Zenas Adkins served in the state senate (he later sat on the circuit bench) and his father represented Alachua County in the Florida House of Representatives. A lawyer, James Sr. in 1922 achieved election as state attorney. From age eleven James Jr. attended court with his father, often sitting on the steps leading up to the judge's bench. As Adkins reminisced, "I was raised with a law book in my hand."[52]

Adkins found primary, secondary, and higher education furnished to him at

Gainesville, although on one occasion he took a slight detour. As a boy he attended public schools until, at age fourteen, his father sent him to business school to learn shorthand and typing. Subsequently he worked in his father's law office and occasionally acted as a court reporter. He graduated from Gainesville High School in the early 1930s, after which, as his father desired, he entered the University of Florida, which Vassar Carlton also attended. There, after Adkins had entered the law program, a touch of rebellion stirred inside him. "I entered in the summer and then the first year, I didn't like it at all. I think it was in 1935. Hitler was making noises, and I was interested in the army and ROTC and decided to go to West Point. I had to lie during the physical, and then when I got to West Point, they found out that I got there by misrepresentation." Eventually discharged thanks to Governor David Sholtz's intercession, Adkins returned to Gainesville and the University of Florida. To get by, he worked for law firms and published a weekly edition of class notes. He graduated with a bachelor of law degree in 1938.[53]

With the Great Depression of the 1930s still plaguing Florida, the soon-to-be attorney found himself in a quandary. "I didn't have any place to go when I graduated," he recorded. So Adkins applied for the position of sole research assistant to the Florida Supreme Court. Meanwhile, he took a temporary job at a Gainesville law firm with a salary of $75 per month. When the court job came through in September, his income doubled. He learned quickly that, aside from family connections, his nonlegal skills had made the difference. "You would not have been hired," assistant librarian Carson Sinclair informed him, "if you couldn't type." The experience impressed Adkins. "Working for six justices gave me an opportunity to associate with all of them and enjoy their friendship and guidance," he noted. "Knowing them made me appreciate the great heritage of the Supreme Court. This will live with me forever." Still, it did not draw the young man to immediate thoughts of court service. "While I learned much from and enjoyed my clerkship, the experience convinced me that I would never wind up as a Justice of the Florida Supreme Court. The last thing I wanted to be was a judge."[54]

Instead, in 1941, after a two-year interlude spent as an assistant attorney general for statutory revision, Adkins retraced his steps to Gainesville where he aimed to make a living in the courtroom. "I looked over the situation and saw that they didn't have any public defenders. I realized that anybody who wanted to get trial experience could do it very easily—just tell the judge, 'I'll represent anybody.'" Fortunately, Adkins's father welcomed his son into his well-established practice. The son assisted his father in revising his classic handbook, *Florida Criminal Law and Procedure*, while also learning the practical aspects of legal work. The partnership continued until James Sr.'s death in 1952. For five years thereafter, the son practiced alone. Among his accomplishments, in 1950 he became the first Florida lawyer to achieve dismissal of charges against a client because no African Americans served on the grand jury.[55]

Adkins enjoyed the life of a small-town lawyer. "I had to know every phase of the law," he explained to an interviewer. "People would come to you for a divorce and later they would have a kid in trouble. Or, later on somebody was charged with a fine or somebody wanted to draw up a will. You became the family lawyer and everybody looked to you. The grandchildren of people I represented come up to me now and say Grandpa thinks so much of you." His small-town ways, honed by years of Gainesville practice, persisted. "He dresses simply, laughs readily, and genuinely listens to others in a way eminent people frequently do not," a reporter noted in 1986. "Adkins hikes down the hall to fetch his own coffee." Supreme court clerk Sid White seconded the reporter's assessment. "He's never become affected. He has a genuine affection for the common man."[56]

At least in his early years, Adkins did not find as much pleasure with or success at marital relations as he did with the practice of law. Seemingly a happy-go-lucky type, he jumped into commitments with less forethought than some others might have given the matter. As a law school student in 1937, he married a woman from Dixie County, only to procure a first divorce the same year. He wed a second time the following year, yet again in the 1940s, and a fourth time in 1950. Sadly, one of the spouses passed away, while the other relationships ended in divorce. A fifth marriage that occurred in the mid-1950s proved more durable. He and Ethel May Fox, a Hawthorne native, would remain together for twenty-three years. The couple shared two children, Linda Rae Adkins and James C. Adkins III.[57]

Not until the late 1950s did Adkins's career of public service begin. In 1957 he took a first step by becoming a part-time assistant state attorney. "I folded up my criminal practice and started prosecuting everybody I had represented," he explained. The work involved Adkins in the creation of a court of record for Alachua County. Believing that service on the bench "might be fun," he applied to fill the position. Governor LeRoy Collins made the appointment in 1959.[58]

Adkins's first experiment with judicial life did not last long, and the low salary of a county judge quickly took its toll. The novice jurist, to make ends meet, continued work on revised editions of his father's criminal law and procedure book, as well as other legal works. "I wrote for a living," he acknowledged. "I didn't write because I enjoyed it." The unhappy experience soon ended. "I resigned after two years so I could make money as a plaintiff's lawyer in negligence cases," he recorded. Four years passed during which the lawyer made money but grew bored with his work. Then, in 1964 a new circuit judgeship offered Adkins an out. He applied for the slot, and Governor Farris Bryant obliged him. The judge remained in the seat for four years.[59]

Then came the 1968 elections when the filling of three supreme court seats required voters' action. By that time Adkins was searching for a way off the circuit bench. "I found that [the] income wasn't much too good either," he related. "It paid $10,000 more on the Supreme Court. I felt I would like to run in the state [in which] I was raised, out of curiosity; but never thought I could ever win—but still I might try." At that point, fate intervened. Adkins's name made its way into state news when he denied bond for two Gainesville "civil rights militants" whom he had charged with contempt for criticizing a grand jury. Two fire bombs thereafter were thrown into his house, greatly enhancing the publicity. Fortunately, no one was home and total damage amounted only to three hundred dollars. Adkins later acknowledged that "there wasn't anything racial relating to the fire bombing," but some quickly saw him as a victim of black radicalism. The incident provided just the boost his candidacy required. "The judicial system is a barrier which will stem the tide of disorder," he proclaimed. "These threats to our society must be faced with a strong experienced judiciary." On May 8 Adkins defeated appeals court judge Woodie A. Liles of Plant City for the Democratic nomination. He went on to best Republican appeals judge David L. McCain in November.[60]

As he mounted the supreme bench, Adkins brought with him a philosophy that he described as "hardnosed, conservative." He opposed efforts to expand the court's jurisdiction and wrote the opinion that reinstated capital punishment. "Some men ought to die," he expressed. "You don't make a pet out of a rattlesnake." Beyond that, he acted subject to what he called "Levy County law," which applied his understanding of "Levy County logic." As the justice explained, "To me, that means down-to-earth and common-sense thinking rather than drifting into legal abstractions." Perhaps most notably, he brought to the panel an immense knowledge of criminal law and procedure, gleaned from his own research and from years of assisting his father. Justice Leander Shaw later identified himself as a "Jimmy Adkins groupie" for his colleague's efforts at "keeping Florida abreast of the ever-changing criminal laws."[61]

Although Justice Adkins made a strong impact on the court during the early years of his tenure, problems soon surfaced. For one thing, his marriage had soured, leaving him "extremely unhappy." He detailed subsequent events. "I was overloaded with work, not making money, unhappy at home, and couldn't see much of a future. So I did my work and had a good time on the side." The good times included heavy drinking, a fact that resulted in Judicial Qualifications Commission proceedings. Compelled to face up to the situation, he thereafter pushed for establishment of schools for drunken drivers and a hot line for attorneys with similar problems.[62]

Then in 1974 Adkins stepped into the chief justice's chair with Vassar Carlton's resignation. He strove to reform traffic courts and to open up judicial proceedings to some coverage by television, but his elevation came just as the court erupted in a series of public controversies and scandals. When Adkins appeared to side with colleagues accused of improper conduct, heavy press criticism ensued. Other negative publicity followed, and depression gripped him again. "I don't have much social life," he complained, adding that "I haven't played golf since I've been here."[63]

Yet Adkins refused to give up. Some of the workload eased with the 1976 end of his term as chief justice. In 1979, conditions improved considerably when his home life took a turn for the better. He met television journalist Elizabeth Ann Lawrence, and the two quickly found themselves attached. He and Ethel, separated for some time, finalized their divorce, leaving Adkins free to marry Beth Lawrence in August. He began to speak out on deeply held beliefs such as "the right to be left alone" and advocated, accordingly, the legalization of marijuana and the right to purchase pornography. Eventually his thinking on the subject compelled him to oppose mandatory membership in the Florida Bar. Adkins's spirits remained high even after a 1986 bout with oral cancer. "I'm having too much fun to leave," he declared.[64]

In 1987 Justice Adkins did leave the court, although not without a fight. Faced with mandatory retirement, he unsuccessfully pursued an age discrimination action. Adkins called the situation "constitutional senility." He remained in Tallahassee and practiced law. He had begun writing murder mysteries during his last court years, and he continued, finding enjoyment at last in writing. In 1992 the Florida Bar Foundation honored him with its Medal of Honor. He died at Tallahassee on June 24, 1994. Upon hearing the news, Justice Leander Shaw spoke of his friend. "Justice Adkins had the finest legal mind that the state has ever known. It combined with his endless empathy for the small person to make him one of the state's greatest justices."[65]

Joseph Arthur Boyd Jr., Supreme Court Justice, 1969–1987; Supreme Court Chief Justice, 1984–1986

Two of the three members of the supreme court's class of 1969 (elected in 1968) boasted extensive judicial experience, but the third newcomer pointed instead to a background in local politics and longtime service on a county governing authority. He could not claim to be a Florida native, nor had he attended the University of Florida or the Stetson University Law School. Joseph A. Boyd Jr. represented something different in these and other ways. In a political sense, he symbolized the emerging power of Miami, Dade County, and the lower Atlantic coast generally. More immediately, his personal habits and perspectives threatened many members of official Tallahassee's top ranks, however acceptable those same traits might have been in flexible, metropolitan Miami. As a result, Boyd's actions sometimes were misunderstood and misconstrued. At a critical juncture they would put Justice Boyd at the center of controversy and public scandal.

Certainly his Georgia origins did not render Boyd the least unusual to the court; in that regard long-standing precedent paved the way. He was born in that state's northern hills near Hoschton in Jackson County on November 16, 1916. His parents, Joseph Arthur Boyd and Esther Puckett Boyd, kept a farm, the income from which Joe Sr. supplemented by circulating as a traveling salesman. The future justice performed the range of chores normally assigned to a child in such a situation, and he reveled in the out-of-doors as also would have been natural. The family adhered closely to the Baptist Church. As an adult Boyd would not drink alcohol or smoke. In years to come he would read the Bible each morning, making it his habit as a Florida justice to do so first thing upon arrival at the court. A sign he posted advised visitors that "prayer changes everything." To those who were interested, he reasoned that "the Sermon on the Mount and the Ten Commandments constitute the basic norms for human conduct." He would add, "Anybody who violates any of these standards is walking into a lot of trouble."[66]

Boyd traced his interest in politics and in the law to events of his boyhood. He recalled, for example, a sheriff dropping by his father's farm when he was about seven to campaign for votes with a jug of moonshine whiskey. Spying the illicit traffic, the lad felt "a deep sense of moral outrage in the knowledge that the sheriff had probably jailed the moonshiner but was freely using the illegal whiskey himself." Joe Sr. told the boy to be patient. "My father said I should grow up," Boyd recalled, "and knock him out of office." The idea stuck.[67]

Joe father's also got him thinking about the law. Once when the child saw a roadside chain gang, he grew fearful that he might be arrested and placed on one for some childish misdemeanor. Joe Sr. comforted his son by explaining carefully the constitutional right to a writ of habeas corpus. "Thus, I was assured, an arrested person who had done no wrong would be immediately released by order of the judge," he recorded. "I have treasured the Great Writ ever since." Joe Sr. also took his son to see his first trial. The case involved a neighboring sharecropper who had run afoul of the locally powerful landowner. Joe Sr. contacted his cousin Joe Quillian, who subsequently served on the Georgia supreme court, to ride to the defense. "We waited in front of the store and we witnessed Joe Quillian's arrival into town," Boyd reminisced. "To our eyes he was dressed 'like a Spanish ambassador.'" He was a most impressive sight as he drove his gleaming black Ford with red wheels through the muddy roads of North Georgia. The mere presence of Joe Quillian was enough to prompt the landowner to dismiss his complaint against the sharecropper."[68]

Certain modern forces influenced the young man as well. Known for his gregarious, amiable nature, Boyd also evidenced a certain feistiness at times. As he put it, "[I am] not afraid of a fight." He attributed the trait to the flicks. "As a child, I used to watch Jimmy Cagney movies," he informed an interviewer. "And the scene which I liked most then, and which I like most now, is when he takes the pistol, knocks the window lights out of the house, and says, 'If you want me, you dirty coppers, come and get me.'"[69]

The young scrapper eventually decided that only college could save him from the hard rural life of his parents. After public high school he attended Piedmont College in Demorest, Georgia, although he spent much of his time there earning enough to survive. He specialized in selling Bibles door to door, but he gained more than a little money by secretly operating a pawn shop out of the college admissions office. His most profound memory of the Piedmont experience involved meeting a fellow student, John Birch, after whom the conservative John Birch Society would be named. "[He was] the most profoundly dedicated person I ever knew," Boyd opined. As soon as he could, the future justice moved on from Piedmont to Macon's Mercer University Law School. To pay expenses, he sold "Bibles, brushes, cleaning equipment, and automobiles." He also "dealt in used appliances and clothing" out of his college dormitory. He lasted one year before he gave up in 1938.[70]

Broke and dispirited, Joe Boyd set out to seek his fortune in Florida. Choosing Miami, he set to work. "I sold bread and cakes on a bread-truck sales route, worked as a hotel night clerk, and sold real estate," he noted. He kept the real estate license and also kept a wife. He met Ann Stripling because she was the assistant Hialeah city clerk, plus a realtor on the side. His close partner, Ann eventually ran his law office and his political campaigns. "Joe's been a wonderful provider," she would joke, "having provided me with steady work since we were married." They eloped in 1938 with fifteen dollars and were married on June 6. Joe borrowed the ten dollars he contributed, leaving Ann thinking fraud had been committed. "Nobody warned me about listening to a Georgia-reared Bible salesman," she commented. The couple shared five children: Joanne, Betty Jean, Joseph, James, and Jane.[71]

World War II soon interrupted the love match. Joe served in the Marine Corps, mostly in the South Pacific and Far East. Following the peace he remained for a time with the army of occupation in Japan, being among the first Americans to visit the destroyed city of Nagasaki. At discharge he carried the rank of sergeant. Back in civilian life, he took immense pride in his military service. He participated actively in the American Legion. In 1953, he achieved election as the organization's state commander. Boyd would admit, though, that not everything had gone well in the service. "I was at Guadalcanal," he once told friends. "Every night at 6, the crabs would march to the sea by the thousands. There seemed to be no end to the crabs. Work at the Supreme Court reminds me of those crabs."[72]

Upon release from the service and with the GI Bill's educational benefits guaranteed to him by a grateful Congress, Boyd hitchhiked to Miami "with only $2 and a wealth of self-confidence." With Ann's support, he enrolled in the University of Miami Law School, from which he earned a juris doctor degree in 1948. Opening a law office as soon as possible thereafter, Boyd specialized in real property, probate, and corporate law. He benefited by gaining appointment in 1951 as Hialeah city attorney, a post he kept until Dade County voters elected him in 1958 to the first Metro commission under its newly established metropolitan charter. He proved quite adept at politics, remaining on the body until his election to the Florida Supreme Court. As Justice Leander Shaw has noticed, "Joe is unnaturally attracted to registered voters." Property investments in the Miami/Dade region meanwhile made Boyd a millionaire.[73]

While rough, Commissioner Boyd's 1968 campaign for the Supreme Court of Florida proceeded far more smoothly than did his eventual transition to court life. His reasons for making the race remain unclear. He sat at the time as chairman of the Dade Metro Commission and enjoyed prominence and prosperity. The fact that Dade County enjoyed no representation on the court bothered him, though, and perhaps that offered enough of a hard reason to surrender to the prestige, respectability, and what appeared to be the less-hectic pace of a justice's life. Boyd found the field to succeed Justice Elwyn Thomas included two others. Large support from his home area helped him lead the Democratic primary and then to defeat Orange County circuit judge Richard Cooper in the runoff. The Democratic nomination no longer ensured automatic election to the court, but Boyd outpolled his Republican opponent, Pinellas County circuit judge C. Richard Leavengood, by a comfortable margin in the November general election.[74]

Then came Tallahassee and the court. Boyd explained his transition difficulties in a *Nova Law Review* article published in 1986. "Life in Tallahassee and working in the supreme court building were drastically different from the style of life and work my family and I had known in the international cosmopolitan setting of Miami," he wrote. "Having no prior judicial experience and being denigrated by some people as just a Miami politician, I felt I had to show my new colleagues that I could fit in and perform court work successfully. At that time the style, manner, and attitudes of a Miamian were so culturally different from those of Tallahassee that I sometimes felt from people's reactions that they regarded me as they would a visitor from a foreign nation." Boyd's court experience proved so distasteful to him that, upon announcing the firm date of his retirement, he asserted, "They couldn't tie me up and drag me back here for another term." He then described service on an appeals court as "like being on a submarine—you're cramped up there together; you learn to like the people even if they disagree with you strongly on some legal issues." He continued: "Disraeli said those who consume them should not see sausages in the making, and I think it's best that people not see court opinions in the making either. No, I'm going to come out of the submarine hatch and be real people again." Nonetheless, Boyd could not resist declaring, "I loved the Supreme Court."

Others' reactions to Boyd's idiosyncrasies contributed to his lack of comfort at Tallahassee and on the court, but he created his major problem. The incident stemmed from a friendship with an attorney who represented a corporation with litigation pending before the court. The attorney composed and supplied to Boyd's office a draft opinion in the case. While Boyd adamantly denied such, the lawyer argued that his justice friend had asked for the improper *ex parte* submission. Whatever, Boyd ultimately ripped up the document and flushed it down his office toilet, but the whole sordid business soon became public knowledge. Against the backdrop of the national Watergate scandal, additional court members were drawn into the affair at essentially the same time as other court members were struggling with questions of ethical lapse. Eventually the court reprimanded Boyd for unethical conduct. The jurist then fought impeachment, in the end by agreeing to a psychiatric examination. Following the procedure, a legislative committee voted against recommending his ouster. One newspaper labeled Boyd "the man who put the whole Florida Supreme Court on trial." He raged, "I survived one of the most vicious political assassination attempts in the history of Florida." Seeing liberals—especially those working for the *St. Petersburg Times*—as his principal foe, Boyd commented further: "I survived because, first of all, I hadn't done anything improper. It was a vicious political conspiracy, not only against me, but against a lot of other people."[75]

This and other problems might have compelled a person of less resolute character to quit the court, but not Justice Boyd. Just as he persisted in fighting impeachment, he fought to stay on the court. Impressive reelections in 1974 and 1980 did not still the unkindness and, perhaps, hostility that he faced from some of his brethren. Every two years from 1976 until 1984 they passed over him for selection as chief justice. This omission occurred even though, in 1981, he and research assistant Randall O. Reder published the respected article "A History of the Florida Supreme Court" in the *University of Miami Law Review*. Two years later, the Florida Bar reissued the history as a bound volume. Finally, in 1984 a less-than-unanimous court agreed to Justice James C. Adkins's motion to allow Boyd to serve as its chief. Of those years, he would declare: "Each one of us is a loner in a way. It's the loneliest job in Florida. Even funeral directors get to see people on funeral day." Boyd added: "You do things because they need to be done. I don't expect to leave a legacy. I came every day and did the best I could."[76]

Boyd eventually found his legacy in finely crafted reasoning and in dissent. "People who laugh at him are usually the people who haven't read his opinions," one Florida State University law professor averred. "The quality of his opinions is very high." The justice's writing, many legal scholars believed, was "concise, to the point, and plain." As one such individual put it, "He has a gift for cutting through the complexities of a case and getting to the heart of an issue quickly and with a minimum of fuss." His dissents seemingly brought him more gratification than his majority opinions. "My views were more in tune with the theme of protection of civil liberties than were those of my colleagues," he related in his final year as chief justice. He reacted with delight when the U.S. Supreme Court upheld his dissenting views in favor of the right to counsel for minor crimes, strictly upholding freedom of the press against state action, and restricting criminal prosecutions for vagrancy. In the end, he said, he wanted to be remembered for helping "the little people," but his accomplishments as chief justice in bringing greater efficiency to the judicial process and in reviving the Florida judicial council also stand out in retrospect.[77]

After his departure from the bench in January 1987, Justice Boyd practiced law and tended to business. He also took life a little easier. To an extent this change was not voluntary for the usually dynamic Boyd. Cancer treatment in 1983 and double-bypass heart surgery three years later had sounded warnings. In April 1993 the supreme court convened at Miami to honor its former chief. Time's passage and a growing appreciation for Boyd's court legacy now permitted humor to replace prior hostility. Boyd listened to gentle barbs and some unstinted praise for his record "as a defender of the first amendment and civil liberties." Still looking and sounding, one report disclosed, "ready to run for statewide office," the former justice summed up the occasion for the *Miami Herald*. "This was like a wedding and a funeral," he said. "You're glad to see all your friends, but you realize it's the last time anybody will know you're around." The Boyds continue to live at Tallahassee.[78]

David Lucius McCain, Supreme Court Justice, 1971–1975

In instance after instance, as the biographical sketches contained in this volume have disclosed, individuals who served on the Supreme Court of Florida had harbored a "lifelong" or, at least, longtime dream of that eventuality. One question raised by that fact involves the lengths to which a potential or sitting justice would go to obtain or keep a seat on the tribunal. Justice David L. McCain's life offers a glimpse of the dark side of the answer. By all appearances McCain was a solid citizen and an ideal candidate for the highest reaches of the judiciary. But his drive engulfed his character and eventually destroyed his career and his life. In doing so, McCain's experience framed one context by which Floridians would measure their supreme court by the mid-1970s. It proved a dismal picture, indeed.

McCain's early life seemed to all who knew him as almost idyllic. Born to Robert G. and Bessie L. McCain at Sebastian on July 23, 1931, he grew up in a home that provided support and encouragement, although perhaps his parents' expectations ran too high. Still, upon his swearing in as a court member in 1970, the proudest person watching was his mother. At the time, her other son, Willie R. McCain, served as chairman of the St. Lucie County Board of Commissioners. During the future justice's childhood, the Great Depression lashed Florida and the nation. Yet David fared well. Beginning in kindergarten, David earned a straight A average. He remained lean, and as he matured, he became handsome. David attended the Baptist church, achieved Eagle Scout status, and eventually ranked as valedictorian of the Vero Beach High School class of 1949. His valedictory theme reflected on the appeal "Friends, may you recall only our virtues, forgetting our faults."[79]

Given that family friend Alto Adams served on the state supreme court during McCain's adolescence, the answer as to why he chose his career path is clear. On hearing news of his own court appointment, McCain would exclaim, "This has been a dream of mine from the time I was a young boy—first to be a lawyer and then be a judge." In the Florida of 1949, the way to accomplish both goals began at the University of Florida. McCain entered the school soon after high school graduation and remained through the award of his LL.B. degree in 1955. He excelled at almost every turn. "He did all those things that Gators do," his stepdaughter Dianne Cossin noted. Among them, McCain served as president of Kappa Sigma fraternity and was honored with selection to Florida Blue Key, the University of Florida Hall of Fame, Alpha Phi Omega, and Phi Delta Phi. He represented the Blue Key speaker's bureau for six years.[80]

His law degree in hand, McCain proceeded to establish a solid professional life. First, he honored his military commitment by serving two years as a captain in the U.S. Air Force judge advocate corps. He spent the greater part of that time as assistant staff judge advocate for the 30th Air Division's headquarters. His work handling court-martials and appeals won him commendation. Released from the military in 1957, McCain quickly joined the Fort Pierce law firm of Thad H. Carlton. Two years later, he became a senior partner in the new firm of Carlton and McCain, subsequently Carlton, McCain, Brennan, and McAliley. As he gained experience, the ambitious young lawyer won the job of Fort Pierce city attorney and emerged, in the eyes of some, as "the best trial lawyer" in the region. As one report had it, McCain worked hard and "was seen as having an uncommonly bright future."[81]

As he grounded himself professionally, so too did McCain attempt to ground himself personally. He married Joyce E. Taquin. Decades later, he still insisted, "I always loved Joycie." They had five children together: Tamara Lee, Cassandra, Laurette, Melanie, and David. By all accounts he devoted himself to his children. "He was the best father," insisted stepdaughter Diane Cossin. "He fixed skinned knees, he drove car pools, and he escorted teenagers to football games. He raised his children to be strong, independent, and eager to learn. He taught us how to get back up after we had been knocked down, and he shared his love of the law and love of life." Beyond immediate family concerns, McCain reached out to perform community service. He associated with local fraternal organizations, the YMCA, the Jaycees, the American Legion, and the United Fund Drive.[82]

All the many calls upon his time and energies did not distract McCain from his professional aspirations. By the early 1960s he had decided to further them by stepping into the political arena as a conservative Democrat. He ran in 1962 for state representative but lost. The experience added to frustrations he felt about changes in the Democratic Party, and four years later he backed Republican Claude Kirk for governor as a "Demokirk." Soon he joined the Republican Party outright. Then Alto Adams reentered the picture. In early 1967, the former justice was assisting the new governor in assessing whether new legislative acts deserved approval or veto. Adams asked McCain to come to Tallahassee and assist. As was his typical pattern, McCain worked, in Adams's words, "exceedingly hard." Both the lawyer and the governor already may have been thinking about a supreme court future for McCain, but the immediate reward came in the form of an appointment to the Fourth District Court of Appeals. Only a few months later, in early 1968, McCain announced his candidacy for the state tribunal on a platform stressing that "criminals should not be coddled." He defeated Miami lawyer Ellis Rubin for the Republican nomination but came in second to Democrat James C. Adkins Jr. in the general election balloting.[83]

Within two years, the appeals court judge's political luck changed. The day after Democrat Reubin Askew ended Governor Kirk's hopes for a second term on November 3, 1970, Justice Campbell Thornal died. The death created a vacancy that Kirk, who remained in office until the new year, could fill. Under a gentlemen's agreement with the Florida Bar, the governor had consented to fill such vacancies from a list submitted by the bar. As the state constitution authorized him, Kirk ignored the arrangement, and on December 9, after encouragement from Alto Adams, he named McCain to the supreme court. The governor explained his selection by pointing out that his designee was a good appellate judge with three years of experience and enjoyed youth that would permit longtime service. "And, then, he will make a good statewide candidate, and that is important," Kirk added. "He will make a good race."[84]

The new justice, who took the oath of office December 15, moved quickly to establish conservative credentials. He observed that, as a "strict constitutional constructionist," he felt that his philosophy would "fit right in with that of the court." McCain declared further, "It is necessary that constitutional and statutory issues be resolved within the meaning of the existing language and not as one person may think it should be." He continued, "Laws and their application should protect not only the rights of an accused but also the rights, lives, and properties of the innocent and the security of our society." Alto Adams, who had returned to the court briefly in 1967–68, thanks to a Kirk appointment, buttressed McCain's conservative credibility. "He's not a reformer type," Adams stated in newspaper interviews. "He will accept tradition and go along with it." The onetime justice assessed his protégé's philosophy as similar to that of Justice B. K. Roberts, especially in the critical area of "property rights."[85]

Right away, signs that something might be amiss began to appear. As the appointment news circulated, one of McCain's 1968 court campaign aides disclosed that the new justice had demanded unreported campaign contributions and other favors from attorneys who had business before his court. The aide, who had just been elected a legislator, provided details. McCain denied the allegations, but a grand jury kept the matter alive. Although most members of the public remained unaware, insiders also knew that McCain's wife had divorced him and that he had remarried since the 1968 campaign. No one had disclosed the justice's drinking problem.[86]

Coverage of campaign finance abuses waned, and Justice McCain settled into court duties. He attempted to influence other panel members to shorten rulings and to write opinions "in words that can be readily and clearly understood." He explained, "I don't see how the press can understand some of those decisions that are full of whereases." These efforts enjoyed limited success, as did his attempts to strike up friendships with other justices. "I was the only one there who was very close to him," recalled Justice Adkins. Adkins also remembered positive aspects of McCain's service. "He had the greatest ability to judge a case," the new arrival's onetime political opponent explained. "He could analyze the case and go into conference and get the meat of it. His mind would just click. He had a beautiful mind. He thought better than he wrote. He wrote some pretty good opinions, but he could really analyze any type of case." McCain's votes, along with Adkins's, offered strong support during the early 1970s for the court's conservative majority. With Republican incumbent president Richard Nixon receiving 72 percent of the state's votes, the electors thanked McCain in 1972 by electing him to a full six-year term.[87]

Less happily, McCain's problems reappeared and mounted. For one thing, the pressures of possible investigations, the press of court business, and reelection concerns dampened his early joy at becoming a court member. His drinking problems grew apace. "When all this heckling started, and all this trouble started, it really got to him," Adkins recorded. "He drank too much, and this just pushed him more into the bottle, and he had a lot of personal problems, too." As cracks began to appear in his new marriage, charges surfaced in 1974 that he had accepted money from a gangster's lawyer and "a union bagman." Then, one after another, new disclosures came to the fore. He had favored certain attorneys in rulings, reports delineated. According to the allegations, McCain also had given preferential treatment for campaign contributions and improperly interfered with judicial processes.[88]

Justice McCain's downward spiral had begun. At first the Judicial Qualifications Commission quietly looked into the concerns, but in February 1975 House Speaker Donald L. Tucker demanded the files and appointed a special committee to look them over. This action led to impeachment hearings that McCain boycotted. Instead, the jurist unsuccessfully sought to have the supreme court interpose its authority to stop the proceedings. When that attempt failed and impeachment seemed certain, he resigned from the court on April 29, 1975, effective August 31. Justice Adkins and Willie McCain had helped him move toward the decision "for the good of the court." His letter of resignation remained defiant. "I do not wish to posture my friends in the legislature of having to vote upon my record of official accomplishments," he wrote. "These I have considered always to be not only defensible but untarnished."[89]

The downward spiral continued. McCain relocated to Orlando and Miami in an attempt to practice law. He watched from afar as the Florida Bar initiated disbarment proceedings. A hearing officer recommended reprimand and a one-year suspension, but the bar pressed in August 1977 for a greater penalty. Meanwhile, McCain took comfort in drink, a fact that led to an arrest for frightening three teenaged girls with a handgun and a separate drunken driving incident. Courts found him guilty of the charges in both cases. In June 1978, the supreme court ordered the former justice disbarred immediately.[90]

The following eight years witnessed profound degeneration. McCain sought to earn a living by performing legal research in Fort Pierce, but in time he turned to drug smuggling. After a Louisiana federal grand jury indicted him for conspiracy to import more than thirty thousand pounds of marijuana, he fled in January 1983 while under one million dollars' bond. His whereabouts for the next three years remain uncertain, but he likely found refuge in South Carolina. Eventually several of his daughters arrived there to offer him care. Mostly, according to reports, he drank, chain-smoked, and ate candy bars. He started calling himself "The Thin Man." In mid-October 1986, Jacksonville physicians operated on him for cancer. On November 11, David L. McCain died, still a fugitive, in a Jacksonville apartment.[91]

That McCain committed serious breaches of judicial ethics and criminal law seems clear from the advantage of hindsight, yet family members believed that journalists and the system had treated him unfairly, if not disgracefully. His stepdaughter, Diane Cossin, voiced some of their sentiments when she wrote to a Tallahassee newspaper following his funeral. "At the services, surrounded by close friends who have stood by us through these difficult years, I felt confident that what is printed does not matter. What does matter is that my father was a strong and good man. No other evidence is necessary than to see these dedicated, sincere, and loyal friends." Cossin added: "To understand another man, you have to sit in his chair. The witch hunt is over."[92]

Hal Peb Dekle, Supreme Court Justice, 1971–1975

The court turmoil that centered on and engulfed Justice David L. McCain in the mid-1970s touched several other panel members including Justice Hal P. Dekle. A man whose background suggested a jurist almost ideally prepared for supreme court service, Dekle would err in a manner serious enough to result in his resignation from the bench. On the other hand, Dekle's actions, response, and after-court life varied markedly from that of Justice McCain. In assessing them, the necessity to examine the details of each man's actions and motivations becomes plain. Justice Dekle's experiences also sound a cautionary note for those who would serve on the supreme court in the modern era of journalism, mass communications, and media frenzy: avoidance of the appearance of impropriety unquestionably constitutes for a court member a responsibility every bit as important as avoiding impropriety itself.

Hal P. Dekle came from a Panhandle family of prominence and pioneer status. Grandfather Matthew Leonidas Dekle arrived with his parents in Jackson County from Thomas County, Georgia, during the Civil War. He entered the mercantile business at Marianna in 1875 and prospered to the point of becoming one of the region's leading bankers and civic leaders. His nine children included M. L. Dekle Jr. who pursued his fortune as a real estate broker and merchant in Jackson and Gadsden counties and married Marianna native Marie Clifford Smith. The young couple would set out to build a large family just as had Dekle Sr. Eventually four girls and four boys would occupy their large Marianna home. The second eldest son, born November 21, 1917, they called Hal Peb.[93]

Childhood for the Dekle progeny involved fortunate times in a small-town north Florida setting. Afternoon play outdoors, walking to and from school, even chapel and its singing produced happy memories. The state's economic bust, which commenced in 1926 and lasted through the 1930s, failed to dampen spirits substantially. Hal's parents were "knocked for a loop" financially, but they responded by teaching their children thrift and frugality while maintaining an optimistic outlook. Education came for the children at home, at the Baptist Church founded by Hal's grandfather, and in Marianna public schools. Favorite subjects included English and history. Studying algebra offered no pleasure. With schooling, particularly high school, also came athletics. Hal Dekle excelled at baseball and basketball while playing "a little" football. His senior basketball team reached the 1935 state finals at Gainesville, a fact that afforded him not only his second trip outside Jackson County but also his first glimpse at a real university. "I thought," he related, "it's a wonderful world out there."[94]

As it turned out, financial concerns directed Dekle away from Gainesville and toward DeLand when he pursued higher education. Stetson University president W. S. Allen, during a preaching visit to the Marianna Baptist Church, encouraged the young man to enroll at Stetson by offering a working scholarship based on high grades at Marianna High School. Grandfather Dekle promised twenty-five dollars per month additional assistance, a benefit maintained by sister Anita Dekle Smith when Dekle died midway through Hal's freshman year. Hal supplemented this income with work managing the college bookstore and collecting dry cleaning.[95]

Dekle fared better at work than at studies. At first he pursued a business degree, but he tired quickly of accounting. Meanwhile, exposure to law students got him thinking about changing focus. Dean Ike Tribble hastened a decision by informing Dekle that "he thought I would do better in law school." A slate of Ds his first semester prompted business faculty members to inform him, "Son, you haven't seen the forest for the trees." The lecture "woke me up," Dekle explained. He graduated from the Stetson University Law School in 1940. His honors included president of the student body, Phi Alpha Delta, and winner of Law Club competitions.[96]

The newly minted lawyer aimed for a career with the Federal Bureau of Investigation, although the future held other directions in store. Initially, Dekle worked in Washington, D.C., for the Justice Department while awaiting results of his FBI examination. With World War II looming, though, he found a draft notice in the mailbox instead of an FBI badge. Quickly, Dekle attempted to enlist in the Marine Corps but was rejected due to poor eyesight. To fill the time before being called to active duty in the army, he accepted the offer of a job with Tallahassee lawyer J. Velma Keen, also a Marianna native. The young lawyer worked for seventy-five dollars per month in an office adjacent to the state capitol.[97]

A stroke of good luck awaited Dekle in Tallahassee. There he encountered Dorothy Clark, then living at Monticello. "She was the best secretary I ever had," Dekle later observed. "I married her to keep her." Born in Colorado to Robert and Laura Josephine Clark, Dorothy had grown up mostly in Venice, Florida, where her engineer father had helped to lay out the city. Their courtship continued after Dekle received his call to active duty in September 1941. The couple wed on Valentine's Day 1943 at Monticello. They would have three children: Patrick, Keith, and Dawn.[98]

Dekle's military service would last from 1941 to 1949. During World War II, he received a commission as a lieutenant in the quartermaster corps before service in the Pacific theater. His movements included a stay in the Philippine Islands. Discharged as a captain in February 1946, he remained in the army reserve for two years. From 1947 to 1949, the captain also served in the 211th Infantry, Florida National Guard.[99]

Peacetime returned him to law practice. First, he settled at Tallahassee, again with J. Velma Keen. The senior attorney, while welcoming the young man back from the war, told him that better opportunities awaited in south Florida. Dekle followed the advice and associated with the Miami firm of Shutts and Bowen. In 1947 he joined attorney M. Lewis Hall Sr. and others to found Hall, Hedrick, and Dekle. By then he drew a salary of three hundred and fifty dollars per month. In 1951–52, he labored as a special assistant U.S. district attorney. In 1957–58, he served on the Florida Judicial Council. All the while, Dekle involved himself in community affairs. The family attended the First United Methodist Church of Coral Gables, where he helped lead the Methodist Men's Club and, from 1960 to 1965, presided over Miami's Methodist Home for the Elderly. He remained active in the American Legion and other veterans, fraternal, and civic organizations.[100]

One community activity, political activism, led a hesitant Dekle onto the bench in 1957. Lewis Hall encouraged his partner to support Governor LeRoy Collins's gubernatorial campaign in 1956. Dekle happily did so, after which he was approached about filling a vacancy on the Dade County Civil Court of Record. Knowing that the move would involve a precipitous drop in his income from $50,000 to $13,500 per year, the lawyer worried about "getting trapped" on the junior bench. At the time he had just managed to purchase his first new automobile. Nonetheless, Dekle accepted the appointment. He and Dade County voters never looked back. In 1958 the judge achieved reelection without opposition. Two years afterward, Governor Collins elevated him to the circuit bench, to which he was reelected without opposition in 1962 and 1966. The Dade County bar consistently ranked him highly among his colleagues, the appellate bench found relatively few occasions to reverse him, and in 1965 the American Trial Lawyers Association honored him with its Award of Merit for Leadership in Judicial Administration.[101]

Just as did his Miami acquaintance Joseph A. Boyd, Dekle saw opportunity in 1968 when three Florida Supreme Court seats came up for election. "Surely," he recalled himself thinking, "I can get one of these." The judge chose to compete for the seat held by Alto Adams and, subsequently, Wade L. Hopping. He established himself as a conservative, although his principal campaign focus ran more to "the importance of providing leadership and stature." Amplifying the theme, he commented, "The Supreme Court is no place to stagnate. It is a place for a man of action, energy, and leadership. It should take the leadership in clearing up criminal dockets in lower courts. The people want something done about this." It turned out that the people were not as interested as Dekle had presumed. Vassar Carlton, a gifted politician, defeated the mostly untried political candidate and his Miami colleague in the Democratic primary. The margin ran almost two to one.[102]

Two years later, Dekle enjoyed far better results when he contested the seat vacated by Justice E. Harris Drew. Former justice Millard Caldwell's Tallahassee law partner, Leo Foster, opposed him for the Democratic nomination. Now Foster stressed facets of judicial reform, while Dekle criticized his opponent as he trumpeted his own conservative philosophy. Particularly, the Miami judge contrasted Foster's wealth and old-line political connections with his own political independence and modest $100,000 net worth. "My one major theme is law enforcement," Dekle also proclaimed. "The people are sick and tired of not being safe in their very homes or on the streets. The people need qualified, dedicated men to stand firm for the law of the land." Rounding out the campaign, Dekle urged a slowdown of public school desegregation efforts, and he also became one of the first to urge implementation of a computer system for the court. This time, Dekle enjoyed the two-to-one advantage in the primary results. Without Republican opposition, he took the oath of office on January 5, 1971.[103]

Unlike Justice McCain's experience, Justice Dekle enjoyed a smooth transition into court life. As he had promised the electorate, he pursued a conservative approach. He later described his philosophy in these words. "I was and am a constitutional conservative, believing in strict construction of the constitution, that the role of the courts as the third branch of government is to interpret the laws, not to create them, which is assigned to the legislative representatives of the people having a voice in creating the laws after due debate and determination." He felt that protection of individual rights fell within a conservative's responsibility. "I believe in the rights of the individual in accordance with the view of Thomas Jefferson, and I strived to uphold these basic rights in my decisions on the court." The cornerstone of proper jurisprudence, he concluded, was *stare decisis,* which meant "following legal precedent for stability in the law." Not surprisingly, Dekle emerged as a court champion of law enforcement and a strong defender of capital punishment. His opinions nonetheless carried little of the formality associated with some of his colleagues. He wrote, an aide related, "in a folksy, conversational style."[104]

Justice Dekle's first term on the court proceeded in a manner that virtually assured his reelection. His positions and philosophy earned him popularity with the bar and public, and he enjoyed his service on the state bench. Then, in late 1974, Dekle's name became enmeshed with the scandal that rocked Justice Boyd's career. Questions of *ex parte* communications and tampering with proper judicial processes soon played in the state press against the backdrop of the Watergate affair. The key problem arose for Dekle because a copy of the legal memorandum prepared by Boyd's lawyer found its way to Dekle's chambers. The longtime judge then either failed to ascertain that it had been routed to him in accordance with proper court procedures or else, if he was aware of the improper arrival of the memorandum, he failed to alert court officials. Available evidence does not indicate that he solicited the legal brief, but he did use it to prepare a court opinion that upheld the lawyer's cause. A court-appointed panel of judges later recommended by a four-to-three vote that Dekle be reprimanded. The remaining three refused to support any punishment. Still, a legislative committee undertook impeachment hearings.[105]

Dekle has maintained that he made a "stupid" mistake, rather than that he acted from improper motives. "It was never challenged that the opinion I wrote for the court in the case was clearly founded upon U. S. Supreme Court cases—just that I, as did the other justices, received a copy of the memo," he declared in a statement written in response to research inquiries undertaken for the preparation of this book. "It was never suggested that I had received any interest in the case, received any benefit, nor that I had any prior knowledge of the deficiency of notice, nor did the other justices, nor had any part in the initiation of the memo. Who needed it!"[106]

A number of Dekle's court colleagues agreed as to their fellow justice's lack of improper motivation or intent. "I thought Dekle was the result of bad circumstances," Chief Justice James C. Adkins Jr. recorded. "They made all these accusations, and Dekle didn't have enough money to fight them. It was just a question of what do you want to do for your family, you know. Judges don't make any money." He concluded, "We lost a good judge."[107]

Having testified before an impeachment panel and facing further proceedings in March 1975, Justice Dekle did resign effective April 30. His legal fees had mounted to $50,000, and he feared for his and his wife's health if the stress of the situation continued. "I can at this point best serve the public interest and my beloved bench and Bar by tendering my resignation, with reservation of retirement benefits, which I hereby do irrevocably," he informed Governor Reubin Askew. Dekle believed that he could survive the impeachment attempt, if it came, but the victory might be a pyrrhic one given the publicity and the fact that he faced reelection the next year. "My effectiveness for the people would be diminished," he explained to Askew, "and I would not wish to fulfill my duties except in the most efficient way possible." He ended his letter: "I harbor no rancor. I look to the future as God grants in his wisdom for me to see it." Privately, Dekle believed himself the victim of "an aggressive liberal press" that was "on attack of our court and me and other conservatives in general at that time." Chief Justice Adkins, who had been out of town when Dekle sent the letter, regretted not knowing of the decision earlier. "I think I could have talked him out of it. I came back and I lost my judge. It affected me terribly." Justice Boyd, who opted to pursue the impeachment fight, survived in office and remained on the court for twelve more years.[108]

Hal P. Dekle returned to the practice of law following his court service. He and wife Dottie eventually settled at Venice, Florida. She died there on April 10, 2003.

Dekle remained in Venice. In 1987 he published *Florida Trial Evidence*, which he subsequently has revised. The former justice died May 23, 2005, at Brandon, Florida. Asked in the year 2000 how he looked back upon his supreme court service, Dekle had responded, "I very much enjoyed my service on the court; I treasure the confidence of the electorate which afforded me this rare opportunity to serve on the highest court of my native state. I feel I made a positive contribution to the jurisprudence of Florida during my term there."[109]

16

Case Decisions, 1964–1972

Florida's executive, legislative, and judicial branches found themselves transformed between 1964 and 1972, changes reflecting even greater alterations that affected the state as a whole. The ouster from power of the Pork Chop Gang, the apportionment of the state legislative seats based upon population, the advent of a viable two-party system, constitutional revision, electoral turnovers, and the march of time and events all combined to exert irresistible influences on public life and, eventually, the state supreme court's direction and impact. Arguably, Florida wrenched itself from the grip of an increasingly irrelevant past to ground itself uneasily in a fast-evolving, exciting, and often troubling modern world.

A hallmark of this era of change, one that soon commanded supreme court attention, aimed to open government to its citizens and to stamp out the legacy of Pork Chop backroom deals and "good old boy" politics. The "Government in the Sunshine Law," brainchild of State Senator Ruebin Askew, achieved enactment in 1967. Its provisions attempted simply to open state and local government deliberations to the public, but many were the critics who preferred the old style of doing things. In *Board of Public Instruction of Broward County* v. *Doran*, the tribunal in 1969 not only dismissed claims of the law's invalidity due to vagueness and denial of due process but expanded its reach. "The right of the public to be present and to be heard during all phases of enactments by boards and commissions is a source of strength in our country," Justice James C. Adkins Jr. proclaimed for the panel. "During past years tendencies toward secrecy in public affairs have been the subject of extensive criticism. Terms such as managed news, secret meetings, closed records, executive sessions, and study sessions have become synonymous with 'hanky panky' in the minds of public-spirited citizens. Regardless of their good intentions, these specified boards and commissions, through devious ways, should not be allowed to deprive the public of this inalienable right to be present and to be heard at all deliberations wherein decisions affecting the public are being made." Adkins concluded, "Statutes enacted for the public benefit should be interpreted most favorably to the public."[1]

Within two years the tribunal again considered the statute and again acted to expand its reach. The *Miami Beach* v. *Berns* ruling disclaimed the necessity of a formal meeting and upheld a district court of appeals determination that the law covered the "entire decision making process." Even informal assemblies came within the court's interpretation. The jurists found no need for voting to trigger the public's right of access and guaranteed public scrutiny, as one legal scholar noted, "from proposals and reports to discussions and recommendations."[2]

Within the court, questions as to which appeals the panel should hear continued to command serious attention as dynamic change swirled outside its doors. Jurisdictional issues, matters arising coincident with the advent of district courts of appeal, immediately had begun to divide the justices. As the state grew wealthier, more populous, and more diverse, the importance of just who decided what matters swelled in significance as well. By 1965 those favoring a more flexible jurisdictional interpretation held a narrow edge as illustrated by *Foley* v. *Weaver Drugs, Inc.* Justices B. K. Roberts, E. Harris Drew, Millard F. Caldwell, and Richard W. Ervin joined in the decision to expand jurisdictional limits. "We hold that this Court may review by conflict certiorari a per curiam judgment of affirmance without opinion," Roberts held, "where an examination of the record proper discloses that the legal effect of such per curiam affirmance is to create conflict with a decision of this Court or another district court of appeal." Justices Campbell Thornal, Elwyn Thomas, and Stephen C. O'Connell dissented strongly. Referring to the jurisdictional lines drawn by the constitutional amendment that created district courts of appeal, Thornal observed, "It appears to me that we now proceed to undo all of this. In our apparent anxiety to emphasize the word 'Supreme' we can easily overlook the fact that the Courts of Appeal are 'supreme' in certain areas."[3]

The divisions and differences of opinion illustrated in *Foley* hinted at a court itself in the spin of evolution within an occasionally volatile atmosphere. New personnel revamped the tribunal's character and its sense of purpose and direction. Firm majorities sometimes slipped away into minorities, as fresh coalitions coalesced and dissolved. The following analysis presents some of the cases considered during this fascinating period.

Consumer Protection

Florida consumers gained a major advantage early in the period when the court determined that "privity [was] not essential to a cause of action by a consumer against the manufacturer where the product is neither a foodstuff nor a dangerous instrumentality." The appeal in *Lily-Tulip Cup Corp.* v. *Bernstein*, decided in 1966, concerned a hospital patient scalded by hot liquid when a paper cup fell apart. "The *Bernstein* decision has ended any conflict over the necessity of privity in an action by the consumer against the manufacturer on breach of implied warranty," one law review reported. "The supreme court has, in effect, held that privity is no longer a part of the law of implied warranty."[4]

Although the decision in 1969's *Shingleton* v. *Bussey* could not be categorized specifically as one related directly to consumer protection, it nonetheless impacted significantly on consumers by placing weight on the interplay between public policy and fair play when it came to consumer interests. The ruling—to which Justices Drew and Roberts dissented—created a direct cause of action by third parties against automobile liability insurers. "Public policy is a molding device available to the judicial process by which changing realities and the attending manifested rules of fair play may be incorporated into our corpus juris," Justice Ervin declared. "It can hardly be denied that one of the fundamental goals of modern procedural jurisprudence is to secure a method of providing an efficient and expeditious adjudication of the rights of persons possessing adverse interests in a controversy."[5] Insurers scored a partial return victory, however, in 1971's *Stecher, et al.* v. *Pomeroy, et al.* Justice Hal P. Dekle there held that policy liability limits should not be mentioned to a jury. "The insurance carrier's position as a real party in interest is a position of continuing interest," he advised, "which includes the trial of the cause which a third party has asserted against its insured."[6]

The purchasers of condominiums, a form of residential housing proliferating in Florida during this period, also claimed a major victory in 1972 as a result of the decision in *Gable* v. *Silver*. This litigation stemmed from the attempt of condominium owners to recover from the builder-seller the costs of repairing a complexwide air-conditioning system. The supreme court, when the appeal made its way to the tribunal, found no fault with a Fourth District Court of Appeals ruling that extended an implied warranty of fitness against the builder to the purchaser of new condominium units. In a *per curiam* opinion, the panel accordingly upheld the lower court.[7]

Environmental Protection

The court in 1962's *Gies, et al.* v. *Fischer, et al.* had taken a major step toward protecting the public's interest when it came to submerged lands sold to private owners, but a divided panel within three years had begun to back away from the precedent, foreshadowing federal court decisions of three decades in the future. Justice Caldwell's decision in *Zabel* v. *Pinellas County Water & Navigation Control Authority* held, "It is our view that a denial of permission to fill in this case amounts to a taking of property without just compensation because it was not established that the granting of the permit would materially and adversely affect the public interest." The four-man majority also determined that the appellant's rights to dredge, fill, and bulkhead—grounded as they were in statute—could not be denied arbitrarily, nor could the beneficial use of their property be restricted without compensation."[8]

Justices Ervin, Thornal, and Thomas disagreed. Ervin predictably sided with government regulation. His lengthy dissent suggested that the new ruling would "emasculate and render sterile the Bulkhead Law and our previous decision upholding it," and his concerns aimed directly at the possibility of environmental damage. "The law was enacted in response to an aroused public interest and alarm concerning the great number, promiscuity, and adverse effects of fills already made in coastal offshore waters of the state and the anticipation of even greater filling of this nature in the absence of any statute regulating indiscriminate filling." As to the case at hand, Ervin noted, "The evidence submitted by the objectors to the application clearly indicate that the proposed fill and the bulkhead line to encompass it are of the character of injurious fills and bulkhead lines which the statute was intended to minimize or prohibit."[9]

A different sense of environmental concern on the part of the panel's majority appeared six years later in the case of *City of St. Petersburg, et al.* v. *Briley, Wild & Associates, Inc., et al.* Acting Associate Justice Ernest E. Mason penned the decision for himself and Justices Ervin, Drew, Vassar B. Carlton, and Joseph A. Boyd Jr. Now the court expressed willingness to accept that the abatement of environmental pollution constituted a "real and substantial" benefit to local residents. It did so to the extent of permitting expenditure of municipal taxes for such a purpose even if the larger part of the benefit accrued to county residents. "Water pollution and the attendant diseases and ills to human habitation that flow therefrom know no city or county lines," Mason observed. "It is impossible to separate as between the various areas of the county the deleterious effect upon the public health of contamination and pollution occurring in a particular area. It is unrealistic to say that the elimination of pollution and contamination of the soils, waters, and streams of the unincorporated areas of Pinellas County will not be of substantial benefit, health-wise and recreation-wise, to the incorporated areas."[10]

A 1971 judgment carried on the theme by limiting the exercise of eminent domain powers where the need to protect natural resources constituted an issue. The court held in *Seadale Industries, Inc.* v. *Florida Power & Light Co.*, in a legal scholar's words, "where independent governmental agencies charged with safeguarding natural resources must ultimately approve a project involving condemnation, the condemning authority must demonstrate a reasonable probability of obtaining approval and that the taking in advance of approval will not result in irreparable harm to natural resources should permission be denied."[11]

Labor Law

A growing public workforce, a state teachers strike, and a new state constitution highlighted issues regarding the right of public employees to unionize and bargain collectively. The 1969 ruling in *Dade County Classroom Teachers' Association Inc.* v. *Ryan, et al.* touched directly on point. For himself and Justices Drew, Carlton, Adkins, and Boyd, Justice Ervin backed the assertion of right by public employees, although he did so subject to certain significant exceptions. "In the sensitive area of labor relations between public employees and public employer," Ervin declared, "it is requisite that the Legislature enact appropriate legislation setting out standards and otherwise regulating the subject within the limits of [the state constitution]. A delicate balance must be struck in order that there be no denial of the guaranteed right of public employees to bargain collectively with public employers without, however, in any way trenching upon the prohibition against public employees striking either directly or indirectly or using coercive or intimidating tactics in the collective bargaining process."[12]

Local Government Law

Numerous matters related to the powers and limitations of local governments received attention during the period. In 1965, for instance, the court again weighed municipal liability for torts committed by an employee. *Hargrove* v. *Town of Cocoa Beach*, decided in 1957, had altered the sovereign immunity doctrine to permit recovery for municipal employee torts under certain circumstances. Now in two cases the justices considered whether intentional torts committed by an employee within the scope of his duties came within the ruling in *Hargrove*. The decision in *City of Miami* v. *Simpson*, to which Justice Caldwell dissented, specified that municipalities are liable in such instances.[13] In *Fisher* v. *City of Miami, et al.*, on the other hand, the court through Justice Thornal decided, absent a legislative pronouncement to the contrary, that municipalities were not liable for punitive damages for such intentional torts.[14]

Also in 1965, the panel examined municipal ordinances—specifically Miami's—that criminalized vagrancy, considered at the time a law enforcement tool effective for use in a tumultuous era. Although earlier decisions had afforded municipalities a good deal of latitude in utilizing general language to define the crime, the court now required more specificity. The ordinance in question had characterized an individual as guilty of disorderly conduct for "standing, loitering, or strolling in the city and not being able to give a satisfactory account of himself." The court reasoned, a commentator explained, that such an ordinance "must be written so that a reasonable man could know with an appreciable degree of certainty what conduct violates its provisions." It also accepted a Third District Court of Appeal ruling that the ordinance must "limit the area involved within the city [and] limit the time of day it was applicable," and it could not be permitted to subject "a person who might be acting lawfully to possible arrest merely because he could not give a satisfactory account of himself."[15]

While tightening requirements for municipal ordinances that criminalized behavior, the tribunal declined to make prosecution and conviction more difficult. The particular case dealing with the matter, *Hilliard* v. *City of Gainesville*, came before the court in 1968 and dealt with whether the right of trial by jury extended to violations of municipal ordinances. Reaffirming previous decisions, the panel members expressed that no such right presently existed because none had existed before the adoption of the constitution.[16]

One ruling issued in 1967 affected municipalities only indirectly while nonetheless limiting the range of their potential activities and programs. *O'Neill* v. *Burns* tested the proper nexus between public purpose and public finance. It concerned a $50,000 legislative appropriation to the "Junior Chamber International for the creation of permanent headquarters in the state of Florida," a grant conditioned upon a pledge of equal value by a Florida municipality. With Justices Ervin, Thornal, and Roberts dissenting, the panel struck the appropriation and authorization as violative of the state constitution. Since the benefit accruing to the state could be seen only as "incidental," and the state retained no appropriate control over the expenditure, then the situation failed to meet the required test of public purpose.[17]

Municipalities naturally held nothing more sacrosanct than their powers of home rule as anticipated by Florida's new constitution of 1968 and implemented pursuant to statute. The test of the potency of the home rule provisions arose in 1972's *City of Miami Beach* v. *Fleetwood Hotel, Inc.* Specifically, Miami Beach enacted rent control ordinances that established rent ceilings for certain leased properties. A court majority consisting of Justices Roberts, Carlton, Adkins, and Boyd rejected the initiative as an unlawful exercise of municipal power. Justice Roberts's opinion declared that municipal authority required a specific delegation of power and that any doubts concerning the authority should be resolved against the city. "The State of Florida through legislative action has enacted statutory provisions to regulate the landlord tenant relationship," he wrote. "Absent a legislative enactment authorizing the exercise of such a power by a municipality, a municipality has no power to enact a rent control ordinance."[18]

Justices Dekle and David L. McCain disagreed with the majority, but Justice Ervin voiced his dissent most strongly. "I am convinced the ordinance is valid," he began. "When spiraling costs and insufficient housing are localized, rent control is properly a municipal matter. Whether we agree with the policy of rent control is immaterial; whether a municipality will adopt a rent control ordinance should be left to the discretion of the local city government." The justice concluded: "Where not superseded by other legislation, municipal ordinances establishing rent control policies must be upheld under Article VIII, Section 2(b) of the Florida Constitution; they can be struck down only if it is shown they violate some other constitutional provision. The ordinance in this case does not."[19]

The Right to Counsel

The stream of litigation that commenced in the early 1960s concerning the right to counsel flowed unabated into the 1970s. In 1969, for example, Justice Ervin's ruling in *Baggett* v. *Wainwright* declared that a trial judge must inform a criminal defendant represented by private counsel of his right to have counsel appointed for appeal when the judge knows that the defendant has become indigent and desires to appeal. One legal scholar noted wryly at the time, "At present, a defendant of intermediate means is not as fully protected as an indigent in provision of counsel on appeal."[20]

One year later, the court majority accepted nudging from the federal judiciary to expand the right of counsel to misdemeanor defendants, but the panel acted in a manner that nonetheless altered the liberal trend suggested by *Baggett*. Writing for the majority, Justice Roberts held in *State ex rel. Argersinger* v. *Hamlin* that an indigent defendant merited court-appointed counsel only for offenses carrying a penalty greater than six months' imprisonment. The opinion's language clearly implied a reluctance even to go so far. Conversely, in dissenting in part, Justices Boyd, Ervin, and Adkins insisted that the ruling did not go far enough. "Any indigent defendant charged with violating any state law or county or municipal ordinance punishable by a jail sentence or imprisonment for any time whatever," Boyd asserted, "is entitled to counsel at the expense of the prosecuting entity of government."[21]

Speedy Trial

Paralleling extensions of the right to counsel were demands for speedy trial rights. Although Florida "functioned under an outdated speedy trial statute," as one critic described it, the court evidenced willingness to put teeth into the measure. The 1967 appeal in *Dickey* v. *Circuit Court, Gadsden County*, for instance, found court members—save Justices Thomas and Caldwell—insisting that the state must use all reasonable means to grant an accused a speedy trial. Justice O'Connell's opinion required the effort even when the defendant remained incarcerated outside the state.[22] The decision in *State ex rel. Johnson* v. *State*, a 1970 appeal, reinforced *Dickey* by permitting only delays caused by the accused to toll the statute (to stop the running of the statute of limitations) other than for delays "necessary to the ends of justice."[23]

The court continued to grapple with related issues until a definitive resolution occurred. In 1970, for example, the panel members took under consideration in *State ex rel. Leon* v. *Baker* whether delays originating in crowded dockets could toll the law's requirements. For a four-member majority—Justices Ervin, Adkins, and Boyd concurred—Justice Carlton found such delays unacceptable. "The State has an obligation to employ all reasonable means available to give a speedy trial," he argued. "This obligation is not met by ignoring defendant's right to speedy trial until the final demand is received at the last term."[24] On the other hand, 1971's *Bates* v. *Amidon* specified that the statute's intent not only protected a defendant but also benefited the state by requiring sufficient notice of a claim for a speedy trial.[25] At that point the legislature acknowledged the statute's weaknesses and vagaries, repealing it outright. The supreme court thereupon promulgated, effective March 1, 1971, Florida Rule of Criminal Procedure 3.191 to replace it. By June 1972, Chief Justice Roberts would inform the bar, "The rule has worked, the dockets have been sharply reduced, and I am ready to compare the currency of our criminal court docket with any in the nation."[26]

Transportation

As the 1965 decision in *Georgia Southern and Florida Railway Company* v. *Seven-Up Bottling Company of Southeast Georgia* illustrated, the era of interstate highways and toll expressways virtually sounded a death knell for the continued financial viability of the nation's onetime transportation mainstay, the railroads. In that case the panel struck down the comparative negligence statute for railroads, as one commentator explained, "reasoning that a railroad comparative negligence statute was reasonably confined to railroads only if railroads were the single major dangerous instrumentality." The commentator added, "The court felt changing circumstances, such as the rise of the automobile and other dangerous instrumentalities, had made it an arbitrary exercise of state power to single out railroads for special liability." Justice Roberts's opinion recognized the reality of the railroads' plight. "It may be that, twenty-three years ago when *Loftin* v. *Crowley* [150 *Florida Reports*, 836] was decided, the imposition of 'comparative negligence' liability upon the railroads by statute was not so unduly burdensome as to amount to a penalty, but today the situation is not the same, as the facts of the case *sub judice* demonstrate."[27]

Women's Rights

The period commenced with the court's conservative stance on women's rights reaffirmed in the 1967 ruling in *Bencomo* v. *Bencomo*. The majority, led by Justice Roberts, denied the right of a divorced woman beaten during marriage to sue her husband for damages. "This Court," Roberts observed, "has long been committed to the proposition that one spouse can not sue the other because, under common law, they are one person." Only Justice Ervin differed. "I think our decisional law should no longer support with pristine force the common law prohibition against actions between *former* husbands and wives for intentional torts committed by one upon the other during coverture, due to subsequent modifying provisions of our Federal and State constitutions and state laws."[28]

By 1971, winds of change had begun to stir. The early 1960s had seen the question of a woman's right to an abortion answered in the court's refusal to invalidate a state statute criminalizing the procedure. Now a different perspective had begun to take hold as suggested by the *Walsingham* v. *State* decision. Justice Adkins's opinion questioned in dictum the law's constitutionality with words far different from those used a few years previously. "Any statute dealing with abortions is heavily weighed with religious teachings and ethical concepts," Adkins observed. "The moral issues are important, but should not exclusively control the judiciary in determining the constitutionality of any statute relating to such a volatile subject. The statute as it is written presently licenses the jury to create its own standard in each case by either applying, or refusing to apply, the nebulous question of whether a certain act was necessary to preserve the life of the mother. As an end result, juries would condemn what they personally disapprove." Adkins added, "The duty and judgment of a physician, the necessity and welfare of the patient, and the rights of both, cannot be subjected to arbitrary and unreasonable legislative interference and infringement. A physician has the right and duty to practice his chosen profession to the best of his ability, which necessarily includes the discretion to perform those procedures which in his expert medical judgment, he deems to be in his patient's best interest."

Justice Ervin, with Adkins's concurrence, would have gone beyond the majority position. "What I have to add relates to the liberty under law of women concerning the instant subject, including privacy, personal control over their bodies, their rights concerning termination of pregnancy, their rights vis-à-vis an unborn child, et cetera, and the extent to which liberties of women in these areas can be abridged by the states," Ervin wrote. "A woman's right to privacy from state intrusion in the personal control of her body is unquestionably a fundamental personal liberty, emanating from what the [U.S. Supreme Court] *Griswold* [v. *Connecticut*] majority calls the penumbra of the specific guarantees of the Bill of Rights. To take away her right to total control of that body, including the elimination of parts of it, the State must show a strong, compelling, and necessary interest. In sum, the [Florida abortion] statute intrudes into the area of personal liberty of women and it does it crudely in vague, uncertain, archaic language."[29]

In 1971 the panel addressed a woman's sexuality, and in so doing it reversed the 1952 judgment in *Ripley* v. *Ewell* that denied a woman compensation for loss of consortium. Justice Adkins, as he had in *Walsingham*, took responsibility for writing the opinion in *Gates* v. *Foley*. In the process he struck a telling note regarding equality before the law. "No reasonable suggestion can be offered any longer to explain the disparity in the spouses' relative rights to secure damages for loss of consortium," he averred. "No reasonable distinctions may be made between the wife's claim for negligent impairment of consortium and a similar claim by her husband. [The law] must keep pace with changes in our society, for the doctrine of *stare decisis* is not an iron mold which can never be changed."[30]

Abbreviations Used in Notes

FSA	Florida State Archives
FSCHS	Florida Supreme Court Historical Society
FSCL	Florida Supreme Court Library
FSU	Florida State University
GS	*Gainesville Sun*
JFT-U	*Jacksonville Florida Times-Union*
LWH	*Lake Wales Highlander*
MH	*Miami Herald*
OS	*Orlando Sentinel*
PKY	P. K. Yonge Library of Florida History
SLF	State Library of Florida
SPT	*St. Petersburg Times*
TD	*Tallahassee Democrat*
TDD	*Tallahassee Daily Democrat*
TFS	*Tampa Florida Sentinel*
TMT	*Tampa Morning Tribune*
TST	*Tampa Sunday Tribune*
TT	*Tampa Tribune*
UF	University of Florida

Notes

Chapter 1. World War I, the Boom, and the Bust

1. *Charlotte (N.C.) Star of Zion*, March 8, 1917; *JFT-U*, February 6, 1916.

2. McRae, *Fourth Census*, 15; Mayo, *Seventh Census*, 9.

3. Mayo, *Fifth Census*, 70; Mayo, *Seventh Census*, 62, 83–84.

4. McRae, *Fourth Census*, 19; Mayo, *Seventh Census*, 9.

5. Brown, *Florida's Black Public Officials*, 55–69.

6. Saunders, *Bridging the Gap*, 3–10.

7. Flynt, *Cracker Messiah*, 40–93; Morris, *Florida Handbook, 1991–1992*, 333–37; Colburn and Scher, *Florida's Gubernatorial Politics*, 12–15; George, "Brokers, Binders, and Builders," 31.

8. Tebeau, *History of Florida*, 368–73.

9. Ibid., 369, 373–75; *Fort Meade Leader*, May 9, November 7, 1918; *TMT*, June 6, 1918.

10. Davis, *History of Jacksonville*, 270; Flynt, *Cracker Messiah*, 188–89; Proctor, "Prelude to the New Florida," 284.

11. Blaine, "South Florida in the Movies," 17–18; Thompson, "Movies Made in the Sunshine," 15; Davis, *History of Jacksonville*, 251–52; *JFT-U*, February 18, 1917, February 23, 1921.

12. Kendrick, *Florida Trails to Turnpikes*, 15; Mohl and Mormino, "Big Change in the Sunshine State," 430.

13. Kendrick, *Florida Trails to Turnpikes*, 15–18; Brown, *In the Midst of All That Makes Life Worth Living*, 240, 243, 257, 272, 274; Mohl and Mormino, "Big Change," 430–31.

14. Rogers, "Fortune and Misfortune," 292–93.

15. *TDD*, October 16, 1925, quoted in Rogers, "Fortune and Misfortune," 292.

16. Tebeau, *History of Florida*, 380, 382–84; Rogers, "Fortune and Misfortune," 290–91; *TDD*, May 24, 1928.

17. Morris, *Florida Handbook, 1991–1992*, 420–21, 423–26, 429, 433; Tebeau, *History of Florida*, 377.

18. Chandler, *Land Title Origins*, 397; Rogers, "Fortune and Misfortune," 293.

19. Mormino and Pozzetta, *Immigrant World*, 280–86; Rogers, "Fortune and Misfortune," 290; Bousquet, "Gangster in Our Midst," 297–309; *Miami Daily News*, March 18, 1930, quoted in Bousquet, "Gangster," 301.

20. Flynt, *Cracker Messiah*, 180, 184; Rogers and Denham, *Florida Sheriffs*, 206–7, 232–33; Brown, *In the Midst*, 267, 295; C. D. Burt to Doyle E. Carlton, November 3, 1930, incoming correspondence of Governor Doyle E. Carlton, RG 102, series 204, box

70, FSA. See also Guthrie, *Keepers of the Spirits*; Guthrie, "Hard Times, Hard Liquor, and Hard Luck."

21. See, for example, Allen, *Big Change.*

22. Vance, *May Mann Jennings*, 89–99, 104–6, 109, 144, 176; Morris, *Florida Handbook, 1991–1992*, 245–47, 597; Vickers, "Congresswoman Ruth Bryan Owen," 123–36; Loquasto, *150: Celebrating Florida's First 150 Women Lawyers*, 17–18; Brown, *In the Midst*, 264–65.

23. Rogers, "Fortune and Misfortune," 289, 293.

24. Orrick and Crumpacker, *Tampa Tribune*, 100.

25. Tierney, *Clarence Darrow*, 354–73.

26. Newton, *Invisible Empire*, 65–68.

27. Ibid., 42–49; Prescott, "White Robes and Crosses," 37–38; Brown, *In the Midst*, 267–70; Chalmers, "Ku Klux Klan," 209–12.

28. Newton, *Invisible Empire*, 46, 49–60; Prescott, "White Robes and Crosses," 18–40; *TMT*, November 1, 1923.

29. Newton, *Invisible Empire*, 69; *TDD*, December 24, 1926, March 4, 1927.

30. *TDD*, October 8, 1939.

31. Vickers, *Panic in Paradise*, 73–97; Hetherington, *History of Polk County*, 116; Rogers, "Fortune and Misfortune," 296–97.

32. Barnes, *Florida's Hurricane History*, 111–40; Rogers, "Fortune and Misfortune," 297–98; *TDD*, November 6, 1929.

33. *LWH*, February 13, December 12, 1930.

34. Rogers, "The Great Depression," 304–6; Brown, *In the Midst*, 297–99; Wright, "Polk County's First Poor Farm," 5; *TDD*, January 1, 1932; Tebeau, *History of Florida*, 394–96.

35. Haas, "Winter Haven," 59; Graf, "Ridge Cities Refunding," 7.

36. Lauderback, *Consolidated, a Partial Story—Much Needs to Be Edited and Added*; Brown, *In the Midst*, 300–301; *Lakeland News*, July 1, 1932.

37. Kennedy, *Freedom from Fear*, 103.

38. *TDD*, June 10, November 9, 1932; *Lakeland News*, July 1, 1932; Morris, *Florida Handbook, 1991–1992*, 603, 608.

Chapter 2. The Supreme Court in Transition

1. *JFT-U*, January 2, 1917; Manley, Brown, and Rise, *Supreme Court of Florida*, 364; Dobson, "Taking the Oath," 7–8; Flynt, *Cracker Messiah*, 78–79, 94–95.

2. *TDD*, January 2, 1917.

3. Manley, Brown, and Rise, *Supreme Court of Florida*, 272–73; Little, "Overview," 16–23; Sebring, "Appellate System," 141; Terrell, "Courts of Florida," 20.

4. Sebring, "Appellate System," 143; Manley, Brown, and Rise, *Supreme Court of Florida*, 330–34.

5. Manley, Brown, and Rise, *Supreme Court of Florida*, 290–93, 346–51, 360–61; Glenn Terrell Jr. to Joseph A. Boyd, February 24, 1982, Reder Files, box 2, FSCHS.

6. Manley, Brown, and Rise, *Supreme Court of Florida*, 334, 340–43, 345–46; DeFoor, "Here's to Jeff Browne," 3.

7. Manley, Brown, and Rise, *Supreme Court of Florida* 291, 340–43, 347–48, 355–56; DeFoor, "Here's to Jeff Browne," 2–3.

8. Ellis, "My Experience," 3; *TDD*, July 27, 1937.

9. *JFT-U*, December 18, 1917.

10. *TDD*, March 29, 1939, September 1, 1940; *JFT-U*, March 30, 1939.

11. *JFT-U*, December 18, 1917.

12. Ellis, "My Experience," 3, 8.

13. *TDD*, July 20, August 22, 1917.

14. Flynt, *Cracker Messiah*, 100–101, 158; *TDD*, August 23, 1917.

15. *TDD*, August 23, 27, 1917; *JFT-U*, August 28, 1917; *TMT* quoted in *TDD*, August 30, 1917.

16. *JFT-U*, August 28, September 2, 1917; *TMT*, June 6, 1918.

17. *TDD*, April 15, 1918; *TMT*, June 2, 1918.

18. *TMT*, June 2, 6, 1918.

19. *TDD*, June 2, July 8, October 9, 1918.

20. *TDD*, April 24, 1919, April 14, May 3, 19, October 12, 1921.

21. *JFT-U*, January 5, 23, October 31, 1921; *TDD*, April 20, 24, October 5, 20, 1920, October 12, November 2, 1921; Ervin, "Stories about Florida Supreme Court Justices," n.p.

22. *TDD*, January 20, April 14, May 1, 11, 1923; *JFT-U*, May 12, 1923.

23. *TDD*, January 20, 1923, January 10, 1935; *JFT-U*, December 5, 1925, *JFT-U*, November 2, 1938, December 24, 1944; *Laws of Florida* (1927), 1261; Buford, "Something about the Supreme Court," 32–33; Whitfield, *Political and Legal History*, 86.

24. *JFT-U*, May 2, September 21, December 9, 1923; *TDD*, April 9, May 25, September 20, 21, October 16, December 8, 1923.

25. *JFT-U*, March 1, 3, 1925.

26. *JFT-U*, June 17, 1922; *Tallahassee Florida Democrat and Weekly Record*, April 25, 1924; *TDD*, August 4, October 19, November 2, 1925; Chapman, "Unauthorized Practice of Law," 179; Sturgis, "Abolition of the Diploma Privilege," 373.

27. Adkins, "Yesterday," 7–8; Buford, "Something about the Supreme Court," 32; Brown, "Brief History," 37–38; Boyd and Reder, *History of the Supreme Court of Florida*, 1051; Manley, Brown, and Rise, *Supreme Court of Florida*, 330.

28. *TDD*, January 18, 1923.

29. Buford, "Something about the Supreme Court," 32; Brown, "Brief History," 37–38; Boyd and Reder, *History of the Supreme Court of Florida*, 1051; *OS*, November 4, 1926; *TDD*, December 9, 1926, January 11, 1927.

30. *Milton Gazette*, June 5, November 24, 1925; *TDD*, June 7, November 24, 1925.

31. *JFT-U*, June 18, July 2, 1925; Brown, "Brief History," 36–37.

32. *Milton Gazette*, November 3, 24, 1925; *JFT-U*, November 2, December 5, 1925; *TDD*, November 24, 1925; Brown, "Brief History," 37.

33. Ellis, "My Experience," 3; *TDD*, July 28, 1929, September 30, 1932; "Proposed Constitutional Amendment," 180–81.

34. Ellis, "My Experience," 9; 94; *Florida Reports*, 1001, 1009.

35. Pudlow, "75 Years of the Bar *Journal*," 12; "Bar Examination Paper," 56; Sebring, "Appellate System," 143; Buford, "Something about the Supreme Court," 32–34; Andrews, "Should We Ratify the Amendment," 251; Jones, "The Question before Us," 256.

36. *TDD*, April 23, July 28, 1929; *JFT-U*, July 28, 1929; *Laws of Florida* (1929), 1080.

37. Brown, "Shall We Have a Supreme Court," 32; Sebring, "Appellate System," 143; Buford, "Something about the Supreme Court," 32–34; Andrews, "Should We Ratify the Amendment," 251; Jones, "The Question before Us," 256.

38. Brown, "Shall We Have a Supreme Court," 32–40; Brown, "Brief History," 38; *TDD*, April 23, 30, 1931, February 19, 1937.

39. *TDD*, January 13, 25, February 15, 22, March 1, 3, 6, 1931, July 28, 1940.

40. *TDD*, April 3, September 30, November 9, 1932; *JFT-U*, November 13, 1932; "Official Vote on the Proposed Constitutional Amendment," 362.

41. DeFoor, "Here's to Jeff Browne," 1–2; Browne, *Key West*, xiii; Manley, Brown, and Rise, *Supreme Court of Florida*, 292.

42. DeFoor, "Here's to Jeff Browne," 102; Browne, *Key West*, xiii; Rerick, *Memoirs of Florida*, 2:449.

43. Browne, *Key West*, xiv, 110–11; 66 *Florida Reports*, 138; 188 *United States Reports*, 720.

44. 34 *Florida Reports*, 311; Ingalls, *Urban Vigilantes*, 36–40; *JFT-U*, June 16, 1891; Brown, *Florida's Black Public Officials*, 86; Denham and Brown, "Black Sheriffs."

45. DeFoor, "Here's to Jeff Browne," 2; Rerick, *Memoirs of Florida*, 2:449–50; Browne, *Key West*, xiii, xxii, 82–83.

46. Manley, Brown, and Rise, *Supreme Court of Florida*, 300; Williamson, *Florida Politics in the Gilded Age*, 173; DeFoor, "Here's to Jeff Browne," 2.

47. *JFT-U*, May 29, 1891; DeFoor, "Here's to Jeff Browne," 2–3; Williamson, *Florida Politics in the Gilded Age*, 174–76; Manley, Brown, and Rise, *Supreme Court of Florida*, 300–301.

48. *MH*, September 22, 1935; Akin, *Flagler*, 211–12.

49. DeFoor, "Here's to Jeff Browne," 2–3; Rerick, *Memoirs of Florida*, 2:449.

50. *Proceedings of the Florida State Bar Association for the Years 1907, 1908, and 1909*, 2, 4; Kabat, "'Everybody Votes for Gilchrist,'" 189, 195–99; *JFT-U*, November 15, 1907; *Tallahassee Weekly True Democrat*, November 22, 1907.

51. DeFoor, "Here's to Jeff Browne," 3–4; Rerick, *Memoirs of Florida*, 2:450; Browne, "Across the Gulf," 203–7; Laramore, *Second Florida Poets*, 24–27; DeFoor, "Poetry of Judge Jefferson B. Browne," 3.

52. Manley, Brown, and Rise, *Supreme Court of Florida*, 345–46; Brown, "Brief History," 36; Boyd and Reder, "History of the Supreme Court of Florida," 1045; *JFT-U*, January 2, 1917.

53. DeFoor, "Here's to Jeff Browne," 3; Leo Foster questionnaire, Reder Files, box 3, FSCHS; Browne, "American Law Institute," 99; Browne, "Super-Constitution," 349; Guthrie, *Keepers of the Spirits*, 25, 28–29, 128; Wiecek, *Lost World*, 79–89, 97–108; Horwitz, *Transformation of American Law*, chapter 1.

54. Browne, "Super-Constitution," 332–37; Browne, "American Law Institute," 84–85; Guthrie, *Keepers of the Spirits*, 29–30; Wiecek, *Lost World*, 199.

55. DeFoor, "Here's to Jeff Browne," 3; Browne, *Key West*, xiv; Leo Foster questionnaire.

56. DeFoor, "Here's to Jeff Browne," 3–4; Browne, *Key West*, xiv, xx.

57. Cash, *Story of Florida*, 3:359; *National Cyclopaedia of American Biography*, 23:363; *TDD*, December 12, 1922.

58. *TDD*, September 6, 1917, February 23, 1931; *Milton Gazette*, November 24, 1925; "In Memoriam to Thomas Franklin West," n.p.; Millard Caldwell questionnaire, Thomas F. West file, Reder papers, box 2, FSCL.

59. "In Memoriam to Thomas Franklin West," n.p.; *TDD*, February 23, 1931; *Milton Gazette*, November 24, 1925; *National Cyclopaedia*, 23: 363; "Ninth President: Thomas Franklin West," 128.

60. Cash, *Story of Florida*, 3:359; *TDD*, December 28, 1927; *National Cyclopaedia*, 23:363.

61. *TDD*, January 2, 1917; *JFT-U*, September 2, 1917; "In Memoriam to Thomas Franklin West," n.p.; Cash, *Story of Florida*, 3:359; Proctor, *Napoleon Bonaparte Broward*, 222–23, 251; Colburn and Scher, *Florida's Gubernatorial Politics*, 162; Dietz, "Sketch," 77.

62. Kerber, "Initiative and Referendum," 302–313.

63. *TDD*, January 2, 1917; *JFT-U*, September 2, 1917; Proctor, *Napoleon Bonaparte Broward*, 251; Colburn and Scher, *Florida's Gubernatorial Politics*, 162.

64. *JFT-U*, September 2, 1917; "In Memoriam to Thomas Franklin West," n.p.; "Ninth President: Thomas Franklin West," 128; 240 *United States Reports*, 328, 342.

65. Flynt, *Cracker Messiah*, 100–101, 158; *JFT-U*, August 28, September 2, 1917; *TMT* quoted in *TDD*, August 30, 1917.

66. "In Memoriam to Thomas Franklin West," n.p.; *TDD*, November 8, 1920, February 23, 1931; Manley, Brown, and Rise, *Supreme Court of Florida*, 342; West, "Citizenship," 13.

67. *TDD*, March 28, April 13, June 6, 1923; "In Memoriam to Thomas Franklin West," n.p.

68. *TDD*, December 12, 1922, December 28, 1927; *Milton Gazette*, June 5, 9, November 24, December 1, 1925; *JFT-U*, March 10, 1925; *National Cyclopaedia*, 23:363.

69. *TDD*, February 23, 24, 1931; "State v. Mock and Mock," 52; "Good v. Bell," 68.

70. *TDD*, February 23, 24, 1931; *JFT-U*, February 24, 1931.

71. *National Cyclopaedia of American Biography*, LII:126; *TDD*, August 23, 1923; "In Memoriam: A Ceremonial Session," 17; "Portrayal of Terrell," 11–12; Nancy Dobson, "Justice Glenn Terrell," 1; and F. Perry Odom, "The Best of Terrell," unpublished type-

scripts, Terrell Papers, box 1; Boyd and Reder, *History of the Supreme Court of Florida*, 1049; Wade L. Hopping interview, May 12, 1982.

72. Dobson, "Justice Glenn Terrell," 1; Odom, "Best of Terrell," 2.

73. *Ocala Banner-Lacon*, January 6, 1883.

74. Valentine, *Looking Back*, 4, 13; *TDD*, October 31, 1943; Yancey, "People's Judge," 1138.

75. "Portrayal of Terrell," 1; Valentine, *Looking Back*, 16; *JFT-U*, May 12, 1923; Yancey, "People's Judge," 1140; Warren, "Yesterday," 12; McKay, *Pioneer Florida*, 2:149–50; Odom, "Best of Terrell," 49.

76. "Portrayal of Terrell," 1; *TST*, July 12, 1981; *National Cyclopaedia*, 52:126; Langum and Walthall, *From Maverick to Mainstream*, 146–47.

77. "In Memoriam: A Ceremonial Session," 11; *TDD*, October 31, 1943; *JFT-U*, May 12, 1923; Danese, "Disfranchisement," 120.

78. *National Cyclopaedia*, 52:126; "In Memoriam: A Ceremonial Session," 9; "Portrayal of Terrell," 2, 13; Yancey, "People's Judge," 1140; Danese, "Disfranchisement," 120–31; Dobson, "Justice Glenn Terrell," 3–4; Stephen C. O'Connell interview, May 2, 2000; Hopping interview, May 12, 1982; Guyte McCord Jr. and Betty McCord interview, May 17, 1982; 87 *Southern Reporter, Second Series*, 504.

79. *JFT-U*, May 12, 1923; Yancey, "People's Judge," 1140; Buford, "Something about the Supreme Court," 31; "Portrayal of Terrell," 5; Flynt, *Cracker Messiah*, 101, 141, 152.

80. *JFT-U*, May 12, 1923; 258 *United States Reports*, 338.

81. *JFT-U*, May 12, 16, 1923; Brown, "Brief History," 37; Buford, "Something about the Supreme Court," 32.

82. Hopping interview, May 12, 1982; *TST*, July 12, 1981; "Portrayal of Terrell," 12–13; 106 *Florida Reports*, 779; "Memorial Proceedings for Judge Louie W. Strum," 25, in John Milton Bryan Simpson papers, PKY, UF; Horwitz, *Transformation of American Law*, 187–92; Hutcheson, "Judgment Intuitive," 274–88.

83. Odom, "Best of Terrell," 15; B. K. Roberts interview, April 21, 1980; Ervin, "Stories," 3; "In Memoriam: A Ceremonial Session," 14, 16.

84. Roberts interview; "Portrayal of Terrell," 13; 118 *Florida Reports*, 253; 83 *Southern Reporter, Second Series*, 20; 146 *Florida Reports*, 491; 140 *Florida Reports*, 610.

85. "In Memoriam: A Ceremonial Session," 10; Warren, "Yesterday," 12; "Portrayal of Terrell," 4; McCord interview; Ervin, "Stories," 7; 141 *Florida Reports*, 804.

86. Dobson, "Visit with Joe Butler," 12; Arnow, "Yesterday," 5; "Portrayal of Terrell," 2, 4–5; Warren, "Yesterday," 12; McCord interview.

87. "Portrayal of Terrell," 3; 43 *Southern Reporter, Second Series*, 179; O'Connell interview, May 2, 2000; Hopping interview, May 12, 1982; Dobson, "Justice Glenn Terrell," 3; Hall, *Judicial Sayings*.

88. Boyd and Reder, *History of the Supreme Court of Florida*, 1049; *TD*, January 12, 13, 1964, February 13, 1989; *JFT-U*, January 12, 13, 14, 1964; *TT*, January 13, 1964.

89. *JFT-U*, March 3, 1925; "In Memoriam: Judge Louie W. Strum," iii; Cutler, *History of Florida*, 2:72; Hall and Rise, *From Local Courts*, 172.

90. *JFT-U*, March 3, 1925; Memorial resolution of the Fifth Circuit Judicial Conference for Louie W. Strum, Simpson Papers, box 4, PKY, UF; "In Memoriam: Judge Louie W. Strum," iii, v; Cutler, *History of Florida*, 2:72.

91. *JFT-U*, March 3, 1925; Memorial resolution; Cutler, *History of Florida*, 2:72.

92. *JFT-U*, March 3, 1925, July 27, 1954; *TDD*, March 21, 1928.

93. Memorial resolution; *JFT-U*, March 3, 1925, July 27, 1954; Cutler, *History of Florida*, 2:72.

94. Memorial resolution; "In Memoriam: Judge Louie W. Strum," v; *TDD*, January 12, March 13, 1928; *JFT-U*, March 3, 1925, July 27, 1954.

95. Leo Foster questionnaire; Bryan Simpson to Glenn Terrell, October 22, 1954, Simpson Papers, box 4; Memorial resolution; "In Memoriam: Judge Louie W. Strum," iv.

96. *TDD*, February 22, 23, 24, 27, March 1, 1931; *JFT-U*, February 23, 1931.

97. *JFT-U*, February 23, 1931, October 9, 1939, July 27, 1954; *TMT*, July 27, 1954; *TDD*, March 1, 1931, June 25, 1940; Hall and Rise, *From Local Courts*, 172.

98. "In Memoriam: Judge Louie W. Strum," iv–v; 57 *Federal Reporter, Second Series*, 313; 103 *Federal Supplement*, 825.

99. Roberts interview; "In Memoriam: Judge Louie W. Strum," iv.

100. *JFT-U*, July 27, 1954; *TMT*, July 27, 1954; "In Memoriam: Judge Louie W. Strum," iii; Florida Bureau of Vital Statistics, death certificate index, available at SLF.

101. *JFT-U*, July 27, 1954; "In Memoriam: Judge Louie W. Strum," vi.

102. "In Memoriam: Justice Armstead Brown," xliii; *National Cyclopaedia*, 39:29; Feibelman, "Memorial Services," 244; "Fifteenth President."

103. Feibelman, "Memorial Services," 244; *National Cyclopaedia*, 39:29; "In Memoriam: Justice Armstead Brown," xliii; Cash, *Story of Florida*, 3:17; Coulter, *Georgia*, 371, 389; Coleman, *History of Georgia*, 213, 222.

104. *JFT-U*, December 5, 1925; *TD*, October 29, 1951; "In Memoriam: Justice Armstead Brown," xliii–xliv; Cash, *Story of Florida*, 3:17; Brown, "Bench and Bar," 189; *National Cyclopaedia*, 39:29.

105. *National Cyclopaedia*, 39:29; *JFT-U*, October 29, 1951.

106. "Fifteenth President"; *National Cyclopaedia*, 39:29.

107. Feibelman, "Memorial Services," 244; *JFT-U*, December 5, 1925; *TD*, October 29, 1951.

108. Brown, "Come to Miami" (typescript in Armstead Brown file, FSCHS); "In Memoriam: Justice Armstead Brown," xliv; Feibelman, "Memorial Services," 244.

109. "In Memoriam: Justice Armstead Brown," xliv; Cash, *Story of Florida*, 3:18; *Proceedings of the Florida State Bar Association* [1923], 171–72; *JFT-U*, June 17, 1922; Brown, "Some Unfinished Business," 4–5.

110. Brown, "Brief History," 36–37; *Milton Gazette*, June 5, 1925; *JFT-U*, June 18, July 2, 1925, December 5, 1925.

111. Ervin, "Stories," 10; Warren, "Yesterday," 12; Adkins, "Yesterday," 9; Roberts interview; "In Memoriam: Justice Armstead Brown," xliv–xlv.

112. Richard W. Ervin questionnaire, Armstead Brown file, Reder Files, FSCHS; Brown, "Individualism and Government," 106–7, 116–17; "In Memoriam: Justice Armstead Brown," xlv.

113. Brown, "Shall We Have a Supreme Court," 38; Brown, "Some Unfinished Business," 4; Brown, "Judicial Section," 5–6; Brown, "Some Observations," 148; Ellis, "New Rules," 551.

114. Brown, "Brief History," 37–38; *TDD*, November 25, 1946; *JFT-U*, November 26, 1946.

115. *JFT-U*, October 30, 1951; *TDD*, October 30, 1951; "In Memoriam: Justice Armstead Brown," 245–46; Warren, "Yesterday," 12; Ervin, "Stories," 10–11.

116. Robert W. Ervin interview, May 15, 2000; Roberts interview; Cutler, *History of Florida*, 2:156.

117. *JFT-U*, December 5, 1925; Buford, "Justice Rivers H. Buford," 2; "Tribute of the Supreme Court," xliii.

118. *TDD*, March 8, 1931; "Tribute of the Supreme Court," xliii.

119. *TDD*, March 8, 1931; Rivers H. Buford autobiographical sketch , Rivers H. Buford file, SLF; *People of Lawmaking in Florida, 1822–1991*, 14.

120. Buford autobiographical sketch; *TDD*, March 8, 1931; Hammond, *Medical Profession*, 446–47; Manley, Brown, and Rise, *Supreme Court of Florida*, 354–57.

121. *JFT-U*, December 5, 1925; *TDD*, March 8, 1931; "Tribute of the Supreme Court," xliv; Buford autobiographical sketch.

122. 63 *Florida Reports*, 16; 64 *Florida Reports*, 32, 381; *JFT-U*, December 5, 1925.

123. *TDD*, January 13, 1943; Buford autobiographical sketch; Richard W. Ervin interview, March 14, 2003.

124. "Tribute of the Supreme Court," xliv; *TDD*, January 13, 1943; Cutler, *History of Florida*, 2:156; Rivers Buford Jr. interview, June 2, 2003; Barbara Buford interview, June 2, 2003.

125. *Report of the Attorney General of the State of Florida, 1921–1922*, 10; *TDD*, February 26, 1921; Ervin, "Stories," 4; Rivers Buford Jr. interview; Barbara Buford interview; *JFT-U*, December 5, 1925; Roberts interview.

126. Leo Foster questionnaire; Robert M. Ervin interview; Roberts interview; "Tribute of the Supreme Court," xliv–lxv; Ervin, "Stories," 9.

127. Leo Foster questionnaire; Robert M. Ervin interview; Roberts interview; "Tribute of the Supreme Court," xliv–lxv; Ervin, "Stories," 9; Adkins, "Yesterday," 9; Buford, "Times and the Courts," 577; Richard W. Ervin interview.

128. Warren, "Yesterday," 11; Adkins, "Yesterday," 9; Roberts interview; 91 *Florida Reports*, 548; Rivers Buford Jr. interview; Barbara Buford interview.

129. *JFT-U*, September 15, 1924; *TDD*, June 3, 1930; *TD*, December 30, 1963; Mary Hollingsworth Buford information card, Florida State College for Women faculty infor-

mation card file, Special Collections, Strozier Library, FSU; Cutler, *History of Florida*, 2:156; Buford autobiographical sketch.

130. A. L. "Jack" Buford interview, June 2, 2003.

131. *JFT-U*, February 17, 1948; *TMT*, February 17, 1948; "Tribute of the Supreme Court," xlv; Roberts interview.

132. *TD*, March 18, 1959; Robert M. Ervin interview; Rivers Buford Jr. interview; Barbara Buford interview; O'Connell interviews, May 2 and 9, 2000; Colburn and Scher, *Florida's Gubernatorial Politics*, 225; Wagy, *Governor LeRoy Collins*, 70, 218; A. L. "Jack" Buford interview.

133. *TD*, March 19, 1959.

134. *TDD*, February 29, 1928; Cash, *Story of Florida*, 3:16–17; Cutler, *History of Florida*, 2:7; *National Cyclopedia of American Biography*, 23:459.

135. "Self-Made," unattributed and undated newspaper clipping, and Evelyn Davis Burns to Joseph A. Boyd Jr., June 2, 1980, Fred Henry Davis biographical file, Reder Papers, box 2, FSCL.

136. Burns to Boyd, June 2, 1980; *TDD*, October 24, 1921, January 17, 1940; *JFT-U*, June 21, 1937; Richard W. Ervin questionnaire, Fred Henry Davis file, FSCHS.

137. Cash, *Story of Florida*, 3:16; "Self Made"; Burns to Boyd, June 2, 1980; Hall and Rise, *From Local Courts*, 178.

138. Burns to Boyd, June 2, 1980; Cutler, *History of Florida*, 2:7; *TDD*, February 29, 1928.

139. Cash, *Story of Florida*, 2:16–17; Burns to Boyd, June 2, 1980; *National Cyclopedia*, 23:459; *TDD*, February 5, 1921; *JFT-U*, February 11, 1921.

140. *JFT-U*, February 10, 1921; *TDD*, February 15, April 14, 1921, February 29, 1928, October 30, 1936, June 21, 1937; France, "Year of Monkey War," 161.

141. *TD*, August 25, 1968; *TDD*, January 24, 1921, June 21, 1937.

142. Burns to Boyd, June 2, 1980; *National Cyclopedia*, 23:459; *TDD*, June 21, 1931.

143. *TDD*, May 10, 19, June 3, 1927.

144. *TD*, August 25, 1968; Burns to Boyd, June 2, 1980; Richard W. Ervin questionnaire.

145. Davis, "Address Delivered," 156.

146. *JFT-U*, June 21, 1937; Richard W. Ervin questionnaire; Roberts interview; Fred Henry Davis file, FSCHS; *TD*, August 25, 1968.

147. Burns to Boyd, June 2, 1980; Roberts interview; *JFT-U*, June 21, 1937; *TDD*, June 21, 1937; *TD*, August 25, 1968.

148. *MH*, December 25, 1973; Burns to Boyd, June 2, 1980.

Chapter 3. Court Decisions for a Tumultuous Era

1. 75 *Florida Reports*, 97; *JFT-U*, January 17, 1918.

2. 88 *Florida Reports*, 196; *JFT-U*, September 11, 1924.

3. 88 *Florida Reports*, 196.

4. 92 *Florida Reports*, 267; *TDD*, July 20, 1926.

5. 95 *Florida Reports*, 530; *TDD*, March 27, 1928.

6. 92 *Florida Reports*, 601; 93 *Florida Reports*, 415; 96 *Florida Reports*, 768; *TDD*, December 15, 1928; *JFT-U*, January 6, 1929.

7. 97 *Florida Reports*, 426; 100 *Florida Reports*, 1349, 1406; *JFT-U*, April 2, 1929; *TDD*, November 21, December 11, 1920.

8. 98 *Florida Reports*, 1044; *JFT-U*, December 8, 1929.

9. 80 *Florida Reports*, 441; 87 *Florida Reports*, 181; *JFT-U*, February 24, 1924.

10. 83 *Florida Reports*, 214; 98 *Florida Reports*, 582; *TDD*, February 10, 1922; *JFT-U*, October 11, 1929.

11. 102 *Florida Reports*, 1105; *TDD*, October 9, 1931.

12. 83 *Florida Reports*, 366; 85 *Florida Reports*, 248, 263; *JFT-U*, March 13, 1922, March 2, 1923.

13. 75 *Florida Reports*, 792; *JFT-U*, December 6, 15, 1917; Guthrie, "Florida Supreme Court," 110–12.

14. 76 *Florida Reports*, 304; *TDD*, August 14, 1918; Guthrie, "Florida Supreme Court," 115–18.

15. 77 *Florida Reports*, 432; *TDD*, April 21, 1919; Guthrie, "Florida Supreme Court," 120–26.

16. 77 *Florida Reports*, 432.

17. 82 *Florida Reports*, 359; *TDD*, November 14, 1921.

18. 83 *Florida Reports*, 606; *TDD*, May 16, 1922.

19. 83 *Florida Reports*, 204; *TDD*, February 10, 1922.

20. 78 *Florida Reports*, 611; 102 *Florida Reports*, 425; *JFT-U*, December 22, 1919; *TDD*, March 26, 1931.

21. 73 *Florida Reports*, 922.

22. 98 *Florida Reports*, 785; *TDD*, October 25, 1929; *JFT-U*, October 26, 1929.

23. 87 *Florida Reports*, 451; *JFT-U*, May 9, 1924.

24. 104 *Florida Reports*, 407; Gramling, "Development of Florida Labor Law," 190–91.

25. 78 *Florida Reports*, 47; *JFT-U*, July 2, 1919.

26. 81 *Florida Reports*, 211; *JFT-U*, February 19, 1921.

27. 101 *Florida Reports*, 429; *TDD*, May 6, 1931.

28. 75 *Florida Reports*, 622.

29. 81 *Florida Reports*, 479.

30. 81 *Florida Reports*, 559; *TDD*, April 22, 1921.

31. 79 *Florida Reports*, 290; *JFT-U*, March 20, 1920.

32. 100 *Florida Reports*, 1027; *TDD*, January 8, 1931.

33. 87 *Florida Reports*, 270; *JFT-U*, March 20, 1924.

34. 87 *Florida Reports*, 270.

Chapter 4. Economic Calamity and War's Challenge

1. *TDD*, January 3, 1933.

2. *Lakeland News*, January 3, 1933; Smith, *Emancipation*, 280; Jones and McCarthy, *African Americans in Florida*, 101–2.

3. Kennedy, *Freedom from Fear*, 116–17; *TDD*, March 20, 1933.

4. *TDD*, August 7, 1933; Newman, *Hugo Black*, 281–83; Saunders, *Bridging the Gap*, 14–15, 17.

5. Egerton, *Speak Now against the Day*, 19.

6. *Fort Meade Leader*, June 15, 1933; *TDD*, January 30, 1933; "Florida and the CWA," 14; unidentified woman to David Sholtz, December 27, 1933, correspondence of Governor David Sholtz, RG 102, series 278, box 91, folder 5, FSA.

7. Burr, *History of Winter Haven*, 164; Hopkins, *Fifty Years of Citrus*, 131–32; Campbell, "Florida in 1934," 10–12, 22–25; Rogers, "The Great Depression," 319–20; Brown, *In the Midst of All That Makes Life Worth Living*, 296–98.

8. Mayo, *Seventh Census*, 9, 10–11.

9. *LWH*, October 31, 1930; *TDD*, September 10, 1937; Irby, "Taking Out the Trailer Trash," 182.

10. Shofner, "Communists, Klansmen, and the CIO," 300–309; Brown, *In the Midst*, 309–10, 320–22.

11. Newton, *Invisible Empire*, 74–105; Shofner, "Communists, Klansmen, and the CIO," 300–309; Brown, *In the Midst*, 320–22.

12. McGovern, *Anatomy of a Lynching*, ix, 15.

13. Saunders, *Bridging the Gap*, 17–19; Green, *Before His Time*, 35–38, 40–41; *TDD*, July 22, 1942; Emmons, "Not a Single Battle," 421–34.

14. *TDD*, January 5, 1937.

15. Colburn and Scher, *Florida's Gubernatorial Politics*, 172–73; Havard and Beth, *Politics of Mis-Representation*, 1–10; *TDD*, May 22, 1935.

16. *JFT-U*, October 28, 1939; Mohl and Mormino, "Big Change in the Sunshine State," 432–33.

17. *TDD*, January 28, May 5, 1940; Stafford, "Sen. Spessard L. Holland," 16; Brown, *In the Midst*, 319; Morris, *Florida Handbook, 1991–1992*, 610.

18. *TDD*, May 2, 3, 1939, April 3, 1944; Dunn, *Black Miami*, 193–94; Green, *Before His Time*, 54; Davis, *Half Century of Struggle*, 144–47; Colburn and Scher, *Florida's Gubernatorial Politics*, 73.

19. Morris, *Florida Handbook, 1991–1992*, 603.

20. Kennedy, *Freedom from Fear*, 131–59; Shofner, "Roosevelt's 'Tree Army,'" 433–56; *TDD*, August 7, 1933, October 20, 1935; *LWH*, March 23, May 4, 1934, October 18, 1935; "$11,000,000 Federal Highway Funds for Florida."

21. *JFT-U*, January 29, 1941; Kennedy, *Freedom from Fear*, 251–53; Linsin, "Something More Than a Creed," 27–30.

22. Pepper and Gorey, *Pepper*, 45; Linsin, "Something More Than a Creed," 41; Jones, "'Without Compromise or Fear,'" 475–83.

23. Kennedy, *Freedom from Fear*, 138–39; *LWH*, May 9, 1933; *TDD*, May 8, December 5, 1933, November 7, 1934; Guthrie, "Rekindling the Spirits," 30–36.

24. Bauer, "Sarasota," 143–45; Branch, "Salesman and His Swamp," 489–91; Brown, *In the Midst*, 310–12.

25. Bauer, "Sarasota," 140–42; Boulard, "State of Emergency," 166–67; *LWH*, September 28, 1934; Tebeau, *History of Florida*, 403–4.

26. Akerman, *Florida Cowman*, 252–53; Brown, *In the Midst*, 313–14; Hetherington, *River of the Long Water*, 127; *TDD*, July 23, 1937.

27. *LWH*, January 1, 1937; Hopkins, *Fifty Years of Citrus*, 163–65, 172–75; *TMT*, September 6, 1939; *TDD*, January 10, 26, 28, 29, 30, 31, 1940.

28. *TDD*, December 29, 1940; *JFT-U*, November 18, 1940, January 29, March 26, 1941; Bennett, "Highways to Heaven," 453.

29. Sage-Gagne, *Pilots in the Sun*, 1–15; Greenhaw, "Defending America," 154–65; Mormino, "World War II," 323; *JFT-U*, May 27, 1941.

30. Revels, "World War II–Era Florida," 140–43; Mormino, "World War II," 328–30; Tebeau, *History of Florida*, 419; Reilly, "Florida's Flying Minute Men," 417–37; *TST*, September 16, 1945; *TT*, June 7, 2000.

31. Tebeau, *History of Florida*, 419; *JFT-U*, November 16, 21, 1944; Jones and McCarthy, *African Americans in Florida*, 118–19. See also Homan and Reilly, *Black Knights*.

32. Mormino, "World War II," 324–35; Coles, "'Hell-by-the-Sea,'" 3–7.

33. Fere, "Crime and Racial Violence"; Mormino, "GI Joe Meets Jim Crow," 23–42.

34. Mormino, "World War II," 328; Mayo, *Seventh Census*, 9, 59.

35. Mayo, *Seventh Census*, 84; *TDD*, April 20, 1940.

36. *TMT*, September 14, 1945.

Chapter 5. The Court in Trying Times

1. *JFT-U*, November 13, 1932; *TDD*, February 19, 1937; Thomas, "Needs of Our Supreme Court," 171.

2. *TDD*, September 30, 1932, January 10, 1933, March 2, November 25, 1934.

3. Brown, "Shall We Have a Supreme Court of Seven Members?" 36; Chapman, "Improved Efficiency," 269.

4. *TDD*, April 25, April 28, May 1, 2, June 16, 18, 1933; B. K. Roberts interview, April 21, 1980.

5. *TDD*, April 1, 24, 26, 27, 1934, January 13, 1935, September 3, 1936, December 23, 1937, June 30, 1938.

6. *TDD*, November 3, December 8, 1933; March 16, April 20, May 25, June 29, October 5, 24, 1934, March 1, 8, June 28, October 4, 17, 1935, May 1, July 24, 1936, July 23, 1937.

7. Chapman, "Improved Efficiency," 270.

8. *TDD*, July 3, 1937, January 4, 6, June 20, 1938; Ingalls, *Urban Vigilantes*, 163–204; Brown, *In the Midst of All That Makes Life Worth Living*, 320.

9. *JFT-U*, July 21, 1937; *TDD*, July 20, 22, 1933; *TMT*, July 20, 21, 1933; "Lynching: 'Negros Remember . . . ,'" 9.

10. *TDD*, January 10, July 13, 1933, February 19, March 16, 25, April 13, May 8, 25, November 25, 1934.

11. *TDD*, November 3, 1933, January 6, 9, 16, June 17, 19, July 7, 1936; Pepper and Gorey, *Pepper*, 50; Pepper, "Practitioner," 8.

12. Davis, "Address Delivered," 156; *TDD*, December 18, 1934, June 24, 1935; Evelyn Davis Burns questionnaire, Fred H. Davis file, Reder Papers, box 2.

13. Kennedy, *Freedom from Fear*, 325–37; *TDD*, March 19, 1937; *TMT*, October 29, 1937.

14. *TDD*, June 1, November 8, 1933, March 29, April 8, 1939; *JFT-U*, March 30, April 1, 1939; Adkins, "Yesterday," 7.

15. Brown, "Brief History," 37; *TDD*, September 5, 1940; Adkins, "Yesterday," 6.

16. *TDD*, June 21, 23, July 9, 27, 1937; Adkins, "Yesterday," 7, 9.

17. *TMT*, October 28, 29, 31, 1937; "Humiliating the Judiciary," 347.

18. *TDD*, April 8, December 6, 1937, May 4, 5, 25, 1938; Bashful, "Florida Supreme Court," 62–79.

19. Richard W. Ervin questionnaire, Rivers H. Buford file, Reder Papers, box 2; *TMT*, November 2, 1937; *TDD*, December 19, 1937, May 2, 4, 5, 1938; *JFT-U*, May 7, 1938; Bashful, "Florida Supreme Court," 79–84.

20. Bashful, "Florida Supreme Court," 84–88.

21. *JFT-U*, September 16, 1938; *TDD*, January 19, February 19, April 28, October 20, 1937, September 16, 1938.

22. Buford, "Times and the Courts," 577; Richard W. Ervin questionnaire, Armstead Brown file, box 2, Reder Papers.

23. *In Memoriam: Honorable Elwyn Thomas and Honorable Campbell Thornal*, 7.

24. *Tampa Daily Times* quoted in *TDD*, November 27, 1940.

25. *JFT-U*, March 16, June 8, 1939; *TDD*, March 24, 1939, November 25, 1940; Thomas, "Needs of Our Supreme Court," 171; "Chief Justice Has Heavy Work under New Set-Up," 145; Little, "Overview," 22.

26. Adams, *Fourth Quarter*, 131; Warren, "Yesterday," 13.

27. *JFT-U*, October 20, 1938, January 19, 1939; *TDD*, February 12, 1939; Thomas, "Needs of Our Supreme Court," 171–72; "New Supreme Court Rules," 159; Chapman, "Improved Efficiency," 269–70; Sebring, "Appellate System," 143–44.

28. Chapman, "Improved Efficiency," 272.

29. *JFT-U*, November 6, 1942, June 9, 1943, January 9, 1946.

30. *TDD*, July 1, 1943.

31. *TDD*, October 7, 1941; *JFT-U*, February 16, 1940, October 7, 1941; Manley, Brown, and Rise, *Supreme Court of Florida*, 346–51.

32. Bashful, "Florida Supreme Court," 89–97; *TDD*, January 14, 1944.

33. *TDD*, March 3, March 11, July 27, 1945; *JFT-U*, March 11, 1945; Chapman, "Improved Efficiency," 271.

34. Chapman, "Improved Efficiency," 272.

35. "In Memoriam: Honorable Roy Harrison Chapman," xxxix–xl; *TDD*, December 24, 1944.

36. *National Cyclopaedia of American Biography*, 44:304; Cash, *Story of Florida*, 2:725; Roy H. Chapman biographical information, Roy H. Chapman file, SLF; *JFT-U*, October 31, 1943; Garwood, *Stetson University*, 194–95; Johnston, "Historic Stetson University Campus," 295.

37. "In Memoriam: Honorable Roy Harrison Chapman," xli; *National Cyclopaedia*, 44:304; Chapman biographical information; 1910 Florida census, Columbia County; *TDD*, June 23, 1937; Proctor, *Napoleon Bonaparte Broward*, 251.

38. Roberts interview; Frank Pepper questionnaire, Roy H. Chapman file; Reder Papers, box 2; *JFT-U*. August 10, 1952.

39. *National Cyclopaedia*, 44:304; Chapman biographical information; Cash, *Story of Florida*, 2:725–26.

40. Keuchel, *History of Columbia County*, 159–87; *National Cyclopaedia*, 44:304.

41. Chapman biographical information; *National Cyclopaedia*, 44:304.

42. *JFT-U*, August 4, 1925; "In Memoriam: Honorable Roy Harrison Chapman," xli.

43. Chapman, "Unauthorized Practice of Law," 178.

44. *TDD*, June 21, 23, July 1, 1937; Roberts interview.

45. Adkins, "Yesterday," 9; Warren, "Yesterday," 12.

46. Roberts interview; *TDD*, July 28, 1937; Frank Pepper questionnaire; "In Memoriam: Honorable Roy Harrison Chapman," xli.

47. *JFT-U*, August 10, 1952.

48. Cash, *Story of Florida*, 2:726; *National Cyclopaedia*, 44:304; Chapman biographical information; *JFT-U*, April 25, 1970.

49. Morris, *Florida Handbook, 1965–66*, 418; *TDD*, January 12, 1947; Cash, *Story of Florida*, 2:646.

50. Morris, *Florida Handbook, 1967–68*, 123; Morris, *Florida Handbook, 1991–1992*, 338; *TDD*, January 12, 1947; *In Memoriam: Honorable Elwyn Thomas and Honorable Campbell Thornal*, 20.

51. *TDD*, January 12, 1944; *TD*, March 1, 1971, January 14, 1998; Cash, *Story of Florida*, 2:646; Morris, *Florida Handbook, 1965–1966*, 418.

52. *TMT*, June 10, 1925; Cash, *Story of Florida*, 2:646; Bashful, "Florida Supreme Court," 62.

53. Bashful, "Florida Supreme Court," 62–79; *TDD*, November 1, 1938; *JFT-U*, November 2, 1938.

54. Roberts interview; Richard W. Ervin questionnaire, Elwyn Thomas file, FSCHS; Ervin and Hilker, "Putnam County Bar Association's Annual Shad Dinner," 13.

55. Warren, "Yesterday," 11.

56. *In Memoriam: Honorable Elwyn Thomas and Honorable Campbell Thornal*, 9.

57. Ibid., 7; *JFT-U*, January 9, 1968.

58. *TD*, March 1, 1971.

59. Thomas, "An Appraisal," 159–60; *JFT-U*, January 29, 1956, January 5, 1957, June 30, 1959. See also Thomas, "Judicial Council History."

60. *TD*, December 14, 1950, March 1, 1971; "The Retiring Justices," 99; Morris, *Florida Handbook, 1967–1968*, 123.

61. *JFT-U*, January 9, 1968; *TD*, March 1, 1971, January 14, 1998; "Retired Justice Elwyn Thomas," 205.

62. *In Memoriam: Honorable Elwyn Thomas and Honorable Campbell Thornal*, 7.

63. *Tampa Daily Times*, April 8, 1952; Morris, *Florida Handbook, 1949–1950*, 113; Adams, "Justice Alto Adams," 8. On Alto Lee Adams's life generally, see Adams, *Fourth Quarter*.

64. *MH*, May 12, 1985; *Tampa Daily Times*, April 8, 1952.

65. *TD*, August 28, 1949; *Bristol Free Press*, November 20, 1941; *Tampa Daily Times*, April 8, 1952.

66. *Tampa Daily Times*, April 8, 1952; *Bristol Free Press*, November 20, 1941; Fennelly, "Alto Lee Adams," 336.

67. Roberts, "Alto Adams," 10; Roberts interview; *JFT-U*, June 14, 1925; *Bristol Free Press*, November 20, 1941; *TD*, February 22, 1988.

68. *Tampa Daily Times*, April 8, 1952; *Bristol Free Press*, November 20, 1941; *MH*, July 15, 1985; Adams, "Justice Alto Adams," 8.

69. *Tampa Daily Times*, April 8, 1952; *MH*, February 21, 1988; Akerman, *Florida Cowman*, 252–53.

70. Adams, *Fourth Quarter*, 121–28; *JFT-U*, November 23, 1938; *TDD*, November 25, 26, 1940.

71. Adams, *Fourth Quarter*, 128; Warren, "Yesterday," 13; Roberts, "Alto Adams," 11; Roberts interview.

72. Stephen C. O'Connell interview, May 2, 2000; B. K. Roberts interview, April 21, 1980; Robert M. Ervin interview, May 15, 2000; *TDD*, February 2, 1947; *JFT-U*, December 13, 1945.

73. *Tampa Daily Times*, April 8, 1952; *MH*, May 12, 1985, February 21, 1988, August 21, 1995.

74. *TT*, October 21, November 11, 1967; *TD*, November 10, 11, 1967; *JFT-U*, November 11, 12, 1967.

75. *TD*, November 14, 1967; *JFT-U*, March 14, July 6, 7, 9, 1968.

76. *MH*, February 21, 1988; *TD*, February 22, 1988, November 2, 1992.

77. *JFT-U*, December 10, 1941; Tindall, *America*, 1:620–22.

78. *TDD*, August 8, 1943; Harold L. Sebring biographical materials included with Bruce R. Jacob to William F. Blews, October 9, 1990, Harold L. Sebring file, Reder Papers, box 2 (hereafter Sebring biographical materials).

79. *JFT-U*, December 10, 1941, April 13, 1942; Sebring biographical materials.

80. *TDD*, August 8, 1943; *JFT-U*, December 10, 1941; Sebring biographical materials; "Tom Sebring Appointed Circuit Judge," 128; Roberts interview.

81. *TDD*, August 8, 1943; "Tom Sebring Appointed Circuit Judge," 128.

82. Braim, *Will to Win*, 46–48; *SPT*, July 27, 1968.

83. *TDD*, August 8, 1943; Sebring biographical materials; *JFT-U*, November 26, 1939.

84. *SPT*, June 29, 1988; *JFT-U*, December 10, 1941.

85. "Tom Sebring Appointed Circuit Judge," 127–28; Sebring biographical materials.

86. *JFT-U*, January 9, 10, 1942.

87. Bashful, "Florida Supreme Court," 89–97; *JFT-U*, November 29, December 10, 1941, January 5, 12, 20, 26, March 12, April 5, 1942; *TDD*, January 11, 13, 22, 1942.

88. *JFT-U*, January 20, April 9, 1942.

89. Warren, "Yesterday," 13.

90. "Honorable Justice Harold L. Sebring," xlvii–xlviii; Mathews, "Remarks," 98; Roberts interview; Richard W. Ervin interview, May 8, 2000.

91. Sebring, "Responsibility of the Lawyer," 29–30.

92. *JFT-U*, October 3, 1946; *TDD*, March 25, August 27, October 19, 1947; *SPT*, July 27, 1968; "Honorable Justice Harold L. Sebring," xlvii; Roberts interview.

93. *JFT-U*, September 16, October 20, 1955; *OS*, October 20, 1955; *SPT*, July 27, 1968.

94. *SPT*, July 27, 1968, June 29, 1988; "In Memoriam: Harold Leon Sebring," n.p.; Sebring biographical materials.

Chapter 6. Case Decisions of the Great Depression and World War II Eras

1. 115 *Florida Reports*, 399.

2. 123 *Florida Reports*, 401.

3. E. E. Callaway to Fred P. Cone, November 12, 1937, Administrative Correspondence of Governor Fred P. Cone, RG 102, series 368, box 71, FSA; 148 *Florida Reports*, 516.

4. 138 *Florida Reports*, 492.

5. 130 *Florida Reports, 465.*

6. *JFT-U*, June 28, 1939; 139 *Florida Reports*, 43.

7. *TDD*, November 28, 1944; 155 *Florida Reports*, 270.

8. *TDD*, May 3, 1939; 137 *Florida Reports*, 808.

9. 119 *Florida Reports*, 833; *TDD*, May 29, 1935.

10. 127 *Florida Reports*, 159; *TDD*, February 18, 1937.

11. *TDD*, June 20, 1939; 139 *Florida Reports*, 54.

12. 117 *Florida Reports*, 594; Wright, "Zoning," 332.

13. 141 *Florida Reports*, 222; Wright, "Zoning," 347.

14. 146 *Florida Reports*, 676; Wright, "Zoning," 349.

15. 121 *Florida Reports*, 683; Wright, "Zoning," 380.

16. 147 *Florida Reports*, 480; Wright, "Zoning," 363–64, 381.

17. 149 *Florida Reports*, 148; Little, "New Attitudes," 503.

18. *JFT-U*, June 4, 1939; *TDD*, May 16, 1939; 138 *Florida Reports*, 32.

19. *TDD*, October 18, 26, 1928; Hughes, "Florida Preachers," 142; Guthrie, "Rekindling the Spirits," 27; 122 *Florida Reports*, 702.

20. 124 *Florida Reports*, 852.

21. *Laws of Florida* (1931), 53; 110 *Florida Reports*, 374; Knight, "Consumer Class Actions," 66.

22. 135 *Florida Reports*, 6; Knight, "Consumer Class Actions," 66.

23. 152 *Florida Reports*, 126; Knight, "Consumer Class Actions," 66.

24. 116 *Florida Reports*, 608; *TDD*, September 26, 1934.

25. 126 *Florida Reports*, 49; *TDD*, November 1, 1936.

26. 120 *Florida Reports*, 1; *TDD*, May 29, 1935.

27. Stephenson, "State Appellate Courts," 194; *TDD*, November 28, 1944; Adams, *Fourth Quarter*, 136–37; 156 *Florida Reports*, 227; 328 *United States Reports*, 331.

28. 153 *Florida Reports*, 84; *JFT-U*, June 2, 1943.

29. 117 *Florida Reports*, 477; *TDD*, December 2, 1934; Starling, "Special District Taxation," 548–59.

30. 135 *Florida Reports*, 463; Starling, "Special District Taxation," 548–49.

31. 137 *Florida Reports*, 188; Starling, "Special District Taxation," 548–49.

32. Shofner, "Militant Negro Laborers," 400–401; Kennedy, *Freedom from Fear*, 274–75, 285, 304–22.

33. 132 *Florida Reports*, 661; Gramling, "Development of Florida Labor Law," 191.

34. 140 *Florida Reports*, 865; Gramling, "Development," 192; *TDD*, December 5, 1939.

35. 152 *Florida Reports*, 378; Stephenson, "State Appellate Courts," 196–97.

36. 153 *Florida Reports*, 672; *TDD*, November 10, 1943.

37. *TDD*, October 30, November 28, 1944; Key, *Southern Politics*, 98; 155 *Florida Reports*, 245.

38. 108 *Florida Reports*, 633; Nachwalter, "Substantive Due Process," 103.

39. 132 *Florida Reports*, 273; Nachwalter, "Substantive Due Process," 102.

40. 133 *Florida Reports*, 590; Nachwalter, "Substantive Due Process," 113.

41. 138 *Florida Reports*, 312; *JFT-U*, May 30, 1939.

42. 116 *Florida Reports*, 120; *TDD*, August 7, 1934.

43. 135 *Florida Reports*, 100; *TDD*, November 30, 1938.

44. 152 *Florida Reports*, 178; *JFT-U*, January 16, 1943.

45. 156 *Florida Reports*, 181; *TDD*, July 27, 1945.

46. 111 *Florida Reports*, 707; *TDD*, August 7, 1933.

47. 117 *Florida Reports*, 642.

48. 123 *Florida Reports*, 734.

49. 136 *Florida Reports*, 568.

50. 309 *United States Reports*, 227; *TDD*, February 12, 1940.

51. *TDD*, December 16, 1940, October 21, 1941, March 10, 1942.

52. 113 *Florida Reports*, 865; *TDD*, February 6, 1934. As to women and their emer-

gence into Florida's political, business, and civic life in the 1930s and early 1940s, see Vance, *May Mann Jennings*, and Vickers, "Congresswoman Ruth Bryan Owen."

53. 151 *Florida Reports*, 253; *TDD*, July 29, 1942.

54. 136 *Florida Reports*, 644; Taylor, "Jury Service for Women," 229.

55. Hall, *Magic Mirror*, 243–44; 140 *Florida Reports*, 677; *JFT-U*, November 15, 1939.

56. 153 *Florida Reports*, 769; *TDD*, August 3, 1943.

57. 154 *Florida Reports*, 633; *TDD*, June 27, 1944.

Chapter 7. The Postwar Boom

1. Joubert, "Florida," 185; "Florida's Building Boom Underway," 5; *TDD*, March 23, June 9, 1947; Derr, *Some Kind of Paradise*, 336–51.

2. Mayo, *Seventh Census*, 9, 84; *Population of Florida*, 1–3; *JFT-U*, November 23, 1958.

3. *Population of Florida*, 4–14; *TD*, July 2, 1950; *JFT-U*, November 23, 1958; Bashful, "Florida Supreme Court," 13–15.

4. Revels, "World War Two–Era Florida," 144; Mohl and Mormino, "Big Change in the Sunshine State," 434–37; Derr, *Paradise*, 340–41; Nolan, *Fifty Feet in Paradise*, 249.

5. Derr, *Paradise*, 340–41; Joubert, "Florida," 185–89; Donovan, "Florida [1949]," 115; Donovan, "Florida [1950]," 101–2; *TD*, June 29, 1950; Hopkins, *Fifty Years of Citrus*, 194–220; Nolan, *Fifty Feet in Paradise*, 250; *TMT*, June 7, 2000.

6. *TDD*, October 29, 1947.

7. Kendrick, *Florida Trails to Turnpikes*, 159–244; Akerman, *Florida Cowman*, 253; Ballinger, "Florida's 'Cowless' Highways," 22, 31–33.

8. *JFT-U*, October 3, 1951, November 3, 1952, January 1, 2, 1953; Kendrick, *Florida Trails to Turnpikes*, 242–43; Rader, "Rickenbacker Causeway Completed," 43, 49–51; Hartley, "Courtney Campbell Parkway," 9–12; Orrick and Crumpacker, *Tampa Tribune*, 301.

9. Danese, *Claude Pepper and Ed Ball*, 11, 82, 85–93, 101–2, 106–7, 183–84, 219; Lincoln, "Terrible-Tempered Mr. Ball," 143–44.

10. Danese, *Claude Pepper and Ed Ball*, 70–71, 74; Lincoln, "Terrible-Tempered Mr. Ball," 145.

11. Danese, *Claude Pepper and Ed Ball*, 82–83, 108, 110; Edward Ball v. Ruth Latham Ball, case file #10304, Leon County Circuit Court records, Tallahassee; Mason and Harrison, *Confusion to the Enemy*, 151–59.

12. Jahoda, *Other Florida*; Mayo, *Seventh Census*, 9, 57–58; *Population of Florida*, 1, 4–14.

13. Havard and Beth, *Politics of Mis-Representation*, 49–51; Mayo, *Seventh Census*, 56–57.

14. Havard and Beth, *Politics of Mis-Representation*, 49–82; *Miami Times*, July 9, 1955; *JFT-U*, May 1, July 2, 1955; *TD*, May 4, 5, 1955, February 3, 1957; *OS*, May 5, 1955; Col-

burn and Scher, *Florida's Gubernatorial Politics*, 31, 77; Sherrill, "Florida's Legislature," 86

15. *MH*, December 9, 1970; Jahoda, *Other Florida*, 14.

16. Sherouse, "Sherouse Years," 410.

17. Gray, *My Story*, 48–49; *TDD*, March 21, May 22, September 12, 1947, August 20, 1948.

18. Key, *Southern Politics*, 99; Orrick and Crumpacker, *Tampa Tribune*, 250; *TD*, August 4, 1985; Havard and Beth, *Politics of Mis-Representation*, 78.

19. Colburn and Scher, *Florida's Gubernatorial Politics*, 101–10.

20. Key, *Southern Politics*, 82–105; Colburn and Scher, *Florida's Gubernatorial Politics*, 73–76; Orrick and Crumpacker, *Tampa Tribune*, 248–49, 187; Halberstam, *The Fifties*, 229–42; Wagy, *Governor LeRoy Collins*, 38–39; John Germany interview, June 14, 2000.

21. See Guthrie, *Keepers of the Spirits*; Orrick and Crumpacker, *Tampa Tribune*, 270, 283–86, 311–13; *TDD*, October 9, 1947; *TMT*, July 6, 1949; Rogers and Denham, *Florida Sheriffs*, 232–81.

22. *TD*, May 25, 26, 28, July 13, 23, August 18, 1950; Orrick and Crumpacker, *Tampa Tribune*, 283; Stephen C. O'Connell interview, May 2, 2000; Iorio, "Political Excess Shaped by a Game of Chance," 30–34.

23. *TDD*, May 15, 18, 23, 30, June 3, July 25, October 5, 10, 22, 24, 1947; *TD*, May 25, 26, 28, 1950; O'Connell interview, May 2, 2000.

24. Brooks, "Winning the Peace," 589; W. Reece Smith Jr. interview, June 13, 2000.

25. Havard and Beth, *Politics of Mis-Representation*, 113.

26. O'Connell interview, May 2, 2000; *SPT*, December 21, 1987.

27. Germany interview; Egerton, *Speak Now against the Day*, 221–22.

28. Germany interview; Havard and Beth, *Politics of Mis-Representation*, 100–101.

29. Havard and Beth, *Politics of Mis-Representation*, 100–101; *TDD*, September 2, 1948.

30. Wills and Morris, *Seminole History*, 55–56; *TDD*, March 7, May 2, 7, 1947.

31. Brooks, "Winning the Peace," 563–76; Green, *Before His Time*, 37–80; Saunders, *Bridging the Gap*, 18–21, 52–57; Neyland and Riley, *History of Florida Agricultural and Mechanical University*, 178–95.

32. *Miami Times*, May 14, 28, 1949; Rivers, *Florida Agricultural and Mechanical University Law School*, 15–26; Neyland and Riley, *History of Florida Agricultural and Mechanical University*, 237–56.

33. *TD*, May 8, 1951; Cooper, "Brown v. Board of Education," 8; *SPT*, July 2, 2000.

34. *Miami Times*, February 5, 1949; Green, *Before His Time*, 1–10, 71–176; Saunders, *Bridging the Gap*, 58–76, 115–19.

35. Danese, *Claude Pepper and Ed Ball*, 202–4; Colburn and Scher, *Florida's Gubernatorial Politics*, 72–75; *TD*, December 29, 1968; Key, *Southern Politics*, 93, 95; Saunders, *Bridging the Gap*, 118; Havard and Beth, *Politics of Mis-Representation*, 30.

36. Danese, *Claude Pepper and Ed Ball*, 185–215.

37. Colburn and Scher, *Florida's Gubernatorial Politics*, 75–78; Wagy, *Governor LeRoy Collins*, 33–83.

Chapter 8. The Postwar Bar

1. Collins, "Law and the Whole Man," 540; Blankenship, "Florida Bar," 38.

2. Brown, "Some Unfinished Business," 3; Richard M. Ervin interview, May 5, 2000; *SPT*, April 8, 1948.

3. Thornal, "I Remember Stephen C. O'Connell," 17; Wigginton, "New Florida Common Law Rules," 1.

4. Sturgis, "Abolition of the Diploma Privilege," 370–76; *Laws of Florida* (1951), 341; *TD*, April 17, 1951.

5. Alloway, "Constitutional Law [1954]," 158; Redfearn, "Amendments to Florida's Constitution," 139–40.

6. David, "Case for Constitutional Revision in Florida," 225–34; Elwyn Thomas to *University of Florida Law Review*, February 7, 1948, *University of Florida Law Review* 1 (spring 1948): n.p.

7. *TD*, February 27, 1949; Richard W. Ervin interview, May 1, 2000; Ervin, "Florida Statutes of 1949," 272–74; *Florida Bar Journal* 24 (July 1950), 245; Henderson, "New Florida Statutes," 348–51.

8. Walker, "Report of the Committee on Law Reporting."

9. Ibid.; "Law Reporting," 133–35.

10. John Germany interview, June 14, 2000; Brown, "Some Unfinished Business," 5.

11. Brown, "Some Unfinished Business," 5; Parker, "President's Annual Address," 166; "Bar Integration Committee Report," 347; "Bar Integration Opinion," 236; Blankenship, "Story of the Florida Bar," 20.

Chapter 9. The Postwar Supreme Court

1. "Bar Integration Opinion," 242; "Proceedings of the 39th Annual Convention of the Florida State Bar Association," 224; Terrell, "Status of the Rules of Civil Procedure," 281–89; Wigginton, "New Florida Common Law Rules," 1–5, 30–32; Wigginton, "Rules of Civil Procedure."

2. Richard W. Ervin interview, May 8, 2000; W. Reece Smith interview, June 13, 2000; Thomas, "Justice without Delay," 1; "Proceedings of the 39th Annual Convention of the Florida State Bar Association," 240.

3. Boyd and Reder, *History of the Supreme Court of Florida*, 1049–62; *TD*, September 7, 1949; Parsons, "Selection and Tenure of Florida Supreme Court Judges," 271–79.

4. *TDD*, August 11, 1946.

5. *TDD*, February 9, 1947.

6. *TDD*, September 7, 9, 1949; Adkins, "Yesterday," 6–7; Boyd and Reder, *History of the Supreme Court of Florida*, n.p.

7. *TDD*, September 26, 1948; *JFT-U*, October 16, 1951, March 29, 1972; Boyd and

Reder, *History of the Supreme Court of Florida*, n.p.; Adkins, "Yesterday," 13; Dobson, "Visit with Joe Butler," 10–14.

8. Richard W. Ervin interview, May 7, 1985; Smith interview.

9. Hall, *Judicial Sayings*, 94; *TD*, November 10, 1946.

10. *JFT-U*, August 1, 1945; Thomas, "Justice without Delay," 1, 4.

11. Sebring, "Appellate System," 141–47; *JFT-U*, January 13, 1954, January 11, 1956, January 8, 1957; Arnow and Brown, "Florida's 1954 Rules of Civil Procedure," 125–42; Truett, "New Florida Appellate Rules," 93–101; Mathews, "Remarks," 96–99.

12. Mayo, *Seventh Census*, 12; *Pittsburgh Courier*, May 11, 1946; Robert W. Saunders Sr. interview, May 25, 2000.

13. Bashful, "Florida Supreme Court," 97–109; *JFT-U*, January 16, March 15, 1946; *TMT*, May 27, 1946.

14. *MH*, December 5, 1982. See Paul D. Barns and T. Frank Hobson biographical sketches in this chapter.

15. *JFT-U*, October 22, 1946; Adams, *Fourth Quarter*, 128–29; *TDD*, May 2, 1947, May 13, 1951.

16. Manley, Brown, and Rise, *Supreme Court of Florida*, 333–34; *Laws of Florida* (1941), 471, (1945), 820; *Tampa Daily Times*, December 10, 1941; Roy H. Chapman to Spessard Holland, November 14, 1944, George B. Howell to Millard F. Caldwell, January 29, 1945, Chapman to Caldwell, January 30, February 7, March 21, April 11, 1945, Guyte P. McCord to Caldwell, March 14, 1945, C. H. Overman to Caldwell, September 13, 1945, Governor Millard Caldwell Administrative Correspondence, RG 102, series, 576, box 70, FSA.

17. B. K. Roberts interview, April 21, 1980; proceedings of the supreme court building commission, April 11, 1946, resolution of the board of commissioners of state institutions and the state budget commission, c. May 1946, memorandum to the governor from John M. Wigginton, September 5, 1946, Governor Millard Caldwell Administrative Correspondence, RG 102, series 576, box 70, FSA; *TDD*, July 19, August 11, 18, September 10, 20, December 13, 1946, January 28, 1947.

18. *TDD*, January 28, February 14, March 18, 31, April 2, 15, 18, 21, 22, 1947; *TMT*, April 16, 1947; telegram, Claude Pepper to Millard Caldwell, May 27, 1947, Governor Millard Caldwell Administrative Correspondence, RG 102, series 576, box 18, FSA.

19. *TDD*, November 25, 1947; "New Supreme Court Building"; *JFT-U*, October 14, December 30, 1948; *TMT*, December 30, 1948; Reed, "Highest Court of a State," 35.

20. *TDD*, March 27, 1949, May 19, 26, 1950; Mathews, "Remarks," 98; *JFT-U*, June 2, 1950; Roberts interview.

21. *SPT*, July 10, 2000; *TDD*, February 2, 28, 1947, October 4, 1948.

22. *TMT*, June 28, July 6, 1949; *JFT-U*, July 6, August 11, 1949; Hewlett, *Jessie Ball duPont*, 199–200; Stephen C. O'Connell interview, May 9, 2000; Burton Thornal interview, July 19, 2000; Wickman, "Honorable B. K. Roberts," 18–21.

23. *JFT-U*, June 2, 22–24, 1950; *MH*, June 22–23, 1950; *TMT*, June 23–24, 1950; *SPT*, June 23, 1950; Pepper and Gorey, *Pepper*, 211–12.

24. *JFT-U*, June 21, 1950, October 3, 16, 1951; *TD*, July 10, October 15, November 7, 1951; *OS*, January 1, 1952; Adams, *Fourth Quarter*, 149; Robert M. Ervin interview, May 15, 2000.

25. *JFT-U*, March 31, 1950, September 18, 1951; Havard and Beth, *Politics of Mis-Representation*, 30; *TD*, September 4, 17, October 7, 1951.

26. "A Negro" to Fuller Warren, October 19, 1951, Governor Fuller Warren Administrative Correspondence, RG 102, series 235, box 91, FSA; Green, *Before His Time*, 157; Colburn and Scher, *Florida's Gubernatorial Politics*, 138; *SPT*, October 18, 1951; *TD*, October 23, 24, 1951.

27. *TD*, October 18, 28, 30, 1951; *JFT-U*, October 18, 19, 31, 1951.

28. Fuller Warren to Board of Governors, Florida Bar, January 11, 1952, *Florida Law Journal* 26 (February 1952): 83; *JFT-U*, February 21, August 10, 12, 16, 1952; *TMT*, August 13, 1952; *OS*, August 13, 1952.

29. *TD*, April 17, May 29, 1951; Sebring, "Appellate System," 141–47; Warren, "Address," 237–42; *JFT-U*, November 2, 1952.

30. *TMT*, August 13, 1952; *JFT-U*, August 19, October 14, 16, 22, November 6, 1952; Bashful, "Florida Supreme Court," 140–50; *OS*, August 13, 1952; Fisher, "Annual Address," 225.

31. *Laws of Florida* (1951), 216; Porter, "Status of Judicial Reform," 104–5; Perlmutter, "Judicial Reform on the March in Florida," 50–56.

32. Perlmutter, "Judicial Reform," 50–57; Feibelman, "Florida's Judicial Council," 73–79; "The Judicial Council of Florida—Statement of Objectives," 56; *JFT-U*, July 13, October 1, 1955, February 23, November 8–9, 1956; Young, "Special Bulletin on Amendment No. 1," 490–91; Dreisbach, "Where to Appeal in Florida," 109–19.

33. John Germany interview, June 14, 2000; *JFT-U*, May 1, 2, July 2, September 16, 20, 1955; *TD*, May 5, 1955; *SPT*, January 16, 1989.

34. Bruton and Bailey, *Plant City*, 305–6; *MH*, September 23, 1973.

35. Paul Dryden Barns Jr. interviews, July 7 and 10, 2000; Warren M. Cason interview, July 14, 2000.

36. *TST*, April 14, 1946; *Bench and Bar of Florida*, 1:31; Barns interview, July 7, 2000; Mary Barns Pruitt interview, July 21, 2000; Bruton and Bailey, *Plant City*, 275.

37. Pruitt interview; "A Visit with Judge Barns," undated clipping from *Coconut Grove Village Post*, Mary Barns Pruitt Collection; Barns interviews; Bruton and Bailey, *Plant City*, 276, 306, 334–35.

38. Barns interviews; Pruitt interview.

39. *Bench and Bar of Florida*, 1:31; Rogers, "Fortune and Misfortune," 290–94; *TST*, April 14, 1946; Barns interview, July 7, 2000. On Justice Barns's judicial service, see also the Paul D. Barns scrapbooks, FSCHS.

40. *Palm Beach Sun*, April 5, 1946; *TST*, April 14, 1946; Roberts interview; Hal P. Dekle interview, July 17, 2000; *JFT-U*, September 24, 1973; *MH*, September 23, 1973.

41. Rogers, "The Great Depression," 308; Barns interviews; Crawford, "Judge Vincent C. Giblin," 7–8.

42. Bashful, "Florida Supreme Court," 101–9; *TMT*, May 15, 1946; *MH*, December 5, 1982; *TDD*, November 25, 1946; *JFT-U*, December 3, 1946.

43. Smith interview; Roberts interview; Richard W. Ervin interview, May 8, 2000; O'Connell interview, May 9, 2000.

44. *TMT*, June 28, July 6, 8, 1949; *JFT-U*, July 6, 1949; *TD*, September 2, 1949; *MH*, September 23, 1973; Barns interview, July 7, 2000.

45. Barns interview, July 7, 2000; *TMT*, July 6, 1949; *MH*, September 23, 1973, December 5, 1982; Paul D. Barns, "Courts, Lawyers, and Taxpayers"; Barns, "Proposed (Consolidated) Rules of Civil Procedure."

46. *MH*, September 23, 1973; Barns interview, July 7, 2000.

47. *Florida Baptist Witness*, September 29, 1960; *JFT-U*, September 23, 1960; Grismer, *Story of St. Petersburg*, 372–73; Frances Hobson Simmons interview, July 18, 2000.

48. *Florida Baptist Witness*, September 29, 1960; Grismer, *St. Petersburg*, 372–73.

49. Simmons interview; *SPT*, March 20, 1948; Grismer, *St. Petersburg*, 373.

50. Simmons interview; Grismer, *St. Petersburg*, 373.

51. Stetson basketball team photograph, with caption, in E. Harris Drew scrapbook, Melanie Drew Mitchell Collection, Tallahassee; Simmons interview; *Bench and Bar of Florida*, 1:177; Grismer, *St. Petersburg*, 373.

52. Straub, *History of Pinellas County*, 333; *SPT*, March 20, 1948; Simmons interview; Grismer, *St. Petersburg*, 373.

53. Straub, *History of Pinellas County*, 333; *SPT*, March 20, 1948; Simmons interview; *Ocala Star-Banner*, June 2, 1948.

54. Simmons interview; Grismer, *St. Petersburg*, 373.

55. *JFT-U*, March 20, April 4, 7, June 3, 1948; *SPT*, March 20, 1948; Bashful, "Florida Supreme Court," 109–26.

56. Roberts interview; Richard W. Ervin interview, May 8, 2000; Robert M. Ervin interview; Wade L. Hopping interview, May 12, 1982.

57. Hopping interviews, May 12, 1982, June 16, 2000; O'Connell interview, May 9, 2000; Dekle interview; Roberts interview.

58. *JFT-U*, March 14, 1953, May 3, 1955, February 14, 1962; T. Frank Hobson to "the Court," c. March 1953, biographical files, SLF; *TD*, February 14, 1962; Roberts interview.

59. *TT*, August 5, 1966, November 11, 1984; *JFT-U*, October 20, 1962; *SPT*, August 4, 7, 1966; *TD*, August 4, 7, 1966.

60. *SPT*, March 11, 1994.

61. *SPT*, August 5, 1966.

62. *Crawfordville Wakulla County News*, June 10, 1949; Hogan, Bradford, and McAden, "Justice B. K. Roberts," 4; *TD*, June 13, 1976; Wickman, " Roberts," 4–5.

63. Hogan, Bradford, and McAden, "Justice B. K. Roberts," 4, 6; *TD*, June 13, 1976; *Crawfordville Wakulla County News*, June 17, 1949; B. K. Roberts interview, September 16, 1986.

64. "Story: B. K. Roberts" in B. K. Roberts biographical file, FSCHS; Wickman, "Roberts," 7–9; Hogan, Bradford, and McAden, "Justice B. K. Roberts," 7–8.

65. Roberts interview, September 16, 1986; Wickman, "Roberts," 9; "Story: B. K. Roberts."

66. Wickman, "Roberts," 9–10; Roberts interview, April 21, 1980; *JFT-U*, September 1, 1949.

67. Hogan, Bradford, and McAden, "Justice B. K. Roberts," 8; Danese, *Claude Pepper and Ed Ball*, 80–82.

68. Hogan, Bradford, and McAden, "Justice B. K. Roberts," 8.

69. "Reminiscing with Justice Alto L. Adams," 10; *Crawfordville Wakulla County News*, July 8, 1949; *TDD*, March 15, 1919, November 16, 1921, February 17, 1923, September 23, 1927.

70. Roberts, "Law Practice in the Depression," 1–4; Danese, *Claude Pepper and Ed Ball*, 82–83; Boyd and Reder, *History of the Supreme Court of Florida*, 1052–53; Roberts interview, April 21, 1980; *TDD*, April 9, 16, 1930, April 25, May 1, June 16, 18, 22, September 19, 1933, June 30, 1983.

71. Roberts interview, September 16, 1986; Boyd and Reder, *History of the Supreme Court of Florida*, 1052–53; Wickman, "Roberts," 11–12.

72. *JFT-U*, May 9, 1971; *Crawfordville Wakulla County News*, June 17, 1949; Roberts interview, April 21, 1980; Wickman, "Roberts," 12–13.

73. *JFT-U*, July 7, 1949; Hogan, Bradford, and McAden, "Justice B. K. Roberts," 8, 10; Drane, "B. K. Roberts," 18; Wickman, "Roberts," 14–15.

74. Hogan, Bradford, and McAden, "Justice B. K. Roberts," 10–11; Drane, "B. K. Roberts," 18; *JFT-U*, August 11, 1949.

75. Roberts interview, September 16, 1986; *TD*, June 13, 1976, February 6, 1994; *MH*, June 13, 1976; Hogan, Bradford, and McAden, "Justice B. K. Roberts," 13.

76. "Society Honors Justice B. K. Roberts," 10–15; *JFT-U*, June 13, 1976; *TD*, November 28, 1990, August 5, 1999.

77. *TD*, January 14, 1991; Hewlett, *Jessie Ball duPont*, 199–200; Hogan, Bradford, and McAden, "Justice B. K. Roberts," 8–9; Hopping interview, June 16, 2000; Robert M. Ervin interview; O'Connell interview, May 9, 2000; Richard W. Ervin interview, May 7, 1985; Burton Thornal interview, July 19, 2000; Leland M. Hawes interview, July 11, 2000.

78. Mark Hulsey to the authors, October 26, 2004.

79. *TD*, February 6, 1994; August 5, 1999; *SPT*, August 5, 1999.

80. *TD*, August 5, 6, 2000; *Crawfordville Wakulla County News*, July 15, 1949.

81. Cutler, *History of Florida*, 2:60; *Book of Florida*, 562; "In Memoriam: Chief Justice John E. Mathews," li; *Ocala Star-Banner*, January 28, 1945.

82. "In Memoriam: Chief Justice John E. Mathews," liii; Cutler, *History of Florida*, 2:60; *JFT-U*, October 31, 1951, July 17, 1966.

83. *JFT-U*, July 17, 1966; "In Memoriam: Chief Justice John E. Mathews," li–lii; Cut-

ler, *History of Florida*, 2:60; Proctor, *Napoleon Bonaparte Broward*, 211, 306; Davis, *History of Jacksonville*, 305–6.

84. "In Memoriam: Chief Justice John E. Mathews," lii; *JFT-U*, January 2, 1953.

85. *JFT-U*, July 17, 1966; *Ocala Star-Banner*, January 28, 1945; "In Memoriam: Chief Justice John E. Mathews," lii.

86. *Ocala Star-Banner*, January 28, 1945; "In Memoriam: Chief Justice John E. Mathews," lii; *TD*, May 8, 11, 1947; William Warren Rogers interview, June 27, 2000; Green, *Before His Time*, 70–72.

87. *TD*, August 4, 1985; Richard W. Ervin interview, May 8, 2000; Roberts interview, April 21, 1980; "In Memoriam: Chief Justice John E. Mathews," lii.

88. "In Memoriam: Chief Justice John E. Mathews," lii; Kendrick, *Florida Trails to Turnpikes*, 169–72; *Miami Times*, May 14, 1949; Tebeau, *History of Florida*, 427–28; *JFT-U*, May 31, 1950, July 17, 1966.

89. *JFT-U*, October 18, 19, 20, 23, 31, 1951, July 17, 1966; *TD*, October 18, 23, 30, 1951; *SPT*, October 18, 1951; Green, *Before His Time*, 90, 157; Colburn and Scher, *Florida's Gubernatorial Politics*, 138.

90. *JFT-U*, December 13, 1953, January 12, 1955; *TD*, February 7, 1953; "In Memoriam: Chief Justice John E. Mathews," liii.

91. Mathews, "Remarks," 96–99; *JFT-U*, January 12, 1955; Darrey A. Davis, "Address," 286.

92. *OS*, May 3, 1955; Roberts interview, April 21, 1980.

93. *JFT-U*, May 1, 3, 1955; *TD*, May 1, 1955.

94. *TD*, January 7, 1968; *Florida from Indian Trails to the Space Age*, 3:798; Hartman and Coles, *Biographical Rosters*, 1:40–41.

95. Melanie Drew Mitchell interview, July 18, 2000; *Supreme Court of Florida*, 12; *Palm Beach Post*, August 12, 1952.

96. Clipping from unidentified West Palm Beach newspaper, January 24, 1921, and Stetson University basketball team photograph in E. Harris Drew scrapbook; Mitchell interview; *Florida from Indian Trails to the Space Age*, 3:798; *Supreme Court of Florida*, 12.

97. *Palm Beach Times*, December 17, 1956; Mitchell interview; *JFT-U*, August 12, 1952.

98. Mitchell interview; *Florida from Indian Trails to the Space Age*, 3:798; Nolan, *Fifty Feet in Paradise*, 164–70, 202–7, 217–18, 229–30, 297–302; Crawford, "Capone Island," 26.

99. *Palm Beach Times*, August 12, 1952.

100. Mitchell interview; Richard W. Ervin interviews, May 7, 1985, May 8, 2000; *TD*, February 10, 1978; O'Connell interview, May 9, 2000; *Palm Beach Times*, August 12, 1952.

101. *TMT*, August 13, 1952; *JFT-U*, August 12, 1952; *Palm Beach Post*, August 12, 1952; *Palm Beach Times*, August 12, 1952; *Bartow Polk County Democrat*, August 12, 1952.

102. Bashful, "Florida Supreme Court," 137–52; Roberts interview, April 21, 1980; Crawford, "Judge Vincent C. Giblin," 8.

103. Hopping interviews, May 12, 1982, and June 16, 2000; Chesterfield Smith and Richard W. Ervin questionnaires on Justice E. Harris Drew, E. Harris Drew biographical file, FSCHS; Roberts interview, April 21, 1980; *TT*, February 10, 1978; *JFT-U*, June 6, 1963.

104. Mitchell interview; Roberts interview, April 21, 1980; *TD*, February 10, 1978.

105. *JFT-U*, September 24, 1963, November 28, 1969; Mitchell interview; "Justice Drew Retires," 22.

106. *TD*, February 10, 1978; Mitchell interview; *SPT*, February 10, 1978.

107. *TT*, February 10, 1978; *SPT*, February 10, 1978; *TD*, February 10, 1978, January 18, 1990.

108. *TD*, November 5, 1970; *SPT*, January 16, 1989.

109. Benjamin Campbell Thornal Jr. biographical materials, SLF; Burton Thornal interview.

110. *OS*, May 5, 1955, November 5, 1970; Burton Thornal interview.

111. *OS*, May 5, 1955; *In Memoriam: Honorable Elwyn Thomas and Honorable Campbell Thornal*, 13; *Supreme Court of Florida*, 13; Yates, "Profile of the New Chief Justice," 917.

112. *OS*, May 5, 1955; *Supreme Court of Florida*, 13; *In Memoriam: Honorable Elwyn Thomas and Honorable Campbell Thornal*, 13.

113. Alyce Thornal Morrison interview, July 17, 2000; Benjamin Campbell Thornal Jr. interview, July 12, 2000; *OS*, May 5, 1955.

114. *OS*, May 5, 1955, November 5, 1970; *Supreme Court of Florida*, 13; O'Connell interview, May 9, 2000; Wayne Todd Jr. interview, May 20, 2004.

115. Morrison interview; Benjamin Campbell Thornal Jr. interview; *OS*, Mary 5, 1955; *TD*, May 5, 1955; *JFT-U*, May 5, 1955; Smith interview.

116. *TD*, May 5, 1955; 96 *So.2d* 130 (Fla. 1957); John Germany interview, June 14, 2000; Elizabeth Pierson questionnaire regarding Justice Campbell Thornal, Thornal biographical file, FSCHS.

117. Chesterfield Smith and Jim Tippin questionnaires regarding Justice Campbell Thornal, Thornal biographical file, FSCHS; *SPT*, January 16, 1989; *OS*, November 5, 1970; Yates, "Profile of the New Chief Justice," 917–18; Sherouse, "Sherouse Years," 412. Copies of Justice Campbell Thornal's Florida supreme court opinions may be found in the Campbell Thornal papers, PKY.

118. William C. Owen interview, April 14, 2003.

119. *Tampa Florida Sentinel*, January 21, 1956.

120. *OS*, November 5, 10, 1970; *TD*, November 5, 1970.

121. *OS*, November 5, 1970; *SPT*, January 16, 1989.

122. O'Connell, "In Memoriam: Mr. Justice Campbell Thornal," n.p.

123. *Fort Lauderdale Daily News*, September 19, 1955; *SPT*, December 21, 1987.

124. "Evening with Stephen C. O'Connell," 4; Dobson, "Justice Stephen C.

O'Connell," n.p.; Leonora M. O'Connell to Nancy Dobson, November 17 [1987?], Stephen C. O'Connell biographical file, FSCHS.

125. O'Connell interview, May 2, 2000; "Evening with Stephen C. O'Connell," 4.

126. O'Connell interview, May 2, 2000; *MH*, September 22, 1987.

127. Dovell, *Florida*, 3:380; O'Connell biographical data, FSCHS; O'Connell interview, May 2, 2000; "Evening with Stephen C. O'Connell," 4–5; Mitchell interview.

128. "Soon Enough If Right," 6; O'Connell interview, May 2, 2000; *TT*, June 8, 1992.

129. *JFT-U*, September 20, 1955; O'Connell interview, May 2, 2000; "Inauguration of Stephen C. O'Connell," 17; "Soon Enough If Right," 6; "Evening with Stephen C. O'Connell," 5–6.

130. "Evening with Stephen C. O'Connell," 4–5; O'Connell interview, May 2, 2000; *Fort Lauderdale Daily News*, September 19, October 21, 1955.

131. *Fort Lauderdale Daily News*, September 19, 1955; *TT*, June 8, 1992; O'Connell interview, May 2, 2000.

132. *TT*, June 8, 1992; Dovell, *Florida*, 3:380; *TD*, August 26, 1977, *JFT-U*, August 28, 1977.

133. O'Connell interview, May 2, 2000; *Supreme Court of Florida*, 14–15; *TT*, June 8, 1992; "Inauguration of Stephen C. O'Connell," 15.

134. O'Connell interview, May 2, 2000; *TT*, June 8, 1992; *JFT-U*, September 20, 1955.

135. *SPT*, December 21, 1987; O'Connell interview, May 2, 2000; *Fort Lauderdale Daily News*, October 21, 1955.

136. *TT*, May 4, 1956, June 8, 1992; Dekle interview; Joe A. McClain to Stephen C. O'Connell, May 5, 2000, Stephen C. O'Connell Collection, Tallahassee; *MH*, August 30, 1957; *Fort Lauderdale Daily News*, April 16, 1957; *JFT-U*, February 1, 1957, June 28, 1961.

137. "Evening with Stephen C. O'Connell," 6–7; *TT*, June 8, 1992.

138. *TT*, June 8, 1992; *TD*, February 8, 1998, April 14, 15, 2001.

139. Thornal, "I Remember Stephen C. O'Connell," 17.

Chapter 10. Case Decisions of the Postwar Era

1. 40 *Southern Reporter, Second Series*, 371; Adams, *Fourth Quarter*, 132.

2. 73 *Southern Reporter, Second Series*, 680; Alloway, "Constitutional Law [1956]," 147.

3. 89 *Southern Reporter, Second Series*, 318.

4. 47 *Southern Reporter, Second Series*, 567; *TDD*, July 7, 1950.

5. 62 *Southern Reporter, Second Series*, 696; Alloway, "Constitutional Law [1954]," 169.

6. 89 *Southern Reporter, Second Series*, 785; Alloway, "Constitutional Law [1958]," 334.

7. 41 *Southern Reporter, Second Series*, 894; Bittan, "Torts: Distinction between Mere Insult and Slander per Quod," 133–35.

8. 67 *Southern Reporter, Second Series*, 434; Bullen, "Torts: Oral Charge That One Is a Communist as Slander per Se," 209–13.

9. 155 *Florida Reports*, 299.

10. 32 *Southern Reporter, Second Series*, 584; "Torts: Res Ipsa Loquitur in Exploding-Bottle Cases."

11. 39 *Southern Reporter, Second Series*, 476; "Sales—Implied Warranty of Fitness in Sale of Food by Restaurant," 638–39.

12. 62 *Southern Reporter, Second Series*, 5; Alloway, "Florida Constitutional Law [1960]," 514.

13. 91 *Southern Reporter, Second Series*, 657.

14. 157 *Florida Reports*, 649; Hunt, "Riparian Rights," 399.

15. 77 *Southern Reporter, Second Series*, 431; Hunt, "Riparian Rights," 400.

16. 44 *Southern Reporter, Second Series*, 899; Gramling, "Development of Florida Labor Law," 195–96.

17. 160 *Florida Reports*, 667; Gramling, "Development," 192–93.

18. 41 *Southern Reporter, Second Series*, 865; Gramling, "Development," 193.

19. 61 *Southern Reporter, Second Series*, 753; Crane, "Labor Law—Right of Non-striking Employees to Enjoin Picketing."

20. 40 *Southern Reporter, Second Series*, 902; "Courts—Inherent Power of the Florida Supreme Court to Integrate the Bar," 111–13; Blankenship, "Story of the Florida Bar."

21. 74 *Southern Reporter, Second Series*, 221; Crockett, "Legal Ethics," 484–86.

22. 82 *Southern Reporter, Second Series*, 657; Davis, "Attorneys," 318–21; Alloway, "Constitutional Law [1958]," 312.

23. 157 *Florida Reports*, 859; Adams, *Fourth Quarter*, 141; Nachwalter, "Substantive Due Process," 104–5.

24. 52 *Southern Reporter, Second Series*, 125; Alloway, "Constitutional Law [1954]," 169.

25. 59 *Southern Reporter, Second Series*, 779; Alloway, "Constitutional Law [1954]," 169.

26. 60 *Southern Reporter, Second Series*, 663; *JFT-U*, October 29, 1952; Alloway, "Constitutional Law [1954]," 169–70; Condon, "Constitutional Urban Redevelopment," 347–48.

27. 75 *Southern Reporter, Second Series*, 765; Alloway, "Constitutional Law [1956]," 157.

28. 72 *Southern Reporter, Second Series*, 655; Alloway, "Constitutional Law [1956]," 158.

29. 75 *Southern Reporter, Second Series*, 832; Alloway, "Constitutional Law [1956]," 158–59, 180.

30. 45 *Southern Reporter, Second Series*, 681; Bartley, "Legal Problems in Florida Municipal Zoning," 382–84.

31. 65 *Southern Reporter, Second Series*, 861; Cheves, "Aesthetic Nuisances in Florida," 56.

32. Hall, *Magic Mirror*, 322–24; Franklin and Moss, *From Slavery to Freedom*, 410–15.

33. 47 *Southern Reporter, Second Series*, 608; Cooper, "Brown v. Board of Education," 1–5; Reed, "Implications of Recent Cases," 362–67.

34. 53 *Southern Reporter, Second Series*, 116; Cooper, "Brown v. Board of Education," 5.

35. 60 *Southern Reporter, Second Series*, 162; Cooper, "Brown v. Board of Education," 6; Alloway, "Constitutional Law [1954]," 186–87.

36. 347 *United States Reports*, 971.

37. 83 *Southern Reporter, Second Series*, 20; Cooper, "Brown v. Board of Education," 6–7; *JFT-U*, October 20, 1955.

38. 46 *Southern Reporter, Second Series*, 880; Lawson, Colburn, and Paulson, "Groveland," 310.

39. 341 *United States Reports*, 50; Lawson, Colburn, and Paulson, "Groveland," 310–11; Green, *Before His Time*, 127–28; Williams, *Thurgood Marshall*, 152–57.

40. 66 *Southern Reporter, Second Series*, 288; Alloway, "Constitutional Law [1954]," 178.

41. 66 *Southern Reporter, Second Series*, 865; Alloway, "Constitutional Law [1954]," 180.

42. 158 *Florida Reports*, 264; Poulton, "Counsel Appointment," 220.

43. 90 *Southern Reporter, Second Series*, 449; Alloway, "Constitutional Law [1958]," 317.

44. Halberstam, *The Fifties*, 588–92; 39 *Southern Reporter, Second Series*, 794; Taylor, "Jury Service for Women," 229.

45. 61 *Southern Reporter, Second Series*, 420; Smith, "Compensation for Loss of Consortium," 198–99.

46. 64 *Southern Reporter, Second Series*, 650; Wickman, "Honorable B. K. Roberts," 27.

Chapter 11. The Civil Rights Era

1. Orrick and Crumpacker, *Tampa Tribune*, 300–301; Kendrick, *Florida Trails to Turnpikes*, 188–91.

2. Colburn and Scher, *Florida's Gubernatorial Politics*, 75–76; Wagy, *Governor LeRoy Collins*, 35–42.

3. Hathorn, "Cramer V. Kirk," 403–7; Klingman, *Neither Dies nor Surrenders*, 155–59; Morris, *Florida Handbook, 1991–1992*, 603, 617.

4. Garrow, *Bearing the Cross*, 1–355; Saunders, *Bridging the Gap*, 71–89, 123–250.

5. Saunders, *Bridging the Gap*, 147–57; Wagy, *Governor LeRoy Collins*, 59–103, 120–43; *JFT-U*, November 12, 1957.

6. *MT*, June 21, 28, 1958, June 20, 1959; *TFS*, September 8, 1962; Motley, *Equal Justice under Law*, 116–17; Wills and Morris, *Seminole History*, 66.

7. Rivers, *Florida Agricultural and Mechanical University College of Law*, 25–34; Neyland and Riley, *History of Florida Agricultural and Mechanical University*, 252; Larry E. Rivers interview, September 4, 2000; *TT*, December 18, 1982; Loquasto, *150: Celebrating Florida's First 150 Women Lawyers*, 106–7; Morris, *Florida Handbook, 1991–1992*, 146.

8. Brown, "1959: The Slow Death of Jim Crow"; Hall, "Civil Rights: The Florida Version," 10–13; Saunders, *Bridging the Gap*, 106, 227–38; *TD*, February 18, 1999, February 20, 2000; Garrow, *Bearing the Cross*, 316–430. For more on the St. Augustine integration crisis, see Colburn, *Racial Change and Community Crisis*.

9. Halberstam, *The Fifties*, 134–35; Derr, *Some Kind of Paradise*, 342–45; Nolan, *Fifty Feet in Paradise*, 261; *OS*, September 10, 2000.

10. Derr, *Paradise*, 342–45; Sherouse, "Sherouse Years," 412.

11. Patterson, "A Special Place, Always," 19–21; Nelson, "Mission Most Perilous," 4–5; Tindall, *America*, 2:1341.

12. Mohl, "Latinization of Florida," 151–68.

13. Colburn and Scher, *Florida's Gubernatorial Politics*, 223–36; *JFT-U*, March 1, 1964.

14. Saunders, *Bridging the Gap*, 159–70; Schnur, "Cold Warriors in the Hot Sunshine," 9–15.

15. Hall, *Magic Mirror*, 312; Wagy, *Governor LeRoy Collins*, 42; Sherrill, "Florida's Legislature," 82; *JFT-U*, November 19, 1962.

16. Colburn and Scher, *Florida's Gubernatorial Politics*, 78–80, 227–28; Warren M. Cason interview, July 14, 2000.

Chapter 12. The Supreme Court, Federal Judicial Activism, and the Civil Rights Era

1. Pepper and Gorey, *Pepper*, 228.

2. Sebring, "Responsibility of the Lawyer," 29–30.

3. Lamar Warren, "Yesterday," 12; Richard W. Ervin interview, May 8, 2000.

4. *JFT-U*, November 17, 1954.

5. *JFT-U*, October 20, 1955; *OS*, October 20, 1955.

6. *OS*, October 22, 1955; Sebring, "Responsibility of the Lawyer," 26.

7. "Reminiscing with Justice Alto L. Adams," 11; W. Reece Smith Jr. interview, June 13, 2000; Robert M. Ervin interview, May 15, 2000; A. Broaddus Livingston interview, June 13, 2000.

8. Livingston interview; Smith interview.

9. Burton Thornal interview, July 19, 2000; Leland M. Hawes interview, July 11, 2000.

10. Richard W. Ervin, "Speech in Honor of Justice B. K. Roberts," October 30, 1986, in B. K. Roberts biographical file, FSCHS.

11. Richard W. Ervin, "Speech in Honor of Justice B. K. Roberts"; Richard W. Ervin interview, May 8, 2000; Robert M. Ervin interview; *JFT-U*, June 14, 1962.

12. John Germany interview, June 14, 2000; Stephen C. O'Connell interview, May 2, 2000; Richard W. Ervin interviews, May 7, 1985, May 8, 2000; *JFT-U*, June 14, 1962.

13. *JFT-U*, October 30, 31, 1960, May 10, June 28, August 1, 1961; *TD*, May 10, 1961.

14. *JFT-U*, August 1, 1961, September 6, 16, 1962, June 15, 1963, July 1, November 7, 1963, September 26, 1964; Germany interview; Laser, "Right to Appointed Counsel," 445–51.

15. *JFT-U*, February 14, 1962, April 2, 1964; *TD*, February 14, 1962; *TMT*, February 14, 1962; Morris, *Florida Handbook, 1965–1966*, 392; Warren M. Cason interview, July 14, 2000; Wagy, *Governor LeRoy Collins*, 140–42. On the Florida Commission on Constitutional Government and its various state and national affiliations, see Dickerson, *Dixie's Dirty Secret*.

16. *JFT-U*, April 1, June 26, 1962, March 26, July 9, 18, 1963; Hall, *Magic Mirror*, 312; *MH*, March 15, 1983; *TD*, June 16, 1964.

17. *JFT-U*, December 14, 1963, February 21, 1964; Caldwell, "Third Legislative Chamber," 327–28.

18. *TD*, September 24, 1964; *JFT-U*, September 25, 1964; *MH*, September 25, 1964; Livingston interview; Smith interview.

19. Harris, "Constitutional Law," 486; Thornal, "Lawyer and the Rule of Law," 1160; *JFT-U*, July 20, 1963.

20. *JFT-U*, January 14, 16, June 16, August 8, 1964; *TMT*, January 14, 1964; *TD*, August 4, 1985; *Florida Bar News*, December 1, 1999; Richard W. Ervin interview, May 1, 2000.

21. Dovell, *Florida*, 4:889; *National Cyclopaedia of American Biography*, G:180; "He Couldn't Throw a Curve," 13; Mary Harwood Caldwell interview, March 1977.

22. *National Cyclopaedia*, G:180; Associated Press dispatch, February 29, 1963, in Millard Caldwell biographical file, SLF.

23. "He Couldn't Throw a Curve," 14; *National Cyclopaedia*, G:180.

24. *TD*, October 24, 1976; "He Couldn't Throw a Curve," 14; *National Cyclopaedia*, G:180.

25. *TD*, October 24, 1976, February 25, 1986; Van Brunt, "Florida's First Family," 15–16; Dovell, *Florida*, 4:890.

26. *TT*, December 18, 1977; Hawes, "'Promising' Politicians"; *TD*, February 24, 1962, December 29, 1968, October 24, 1976.

27. *TT*, December 18, 1977; Sikes, *He-Coon*, 102.

28. Sikes, *He-Coon*, 70, 72, 97, 102; *TT*, December 18, 1977; "He Couldn't Throw a Curve," 35; Dovell, *Florida*, 4:890; Green, "Blackwater River State Forest," 3; Nathan Woolsey to Canter Brown Jr., July 5, 2000; *TDD*, April 16, 1944; *TD*, October 24, 1976.

29. *TD*, December 29, 1968; Hawes, "'Promising' Politicians"; Millard F. Caldwell gubernatorial campaign press release, October 14, 1943, Millard F. Caldwell biographical

file, SLF; Morris, *Florida Handbook, 1991–1992,* 610. Millard Caldwell's personal papers as governor are deposited in the mss. collection, FSA.

30. Hawes, "Caldwell Disdains Timid, Honeyed Talk"; Hawes, "Caldwell Says Too Many Indifferent to, Neglectful of Public Responsibility"; William Warren Rogers interview, June 27, 2000; *TD*, October 24, 1976, October 24, 1984; "'Tax Revenue Spent for Public Education, a Sound Investment,' Says Caldwell"; Egerton, *Speak Now against the Day*, 390, 430–31, 511.

31. *TD*, September 2, 1949, September 23, 1951; "Remembering Millard Fillmore Caldwell," 10; *TT*, February 18, 1977; Hawes, "Caldwell Says Too Many Indifferent to, Neglectful of Public Responsibility."

32. Cason interview; Germany interview; *JFT-U*, February 14, 1962; *TD*, February 14, 1962; *TT*, February 13, 15, 1962.

33. O'Connell interview, May 9, 2000; Smith interview; Richard W. Ervin interview, May 8, 2000; *JFT-U*, December 14, 1963, February 21, 1964, Caldwell, "Third Legislative Chamber," 328; *TT*, December 18, 1977: Livingston interview; Burton Thornal interview; Gray, *My Story*, 299.

34. "Remembering Millard Fillmore Caldwell," 10–11; *TD*, October 24, 1984, February 25, 1986; *MH*, October 24, 26, 1984, February 26, 1986.

35. *TD*, August 4, 1985; Richard W. Ervin interview, May 1, 2000.

36. Dovell, *Florida*, 3:320; Ervin, "Memoirs," 10.

37. *TD*, August 4, 1985; Ervin, "Memoirs," 9–11; Dovell, *Florida*, 3:320.

38. Richard W. Ervin interview, May 7, 1985, May 1, 2000; Wills and Morris, *Seminole History*, 40–43; Richard W. Ervin questionnaire regarding Robert Spratt Cockrell, Robert Spratt Cockrell biographical file, FSCHS; Manley, Brown, and Rise, *Supreme Court of Florida*, 344–46.

39. Richard W. Ervin interview by Russell Troutman, no date.

40. "Personal History and Background for Richard W. Ervin" in Richard W. Ervin biographical file, SLF; Richard W. Ervin interviews, May 7, 1985, May 1, 2000; Ervin, "Memoirs," 11, 14–15.

41. Richard W. Ervin interviews, May 7, 1985, May 1, 2000; Richard W. Ervin campaign press release, July 17, 1948, in Ervin biographical file, SLF; Dovell, *Florida*, 3:320.

42. Ervin, "Memoirs," 1, 4, 19–20; Dovell, *Florida*, 3:320.

43. *JFT-U*, December 22, 1974; *TD*, September 16, 1951, August 4, 1985; *Florida Bar News*, December 1, 1999.

44. Richard W. Ervin interviews, May 7, 1985, May 1, 2000; Robert M. Ervin interview; *Florida Bar News*, December 1, 1999; Morris, *Florida Handbook, 1991–1992,* 620.

45. *TD*, February 27, 1949, June 18, 1950, September 17, 1951; *JFT-U*, February 13, May 5, 1956, December 22, 1974; "Florida Supreme Court Historical Society Honors Richard W. Ervin," 10–12; "Justice Richard W. Ervin, 1964–1975" in Ervin biographical file, FSCHS.

46. Wagy, *Governor LeRoy Collins*, 86–88; *TT*, January 16, 1964; *JFT-U*, December 22, 1974; "Florida Supreme Court Historical Society Honors Richard W. Ervin," 12.

47. Richard W. Ervin interview, May 1, 2000; *JFT-U*, January 14, 15, 1964; *TT*, January 14, 16, 1964; *TD*, January 15, 1964.

48. *TD*, January 17, 1964; Brown and Haddad, "Judicial Decision-Making," 581–82; Richard W. Ervin interview, May 7, 1985; William C. Owen interview, April 14, 2003; *JFT-U*, December 22, 1974; *Florida Bar News*, December 1, 1999.

49. Richard W. Ervin interview, May 1, 2000; "Florida Supreme Court Historical Society Honors Richard W. Ervin," 13.

50. Richard W. Ervin interview, May 7, 1985; *JFT-U*, February 27, 1964, December 22, 1974.

51. Owen interview.

52. *TD*, August 4, 1985; *Florida Bar News*, December 1, 1999; remarks of Robert M. Ervin, May 9, 1997, at the presentation of an honorary doctor of laws degree by Florida State University on Richard William Ervin, collection of Robert M. Ervin, Tallahassee; Owen interview.

53. *TD*, August 26, 2004; Barbara Pariente, *Florida Bar News*, September 14, 2004; "Remarks of Bob Butterworth at Memorial Service for Richard M. Ervin" and "Remarks of Ben Overton at Memorial Service for Richard M. Ervin," collection of Robert M. Ervin, Tallahassee.

Chapter 13. Case Decisions of the Civil Rights Era

1. 125 *Southern Reporter, Second Series*, 554; Alloway and Knight, "Trends," 706.

2. 126 *Southern Reporter, Second Series*, 133; Alloway and Knight, "Trends," 704.

3. 126 *Southern Reporter, Second Series*, 129; Alloway and Knight, "Trends," 705.

4. *JFT-U*, March 26, 1963.

5. 352 *United States Reports*, 380.

6. 102 *Southern Reporter, Second Series*, 386.

7. 130 *Southern Reporter, Second Series*, 605; Alloway and Knight, "Trends," 700.

8. 127 *Southern Reporter, Second Series*, 98; Gay, "High Water Mark," 570.

9. 334 *United States Reports*, 1; 116 *Southern Reporter, Second Series*, 622; Alloway and Knight, "Trends," 732.

10. 154 *Southern Reporter, Second Series*, 169; Semet, "Sales," 502–9.

11. 146 *Southern Reporter, Second Series*, 361; Gay, "High Water Mark," 571.

12. 108 *Southern Reporter, Second Series*, 33; Alloway, "Constitutional Law [1960]," 519.

13. 92 *Southern Reporter, Second Series*, 415; Alloway, "Constitutional Law [1958]," 329.

14. 141 *Southern Reporter, Second Series*, 269; Ross, "Labor Law—Agency Shop Violates Florida Constitution," 204.

15. 86 *Southern Reporter, Second Series*, 799; Alloway, "Constitutional Law [1958]," 294.

16. 145 *Southern Reporter, Second Series*, 871; Semet, "Florida Constitutional Law," 911–12.

17. 84 *Supreme Court Reports*, 529; Semet, "Florida Constitutional Law," 912.

18. 96 *Southern Reporter, Second Series*, 130; Cobb, "Municipal Tort Liability," 121–23; Roscow, "Municipal Corporations," 174.

19. 95 *Southern Reporter, Second Series*, 912; "Contributions of Justice Campbell Thornal to the Jurisprudence of Florida," Campbell Thornal file, FSCHS.

20. 115 *Southern Reporter, Second Series*, 745; Condon, "Constitutional Urban Redevelopment," 350; Alloway and Knight, "Trends," 716.

21. 122 *Southern Reporter, Second Series*, 611; Nachwalter, "Substantive Due Process," 118–19.

22. 350 *United States Reports*, 43.

23. 93 *Southern Reporter, Second Series*, 354; Cooper, "Brown v. Board of Education," 8–9.

24. 93 *Southern Reporter, Second Series*, 354.

25. 87 *Southern Reporter, Second Series*, 501; Alloway, "Constitutional Law [1956]," 181–82; Nachwalter, "Substantive Due Process," 141.

26. 92 *Southern Reporter, Second Series*, 621; Alloway, "Constitutional Law [1958]," 328; Nachwalter, "Substantive Due Process," 141.

27. 160 *Southern Reporter, Second Series*, 114.

28. 153 *Southern Reporter, Second Series*, 1; Semet, "Florida Constitutional Law," 910–11.

29. 85 *Supreme Court Reports*, 283.

30. 143 *Southern Reporter, Second Series*, 21; Semet, "Florida Constitutional Law," 895; Harris, "Constitutional Law," 484–85.

31. 143 *Southern Reporter, Second Series*, 21.

32. 374 *United States Reports*, 487; Harris, "Constitutional Law," 484–85.

33. 160 *Southern Reporter, Second Series*, 97; Harris, "Constitutional Law," 484–85.

34. 84 *Supreme Court Reports*, 1272; Harris, "Constitutional Law," 485.

35. 135 *Southern Reporter, Second Series*, 746; 372 *United States Reports*, 335. On the story of *Gideon*, generally, see Lewis, *Gideon's Trumpet*.

36. 372 *United States Reports*, 335; Hall, *Magic Mirror*, 321; Newman, *Hugo Black*, 526–28.

37. 153 *Southern Reporter, Second Series*, 299.

38. 159 *Southern Reporter, Second Series*, 866; Dunaj, "Will the Trumpet of Gideon Be Heard," 470; Manly, "Criminal Law," 639–43; Kantor, "Constitutional Law," 430.

39. 166 *Southern Reporter, Second Series*, 892; Laser, "Right to Appointed Counsel," 445, 449.

40. 176 *Southern Reporter, Second Series*, 331.

41. 119 *Southern Reporter, Second Series*, 691; Eaton, "Equal Protection in Florida," 144.

42. 155 *Southern Reporter, Second Series*, 787; Bishop, "Florida Abortion Law," 347.

Chapter 14. A Peaceful Revolution of Earthquake Proportions

1. Zibart, *Unofficial Disney Companion*, 15–19; Brown, "Welcome to Reedy Creek," 36; *SPT*, May 30, 1965.

2. "East Coast Disneyland to Rise near Orlando," undated *New York Times* clipping in Disney World file, University of South Florida Library subject files; *MH*, November 7, 1965; *TMT*, May 12, 1967; *OS*, August 29, 1971; *TD*, September 26, 1971.

3. Mayo, *Seventh Census*, 9; Morris, *Florida Handbook, 1991–1992*, 562–65.

4. Tebeau, *History of Florida*, 459–60.

5. Tindall, *America*, 2:1394–99.

6. Wills and Morris, *Seminole History*, 69–72; *TT*, June 8, 1992; Tindall, *America*, 2:1389–94, 1405–7.

7. *JFT-U*, August 4, 1966; *TD*, May 14, 1971.

8. Colburn and Scher, *Florida's Gubernatorial Politics*, 80–81; Kallina, *Claude Kirk*, 27–28; Klingman, *Neither Dies nor Surrenders*, 164–65; Morris, *Florida Handbook, 1991–1992*, 611, 620.

9. Kallina, *Claude Kirk*, 19–43; Colburn and Scher, *Florida's Gubernatorial Politics*, 82–84; Klingman, *Neither Dies nor Surrenders*, 165–67.

10. 385 *United States Reports*, 440; Colburn and Scher, *Florida's Gubernatorial Politics*, 111; *SPT*, June 11, 2000.

11. Barnes, "Government in the Sunshine," 361; Kallina, *Claude Kirk*, 57–67.

12. *JFT-U*, January 6, 12, December 4, 9, 12, 14, 1966.

13. Kallina, *Claude Kirk*, 122–23; Wade L. Hopping interview, June 16, 2000; *JFT-U*, July 28, 1967, July 8, 1968.

14. *JFT-U*, June 29, July 4, 8, September 10, November 6, 1968, March 17, 1969; "Constitution Committee Works to Erase Conflict over Article V," 113; Kallina, *Claude Kirk*, 123–24; Hopping interview, June 16, 2000.

15. *JFT-U*, November 6, 11, 1968; Colburn and Scher, *Florida's Gubernatorial Politics*, 55, 84–86; Klingman, *Neither Dies nor Surrenders*, 187–89; Kallina, *Claude Kirk*, 126–200; Morris, *Florida Handbook, 1991–1992*, 146, 615, 608.

16. Orrick and Crumpacker, *Tampa Tribune*, 370; Tscheschlok, "Long Time Coming," 440–60; "Florida Electorate Turns Down Judicial Article V"; D'Alemberte, "Judicial Reform," 68.

17. D'Alemberte, "Judicial Reform"; *JFT-U*, November 19, 1971, January 19, 21, February 11, 13, March 9, 16, 1972.

Chapter 15. The Supreme Court and Its Own Revolution

1. "Evening with Stephen C. O'Connell," 15; Brown and Haddad, "Judicial Decision-Making," 582; Burton Thornal interview, July 19, 2000.

2. Brown and Haddad, "Judicial Decision-Making," 569.

3. *JFT-U*, August 16, 1953; *TD*, March 30, April 14, 1999.

4. *JFT-U*, July 23, 29, 1965.

5. "Soon Enough If Right," 7; "Judicial Council Releases Court Caseloads in Annual Report," 351; Roberts, "State of the Judiciary," 394–95.

6. *JFT-U*, January 7, 1966.

7. Brennan, "State Supreme Court Judge versus United States Supreme Court Justice," 227.

8. Eaton, "Equal Protection in Florida," 141.

9. Wade L. Hopping interviews, May 12, 1982, June 16, 2000; *TMT*, October 21, 1967; *TD*, November 10, 1967; Adams, *Fourth Quarter*. 138.

10. *TMT*, November 11, 1967; *TD*, November 10, 11, 1967; *JFT-U*, November 11, 12, 1967.

11. *JFT-U*, January 9, March 12, 14, 21, April 12, 14, May 29, November 3, 1968.

12. *TD*, August 1, 1968; *JFT-U*, April 12, May 29, July 6, 7, 9, 11, September 11, November 1, 6, 9, 1968.

13. *JFT-U*, November 9, 1968, January 5, 1969.

14. Morris, *Florida Handbook, 1973–1974*, 562; *JFT-U*, November 28, 1969, August 14, 23, 1970.

15. *OS*, November 6, 7, 1970; *JFT-U*, November 5, 7, December 2, 9, 10, 15, 1970, January 6, 1971.

16. Burton Young to Walter Manley, August 6, 2003.

17. *OS*, November 6, 7, 1970; *JFT-U*, November 5, 7, December 2, 9, 10, 15, 1970, January 6, 1971; *Jacksonville Journal*, December 9, 1970.

18. *TMT*, December 1, 1970; *OS*, December 1, 1970; *JFT-U*, December 2, 1970.

19. *MH*, December 10, 11, 1970; *JFT-U*, January 16, 1971.

20. "Judicial Nominating Councils Named"; D'Alemberte, "Judicial Reform," 68.

21. D'Alemberte, "Judicial Reform," 68–70.

22. *JFT-U*, March 15, 26, April 12, June 1, December 14, 1972; "Supreme Court Appoints Ueberhorst Chief Administrator of State Courts," 417.

23. Hopping interview, August 1, 2000; Hopping biographical materials, collection of Wade L. Hopping, Tallahassee.

24. Hopping interview, August 1, 2000.

25. Ibid.

26. Hopping biographical materials; Hopping interviews, May 12, 1985, August 1, 2000.

27. *JFT-U*, November 3, 1968; Hopping interviews, June 16, August 1, 2000.

28. *JFT-U*, November 3, 1968; Hopping biographical materials; Hopping interviews, June 16, August 1, 2000.

29. Hopping interviews, May 12, 1982, June 16, August 1, 2000.

30. "Wade L. Hopping Named CLE Director," 86; Hopping interview, August 1, 2000.

31. Hopping interviews, May 12, 1982, June 16, 2000.

32. "Wade L. Hopping Named CLE Director," 86; Hopping interview, June 16, 2000. On Governor Claude Kirk, his administration, and Wade Hopping's role in it, see also Kallina, *Claude Kirk*.

33. *JFT-U*, November 12, 1967, March 12, April 12, May 29, July 6, 7, 11, September 10, 1968; *TT*, November 10, 1967; *TD*, August 1, 1968; Dobson, "Justice Wade Hopping," n.p.; Hopping interview, June 16, 2000.

34. Morris, *Florida Handbook, 1973–1974*, 562; Hopping interviews, May 12, 1982, June 16, 2000.

35. Hopping interview, June 16, 2000.

36. *JFT-U*, December 13, 1968; *SPT*, April 23, 2000; *TD*, November 3, 1985; Hopping interview, June 16, 2000; Hopping biographical materials.

37. Dovell, *Florida*, 4:620; Stone, *Lineage of John Carlton*, 88; Brown, *Florida's Peace River Frontier*, 102, 108, 113, 117, 126, 129, 169, 209, 289; Brown, *Fort Meade*, 22–23, 27; Carlton, *Settlin' Judge*, 2–3; Morris, *Florida Handbook, 1991–1992*, 337.

38. Carlton, *Settlin' Judge*, 10, 15–16, 22, 31–32.

39. *TT*, May 8, 1973; Carlton, *Settlin' Judge*, 16–27, 43–58.

40. Carlton, *Settlin' Judge*, 33–37.

41. Ibid., 63–67.

42. Ibid., 67–70; Dovell, *Florida*, 4:620; *TT*, May 8, 1973.

43. Carlton, *Settlin' Judge*, 77–80; *JFT-U*, November 13, 1940.

44. *JFT-U*, November 13, 1940, April 12, 1968; Carlton, *Settlin' Judge*, 80–87.

45. *TT*, May 8, 1973, January 27, 1974; *Cocoa Tribune*, February 1, 1966; Carlton, *Settlin' Judge*, viii, 89–104, 123.

46. Carlton, *Settlin' Judge*, 33; Saunders, *Bridging the Gap*, 111–19; *TD*, December 26, 1951; *OS*, December 27, 1951. On Harry T. Moore, see also Green, *Before His Time*.

47. Carlton, *Settlin' Judge*, 90–91, 109; Dovell, *Florida*, 4:620; *JFT-U*, January 13, 1954.

48. *TT*, May 8, 1973; *Cocoa Today*, September 25, 1967; *JFT-U*, April 12, November 3, 6, 1968; Carlton, *Settlin' Judge*, 125–33.

49. *TT*, May 8, 1973; W. Reece Smith interview, June 13, 2000; Carlton, *Settlin' Judge*, 138–39.

50. Carlton, *Settlin' Judge*, 139–46; *TT*, December 5, 1972, January 18, 1973, January 27, February 10, November 24, 1974.

51. *TT*, May 8, 1973, February 16, 1974, April 11, 1988; Carlton, *Settlin' Judge*, 146–50.

52. Stobbie, "Down Home Justice," 13; James C. Adkins Jr. interview, August 16, 1987; *GS*, January 26, 1987.

53. Adkins interview; Stobbie, "Down Home Justice," 14; Dovell, *Florida*, 4:815.

54. Adkins, "Yesterday," 6–7, 9; Adkins interview; Adkins, Samuels, and Crockett, "Eighteen Years," 2.

55. Stobbie, "Down Home Justice," 14; *SPT*, January 4, 1987; Adkins interview; *TD*, June 25, 1994.

56. Stobbie, "Down Home Justice," 14–15; *TD*, November 23, 1986.

57. *SPT*, January 4, 1987; Florida marriage and divorce indexes, Office of Vital Statistics, Florida Department of Health; Dovell, *Florida*, 4:815; *JFT-U*, November 3, 1968; *TD*, October 19, 1975.

58. Adkins interview; Adkins, Samuels, and Crockett, "Eighteen Years," 2; Stobbie, "Down Home Justice," 15.

59. Adkins interview; *GS*, September 11, 1960; *JFT-U*, January 11, 1964; *TT*, January 11, 1964. On Adkins's legal publications of the period, see, for example, *Florida Real Estate Law and Procedure*.

60. Adkins interview; *GS*, January 17, 18, 20, 1968; *MH*, May 9, 1968; *TT*, February 17, 1968; *GS*, January 26, 1987; Morris, *Florida Handbook, 1973–1974*, 562.

61. "Florida Supreme Court Historical Society Honors Richard W. Ervin," 13; *SPT*, January 4, 1987; Adkins, Samuels, and Crockett, "Eighteen Years," 3.

62. *SPT*, January 4, 1987; *GS*, January 26, 1987; *TD*, October 19, 1975.

63. *TT*, January 29, 1974, December 5, 1975; *MH*, January 6, 1975; *TD*, October 19, 1975; *SPT*, January 4, 1987; *GS*, January 26, 1987.

64. *SPT*, January 4, 1987, June 25, 1994; Florida marriage and divorce indexes, Office of Vital Statistics, Florida Department of Health; *TD*, June 25, 1994; *TT*, September 13, 1986.

65. *TD*, November 23, 1986, April 8, 1993, June 25, 1994; *SPT*, November 1, 1986, January 4, 1987, June 25, 1994; *TT*, January 29, 1985, November 5, 1986; *GS*, January 26, 1987.

66. "Supreme Court of Florida," 15; *JFT-U*, November 3, 1968; *TD*, October 20, 1975, July 22, 1984; *TT*, November 24, 1974.

67. Boyd, "Looking Back," 26–27; *MH*, December 8, 1986.

68. Boyd, "Looking Back," 26.

69. *TD*, July 22, 1984.

70. Boyd, "Looking Back," 27; *MH*, December 8, 1986.

71. *MH*, April 24, 1993; *TD*, June 8, 2003; Boyd, "Looking Back," 27; "Supreme Court of Florida," 15.

72. Boyd, "Looking Back," 27; *MH*, December 8, 1986.

73. Boyd, "Looking Back," 27; *MH*, April 24, 1993.

74. Boyd, "Looking Back," 27–28; *JFT-U*, April 12, 14, May 29, November 3, 1968; Morris, *Florida Handbook, 1973–1974*, 562.

75. *TD*, November 24, 1974, June 14, October 20, 1975, July 22, 1984; *TT*, November 24, 1974, January 30, 1975, February 4, 1985; *SPT*, July 27, 1980, January 4, 1987.

76. *SPT*, May 1, 3, 1984, January 4, 1987; *TD*, July 22, 1984; Boyd and Reder, *History of the Supreme Court of Florida*.

77. *TD*, July 22, 1984; *SPT*, January 4, 1987; Boyd, "Looking Back," 29.

78. *TT*, January 11, 1986; *MH*, April 24, 1993; *TD*, June 8, 2003.

79. *TD*, December 1, 1986; *OS*, December 15, 1970; Adams, *Fourth Quarter*, 139; David L. McCain biographical materials, SLF.

80. *MH*, December 10, 1970; *OS*, December 9, 1970; *TD*, December 1, 1986; McCain biographical materials.

81. *TT*, December 10, 1970; *OS*, December 9, 1970; *SPT*, November 14, 1986; McCain biographical materials.

82. *JFT-U*, November 3, 1968; *TD*, December 1, 30, 1986; McCain biographical materials.

83. *MH*, December 10, 1970; Adams, *Fourth Quarter*, 139; Morris, *Florida Handbook, 1973–1974*, 562; *JFT-U*, April 14, November 3, 1968.

84. *OS*, December 9, 1970; *TT*, December 10, 15, 1970; *MH*, December 9, 10, 1970.

85. *OS*, December 9, 15, 1970; *MH*, December 10, 1970; *TT*, December 15, 1970.

86. *TD*, December 1, 1986; *MH*, December 10, 11, 1970; McCain biographical materials.

87. *MH*, December 10, 1970; *TD*, December 1, 1986; Adkins interview.

88. *TD*, April 27, 1975, December 1, 1986; Adkins interview.

89. *TT*, February 13, April 29, 1975; *TD*, April 23, 27, 1975; *SPT*, April 4, 29, 1975; Adkins interview.

90. *TD*, August 28, 1977, June 16, 1978; *TT*, June 16, 1978.

91. *TD*, November 13, December 1, 30, 1986.

92. *TD*, November 13, December 1, 30, 1986; *SPT*, November 14, 1986.

93. *Makers of America, Florida Edition*, 2:209–11; Shofner, *Jackson County*, 347, 354, 359, 368, 386, 396–97, 402–3, 435–26; Hartman and Coles, *Biographical Rosters*, 4:1608; Hal P. Dekle interview, July 17, 2000; Hal P. Dekle biographical materials, SLF.

94. Dekle interview.

95. Dekle biographical materials; Dekle interview.

96. Dekle interview; Dekle biographical materials.

97. Dekle interview.

98. Ibid.; Dekle biographical materials.

99. *JFT-U*, November 24, 1969; Dekle interview; Dekle biographical materials.

100. Dekle biographical materials; Dekle interview.

101. *JFT-U*, November 24, 1969; Dekle interview; Dekle biographical materials.

102. *JFT-U*, April 12, 1968; Morris, *Florida Handbook, 1973–1974*, 562; Dekle interview.

103. *JFT-U*, November 24, 28, 1969, August 14, 23, 1970; Morris, *Florida Handbook, 1973–1974*, 562; *TT*, December 29, 1970.

104. Hal P. Dekle Jr. to Canter Brown Jr., July 17, 2000; *TD*, November 24, 1974.

105. *TT*, November 24, 1974, March 10, 1975; *TD*, November 24, 1974.

106. Dekle to Brown, July 17, 2000.

107. Adkins interview.

108. *TT*, March 10, 1975; Dekle to Brown, July 17, 2000; Adkins interview; Robert M. Ervin interview, May 15, 2000.

109. Dekle to Brown, July 17, 2000; *TD*, April 12, 2003; Dekle, *Florida Trial Evidence*.

Chapter 16. Case Decisions, 1964–1972

1. 224 *Southern Reporter, Second Series*, 693; Barnes, "Government in the Sunshine," 364.

2. 245 *Southern Reporter, Second Series*, 38; Barnes, "Government in the Sunshine," 366.

3. 177 *Southern Reporter, Second Series*, 221.

4. 181 *Southern Reporter, Second Series*, 641; Spencer, "Implied Warranty," 195.

5. 223 *Southern Reporter, Second Series*, 713; Marsee, "Civil Procedure," 145–54.

6. 253 *Southern Reporter, Second Series*, 421; Tudhope, "Civil Procedure," 820–26.

7. 264 *Southern Reporter, Second Series*, 418; Smith-Adam, "Implied Warranties in Housing," 619–24.

8. 171 *Southern Reporter, Second Series*, 376; Gay, "High Water Mark," 572.

9. 171 *Southern Reporter, Second Series*, 376.

10. 239 *Southern Reporter, Second Series*, 817; Little, "New Attitudes," 485–86.

11. 245 *Southern Reporter, Second Series*, 209; Fawsett, "Eminent Domain," 392–93.

12. 225 *Southern Reporter, Second Series*, 906.

13. 172 *Southern Reporter, Second Series*, 435; Roscow, "Municipal Corporations," 173–74.

14. 172 *Southern Reporter, Second Series*, 455; Roscow, "Municipal Corporations," 174.

15. 171 *Southern Reporter, Second Series*, 368; Robinson, "Constitutional Law," 169–73.

16. 213 *Southern Reporter, Second Series*, 689; Schram, "Municipal Ordinance Violations," 485.

17. 198 *Southern Reporter, Second Series*, 1; Kirk, "Public Finance."

18. 261 *Southern Reporter, Second Series*, 801; Riedel, "Municipal Powers," 597–602; Sparkman, "History and Status," 305–6.

19. 261 *Southern Reporter, Second Series*, 801.

20. 229 *Southern Reporter, Second Series*, 239; Smiljanich, "Right to Counsel on Appeal," 215.

21. 236 *Southern Reporter, Second Series*, 442; Dunaj, "Will the Trumpet of Gideon Be Heard," 472; Boyd, "Looking Back," 29.

22. 200 *Southern Reporter, Second Series*, 521; Hahn, "Speedy Trial," 518; Earl, "Criminal Law," 606.

23. 233 *Southern Reporter, Second Series*, 393; Earl, "Criminal Law," 606.

24. 238 *Southern Reporter, Second Series*, 281; Earl, "Criminal Law," 603.

25. 249 *Southern Reporter, Second Series*, 1; Hahn, "Speedy Trial," 519.

26. Hahn, "Speedy Trial," 518–20; Roberts, "State of the Judiciary [1972]," 458.

27. 175 *Southern Reporter, Second Series*, 39; Nachwalter, "Substantive Due Process," 135.

28. 200 *Southern Reporter, Second Series*, 171; *Florida Bar News*, December 1, 1999.

29. 239 *Southern Reporter, Second Series*, 817.

30. 247 *Southern Reporter, Second Series*, 40; Smith, "Compensation for Loss of Consortium," 198–99.

Bibliography

Manuscripts

Barns, Paul D. Scrapbooks. Florida Supreme Court Library, Tallahassee.

Biographical files. Florida Supreme Court Historical Society, Tallahassee.

Biographical files. State Library of Florida, Tallahassee.

Caldwell, Millard Fillmore. Papers. Florida State Archives, Tallahassee.

———. Scrapbooks. Florida Supreme Court Library, Tallahassee.

Drew, E. Harris. Papers. Florida Supreme Court Library, Tallahassee.

———. Scrapbook. Collection of Melanie Drew Mitchell, Tallahassee.

Ervin, Richard W. Personal papers. Tallahassee.

Ervin, Robert M. Personal papers. Tallahassee.

Florida State College for Women. Faculty information card file. Strozier Library, FSU.

Hopping, Wade L. Personal papers and biographical materials. Tallahassee.

O'Connell, Stephen C. Personal papers. Tallahassee.

Pruitt, Mary Barns. Personal papers. Orlando and Stuart, Fla.

Reder, Randall O. Files. Florida Supreme Court Historical Society, Tallahassee.

Reder, Randall O. Papers. Florida Supreme Court Library, Tallahassee.

Simpson, John Milton Bryan. Papers. P. K. Yonge Library of Florida History, University of Florida.

Subject files. University of South Florida Library, Tampa, Fla.

Terrell, Glenn. Papers. Strozier Library, Florida State University.

Thornal, Campbell. Papers. P. K. Yonge Library of Florida History, University of Florida.

Whitfield, James Bryan. Papers. Florida State Archives, Tallahassee.

Thomas, Elwyn. Papers. Florida Supreme Court Library, Tallahassee.

Thornal, Campbell. Album. Florida Supreme Court Library, Tallahassee.

———. Papers. P. K. Yonge Library of Florida History, University of Florida, Gainesville.

Whitfield, James Bryan Collection. Florida Supreme Court Library, Tallahassee.

Public Documents and Public Records

Florida. Attorney General. *Report of the Attorney General of the State of Florida, 1921–1922.* Tallahassee: State Printer, 1923.

Florida. Department of Health. Office of Vital Statistics. Florida marriage and death records.

———. *Laws of Florida*, 1917–72.

———. Office of the Governor. Governors' Correspondence, 1929–71. RG 102, FSA.
Florida Reports.
Florida Supreme Court. Case Files, 1825–1997. RG 1100, series 49, FSA.
———. Minutes, 1917–72.
Leon County. Circuit court records. Leon County courthouse, Tallahassee.
Mayo, Nathan. *The Fifth Census of the State of Florida Taken in the Year 1925.* Tallahassee: T. J. Appleyard, 1925.
———. *The Seventh Census of the State of Florida 1945.* Tallahassee: Florida Department of Agriculture, 1945.
McRae, W. A. *The Fourth Census of the State of Florida Taken in the Year 1915.* Tallahassee: T. J. Appleyard, 1915.
The People of Lawmaking in Florida, 1822–1991. Tallahassee: Office of the Clerk of the House of Representatives, 1991.
Southern Reporter.
United States Reports.

Newspapers and Periodicals

Bartow Polk County Democrat, 1952.
Bristol Free Press, 1941.
Cocoa Today, 1967.
Cocoa Tribune, 1966.
Crawfordville Wakulla County News, 1949–50.
Florida Baptist Witness, 1960.
Florida Bar News, 1999–2004.
Fort Lauderdale Daily News, 1955–57.
Fort Meade Leader, 1918, 1933.
Gainesville Sun, 1960–87.
Jacksonville Florida Times-Union, 1891–2000.
Jacksonville Journal, 1970.
Jacksonville Times-Union and Journal, 1971.
Lakeland News, 1932–33.
Lake Wales Highlander, 1930–37.
Miami Daily News, 1930.
Miami Herald, 1935–2000.
Miami Times, 1949–56.
Milton Gazette, 1925.
Ocala Banner-Lacon, 1883.
Ocala Star-Banner, 1945–48.
Orlando Sentinel, 1949–72.
Palm Beach Post, 1952.
Palm Beach Sun, 1946.

Palm Beach Times, 1952–56.
Pittsburgh Courier, 1946.
St. Petersburg Times, 1948–2003.
Tallahassee Daily Democrat, 1917–49.
Tallahassee Democrat, 1949–2003.
Tallahassee Florida Democrat and Weekly Record, 1924.
Tampa Daily Times, 1941, 1952.
Tampa Florida Sentinel, 1956.
Tampa Morning Tribune, 1918–50.
Tampa Sunday Tribune, 1946–2000.
Tampa Tribune, 1950–2000.

Secondary Sources

Adams, Alto Lee. *The Fourth Quarter*. Ft. Pierce: privately published, 1975.

———. *The Law of the Land*. Miami: Florida Flair, 1988.

Adams, Alto Lee, Jr. "Justice Alto Adams." *Florida Supreme Court Historical Society Review* 3 (1987–88): 8.

Adkins, James C., Jr. *Florida Criminal Law and Procedure, Annotated, with Forms*. Norcross, Ga.: Harrison, 1954.

———. *Florida Motor Vehicle Liability Law*. Clearwater: D & S, 1981.

———. *Florida Real Estate Law and Procedure, with Forms; A Complete Narrative Treatise on the Florida Law of Real Estate, Including the Examination of Titles, Conveyancing, and the Practice and Procedure Relating to Actions for Land*. Atlanta: Harrison, 1959–60.

———. "Yesterday." *Florida Supreme Court Historical Society Review* 2 (Fall 1985): 6–9.

Adkins, James C., Jr., and Richard T. Jones. *Florida Civil and Criminal Discovery*. Norcross, Ga.: Harrison, 1976.

Adkins, James C., Jr., Leonard R. Samuels, and Paul Hampton Crockett. "Eighteen Years in the Judicial Catbird Seat." *Nova Law Review* 11 (Fall 1986): 1–24.

Akerman, Joe A., Jr. *Florida Cowman: A History of Florida Cattle Raising*. Kissimmee: Florida Cattlemen's Association, 1976.

Akin, Edward N. *Flagler: Rockefeller Partner and Florida Baron*. Kent, Ohio: Kent State University Press, 1988.

Allen, Frederick Lewis. *The Big Change: America Transforms Itself, 1900–1950*. New York: Harper, 1952.

Allison, John M. "Annual Address of John M. Allison, President of the Florida Bar." *Florida Law Journal* 26 (June 1952): 231–37.

Alloway, Clifford C. "Constitutional Law." *Miami Law Quarterly* 8 (Winter/Spring 1954): 158–203.

———. "Constitutional Law." *Miami Law Quarterly* 10 (Spring 1956): 143–97.

———. "Constitutional Law." *University of Miami Law Review* 12 (Winter 1958): 288–335.

———. "Florida Constitutional Law." *University of Miami Law Review* 14 (Summer 1960): 501–20.

Alloway, Clifford C., and Richard B. Knight. "Trends in Florida Constitutional Law." *University of Miami Law Review* 19 (Summer 1962): 685–744.

Andrews, Charles O. "Should We Ratify the Amendment Providing for Seven Supreme Court Justices?" *Florida State Bar Association Law Journal* 6 (October 1932): 251–53.

Ansbacher, Sidney F., and Joe Knetsch. "The Public Trust Doctrine and Sovereignty Lands in Florida: A Legal and Historical Analysis." *Journal of Land Use and Environmental Law* 4 (1989): 337–75.

Arnow, Winston E. "Yesterday." *Florida Supreme Court Historical Society Review* 1 (Fall 1984): 4–5.

Arnow, Winston E., and Clarence E. Brown. "Florida's 1954 Rules of Civil Procedure." *University of Florida Law Review* 7 (Summer 1954): 125–42.

Ballinger, J. Kenneth. "Florida's 'Cowless' Highways." *Florida Highways* 19 (December 1951): 22, 31–33.

"Bar Examination Paper." *Florida State Bar Association Law Journal* 3 (March 1930): 56.

"Bar Integration Committee Report to Mid-Year Conference of Bar Delegates." *Florida Law Journal* (December 1948): 347.

"Bar Integration Opinion." *Florida Law Journal* 23 (July 1949): 236–42.

Barnes, Jay. *Florida's Hurricane History*. Chapel Hill: University of North Carolina Press, 1998.

Barnes, Ruth Mayes. "Government in the Sunshine: Promise or Placebo?" *University of Florida Law Review* 23 (Winter 1971): 361–75.

Barns, Paul D. "Courts, Lawyers, and Taxpayers and the Proposed Revision of the Judiciary Article V of the State Constitution to Be Voted On in November, 1956, as Amendment 'No. 1.'" *Florida Bar Journal* 30 (March 1956): 162–73.

———. "Proposed (Consolidated) Rules of Civil Procedure for Florida." *Miami Law Quarterly* 8 (Fall 1953, supp.): 1–53.

Barns, Paul D., and Taylor Mattis. "1962 Amendments to the Florida Rules of Civil Procedure." *University of Miami Law Review* 17 (Spring 1963): 276–305.

Bartley, Ernest R. "Legal Problems in Florida Municipal Zoning." *University of Florida Law Review* 6 (Fall 1953): 355–84.

Bashful, Emmett Wilfort. "The Florida Supreme Court: A Study in Judicial Selection." PhD diss., University of Illinois, 1955.

Bauer, Ruthmary. "Sarasota: Hardship and Tourism in the 1930s." *Florida Historical Quarterly* 76 (Fall 1997): 135–51.

Bench and Bar of Florida: A Pictorial and Biographical Directory of the Members of the Bench and Bar of Florida. Vol. 1. Tallahassee: Horace Evans, 1935.

Bennett, Evan P. "Highways to Heaven or Roads to Ruin? The Interstate Highway System and the Fate of Starke, Florida." *Florida Historical Quarterly* 78 (Spring 2000): 451–67.

Bishop, C. Ken. "The Florida Abortion Law—Reform or Regression in 1972?" *University of Florida Law Review* 24 (Winter 1972): 346–52.

Bittan, B. A., Jr. "Torts: Distinction between Mere Insult and Slander per Quod." *University of Florida Law Review* 3 (Spring 1950): 133–35.

Blaine, Michael, comp. "South Florida in the Movies." *Marquee: South Florida's Magazine of the Arts and Entertainment* 2 (August–September 1982): 17–25.

Blankenship, Gary. "The Florida Bar: Changing through Technology." *Florida Bar Journal* 73 (April 2000): 37–40.

———. "The Story of the Florida Bar." *Florida Bar Journal* 73 (April 2000): 18–30.

The Book of Florida: An Illustrated Description of the Advantages and Opportunities of the State of Florida and the Progress That Has Here Been Achieved with a Biographical Record of Those Citizens Whose Endurance Has Produced the Superb Structure—Commercial, Industrial, Agricultural, and Political—Which Comprises the Strength of This Charming Section. Jacksonville: James O. Jones Co., 1925.

Bousquet, Stephen C. "The Gangster in Our Midst: Al Capone in South Florida, 1930–1947." *Florida Historical Quarterly* 76 (Winter 1998): 297–309.

Boulard, Garry. "'State of Emergency': Key West in the Great Depression." *Florida Historical Quarterly* 67 (October 1988): 166–83.

Boyd, Joseph A., Jr. "Looking Back on Eighteen Years as a Justice of the Supreme Court of Florida." *Nova Law Review* 11 (1986): 25–44.

———. "Staring Down." *Florida Supreme Court Historical Society Review* 1 (Winter 1985): 6.

Boyd, Joseph A., and Randall O. Reder. *A History of the Supreme Court of Florida*. Tallahassee: Florida Bar, 1983. The greater part of this work originally appeared in *University of Miami Law Review* 35 (September 1981): 1019–66.

Braim, Paul F. *The Will to Win: The Life of General James A. Van Fleet*. Annapolis: Naval Institute Press, 2001.

Branch, Stephen E. "The Salesman and His Swamp: Dick Pope's Cypress Gardens." *Florida Historical Quarterly* 80 (Spring 2002): 483–503.

Brennan, William J., Jr. "State Supreme Court Judge versus United States Supreme Court Justice: A Change in Function and Perspective." *University of Florida Law Review* 19 (Fall 1966): 225–37.

Brooks, Jennifer E. "Winning the Peace: Georgia Veterans and the Struggle to Define the Political Legacy of World War II." *Journal of Southern History* 66 (August 2000): 563–604.

Brown, Armstead. "The Bench and Bar of Florida." *Florida Law Journal* 19 (June 1945): 184–91.

———. "Brief History of the Supreme Court of Florida." *Florida Law Journal* 17 (January 1943): 34–38.

———. "Come to Miami." Typescript, 1923.
———. "Individualism and Government." In *Proceedings of the Florida State Bar Association*. Miami: Florida State Bar Association, 1923.
———. "The Judicial Section of the Florida State Bar Association." *Florida State Bar Association Law Journal* 2 (January 1929): 4–7.
———. "Shall We Have a Supreme Court of Seven Members?" *Florida Law Journal* 3 (April 1930): 32–40.
———. "Some Observations on the Canons of Professional and Judicial Ethics." *Florida Law Journal* 11 (April 1937): 145–48.
———. "Some Unfinished Business." *Florida Law Journal* 20 (January 1946): 3–7.
Brown, Canter, Jr. "A Florida Welcome to Reedy Creek." In *Program of the 1998 Annual Meeting of the Society of American Archivists, Orlando, Florida, August 31–September 6*. Chicago: Society of American Archivists, 1998.
———. *Florida's Black Public Officials, 1867–1924*. Tuscaloosa: University of Alabama Press, 1998.
———. *Florida's Peace River Frontier*. Orlando: University of Central Florida Press, 1991.
———. *Fort Meade, 1849–1900*. Tuscaloosa: University of Alabama Press, 1995.
———. *In the Midst of All That Makes Life Worth Living: Polk County, Florida, to 1940*. Tallahassee: Sentry Press, 2001.
———. "1959: The Slow Death of Jim Crow." *Forum: The Magazine of the Florida Humanities Council* 22 (Summer 1999): 4–6.
———. *None Can Have Richer Memories: Polk County, Florida, 1940–2000*. Tampa: University of Tampa Press, 2005.
Brown, Patrick, and William A. Haddad. "Judicial Decision-Making on the Florida Supreme Court: An Introductory Behavioral Study." *University of Florida Law Review* 19 (Winter 1966–67): 566–90.
Browne, Jefferson B. "Across the Gulf by Rail to Key West." *National Geographic* 7 (June 1896): 203–7.
———. "The American Law Institute, Its Organization and Purposes." In *Proceedings of the Florida State Bar Association*. Miami: Florida State Bar Association, 1923.
———. *Key West, the Old and the New*. St. Augustine: Record, 1912. Reprint, Gainesville: University of Florida Press, 1973.
———. "The Super-Constitution." *American Law Review* 54 (May–June 1920): 332–49.
Bruton, Quintilla Geer, and David E. Bailey Jr. *Plant City: Its Origin and History*. Winston-Salem, N.C.: Hunter, 1984.
Buford, Barbara. "Justice Rivers H. Buford." *Historia Juris: Quarterly Newsletter of the Florida Supreme Court Historical Society* (July 2002): 2.
Buford, Rivers. "Something about the Supreme Court of Florida." *Florida State Bar Association Law Journal* 6 (May–June 1932): 29–35.
———. "The Times and the Courts." *Florida Law Journal* 9 (December 1935): 577–89.

Bullen, Dana. "Torts: Oral Charge That One Is a Communist as Slander per Se." *University of Florida Law Review* 7 (Summer 1954): 209–13.

Burr, Josephine G. *History of Winter Haven, Florida.* Winter Haven: Larry Burr Printing, 1974.

Caldwell, Millard F. "The Third Legislative Chamber." *Florida Bar Journal* 38 (June 1964): 327–36.

Campbell, A. Stuart. "Florida in 1934." *Florida Municipal Record* 7 (February 1935): 10–12, 22–24.

Carlton, Sue Collins. *The Settlin' Judge: The Life of Vassar B. Carlton.* N.p.: privately published, 1984.

Carruthers, R. Bruce. "*Gideon, Escobedo, Miranda*: Begrudging Acceptance of the United States Supreme Court's Mandates in Florida." *University of Florida Law Review* 21 (Winter 1969): 346–59.

Cash, William T. *The Story of Florida.* 4 vols. New York: American Historical Society, 1938.

Chalmers, David. "The Ku Klux Klan in the Sunshine State: The 1920s." *Florida Historical Quarterly* 42 (January 1964): 209–15.

Chandler, Alfred N. *Land Title Origins: A Tale of Force and Fraud.* New York: Robert Schalkenbach Foundation, 1945.

Chapman, Roy H. "Improved Efficiency of Supreme Court under Amendments of Judiciary Article Florida Constitution." *Florida Law Journal* 19 (November 1945): 268–72.

———. "Unauthorized Practice of Law." *Florida Law Journal* 13 (May 1939): 178–80.

Cheves, Charles J., Jr. "Aesthetic Nuisances in Florida." *University of Florida Law Review* 14 (Spring 1961): 54–62.

"Chief Justice Has Heavy Work under New Set-up." *Florida Law Journal* 15 (April 1941): 145.

Clark, Thomas D. *The Emerging South.* 2nd ed. New York: Oxford University Press, 1968.

Cobb, Warren H. "Municipal Tort Liability: Proprietary-Governmental Distinction Discarded." *University of Florida Law Review* 11 (Spring 1958): 121–23.

Colburn, David R. "Florida Politics in the Twentieth Century." In *The New History of Florida*, ed. Michael Gannon. Gainesville: University Press of Florida, 1996.

———. *Racial Change and Community Crisis: St. Augustine, Florida, 1877–1980.* Gainesville: University of Florida Press, 1991.

Colburn, David R., and Jane L. Landers, eds. *The African American Heritage of Florida.* Gainesville: University Press of Florida, 1995.

Colburn, David R., and Richard K. Scher. *Florida's Gubernatorial Politics in the Twentieth Century.* Tallahassee: University Presses of Florida, 1980.

Coleman, Kenneth, ed. *A History of Georgia.* Athens: University of Georgia Press, 1977.

Coles, David J. "'Hell-by-the-Sea': Florida's Camp Gordon Johnston in World War II." *Florida Historical Quarterly* 73 (July 1994): 1–22.

Collins, LeRoy. "Law and the Whole Man." *Florida Bar Journal* 32 (November 1958): 539–41.

———. "Stephen C. O'Connell Served His State with Vision and Dedication." *St. Petersburg Times* (December 21, 1987).

Condon, Alphonse G., Jr. "Constitutional Urban Redevelopment." *University of Florida Law Review* 13 (Fall 1960): 344–53.

"Constitution Committee Works to Erase Conflict over Article V." *Florida Bar Journal* 43 (February 1969): 113.

Cooper, Algia R. "Brown v. Board of Education and Virgil Darnell Hawkins: Twenty-Eight Years and Six Petitions to Justice." *Journal of Negro History* 64 (Winter 1979): 1–20.

Coulter, E. Merton. *Georgia: A Short History*. Chapel Hill: University of North Carolina Press, 1960.

"Courts—Inherent Power of the Florida Supreme Court to Integrate the Bar." *Miami Law Quarterly* 4 (December 1949): 111–13.

Crane, Nicholas A. "Labor Law—Right of Non-striking Employees to Enjoin Picketing." *Miami Law Quarterly* 7 (April 1953): 434–35.

Crawford, William G., Jr. "Capone Island: From Swampland to Broward County's Deerfield Island Park, 150 Years of Florida Land History." *Broward Legacy* 19 (Summer/Fall 1996): 2–35.

———. "Judge Vincent C. Giblin: Broward's First Circuit Judge Was Capone's Lawyer, Dade Judge in the '50s." *Broward Legacy* 18 (Summer/Fall 1995): 2–12.

Crockett, Jerry B. "Legal Ethics: Solicitation as Ground for Disbarment." *University of Florida Law Review* 7 (Winter 1954): 484–86.

Cutler, Harry Gardner. *History of Florida Past and Present: Historical and Biographical*. 3 vols. Chicago: Lewis, 1923.

D'Alemberte, Talbot. "Judicial Reform—Now or Never: Lawyers Can Lead the Way to Judicial Reform." *Florida Bar Journal* 46 (February 1972): 68–71.

Danese, Tracy E. *Claude Pepper and Ed Ball: Politics, Purpose, and Power*. Gainesville: University Press of Florida, 2000.

———. "Disfranchisement, Women's Suffrage, and the Failure of the Florida Grandfather Clause." *Florida Historical Quarterly* 74 (Fall 1995): 117–31.

Datz, Albert J. "Florida's New Rules of Criminal Procedure." *Florida Bar Journal* 42 (May 1968): 285–92.

David, Thomas E. "The Case for Constitutional Revision in Florida." *Miami Law Quarterly* 3 (February 1949): 225–34.

Davis, Darrey A. "The Address of Honorable Darrey A. Davis." *Florida Bar Journal* 29 (May 1955): 282–88.

Davis, David A. "Attorneys: Refusal to Answer Charges of Communism as Ground for Disbarment." *Miami Law Quarterly* 8 (Fall 1955): 318–21.

Davis, Edward C. *A Half Century of Struggle for Freedom in Florida*. Orlando: Drake's, 1981.

Davis, Fred Henry, "Address Delivered by Hon. Fred H. Davis, Chief Justice of Supreme Court of Florida, at October Meeting of the Volusia County Bar Association." *Florida State Bar Association Law Journal* 7 (December 1933): 156–57.

Davis, Mattie Belle. *A History of the Florida Association for Women Lawyers, 1951–2002.* Miami: privately published, 2003.

Davis, T. Frederick. *History of Jacksonville, Florida, and Vicinity, 1513–1924.* Jacksonville: Florida Historical Society, 1925. Reprint, Jacksonville: San Marco Bookstore, 1990.

DeFoor, J. Allison, II. "Here's to Jeff Browne." *Florida Supreme Court Historical Society Review* 2 (1986): 1–4.

———. "The Poetry of Judge Jefferson B. Browne." Manuscript, n.d.

Dekle, Hal P. *Florida Trial Evidence.* New York: Wiley Law, 1987.

Denham, James M., and Canter Brown Jr. "Black Sheriffs of Post-Civil War Florida." *Sheriff's Star* 42 (September–October 1998): 12–15.

Derr, Mark. *Some Kind of Paradise: A Chronicle of Man and the Land in Florida.* New York: William Morrow, 1989.

Dickerson, James. *Dixie's Dirty Secret: The True Story of How the Government, the Media, and the Mob Conspired to Combat Integration and the Vietnam Antiwar Movement.* Armonk, N.Y.: M. E. Sharpe, 1998.

Dietz, George A. "Sketch of the Evolution of Florida Law." *University of Florida Law Review* 3 (Spring 1950): 74–81.

Dobson, Nancy. "Justice B. K. Roberts, 1949–1976." Typescript, Florida Supreme Court Historical Society, 1995.

———. "Justice Stephen C. O'Connell, 1955–1967." Typescript, Florida Supreme Court Historical Society, n.d.

———. "Justice Wade Hopping: August 1, 1968–January 7, 1969." Typescript, Florida Supreme Court Historical Society, n.d.

———. "Taking the Oath of Office, 1917–1985." *Florida Supreme Court Historical Society Review* 2 (Winter 1986): 7–10, 13.

———. "A Visit with Joe Butler." *Florida Supreme Court Historical Society Review* 3 (1987): 10–14.

Donovan, C. H. "Florida." *Southern Economic Journal* 16 (July 1949): 115.

———. "Florida." *Southern Economic Journal* 16 (January 1950): 373.

———. "Florida." *Southern Economic Journal* 17 (July 1950): 101–2.

Dovell, J. E. *Florida: Historic, Dramatic, Contemporary.* 4 vols. New York: Lewis Historical, 1952.

Drane, Hank. "B. K. Roberts." *Jacksonville Florida Times-Union and Journal* (February 21, 1971): 17–18, 27 (magazine section).

Dreisbach, William G. "Where to Appeal in Florida." *Florida Bar Journal* 32 (March 1958): 109–19.

Dunaj, Sherryll Martens. "Will the Trumpet of Gideon Be Heard in All the Halls of Justice?" *University of Miami Law Review* 25 (Spring 1971): 450–75.

Dunn, Marvin. *Black Miami in the Twentieth Century*. Gainesville: University Press of Florida, 1997.

Earl, William L. "Criminal Law: Crowded Dockets No Longer Justify Denial of Speedy Trial." *University of Florida Law Review* 23 (Spring 1971): 603–8.

———. "The Rulemaking Power of the Florida Supreme Court: The Twilight Zone between Substance and Procedure." *University of Florida Law Review* 24 (Fall 1971): 87–105.

Eaton, William. "Equal Protection in Florida Constitutional Law." *University of Miami Law Review* 21 (Fall 1966): 132–44.

Egerton, John. *Speak Now against the Day: The Generation before the Civil Rights Movement in the South*. New York: Alfred A. Knopf, 1994.

"$11,000,000 Federal Highway Funds for Florida." *Florida Public Works* 12 (April 1935): 1.

Ellis, William H. "My Experience as a Supreme Court Judge." *Florida State Bar Association Law Journal* 1 (January 1928): 3–8.

———. "The New Rules." *Florida State Bar Association Law Journal* 4 (March 1931): 549–53.

Emmons, Caroline. "'Not a Single Battle but Rather a Real War': The Fight to Equalize Teachers' Salaries in Florida in the 1930s and 1940s." *Florida Historical Quarterly* 81 (Spring 2003): 418–39.

Ervin, Richard W. "Florida Statutes of 1949." *Florida Law Journal* 23 (October 1949): 272–74.

———. "The Law—An Honorable Profession." *Florida Bar Journal* 38 (July 1964): 410–11.

———. "The Memoirs of Richard W. Ervin." Typescript, Tallahassee, 1999.

———. "Stories about Florida Supreme Court Justices." In *A Journal: 150 Years of History, the Supreme Court of Florida, 1846–1996*, comp. Nancy Dobson. Tallahassee: Florida Supreme Court Historical Society, n.d.

Ervin, Richard W., and Stephen E. Hilker. "The Putnam County Bar Association's Annual Shad Dinner." *Florida Supreme Court Historical Society Review* 4 (1991–94): 12–15.

Ervin, Richard W., and Bruce R. Jacob. "'Sit-In' Demonstrations: Are They Punishable in Florida?" *University of Miami Law Review* 15 (Winter 1960): 123–37.

"An Evening with Stephen C. O'Connell." *Florida Supreme Court Historical Society Review* 3 (1987–88): 4–7, 12–15.

Fawsett, Patricia Combs. "Eminent Domain: Public Purpose and Conservation of Natural Resources." *University of Florida Law Review* 24 (Winter 1972): 392–96.

Feibelman, Herbert U. "Florida's Judicial Council." *Florida Bar Journal* 28 (March 1954): 73–79.

———. "Memorial Services for Justice Armstead Brown." *Florida Law Journal* 26 (June 1952): 243–46.

Fennelly, John E. "Alto Lee Adams: Passion for Justice." *Journal of Southern Legal History* 3 (1994): 335–53.

Fere, Catherine. "Crime and Racial Violence in Tampa during World War II." *Tampa Bay History* 17 (Spring/Summer 1985): 65–82.

"Fifteenth President, 1922–23: Justice Armstead Brown, Tallahassee." *Florida Law Journal* 8 (August 1934): 103.

Fisher, Horner C. "The Annual Address of Honorable Horner C. Fisher, President of the Florida Bar 1953–1954." *The Florida Bar Journal* 28 (June 1954): 220–25.

"Florida and the CWA." *Florida Municipal Record* 6 (December 1933): 14, 22.

"Florida Building Boom Well Underway." *Florida Builder* 2 (February 1947): 5.

"Florida Electorate Turns Down Judicial Article V." *Florida Bar Journal* 44 (December 1970): 579.

Florida from Indian Trails to the Space Age. 3 vols. Delray Beach: Southern, 1965.

"Florida Supreme Court Historical Society Honors Richard W. Ervin." *Florida Supreme Court Historical Society Review* 2 (Fall 1985): 10–15.

Flynt, Wayne. *Cracker Messiah: Governor Sidney J. Catts of Florida*. Baton Rouge: Louisiana State University Press, 1977.

France, Mary Duncan. "'A Year of Monkey War': The Anti-Evolution Campaign and the Florida Legislature." *Florida Historical Quarterly* 54 (October 1975): 156–77.

Franklin, John Hope, and Alfred A. Moss Jr. *From Slavery to Freedom: A History of African Americans*. 7th ed. New York: McGraw-Hill, 1994.

Gannon, Michael, ed. *The New History of Florida*. Gainesville: University Press of Florida, 1996.

Garrow, David J. *Bearing the Cross: Martin Luther King Jr. and the Southern Christian Leadership Conference*. New York: William Morrow, 1986.

Garwood, Harry C. *Stetson University and Florida Baptists: A Documentary History of Relations between Stetson University and the Florida Baptist Convention*. DeLand: Florida Baptist Historical Society, 1962.

Gay, Norwood. "The High Water Mark: Boundary between Public and Private Lands." *University of Florida Law Review* 18 (Spring 1966): 553–76.

George, Paul S. "Brokers, Binders, and Builders: Greater Miami's Boom of the Mid-1920s." *Florida Historical Quarterly* 65 (July 1986): 27–51.

"Good v. Bell." *Florida State Bar Association Law Journal* 2 (October 1928): 68.

"The Governor Looks Ahead . . ." *Florida Highways* 13 (January 1945): 11–12, 35.

Graf, Max D. "Ridge Cities Refunding." *Florida Municipal Record* 5 (June 1932): 7, 21.

Gramling, J. Carrington, Jr. "The Development of Florida Labor Law." *Miami Law Quarterly* 7 (February 1953): 188–204.

Gray, R. A. *My Story: Fifty Years in the Shadow of the Near Great*. Tallahassee: Rose Printing, n.d.

Green, Ben. *Before His Time: The Untold Story of Harry T. Moore, America's First Civil Rights Martyr*. New York: Free Press, 1999.

Green, Laurie. "The Blackwater River State Forest." *Santa Rosa Historical Society Newsletter* 4 (February 1980): 1, 3.

Greenberg, Mark I., William Warren Rogers, and Canter Brown Jr., eds. *Florida's Heritage of Diversity: Essays in Honor of Samuel Proctor*. Tallahassee: Sentry Press, 1997.

Greenhaw, Thomas D. "Defending America by Aiding the Allies: The British Student Pilots at Arcadia and Clewiston, 1941–1945." *Florida Historical Quarterly* 74 (Fall 1995): 154–65.

Grismer, Karl H. *The Story of St. Petersburg: The History of Lower Pinellas Peninsula and the Sunshine City*. St. Petersburg: P. K. Smith, 1948.

Guest, David. "The Ordinary High Water Boundary on Freshwater Lakes and Streams: Origin, Theory, and Constitutional Restrictions." *Journal of Land Use and Environmental Law* 6 (1991): 205–40.

Guthrie, John J., Jr. "The Florida Supreme Court and the Intoxicating Liquor Laws: From Local Option to National Prohibition, 1885–1920." *Georgia Journal of Southern Legal History* 2 (Spring/Summer 1993): 99–137.

———. "Hard Times, Hard Liquor, and Hard Luck: Selective Enforcement of Prohibition in North Florida, 1928–1933." *Florida Historical Quarterly* 72 (April 1994): 435–52.

———. *Keepers of the Spirits: The Judicial Response to Prohibition Enforcement in Florida, 1885–1935*. Westport, Conn.: Greenwood Press, 1998.

———. "Rekindling the Spirits: From National Prohibition to Local Option in Florida, 1928–1935." *Florida Historical Quarterly* 74 (Summer 1995): 23–39.

Haas, Russell N. "Winter Haven—Then and Now." *Florida Municipal Record* 5 (January 1933): 10–12, 59.

Hahn, William E. "Speedy Trial in Florida: Has the Defendant's Shield Become His Sword?" *University of Florida Law Review* 24 (Spring 1972): 517–33.

Halberstam, David. *The Fifties*. New York: Fawcett Columbine, 1993.

Hall, Kermit L. "Civil Rights: The Florida Version." *Florida Humanities Council Forum* 18 (Winter 1994): 10–13.

———. *The Magic Mirror: Law in American History*. New York: Oxford University Press, 1989.

Hall, Kermit L., and Eric W. Rise. *From Local Courts to National Tribunals: The Federal District Courts of Florida, 1821–1990*. Brooklyn, N.Y.: Carlson, 1991.

Hall, M. Lewis, comp. *The Judicial Sayings of Justice Glenn Terrell*. Atlanta: Harrison, 1964.

Hammond, E. Ashby. *The Medical Profession in Nineteenth-Century Florida: A Biographical Register*. Gainesville: George A. Smathers Libraries of the University of Florida, 1996.

Harris, Gordon H. "Constitutional Law: Religious Practices in Public Schools." *University of Florida Law Review* 17 (Winter 1964): 484–88.

Hartley, Howard W. "Courtney Campbell Parkway." *Florida Highways* 16 (February 1948): 9–12.

Hartman, David W., and David J. Coles, comps. *Biographical Rosters of Florida's Confederate and Union Soldiers, 1861–1865*. 6 vols. Wilmington, N.C.: Broadfoot, 1995.

Hathorn, Billy B. "Cramer V. Kirk: The Florida Republican Schism of 1970." *Florida Historical Quarterly* 68 (April 1990): 403–26.

Havard, William C., and Loren P. Beth. *The Politics of Mis-Representation: Rural-Urban Conflict in the Florida Legislature*. Baton Rouge: Louisiana State University Press, 1962.

Hawes, Leland. "Caldwell Disdains Timid Honeyed Talk; Once Jolted Tampans in Blunt Speech." *Tampa Morning Tribune* (April 24, 1958).

———. "Caldwell Says Too Many Indifferent to, Neglectful of Public Responsibility." *Tampa Morning Tribune* (April 25, 1957).

———. "'Promising' Politicians No Better than Confidence Men, Millard Caldwell Says." *Tampa Morning Tribune* (April 23, 1957).

"'He Couldn't Throw a Curve . . .': Biography of Millard F. Caldwell." *Florida Highways* 13 (January 1945): 13–14, 35.

Henderson, Charles Tom. "The New Florida Statutes What—When—and How Much." *Florida Law Journal* 23 (December 1949): 348–51.

Hetherington, Alma. *The River of the Long Water*. Chuluota: Mickler House, 1980.

Hetherington, M. F. *History of Polk County, Florida*. St. Augustine: Record, 1928. Reprint, Chuluota: Mickler House, 1971.

Hewlett, Richard Greening. *Jessie Ball duPont*. Gainesville: University Press of Florida, 1992.

Hogan, Paul, Duane Bradford, and Fitz McAden. "Justice B. K. Roberts: From the Piney Woods to the Halls of Power." *Tampa Sunday Tribune* (Florida Accent Section, October 5, 1975).

Homan, Lynn M., and Thomas Reilly. *Black Knights: The Story of the Tuskegee Airmen*. Gretna, La.: Pelican, 2001.

"Honorable Justice Harold L. Sebring." 86–89 *Southern Reporter, Second Series (Florida Cases)*: xlv–xlix.

Hopkins, James T. *Fifty Years of Citrus: The Florida Citrus Exchange, 1909–1959*. Gainesville: University of Florida Press, 1960.

Horwitz, Morton J. *The Transformation of American Law, 1870–1960: The Crisis of Legal Orthodoxy*. New York: Oxford University Press, 1992.

Hughes, M. Edward. "Florida Preachers and the Election of 1928." *Florida Historical Quarterly* 67 (October 1988): 131–46.

"Humiliating the Judiciary." *Florida Law Journal* 11 (November 1937): 347.

Hunt, Richard H. "Riparian Rights in Florida." *University of Florida Law Review* 8 (Winter 1955): 393–410.

Hutcheson, Joseph C., Jr. "The Judgment Intuitive: The Function of the 'Hunch' in Judicial Decision." *Cornell Law Quarterly* 14 (1929): 274–88.

"In Memoriam: A Ceremonial Session Dedicated to the Memory of the Late Justice Glenn Terrell." 160–63 *Southern Reporter, Second Series (Florida Cases)*: 7–20.

"In Memoriam: Chief Justice John E. Mathews." 86–89 *Southern Reporter, Second Series (Florida Cases)*: li–liv.

"In Memoriam: Harold Leon Sebring, 1898–1968." *University of Florida Law Review* 21 (Summer 1968): n.p.

In Memoriam: Honorable Elwyn Thomas and Honorable Campbell Thornal, Justices, Supreme Court of Florida. Tallahassee: Supreme Court of Florida, 1971.

"In Memoriam: Honorable Roy Harrison Chapman." 102–4 *Southern Reporter, Second Series (Florida Cases)*: xxxix–xliii.

"In Memoriam: Judge Louie W. Strum." 71–74 *Southern Reporter, Second Series (Florida Cases)*: iii–vi.

"In Memoriam: Justice Armstead Brown." 58–60 *Southern Reporter, Second Series (Florida Cases)*: xliii–xlv.

"In Memoriam to Thomas Franklin West." 101 *Florida Reports*, n.p.

"The Inauguration of Stephen C. O'Connell." *Florida Alumnus* 18 (June 1966): 5–8.

Ingalls, Robert P. *Urban Vigilantes in the New South: Tampa, 1882–1936*. Knoxville: University of Tennessee Press, 1988.

Iorio, Pam. "Political Excess Shaped by a Game of Chance: Tampa, *Bolita*, and the First Half of the Twentieth Century." *Sunland Tribune* 26 (2000): 27–35.

Irby, Lee. "Taking Out the Trailer Trash: The Battle over Mobile Homes in St. Petersburg, Florida." *Florida Historical Quarterly* 79 (Fall 2000): 181–200.

Jahoda, Gloria. *Florida, a Bicentennial History*. New York: W. W. Norton, 1976.

———. *The Other Florida*. New York: Charles Scribner's Sons, 1967.

Johnston, Sidney. "The Historic Stetson University Campus in DeLand, 1884–1934." *Florida Historical Quarterly* 70 (January 1992): 281–304.

Jones, Hugh Gilbert. "The Question Before Us Is: Should the People of Florida Adopt the Constitutional Amendment Providing for a Seventh Supreme Court Judge and a New System and Procedure for Our Appellate Court?" *Florida State Bar Association Law Journal* 6 (October 1932): 256.

Jones, Maxine D. "'Without Compromise or Fear': Florida's African American Female Activists." *Florida Historical Quarterly* 77 (Spring 1999): 475–502.

Jones, Maxine D., and Kevin M. McCarthy. *African Americans in Florida*. Sarasota: Pineapple Press, 1993.

Joubert, William H. "Florida." *Southern Economic Journal* 12 (October 1945): 184–93.

"The Judicial Council of Florida—Statement of Objectives." *Florida Bar Journal* 28 (February 1954): 56.

"Judicial Council Releases Court Caseloads in Annual Report." *Florida Bar Journal* 44 (June 1970): 351–52.

"Judicial Nominating Councils Named; Judges Appointed by Specific Criteria." *Florida Bar Journal* 45 (October 1971): 507–8.

"Justice Drew Retires." *Florida Bar Journal* 45 (January 1971): 22.

Kabat, Ric A. "'Everybody Votes for Gilchrist': The Florida Gubernatorial Campaign of 1908." *Florida Historical Quarterly* 67 (October 1988): 184–203.

Kallina, Edmund F., Jr. *Claude Kirk and the Politics of Confrontation*. Gainesville: University Press of Florida, 1993.

Kantor, Hal. H. "Constitutional Law; Indigent Misdemeanant's Right to Appointed Counsel: Lifting the Poverty Bar—A New Florida Standard." *University of Florida Law Review* 23 (Winter 1971): 428–37.

Kaplan, Stanton S. "Certification of Questions from Federal Appellate Courts to the Florida Supreme Court and Its Impact on the Abstention Doctrine." *University of Miami Law Review* 16 (Spring 1962): 413–33.

Kendrick, Bayard. *Florida Trails to Turnpikes, 1914–1964*. Gainesville: University of Florida Press, 1964.

Kennedy, David M. *Freedom from Fear: The American People in Depression and War, 1929–1945*. New York: Oxford University Press, 1999.

Kerber, Stephen. "The Initiative and Referendum in Florida, 1911–1912." *Florida Historical Quarterly* 72 (January 1994): 302–15.

Keuchel, Edward F. *A History of Columbia County, Florida*. Tallahassee: Sentry Press, 1981.

Key, V. O., Jr. *Southern Politics in the State and Nation*. New York: Alfred A. Knopf, 1949.

Kirk, William L., Jr. "Public Finance: A New Test for Public Purpose." *University of Florida Law Review* 19 (Spring 1967): 747–51.

Klingman, Peter D. *Neither Dies nor Surrenders: A History of the Republican Party in Florida, 1867–1970*. Gainesville: University of Florida Press, 1984.

Knight, Gerald L. "Consumer Class Actions: A Proposal for Florida." *University of Florida Law Review* 26 (Fall 1973): 58–77.

Langum, David J., and Howard P. Walthall. *From Maverick to Mainstream: Cumberland School of Law, 1847–1997*. Athens: University of Georgia Press, 1997.

Laramore, Vivian Yeiser. *Second Florida Poets: An Anthology of 42 Contemporaries*. New York: H. Harrison, 1932.

Laser, Gary S. "The Right to Appointed Counsel at Collateral Attack Proceedings." *University of Miami Law Review* 19 (Spring 1965): 432–55.

Lauderback, Martha. *Consolidated, A Partial Story–Much Needs to Be Edited and Added*. Jacksonville: Consolidated Naval Store Company, n.d.

"Law Reporting." *Florida Law Journal* 24 (April 1950): 133–35.

Lawson, Steven F., David R. Colburn, and Darryl Paulson. "Groveland: Florida's Little Scottsboro." In *The African American Heritage of Florida*, ed. David R. Colburn and Jane L. Landers. Gainesville: University Press of Florida, 1995.

Lewis, Anthony. *Gideon's Trumpet*. New York: Random House, 1964.

Lincoln, Freeman. "The Terrible-Tempered Mr. Ball." *Fortune* 46 (November 1952): 142–62.

Linsin, Christopher. "Something More than a Creed: Mary McLeod Bethune's Aim of Integrated Autonomy as Director of Negro Affairs." *Florida Historical Quarterly* 76 (Summer 1997): 20–41.

Little, Joseph W. "New Attitudes about Legal Protection for Remains of Florida's Natural Environment." *University of Florida Law Review* 23 (Spring 1971): 459–513.

———. "An Overview of the Historical Development of the Judicial Article of the Florida Constitution." *Stetson Law Review* 19 (Fall 1989): 1–41.

Loquasto, Wendy S., comp. *150: Celebrating Florida's First 150 Women Lawyers.* Charlottesville, Va.: LEXIS, 2000.

"Lynching: 'Negros Remember . . .'" *Newsweek* 10 (July 31, 1937): 9.

Makers of America, Florida Edition. 4 vols. Atlanta: A. B. Caldwell, 1909–11.

Manley, Walter W., II, Canter Brown Jr., and Eric W. Rise. *The Supreme Court of Florida and Its Predecessor Courts, 1821–1917.* Gainesville: University Press of Florida, 1997.

Manly, Robert L. "Criminal Law: Indigent's Right to Appointed Counsel When Accused of Misdemeanors." *University of Florida Law Review* 27 (Spring 1965): 639–43.

Marsee, Howard R. "Civil Procedure: Judicial Creation of Direct Action against Automobile Liability Insurers." *University of Florida Law Review* 22 (Summer 1969): 145–54.

Mason, Raymond K., and Virginia Harrison. *Confusion to the Enemy: A Biography of Edward Ball.* New York: Dodd, Mead, 1976.

Mathews, John E. "Remarks of Mr. Chief Justice John E. Mathews." *Florida Bar Journal* 29 (February 1955): 96–99.

McGovern, James R. *Anatomy of a Lynching: The Killing of Claude Neal.* Baton Rouge: Louisiana State University Press, 1982.

McKay, Donald B. *Pioneer Florida.* 2 vols. Tampa: Southern, 1959.

Means, Ernest E. "Florida's District Courts of Appeal: A Tentative Appraisal." *Florida Bar Journal* 33 (December 1959): 1208–12.

Mohl, Raymond A. "The Latinization of Florida." In *Florida's Heritage of Diversity: Essays in Honor of Samuel Proctor*, ed. Mark I. Greenberg, William Warren Rogers, and Canter Brown Jr. Tallahassee: Sentry Press, 1997.

Mohl, Raymond A., and Gary R. Mormino. "The Big Change in the Sunshine State: A Social History of Modern Florida." In *The New History of Florida*, ed. Michael Gannon. Gainesville: University Press of Florida, 1996.

Mormino, Gary. "GI Joe Meets Jim Crow: Racial Violence and Reform in World War II Florida." *Florida Historical Quarterly* 73 (July 1994): 23–42.

———. "World War II." In *The New History of Florida*, ed. Michael Gannon. Gainesville: University Press of Florida, 1996.

Mormino, Gary R., and George E. Pozzetta. *The Immigrant World of Ybor City: Italians and Their Latin Neighbors in Tampa, 1885–1985.* Reprint, Gainesville: University Press of Florida, 1998.

Morris, Allen, comp. *The Florida Handbook, 1947–1948.* Tallahassee: Peninsula, 1947.

———. *The Florida Handbook, 1949–1950.* Tallahassee: Peninsular, 1949.

———. *The Florida Handbook, 1965–1966.* Tallahassee: Peninsular, 1965.
———. *The Florida Handbook, 1967–1968.* Tallahassee: Peninsular, 1967.
———. *The Florida Handbook, 1973–1974.* Tallahassee: Peninsular, 1973.
———. *The Florida Handbook, 1991–1992.* Tallahassee: Peninsular, 1991.
Motley, Constance Baker. *Equal Justice under Law.* New York: Farrar, Straus and Giroux, 1998.
Nachwalter, Michael. "Substantive Due Process in Florida." *University of Miami Law Review* 21 (Fall 1966): 99–131.
The National Cyclopaedia of American Biography, Being the History of the United States. 63 vols. New York: James T. White, 1898–1984.
Nelson, Bill. "Mission Most Perilous: Risks? 'You Don't Dwell on That.'" *Forum: The Magazine of the Florida Humanities Council* 20 (Winter 1997): 4–7.
"New Supreme Court Building." *Florida Law Journal* 22 (April 1948): 107–8.
"New Supreme Court Rules." *Florida Law Journal* 13 (April 1939): 159.
Newman, Roger K. *Hugo Black: A Biography.* New York: Pantheon Books, 1994.
Newton, Michael. *The Invisible Empire: The Ku Klux Klan in Florida.* Gainesville: University Press of Florida, 2001.
Neyland, Leedell W., and John W. Riley. *The History of Florida Agricultural and Mechanical University.* Gainesville: University of Florida Press, 1963.
"Ninth President: Thomas Franklin West, 1874–1931." *Florida Law Journal* 8 (October 1934): 128.
Nolan, David. *Fifty Feet in Paradise: The Booming of Florida.* San Diego: Harcourt Brace Jovanovich, 1984.
O'Connell, Stephen C. "Convention Report of the Judicial Council to the Florida Bar." *Florida Bar Journal* 34 (June 1960): 355–60.
———. "In Memoriam: Mr. Justice Campbell Thornal." *University of Florida Law Review* 23 (Winter 1971): n.p.
———. "Report on the Judicial Council of Florida." *Florida Bar Journal* 32 (June 1958): 350–56.
"Official Vote on the Proposed Constitutional Amendment Providing for an Additional Judge of the Supreme Court." *Florida State Bar Association Law Journal* 6 (December 1932): 362.
Orrick, Bentley, and Harry L. Crumpacker. *The Tampa Tribune: A Century of Florida Journalism.* Tampa: University of Tampa Press, 1998.
Parker, Julius F. "President's Annual Address." *Florida Law Journal* 20 (June 1946): 163–68.
Parsons, Malcolm B. "The Selection and Tenure of Florida Supreme Court Justices." *Miami Law Quarterly* 9 (Spring 1955): 271–79.
Patterson, Gordon. "A Special Place, Always: The Edge of the Continent Has Long Been on the Edge of History as Well." *Forum: The Magazine of the Florida Humanities Council* 20 (Winter 1997–98): 19–21.

Pepper, Claude. "A Practitioner from the Past Returns to the Court." *Florida Supreme Court Historical Society Review* 1 (Spring 1985): 6–8, 15.

Pepper, Claude, and Hays Gorey. *Pepper: Eyewitness to a Century*. San Diego: Harcourt Brace Jovanovich, 1987.

Perlmutter, Julius J. "Judicial Reform on the March in Florida." *Miami Law Quarterly* 9 (Fall 1954): 50–72.

Perret, Geoffrey. *Eisenhower*. New York: Random House, 1999.

Polley, Brian, and Isabel Kirwood. "Seals." *Florida Supreme Court Historical Society Review* 1 (Winter 1985): 8–9.

Poore, Caroline Emmons. "Striking the First Blow: Harry T. Moore and the Fight for Black Equality in Florida." Master's thesis, Florida State University, 1992.

Population of Florida. Tallahassee: Florida Development Commission, 1959.

Porter, Lawrence C. "The Status of Judicial Reform in the State of Florida." *University of Miami Law Review* 12 (Fall 1957): 104–13.

"Portrayal of Terrell: Family Man, Mentor, Jurist." *Florida Supreme Court Historical Society Review* 1 (Spring 1985): 1–4, 11–13.

Poulton, Timothy P. "Counsel Appointment for Indigent Defendants in Noncapital Cases." *University of Florida Law Review* 11 (Summer 1958): 220– 24.

Prescott, Stephen R. "White Robes and Crosses: Father John Conoley, the Ku Klux Klan, and the University of Florida." *Florida Historical Quarterly* 71 (July 1992): 18–40.

Proceedings of the Florida State Bar Association. Miami: Florida State Bar Association, 1923.

Proceedings of the Florida State Bar Association for the Years 1907, 1908, and 1909. Jacksonville: Florida State Bar Association, 1909.

"Proceedings of the 39th Annual Convention of the Florida State Bar Association." *Florida Law Journal* 20 (July 1946): 222–43.

Proctor, Samuel. *Napoleon Bonaparte Broward: Florida's Fighting Democrat*. Gainesville: University Press of Florida, 1950.

———. "Prelude to the New Florida, 1877–1919." In *The New History of Florida*, ed. Michael Gannon. Gainesville: University Press of Florida, 1996.

"The Proposed Amendment to the Judiciary Article of the Constitution Should Be Adopted." *Florida Law Journal* 26 (October 1952): 337–43.

"Proposed Constitutional Amendment Increasing Number of Justices of the Supreme Court of Florida." *Florida State Bar Association Law Journal* 6 (September 1932): 180–81.

"Proposed Revisions for Florida's Trial Court System." *Florida Bar Journal* 35 (January 1961): 21–24.

Pudlow, Jan. "75 Years of the Bar *Journal*." *Florida Bar Journal* 76 (December 2002): 12–15.

Rader, Earle M. "Rickenbacker Causeway Completed." *Florida Highways* 15 (November 1947): 43, 49–51.

Redfearn, D. H. "Amendments to Florida's Constitution." *Florida Bar Journal* 36 (March 1962): 138–41.

Reed, Nadine Neil. "Implications of Recent Cases on Education of Minority Racial Groups." *University of Florida Law Review* 3 (Fall 1950): 358–67.

Reed, Stanley. "The Highest Court of a State." *Florida Law Journal* 23 (February 1949): 32–35.

Reilly, Thomas. "Florida's Flying Minute Men: The Civil Air Patrol, 1941–1943." *Florida Historical Quarterly* 76 (Spring 1998): 417–38.

"Remembering Millard Fillmore Caldwell, 1897–1984." *Florida Supreme Court Historical Society Review* 1 (Spring 1985): 9–11.

"Reminiscing with Justice Alto L. Adams." *Florida Supreme Court Historical Society Review* 3 (1987–88): 8–11.

Rerick, Roland W. *Memoirs of Florida*. 2 vols. Atlanta: Southern Historical Association, 1902.

"Retired Justice Elwyn Thomas Dies After Long Illness." *Florida Bar Journal* 45 (April 1971): 205.

"The Retiring Justices." *Florida Bar Journal* 43 (February 1969): 98–99.

Revels, Tracy Jean. "World War II–Era Florida: Change in the 1940s." In *Florida's Heritage of Diversity: Essays in Honor of Samuel Proctor*, ed. Mark I. Greenberg, William Warren Rogers, and Canter Brown Jr. Tallahassee: Sentry Press, 1997.

Riedel, Harley E. "Municipal Powers in Florida: By Constitutional Right or Legislative Grace?" *University of Florida Law Review* 25 (Spring 1973): 597–602.

Rigot, Linda M. "Current Amendments to the Florida Rules." *University of Miami Law Review* 23 (Summer 1969): 815–27.

Ripley, Wayne E., Jr. "Gideon's Encore." *University of Miami Law Review* 26 (Summer 1972): 828–33.

Ritter, Paul. "The Florida Supreme Court and the Gubernatorial Election." *University of Florida Law Review* 7 (Spring 1954): 35–46.

Rivers, Larry O. *Florida Agricultural and Mechanical University College of Law, 1949–2000*. Tallahassee: Florida Agricultural and Mechanical University, 2000.

Roberts, B. K. "Alto Adams." *Florida Supreme Court Historical Society Review* 3 (1987–88): 10–11.

———. "Law Practice in the Depression Decade of the 30's." *Florida Supreme Court Historical Society Review* 1 (Fall 1984): 1–4.

———. "The State of the Judiciary." *Florida Bar Journal* 45 (July 1971): 394–98.

———. "The State of the Judiciary." *Florida Bar Journal* 46 (August 1972): 457–61.

Robinson, R. M. "Constitutional Law: Vagrancy Ordinance Held Unconstitutional for Vagueness." *University of Florida Law Review* 18 (Summer 1965): 169–73.

Rogers, William Warren. "Fortune and Misfortune: The Paradoxical Twenties." In *The New History of Florida*, ed. Michael Gannon. Gainesville: University Press of Florida, 1996.

———. "The Great Depression." In *The New History of Florida*, ed. Michael Gannon. Gainesville: University Press of Florida, 1996.

Rogers, William Warren, and Canter Brown Jr. *Florida's Clerks of the Circuit Court, Their History and Experiences*. Tallahassee: Sentry Press, 1996.

Rogers, William Warren, and James M. Denham. *Florida Sheriffs: A History, 1821–1945*. Tallahassee: Sentry Press, 2001.

Roscow, John. "Municipal Corporations: Liability for Intentional Torts and Punitive Damages." *University of Florida Law Review* 18 (Summer 1965): 173–77.

Ross, Donald H. "Labor Law—Agency Shop Violates Florida Constitution." *University of Miami Law Review* 17 (Winter 1962): 204–12.

Sage-Gagne, Waneta. *Pilots in the Sun: Primary Pilot Training Schools in Lakeland and Avon Park, Florida, 1940–1945*. Lakeland: Friends of the Library, 1990.

"Sales—Implied Warranty of Fitness in Sale of Food by Restaurant." *Miami Law Quarterly* 3 (June 1949): 638–39.

Saunders, Robert W., Sr. *Bridging the Gap: Continuing the Florida NAACP Legacy of Harry T. Moore, 1952–1966*. Tampa: University of Tampa Press, 2000.

Schnur, James A. "Cold Warriors in the Hot Sunshine: USF and the Johns Committee." *Sunland Tribune* 18 (November 1992): 9–16.

Schram, Ronald Young. "Municipal Ordinance Violations in Florida: Selected Due Process Considerations." *University of Florida Law Review* 22 (Spring/Summer 1970): 580–95.

Sebring, Harold L. "The Appellate System of Florida." *Florida Law Journal* 25 (April 1951): 141–47.

———. "The Responsibility of the Lawyer." *Miami Law Quarterly* 10 (Fall 1955): 26–33.

Semet, Barry N. "Florida Constitutional Law." *University of Miami Law Review* 18 (Summer 1964): 888–916.

———. "Sales—Implied Warranty Liability of Cigarette Manufacturers." *University of Miami Law Review* 18 (Winter 1963): 502–9.

Sherouse, Kenneth. "The Sherouse Years (Editor 1954–1957)." *Florida Bar Journal* 51 (July–August 1977): 410–13.

Sherrill, Robert. "Florida's Legislature: The Pork Chop State of Mind." *Harper's* 9 (November 1965): 82–97.

———. *Gothic Politics in the Deep South: Stars of the New Confederacy*. New York: Grossman, 1968.

Shofner, Jerrell H. "Communists, Klansmen, and the CIO in the Florida Citrus Industry." *Florida Historical Quarterly* 71 (January 1993): 300–309.

———. *Jackson County, Florida—A History*. Marianna: Jackson County Heritage Association, 1985.

———. "Militant Negro Laborers in Reconstruction Florida." *Florida Historical Quarterly* 39 (August 1973): 397–408.

———. "Roosevelt's 'Tree Army': The Civilian Conservation Corps in Florida." *Florida Historical Quarterly* 65 (April 1987): 433–56.

Sikes, Robert. *He-Coon: The Bob Sikes Story*. Pensacola: Perdido Bay Press, 1984.

Sinclair, Carson F. "Yesterday." *Florida Supreme Court Historical Society Review* 1 (Winter 1985): 7–8.

Smiljanich, Terrance A. "Advisory Opinions in Florida: An Experiment in Intergovernmental Cooperation." *University of Florida Law Review* 24 (Winter 1972): 329–41.

———. "Right to Counsel on Appeal: The Defendant of Intermediate Means." *University of Florida Law Review* 23 (Fall 1970): 211–15.

Smith, J. Clay, Jr. *Emancipation: The Making of the Black Lawyer, 1844–1944*. Philadelphia: University of Pennsylvania Press, 1993.

Smith, Frederick D. "Compensation for Loss of Consortium: The Wife's Cause of Action." *University of Florida Law Review* 24 (Fall 1971): 198–202.

Smith-Adam, Louisa. "Implied Warranties in Housing: Let the Buyer Rejoice." *University of Florida Law Review* 25 (Spring 1973): 619–24.

"Soon Enough If Right." *Florida Alumnus* 18 (June 1966): 5–8.

Sparkman, Stephen L. "The History and Status of Local Government Power in Florida." *University of Florida Law Review* 25 (Winter 1973): 271–307.

Spencer, John C. "Implied Warranty: Strict Liability of the Manufacturer in Absence of Privity for All Products." *University of Florida Law Review* 19 (Summer 1996): 193–97.

Stafford, Charles. "Sen. Spessard L. Holland: Statesman and Southerner." *Floridian: The St. Petersburg Times Magazine* (October 11, 1970): 14–20.

Standley, Fred L. "Justice Glenn Terrell: A Brief Analysis of His Legal Opinions." *Florida Bar Journal* 41 (February 1967): 103–7.

Starling, John M. "Special District Taxation." *University of Florida Law Review* 13 (Winter 1960): 531–55.

"State v. Mock and Mock." *Florida State Bar Association Law Journal* 1 (November 1927): 52.

Stephenson, D. Grier, Jr. "State Appellate Courts and the Political Process: Florida and the Public Forum." *University of Miami Law Review* 23 (Fall 1968): 182–210.

Stobbie, Denise. "Down Home Justice." *Florida Lawyer* 24 (Fall 1987): 13–15.

Stone, Spessard. *Lineage of John Carlton*. Wauchula: privately published, 1998.

Straub, W. L. *History of Pinellas County, Florida, Narrative and Biographical*. St. Augustine: Record, 1929.

Sturgis, Wallace E., Jr. "Abolition of the Diploma Privilege." *University of Florida Law Review* 4 (Fall 1951): 370–81.

"Supreme Court Appoints Ueberhorst Chief Administrator of State Courts." *Florida Bar Journal* 46 (July 1972): 417.

The Supreme Court of Florida. Tallahassee: Supreme Court of Florida, 1969.

"'Tax Revenue Spent for Public Education, a Sound Investment,' Says Caldwell." *Journal of the Florida Education Association* 22 (January 1945): n.p.

Taylor, Grace Elizabeth Woodall. "Jury Service for Women." *University of Florida Law Review* 12 (Summer 1959): 224–31.

Tebeau, Charlton W. *A History of Florida*. Coral Gables: University of Miami Press, 1971.

Terrell, Glenn. "The Courts of Florida." In *Florida Handbook, 1947–1948*, comp. Allen Morris. Tallahassee: Peninsular, 1947.

———. "Rules of Civil Procedure." *Florida Law Journal* 23 (July 1949): 230–35.

———. "Status of the Rules of Civil Procedure." *Florida Law Journal* 20 (July 1946): 281–89.

Thomas, Elwyn. "An Appraisal of Progress Made." *Florida Bar Journal* 30 (March 1956): 159–61.

———. "Judicial Council History." *Florida Bar Journal* 33 (February 1959): 59–64.

———. "Justice without Delay." *University of Florida Law Review* 2 (Spring 1949): 1–11.

———. "The Needs of Our Supreme Court." *Florida Law Journal* 13 (May 1939): 170–74.

Thompson, Sandra. "Moves Made in the Sunshine." *Floridian: The St. Petersburg Times Magazine* (November 14, 1982): 15–16.

Thornal, Campbell. "I Remember Stephen C. O'Connell . . . as Supreme Court Justice." *Florida Alumnus* 20 (Fall 1968): 17.

———. "The Lawyer and the Rule of Law." *Florida Bar Journal* 36 (December 1962): 1159–61.

Tierney, Kevin. *Clarence Darrow: A Biography*. New York: Thomas Y. Crowell, 1979.

Tindall, George Brown. *America: A Narrative History*. 2 vols. New York: Norton, 1988.

"Tom Sebring Appointed Circuit Judge." *Florida Law Journal* 8 (October 1934): 127–28.

"Torts: Res Ipsa Loquitur in Exploding-Bottle Cases." *University of Florida Law Review* 1 (Fall 1948): 470–71.

"Tribute of the Supreme Court of Florida to Mr. Justice Rivers Henderson Buford on His Retirement March 1, 1948." 100–101 *Southern Reporter, Second Series (Florida Cases)*: xliii–xlv.

Truett, Lawrence A. "The New Florida Appellate Rules of Practice." *University of Florida Law Review* 9 (Spring 1955): 93–107.

Tscheschlok, Eric. "Long Time Coming: Miami's Liberty City Riot of 1968." *Florida Historical Quarterly* 74 (Spring 1996): 440–60.

Tudhope, Wallace W. "Civil Procedure: Joiner of Liability Insurers—A Welcome Clarification of *Shingleton* and *Beta Eta*." *University of Florida Law Review* 24 (Summer 1972): 820–26.

Valentine, Doris, comp. *Looking Back, Sumter County: A Photographic Essay*. Bushnell: Sumter County Historical Society, 1981.

Van Brunt, "Florida's First Family." *Florida Highways* 13 (January 1945): 15–18, 35, 63.

Vance, Linda D. *May Mann Jennings, Florida's Genteel Activist*. Gainesville: University Press of Florida, 1985.

Vickers, Raymond B. *Panic In Paradise: Florida's Banking Crash of 1926*. Tuscaloosa: University of Alabama Press, 1994.

Vickers, Sally. "Congresswoman Ruth Bryan Owen: The Spirit of Florida." In *Florida's Heritage of Diversity: Essays in Honor of Samuel Proctor*, ed. Mark I. Greenberg, William Warren Rogers, and Canter Brown Jr. (Tallahassee: Sentry Press, 1997).

"Wade L. Hopping Named CLE Director." *Florida Bar Journal* 38 (February 1964): 86.

Wagy, Tom R. *Governor LeRoy Collins of Florida: Spokesman of the New South*. Tuscaloosa: University of Alabama Press, 1985.

Walker, Donald. "Report of the Committee on Law Reporting." *Florida Law Journal* 21 (May 1947): 116–18.

Warren, Fuller. "Address by Governor Fuller Warren at the Florida Bar Convention." *Florida Law Journal* 26 (June 1952): 237–42.

———. "Appellate Procedure . . . in Florida . . . Adjusted to the New 1955 Supreme Court Rules." *Miami Law Quarterly* 9 (Summer 1955): 375–84.

Warren, Lamar. "Yesterday." *Florida Supreme Court Historical Society Review* 2 (Winter 1986): 11–13.

Waybright, Roger J. "Florida's New Juvenile Court Act." *Miami Law Quarterly* 6 (December 1951): 1–23.

———. "A Proposed Juvenile Court Act for Florida." *University of Florida Law Review* 4 (Spring 1951): 16–39.

West, Thomas F. "Citizenship—Its Rights—Its Obligations." *Florida State Bar Association Law Journal* 3 (March 1930): 13.

Wiecek, William M. *The Lost World of Classical Legal Thought: Law and Ideology in America, 1886–1937*. New York: Oxford University Press, 1998.

Whitfield, James Bryan. *Political and Legal History of Florida*. Atlanta: Harrison, 1943.

Wickman, Patricia R. "Honorable B. K. Roberts: Biographical Report." Typescript, Museum of Florida History, 1988.

Wigginton, John T. "New Florida Common Law Rules." *University of Florida Law Review* 3 (Spring 1950): 1–32.

———. "Rules of Civil Procedure." *Florida Law Journal* 24 (April 1950): 148–49.

Williams, Juan. *Thurgood Marshall, American Revolutionary*. New York: Random House, 1998.

Williamson, Edward C. *Florida Politics in the Gilded Age, 1877–1893*. Gainesville: University of Florida Press, 1976.

Wills, Martee, and Joan Perry Morris. *Seminole History: A Pictorial History of Florida State University*. Jacksonville: South Star, 1987.

Wilson, James R., William G. Dreisbach, Samuel A. Broadnax, and Reeves Bowen. "The Florida Appellate Rules." *University of Florida Law Review* 11 (Spring 1958): 1–67.

Wilson, Julie. "Chief Justice and Mrs. B. K. Roberts." *Jacksonville Times-Union and Journal* (May 9, 1971).

Wright, Floyd A. "Zoning under the Florida Law." *Miami Law Quarterly* 7 (April 1953): 324–57.

Wright, Freddie. "Polk County's First Poor Farm." *Polk County Historical Quarterly* 8 (March 1982): 5.

Yancey, Susan, "The People's Judge." *Florida Bar Journal* 33 (November 1959): 1138–43.

Yates, Linda H. "A Profile of the New Chief Justice." *Florida Bar Journal* 39 (September 1965): 917–19.

Young, George C. "Special Bulletin on Amendment No. 1." *Florida Bar Journal* 30 (October 1956): 490–91.

Zibart, Eve. *The Unofficial Disney Companion: The Inside Story of Walt Disney World and the Man behind the Mouse*. New York: Macmillan, 1997.

Interviews

Adkins, James C., Jr. Interviewed by Harold Bryan Crosby, August 16, 1987, Tallahassee. Transcript in James C. Adkins Jr. biographical file, FSCHS.

Barns, Paul Dryden, Jr. Interviewed by Canter Brown Jr., July 7 and 10, 2000, Coral Gables, Fla.

Buford, A. L. "Jack." Interviewed by Walter W. Manley II, June 2, 2003, Tallahassee.

Buford, Barbara. Interviewed by Walter W. Manley II, June 2, 2003, Tallahassee.

Buford, Rivers, Jr. Interviewed by Walter W. Manley II, June 2, 2003, Tallahassee.

Caldwell, Mary Harwood. Interviewed by M. McKory, March 1977, Tallahassee. Notes in Millard Caldwell biographical file, State Library of Florida, Tallahassee.

Cason, Warren M. Interviewed by Canter Brown Jr., July 14, 2000, Tampa.

Dekle, Hal P. Interviewed by Canter Brown Jr., July 17, 2000, Venice, Fla.

Ervin, Richard W. Interviewed by Ditti Davis, May 7, 1985, Tallahassee. Transcript in collection of Florida Supreme Court Historical Society.

———. Interviewed by Walter W. Manley II and Canter Brown Jr., May 1 and 8, 2000, Tallahassee.

———. Interviewed by Walter W. Manley II, March 14, 2003, Tallahassee.

———. Interviewed by Russell Troutman, n.d. Videotape in collection of Florida Supreme Court Historical Society.

Ervin, Robert M. Interviewed by Walter W. Manley II and Canter Brown Jr., May 15, 2000, Tallahassee.

Folsom, John K. Interviewed by Canter Brown Jr., April 3, 2000, Tallahassee.

Germany, John. Interviewed by Canter Brown Jr., June 14, 2000, Tampa.

Hawes, Leland. Interviewed by Canter Brown Jr., July 11, 2000, Tampa.

Hopping, Wade L. Interviewed by Randall Reder, May 12, 1982, Tallahassee. Notes in collection of Florida Supreme Court Historical Society.

———. Interviewed by Canter Brown Jr., June 16, August 1, 2000, Tallahassee.

Livingston, A. Broaddus. Interviewed by Canter Brown Jr., June 13, 2000, Tampa.
McCord, Guyte, Jr., and Betty McCord. Interviewed by Randall Reder, May 17, 1982, Tallahassee. Notes in collection of Florida Supreme Court Historical Society.
Mitchell, Melanie Drew. Interviewed by Canter Brown Jr., July 18, 2000, Tallahassee by phone.
Morrison, Alyce Thornal. Interviewed by Canter Brown Jr., July 17, 2000, Orlando.
O'Connell, Stephen C. Interviewed by Walter W. Manley II and Canter Brown Jr., May 2 and 9, 2000, O'Connell's ranch near Tallahassee.
Owen, William C. Interviewed by Walter W. Manley II, April 14, 2003, Tallahassee.
Pruitt, Mary Barns. Interviewed by Canter Brown Jr., July 21, 2000, Stuart, Fla.
Rivers, Larry E. Interviewed by Canter Brown Jr., September 4, 2000, Tallahassee.
Roberts, B. K. Interview by Randall O. Reder, April 21, 1980, Tallahassee. Transcript in Randall O. Reder Papers, Florida Supreme Court Library, Tallahassee.
———. Interview by Ditti Davis and Brian Polley, September 16, 1986, Tallahassee. Notes in Florida Supreme Court Historical Society biographical files.
Rogers, William Warren. Interviewed by Canter Brown Jr., June 27, 2000, Tallahassee.
Saunders, Robert W., Sr. Interviewed by Canter Brown Jr., May 25, 2000, Bartow, Fla.
Simmons, Frances Hobson. Interviewed by Canter Brown Jr., July 18, 2000, Wauchula, Fla.
Smith, W. Reece, Jr. Interviewed by Canter Brown Jr., June 13, 2000, Tampa.
Thornal, Benjamin Campbell, Jr. Interviewed by Canter Brown Jr., July 12, 2000, Orlando.
Thornal, Burton. Interviewed by Canter Brown Jr., July 19, 2000, Franklin, N.C.
Todd, Wayne Jr. Interviewed by Walter W. Manley II, May 20, 2004, Tallahassee.

Index

Walter W. Manley II is professor of business administration at Florida State University. A visiting professor at Oxford and Cambridge, he was a member of five faculties including that of law at Oxford University and law and social and political science at Cambridge University. In addition to *The Supreme Court of Florida and Its Predecessor Courts, 1821–1917*, coauthored with Canter Brown Jr., Manley is the author of several books including *The Handbook of Good Business Practice* and *Critical Issues in Business Conduct.*

Canter Brown Jr. is special assistant and counsel to the president, and professor of history, at Fort Valley State University, Fort Valley, Georgia. He is the author or coauthor of numerous books, including *Florida's Peace River Frontier*, *Cracker Times and Pioneer Lives*, and *Florida's Black Public Officials, 1867–1924*. Brown's work has been honored by the Florida Historical Society with its Rembert Patrick Book Award, Harry T. and Harriette V. Moore Award, and Governor LeRoy Collins Prize; by the Southern Jewish Historical Society with its B. H. Levy Prize; and by the American Association of State and Local History with its Certificate of Commendation.